Imperial Challenge

Supplementary Volumes to
The Papers of Woodrow Wilson
Arthur S. Link, Editor

The Editorial Advisory Committee

Katherine E. Brand, *Emeritus*
Henry Steele Commager, *Emeritus*
John Milton Cooper, Jr.
William H. Harbaugh
August Heckscher
Richard W. Leopold
Arthur M. Schlesinger, Jr.
Betty Miller Unterberger

A list of volumes in this series
will be found at the back of the book.

Johann Heinrich Count von Bernstorff, German Ambassador to the United States, 1908–17 (author's collection; gift of Alexandra Princess Lowenstein Wertheim Rosenberg)

REINHARD R. DOERRIES

IMPERIAL CHALLENGE

Ambassador Count Bernstorff

and German-American Relations, 1908–1917

Translated by Christa D. Shannon

The University of North Carolina Press

Chapel Hill and London

© 1989 The University of North Carolina Press
All rights reserved
Manufactured in the United States of America

The paper in this book meets the guidelines for permanence and durability of the Committee on Production Guidelines for Book Longevity of the Council on Library Resources.

93 92 91 90 89   5 4 3 2 1

Library of Congress Cataloging-in-Publication Data

Doerries, Reinhard R.

Imperial challenge: Ambassador Count Bernstorff and German-American relations, 1908–1917 / by Reinhard R. Doerries; translated by Christa D. Shannon.

p.   cm. — (Supplementary volumes to the papers of Woodrow Wilson)

Rev. ed. of: Washington-Berlin, 1908/1917, 1975.

Bibliography: p.

Includes index.

ISBN 0-8078-1820-8 (alk. paper)

1. United States—Foreign relations—Germany. 2. Germany—Foreign relations—United States. 3. World War, 1914–1918—Diplomatic history. 4. Bernstorff, Johann Heinrich, Graf von, 1862–1939. I. Doerries, Reinhard R. Washington-Berlin, 1908/1917. II. Title.

III. Series.

E183.8.G3D63   1989   88-20907

327.43073—dc19   CIP

For Elaine

CONTENTS

Foreword by Arthur S. Link   xiii

Acknowledgments   xvii

Introduction   1

ONE | The Prewar Years in Washington   14
 Count Bernstorff and American Public Opinion, 1908–1914   15
 Negotiations for an Arbitration Treaty   25
 Germany's Policy South of the Rio Grande   32

TWO | The War Years, 1914–1917:
         Propaganda for Germany   39
 The Press Office in New York   41
 Acquisition and Financial Support of American Press
   Organs   50
 German Propaganda among Jews in America   57
 German Propaganda among Americans of German Descent   67
 German Propaganda among Americans of Irish Descent   72

THREE | The War Years, 1914–1917:
         Submarine Warfare and the Possibilities for
         Peace from August 1914 to June 1915   77
 U-boat Warfare from the Beginning of the War until the
   Torpedoing of the *Lusitania*   78
 Peace Efforts between Germany and the United States until the
   Spring of 1915   85

FOUR | The War Years, 1914–1917:
         Submarine Warfare and the Possibilities for
         Peace from May 1915 to the Summer of 1916   98
 The U-boat War on Commerce from the Sinking of the *Lusitania*
   until the *Sussex* Crisis   99

Mediation Possibilities from the Spring of 1915 until the
Summer of 1916   127

FIVE | The War Years, 1914–1917:
Unofficial and Covert Activities of German
Representatives and Agents in the United States   141
Forged Passports for Reservists and Agents   144
Measures against the British Colonial Empire in India
Undertaken from American Soil   146
Sir Roger Casement in the Web of German War Policy   155
German Interests and the Civil War South of the Border   165
In the Twilight of Intelligence Operations   174

SIX | The Break with the United States   191
Berlin's Urging for an American Peace Appeal in the Early Fall
of 1916   192
The So-called German Peace Offer of December 12, 1916, and the
Rejection of the American Mediation Attempt   199
Bernstorff's Stand vis-à-vis Berlin in the Battle for the Neutrality
of the United States   210

Notes   233

Bibliography   367

Index   425

ILLUSTRATIONS

Johann Heinrich Count von Bernstorff, German Ambassador to the United States, 1908–17   frontispiece

Count and Countess Bernstorff, ca. 1908   9

Count and Countess Bernstorff, 1930s   13

Hermann Freiherr Speck von Sternburg, Bernstorff's predecessor as Ambassador to the United States   29

Count Bernstorff as Imperial Ambassador   35

Colonel Edward M. House and President Woodrow Wilson   89

Chancellor Theobald von Bethmann Hollweg at Charleroi   208

FOREWORD

I am happy to welcome Reinhard R. Doerries's *Imperial Challenge: Ambassador Count Bernstorff and German-American Relations, 1908–1917* to the Supplementary Volumes Series.

Imperial Challenge is, first of all, a translation of Professor Doerries's *Washington-Berlin 1908/1917* (Düsseldorf, 1975). We would have been glad to publish *Imperial Challenge* if it had been only a good translation of *Washington-Berlin 1908/1917*, if for no other reason than to make this important book available to the worldwide community of scholars in the field of twentieth-century diplomatic history. Indeed, the approach, emphasis, and findings of *Imperial Challenge* are the same as those of *Washington-Berlin 1908/1917*. Bernstorff, a seasoned diplomat, came to Washington as Imperial German Ambassador during a placid and superficially cordial period in German-American relations and played very well what was largely a ceremonial role before the summer of 1914. However, the outbreak of the World War, and particularly his government's decision in early 1915 to launch an unrestricted submarine campaign against merchant shipping, thrust Bernstorff into the center of a diplomatic firestorm that grew in intensity and culminated in an American declaration of war against the German Empire in April 1917.

Whatever superciliousness about German-American relations Bernstorff may have demonstrated before 1914 quickly vanished as he confronted the diplomatic and strategic realities of the period 1914–17. By 1914, Bernstorff knew the United States well. He knew that it had immense economic and manpower resources which could be rapidly mobilized, and that American entry into the war on the side of the Allies could result only in the defeat of Germany. He also was convinced that President Wilson was genuinely neutral vis-à-vis the two alliances and sincerely wanted to end the war through his personal mediation and to bring into being a new postwar community dedicated above all to the prevention of future wars.

These were not popular views anywhere in Europe, and particularly not in Berlin, where the Emperor, the military and naval high commands, and the Foreign Office, so inordinately proud of their prowess in realpolitik, obtusely closed their eyes to the most important reality of world politics in this period: the United States of America was in fact potentially the strongest power in the world. Given Berlin's mentality from 1914 to 1917, there was no way that Bernstorff could have reoriented German foreign policy from antagonism toward friendship with the United States. To be sure, Bernstorff sustained a desperate and successful campaign before 1917 to avert a German-American break. Probably no other German diplomat could have done as well as he did. However, Bernstorff fought from a position of weakness, and his efforts were sooner or later bound to fail, because Berlin's decisions vis-à-vis the United States were based, not upon a desire for a peace without victory but for a postwar world in which Germany would stand as a colossus astride Europe and the world. More immediately to the point was the fact, which made Bernstorff's bargaining position always tenuous, that German policy toward the United States from 1915 to 1917 was based upon calculations, very precise, very mathematical, and very cold (so the German leaders thought) of whether Germany had enough submarines to maintain an effective blockade of the Allied countries. Bernstorff succeeded as he did before 1917—often narrowly and sometimes by taking huge personal risks—only because the German navy could not guarantee a quick victory in Europe. When the Admiralty, in December 1916–January 1917, guaranteed such a victory, Bernstorff was helpless, impotent, a cipher.

Meanwhile, the German government, certainly with Bernstorff's knowledge but probably not with his complicity, mounted a massive campaign on American soil of intrigue, espionage, and sabotage unprecedented in modern times by one allegedly friendly power against another. It revealed better than anything else the true attitude of the German leaders toward the United States. It was an attitude of hostility and contempt.

It would be an exaggeration to say that, as compared with *Washington-Berlin 1908/1917*, *Imperial Challenge* is a new book. It is more accurate to say that the latter enriches the narrative and findings of the former through extensive new research. *Washington-*

Berlin 1908/1917 was based primarily upon research in German archival sources and, on the American side, almost exclusively on printed sources. In preparing *Imperial Challenge*, Professor Doerries cast a much wider net. To his earlier researches, he added, among other sources, careful work in *The Papers of Woodrow Wilson*, the files of the Department of State in the National Archives, relevant files of the British Foreign and War Offices in the Public Record Office, and additional private manuscript collections. The reader will find new or expanded discussions in the text of *Imperial Challenge*, for example, on the attitudes toward the war in Europe of American Jews of German descent, the Gildemeester mission, the Rintelen affair, and most especially on the Casement affair and other German and Irish-American intrigues in the United States.

The reader's attention is drawn particularly to the notes and bibliography of *Imperial Challenge*. Professor Doerries has added many new notes and expanded the notes in *Washington-Berlin 1908/1917*. He has also expanded the bibliography in the latter book. While the emphasis of *Imperial Challenge* is on the Anglo-American-German connection from the German side, the book is as definitive a treatment of the subject as can be written and probably ever will be written.

>Arthur S. Link
>George Henry Davis
>1886 Professor of American History and
>Director and Editor of *The Papers of Woodrow Wilson*,
>Princeton University

>Princeton, New Jersey
>September 29, 1987

ACKNOWLEDGMENTS

The original German study as well as the numerous additions and alterations made to this American edition would not have been possible without the assistance beyond any call of duty of a great number of archivists and librarians on both sides of the Atlantic. At the Foreign Office, in Bonn, I benefited from the help and counsel of Dr. Heinz Günther Sasse, Dr. Theodor Gehling, Mrs. Eva Magka and, most recently, Dr. Eva Maria Keipert, who aided me in finding specific documents needed for the revision. I am also very much indebted to the archivists at the Public Record Office in London, the Library of Congress and the National Archives in Washington, D.C., the Bundesarchiv in Koblenz, and the Geheime Staatsarchiv and the Kriegsarchiv in Munich. Milton O. Gustafson, John Mendelsohn, Timothy K. Nenninger, and Robert A. Wolfe of the National Archives over the years have graciously put up with never-ending queries and patiently assisted me in the difficult research for a yet unfinished study of German intelligence activities, from which a few data have been used in this revised edition. A special thank-you is due to Judith A. Schiff of the Yale University Library who was always available even when the transatlantic traveler was unable to keep to regular opening hours. The generous lending policy of Mr. Helmut Vogt, Director of the Niedersächsische Staats- und Universitätsbibliothek in Göttingen, and the ceaseless support there particularly from Mrs. Ellen Machleidt and Dr. Hans-Joachim Kiefert were almost a conditio sine qua non in my search for unusual publications. Other institutions that assisted me or kindly supplied documents and photocopies include Brown University, the University of Chicago, Columbia University, Franklin and Marshall College, Germania Judaica, The Johns Hopkins University, Institut für Zeitgeschichte, Kreisarchiv Herzogtum Lauenburg, the Leo Baeck Institute, the New York Public Library, the University of Pennsylvania, the University of Pittsburgh, Princeton University, the Wiener Library, and the University of Wisconsin. Eric M. Warburg generously gave me access to the papers of his father, Max M. Warburg. Use of the papers of Ambassador Rudolf Nadolny was permitted by Mrs. Änny Nadolny. Mrs. Hildegard Ahrens repeatedly shared with me her memories of another age and allowed me to see what remained of the papers of her husband, Minister Georg Ahrens.

A large number of persons granted interviews and freely assisted me with all kinds of detailed information without which my study would have remained an all too sober interpretation of the records. May they forgive me the impersonal listing which appears in sharp contrast to the many delightful encounters and conversations about their lives and personal memories. For such meetings and helpful correspondence I thank Anna Countess von Bernstorff, Oberlandesgerichtsrat Werner Count von Bernstorff, Professor Fritz T. Epstein, Kapitän zur See a.D. Dr. Walter Forstmann, Professor Heinz Mosche Graupe, Oberstudienrat Hermann Harms, Botschafter a.D. Dr. Werner Otto von Hentig, Kreisarchivar Dr. Kurt Langenheim, Alexandra Princess zu Loewenstein Wertheim Rosenberg, Kirchenpräsident a.D. D. Martin Niemöller, Dr. Arnold Paucker, Dechant Manfred Count von Pourtalès, Director Riccardo Posani, Professor Johann Albrecht von Rantzau, Mrs. Oda Rolleri, Dr. Eduard Rosenbaum, Professor Kurt Freiherr von Stutterheim and his wife, Luise-Henriette von Stutterheim, née Countess von Bernstorff. At an early stage of my research, Sister Ethel Mary Tinnemann graciously let me see a copy of her unpublished dissertation "Count Johann von Bernstorff and German-American Relations, 1908–1917."

Friends and colleagues who over the years have shared Bernstorff and in various ways through counsel and criticism have contributed to the present book are Erich Angermann, John B. Duff, Gerald D. Feldman, Fritz Fellner, Fritz Fischer, William D. Griffin, William H. Harbaugh, David W. Hirst, Konrad H. Jarausch, Detlef Junker, George O. Kent, Fritz Klein, Frederick C. Luebke, Hans Mommsen, Klaus Schwabe, Fritz Stern, Henry A. Turner, Rudolf Vierhaus, Gerhard Weinberg, and Kurt Wimer. Robert H. Ferrell helped with technical matters and graciously gave his time to read a complete earlier version of the translated text with his well-known discerning eye.

My very special gratitude goes to Arthur S. Link, who has furthered my understanding of Woodrow Wilson and his policies in the difficult years from 1914 to 1917. His unparalleled knowledge of Wilson has been an essential factor for the interpretation of numerous issues confronted by Bernstorff. His patience knew no limits

Acknowledgments

when the younger European historian took positions at variance with his own tested views. Without Arthur's support and warm encouragement this revised and expanded edition would have been inconceivable. His remarkable interest in European scholarship and interpretation of American history have been a most welcome lifeline across the Atlantic. I thank him also for meticulously editing the manuscript of this book.

The translation of the German edition was made possible by a generous grant from Inter Nationes, Bonn. Mrs. Christa D. Shannon was commissioned to do the first translation; for the final prose I assume the responsibility.

Finally, it should be emphasized that while all those mentioned here and countless others, who will forgive me for not having been named specifically, have with their support made this book possible, any shortcomings that may be registered are entirely my own.

Reinhard R. Doerries
Hamburg and New York
October 1983

INTRODUCTION

This study of German-American diplomatic relations during the years prior to America's entry into the First World War in 1917 has its early origins in a research paper done for Alfred H. Kelly at Wayne State University, further work pursued under the guidance of William E. Emerson at Yale University, and numerous inspiring conversations with Hajo Holborn. Graduate seminars of Leonard Krieger at Yale University helped me better to understand the cultural differences reflected in European and American diplomacy. Intensive work in European and American archives later led to a Ph.D. dissertation under Rudolf Vierhaus at the Ruhr-Universität Bochum that was published in Germany in 1975 under the title *Washington-Berlin 1908/1917: Die Tätigkeit des Botschafters Johann Heinrich Graf von Bernstorff in Washington vor dem Eintritt der Vereinigten Staaten von Amerika in den Ersten Weltkrieg.*

As there can be little doubt that the outcome of the World War in large degree was influenced by the United States, I wished to show the developments that led to the break between the United States and the German Empire. Previous publications had cast light on aspects of such specific issues as the submarine war or the mediation efforts,[1] but German-American relations during this period had neither been treated as a unified topic nor examined on the basis of the vast amount of documentary evidence available after the release of the so-called Captured German Documents to the German Federal Republic. Most of the German authors concerned with World War I have emphasized other questions, which from a purely national perspective seemed to them more significant, and therefore in effect they have treated German-American relations as a matter of secondary interest. Even Fritz Fischer's *Griff nach der Weltmacht*, destined to unleash a fierce but fruitful debate among historians, perhaps because the author focuses on issues closer to home, does not fully relate the tragic sequence of German decisions leading to the eventual breakdown of relations in 1917.[2] Other publications, such as the monumental *Staatskunst und Kriegshandwerk* by Gerhard Ritter, contain a number of what to me appeared to be serious misinterpretations and, in fact, in several cases plain errors.[3]

Although my study was conceived, prepared, and written free from any of the combative spirit characterizing a sector of German historiography following the publication of Fritz Fischer's important book, the documentary evidence particularly from the files of the German Foreign Office precluded the book from becoming a pleasantly descriptive diplomatic history. From the earliest stages of the research, it has been my purpose to weigh all evidence in the most impartial fashion and consciously to avoid a charted revisionist path. My book therefore was not intended, as a French colleague sympathetically has surmised, to be part of a grand campaign of a "révision systematique," but the same reviewer certainly has perceived the burden that is part of writing modern German history when he speaks of the "prise de conscience, certes douloureuse."[4] The often revealing and in some cases perturbing evidence from the German files is not presented to back up a moralistic judgment but to clarify the historical record.[5] Though it was not my purpose to demonstrate a continuity of development in Germany, there is much that would appear to support the thesis that German leaders and the German government under the Emperor Wilhelm II and under Adolf Hitler exhibited an astonishing degree of confidence in their nation's military and economic power as well as cultural superiority, coupled with a devastating ignorance or underestimation of American military and economic strength.[6]

For the first time in Germany, my study placed the figure of the German Ambassador in Washington, Count Johann Heinrich von Bernstorff, in the center of attention.[7] He was among those few German leaders who recognized the immense potential of the United States. Because, in contrast to his government and his superiors, he quickly perceived Washington's importance for Germany's future development, he often found no support in the Wilhelmstrasse for his policy suggestions and, as this study shows, at times even felt obliged to act on his own and to pursue a more conciliatory policy than Berlin intended.

The German government had made no secret of the fact that it did not consider the United States a world power. The post of ambassador in Washington was not among the prestige positions of the German Empire. Imperial Germany, still Prussia-oriented and tradition-laden, found it difficult to accept the quickly rising, apparently unaristocratic, and rather rough-hewn United States as a partner among the leading nations of the Western world. Even in the competitive contests among the expansionist nations prior to the World War, Germany does not appear to have viewed America as an adversary worthy of consideration. When American resistance was encountered in the Pacific and in Latin America, the responsible authorities in Germany did not develop new overall analyses of the real and the potential world balance of power that included the United States.

While Germany, in marked contrast to Great Britain, continued to base its policy on a dangerous underestimation of the United States, Americans, after initial support of the Prussian-German efforts in the war of 1870, became, as Walter LaFeber emphasizes, increasingly doubtful of the militaristic mentality that seemed to dominate in Berlin.[8] When Wilhelm II attempted to establish a German sphere of influence in the Pacific and in evident disregard of the Monroe Doctrine began to apply military pressure in Latin America, fear and suspicion took hold in the United States that one day it might become necessary to defend American interests against the newest of the colonial powers.

Toward the end of the nineteenth century, the United States had clearly begun to abandon its foreign policy position of relative modesty and reserve and to fill the role of a leading power in the Americas that had become vacant due to the rapid decline of the older European colonial nations. Hawaii and Samoa were warning signals that the United States would no longer be merely a spectator at the heated game of the imperialist contestants. As early as 1890, Alfred Thayer Mahan had explained to Americans—and not only to them—that a strong fleet was the most essential factor in achieving desired expansion in the future.[9] Surely, it was not accidental that a new feeling of mission began to assert itself in American foreign policy precisely at the time when the continental expansion had reached the Pacific and the very structures of American society had been questioned in a grave economic crisis.

When Theodore Roosevelt became President in 1901, the United States was well on its way to assuming its foreseeable role as a world power. In the search for new frontiers, Americans had hoisted the Stars and Stripes over the Philippines, and the suppression of the Aguinaldo guerrillas who were fighting for the independence of their country would only be a matter of time. Spain had been instrumental in the rise of the world power: besides the Philippines, it had also ceded Guam and Puerto Rico to Washington in 1898. Even European statesmen who previously may not have been particularly impressed by the military potential of the Yankee nation now had been served notice that the United States would defend its international interests, if need be with armed force. Attentive Europeans could hardly fail to register that Roosevelt was now determined to put a share of the "white man's burden" on the United States and to pursue his foreign policy goals with a "Big Stick" policy, if necessary.

When Roosevelt showed an interest in negotiating arbitration treaties with the great powers, the Emperor gave him the cold shoulder and refused to conclude such an agreement, although it would have expressed little more than the good will that presumably existed between the two nations. In Latin America, nothing was done to avoid a direct conflict with the United States; prior experiences in the region apparently did not serve as a lesson. That the German government had no wish to appreciate the sufficiently blunt message of the "Roosevelt Corollary" to the Monroe Doctrine became evident, among other things, in Berlin's Mexican policy following the downfall of Porfirio Díaz. It must be considered a serious misjudgment on the part of the German government not to have realized just how much the situation had changed. Long before the outbreak of the World War, at the latest during the presidency of Theodore Roosevelt, the United States had entered the arena of international politics, informing the world at large that henceforth the country would not remain a passive observer during serious conflicts. Those in Germany who arrived at a more realistic appraisal of America's power and therefore advocated a policy of understanding toward Washington found little resonance at the Imperial court and in influential German governmental circles. It was unfortunate for Germany that its two representatives in Washington prior to the war, Hermann Speck Baron von Sternburg and Johann Heinrich Count von Bernstorff, who were both very popular in the United States and thus well suited to prepare the way for establishing friendly relations between the two countries, did not command much influence in Berlin and hence were at the mercy of the inflammatory tirades and libel campaigns of the Pan-Germans and their following.

Although in the decade before the war, the United States visibly participated as a great power in international politics and firmly stood up for its interests, it would be misleading to interpret the American stance from the present perspective of U.S. global power. The foreign policy of Woodrow Wilson cannot be understood or evaluated with the criteria of our time. America, having just left behind the relative political isolation of the nineteenth century, did not consider war as an integral part of foreign policy as lightly as was common in the capitals of the Old World. On the contrary, at least as far as the foreign policy of the United States is concerned, the prewar era in retrospect appears as the last period of a different America, of an America that only later, through participation in two world wars and through its own military adventures in Asia, fundamentally changed its political character.

The present study is clearly a slice of diplomatic history and cannot be the long-overdue biography of the controversial German diplomat. Any attempt to write Bernstorff's biography would be severely impeded by the fact that the Ambassador's personal papers, reportedly destroyed during the Second World War, have not been found.[10] Thus, only the most important stations of an eventful life can be briefly summarized here. Sensational reports about the private life of Bernstorff appearing in the press after he left the United States and used by his political enemies during the Weimar Republic are not treated because such matters did not influence his diplomatic efforts in Washington or his standing in the German Foreign Office.

Johann Heinrich Andreas Hermann Albrecht Count von Bernstorff was born in London on November 14, 1862. His father was Albrecht Count von Bernstorff, Ambassador to the Court of St. James's and former Royal Prussian Foreign Minister.[11] The boy spent the first ten years of his life in the British capital. English became his second mother tongue, and England in many ways formed the man whose entire political life was to become based on the premise that Germany's interests were best served by a policy of peace and understanding toward the West.[12] In 1873 he lost his father; his mother[13] returned to the northern German family estate, Stintenburg, in the Schaalsee, and after brief stays in Sulza, Thuringia, and at the Vitzthum Gymnasium in Dresden, he was finally sent to the Lauenburgische Gelehrtenschule in Ratzeburg. His accomplishments in school were average to good, and his "Ordnungsliebe" (love for order) was judged by his teachers as "not always satisfactory"; in contrast, in history, he was the only pupil in his graduating class to receive the grade "very good."[14] Although young Bernstorff would have liked to prepare for a diplomatic career and thus to follow in his father's footsteps, his family at the time decided against such plans because a family quarrel with the Bismarcks made his prospects in the foreign service look rather dim.[15] Instead, he entered the First Guard Field Artillery Regiment in Berlin, although he had no doubt that he was "not cut out to be a soldier." He was only "grudgingly" in the military and later in his memoirs had little to say about the eight years spent there. Nevertheless his time in the military apparently helped to introduce him to the social circles at the Court and to the Berlin salons. A passionate Wagnerian, he frequently visited the home of Mathilde Wesendonk, whose American niece, Jeanne Luckemeyer, descendant of a Krefeld merchant family, he married in 1887.[16] A year later, the restored favor of Herbert von Bismarck made it possible for the young lieutenant to be stationed with the embassy in Constantinople.[17]

The German Ambassador at the Bosporus was Joseph von Radowitz, who had known Bernstorff's parents well, but was unable to appreciably further the young Attaché's career, because by this time he himself had fallen out of favor in Berlin. Karl Max Prince von Lichnowsky, later controversial Ambassador in London, was the Second Secretary at the Embassy. The collaboration between Lichnowsky and Bernstorff in Constantinople was to become the foundation for a life-long friendship.[18] Toward the end of 1890, Bernstorff was transferred to the Foreign Office in Berlin in order to take the two-year course prior to the diplomatic examination, which he passed in February 1892 with the grade of "Good." Subsequently, he was sent as Legation Secretary to Belgrade, where Ludwig Baron von Waecker-Gotter served as Envoy. The Guard Officer, spoiled by the lively cultural and social life of Berlin and Constantinople, saw Belgrade as "only a village," and, apart from his friendship with Johann Margrave von Pallavicini, very little of his experience in Belgrade later appeared memorable to Bernstorff.[19]

From June 1894 until December 1895, Bernstorff was Legation Secretary in Dresden. "There were no politics at all in Dresden," Bernstorff later wrote, and he was delighted when he was transferred to the embassy in Petersburg as Second Secretary. Friedrich von Holstein had selected him to smooth over the personal wranglings between the Ambassador, Hugo Prince Radolin, and the highest Russian court circles. As it was, Bernstorff apparently was not blessed with success on this less than enviable assignment, and such tensions developed between him and Radolin that the Ambassador requested Berlin to recall his Secretary.[20]

In October, 1897, Bernstorff was named Legation Secretary at the Prussian legation in Munich. The five years spent with Ambassador Anton Count von Monts were not years of gripping political activity but in many respects they formed the young diplomat intellectually. Concerts, political cabarets, and poetic readings were the order of the day, and Bernstorff's preference for *Jugendstil* art dates from this time. Among the numerous personalities of culture and society whom he met in Munich was also the well-known political economist, Lujo Brentano. Bernstorff visited him often, and his later economic views decidedly show the influence of the liberal scholar.[21] Also during this time in Munich, Countess Bernstorff became interested in the teachings of Buddhism; here she began her collection of Asiatic art.[22]

Bernstorff received his first significant post in the autumn of 1902, when he was named Counselor of the Embassy in London. The Imperial Ambassador in London was Paul Count von Wolff-Metternich zur Gracht, who from 1901 to 1912 left no stone unturned to reach an agreement between Germany and Great Britain. It is difficult to avoid comparing Metternich's frustrated attempts in London with Bernstorff's fruitless efforts in Washington. Both diplomats only reaped disdain from circles around the German navy, who, in the final analysis, caused the failure of all conciliatory policy. Although his predecessor, Hermann Baron von Eckardstein, stayed on in London and intrigued against him,[23] the Counselor evidently succeeded in shoring up his position[24] and was able to carry out his assignment calling for a public relations campaign in behalf of Germany's interests.[25] The eloquent Bernstorff almost perfectly complemented the taciturn and reserved Metternich, who preferred a more withdrawn life and made no secret of his distaste for public appearances and social gatherings.[26]

Bernhard Prince von Bülow was so impressed by the performance of his young protégé in London that he helped him to obtain his first top post in the spring of 1906.[27] Bernstorff was named Consul General in Cairo, a sort of last trial before becoming an ambassador. His time in Cairo, however, was rather uneventful, and, concerning politics, Bernstorff later remembered that "it was only a question of trying to diminish British mistrust toward us." With the Turks, who at that point already looked to the German Emperor as a protector of their interests he had no problems; with the wary British he was able to reach a modus vivendi.[28] The Bernstorffs appreciated the pleasant climate of North Africa and enjoyed the extended summer vacations granted to heads of missions. His favorable prospects for further promotion also allowed Bernstorff to seek a more permanent refuge from the wandering life of a diplomat, and, in the summer of 1907, the family moved to the *Grillenhaus* (Cricket House) in Starnberg, furnished for them by a well-known Munich antique dealer.[29]

Bernstorff's appointment as Imperial Ambassador to Washington followed in the autumn of 1908.[30] His opponents in Berlin, who had successfully blocked him from becoming Under Secretary at the Foreign Office, found themselves outmaneuvered this time.[31] However, it is doubtful whether, after Sternburg's death, Berlin had a more qualified diplomat at its disposal for the post in Washington[32]—provided that Germany's assurances of wanting to maintain good relations with the United States were meant in earnest. At the last moment, Holstein attempted to sway Bülow against Bernstorff,[33] but the diplomat was welcomed in Washington as German Ambassador.[34]

Undoubtedly Bernstorff's career reached its zenith in Washington, but the battle for America's neutrality between 1914 and 1917, so thoroughly sabotaged by Berlin, broke his willpower and optimism so that after his return to Europe he increasingly avoided the spotlight of public politics. If before 1914 the Liberals had looked upon him as a possible Foreign Secretary or even Chancellor,[35] he later lacked the necessary drive to play for high political stakes. The humiliating wait for an audience with Wilhelm II in the spring of 1917[36] could only confirm to him what he had probably suspected for some time, namely that his ceaseless efforts in America were not acknowledged or appreciated in Berlin and that he had fallen into disfavor at the court.[37] Nevertheless, he agreed to accept another position abroad[38] and, in the final year of war, took over the difficult post of Ambassador in Constantinople.[39]

In October 1918, at the same time when some military leaders in Germany seriously considered unleashing a final "desperate battle" and "in case of further retreat turning France and Belgium into a field of rubble,"[40] some people in Berlin remembered the Ambassador and asked him to succeed Paul von Hintze as Foreign Secretary.[41]

Bernstorff refused the offer, because, although he was convinced that the monarchy should be preserved, he also knew that a government headed by Wilhelm would not be able to initiate peace nego-

*Count and Countess Bernstorff, ca. 1908
(reproduced by permission of Oda Rolleri)*

tiations with Washington.⁴² Since he was one of the few Germans with first-hand knowledge of Woodrow Wilson, he was nevertheless ordered to Berlin on October 26, "to be on hand for negotiations with President Wilson, which were hoped for in Berlin."⁴³ That same night Bernstorff left the Turkish capital aboard a submarine accompanied by his "best colleague," the Legation Secretary, Hans Heinrich Dieckhoff, and thus escaped capture by the British.⁴⁴ Arriving in Berlin on October 31, he immediately conferred with the new Imperial Chancellor, Max Prince von Baden, who in his opinion "one year earlier would have been the right man to bring about a tolerable peace." Once more Bernstorff's old temperament, replaced by apathy since February 1917, came to the fore. In response to a statement of Prince Max that, as a German Prince, he could not cause the German Emperor to step down, Bernstorff exploded: "Then you should not have become Chancellor."⁴⁵ Bernstorff, of course, was eager to prevent the impending revolution, but he was also in full agreement with Philipp Scheidemann—influential Social Democratic Member of the Reichstag, and, since October 1918, Minister without portfolio—that this could be done only if the Emperor abdicated. It was to this end that he tried to persuade Prince Max to take the wheel of state as regent (Reichsverweser).⁴⁶

The pending negotiations with the Allies again motivated the Ambassador to enter the fray. Rejecting the idea of a delegation, he offered to face the Allies alone.[47] He was overruled, and after Reichspräsident Friedrich Ebert tried to entrust him with the leadership of the German delegation,[48] Bernstorff instead, as a sort of counterpart to his cousin, the Foreign Minister Ulrich Count von Brockdorff-Rantzau, became chief of the Preparatory Commission for the Peace Negotiations.[49]

Expectedly, the collaboration between the two differently inclined diplomats turned out to be somewhat less than fruitful. The root of the problem was that Bernstorff, at least for a time, agreed with Matthias Erzberger, the powerful Center politician who since October 1918 had served as Parliamentary Secretary, that the Allied conditions would have to be accepted. The conservative Foreign Minister, suffering from a persecution complex, suspected his cousin of intriguing with Erzberger against him during his absence from Berlin.[50]

Bernstorff not only was among those who tried to reach a workable compromise by advocating acceptance of the peace treaty, but in the aftermath of Versailles he took a public stand on the side of the much derided "Erfüllungspolitiker" (politicians fulfilling or giving in). Before the German Democratic Party (Deutsche Demokratische Partei, DDP), which he had helped to organize, he declared on July 20, 1919:

> We cannot disregard the fact that world politics as it was practiced before the war is now impossible. The peace treaty has been signed by the Government under protest, because it is intolerable and unfulfillable. This protest is valid. However, the loyalty and honesty that henceforth should be the watchword of German foreign policy demand that we honestly fulfill the treaty to the best of our ability.... We do not want to and indeed cannot wage a war of revenge. In place of power and revenge we shall place real striving for justice and morality. This path leads to the League of Nations and to a revision of the peace treaty by peaceful diplomatic means.[51]

As a staunch supporter of the Republic, Bernstorff decided to run for office and represent his party in Parliament.[52] His first attempt in the electoral district of Düsseldorf-West proved a failure, but, with the support of the well-known theologian and Democrat, Otto

Baumgarten, he was nominated in electoral district thirteen in Schleswig-Holstein.[53] Here he won the election and represented his party in the Reichstag from 1921 to 1928.[54]

On the international level, Bernstorff limited his efforts to the League of Nations, above all as cofounder of the German Association for the League of Nations.[55] He served the association as president for ten years and for a time also was president of the World Federation of Associations for the League of Nations. In sharp contrast to his cousin, Brockdorff-Rantzau, he became one of the main advocates for the League of Nations in Germany. Indeed, his political concepts were rather ahead of their time: "As far as the United States of Europe is concerned, you know of course that I defend the idea. . . . Larger areas without customs-barriers simply *must* be created. And if the League of Nations in Geneva will transform itself into the United States of Europe, À qui la faute? I am thinking of Europe, Asia, and America united into three Leagues of Nations which in turn will come together."[56] From 1926 until 1933, he led the German delegation to the Preparatory Conference for Disarmament in Geneva. Yet, in retrospect, it is evident that time was working against the diplomat, who was convinced that a policy based on peace and international understanding would lead to a solution of Germany's problems.

The foes of the young Republic murdered the gifted industrialist-politician Walther Rathenau, who had served the Empire and the Republic in crucial times and whom Bernstorff held in high esteem. The same radical elements assassinated Matthias Erzberger, whose views he had often shared during the difficult negotiations at Versailles. His friend and close adviser Maximilian Harden, editor of the critical journal *Die Zukunft*, was severely beaten in an attack by a gang of rightist rowdies. Since Bernstorff was also maligned as an "Erfüllungspolitiker," spoke out in favor of Jewish interests, and was viewed as a traitor by the radical right because of his activities in Washington,[57] he, too, had now to live in fear for his life.[58] At Rathenau's death he said: "Now the avalanche will begin to roll."[59] Regrettably the few scattered notes and letters of Bernstorff that have been preserved contain no clues as to what he felt when he saw the irresponsible Military Attaché of his Washington time, Franz von Papen, rise to power in the new German state. Bernstorff indeed had lost his place in Germany; his services were no longer needed. In silent defeat, he went into exile in Geneva in 1933 and thus escaped the almost certain persecution that would have been in store for him in Hitler's Third Reich. He was never to return to Germany.

His second volume of memoirs had to be published in Switzerland. The official verdict of the German historical profession appeared in the *Jahresberichte für Deutsche Geschichte* of 1936: "In its political views, however, the book, in which the author takes a position in sharp opposition to the Third Reich, must be absolutely rejected."[60] In an unusual lapse of tact, the prestigious *Historische Zeitschrift* in 1938 printed a review of Bernstorff's memoirs written by the ambitious National Socialist historian, Professor Erwin Hölzle. In the year of the Reichskristallnacht, Hölzle wrote:

> But Count B. has learned nothing. Even today he thinks, as he did in his youthful days, that Germany belongs to Western Europe and should seek a Western orientation—, he knows nothing of the Empire of the Center of Europe, that from war and decline has just had to return to its nature-given destiny (Aufgabe). Even today he still has hopes for the League of Nations and disarmament, still sees anti-Semitism as a "mark of disgrace," the November-revolt as "not finished," and he awaits the "next German republic." A pure soul from the beginning, he believes that he must not go through purgatory with his nation. Thus the "confession" of the book is closely related to an unedifying emigrant spirit and only suited to cast further shadows on the personality of Count B. . . . It is incomprehensible why B. in the middle of the war had to engage himself for the Jews in Turkey and promote a "Jewish National Home" in Palestine, most likely supported in this by Emil Ludwig, Ullstein, and Georg Bernhard. With Erzberger too, B. corresponded assiduously, especially during the days of Brest Litovsk about a democratic peace with Russia as a preparation for a general peace that would lead to democracy and international understanding.[61]

It was left to a foreigner, the well-known Harvard historian William L. Langer, to conclude: "This book will help, if necessary, to recall to the world the upright efforts of a man, a true patriot and statesman of vision."[62]

On October 6, 1939, a lonely Bernstorff died in Geneva. Notably, obituaries appeared only in foreign newspapers.[63] Only ten years later, and after the collapse of the Third Reich, the German silence

*Count and Countess Bernstorff, 1930s
(reproduced by permission of Oda Rolleri)*

was broken by an article in the *Frankfurter Rundschau*. On October 28, 1949, Bernstorff's loyal friend, Georg Ahrens, told German readers:

> Ten years ago Johann Heinrich Count von Bernstorff died in exile in Geneva, driven from his German home by threats against his life and property. He was one of the most eminent diplomats of the era of Wilhelm II and the German Republic. No *in memoriam* was heard then in his fatherland for him, the Democrat.... The tragedy of futility surrounds the efforts of this personality, who thus has become the prototype of the futile battle of German democracy in the past. The very tragedy, however, commits us to keep alive in our days the memory of the diplomat of great stature, as an example for our coming generation of diplomats whom one may wish more fortune.[64]

O N E

THE PREWAR YEARS IN WASHINGTON

When the forty-six-year-old Count Bernstorff and his family left Cherbourg for New York in December 1908, much German public opinion was still characterized by an optimistic outlook toward the future. Indeed, in some quarters the optimism, perhaps mixed with a little naiveté, was so overwhelming that the local newspaper in the Ambassador's home region of Lauenburg forecast the dawn of a new era with a German-American alliance "as a counterbalance to the English-French-Russian alliance." The paper expressed the hope that Bernstorff would "succeed in persuading the American government of the advantage of an alliance with Germany."[1] Theodore Roosevelt, at this point already at the end of his term of office, seemed to share these hopes when he wrote to Wilhelm II: "The combination of your personality and your position render you the most influential and powerful of living men; and your hearty good will to America has been of real moment to my fellow countrymen."[2]

In fact, the Imperial Ambassador, Hermann Freiherr Speck von Sternburg, who had died in Germany in August 1908 and whom Bernstorff was succeeding in Washington, had been on extraordinarily friendly terms with the White House. Except for a few unpleasant memories, such as perhaps Venezuela and Manila, no particularly serious conflicts disturbed the relations between the two countries when Bernstorff took over the embassy in December 1908. On the other hand, there are no documents which would even suggest the likelihood of a German-American alliance, particularly as a countermeasure against the English-French-Russian connection. To the contrary, the sources rather give the impression of a relationship which on the whole seemed to go smoothly but under the surface concealed a number of opposing interests, some of which were still unresolved by 1914.[3]

Theodore Roosevelt was still in office when Bernstorff paid his first visit to the White House on New Year's Eve 1908. For more than an hour they conversed in the President's private study, and the Ambassador presented a gift from Wilhelm II, a book about the adventures of German cavalry troops in Southwest Africa, along with a personal letter.[4] Things were off to a good start for the new Ambassador, and it was seen as positive that Countess Bernstorff was a native American and that the years of his youth spent in England seemed to have shaped him.[5] Bernstorff had time to consolidate his position, since there appeared to be no urgent business at hand, and the new American President, William Howard Taft, was not to take office until March 4, 1909. At a reception of the New York Chamber of Commerce, he met leading men from the business world, and Herman Ridder of the *New Yorker Staats-Zeitung* organized a banquet in his honor. On both occasions, Bernstorff gave speeches which were well received. He himself was quite pleased with his reception in the United States. His public appearances were cheered, and, after a two-month stay, he had "not yet found an unfriendly word about Germany in the newspapers here."[6]

With respect to the relationship between Bernstorff and Roosevelt, it is understandable that any important matters which had been left unfinished by Sternburg were not brought up during the few weeks before March 4. In the course of his presumably rather superficial conversations with the retiring American President, Bernstorff gained the impression that Roosevelt "was an admirer of the German people" and regarded the German Empire "as the first nation of the Old World."[7]

COUNT BERNSTORFF AND AMERICAN PUBLIC OPINION, 1908–1914

If such a friendly spirit indeed prevailed in Washington, it is all the more surprising that the Ambassador soon was engaged in a not always successful public relations campaign. In fact, Bernstorff had a specific assignment in this respect: "When I was appointed Ambassador to Washington, my main instructions from the Emperor and the Chancellor were to inform the American public about the peaceful and friendly intentions of German foreign policy."[8] From the records of the German Foreign Office, it is evident that "the use of official funds for press purposes" had been a common practice for years. Thus, since at least 1905, 20,000 marks per annum had been granted to the Imperial Embassy in Washington for such purposes, and Bernstorff found it only appropriate that the same sum should be at his disposal. As early as April 1909, he also recommended improving contacts with the American press through an intermediary, provided this could be done without public knowledge.[9]

In 1909, the journalist J. D. Whelpley took care of contacts and was paid 17,000 marks by the German Embassy for his services that year. Another sum of about 3,000 marks went to Dr. A. D. Jacobson.[10] These gentlemen planted articles in the American press which Bernstorff for various reasons deemed favorable to Germany, but which he had not written himself. Thus, for instance, an anonymous piece made available to the Ambassador by the *Reichsmarineamt* appeared at his instigation in the *North American Review* in August 1909. Supposedly it was written by a former German naval officer who, now that he was no longer in the military service, wanted to reveal the truth. This story, which in 1909 Bernstorff was still willing to publish under his own name,[11] maintained, among other things, that it had not been the German naval construction policy which prompted Britain to reinforce its fleet but that, on the contrary, "in view of the comparative strength of both sides, the tense atmosphere in England and the lessons of English politics over the last three centuries . . . it was actually Germany that [was] threatened."[12] From his readiness to adopt such statements, one might be led to conclude that Bernstorff was in full agreement with the influential, politically conservative groups in Germany and enjoyed their support. In reality, however, matters were quite different.

Additional, less desired assistance came to the Ambassador directly from Germany. In June 1909, the Freiburg political economist Gerhart von Schulze-Gaevernitz had turned to Bülow with a plan to bring Bernstorff together with the Germanophile Edward E. Rumely. According to the German scholar, Rumely was to join forces with Bernstorff and consider "the question of a better representation of German points of view in the American press."[13] Schulze-Gaevernitz, however, was not satisfied with giving well-meant advice and, without the Ambassador's knowledge, he wrote a circular letter, which he dispatched to a number of German-Americans. The letter caused such a stir that Bernstorff thought it wise to ask the Imperial Chancellor, Theobald von Bethmann Holl-

The Prewar Years

weg, to see to it that further such inappropriate circulars would not appear, because "the press here . . . during the last years has not given us any reason for complaint."[14] Actually, Bernstorff had recognized the danger of interference from outsiders like Schulze-Gaevernitz very early and had written to the Imperial Chancellor in March 1909: "The prevailing mood here is thoroughly favorable and there is no need for artificial assistance, especially not from political *franctireurs* who . . . deem it necessary to indulge here publicly in tasteless praise of conditions in Germany."[15] Although through Whelpley's articles the Ambassador launched ideas into the American press that appeared justifiable to him, he became very disturbed when unauthorized persons tried to take the publicity campaign in the United States into their own hands. He was aware that the political institutions of Britain and America "were founded on the same democratic basis" and that public opinion in both countries was acknowledged as a highly important factor.[16] His recognition that public opinion in America was not to be treated arbitrarily and condescendingly led to repeated bitter conflict with certain circles in Germany during the peaceful years of the prewar period. Difficulties with some German-Americans were added during the war years. Bernstorff not only took a stand against some of the reports reaching America from the Old World, he also actively gave his support to those interests in Germany whose liberal-democratic sentiments he shared. Clashes with the vociferous right in Germany were therefore bound to develop sooner or later.

In fact, Bernstorff did not have to wait long for an argument. On November 6, 1909, he spoke before the American Academy of Political and Social Sciences in Philadelphia on "Germany as a World Power." An audience of more than a thousand applauded his address, and a lively discussion developed afterwards. The following day many Americans read in their Sunday papers Bernstorff's words:

> In speaking of Germany as a World Power I am obliged to begin by saying that our World Policy has often been intentionally or unintentionally misrepresented abroad and this particularly because foreign authors and journalists have taken or pretended to take seriously the flights of fancy of the so-called Pangermanists [*sic*], who are of no importance at all. They have hardly any representatives in our Parliament and not the slightest in-

fluence on the Government. By the latter the Pangermanists [sic] are even considered a very undesirable element of German journalism, because they stir up ill feeling abroad against Germany by putting forth questions and aims which are quite beyond the scope of practical politics."[17]

While in their Sunday and Monday editions American newspapers reported "a tone of sincerity in the remarks" and "much more than polite conventionality in the cordial expressions,"[18] the *Rheinisch Westfälische Zeitung* claimed that Bernstorff, in order to gain approval, had delivered "an unintelligible as well as undignified speech," and that to all appearances he had completely forgotten why he was actually in the United States, namely in order "to represent German interests in a dignified manner and to increase Germany's power." He might perhaps be the right representative for a "social-democratic liberal government," but he was hardly suitable as Ambassador for the Germany of Wilhelm II.[19]

Understandably, the reaction of the Pan-Germans, whom Bernstorff had especially addressed in his speech, was hardly friendly. Heinrich Class, the leader of the Pan-Germans, who states in his memoirs that at the latest by April 1909, he had "the reins absolutely in his hands" in the Pan-German Association,[20] had the author and fellow Pan-German, Count Ernst zu Reventlow, obtain an appointment for him with the Foreign Secretary Wilhelm von Schoen on November 26, 1909, in order to file his complaint. Schoen appeased the angry Pan-German and declared that he had already expressed his disapproval in a cablegram to Bernstorff. The visit was marked by such harmony that the Foreign Secretary went so far as to give Class the original copies of his telegram to the Ambassador in Washington and of an order to all German representatives abroad. It said that German diplomats should exercise more caution when discussing matters of domestic policy with foreigners. Class later could proudly report that the chief of the Foreign Office had told him that he always replied to people who insulted the Pan-Germans by saying: "Be glad that we have the Pan-Germans! Without them we would be even deeper in the morass!"[21] On November 27 the directors of the Pan-German Association met in order to deal with the remarks of the unpopular Ambassador. Heinrich Class presented them with Schoen's telegram to Bernstorff and the order to the diplomatic representatives. Those assembled were satisfied with the content of the documents but nevertheless deemed it appropriate to write a biting reply to Bernstorff, which was given to the press for publication.[22]

Bernstorff thus had his first scandal during his period of office in America, and quite a few Germans may have doubted whether this protégé of Bülow really was the best choice to serve as Germany's representative in Washington.[23] It would be of interest to know more about the Emperor's reaction to Bernstorff's speech in Philadelphia. Bernstorff, who had little sympathy for the ultranationalistic elements in Germany, especially those of the Pan-German Association, could only interpret the Emperor's instructions to inform America about the peaceful intentions of German politics to mean that he should steadfastly oppose Pan-German propaganda in the United States. Whether the Emperor had indeed intended his instructions to be so interpreted cannot be ascertained in retrospect; in any case, he decorated his Ambassador with the "Roter Adler Orden II. mit Eichenlaub" just one month after the clash with the Pan-Germans. The American press was led to conclude from this that Wilhelm had not only approved of Bernstorff's words, but that he also wanted the conferral of the medal to be understood as his answer to the attacks of the German press.[24] This assumption is reinforced by the "ja" which the Emperor personally wrote in the margin of Bernstorff's report of December 30, 1909, to Bethmann Hollweg: "Even the *New York Daily Tribune*, which is known to be highly anglophile, writes about the decoration which was bestowed upon me.... It is pointed out that my words obviously gave expression to the personal views of His Majesty the Emperor."[25]

While Bernstorff's denunciation of the Pan-Germans may have been motivated at least partly by personal antipathy, he undoubtedly regarded his statements in Philadelphia referring to Germany's foreign policy as fully justifiable in terms of realpolitik. Before the American political and social scientists Bernstorff, who in Germany had known and exchanged views with the liberal political economist, Lujo Brentano,[26] had declared:

> I would like to explain to you ... that the world policy of the German Empire is purely commercial and without territorial ambitions or deep-seated designs against other states and the existing balance of power in the world. We do not strive to acquire further colonies ... and are quite content to develop the resources of those colonies we have.... we do not desire to

"rule the waves," and the development of our navy need therefore not be regarded with suspicion by anybody. . . . Colonies do not increase the power of the mother country because they are its possessions, nor yet because a few millions of its emigrants with their descendants live in them, but because by the trade with them the wealth and with it the defensive strength of the mother country are increased. Colonies which do not produce that result are of little value; and countries which possess this importance for a nation, even though they are not its colonies, are in this decisive point a substitute for colonial possessions in the ordinary sense. Moreover in our days we notice symptoms in all great colonies and dependencies which seem to prove that the era of colonial expansion is past. In nearly all colonies and dependencies we notice a growing spirit of independence which must some day lead from self-government to political independence. [!] . . . In these modern days there is no better way to bring about amity between nations than to bind them by commercial ties which shall be to the advantage of both.[27]

Such statements had a calming effect in America but certainly were not compatible with the opinions of those back home who still indulged in dreams of a far-flung German colonial empire and the opening of ever new areas for settlement. It is not surprising that such a contrast of opinion should be a permanent source of conflict during Bernstorff's years in Washington.

While Bernstorff went out of his way during the prewar years to seek America's friendship or at least understanding, the general climate of relations between the two nations was of course not solely determined by the efforts of the Ambassador. Friedrich von Bernhardi's[28] *Deutschland und der nächste Krieg* was published in Berlin in 1912. Americans could read that the author wished to "examine for their true moral content the peace movements which seem to dominate our time and which threaten to also poison the soul of the German people," and that he wanted to demonstrate "that war is not only a necessary element in the life of nations but also an indispensable factor of culture, yes, indeed the highest expression of strength and life in truly civilized nations."[29] Surely, pronouncements of such nature were not suited to increase the understanding of the German viewpoint abroad. Moreover, Bernhardi's thoughts did not seem to be just the expression of one individual outside the mainstream of German public opinion.³⁰ On the contrary, it was easy to establish that numerous parallels could be drawn with other contemporary German writings.³¹

Statements of this kind were particularly embarrassing when they surfaced abroad as the Emperor's very own words. In the late autumn of 1908, Wilhelm had granted the well-known American journalist William Bayard Hale an interview during which he allowed himself a number of slips of the tongue and which for that reason was not fit for publication abroad.³² Nonetheless the hot item had already made its way to Britain and North America, and all indications seemed to point toward a new *Daily Telegraph* Affair.³³ In this case it was only thanks to the decisive action taken by the Foreign Office that much greater damage could be prevented. The German Ambassador in London, Count Wolff-Metternich, and Bernstorff were instructed to forestall the publication under any circumstances, and the tactful understanding of Sir Edward Grey, Lord Charles Hardinge, and especially Theodore Roosevelt helped the dismayed Imperial diplomats avoid disaster at the last minute. While Wolff-Metternich, who could not fathom how "one could ever have considered publishing this article," intervened in Britain through Grey's mediation, the affair was not so easily settled in America, because several versions of the Hale article existed.³⁴ Nevertheless, after some debate Hale was persuaded to withdraw his article from publication in *Century Magazine*, and Roosevelt through personal pressure prevented the appearance of a second version which Hale had sent to the *New York Times*.³⁵

One is not surprised to learn that from the very beginning a considerable part of the Ambassador's propaganda effort concerned the German-Americans. The German immigrants had settled quite densely in certain regions. In several major cities ethnic groups were so strongly represented that their influence could not be overlooked. Bernstorff writes in his memoirs that the Empire expected too much of its emigrant sons in America, "for the Americans of German descent have preserved in their new homeland all the faults and good qualities of the German people." The Ambassador goes on to say that the German-Americans had "less political interest and understanding" than other Americans, but had been noted for "their respect for public order, their loyalty, and their diligence in their professions." In his view, because of this, the Germans in America did not gain the political power proportionate to their numbers.³⁶ Bernstorff may not have been entirely wrong in this appraisal, written right after the First World War, but it is a dangerous prejudice to consider as a homogenous whole an ethnic group which is comprised of people who emigrated at different times and from different areas. After all, a number of German-Americans had succeeded, at least on a local and regional level, in attaining influential positions.

During the war the relationship between the German diplomatic representatives and the German-Americans of course underwent changes, and frantic efforts were made to gain more recognition for the German point of view. Before the war Bernstorff had already correctly realized that on the whole it would indeed be best to simply write off the immigrants as a loss.[37] It is true that the Ambassador took pains to maintain social contacts with German associations in the country, but he refrained from any effort to activate politically those groups for German purposes. He thought that the most valuable contribution they could make to their country of origin was on the commercial level and that, for this purpose, it was important that they adapt as quickly as possible to life in America in order to participate in the country's socioeconomic development.[38] Besides, Bernstorff observed: "We must never forget that the Germans here are all American citizens.[39] This crucial fact is at the heart of the problem. If we would openly use the German-Americans for purely national purposes, this would certainly create discontent in the American government and among the other citizens of this country. The Germans here would then be looked upon as a foreign body in the country, and they would lose the political influence, which is useful for us."[40] As to the possibility of regarding the Germans in America as peaceful harbingers of German culture and of supporting them as such, the Ambassador soberly noted that the immigrants did not come into question "as representatives of German culture, because coming from the lower classes, they had not brought any culture with them."[41] On the whole, after more than five years in the United States, Bernstorff had to admit "that comparatively speaking our American policy had the least success on the cultural level." Quite correctly, he saw the main reason for this development in the closed character of the English-language community, but he also felt the influence of "French taste." Somewhat brashly, the Ambassador nevertheless pointed to "the German nation's universal historical duty to insure that the American culture of the future would not become exclusively Anglo-Saxon." In line with this, he suggested promoting the exchange of artists and writers in order to "create an appropriate regard for German culture—something to which it is by all means entitled as the first culture of the world."[42] The records contain no evidence whether suggestions of this nature found a significant echo in Germany prior to the war.[43]

Bernstorff personally did his best to represent Germany in America in every way possible, and on his trips through the country he tried to get to know influential representatives of American business and cultural life. The fact that during the prewar years he was awarded no fewer than ten honorary degrees by American universities may be seen as evidence of his considerable personal success. Among the universities that honored Bernstorff were internationally renowned institutions of higher learning such as Columbia University (1909), Brown University (1910), The Johns Hopkins University (1910), the University of Pennsylvania (1911), the University of Chicago (1911), and Princeton University (1913).

Before President Nicholas Murray Butler conferred the honorary doctorate of Columbia University upon the new Ambassador in 1909, Professor Harry Thurston Peck said: "To Americans the very name of Germany is redolent of a fine idealism. Germany has given to us freely of its art, its science, its literature and the inspiration of its constructive scholarship."[44] To the festive assembly at Brown University the next year Bernstorff spoke of the possibility of opening a new era of international understanding by exchanging students and professors more frequently.[45] In 1910, President Ira Remsen of The Johns Hopkins University wrote to Bernstorff in a private letter: "I have for some time been desirous that the Degree of Doctor of Laws in this University should be conferred upon Your Excellency, in recognition of the distinguished services which you have performed, and are performing, in bringing your nation and our own closer together. This feeling is enthusiastically shared by my colleagues."[46] Before the commencement assembly in Philadelphia in 1911 Bernstorff said: "Those German settlers and the many millions of others who came here in later days have since been Americanized and proved to be very good citizens. They now form a natural bond of an ever increasing friendship between Germany and the United States."[47] A year before the outbreak of the war, in June 1913, Bernstorff received his last academic honors in Princeton, New Jersey, and Dean Andrew F. West lauded the Ambassador: "In five years here he has quietly maintained and noticeably strengthened the many attachments which bind his land with ours, and by his modesty, courtesy and efficiency most worthily stands in his high place as an authoritative international messenger of peace and goodwill."[48]

The possibility of personally influencing public opinion in the United States was, however, by no means limited to academic festivities.[49] In America, well-known public figures, often including diplomatic representatives, are generally expected to make themselves available as speakers to all kinds of political and social organizations. It goes without saying that an ambassador cannot respond to every opportunity to appear in public which presents itself. Yet there are in the United States, as everywhere, interest groups which exercise a recognizable influence on the political trends of the nation and whose invitations are therefore treated with appropriate tact. Since America was "the motherland of the peace movement" and since for quite some time there had been several powerful peace societies in the country, it was difficult to decline offers from the pacifists.[50] Certainly, at public appearances an ambassador may only represent the standpoint of his government instead of voicing his own personal, perhaps divergent opinion, yet it is astonishing how little understanding the German Foreign Office showed of the American peace movement.

After the Ambassador had tried to outline the German viewpoint on arbitration and disarmament before delegates to the Second National Peace Congress in May 1909 in Chicago, he was repeatedly invited on similar occasions.[51] The Lake Mohonk Conference of International Arbitration, for instance, turned to him in 1909 and 1910. He refused the invitation in 1909 because he had already spoken on the subject in Chicago. In 1910 he checked with Berlin whether he should talk before the Mohonk Conference on the topic of the International Court of Justice in The Hague,[52] but Wilhelm Stemrich in the Foreign Office advised him that it was not yet appropriate to discuss the matter in public. In 1911, Berlin did not even wait until the Ambassador received the prospective invitations to the annual peace conventions. Instead, Foreign Secretary Alfred von Kiderlen-Wächter informed him in no uncertain terms in February, three months before the conventions, that attendance at the meetings of the pacifists was not in the interest of German policy.[53]

In order to secure goodwill even at the highest level, Bernstorff from the very beginning sought close contact with the American Presidents. Theodore Roosevelt avoided any disagreements during his last months in office. Questions that might have given rise to conflict were postponed for President Taft, and the conversations during the visits of the Ambassador to the White House were largely confined to general topics and the preparation of Roosevelt's trip to Africa in March 1909. With Roosevelt's successor, the Ambassador had a good relationship, and Bernstorff wrote that the new President "liked a jovial, casual tone and dealings." As William Howard Taft's personal guest, Bernstorff went to Cincinnati, the President's home town, and there participated with him in the local festivities. On another occasion, the American head of state honored the German diplomat by unexpectedly turning up at an embassy ball, even though, for reasons of protocol, he had not been invited.[54]

Bernstorff also soon was able to establish good connections with numerous leading families in the country. Even into the war years he kept in close contact with the banker James Speyer.[55] A personal friendship connected him with the American Warburgs, and he knew numerous industrial families in the Midwest, such as the McCormicks and the Armours. As we know from the Ambassador's memoirs, it became more and more difficult after the beginning of the war to maintain a great number of those valuable connections. In the end there were very few who stayed close to the man in whom they could not help but see the representative of Wilhelm II.

In short, during the prewar years the Ambassador cultivated numerous social friendships, entertained extensively, and his house soon became one of the top addresses in Washington society. Countess Bernstorff cherished the company of people, and from time to time the Ambassador's two adult children would also be in Washington. Beyond that, Bernstorff had acquired the habit of traveling to New York every week in order to foster important political and social contacts in the metropolis. During the hot summer months, many of the elite moved to the New England resorts, and there too the Bernstorffs quickly and without difficulty found their way to the top of the American oligarchy.

NEGOTIATIONS FOR AN ARBITRATION TREATY

On March 4, 1909, shortly after the Hale interview affair, Theodore Roosevelt handed over the helm of state to William Howard Taft. After that, Roosevelt set out on an extended trip to the tropics and

Europe, perhaps not to be in the way of his former Secretary of War during his first weeks in office, but more likely because the Roughrider in him really wanted to see Africa. With his departure and the taking over of the affairs of government by Taft and his cabinet, Bernstorff's diplomatic work could begin. Two weeks after Taft's inauguration, the Ambassador had his first long talk with Philander C. Knox, the new Secretary of State. Quite casually the American remarked that with the friendly relations between the United States and Germany he would have to negotiate with the Ambassador "probably for the most part only arrangements such as patent, trade and arbitration agreements."[56] Diplomatic records of the time show that Knox's optimism was not totally unjustified. Indeed, there were no or almost no unsolvable diplomatic differences between the two nations. Only after the battle of the Marne was it realized in some quarters that perhaps during the last prewar years and the first weeks of the war an opportunity had been missed which would not offer itself again under such favorable international conditions. It was the question of an arbitration treaty with the United States, seemingly mentioned only in passing by Knox, that in later years was often raised in connection with serious reproaches against the foreign policy of the German government during the prewar years. There seems little point here in investigating whether an arbitration treaty might have prevented Germany and America from becoming bitter enemies only a few years later. Instead it seems important to establish at least the official reasons[57] why Germany did not feel itself in a position to conclude an arbitration treaty with the United States, as many other countries had done before the war and did even as late as the fall of 1914. After all, the significance of an international treaty is to be found not only in its wording but also in the spirit in which negotiations leading to its signing are carried out and in the psychological effect on the relationship between the concerned nations.

When Bernstorff established his first contacts with the Taft administration, the question of an arbitration treaty was by no means a new issue. In order to put the precarious development of the German negotiations with America under Bernstorff into the proper light, it is necessary to briefly examine the historical background. In fact, President Roosevelt had offered Ambassador Speck von Sternburg a German-American arbitration treaty as early as the fall of 1904, after such a treaty had been concluded with Britain in the summer of that year. Sternburg immediately reported to Berlin, and

Chancellor von Bülow replied at once that the Emperor "is 'very glad' to take up the idea of an arbitration treaty."[58] On November 4, 1904, Sternburg handed the Emperor's answer to the American President. Roosevelt instructed his Secretary of State to begin immediately to negotiate the text of such a treaty with the German Ambassador. Secretary of State John Hay thought that the wording of the already existing British-French arbitration treaty could be used here too. At the end it should read: "To go into effect after ratification of Senate of United States." Sternburg wired Bülow that, with exception of the ratification provision, the text resembled the British-French arbitration treaty of October 14, 1903, and that Roosevelt would be happy to see the treaty signed soon.[59] On November 17, Sternburg telegraphed that at Hay's request the treaty should be valid for five years and that concurrently with the treaty a secret agreement should be signed which determined that the treaty only become effective after ratification by the Senate. On November 22, 1904, the treaty was signed.[60]

As it was, however, the Senate wished to make certain that its treaty ratification rights would also apply to the later individual compromises. It therefore refused to approve the arbitration treaties, including the agreement between Germany and the United States, without alterations.[61] Not until January 20, 1908, was the matter brought up again. Elihu Root, formerly Roosevelt's Secretary of War and now John Hay's successor in the State Department, wrote to Sternburg and suggested the adoption of the old treaty text of 1904 with a change in Paragraph II. De facto the new text said that every agreement resulting from the arbitration treaty in each individual case would have to be ratified by the Senate.[62] Thereby, it became questionable whether an arbitration treaty in this form still represented a valuable diplomatic instrument, and it is not surprising that Germany had the feeling that a practically useless treaty was being put together. The reaction from Berlin reflected this: first, the fact that under the general arbitration treaty a special treaty had to be agreed on in each individual case would be much more advantageous to America than to Germany, because under constitutional law the German government, as opposed to the U.S. Senate, would not regard these individual treaties as new international treaties; second, the condition that the Senate had to give its consent was "hardly desirable," since it was doubtful that it would accept arbitration court decisions which were not to the advantage of the United States.[63] Secretary of State Root, despite his difficulties with the Senate, exhibited more sensitivity for other political considerations which tended to play a role in treaty negotiations: "It is not so much the treaty itself but the public sentiment connected with it. After France and England have accepted, it would create much surprise and disappointment if Germany should stand aside." The President took such personal interest in the matter that he summoned the Ambassador for talks on April 3 and 4, 1908. Once again Roosevelt tried to explain to the German government that, from the international point of view, it would create an extremely unfavorable impression if Berlin did not consider itself in the position to accept a treaty which France and other powers had readily approved. Roosevelt went so far as to suggest to Sternburg that Germany could publicize a memorandum immediately after conclusion of the new treaty to the effect "that ... the treaty hardly represented more than the expression of good will, but that the German Government was of the opinion that even a treaty of this nature had its value." Sternburg obviously understood Roosevelt and cabled to Bülow: "President evidently attaches greatest importance to conclusion of the treaty with Germany ... and closed with the remark: 'I should regret to see Germany refusing such a treaty when England and France accept.' "[64] A few days later the Americans moved toward the German position by offering to change the text of Paragraph II in such a way that it would grant both parties to the agreement equal advantages in the acceptance of the special treaties. This was supposed to be attained by having the special treaties take effect only after an exchange of notes between Germany and the United States.[65]

Despite all of Sternburg's warnings, Berlin reacted most unfavorably to the American proposals. Goodwill, it was felt, could just as well be expressed by a simple exchange of notes. If that were not enough for the Americans, one could include in the arbitration treaty a reference to the competent authority of the Permanent Court of Arbitration to provide for cases where an agreement was not reached. This was suggested, even though it must have been known that the Senate would hardly approve. The responsible parties in Germany apparently did not consider that such suggestions could only serve to arouse new suspicion in Washington concerning the aims of German foreign policy. Or had Bülow decided now to count the United States among those "smaller" nations which, in the words of the editors of the *Grosse Politik*, one "would hope to handle diplomatically without difficulty"?[66]

Hermann Freiherr Speck von Sternburg, Bernstorff's predecessor as Ambassador to the United States (Library of Congress)

Root's reaction to the German suggestions accordingly turned out to be reserved, and once again the Secretary of State besought the German Ambassador to take the potential consequences of the German refusal fully into account. Sternburg wired back immediately and once more pointed out in detail the disadvantageous consequences for Berlin's foreign policy if Germany maintained a negative attitude.[67] Schoen's reply, however, only demonstrated a complete lack of understanding on the part of the Foreign Office for the American standpoint, and he insisted in a less than diplomatic tone on the alternative offered by the Germans.[68] Sternburg, whose position meanwhile had become less than enviable, continued his negotiations with Roosevelt and Root. However, as was to be expected, the German viewpoint did not find acceptance, and on May 7, 1908, Sternburg had to report to Schoen that Root had told him Germany should quite frankly declare that it did not wish a treaty, if that were the case. Moreover, Root had informed him, arbitration treaties had been concluded with eleven nations.[69] A week later, Roosevelt personally broke off the negotiations with Germany for an arbitration treaty.[70]

Thus came the sad ending of a long-drawn-out exchange of viewpoints. There is little doubt that an arbitration treaty, even in the last watered-down version, would have created a certain amount of goodwill, if only by the mere declaration of such goodwill in the text of the agreement.[71] For Ambassador Sternburg, these were the last important negotiations conducted in the United States. The man who had succeeded in winning Theodore Roosevelt's personal friendship was not able to convince Berlin of the importance of the concept of arbitration before he bade farewell to Washington in the early summer of 1908. Shortly before his departure, he called on the President once more, and the two men talked about the failure to conclude an arbitration treaty for whose conclusion they had worked. Roosevelt lamented "that a going together with Germany in all questions of significance had always been important to him. ... What would Congress and public opinion think of him if now, after the failure to conclude an arbitration treaty, he would try to go along with Germany on major world issues?"[72]

When Bernstorff succeeded Sternburg in December 1908, the Americans had by no means forgotten the matter. By the same token, the views in Berlin concerning an arbitration treaty with the United States did not seem to have changed significantly either. From the records, it is difficult to discern exactly what kind of instructions Bernstorff was given concerning this question. A cablegram of January 17, 1909, from the Ambassador, however, seems to indicate that he had at least been directed not to bring up the matter of an arbitration treaty on his own.[73] Although in 1908 the Foreign Office had worked out a memorandum which in fact recognized the advantages of an arbitration treaty between Germany and the United States,[74] a new means of procrastinating had been found in the revival of the so-called Georgia Case. When at the beginning of Taft's term of office in March 1909, Secretary of State Knox wanted to resume negotiations regarding the treaty, Bernstorff was not in possession of any positive instructions and could only point toward the difficulties encountered up to then which were still unresolved,[75] and to the pending Georgia Case.[76] Only one month later, the Foreign Office formulated its opinion much more precisely and indeed demanded settlement of the Georgia quarrel in favor of Germany as a precondition for the conclusion of an arbitration agreement.[77] Berlin had thus found a reason to keep Germany out of the group of signatories to the "goodwill" declarations which between 1908 and 1910 grew to no less than twenty-two nations.[78] In retrospect, the motives of the German government are not very convincing, especially since the arguments against a treaty in no way outweighed the obvious value of such manifestation of international goodwill. Instead, Bernstorff probably touched upon the heart of the matter when, shortly before Christmas 1909, he reported to the Foreign Office that Ambassador David Jayne Hill had told him that the Georgia Case and German "craftiness" had prevented the conclusion of an arbitration agreement for the time being.[79]

Germany continued to maintain its reserve. Bernstorff adhered to the official line and gave the Americans no reason for speculation that Berlin might deviate from its standpoint. The Ambassador did report that the arbitration agreements were brought up again and again at all possible occasions,[80] that they also played a part in President Taft's domestic politics, and that American public opinion would draw its own conclusions in case Germany rejected an agreement which had been signed by Britain and France.[81] But there is no indication that the Wilhelmstrasse felt in any way inclined to show the least willingness to meet the Americans halfway.[82] Nonetheless, Bernstorff thought the matter precarious enough to address a long personal message to the head of the Political Department in the Foreign Office, Wilhelm von Stumm, in February 1912, in which he tried to persuade Berlin that on the whole it would be advantageous to conclude a treaty with Washington. Once again the Ambassador declared that while the arbitration agreements with Britain and France were most likely without practical value, this was no reason "why we should not conclude a quite similar treaty with the United States since serious disadvantages would result for us if such treaty were not reached."⁸³ At the same time Bernstorff asked for new instructions which should be free of previous conditions. Germany would never be involved in a war with the United States anyway, he felt, and "other differences were bound to become better rather than worse through an arbitration treaty."⁸⁴

There is no new German proposal on record. Expectedly, President Woodrow Wilson and his new Secretary of State, the leading pacifist, William Jennings Bryan, took up the question of the arbitration treaties soon after they entered office. Late in January 1913, Bernstorff had to inform the Imperial Chancellor that the Senate Committee on Foreign Relations, in agreement with the President, had recommended ratification of the already signed arbitration agreements.⁸⁵ When in May 1914 the Ambassador telegraphed to Chancellor Bethmann Hollweg that Bryan had approached him again on the arbitration treaty, the curt and unmistakable reaction of the Emperor himself was: "We shall not acquiesce."⁸⁶

And so it remained. Bryan was able to sign the so-called Bryan Treaties with many countries in 1913 and 1914, but Germany remained aloof.⁸⁷ Again and again the German Ambassador was urged by the American government,⁸⁸ but Germany and Austria-Hungary did not want to have any part in the worldwide peace efforts of the United States.⁸⁹ Britain and France signed the convention as late as September 15, 1914, one and a half months after the European equilibrium had collapsed.⁹⁰ Undoubtedly, Germany had maneuvered itself outside the international community of nations and thereby confirmed an old American suspicion "that the German government was militaristic, hostile to democracy, and unfriendly to the United States."⁹¹ Bernstorff expresses himself very cautiously in his memoirs, when he sums up the results of the German refusal of an arbitration treaty with the United States before the war as follows: "The effect which our obstruction in this matter had on the feelings of the Americans is by no means to be underestimated. It contributed essentially toward convincing public opinion in the United States of Germany's supposed belligerent intentions."⁹²

GERMANY'S POLICY SOUTH OF THE RIO GRANDE

Besides Bernstorff's efforts to influence American public opinion and the attempt to conclude an arbitration treaty as an expression of goodwill, the question of Germany's policy toward America's neighbors to the south was perhaps one of the more important issues in the prewar German-American relationship, especially in regard to later developments in the World War. The foreign policy of the United States toward the Latin American nations essentially relied on the precedent of the doctrine that President James Monroe had proclaimed in 1823, according to which attempts by European powers to extend their influence in the Western Hemisphere were regarded as a threat to the security of the Union.[93] It may be presumed that the United States, at least since Theodore Roosevelt, thought it had to preserve and protect an actual self-interest in Latin America. Roosevelt was certainly aware of the growing imperialist competition of the European powers on the South American continent, and he looked with discomfort toward Germany, which among other things expressed its intentions by pushing the construction of a great navy. If Germany were considering an expansion of its sphere of power in the Americas, it would first have to defeat the United States, Roosevelt wrote to Sir Cecil Arthur Spring Rice as early as 1897.[94] On December 6, 1904, the President formulated the so-called Roosevelt Corollary before the American Congress: "Chronic wrongdoing, or an impotence which results in a general loosening of the ties of civilized society, may in America, as elsewhere, ultimately require intervention by some civilized nation, and in the Western Hemisphere the adherence of the United States to the Monroe Doctrine may force the United States, however reluctantly, in flagrant cases of such wrongdoing or impotence, to the exercise of an international police power."[95] With such an interpretation of American prerogatives and in view of the simultaneously growing interest in the Germans[96] overseas by openly imperialist currents in Germany, it is hardly surprising that it was particularly in Latin America where Berlin and Washington would collide.[97] America's pride was particularly vulnerable in all questions concerning Mexico, its direct neighbor to the south. Thus it was not without reason that Mexico especially should play a significant role in the German-American confrontation before and during the First World War.

Since 1877, Porfirio Díaz, a follower of Benito Juárez, had been in total control in Mexico. Through the influx of capital from abroad, especially from the United States,[98] the Mexican economy had received a considerable impetus under the brutal dictator, but at the same time exploitation of the country by foreign interests had increased considerably. Despite diplomatic support of the regime by President Taft, rapidly growing unrest among the underprivileged masses, especially among the peasants,[99] and the thriving agitation of revolutionary movements led by Pascual Orozco,[100] Francisco Villa, and Emiliano Zapata culminated in the overthrow of Porfirio Díaz.[101] His successor, elected by the people, was Francisco Indalecio Madero.[102] More conservative than revolutionary, he came from a wealthy family and had been trained in Paris and Berkeley. His brief period of office was ended abruptly less than two years later, when he was treacherously slain by Gen. Victoriano Huerta. With the help of the large landholders and foreign capital and with the questionable backing by the American Ambassador, Henry Lane Wilson, the General was able to seize power.[103] With the assistance of the Catholic church, landholders, and groups of foreign residents, the counterrevolution tried to establish itself,[104] but the social upheaval had gained enormous momentum, and the state of the country could only be described as civil war. Emiliano Zapata[105] led his guerrillas from Morelos against the usurper; Venustiano Carranza, Governor of Coahuila, organized the so-called Constitutionalists, who also maintained their own army. Francisco Villa returned from exile in the United States and gathered a force of adventurers and fortune hunters with whom he too fought against General Huerta, the new Caudillo.

This situation was aggravated by the fact that Taft, America's "lame duck" President, and Wilson, his successor (inaugurated only on March 4, 1913, and evidently an opponent of dollar diplomacy), could not bring themselves to adopt a clear position concerning the catastrophic conditions in the neighboring country.[106] An added problem was the attitude of a number of other nations, who showed no hesitation to stoke the fire in various ways. The foreign industrial investors in Mexico played no small part in these political activities.[107]

Bernstorff certainly exaggerated when he wrote in his memoirs that for Woodrow Wilson the relationship with Europe in general and with Germany in particular "became completely secondary"[108] in view of the Mexican crisis. Nevertheless, the American President, who steadfastly refused to recognize the Huerta government,[109] suddenly saw himself surrounded by enemies in his Mexican policy. Together with the British, who had very large investments in Mexico and through their envoy entertained friendly

*Count Bernstorff as Imperial Ambassador
(Library of Congress)*

relations with Huerta,[110] Wilson succeeded in achieving a modus vivendi. Because of the less than friendly Japanese-American relations, Japanese intentions gave Washington reason to be at least suspicious, especially since it was soon to become apparent that the Japanese were supplying Huerta with arms.[111] Germany, which had been trying for years to gain a larger share of military[112] and economic influence in Mexico, also wanted to participate in Mexican affairs and at least be considered an equal partner among the big nations concerned. As it turned out, however, the interested German parties in the long run were speculating in rather unprofitable stocks. In November 1913, Bernstorff reported to his Chancellor that in Latin America the European powers would have to be satisfied with the role of inactive spectators. If Wilson were to take up arms in Mexico, this would mean a considerable strengthening of the "imperialistic tendencies" in the United States. However, Bernstorff wrote, the "pure idealist," Secretary of State Bryan, was opposed to a possible American intervention in Mexico.[113]

Germany decided to support Huerta, and the Emperor expressed his opinion "There you are!" on the news "that Huerta was the only personality who could restore order." "Just what I intended," was Wilhelm's comment on the same report from London, which went on to say: "In Mexico it would not be a matter of creating a capable system of government but simply of finding an energetic personality who *like Porfirio Díaz, would be able to force his will on the half-savage* population, *three quarters of which are Indians. But Villa and Carranza are bandits from whom nothing is to be expected.*"[114]

The German shipping magnate, Albert Ballin, put those attitudes into practice and sent ammunition and guns for Huerta to Mexico. The *Ypiranga*, a steamer of the Hamburg-American Line (HAPAG), carried to Veracruz the weapons, which Ballin had earlier shipped from New York to Odessa and from there to Hamburg, in order to conceal the eventual port of destination.[115] The documents do not reveal with absolute certainty whether Arthur von Kemnitz, the responsible expert in the Foreign Office, who was worried "because of Germany's important economic interests in Mexico,"[116] had been completely informed about the ammunition shipments and the dates of their arrival in Mexico. The American Department of the Navy, which after the unnecessarily exaggerated flag incident felt inclined to settle a debt with the Mexicans,[117] learned about the planned landing of German arms and literally got President Wilson out of bed during the night of April 21, 1914, to prevent the unloading of the cargo. Admiral Frank F. Fletcher, who commanded the American warships in the Gulf of Mexico off the shores of Veracruz,[118] was directed by Washington at dawn on April 22 to have his sailors occupy the customs office at Veracruz and to prevent the landing of the *Ypiranga*'s cargo.[119] The German authorities reacted very quickly and placed the *Ypiranga*, which had been stopped by the American warship *Utah*, under the command of the cruiser *Dresden*, already in position off the coast of Mexico. Officially, the captain of the *Dresden* commandeered the *Ypiranga* for the removal of refugees and thereby saved the shipment of weapons from the impending American confiscation.[120] Although Bryan urged Bernstorff not to allow the arms to reach Huerta and even held out the prospect of American compensation to the German shipping company,[121] the captain of the *Dresden* dismissed the *Ypiranga* from Imperial service, leaving the steamer, now once again sailing under the flag of the Hamburg-American Line, to unload its arms cargo shortly thereafter in Puerto México.[122] President Wilson, who had thought that the German arms would be directed back to Hamburg and through Bernstorff had already officially thanked the German Government,[123] now assumed correctly that the Germans were not laying all their cards on the table. Bernstorff, who had been asked by Bryan for an explanation, also had not been sufficiently informed and, even after consulting with representatives of the Hamburg-American Line, was able to give the American government only the rather meager explanation that unloading the *Ypiranga*'s arms was the sole responsibility of HAPAG representatives in Mexico.[124]

The entire handling of the affair by the Foreign Office and the German Admiralty shows clearly that Berlin, at least temporarily, had opted for Huerta and, despite America's expressed interest and obvious distrust, could not be swayed from its position. The Foreign Office, which was in contact with the Hamburg-American Line, revealed that consideration for the political views of the United States, at least in Mexico, was not necessarily a determining factor for German actions. Thus it happened that, even before the outbreak of the World War, Count Bernstorff, who was the most important German diplomatic representative on the American continents, was maneuvered into a very unpleasant, if not to say somewhat discreditable position vis-à-vis the American government. In any case, such an inconsiderate attitude toward the American point of view, irrespective of one's estimation of its merits, was hardly apt to increase confidence in Bernstorff or to buttress the prestige of the German Empire in the White House and on Capitol Hill.

TWO

THE WAR YEARS, 1914–1917

Propaganda for Germany

Bernstorff was in Washington on June 28, 1914, when the Austro-Hungarian successor to the throne, Archduke Franz Ferdinand, and his wife were slain by Serbian assassins. No news or instructions about possible consequences reached Bernstorff from Berlin, and thus on July 7 he began his customary European vacation.¹ He sailed to Germany on the *Vaterland* in order to spend the summer weeks at St. Johann, his estate on Lake Starnberg. Shortly after his arrival in Starnberg, he learned of the death of his son-in-law, Raimund Count Pourtalès. Funeral services were scheduled to take place in Yvoire on the French side of Lake Geneva on July 28, the day that turned out to be the date of the Austro-Hungarian declaration of war against Serbia. Bernstorff and his son Günther attended the burial and only narrowly escaped capture by the French. When the mayor of Yvoire was about to arrest the German Ambassador and the young officer of the Guards, the two fled under the cover of darkness and in a motorboat crossed the lake to Vevey.²

Bernstorff was spending the evening of August 1 at St. Johann when the ominous sound of drums from the surrounding villages announced the general mobilization. The next day saw him hurrying off to Berlin on a military train. There he was to receive last-minute briefings on how the German government wanted him to deal with the new situation in Washington. According to his memoirs, he had "talks with the influential people, and the quintessence of these talks was to make the German standpoint clear to the government and the people of the United States." Opinion in Berlin had it that one would soon seek an understanding with London and that therefore a tough stand against Great Britain would not be appropriate. Russia, by contrast, according to the Berlin stance, was "the one who had started the war."³

At the Wilhelmstrasse, Bernstorff learned that the former chief of the German Colonial Office, Bernhard Dernburg, and Heinrich Albert of the Imperial Ministry of the Interior would be sent to Washington with him.[4] According to Bernstorff's memoirs, the activities of these two men, who officially came to America as a representative of the German Red Cross and as an envoy of the so-called Zentral-Einkaufs-Gesellschaft (Central Purchasing Company) respectively, were supposed to be limited to financial and business matters. The treasury bonds with which Dernburg wanted to float a loan in the United States in order to pay for Albert's purchases were—according to Bernstorff—not meant to finance German propaganda in America.[5] Unfortunately, the records of the German Foreign Office do not furnish any additional, more specific information concerning the Ambassador's instructions. Only the details concerning the financial transactions of Dernburg and Albert are documented rather extensively.

When Bernstorff arrived in New York on August 25, 1914, the German armies were on the advance everywhere on the western front. The American public, whose participation in the war during those first weeks was generally limited to reading newspaper reports, was still shocked by the turn of events in Europe. While in Germany patriotic frenzy was driven to new heights by glowing reports of victory and the German General Staff was carrying out the steps of the Moltke-Schlieffen Plan, which it had so often practiced on paper, in the United States the first sounds of a propaganda campaign were heard, and early attempts were made to win public favor. A generation of Americans who had strongly believed in the inevitability of progress was now, in August 1914, left with little but gratitude for the geographical distance from Europe and America's independence from treacherous alliances.[6] Most studies that have dealt with public opinion in the United States and with what is generally referred to as the American image of Germany[7] seem to indicate that American public attitude was less than favorably disposed toward what may have been seen as the German character. Americans had little or no understanding of the German political system, which appeared so totally different from the American ideal. To them, the German social structure often seemed "stuffy and title-ridden," and the German nation, with its military spirit, appeared "brutal and dangerous."[8]

To influence this people, to explain the official German standpoint and, above all, to find effective media to reach the average American would be difficult tasks. In the following sections we will examine what steps Bernstorff himself undertook to help improve Germany's image in the United States and what actions were taken during the years 1914 to 1917 in the area of public relations by the officials under his authority or by agents who were not attached to the embassy.

THE PRESS OFFICE IN NEW YORK

When Bernstorff arrived in New York at the end of August 1914, he found a publicity office already in operation. It had been set up by the second man in the German embassy, Botschaftsrat Dr. K. A. Haniel von Haimhausen, and was directed by Heinrich Charles, the Secretary of the German-American Chamber of Commerce in New York. The Ambassador decided that it was advisable to close this press office, since all the articles launched in the American press by Charles were marked as coming from the German-American Chamber of Commerce.[9] A new office under the general management of Bernhard Dernburg was opened on Broadway. Dernburg was available because under the circumstances he was unable to carry out the financial transactions with which he had been entrusted in Berlin.[10] The first work session of the newly created propaganda organization[11] took place in the New York offices of the Hamburg-American Line apparently on September 28, 1914, and was attended by Bernhard Dernburg, Heinrich Albert, Anton Meyer-Gerhard, J. P. Meyer, George Sylvester Viereck, F. F. Schrader, A. Rau, M. B. Claussen, and Karl Alexander Fuehr.[12]

Under the direction of Dernburg, a program and general guidelines were worked out. The preparation of the material was to be done at an office rented for this purpose by Karl A. Fuehr in the Townsend Building at 1123 Broadway. It was decided that control over the propaganda dissemination would be placed with a special commission consisting of Albert, Viereck, and Claussen.[13] Just how insufficient the information material of the propaganda organization would be is evidenced by their news sources. The following possibilities for obtaining information were contemplated: first, the few German newspapers reaching America; second, English newspapers; third, material from the editor's office of the pro-German journal *Fatherland*, which appeared in English; fourth, information supplied by the German embassy; and finally, original contributions by members of the press office.[14] The products of the propaganda group were to be disseminated through newspaper articles as well as brochures. As for the financial base of this not very impressive enterprise, Dernburg "especially emphasized" that the "limited" funds did not come from the embassy but from private donations of "friends of the German cause." Viereck estimated weekly costs for the preparation of the material to come to about $500, including rental expenses for the New York office. Claussen predicted weekly expenses for his work at about $700, most of this going for salaries to eight to ten persons doing "confidential work" for him. Concerning the slant of the articles to be written, Dernburg felt that it would be wise to avoid becoming embroiled in newspaper polemics. Consequently, there were to be no reports "about atrocities by soldiers, about the violation of Belgian neutrality, about Serbia, and about German militarism."[15]

In his earlier memoirs, Bernstorff reports that the propaganda office was subordinate to the Zentralstelle für Auslandsdienst (Central Office for Service Abroad) of the German Foreign Office[16] and that its financial operations were completely independent of the embassy.[17] Whether and how this dividing line between embassy and press office was actually drawn in daily operations cannot be determined with certainty for most individual undertakings. In contrast, the records clearly show that the relatively small number of men who could be entrusted with propaganda assignments did not work without supervision or without financial support from the embassy in Washington. It is therefore in no way surprising that Bernstorff's name was repeatedly involved, directly or indirectly, with the diverse activities of the New York press office.[18]

First of all, the press office strove to convince the American people that, against its own will and without any provocation on its part, Germany had been plunged into a defensive war by the Entente powers, a war which now had to be brought to the best possible conclusion. In contrast with the minutes of the first meeting of the propaganda group on September 28, which clearly stated that German propaganda was not to deal with the so-called atrocities, the invasion of Belgium, etc., it soon became apparent that these topics could not be avoided.[19] Whether the lack of a well-planned and effectively organized publicity program[20] in the United States was the consequence of the limited abilities of the individual German representatives or whether it must be attributed to the apparently complete impossibility of coordinating these different temperaments is difficult to ascertain in retrospect. Our main sources are the diplomatic correspondence of the Ambassador, who frequently reported to Berlin on American public opinion, and the minutes of the Senate Subcommittee on the Judiciary for the investigation of "Brewing and Liquor Interests and German and Bolshevik Propaganda."[21] One might also examine in greater detail the articles, speeches, and brochures of this organization and their possible impact on the American public.[22] Ultimately the publicity campaign of the press office did not produce any tangible, positive results, and a more detailed investigation into the individual propaganda measures would only be of journalistic interest. It also goes without saying that the New York press office could hardly score any successes as long as every measure taken was immediately thwarted, or at least offset, by the events of the war, such as the constant sinkings of neutral ships. Bernstorff even remembers: "With the sinking of the *Lusitania*, the clarifying purposes of our propaganda in the United States essentially came to an end. Henceforth the main goal of our propagandistic efforts there was ... to keep the United States out of the war."[23]

Despite the considerable damage caused by its often inept actions, the German press office in New York continued operations until the breaking off of diplomatic relations in February 1917. Dernburg appears to have directed the general management of the office until June 1915. The organization of his associates is not quite clear. It seems that until approximately December 1914 Karl Alexander Fuehr held the leading position under Dernburg, including the responsibility for the daily propaganda or news bulletin which was edited by Matthew B. Claussen and distributed to the newspapers. Although a successful personnel policy was out of the question because only a few German citizens managed to cross the Atlantic in the years from 1914 to 1917, personal differences within the group[24] and the wish to improve the organization led to some changes. In the late fall of 1914, the American journalist William Bayard Hale, for instance, took over part of the work of the press office. Under contract from the German Ambassador, he was employed until June 1918 and was promised a yearly salary of $15,000.[25]

The other persons connected with the press office do not give the impression of having been experienced propaganda functionaries. Heinrich Albert was a civil servant with previous experience in the commercial sector. Fuehr had worked as an interpreter for the German diplomatic service in Japan. Dernburg's time spent in banking and his former position as chief of the German Colonial Office certainly did not qualify him for his delicate assignment in the United States.[26] In fact, there is little or no supporting evidence anywhere for the opinion spread by the Entente and later also held in America that, at the outbreak of the war in 1914, Germany had "gathered the most capable propaganda experts from Europe and East Asia in New York" and with these men had established an effective propaganda network covering the entire United States.[27]

Quite to the contrary, the impression is rather that of a handful of amateurs with goodwill and much patriotism, but without any solid knowledge of propaganda techniques. Shocking also is the degree to which the German agents misjudged the structure of public opinion in America and therefore repeatedly allowed themselves to be carried away by outbursts of unjustified optimism. Thus, in October 1914, Anton Meyer-Gerhard, an associate of Dernburg, reported to Wilhelm Solf, chief of the Berlin Colonial Office, that Dernburg's presence in the United States was "an assurance for Germany that America would help Germany if Germany were ever in a poor military situation. . . . Should we ever be the 'underdog,' we can expect much from America."[28] Dernburg, in fact, demonstrated very few qualities which would have made him appear particularly suited for public relations work. The Frenchman G. Lechartier calls him "le verbeux, pédant, prétentieux et fastidieux docteur Dernburg."[29] In his study about war propaganda, H. C. Peterson writes that Dernburg seldom was in possession of reliable news and data and therefore was in no way informed as to which steps the American, the British, or even his own government were contemplating. As a matter of fact, he was not even up to date about the actions of his colleagues in the United States. In the words of H. C. Peterson, "Dernburg's force was blind, deaf and dumb."[30] Nevertheless, it would appear that, at least in the early phase of his work, Dernburg was able to claim some measure of success. Many of the articles which he wrote at that time found a ready market and certainly helped to bring before the American public what he and his agents looked upon as the German point of view.[31]

Although it proved detrimental to his goals, the director of the German publicity campaign did not limit himself to newspaper articles, but also tried to improve the American image of Germany through personal public appearances.[32] Here it became evident that Dernburg, who had already criticized American pacifism and the "flaccidity of a nation which has not seen a war for over fifty years,"[33] obviously lacked any psychological understanding of the American mentality. Perhaps he had already aroused astonishment among American readers with his articles proclaiming that Belgium clearly belonged to Germany geographically, that Antwerp was a German harbor, and that Germany after the war needed areas, such as Morocco, for settlement. He certainly incurred more than the displeasure of his audience when, during a public speech in Cleveland after the sinking of the *Lusitania*, he informed the already upset Americans that the sinking of the passenger ship was a justified measure. Oswald Garrison Villard, owner and editor of *The Nation* and son of the famed German-American financier Henry Villard, lunched with Bernstorff in the German embassy on May 15, 1915, and the Ambassador apparently spoke rather frankly about the verbal derailment in Cleveland of his chief of propaganda. Villard noted: "He could not understand why Dernburg had made any speech at Cleveland at all, much less make the terrible breaks that he did." With the appearance in Cleveland, Dernburg's career in the United States came to an abrupt end, and he left the country before Washington could order his expulsion.[34]

All in all there is sufficient evidence to doubt whether, as the well-known German historian Gerhard Ritter writes, Dernburg directed the German propaganda until June 1915 "with much success and skill."[35] Neither the records nor the actual results of the German campaign can be cited as proof of an appreciable success of the activities of the press office. The Ambassador's own reminiscences about "German Propaganda in the United States" appeared soon after the end of the war and only represent a very incomplete account. With a naiveté which can only be explained by the time of publication, Bernstorff in fact blames American lack of receptivity for the failure of the publicity campaign: "The American does not wish to be instructed. He was not interested in learning the 'truth' which the German press news and informative literature were eager to bring him."[36]

When looking for the real reasons for the failure of the German agents, one cannot quite overlook the fact that the propaganda machine in America was almost completely cut off from its home base. Direct and prompt transmission of news and information material from Germany soon became extremely difficult and the wireless could not replace normal peacetime communications.[37] The obvious lack of a German plan of action[38] for such an eventuality led various, often completely unqualified persons to undertake projects which were characterized above all by their ignorance of American mentality.[39] German and American public personalities who all too openly sympathized with the German cause traveled throughout the country and propagated the German point of view. German war films were shown before audiences which had no enthusiasm for the war. Considerable sums were invested in order to acquire well-known newspapers or to keep publications which were throttled by financial difficulties on a pro-German course. Various types of propaganda material and mail were brought into the country by sailors and countless other messengers presumably traveling on neutral steamers. American journalists such as William Bayard Hale, Edward Lyell Fox, or Albert Dawson, who seemed suitable to the Germans, were sent to the battlefields of Europe and to Berlin in the hope of planting positive news in the press by way of the syndicates.[40] Ethnic groups which in any way appeared to have Germanophile or anti-Entente sentiments were given special attention. Propaganda for peace in the world was mixed with tirades of agitation against the Entente. The same agents whose names and reputations served the publicity campaign also acted as operatives in the illegal arms trade and indeed sabotage.[41]

When one looks at the motley group of people who played the propaganda game in America, it does not seem surprising that overall cooperation, even disregarding the lack of a master plan in Berlin, was not always achieved. The Ambassador, in his capacity as the leading German diplomat in the United States, could not engage himself publicly in the propaganda campaign. Although the State Department could have no doubt that Bernstorff was at least informed about the official publicity work of the German agents, it was impossible for the Ambassador to appear as a speaker at propaganda meetings, to write tendentious newspaper articles, or to appear openly as coordinator of the various activities. The fact that in retrospect Bernstorff still has largely been looked upon as the leader of the German propaganda organization and as responsible for even the less acceptable undertakings of various agents was at least in part caused by the American war psychosis, which in 1917 and 1918 led to widespread public concern over the so-called German conspiracies in the United States. Undoubtedly, a considerable portion of the blame must be put on Bernstorff himself, for time and again his name appeared in connection with some sensational disclosure, and Entente and American intelligence services managed to link him with dubious projects. His book, *Deutschland und Amerika* which was subtitled *Erinnerungen aus dem fünfjährigen Krieg* and appeared shortly after the war, regrettably furnishes very little concrete evidence about his actual role in propaganda and merely reveals a measure of bitterness.

Nevertheless, the picture can to a certain extent be completed from the remaining records and the memoirs of some of the people involved.[42] Thus, one discovers that German propaganda activities, which had been carried on from September 1914 without noticeable success but also without major scandals, suffered a stunning blow through the—at least—imprudent sinking of the British passenger liner *Lusitania* in May 1915. The blow was so severe that the German propaganda machine did not fully recover from it during the remaining two years of American neutrality. Although Dernburg was forced to leave the country, neither the German government nor its representatives in the United States appear to have fully realized in the summer of 1915 that the death of 1,200 civilians, among them many Americans, off the coast of Ireland was a decisive turning point. It goes without saying that the Allies used the sinking of the *Lusitania* for maximum returns in their own propaganda campaign. In view of the political climate in Germany, it is not surprising that Bernstorff seldom saw eye to eye with the German naval authorities and that Germany's official notes to the American government often used a tone which made the Ambassador's work most difficult. In spite of all this, one is justified in asking whether the propagandistic activity of the Germans was sufficiently attuned to the specific American circumstances.

It is true that it was only a small group of people who officially dealt with propaganda in America,[43] but it is still striking how large the number of those was who spoke and wrote for Germany and who therefore were associated by the Americans with the propaganda machine. The inflammatory speeches and exaggerations of some people went so far that even the Military Attaché, Capt. Franz von Papen, who was not exactly known in the United States for his diplomatic sensitivity, complained to the Ministry of War in Berlin about the way in which "gentlemen such as Professor Eugen Kühnemann carry out 'publicity work' in this country."[44] Kühnemann, a professor of philosophy, traveled around the United States and made speeches before German-American groups.[45] He declared that "in no army in the world are there so many good-hearted and highly civilized men as in the German army" and that, therefore, "atrocities are more improbable, not to say more impossible, in the German army than in any other army in the world."[46] Among those less successful representatives of the German cause in the United States was also Hugo Münsterberg, who frequently supported the German Information Service and who tried to reach the American reader through numerous publications. His contributions, however, were so transparent in their intentions that they soon appeared to be less the opinion of a Harvard professor than those of "an agent of the German Government."[47] He was assisted by Edmund von Mach, whose position until 1915 was that of professor of art history at Bradford Academy in Cambridge, Massachusetts.[48] Another propaganda agent was the Celticist Kuno Meyer, professor in Berlin and member of the Akademie der Wissenschaften. Granted a leave of absence from his teaching duties by the Minister of Spiritual and Educational Affairs, August von Trott zu Solz, and supplied with false papers of a merchant, he had been sent by the Foreign Office to the United States to "make propaganda in our interest in Irish circles." Bernstorff had been instructed by the Foreign Office to "receive him courteously" upon his arrival and to "supply him with further recommendations."[49] It must be remembered that, quite independently of the efforts of these gentlemen, a large group of well-known personalities in Germany publicly treated the horrors of war in euphemistic terms, simultaneously outlined Germany's exaggerated war goals, and conjured up the superiority of German culture in the world. One of the best-known examples was the so-called "Declaration of the 93," a document signed at first by ninety-three personalities of academic and cultural life in Germany. The text began with the statement: "We as representatives of German science and art protest herewith before the entire world of culture against the lies and defamations with which the enemies of Germany strive to dirty the pure intentions of Germany in the difficult battle for existence which has been forced upon it."[50] American journalists, who as neutrals were able to stay in Germany, of course reported about the annexationist agitation to their newspapers, which in many cases were not favorably disposed toward Germany anyway. One notes with all the more surprise that the German authorities permitted men like Eugen Kühnemann and Kuno Meyer to speak in the same aggressive tone in America that they had become accustomed to in Germany. On the other hand, there were certainly German academicians who did not volunteer their names for the propaganda machine. One of those was Wilhelm Conrad von Röntgen. Cyril Brown, an American journalist in Berlin, had suggested to the General Staff that hostile news about German atrocities could be effectively countered by an interview with a well-known German scientist such as Röntgen. The General Staff immediately furnished the scholar with information, but Röntgen, having looked at the things sent to him, frankly declared that he thought he would not be the right man for this type of activity.[51]

In connection with the undertakings of the German Information Service, a particularly delicate subject for the people concerned was the origin rather than the amount of the monies used. Bernstorff, whose memoirs are otherwise meager on information about propaganda, here suddenly feels inclined to provide details. He defends himself against the claim that a high percentage of total German expenses in the United States from 1914 to 1917 was used for propaganda purposes. The largest portion of the expenses, according to the Ambassador, arose in connection with the purchase of war materiel by Heinrich Albert and only a relatively small part of the total sum was spent on propaganda. The press office was especially hampered by the fact "that approval had to be obtained from Berlin in advance for very insignificant expenses which went beyond the budget that had been established." And he states: "During the two and a half years between the outbreak of the war and the rupture of German-American relations, all in all not even one million dollars were spent for propaganda purposes in the Union, including smaller amounts for other countries, as for example the picture service, which had been extended from New York to South America and East Asia." With regard to the often-voiced charges that Germany spent for propaganda projects the funds which had been raised in America for the Red Cross, Bernstorff writes that these amounts although first deposited in different checking accounts in New York, were transferred regularly and in full to Germany. Yet it appears that considerable amounts of cash were first used by German representatives in the United States, and only later were credits for those sums transferred to Germany. How large the sums were which became available to the Ambassador in this way is indicated, for instance, by the fact that until January 31, 1915, the German-American National Alliance alone had collected $319,087.48, of which $233,000 was "delivered" to Bernstorff and $67,000 to the Austro-Hungarian Ambassador Constantin Dumba.[52] The total amount cited of one million dollars in expenditures for propaganda purposes by Bernstorff in no way corresponds to the facts, as can be seen from the examination below of select individual projects.[53]

The problems of the press office were not eased by the fact that members of the propaganda team wasted a great deal of their energy in trying to expand their less-than-effective propaganda activities to South America and East Asia.[54] Too many projects were undertaken, and too few were successfully completed. One example of a particularly unsuccessful project was the attempt to influence the American public through films. First of all, the production and preparation of film material was connected with much higher costs than propaganda through planted newspaper articles. In the end this attempt at film propaganda failed because the American Correspondent Film Company,[55] a New York firm founded by Heinrich Albert for this purpose in the spring of 1915, could not persuade the German Central Film Agency to make available for America anything other than purely military films, which consisted "mostly of battle scenes." At considerable expense, the films had to be reworked by Albert's people in America, and the "moving picture propaganda" (*Wandelbildpropaganda*) coming from Germany, was, in Bernstorff's words, so useless that they decided to send their own correspondents from America to Germany and Austria in order to obtain material which could actually be used. Clearly, this undertaking failed because of lack of support on the part of the authorities in Berlin.[56]

Other propaganda projects such as the attempts to influence ethnic groups and the acquisition of newspapers were in some cases carried out by the same agents. Since, on the whole, these activities were organized independently of the routine work in the press office and since the embassy in Washington pursued some of these projects directly, they are examined separately in the following sections.

ACQUISITION AND FINANCIAL SUPPORT OF AMERICAN PRESS ORGANS

Although there existed in the United States a considerable number of German-language newspapers,[57] Bernstorff's diplomatic reports contain no evidence which would suggest particularly close ties between most of these journals and the official German representatives in Washington. It was quite natural and not surprising that from 1914 until 1917 German-language newspapers came out more or less in support of the German cause and that some of these papers, especially in cities where large portions of the population were of German descent, should maintain cordial relations with the German consulates. In the embassy and on the team which was responsible for the German Information Service, close contacts with the smaller and local German-language publications in the country were not thought very useful, particularly since these had only limited access to the American public at large. Instead, the Germans attempted to reach the general public by influencing certain English-language papers.

An important exception was made in New York City. Even before the war, Herman Ridder and his *New Yorker Staats-Zeitung*, which had been published since 1834, maintained good relations with Bernstorff. In spite of the relatively large number of German-Americans in New York, this newspaper operated continually in the red during the First World War, and there was a real danger that the Ridder family might lose control. Even though the business had already received a financial boost from the German authorities in the fall of 1914,[58] Bernstorff was forced to bring up the matter again with the Foreign Office on December 19, 1914. This time he asked for the approval of a large sum to keep the *Staats-Zeitung* above water, "since its collapse would be most disadvantageous to our interests." He mentioned debts amounting to $550,000 which would have to be financed "in order to save Ridder." For security, he suggested holding stocks of the *Staats-Zeitung*. Dernburg, who had handled negotiations with New York German-American business interests in order to salvage the company, had indicated to Bernstorff that he could raise half of the amount in the United States, if Berlin would cover the other half.[59] Under Secretary Arthur Zimmermann of the Foreign Office apparently was less intrigued by the plan and told Bernstorff that Berlin was not willing to cover half of the debts; at most a *Restbetrag* (a remaining amount) could be considered.[60] The embassy, however, insisted on an "urgent financial need" for $200,000 from the government, "since otherwise [there is] danger of [the] paper going into hands that try to move the Germans here in another direction."[61] That apparently did it in Berlin, and on December 31, 1914, Zimmermann wired: "Agreed."[62] The assurance of the German credit brought the desired result, and two weeks later Bernstorff was able to report to Berlin that the well-known German-American paper had not been lost to German interests. Bernstorff's straw man, Adolf Pavenstedt, had gone to the creditors with the pledge from Berlin and succeeded in persuading them "to extend the due notes for a few years."[63] Thus, for the time being the ownership of the *Staats-Zeitung* was secured in line with German interests.[64]

How far the German authorities controlled the *Staats-Zeitung* becomes evident in a report from Bernstorff to the Imperial Chancellor in November 1915. The Ambassador wrote that, although Mr. Ridder had died, the paper would remain in the family's hands; he himself would discuss all relevant questions with Adolf Pavenstedt. Furthermore, Reginald Schroeder, "for years confidant of the Embassy," would "take over the management of the morning paper."[65]

The official German interest in George Sylvester Viereck's weekly, *The Fatherland*, was just as undisguised as the influence on the *New Yorker Staats-Zeitung*.[66] Viereck so thoroughly engaged himself for the Central Powers[67] that his journal soon had acquired the reputation of being a distinctly propagandistic paper.[68] The "courageous weekly," as Bernstorff called it, had come to life only at the outbreak of the European war[69] and is already mentioned as a news source in the October minutes of the German Information Service. The close connection between the German propaganda agents and Viereck's enterprise thus had been obvious since the autumn of 1914,[70] especially since the fact that Viereck received subsidies from the Germans was not even kept secret in America.[71] As time went on, however, Viereck's paper struck a tone which seemed exaggerated even to the German propagandists.[72] When Heinrich Albert attempted to exert a moderating influence on Viereck and to enforce somewhat stronger controls over the newspaper, he encountered the publisher's resistance. Things went so far in October 1916 that Bernstorff expressed his dismay to the Foreign Office: "I also would like to get rid of *The Fatherland*, for this publication too has proved a failure."[73]

The cooperation with Marcus Braun and his journal *Fair Play* took a similarly disappointing turn. Braun also encountered financial difficulties and thought of salvaging his paper with money from the embassy. According to documents submitted later to the Subcommittee on the Judiciary by the federal agent A. Bruce Bielaski, it would appear that, at least for a time, Braun received a monthly subsidy of $1,200 approved by Berlin. By the beginning of 1916,

Braun was evidently doing so badly that he decided to put the embassy under pressure with new financial demands. At first he asked for $4,600 and threatened unfavorable publicity for the Ambassador in case *Fair Play* and his firm, the Universal Press Association, were forced to declare bankruptcy. After some consultations between Bernstorff, Albert, and the attorney Norvin R. Lindheim, it was decided that Braun should be paid approximately $3,000.[74] In October 1916 a somewhat relieved Bernstorff was able to report that he had succeeded "in getting out of the relations with Mr. Marcus Braun's *Fair Play*."[75]

Far more complicated was the German effort to acquire a large English-language daily newspaper in New York. The mere size of the investment necessary in connection with a project of this nature brought well-known personalities such as the Freiburg national economist Gerhart von Schulze-Gaevernitz, the American businessman Hermann Sielken, and Albert Ballin of the Hamburg-American Line into the financial negotiations.[76] The preparatory discussions for the takeover of the *New York Evening Mail* began immediately after the outbreak of war. In agreement with Edward Rumely,[77] Bernstorff had come to the conviction that the *Evening Mail* was a suitable object for acquisition. Mentioning possible "moral and financial support" by the Reichskolonialamt, the Ambassador wrote to Berlin: "I consider it urgently necessary for the future to make up for the earlier failure and to bring an English-language newspaper under our control." Bernstorff estimated the cost at about $1,000,000 and asked the Foreign Office: "How far may I go with a promise to buy stocks or to subsidize?"[78] Three weeks later, Zimmermann let him know that the project had been approved on the condition that German influence would also be assured in peacetime.[79] In the course of the secret negotiations, in which Dernburg represented the interests of the embassy, it soon became clear that the actual purchase would have to be made through various straw men. Bernstorff cabled Berlin that political reasons made "immediate action absolutely necessary" and asked for a first allocation of up to $500,000.[80]

For reasons unknown, the Foreign Office at this point suddenly decided to drop the Ambassador's plans and to create an American press office[81] instead.[82] But Bernstorff and Dernburg insisted that "the planting of news" was far more important than the "organization of the news service" and went ahead to secure an option to purchase the paper, it would appear, for the time being, without a green light from the Foreign Office. The total cost of the acquisition was now assessed at $1,200,000 or $1,300,000, and Bernstorff asked for authorization from Berlin to make a downpayment of $325,000 or $650,000. The *Evening Mail* was praised as "a distinguished local newspaper with a daily circulation of 145,000 paid copies."[83] At the same time in Germany, Schulze-Gaevernitz was mobilized for the project at the instigation of Rumely and with the apparent approval of Bernstorff. He was to establish contact with Hermann Sielken in order "to secure a subscription of at least $100,000 in 6% preference shares."[84] Albert Ballin, a personal friend of both Bernstorff and Dernburg, was drawn into the negotiations through the Foreign Office.[85] Such efforts and the powerful commercial contacts obviously furnished the necessary financial basis for Bernstorff's plan, for only a few days later Zimmermann telegraphed to Washington that the "deal" could be concluded.[86] The Ambassador instructed Heinrich Albert to make the payments to Rumely in the name of the German government as a "fiscal agent"; Rumely appeared as the buyer of the newspaper shares.[87] The control of the *Evening Mail* was to remain in German hands until 1917.

After Dernburg's departure from the United States, Bernstorff had to transfer the supervision of this enterprise to Heinrich Albert.[88] Control became more difficult because Rumely, whose private interests now of course were closely tied to the paper, remained the legal owner of the newspaper company.[89] In order to bring the business out of its insecure financial position, the Ambassador had to try above all to maintain the image of a normal, independent American daily newspaper and to prevent the *Evening Mail* from becoming discredited as a German propaganda sheet. Albert claims that on the whole he was successful in this respect; in consequence, however, it was impossible to strongly support the political line of the Central powers. "No American would have read an exclusively German newspaper anymore." The fact that the paper was "in a rather desolate state" does not seem to have convinced the banker Dernburg and the businessman Albert of the uselessness of this transaction.[90] In October 1916, a contract was drawn up between the German Empire and the *Evening Mail;* Foreign Secretary Gottlieb von Jagow signed the document for the Foreign Office, and the financial interests of Mrs. Adolphus Busch were represented by Hermann Sielken.[91] The money that was spent for the newspaper reportedly came from the proceeds of the sale of treasury bonds in the United States. According to later statements before the Subcommittee on the Judiciary, the amounts were paid from Albert's account at the Equitable Trust Company and the Columbia Trust Company through the law firm Hays, Kaufmann and Lindheim[92] to Walter Lyon of the firm of Senskorf, Lyon and Company, who then took care of the payments to the McClure Newspaper Corporation or rather Edward Rumely. Although it did not remain a secret that the newspaper had become German property,[93] and although the purpose of the whole undertaking was therefore jeopardized, the $200,000 which the Ambassador had deposited with Hays, Kaufmann and Lindheim were paid to Rumely as late as April 1917, in other words after Bernstorff's departure from the United States.[94]

Although, or perhaps because, the *Evening Mail* project did not produce any notable success, Bernstorff contemplated the purchase of further newspapers. Reportedly the *Washington Post* and the *New York Sun* were the objects of such consideration. Efforts to buy the *Washington Post* came to nothing. The takeover of the *New York Sun* was to be arranged through a man referred to in the sources only as von Hamm,[95] with the support of his friend, the wealthy New York lawyer Samuel Untermyer. Although Bernstorff had been instructed by the Foreign Office to break off negotiations concerning this matter, he insisted on pursuing the project and reported to Berlin that the purchase price was $2,000,000, plus additional expenses of $500,000 for the "reconstruction of the newspaper." Despite the negative experiences in his other press ventures, Bernstorff was convinced that in this instance German control could be kept absolutely secret.[96] Later, before the Subcommittee on the Judiciary, Untermyer denied having had any knowledge of Bernstorff's interests in purchasing the newspaper and maintained that he had never discussed newspaper questions with the Ambassador. On the contrary, he said, he had been of the opinion that Heinrich Albert had a purely private business interest in the *New York Sun*. Untermyer told the committee that he had regarded the business proposition as profitable, but that he had not been willing to put up the amount of $1,250,000 by himself. In the end, Bernstorff was unable to convince the Foreign Office in time of the advisability of purchasing the *New York Sun*, and the newspaper was acquired by other interests.[97]

Completely different in its objectives was the cooperation of Bernstorff with the agent Bolo Pascha in yet another newspaper project. Paul Bolo, who was born in Marseilles, was a French citizen and had at one time worked for Abbas Hilmi, the Khedive of Egypt. In the United States, he succeeded within a few days in establishing contact with such different influential persons as E. G. Grace, president of the Bethlehem Steel Company; the newspaper magnate, William Randolph Hearst; and Count Bernstorff. According to later testimony before the Subcommittee on the Judiciary, Bolo was introduced to Grace and Hearst by Charles F. Bertelli, an Italian correspondent for Hearst in Paris, who came to America with Bolo. While Bolo's efforts to obtain through Grace financial support for the purchase of the *Journal*, a large Paris newspaper, were unsuccessful, his negotiations with the German Ambassador proved to be much more fruitful. Adolf Pavenstedt, who apparently had met Bolo in Cuba in 1914, served as intermediary in Bolo's dealings with Bernstorff. Bolo, who arrived in New York on February 22, 1916, sent Pavenstedt to Washington on February 24 to discuss this propaganda scheme with Bernstorff. On February 26, the Ambassador cabled to Berlin and asked for permission to support a political action in an enemy country with a financial contribution of $1,700,000. The action would contribute toward bringing about peace. Bernstorff did not mention any names. On February 29, the Foreign Office replied that the Ambassador's proposal would be acceptable, if indeed it was a promising project, and as long as the country concerned was not Russia, since the amount mentioned would be too small to achieve anything of consequence there. In Italy, on the other hand, it would not be worthwhile spending such a large sum. On March 3, Bernstorff met with Pavenstedt in New York and told him of the approval by the German government. While some sources speak of a payment by Bernstorff amounting to $1,700,000, the minutes of the Subcommittee on the Judiciary mention the sum of $1,683,500. According to this source, the transfer of the funds was arranged by Hugo Schmidt, a representative of the Deutsche Bank in New York. The payments were made by the Deutsche Bank via the Guaranty Trust Company in New York and G. Amsinck & Co. to the Royal Bank of Canada. In addition, smaller amounts apparently were transferred to the accounts of Charles Humbert and Madame Bolo.[98] The project is especially surprising since, at least officially, Berlin does not seem to have been informed about Bolo or about the details of the Paris transaction before approving the sizable sum. Incidentally, Bolo apparently succeeded almost simultaneously in persuading agents of Matthias

Erzberger to pay him another 10,000,000 francs for the same purpose.[99]

Apart from these rather sensational projects, there were still other efforts to bring newspapers in the United States under German influence. For instance, Bernstorff granted financial support to Theodore Lowe for his Washington weekly *The National Courier*.[100] After prompting from the intelligence section of the General Staff, the Foreign Office also authorized the Ambassador to make funds available to the *New York Irish World*, if the British should try to buy the business.[101] Finally, the records show that Bernstorff also paid $220,000 "for the purchase of a Jewish newspaper."[102]

On the whole, it is evident from the documents of the German Foreign Office and other records that Bernstorff not only carried out instructions from Berlin to influence American newspapers financially, but that he also made suggestions on his own and repeatedly spoke out in favor of more projects of this nature. The Ambassador's rather unpleasant experiences in most of these cases and his knowledge that in the long run foreign control of American newspapers could not be kept secret apparently did not discourage his engagement.[103] Thus, large amounts were spent at Bernstorff's instigation or with his consent.[104]

GERMAN PROPAGANDA AMONG JEWS IN AMERICA

Possibly due to the overwhelming effect of the systematic extermination of the Jews in National Socialist Germany, the temporary close political cooperation of the German Imperial Government with some Jewish organizations during the First World War has received relatively little attention in German historical research since 1945. Only a few studies have been published on that subject.[105] But since the General Staff, the Reichsmarineamt, and the Foreign Office instigated a variety of measures with the purpose of using the Jews in America for German ends, a consideration of this propagandistic activity must be included in the present study.

It should be pointed out that Bernstorff himself, in contrast to many leading men of his generation, had always had close contact with Jewish circles in Germany.[106] His personal connections with Jewish families had, however, nothing in common with the ultimately rather superficial and insubstantial relations which some leading Jews cultivated at the Imperial court.[107] The Ambassador, who "considered anti-Semitism as a shameful blot on the shield of honor of German culture,"[108] had soon found Jewish friends in the United States as well. These connections, which had not gone unnoticed in Berlin, made him appear most suitable to win the American Jews for the aims of the Central Powers. That the Germans should make such an effort to address American Jews in their propaganda campaign seems understandable for a number of reasons. Jewish families of German descent controlled a large sector of the wealthy private financial houses of America, some of which, like Kuhn, Loeb & Co., because of international business links, also pursued financial interests in Germany.[109] In other circumstances, those financial groups certainly might have been in a position to bolster Germany with urgently needed credits. That personal considerations and the course of political events in the war would lead them to lose every interest in Germany was something that could hardly be foreseen by German governmental officials in August 1914.[110]

Beyond that, it was quite natural that even these often anti-Semitic officials of Imperial Germany should seek access to the American Jews, among whom anti-Russian sentiments were clearly evident, especially in view of the Russian pogroms. Curiously enough, it does not seem to have occurred to either the authorities in Berlin or to the Jewish circles in Germany favoring assimilation that, as a precondition for a fruitful German-Jewish campaign in America, the deeply rooted anti-Semitism in Germany would first have to be eliminated, or at least the appearance of official approval of anti-Semitic tendencies would have to be avoided.[111] In any case, the Foreign Office perhaps overestimated the international influence of the Jews loyal to the Emperor and therefore assumed that their siding with Germany would suffice as a basis for public relations work among America's Jews.

Moreover, it must be remembered that the German government, which looked forward so expectantly to a fruitful collaboration with American Jews, in August and September 1914 registered voices from the German Jewish community which hardly differed from the war enthusiasm of the general public. Fully in harmony with the all-encompassing German public spirit of those weeks, the Central Association of German Citizens of the Jewish Faith[112] called upon its members: "It is *self-evident* that *every German Jew* is ready for the *sacrifices of property and life* which duty demands. Fellow believers! We call upon you to devote all your *energy to the fatherland beyond the measure of duty! Hurry to the banners voluntarily!* ... Place yourselves *in the service of the fatherland* through *personal assistance* of every kind and by *giving money and property!*"[113] If therefore a certain optimism about propagandistic cooperation may appear justified, it is less understandable that the officials in Berlin had not bothered to inform themselves more thoroughly concerning either the prevailing ideological divisions among German Jews or the prospective attitude of the American Jews toward the events of the war.

As early as August 4, 1914, the Berlin Justizrat Max I. Bodenheimer,[114] apparently on his own initiative, had contacted representatives of the General Staff and subsequently conferred with Carl-Ludwig Diego von Bergen and Bogdan Count Hutten-Czapski, a friend of Count Bernstorff.[115] It was "as a consequence of these consultations" that the decision was made to found the German Committee for the Liberation of the Russian Jews (Deutsches Komitee zur Befreiung der russischen Juden) and to establish this organization in an office in Berlin.[116] Soon afterwards came the dispatch of "an expedition to America of three gentlemen under the leadership of Dr. Straus, in order to spread a favorable opinion about Germany in the Jewish press and in financial circles in the United States."[117] Not surprisingly, this group was not only sent to influence Jewish public opinion in America, but expansionist plans for border changes in Eastern Europe after an expected German victory also played a role in the mission. The German Committee for the Liberation of the Russian Jews in fact was "to represent the bringing together of all those groups which in the interest of the fatherland strive to tear away from Russia her western and southwestern provinces." Thus the three delegates also went to the United States "to awaken" in the respective Jewish circles "interest ... in a future political structuring of the conquered regions and the liberation of the oppressed peoples of northern Russia."[118]

The political mood among the leading Jews in America was such that, justifiably or not, they were often mentioned in the same breath with pro-German elements. Both Roosevelt and the British Ambassador, Cecil Spring Rice, at times thought that the Jewish banking houses had fully taken sides with Germany—a wholly incorrect appraisal even at the outset of the war.[119] The misinterpretation in part may have been caused by the friendly relationship which Bernstorff maintained with the Warburgs and the Speyers,[120] and it may have been reinforced by the fact that the German propaganda chief and financial expert, Bernhard Dernburg, himself came from the banking world. Behind much of the erroneous German appraisal was the undeniable fact that a considerable sector of the American Jews harbored a bitter antagonism against tsarist Russia.[121]

In order to take advantage of these anti-Russian leanings, Imperial propaganda from the very beginning stressed the idea of the German fight for culture and progress, a final battle between "German civilization and Russian barbarism." To buttress the German propaganda campaign, both the Foreign Office and the General Staff tried to disseminate news regarding "the mistreatment of Jews by the Russians."[122] Here the German effort was not only in full accord with the voices of numerous public personalities and academic leaders, who were not unknown even in far-off America, such as Friedrich Meinecke, Eduard Meyer,[123] Hans Delbrück,[124] and others, but it also was very much in line with the published opinion of a number of influential Jews in Germany. The historian Meinecke wrote: "The wild, unbridled passion of Pan-Slavism . . . working through assassination, hypocrisy, and breach of faith has ignited this war," and "the Slavic peoples will then have to show the world whether their wild, primitive nationalism and their semi-barbaric ethics will be able to develop a culture that is equal to Germany's."[125] The Central Association of German Citizens of the Jewish Faith implored its readers in September 1914: "Russia, which has also treated your fellow believers so inhumanely, is threatening Germany's borders, Russia, which has incited Serbia's assassins against our ally Austria. The loyalty toward our friend Austria, the protection of German thought and culture against Russian crudity and lack of culture makes the war a holy one. We are on God's side, therefore, God will be on ours."[126] Certainly being one of the more Western-oriented German diplomats, Bernstorff himself, though in a more moderate tone, also addressed this hatred of the presumably barbaric Slavs and particularly of the Russians. In November 1914, he wrote to the editor of the New York Jewish paper *Der Tag*: "Germany is offering the Jews in Russian Poland openly and without reservation everything that they have been deprived of under the Russian regime and which even today Russia has not begun to give them."[127]

Isaac Straus, Arthur Meyrowitz, and S. M. Melamed,[128] who were organizing the German propaganda among America's Jews, originally had been dispatched in accordance with an arrangement with Ernst Jaeckh of the Reichsmarineamt. The German navy also paid their travel expenses.[129] Shortly afterwards, still in the fall of 1914, this project passed into the sphere of competence of the Zentralstelle für Auslandsdienst of the Foreign Office[130] and thus, in fact, belonged to Dernburg's area of responsibility, since Bernstorff had entrusted the latter with the overall direction of German propaganda in the United States. As the records show clearly, the Jewish propaganda group indeed operated as an integral part of the Imperial public relations work in America.

At first sight the undertaking seems to have been no more than a simple propaganda project of a nation aiming to use to its advantage the political orientation of a minority group in another nation. As it turned out, however, in daily practice the mission was hampered by circumstances which had already been a basic organizational problem of the Jews within Germany. Despite special efforts, Bodenheimer and Oppenheimer had not succeeded in winning well-known personalities from other factions, such as Paul Nathan and James Simon, for the work of the Committee for the Liberation of the Russian Jews.[131] At the root of the problem were the usual differences between Zionists, non-Zionists, assimilationists, and still other groups that had made it impossible to represent a more united Jewish front in the contacts with the authorities of the Imperial government.[132] Hence, the delegates in America could not speak for all German Jews, not even for a clear majority, but only for one of several factions. The fact that Hindenburg, the commander in chief of the German eastern troops, declared in the fall of 1914 that he "looked upon the endeavors of the Committee with a positive interest" and that he was prepared "to further its goals"[133] may have impressed some Jews in Germany who were given to German nationalist views. Testimonials of this nature, however, would hardly suffice to win the cooperation of German-Americans of such caliber as Jacob Henry Schiff of Kuhn Loeb & Co. Schiff's standpoint, for instance, is evident from a letter to Max Warburg in the autumn of 1915: "I cannot arouse any enthusiasm for a system which permits the free development of the individual only in so far as that development helps the state.... Nor am I willing to give my approval to a system under which everything is dependent upon the approval of the military element, and subsidiary thereto."[134]

Even the choice of personnel for the propaganda campaign in the United States was not particularly fortunate. In the initial discussions with Ernst Jaeckh of the Reichsmarineamt, it had been agreed to dispatch as agents to America two representatives of the Committee for the Liberation of the Russian Jews, and likely candidates, considered for the mission, had been the author Adolf Friedemann and the North German Lloyd employee, Arthur Meyrowitz. Later it had been decided to send Isaac Straus, a member of a banker's family, instead of Friedemann, who was thought too nervous for the assignment.[135] A Russian-born journalist named S. M. Melamed was hired as translator and assistant to the two men. The emissaries were supposed to represent the Committee for the Liberation of the Russian Jews (later, following an ultimatum by the Zionists, renamed Committee for the East)[136] in America, to collect donations for needy Jews in Eastern Europe,[137] and, above all, to win the American Jews for Wilhelminian Germany. In this, however, they not only did not represent the majority of German Jews, but they also worked against the will and the declared positions of many European Jews, who could not bring themselves to view Wilhelm II and his generals as protectors of the Jewish people.[138] What is more, Straus and Meyrowitz were not able or willing to cooperate in the United States, but in fact hindered each other. At least in part, this may have been a consequence of the very diverse Jewish currents in America.[139] Whatever the exact underlying reasons, certainly the internal conflict did not contribute to improving the performance of the Jewish press office. After only a few months, the working climate within the group had become so intolerable that Bernstorff asked Berlin to recall Meyrowitz immediately.[140]

In spite of the complications mentioned here, Isaac Straus apparently succeeded in influencing at least a part of the American press in the Germans' favor.[141] Bernstorff, in fact, was so taken by Straus's advertising campaign that he reported to the Chancellor that Straus had, "judged from our point of view, developed very useful activities here."[142] Apart from the already indicated difficulties with Meyrowitz, cooperation between Straus's office and the German authorities seemed to run smoothly. The Reichsmarineamt advanced the initial funds for the group. After their arrival in the United States, they contacted Dernburg's office and were given valuable support. Dernburg's German Information Service also made available the "technical apparatus" for Straus's undertakings. From the beginning Straus also worked hand in hand with Bernstorff, who offered assistance "at any time."[143] From June 1915 to January 1916 alone, Straus presumably received $28,000 from the German government. Beyond that, the records of the Subcommittee on the Judiciary speak of $4,000,000 to $5,000,000, which were paid to Straus by Heinrich Albert.[144] Sums of this order of magnitude appear less incredible when one takes into account, for instance, that Bernstorff reported to Berlin the expenditure of $220,000 for the purchase of one Jewish newspaper alone.[145]

Straus even managed to arrange "several personal conferences" with Jacob H. Schiff and to talk him into calling "a conference of the most prominent members of the Executive Council of the American Jewish Committee."[146] On October 8, 1914, Straus met with these people at Schiff's office in order to discuss promising propaganda possibilities. On October 9, he talked with Albert and Dernburg, and the next day he was off to Washington to win over the Ambassador for one of his projects. Straus had already talked with Bernstorff in September about the possibility of "an official German declaration on the Jewish question," and the Ambassador had then recommended to the Foreign Office a "declaration of the Imperial Government in favor of Russian Jews or Jews in general."[147] Now too, the Ambassador was not opposed to an official German statement, and it was agreed that Consul General Richard Kiliani, scheduled to travel to Germany shortly, should take along an appropriate document for the German government. This memorandum was drafted by Straus and on October 14 given to the Ambassador, who deemed such a declaration "very useful."[148]

Although the Straus mission on the whole achieved rather little for Germany, and although America's large financial institutions increasingly turned toward the Entente,[149] it may be of interest to briefly look at the reasons for the failure of this undertaking. We have already mentioned the difficulty in selecting suitable agitators for the propaganda work among American Jews, and the feud between Straus and Meyrowitz, carried out before the eyes of the American public, turned out to be an additional obstacle of some magnitude. The lack of a clear mandate from all Jews in Germany probably compounded Straus's difficulties. Moreover, Germany grossly overestimated the prospects for successful agitation among the Jews in America, even taking into account that many of them were as pro-German as they were anti-Russian.[150] The same careless optimism that characterized a number of other German operations is visible here, too. There seems to be no other way to explain the conclusion reached by the German Information Service during its session in New York on November 5, 1914, that relations with the American Jewish press had "come off to a good start" and were being "carefully cultivated."[151] In addition, the German propagandists apparently labored under the curious misconception that in order to convince other countries of the nonexistence of the ill-reputed German anti-Semitism nothing more needed to be done than "to raise Jewish self-esteem, for example by appointing Jewish officers, by employing and honoring Jewish professors."[152] Heinrich Albert, chief of the German propaganda operations after Dernburg's demise in the wake of the *Lusitania* crisis, thought himself qualified for the work with the "special organization . . . for Jewish propaganda" simply because he had had "school lessons in Hebrew."[153] Evidently such a dilettantish approach was hardly sufficient to hitch the American Jewish leaders to the Kaiser's wagon.

A personal letter from Schiff to Arthur Zimmermann, Under Secretary in the German Foreign Office, may serve here as an example of the attitude of some Jews in America.[154] After having arranged the above-mentioned sessions with the German Jews, which Straus reported to have been very useful meetings, the senior director of Kuhn, Loeb & Co., who was often regarded as pro-German, wrote on October 19, 1914:

> In these difficult days when Germany's fortunes and misfortunes are the concern of everyone in whose veins German blood flows . . . I feel the urge to write to you in order to bring up a matter which not only gravely concerns me and many others in this country, but which is also of such far-reaching importance for Germany that this in itself must serve as my excuse for speaking out about it without reservation. . . . These gentlemen [Straus and Meyrowitz] have explained to me that their coming here is intended to awaken the full sympathy of the German Jews for Germany, by pointing out what Germany has become for its own citizens of the Jewish faith and, moreover, to determine in what way Germany could further the interests of the Eastern, especially the Polish, Jews in the situation which is likely to be created by the now prevailing conflict. . . . On the other hand, with respect to the mission of these two gentlemen, I feel that it might appear desirable in the interest of Germany that influential circles in Germany receive information about the position which American Jews, who are significant in number and influence, are taking toward the European war of nations. . . . In Germany—it is probably correct—

citizens of Jewish faith have full equality before the law... but in practice—as you undoubtedly know—the letter of the law is not followed in many respects. Thus a German of Jewish faith is almost completely denied the right to enter civil service [*Beamtenstand*], not to mention that the aspirations of German Jews for a professorship, for higher or the highest judicial offices, for the career of an officer, for almost all governmental positions, must remain completely unfulfilled, or their fulfillment is made so exceedingly difficult that the nomination of a Jew to most positions is made dependent on renunciation of his faith.... We Americans of the Jewish faith cannot believe that Germany is really willing to be less advanced in this question than our own country, England, and other countries, and that the great word of the German Emperor... : 'I know only Germans and no parliamentary parties' should not also be interpreted to mean: 'I know only Germans and no religions' and that, accordingly, these words should also apply to Germans of the Jewish faith. The sympathies of a majority of American Jews, who are in the main of Russian origin, decidedly are on the side of Germany, but I cannot but state that a great number of Jews, especially those born in this country, whose parents came here from Germany many years ago, do not completely share this sympathy, because the members of this younger generation, very much convinced of their human dignity, cannot forget that Germany has been the breeding ground of anti-Semitism and that this irresponsible movement has spread out further from Germany. As I firmly assume, it will be of the furthest reaching moral value for Germany if *all* American Jews can be taught that the prejudices against Germans of Jewish faith, which have asserted themselves until modern times in Germany, will soon cease to exist, but to this end it will not be enough to appoint a number of Jews as officers or to select in the near future perhaps a dozen or more professors from scholarly circles. However, besides such possible and probably desirable steps, a new spirit would have to be raised systematically in the German people, which naturally has to be initiated by the government, so that the harm which anti-Semitism has wrought will first of all be completely banned and, in the course of time, the virus which in this connection has gone into the blood of the German people will be completely eradicated. Since, although I have been an American citizen for almost half a century, the weal and woe of Germany, the country of my birth, the country in which my ancestors lived for many centuries, concerns me deeply, and since I want to secure on its behalf the good opinion of the whole world, but especially of *all* my fellow American citizens—as far as this is feasible—I do not hesitate to write to you so candidly, and it would give me the greatest satisfaction if I could hope that what has been said here could be expressed in the right place.[155]

These were the thoughts of a wise old Jew in America who held the land of his fathers in high regard and was willing to stand up for that country. In all courtesy and firmness, however, he demanded what to him as a citizen of the liberalistic, constitutional, democratic society of America seemed self-evident, but had never become part of the static German social structure. The documents give no indication whether Zimmermann gave expression to this important American opinion "in the right place." If Jagow, Bethmann Hollweg, or even persons at General Headquarters took notice of such opinions of leading foreign Jews, it obviously had little or no effect on the way in which German troops conducted themselves in the occupied eastern areas, precisely those places where Germans expressed the expectation that the Jewish population would place itself at the service of the German Empire.

Was it enough that German troops invading Poland posted a proclamation[156] in Hebrew and Yiddish on the walls saying that the German flags would bring a new era of civil rights?[157] And what did it mean to the American Jews when Bernstorff, quoting this proclamation, personally spoke out against Russian reports of German massacres, and even claimed that such promises had not just been mere words? Did the New York Jews, who now saw their relatives freed from Russian rule by German and Austrian armies, believe Bernstorff when he asked publicly: "Can it be that the world-famous discipline of the German army is not able to prevent soldiers from committing atrocities, especially here, where in addition to humaneness, important political considerations prohibit them?"[158] The embarrassment was on Bernstorff's side when he attempted to tell the American public that anti-Semitism would largely come to an end in Germany after the war,[159] and the *Deutschvölkische Blätter* bluntly countered: "We do not understand how Count Bernstorff could contend that the antipathy of large circles against the Jews would completely disappear after the war. He should just wait and see. We believe that exactly the opposite will be the case."[160] As it was, American Jews certainly were not dependent on Bernstorff's official statements if they wished to know about German measures in Eastern Europe. It would be surprising if the generally well-informed American Jewish leadership[161] had not learned that living conditions of the Jews under German occupation were such that even the Committee for the East, otherwise following the line of General Erich Ludendorff and Field Marshall Hindenburg, had to consider "the moral support of the Jews in Poland in the face of ignorance, the prejudices, and the arbitrariness[162] of the German-Austrian occupation authorities"[163] as a "special task."[164] All the same, in December 1914 Franz Oppenheimer wrote to Diego von Bergen that Bernstorff's letter to *Der Tag* had contributed to "winning the sympathies of the American Jews."[165]

Evidently not all the Jews in America, nor even a portion of the splinter groups large enough to mention, were won for the German cause. The American Jews, it would appear, were American above all and, disregarding a perhaps stronger feeling of international solidarity, in this were not very different from other ethnic minorities in the United States. Moreover, they found it difficult to accept the harshness that had become part of German warfare. The dead of the *Lusitania* also cost Bernstorff his Jewish friends.[166]

GERMAN PROPAGANDA AMONG AMERICANS OF GERMAN DESCENT

Although in recent German scholarship there has been some interest in the development of the German ethnic group in the United States prior to and during the World War, the extensive and conclusive study which would have to take into consideration especially the documents and sources which have become available during the past decades has yet to be written.[167] The purpose here is to attempt to clarify the relationship of German-Americans to the European war, and their propaganda activities in cooperation with the representatives of the Empire in America.[168] A sociostructural analysis of the so-called German-Americans, who are generally treated as a coherent interest group, but who have in fact emerged from quite different waves of immigration, does not belong here.

When speaking of "German-Americans," one generally refers to two not quite similar groups, namely, Americans who were born in

Germany and those who are of more or less direct German origin. Concerning the latter group, identification beyond the first generation of immigrant children is difficult, since any other association with the German-American population appears to be personally motivated. In short, it can be argued that the immigrants' children were frequently already fully assimilated, but, by the same token, one often discovers a lively interest in German matters after several generations, in many cases even after the German language has been lost.[169]

It has often been emphasized that to a large extent the German-American population was organized into clubs and associations even before the war, a claim entirely supported by statistics and membership figures.[170] Strong doubts, however, arise concerning the importance and the cohesiveness of these groups in their orientation toward Germany, when one notes how in 1917 the German-American sector of the American population in no way prevented the government of the United States from entering the war on the side of the Entente and from contributing directly in the course of the next two years to the military collapse of Germany. Even taking into account the pressures of public opinion on German-Americans after the American declaration of war and the considerable effect of the American propaganda machine, the resistance of German-Americans to Washington's entry into the war seems rather mild and moderate, especially when measured against their relatively large numbers.[171] One must therefore caution against an all-too-hasty overestimation of the political influence of these associations and clubs, particularly on American foreign policy.

Even before the war, Bernstorff had realized and informed the Wilhelmstrasse that the majority of German-Americans were lost for the German cause as far as direct engagement was concerned.[172] True to his liberal views, he had gone on to suggest looking upon the Americans of German descent more appropriately as an important link in the German efforts to achieve increasingly better trade relations with the United States. Under the pressures of the outbreak of the war, this insight seems to have been forgotten and, contrary to Bernstorff's earlier appraisal, a serious effort was made to incorporate the German-Americans into the propaganda machine.

Indeed, the German-Americans themselves were not quite immune to the "spirit of 1914." In the initial frenzy of patriotic enthusiasm, they gathered for mass demonstrations in many cities throughout the country. Fiery speeches were delivered, and the texts were given to the press for publication. The German-American reservists who had reported for military duty to serve the distant Empire marched through the streets of Chicago with flying colors. People sang "Die Wacht am Rhein" and sent telegrams to the Emperor.[173] During the first days of August "an immense number of German men" from all the states of the Union and a little later even from South and Central America and East Asia traveled to New York. They were evidently driven by their enthusiasm for the cause of the fatherland, but, it should be remembered, they were also called upon by the German consulates to be ready for shipment to Europe as military reservists.[174] When Bernstorff arrived in America, it was his unpleasant task to see to it that these reservists went home quietly, since the Germans had no means to send troop-transports—estimates spoke of a troop strength of up to two army corps—to Germany.[175]

If the strange encampment of German military men in New York City had already caused some sensation, the American press now began to observe with growing attention any further official steps taken by the German representatives. As early as October, American newspapers carried reports that Matthew B. Claussen's press propaganda activities in New York City had been organized "at the request of prominent German-Americans";[176] in other words, in the eyes of the public, a connection between German-Americans and the Imperial propaganda campaign was established early. Yet this was to be only the beginning. During a conference of the German press office on November 5, 1914, to which Bernstorff had also come from Washington, it was officially stated that the time had now come to fully involve the German-Americans in the public relations campaign. The chief of propaganda, Bernhard Dernburg,[177] argued that, in his view, German-Americans wished "to strike a stronger tone now," and that it would be appropriate not to prevent them from doing so. The German representatives and agents even thought they recognized that "among many indifferent people of German descent, German sentiment [Deutschtum] in these times has been reawakened,"[178] and it was decided that this new movement could and should be encouraged. Accordingly, two measures were adopted: support of the German-language press and speeches before German gatherings.[179] In other words, as the later German Ambassador Friedrich Wilhelm von Prittwitz und Gaffron wrote in his memoirs, they furthered "the mentality... which in America somewhat disparagingly is called hyphen mentality."[180] As it turned out, during the war years Americans of German descent were to suffer severely from the consequences of this "hyphen mentality."

The German-language press was represented most outspokenly by George Sylvester Viereck's propaganda sheet, *The Fatherland*, and the *New Yorker Staats-Zeitung* of the Ridder family. In both cases the tendentious tone was not likely to convince a majority of Americans who were not of German descent of the impartiality of the reports printed. Since Viereck's financial dependence on the embassy became known, the propagandistic value of this publication, too, was limited. The *Staats-Zeitung* was an old German paper and known as such; even if Americans who were not of German descent but read German may not have suspected the official German influence, it is still doubtful whether this paper was particularly suitable as an advertising medium for the Central Powers.

Clearly, the German-language newspapers had to do their work under most unfavorable conditions. During the war it became more and more difficult for them to justify to Americans and probably also to many German-Americans the illegal activities and offenses of German agents which repeatedly drew public attention. All the same, specific criminal acts by the German intelligence services, such as the blowing up of a bridge by the German reservist, Werner Horn, discussed elsewhere, could somehow be explained as the deeds of irresponsible individuals whose sanity indeed might be questioned.[181] Again, other German endeavors, such as certain conspiracies in Mexico, which took place far enough away, were declared to be slanderous rumors manufactured by a libelous Entente.[182] The end of this kind of journalistic activity came only when Lt. Walter Schwieger torpedoed the *Lusitania* on May 7, 1915. The death of 124 neutral American citizens was a heavy blow to America's national pride, and the majority of Americans reacted with disgust to the news of this German action. Germany had suddenly become "an outlaw among civilized nations."[183]

While in early 1915 many German-Americans had still hoped for "a more just evaluation of Germany" by their fellow citizens, all prospects for a friendly attitude on the part of the American public toward Germany were dashed at least temporarily with the sinking of the passenger liner. German-Americans found themselves in a rather hopeless situation. It is true, the two cornerstones of German-American propaganda, Ridder and Viereck, explained to their readers that the American victims of the *Lusitania* were themselves to be blamed for their deaths because they had booked a trip on a steamer which was loaded with war material,[184] and Dernburg, in his own inimitable manner, voiced similarly inappropriate opinions in public. But these German reactions turned out to be empty speeches which could hardly hope for a positive echo.[185] Certainly, the majority of Americans did not want a war, but as never before, the tension of public opinion was nearing the breaking point.

Bernstorff himself at this time thought it advisable to remain silent in public. The more the chorus of propagandists talked of Britain's guilt, of the *Lusitania*'s cargo of ammunition, and of the risk of traveling on a British passenger ship, the stronger became the reactions of those who pleaded for an American intervention against Germany.[186] Since Heinrich Albert was already overburdened with work, the German-Americans were for the most part left to themselves after Dernburg had to depart. The possibility that under the new conditions German-Americans could still exert an influence worth mentioning on public opinion in favor of Germany could only be considered small.[187] Uneasy silence or loyalty to America had now become the alternatives for many of them.[188]

As it was, the German-Americans recovered from the emotional low of the *Lusitania* crisis, and, in the following one and a half years before the German declaration of unlimited submarine warfare, there were repeated occasions when German-American voices were heard loudly and clearly on the American political scene. These comments came from the host of more or less insufficiently informed German-American local newspapers, as well as from some associations which could not be silenced, especially Charles Hexamer's vociferous German-American National Alliance. Thus, in some areas German-Americans remained an important factor during elections. Large numbers also participated in political organizations, which, in some cases at the direct instigation of agents of the German embassy, agitated for an embargo[189] or which for a variety of reasons supported peace movements. The vague possibility, however, of the entry of the United States into the war on the side of the Central Powers, something which isolated groups may have hoped for at the beginning of the war, was no longer a topic of the propaganda. The goal of most German-Americans, if they were at all politically engaged, was to keep America at least out of the camp of the Entente.[190] However, German-Americans not only joined all kinds of organizations which were questionable with regard to their intentions in neutral America and were influenced by

Imperial German propaganda, but they also in many cases served as patriotically inspired or simply as paid agents of the so-called "propaganda of action." If their participation in German propaganda lent itself to the anti-German campaign of the pro-Entente newspapers, the much-discussed actual and suspected acts of sabotage and the strike movements instigated with German funds did much damage to the German image in American public opinion.

On the whole, the tragedy of the situation for German-Americans was that the war led a minority of immigrants, who actually had fully assimilated in their new home, back to a nationalistic, vulgarly patriotic group consciousness. Still it must be remembered that they had little or no political power and organizational base in America upon which they could have built their new patriotic stance.[191] Bernstorff had recognized this, but was so overtaken by the events of war that he did not offer strong personal opposition and in some cases even contributed to the ruthless exploitation of the German-Americans for German interests.

GERMAN PROPAGANDA AMONG AMERICANS OF IRISH DESCENT

At the time of the First World War, the Irish ethnic group was different from the German-Americans, the Russian Jews, and the Americans of Austro-Hungarian descent in having a lively political tradition in the United States.[192] The Irish played leading roles in America's trade union movement, they had an extremely influential voice in the American Catholic church, and they held powerful positions in the Democratic party.[193]

The antecedents of the German-Irish cooperation during the war go far back.[194] Seven years before the war broke out, contacts were made through the mediation of Theodor Schiemann, professor for Eastern European history in Berlin, between the Wilhelmstrasse and Irish groups in New York which reflected on the possibility of a British-German confrontation and for that eventuality considered an Irish-German collaboration in America.[195] Even this early, Schiemann replied to the Irishman George Freeman, associated with the *Gaelic American*: "The cooperation of your countrymen with the Germans of America for the welcome purpose which you have in mind is naturally in the highest degree desirable," although he added that he would advise against establishing any connections with Ambassador Sternburg in order to avoid possible embarrassment.[196] The documents, however, show clearly that Sternburg certainly kept his lines of communication with the Irish open and was completely informed about the Irish-German efforts. Direct contact in public with personalities of the German-Irish movement was avoided; the way for "fraternization" instead was prepared by Charles J. Hexamer[197] in Philadelphia. Sternburg, for his part, feared: "The slightest suspicion could cause the loss of the trust which we enjoy here."[198]

Bernstorff of course knew of the position of the Irish in America and expressed his view to the Foreign Office that they were "a stronger counterbalance against the British influence than the German-Americans."[199] Still, in January 1914 he reported to Berlin that the leadership of the German-Americans had "gotten into the hands of demagogic elements," and he felt that this was so "particularly since common interests had been established with the Irish."[200] By the same token, just as in the case of the German-Americans, new conditions were created by the war, and it was not long until Bernstorff practically functioned as a go-between for the Irish revolutionaries in Ireland and America and the German General Staff,[201] or rather, Roger Casement in Berlin.

Even before the Ambassador had returned to Washington in the summer of 1914, the German Military Attaché, Capt. Franz von Papen, had first conversations with Roger Casement, who was in America at that time. As a result of these discussions, the Foreign Office on August 27 asked Bernstorff about his views regarding the advisability of an official German announcement in support of the Irish liberation movement.[202] His answer, which incidentally was intercepted by the British intelligence service and (probably somewhat later) deciphered, read: "In this case I do not think it is necessary to take American public opinion into consideration, since here we are most likely to find friends, if we free oppressed peoples such as Poles, Finns, and Irish. . . . It seems to me that the crucial question is whether there is any prospect of reaching an understanding with England or whether we have to prepare for a battle of life and death. In the latter case, I recommend compliance with Irish wishes, provided that there are really Irish who will help us."[203] Direct help for Germany seemed to become a real possibility through the organization of the Irish Brigade, a project which at least officially met with Bernstorff's hearty approval.

In neutral America, Bernstorff sought to support the anti-English mood of the Irish, particularly through his relations with the spokesmen of the revolutionary movement in New York. He maintained contact with John Devoy, the most prominent leader of the Irish and publisher of the *Gaelic American*, with the New York judge, Daniel F. Cohalan, one of the leading men in the Irish revolutionary organization, with members of the Clan na Gael, and with other important persons.[204] Aside from the direct relations with the revolutionaries in connection with the Easter Rising in Dublin in 1916, which will be examined later, there is, despite many uncertainties and open questions, no doubt that during the period of American neutrality from 1914 to 1917 the German government carried out systematic, though not very successful, propaganda work among the Irish.

Dernburg's previously discussed press office even maintained a special Irish Press and News Service in New York, which was run by James McGuire, and two to three times a week provided eighteen to twenty Irish newspapers with information favoring the Central Powers.[205] The *Gaelic American* published German propaganda, and German-American companies and the *New Yorker Staats-Zeitung* supported the Irish press through advertisements. The *Gaelic American*, as well as the *Irish World*, followed a propaganda line which hardly differed from that of the German-language newspapers. So-called peace rallies were held together, and Germans and Irish marched in the same demonstrations.[206] Many of these organized expressions of opinion may indeed have come about independently of the official German propaganda; many an American of Irish descent may have joined German protest movements entirely on his own, merely to vent his antagonism against Britain. In retrospect, it is nearly impossible to determine with any degree of accuracy how much of the Irish-German cooperation in the peace, embargo, and anti-British agitation would have been supported by the Irish anyway, and to what extent agents of the German government were responsible for the actions of these movements. The sparse documents of the intelligence services which escaped destruction toward the end of the war and found their way into the records of the Foreign Office are nevertheless proof enough to state that Berlin did consciously work on the Irish population, especially in the eastern United States. In the final analysis, the accusations voiced on the American side agree surprisingly well with the facts which can be sifted from the remaining records.[207]

The official sources leave no doubt that Bernstorff, Papen, and others were not only completely informed about the actions planned by the Irish revolutionaries, but also that they supported these undertakings in many ways. After Papen had been expelled from the United States in December 1915, a considerable part of his functions, among them the work with the Irish, was continued by Wolf von Igel, who even at the outset of his activities can hardly have worked without Bernstorff's knowledge.[208] In addition to the activities of Bernstorff, Papen, Igel, and Georg von Skal, which emanated from the embassy and were directed from Berlin, the intelligence services in Berlin also paid close attention to the Irish question; the exact extent of cooperation between the intelligence agents and the embassy in Washington can no longer be clarified. From the Foreign Office records we do know that the German authorities sent a number of agents to the United States. From February 1915 onward Major Hans Boehm of Department IIIb of the General Staff, who at the beginning of the war had gone to the United States on sabotage missions, traveled "several times" to America on Irish matters.[209] Even after the tragic uprising in Dublin, the propaganda among the Irish was by no means abandoned; instead, new agents were sent as late as the fall of 1916 to stir up the Irish opposition.[210]

Capt. Paul Reichardt, who from August 1916 until March 1917 directed the Sabotage Section N IV of the intelligence department of the Admiralty on Lützowstrasse in Berlin under the cover name of "Agatit-Werke," informed the Imperial Ministry of Defense (Reichswehrministerium) after the war that as late as September 1916 there had been plans "to operate against England with the help of the Irish living in America, that is, to win over Irishmen in the United States who were supposed to perform acts of sabotage in England or in the English fleet." For this purpose two agents, Hermann Wessels[211] and a woman named Dr. Simon, née Kretzschmann[212] were sent to America by the above-mentioned office. Wessels, who traveled with a forged Swiss passport, went first; the woman agent was supposed to help him with his tasks. Shortly thereafter, the Admiralty sent a third agent by the name of Kircheisen, who was to work as a contact man for Wessels.[213]

Independently of the work of the German representatives and their agents or the intelligence service operatives among the Irish, this ethnic group gave tangible expression to its anti-English sentiment on various occasions. Thus, soon after the beginning of the war, they reacted with unbridled indignation when they thought they noticed that Wilson's neutrality permitted arms deliveries to the Entente powers, but that he was unwilling or unable to insure that Germany should profit in the same way from American industrial output.[214] As an answer to Wilson's policy, they voted together with the German-Americans against the Democrats in many areas in the congressional elections in November 1914.[215] The American Truth Society was especially active in the joint propaganda efforts of Irish and Germans in the eastern states.[216] Directed by the Irish-American leader, Jeremiah A. O'Leary, this organization had been founded in 1912, but during the war it counted among its well-known members such prominent personalities as Viereck, Ridder, and F. F. Schrader, who were clearly in the service of the Germans.[217] In the election battle in November 1916, Germans and Irish joined forces in many cities in order to try to bring the Republican candidate Charles Evans Hughes to the White House.[218]

In spite of a wide variety of activities, the German campaign among the Irish in America was a failure. It was not able to win the Irish en masse over to the side of the Central Powers, nor did it succeed in mobilizing an effective movement for an arms embargo, against the availability of credits to the Allies, or against America's entry into the war in 1917. Kuno Meyer's public appearances under the motto "The golden age of Irish civilization and its influence on Germany"[219] and the efforts of the Irish press office could not weld the divided Irish into a political front. If the militant Irish did not manage among themselves to pool their strength for the common goal of an Irish state, the differences of opinion between the radical Sinn Fein group around John Devoy's *Gaelic American* and the followers of John Redmond (who were willing to make their peace with England, for the time being at least) were almost irreconcilable.[220]

THREE

THE WAR YEARS, 1914−1917

Submarine Warfare and the Possibilities for Peace

from August 1914 to June 1915

In spite of the numerous studies about the submarine war,[1] it is necessary to ask what effects the U-boat, which in 1914 was still a very new weapon and untested as an instrument of power, had on Bernstorff and his diplomatic conduct. Historians until now have agreed that, besides the so-called Zimmermann telegram, submarine warfare, with the accompanying exchange of notes between Berlin and Washington, was the cause for the rupture of diplomatic relations in February 1917. In addition to this conflict about the use of submarines and in some respects dependent on this question, there was also a constant exchange of messages between Berlin and the Embassy in Washington in which the possibility of an American mediation was discussed. While in Berlin in the summer of 1914, Bernstorff apparently did not receive any specific instructions regarding possible American reactions to submarine warfare or the exploration of the possibilities of mediation.[2] Yet during the first phase of the war, both questions gained considerable importance for Germany's attitude toward the most powerful of the neutral countries, as well as for the American government in the formulation of its thoroughly serious policy of neutrality. Although this author does not count himself among those interpreters who would see submarine warfare as the final or only decisive issue in the German-American conflict, he has no doubt that the use of the new weapon greatly contributed to preparing the American public and government for war with the Central Powers. However, to the United States, German submarine warfare was not the sole threat to its neutrality; American opposition to German actions or announcements in the naval sector has to be seen in connection with measures taken by Germany in quite different areas of modern warfare.

U-BOAT WARFARE FROM THE BEGINNING OF THE WAR UNTIL THE TORPEDOING OF THE *LUSITANIA*

Although officially the German declaration of submarine warfare on February 4, 1915, was announced as a countermeasure to the British blockade, it came in fact not only as a retaliatory step but also as a result of considerations which since the outbreak of the war had found eager advocates in Germany. As early as August 1914, ten U-boats had been sent to the North Sea to track down the British fleet, and at the end of September Lt. Otto Weddigen and his *U-9* had sunk three British cruisers off the Dutch coast. After such successes from a single submarine,[3] it was not surprising that on October 8 Lt. Cdr. Hermann Bauer, chief of the German U-boat fleet, suggested countering British mine warfare with an unrestricted submarine war against commercial shipping. Bauer was well aware of the fact that his weapon could not be deployed according to international rules of capture, but he felt that a special status could be claimed for submarine warfare.[4]

Use of the U-boat weapon against commerce was thus considered at a time when, it is true, the battle of the Marne had come to a halt, but when, on the other hand, German troops were about to break the last resistance in Belgium. Antwerp fell on October 9, Ostend on October 15. Although the German navy did not have more than twenty-one submarines at its disposal,[5] of which only nine were fit for long-distance voyages, Bauer's suggestion soon found approval in navy circles, despite initial reservations. After Britain declared the entire North Sea a war zone on November 2, Admiral Hugo von Pohl, Chief of the Naval Staff, gave his support to the plan. On November 21, the State Secretary in the Reichsmarineamt, Admiral of the Fleet Alfred von Tirpitz, spoke to the American journalist, Karl H. von Wiegand, about an impending blockade of Britain by German submarines. This interview, published on December 22,[6] was the beginning of a development that was to have a disastrous influence on German submarine decisions up to that fateful encounter in Pless in January 1917. It was at this time that the so-called U-boat movement (*U-Boot-Bewegung*) started. "From then on," as Gerhard Ritter remarks, "submarine warfare was no longer a military problem, which had to be dealt with by experts, but a political question of the first order, on which the whole world wished to have a say."[7]

As was to be expected, the ensuing discussion in Germany was concerned, among other things, with the possible reaction of the neutral countries in the event that their cargo vessels fell victim to German submarines. One would have thought that the United States, being the big power among the neutral nations, would have been the object of special attention. But during the early months of the war, considerations in Berlin were characterized by the same curious underestimation of America which was to have such a fateful effect on Bernstorff's later endeavors. Even though the military and the government thoroughly reckoned with the possibility that the United States might support the Entente with shipments of war material in the event of a German-American break, the prevailing opinion was that America would not declare war, since, due to its lack of combat-ready troops, Washington would be forced to observe restraint.[8] As for the violation of international law, Bethmann Hollweg did have certain reservations "that the torpedoing of neutral ships was not quite reconcilable with the general rules of international law."[9] For Tirpitz the matter was much simpler, namely submarines had not been in existence when the present regulations were formulated; furthermore, Tirpitz knew that international law only stipulated that a blockade had to be effective, and it was precisely this which he felt the new weapon promised.[10] Nevertheless, it was the Chancellor who won the first round when he appeared with Admiral von Pohl before the Emperor on January 9, 1915. Declaration of the blockade was postponed "until the presently existing unclarity of the political situation is eliminated."[11]

The postponement was to be of only short duration; by January 20, Pohl could "no longer consider the reservations against the submarine blockade well founded." While the neutral countries would see in Germany's declaration a sign of strength which would keep them from joining the Entente, "the German people" demanded that this weapon, "which they expected to be a means of inflicting heavy damage on England," no longer remain unused.[12] Officially, Pohl founded his new demand, which he wanted to present to the Emperor, on the necessity of preventing the expected transport of troops from Britain to France.[13] In fact, however, as Jagow correctly informed the Chancellor,[14] Pohl's plan was tantamount to the just postponed submarine blockade. Some representatives of the "German people" cited by Pohl wasted no time in expressing their opinions. On January 26, 1915, eight well-known university professors submitted a petition to the Imperial Chancellor in which they demanded air raids on unfortified harbors, such as Liverpool, and the blockade of Britain by submarines. They argued that the effectiveness of the blockade should be the only recognized principle; "humanitarian scruples concerning the perhaps unavoidable hardships caused by destroying blockade-runners" were to be considered "less important" in view of the sufferings inflicted on German citizens by the British blockade.[15] These professors did not speak for their group alone, but they could be viewed, as they emphasized in their petition, as representatives of a significant portion of the German people. As Karl Birnbaum has written,[16] these Germans, probably as a consequence of the successes of German submarines in the fall of 1914 and of Tirpitz's encouraging information to Wiegand, had become convinced that the new weapon would help Germany to bring the war to a quick and successful end. It is difficult to say whether the Chancellor was really "under unusually strong pressure from public opinion"[17] and for that reason gave in to the military leaders on February 1, 1915,[18] or whether Bethmann Hollweg, who at the same time was not at all anxious to enter into peace negotiations not dictated by Germany, trusted the military experts and hoped for an early German victory.[19]

On February 4, 1915, in the words of Thomas A. Bailey and Paul B. Ryan "a fateful day in world history," Pohl delivered the proclamation, which had been discussed on February 1, to the Emperor in Wilhelmshaven in the presence of the Chancellor, and Wilhelm II affixed his signature to this first declaration of submarine warfare.[20] To enemy and neutral nations alike the German Empire declared a blockade area around the British Isles, where it reserved the right to sink any merchant vessel after February 18, regardless of nationality, without ensuring the safety of passengers and crew. James W. Gerard, the American Ambassador in Berlin, had already received news of the impending announcement from Zimmermann on February 4 and had immediately wired Secretary of State Bryan. On that evening, Gerard cabled the final text of the German decision, which was also conveyed to the American Secretary of State on February 7 by Count Bernstorff. The proclamation stated that Germany was forced into the blockade by the unlawful measures taken by Britain, especially since the neutral powers—that is, America—had not succeeded in influencing Britain's behavior. "Beginning February 18, 1915, . . . [Germany] will endeavor to destroy every enemy merchant ship that is found in this area of war without its always being possible to avert the peril that thus threatens persons and cargoes. Neutrals are therefore warned against further entrusting crews, passengers and wares to such ships. Their attention [is] also called to the fact that it is advisable for their ships to avoid entering the area."[21] In his memoirs, Bernstorff recalls that at first Bryan had been completely incredulous and apparently had taken the German declaration to be a "bluff." "Accordingly," Bernstorff writes, Washington had not taken any "preventive measures," but on February 12[22] had sent a note of protest to Germany.[23] In fact, Gerard's warning had not arrived at the State Department until February 4, and Wilson was not informed until February 5. Indeed the American President had first learned about the German decision from reports in the morning newspapers. The answer to the Germans, prepared by Lansing and Wilson,[24] was clear enough: "If the commanders of German vessels of war should act upon the presumption that the flag of the United States was not being used in good faith and should destroy... an American vessel or the lives of American citizens, it would be difficult for the Government of the United States to view the act in any other light than as an indefensible violation of neutral rights.... If such a deplorable situation should arise, the Imperial German Government can readily appreciate that the Government of the United States would be constrained to hold the Imperial German Government to a strict accountability for such acts."[25]

America's "menacing note of protest"[26] evidently made enough of an impression on German governmental circles for them to postpone once again the beginning of the campaign set for February 18. While Berlin did not treat the emotions of the neutral world with kid gloves, it did hesitate at this point to provoke the break with the United States which had suddenly become a real possibility.[27] When Jagow replied on February 16, the tone was accordingly milder. After the illegal use of neutral flags by British ships and the intolerability of the British blockade had been pointed out once more, the Germans said they were willing to spare from attack American ships which were clearly recognizable as such, did not carry contraband, and possibly moved in convoys.[28] In the meantime, the provisional order of February 2 to the submarines to sink all merchant ships was replaced by a new order on February 18, according to which recognizably neutral ships, especially those in convoys, were to be spared.[29] On February 22 the U-boats finally received orders from the new Chief of Naval Staff, Adm. Gustav

Bachmann, to start operations in the war zone.[30] Two German submarines were already stationed there, and four more left port in February.

The U-boat war on commercial shipping was now a reality, and the sinking of neutral merchant ships, including American vessels, had thus become a foreseeable possibility, with all the expectable consequences. Nevertheless, the originally planned use of submarines and the impact of this weapon, if one can speak at all of such, given the small number of boats available, had been limited considerably due to the American opposition. Bernstorff thought the German note of February 16 to have been a success,[31] because it had prompted the American government to ask the warring nations[32] not to misuse neutral flags and to suggest to Britain that it let food supplies go through to Germany as long as they were destined to be sold solely to the civilian population. Against the navy's massive protest,[33] the Emperor agreed with Bethmann Hollweg and Jagow to respond in generally positive terms to these suggestions.[34] As it was, the American initiative was to be unsuccessful, because the British, as might have been expected, declared the suggestions impracticable. The British cruiser blockade, they argued, had basically the same purpose as the German blockade, but differed essentially from it in that neutral lives and goods were not destroyed.[35] It remains to be noted that the American suggestion probably would not have proved practicable for Germany's intensive war economy anyway, especially as far as imports of raw material were concerned.

For the German military leadership, these ineffectual negotiations between the United States and Great Britain were less important than the disappointing results of the first weeks of submarine warfare. Whereas the Germans had expected that a large number of ships would be destroyed by the U-boats and even more that the expected losses of ships would cause a paralyzing shock on the enemy side, the Admiralty was only able to register a mere total of 22,184 tons, nine small ships, sunk in February. In March, too, enemy losses were relatively small, compared to the number of ships safely crossing the war zone.[36] Strictly speaking, this should not have surprised a naval command which could only throw a handful of ships into the battle. While the failure of the submarines caused much disappointment, Britain did not miss the opportunity to rub salt into the wounds by announcing in early March the complete halt to *all* shipments bound for Germany, both directly to German ports as well as through neutral countries. The purpose of the Order in Council of March 11, 1915, was to force the shipping companies to give up all trade with Germany.[37] The Americans, who so far had suffered relatively little from the events of war, responded to this British measure with a statement to the effect that they would tolerate the blockade, although it lacked any legal basis, as long as the British remained within the framework of international agreements as far as American commerce was concerned. In other words, in the case of the German declaration of a war zone on February 4, as well as in the case of the British declaration of the total blockade, Woodrow Wilson accepted the use of an instrument of war that so far had not been customary. At the same time, he tried, although more strongly in the case of Germany, to safeguard American rights by holding the warring nations responsible for any eventualities. "Both sides are seeing red on the other side of the sea, and neutral rights are left, for the time being, out of their reckoning altogether."[38]

Unfortunately, German tactics entailed that ships were to be sunk instead of handed over to a prize court. In the one case, it was a matter of the temporary loss of goods, but in the other it was a matter of destruction of life and property, a difference the British never tired of stressing. The American response to the British measure certainly did not help to create a better climate for German-American relations, which at that time had already suffered considerable setbacks because of the activities of German intelligence operatives inside the United States. Strangely enough, the imminent danger of the destruction of American ships and of possible deaths of American citizens played a relatively small role in the American deliberations during those first few weeks of the submarine war on commerce. Bernstorff, Dernburg, and a few other German representatives appear to have been the only ones who were seriously worried about the consequences of the loss of American lives.[39] By the middle of April 1915, they had decided to publish a warning in the American press that was intended to keep American citizens from traveling on enemy passenger ships and thus risking their lives. The warning, under the heading "NOTICE!," read: "Travelers intending to embark on the Atlantic voyage are reminded that a state of war exists between Germany and her allies and Great Britain and her allies; that the zone of war includes the waters adjacent to the British Isles; that, in accordance with formal notice given by the Imperial German Government, vessels flying the flag of Great Britain, or any of her allies, are liable to destruction in those waters and that travelers sailing in the war zone on ships of

Great Britain or her allies do so at their own risk. IMPERIAL GERMAN EMBASSY. Washington, D.C., April 22, 1915." Bernstorff writes in his memoirs that the plans called for publication of this notice on three consecutive Saturdays beginning April 24; due to technical difficulties, he explains, it did not appear in the newspapers until May 1.[40]

On that day the large British passenger liner *Lusitania* was docked at a pier in New York harbor; departure time had been set for 10 A.M. The German Ambassador writes that he never considered the possibility of German submarines sinking passenger ships, and it does seem plausible that the publication of the official warning on this date did not have any direct connection with the departure of the *Lusitania*. Bernstorff was, as many others, convinced that the *Lusitania*'s high speed made it technically impossible to attack her.[41] That also seems to have been the opinion of the passengers who boarded the vessel that morning. Indeed, the harbor was swarming with reporters who had been driven there by the German warning, and much time was lost because authorities thoroughly checked each passenger's luggage, but in the end only one passenger, a pastor from New England, decided to cancel his trip. The other passengers—among them the well-known multimillionaire Alfred Gwynne Vanderbilt, who crossed the gangway with a carnation in his buttonhole—celebrated the departure. To be sure, the German notice was not a customary occurrence, and for Robert Lansing, Counselor and second man in charge of the State Department, it was further proof of Germany's carelessness regarding a break with the United States. Bryan, on the other hand, the pacifist and idealist, saw it as Bernstorff seems to have done, namely as an effort to avoid a possible German-American conflict.[42]

One week later the luxury liner was traveling through the war zone at a speed of eighteen knots and heading for Queenstown. The passengers were having lunch when Lt. Walter Schwieger, commander of the *U-20*, attacked the ship with a single torpedo from a distance of 700 meters. After less than an hour, nothing of the proud steamer was left on the surface but a few life boats and 761 people who had been able to save themselves during the sudden catastrophe. Among the 1,198 passengers and crew who went down with the ship were 124 American citizens.[43]

PEACE EFFORTS BETWEEN GERMANY AND THE UNITED STATES UNTIL THE SPRING OF 1915

Bernstorff recalls in his memoirs that until the sinking of the *Lusitania* he had not directly been drawn into negotiations about submarine warfare.[44] Indeed, this first phase of the U-boat conflict was handled from Berlin, and Bernstorff only served as the courier in the exchange of notes between the two governments. Nevertheless, the previously described developments are of great importance if one takes into consideration the fact that concurrently with the dispute over the use of the new weapon and the following initial phase of submarine warfare, the Ambassador was involved in negotiations to bring about an early peace through America's mediation or at least to explore the warring parties' viewpoints concerning terms under which they could come to the peace table.

Since the United States, contrary to the opinion of a number of influential German political and military leaders, already held a position of international power and influence, it was not surprising that Woodrow Wilson felt called upon to offer his mediation. Count Bernstorff recognized America's special status at a time when under the first impression of early military successes the often naive propaganda campaign in Germany could hardly foresee any other end to the war than a clear German victory. Although it cannot be overlooked that Bernstorff, especially during the initial months of the war, launched an equally heated propaganda campaign in America and in its takeoff phase did not hesitate personally to enter this battle of words, we have a number of indications that very early he had few illusions about the true distribution of political and economic weight in the power constellation of 1914. The Ambassador's insight may serve as a possible explanation for his repeated involvement in mediation talks during the fall and winter of 1914–15. Again and again he attempted to convince Americans that Germany was not opposed to a peace under acceptable conditions. In so doing, he often exposed himself to scorn, because Berlin at that time evidently was not searching for peace, and certainly not a status quo ante peace, and thus deemed it advisable to nip in the bud any mediation attempts, at least those emanating from America. Independent of the momentary military situation, Bernstorff seriously explored all possible avenues that might lead to peace. Occasional contradictory utterances, which probably should be written off as propaganda, do not alter this impression of his basic attitude.

Moreover, from the beginning of the war Bernstorff was convinced, and not without reason, that, despite evident sympathy for the Allies, Wilson was sincere in his mediation efforts.[45]

As early as August 4, 1914, Woodrow Wilson sent an offer of good offices to the heads of state of Germany, Britain, France, Austria-Hungary, and Russia: "I should welcome an opportunity to act in the interest of European peace, either now or at any other time that might be thought more suitable."[46] As was to be expected, hardly anyone in Europe was thinking of peace in those emotionally charged days.[47] France and Russia deplored the fact that they had been forced into a defensive war, Britain did not think the time was ripe to speak of peace, and, in the presence of Ambassador Gerard in the garden of the Imperial residence, the German Emperor wrote a detailed note demanding that Germany be exonerated of all responsibility for the war.[48] There was indeed very little prospect for rousing general interest in peace negotiations in Europe at this stage of the conflict. Yet Wilson's desire to bring peace to the world seems not to have been affected by this, and Washington kept searching for new opportunities.

During the next weeks there ensued a lively exchange of offers and refusals largely set in motion at the instigation of Colonel Edward Mandell House, but also made possible by the complete agreement of President Wilson. On September 5, House wrote Under Secretary Zimmermann and suggested that the peace-loving Emperor could, now that his armies had so clearly proved their strength, take the opportunity to consent to possible peace feelers. House said that he would be happy to serve as a "medium" of such efforts.[49] That same evening, while House was sitting down to dinner with the Austro-Hungarian Ambassador, Constantin Dumba, and was using the occasion to sound him out, another dinner was taking place in New York at the home of the banker, James Speyer, which was attended by the former American Ambassador to Turkey, Oscar S. Straus, and Count Bernstorff.[50] Speyer had had a long friendly relationship with Bernstorff, and Straus, too, had known the German Ambassador for many years. While German troops on the western front were threatening the French capital, the guests at the Speyer home discussed the possibilities for peace. One can no longer reliably reconstruct what was said by whom, but it would appear that Straus made the first move[51] by broaching the question of mediation: since France was now on its knees, the moment would be most favorable. Bernstorff, who obviously did not have instructions from Berlin for such an eventuality, and who, as Karl E. Birnbaum observes, "seems to have judged the whole peace problem in a different way from that of his superiors,"[52] replied that Germany "certainly [would be] ready for a negotiated peace at the earliest appropriate opportunity."[53] At Straus's insistence, he added that he did not object to having his opinion reported to Bryan. Later that same night, Straus traveled to Washington to quickly convey the favorable news to the Secretary of State.[54] Wilson shared Bryan's view that the German Foreign Office should be consulted immediately, and, with Bernstorff's consent,[55] Bryan instructed Gerard on September 7 to inform the government in Berlin about the conversation. If the Emperor was positively inclined toward a mediation offer by the United States, Wilson would appeal to the governments of the Allies.[56] As it was, Washington did not wait for the German answer. After the arrival of a report from Walter H. Page, the American Ambassador in London, that the Entente powers had decided not to consider any peace suggestions separately, Bryan informed Page and Myron T. Herrick in Paris, as well as the Ambassadors of Britain and France in Washington.[57] Bernstorff reported to the Foreign Office that he knew what great importance America placed on the restoration of peace; therefore, he said, he had not wanted to refuse the offer. In fact, he advised Berlin to accept, because public opinion in America would turn against the power that appeared responsible for the prolongation of the war.[58]

But the effort was in vain. While Edward Grey intimated during a confidential conversation with Page that Britain was in principle willing to negotiate, provided that an end was put to German militarism and reparations were paid to an evacuated Belgium,[59] Bethmann Hollweg replied that Germany first wished to hear the suggestions of its enemies: "If we accepted America's offer of mediation now, our enemies would interpret it as a sign of weakness and the German people would not understand it."[60] Nevertheless, the German answer did not conclusively refuse American peace mediation,[61] and Wilson felt inclined to pursue Straus's initiative. A change in Wilson's method, not in his goals, came about in so far as he now transferred the negotiations to his trusted adviser,[62] Colonel House.

House had succeeded in developing a somewhat personal relationship with both Spring Rice and Bernstorff. The opinion prevails that, of the two men, he knew Spring Rice the better.[63] This is not surprising if one keeps in mind how the German national image and its military elements[64] appeared to many Americans, including House, and if one also recalls Bernstorff—certainly not a military man, but, from an American perspective, rather Prussian in appearance, with a very proper manner of dress and great self-assurance, if not at times conceited ways.[65] He indeed seemed to represent all those things which Americans would connect with the ambassador of Wilhelm II and a member of the German noble and Junker class.[66] Still, despite some differences, Bernstorff and House learned to work together closely during the war years, and one cannot help but have the impression that their negotiations took place in an atmosphere of mutual trust hardly to be expected in the circumstances. Over the years the influential Texan and the German diplomat developed a relationship which can certainly be called a friendship of two men guided by similar goals.[67]

House tried to win Bernstorff and Spring Rice for secret negotiations, as Charles Seymour says, "a highly unconventional proceeding," but in the considered opinion of House, perhaps the only step that held any promise in view of the refusals from Europe. The Colonel's efforts were not made easier by the deep mistrust between Spring Rice[68] and Bernstorff, two basically different personalities. The Englishman, in particular, could not find anything positive in Germany or the Germans. A further difficulty was that, although neither Germany nor Britain had expressed a readiness for peace, in the long run it would become necessary to talk about points of detail going beyond a general preparedness to negotiate. House operated on the premise that Britain still played the role of the leading power among the Allies and would be satisfied with a disarmament agreement and reparation payments to Belgium, and he assumed that Germany would not be disinclined to consider such conditions.[69] To what extent his ideas corresponded with reality cannot be examined in detail here. Suffice it to say that House's evaluation appears somewhat optimistic in view of the war aims which both nations had formulated up to then. No matter how one judges its significance, Bethmann Hollweg's "September Program" spoke of a France to be degraded for years to the status of a second-class nation dependent on German trade and deprived of its ore region in Briay, and of a Belgium which through the surrender of its territory and considerable limitations on its sovereignty was to become de facto a province of Germany. Luxembourg's end as an independent country was to be brought about by its incorporation as a German federal state.[70] On the British side, the willing-

*Colonel Edward M. House and President Woodrow Wilson
(courtesy of the Woodrow Wilson Papers)*

ness for peace was no more promising. Ambassador Page told Wilson on September 22, 1914, that the British would hardly be willing to sit down at the peace table unless it were in Berlin. "In other words, they will reject any terms that Germany will offer except on the basis of defeat."[71] Of course, this was the opinion of the less than impartial American Ambassador to the Court of St. James's. Still, there is no doubt that, at the time, Britain would not have been willing to negotiate until the German government had at least declared its intention to evacuate Belgium and to pay suitable reparations for war damages.[72] Such thoughts, however, had not entered into the political considerations of the German leaders.

Even though the conditions for successfully paving the way for steps toward peace appeared unfavorable, a series of confidential talks began in Washington in September 1914. Unfortunately, Bernstorff does not say anything about these negotiations in the memoirs he published right after the end of the war, and the historian therefore has to rely on information from the Americans and the Allied side.

It was Bernstorff who took the initiative[73] by calling on House in New York on September 18 and expressing his willingness to confer with Spring Rice. They decided that the first contacts should be kept completely confidential, and that besides Bernstorff, Spring Rice, and House, only President Wilson should be informed.[74] On September 20 House met Spring Rice and tried unsuccessfully to persuade him to confer with the German Ambassador. Spring Rice emphasized that Britain was bound by treaty not to enter discussions on any offer of peace which had not been accepted by her three major allies. Besides this, they talked about British conditions, such as the end of militarism and reparations to Belgium. On the whole, Spring Rice interpreted the efforts of House as a German attempt to shuffle the cards in such a way that it would look as if Britain were rejecting Germany's peaceful offers.[75] Neither Bernstorff nor House seems to have been particularly disappointed with the outcome of the conversation. House reports that Bernstorff had understood that Spring Rice needed the consent of his government and of the Allies for a conference. As House saw the matter, Bernstorff, for his part, had thought that, within the framework of his instructions, he was empowered to conduct negotiations of this kind.[76]

On September 25 Bernstorff met one of House's close friends, Hugh Campbell Wallace,[77] at the New York Ritz Carlton and tried to find out whether there had been any development in the contacts. Once more he stated frankly that he was very much in favor of starting negotiations as quickly as possible and again he let it be known that Germany's cooperation could be counted on. Although the Ambassador stressed the confidential nature of this information, one may assume that he expected not only House and Wilson to be apprised of his statements. In the course of the conversation, Wallace remarked that Edward Grey probably had more conciliatory views than Winston Churchill, the First Lord of the Admiralty. Bernstorff replied that, if this were true, it was perhaps advisable for Wilson to send someone to Europe as a mediator. Understandably, he suggested that the mediator should first go to London and then to the Continent, hardly a coincidence, since all belligerents were very concerned not to appear as the power to ask for negotiations first.[78] It was on this point that Bernstorff's repeated efforts were bound to fail, not to mention the fact that not all those who knew about this affair thought it advisable to lend their support to the peace feelers of the German Ambassador. Thus Page, for instance, fully sympathized with the British view that only a defeated Germany would guarantee the end of German militarism, and Spring Rice too had a very hostile attitude toward Germany. Indeed, as chief of a malicious propaganda campaign against the Entente in the United States, Bernstorff must have appeared to his partners in possible negotiation rather dubious in his role as mediator. It is true that Germany had at least taken a first step through Bernstorff, but the negotiations made no progress because London was unwilling to openly formulate an answer which would have forced the German government either to publicize its war aims or to agree to discuss the British suggestions.

House brought up the hopelessness of the endeavor with Wilson and mentioned that Bernstorff had suggested that House travel to Europe. Wilson, who was not in favor of the idea, instead advised House to put pressure on Grey in writing by explaining to him that it would not be in Britain's interest to destroy Germany and Austria completely, since otherwise there would be no way to block Russian ambitions on the Continent.[79] In this spirit and probably influenced by Bernstorff's assurance that Germany would be willing to negotiate, House wrote to Page on October 3: "I have a feeling that Germany will soon be willing to discuss terms. I do not agree that Germany has to be completely crushed and that terms must be made either in Berlin or London. It is manifestly against England's interest and the interest of Europe generally for Russia to become the dominant military force in Europe, just as Germany was. The dislike which England has for Germany should not blind her to actual conditions. If Germany is crushed, England cannot solely write the terms of peace, but Russia's wishes must also largely prevail."[80]

Britain, however, could not be brought to declare its willingness to negotiate. On the contrary, Wilson received news from his Ambassador in London which clearly indicated that the British government was not inclined to give in, unless the German Empire were to express its readiness to restore Belgium and to pay reparations for war damage. Since Berlin was still very much under the impression of the victorious first weeks of the war and therefore no such German offer was forthcoming, the peace efforts of the American President had failed for the time being. Bernstorff did not think the British ideas to be totally unacceptable, at least as a point of departure, thus demonstrating that his views were somewhat more realistic than those of the German military leaders and influential government officials. It should not be forgotten, however, that the Ambassador, with his anticolonialism, his friendly relations with Jewish circles, and his tendencies toward liberalism,[81] was always held in low esteem by precisely those Germans who held rather illusory notions about the objectives of the war. One might justifiably say that, with his peace efforts in the autumn of 1914, Bernstorff did not represent the policy of the German government.[82]

On December 3, 1914, Under Secretary Zimmermann finally wrote his answer to House's suggestion of September 5. But the content of the letter did not offer the slightest ground for hopes for a German willingness to negotiate: "The question of mediation has not yet reached the stage for action.... The war has been forced upon us.... This makes it impossible for us to take the first step towards making peace. The situation might be different if such overtures came from the other side."[83] In mid-December, Bernstorff and House met again, and House told the Ambassador that he had been empowered by the President to initiate steps toward peace. Bernstorff was still convinced, or at least spoke to Colonel House on the assumption that Germany would be willing to discuss possibilities for peace, even if the Entente were only open to contacts under the conditions of the evacuation of Belgium and a disarmament agreement. Nevertheless, he did not deem it opportune to inform the Foreign Office about this question.[84] The intelligent House was aware that Bernstorff at least in part was pursuing his own politics, but as long as the Ambassador took this position, House was able to continue the mediation efforts for Wilson. When a few days later Sir Edward Grey let the American government know through Spring Rice that Britain would not necessarily oppose mediation on the basis of disarmament and the restoration of Belgium, House was so elated that he discussed the matter with Wilson, and the two men agreed on the necessity of an immediate trip to Europe by the Colonel.[85]

But only three days later, Spring Rice had less positive news for the eager House. Grey, it turned out, had only expressed his own personal opinion, which had not yet been discussed by the cabinet. Also, the Allies had not yet been informed. Besides, Spring Rice now had negotiations in mind which were to lead to what House refers to in his diaries as a plan allowing a "permanent settlement." There was also talk about additional wishes by the Entente, such as Russia's claims to Constantinople and France's to Lorraine. Nonetheless, House felt encouraged to ask Spring Rice to find out from Grey whether his visit would be welcomed by the British.[86] The welcoming note from London did not arrive until a month later, before the beginning of the spring offensives expected by all sides. Grey let it be known that he would be in favor of House's trip to Europe, but that he could only promise to negotiate with England's allies if Germany "seriously and sincerely" wanted peace. Besides, he wrote, English public opinion was becoming increasingly upset because it was felt that, under German influence, the United States was acting against the interest of the Allies and especially of Great Britain.[87] House had meanwhile decided to go on his trip and had negotiated accordingly with Bernstorff and Spring Rice. On January 12 he and Wilson agreed that he would depart for Europe on January 30. To the Englishman, he had made his project attractive by telling him that he was going to Europe less to talk about definite peace terms with Germany than "to discuss a plan which would ensure permanent peace." At Spring Rice's urging, House tried to convince Jusserand and George Bakhmeteff, the Russian Ambassador to Washington, neither of whom thought that Germany could be trusted, of the practicality of his plan.[88] By contrast, Bernstorff was delighted that his efforts now should finally lead to a concrete step, and he promised to notify the Foreign Office immediately. In his telegrams to Berlin of January 15 and 21, he correctly reported that the ambassadors of Great Britain, France, and Russia had given House little hope and that all three were of the opinion that "a permanent peace cannot be counted on if we are not defeated." But also: "House is decidedly well-disposed toward us. With his journey he has no other ambition than to make a first move to cause both camps to talk openly with each other. He has no conditions and no conference in mind."[89]

It has later been frequently and unabashedly argued that Bernstorff had allowed himself to be led astray by House, that House had always taken a clear pro-Allied stance, and that therefore it was far from his intention to be part of a mediation effort that was also satisfactory to Germany.[90] Undeniably House, like most important American political figures of the time, harbored greater sympathies for Britain than for the Prussian-German state and the German cause. But this is of little importance to the question whether early in the war Germany could not have gained greater long-term advantages from peace negotiations, regardless of the conditions under which they would have taken place, than its economic and military capacity—disregarding the domestic situation—could have achieved. The precondition, however, for a positive appraisal of negotiations was the recognition, painful as it no doubt was for Germany, that in the late fall of 1914 a "German peace"—a peace through victory—had already become a fata morgana. To those who for various reasons had not yet come to this viewpoint it must indeed have appeared superfluous to negotiate with the Entente on the basis of a restoration of Belgium and against the background of disarmament plans. Bernstorff, though, was not held back by such considerations; he had recognized "that since the first battle of the Marne we were no longer in a position to win a military victory."[91] Indeed, he went even further and came to the conviction that to "aim at a conclusion of peace" was necessary, even if its relatively unfavorable conditions perhaps would have temporarily baffled German public opinion and roused its indignation. Consideration of public opinion, however, should not have been as dominating a concern as was the case.[92] To Germany's detriment, the situation was appraised less realistically by its leaders, a fact which was to have devastating consequences on the further course of the war.

House left New York on January 30 on the *Lusitania*. When the ship approached Ireland on February 5, the captain, fearing a torpedo attack, hoisted the Star Spangled Banner, and House was able personally to observe a British action against which the German government had raised constant objections.[93] The voyage otherwise went without incident,[94] and, immediately after his arrival in London, House went into conference with Sir Edward Grey. The latter spoke of French plans in Alsace-Lorraine and Russia's desire for

Constantinople, but apparently he did not demand any territorial gains for Britain. More interesting than the discussion of war aims, however, was the agreement of the two men that some means would have to be found to guarantee peace, or, that is, to develop certain principles for "civilized warfare."[95] House quite evidently was impressed with Grey: "If every belligerent nation had a Sir Edward Grey at the head of its affairs, there would be no war; and if there were war, it would soon be ended upon lines broad enough to satisfy any excepting the prejudiced and selfish."[96]

Any possibilities which the British intentions might have held forth were curtailed, however, by the German declaration of submarine warfare on February 4, 1915, even before House received the news from Germany that his visit was welcome. In fact, the German invitation did not reach him until February 12; it came in the form of a note from Zimmermann, dispatched from Berlin the same day as the declaration of submarine war and stating that Germany was ready "to do our share to bring about the desired termination of the war," but also that he saw no way to pay Belgium any reparations. "Our campaign in that country has cost the German nation such infinite sacrifices of human lives that anything in the form of such a decided yielding to the wishes of our opponents would cause the most bitter feeling among our people."[97] Seen from Berlin's standpoint, the German Under Secretary probably was quite correct in fearing the reaction of a roused German public; but it must be remembered that Bernstorff had always operated on the assumption that the matter of Belgium could at least be discussed.

After consultations with Grey and Prime Minister Herbert Asquith, it was decided in London that House should postpone his trip to Germany until the military situation in the East could be better evaluated.[98] From Berlin, Ambassador Gerard urged that the time was right and that influential circles in Germany would put pressure on the government as soon as acceptable negotiation offers were in sight.[99] But for the time being House stood by his decision and on February 17 once again tried to make it clear to Zimmermann that the question of Belgium would have to be the opener of any talks: "All of our conversations with the Ambassadors in Washington representing the belligerent nations were based upon the supposition that Germany would consent to evacuate and indemnify Belgium and would be willing to make a settlement looking towards permanent peace."[100] The German government, however, had made the "incorporation of Belgium into the German power sphere"[101] a firm part of its annexionistic war policy,[102] and accordingly Zimmermann replied on March 2 that House had apparently based his opinion on the false premise that Germany was at the end of its strength. Also, he wrote, Germany could not forget the "terrific cost" that had been paid in order to occupy Belgium.[103] Evidently, at this moment, the German government was not in the least thinking about seriously discussing peace possibilities with the United States.[104] No effort was made to keep America favorably disposed toward a future role in the mediation process. How little Berlin was concerned with this becomes clearer when one recalls that, particularly during the first weeks of 1915, the German intelligence services, with the full knowledge of the Foreign Office, attempted to stage in the United States a sabotage campaign of hitherto unknown dimensions and to reinstate the regime of General Victoriano Huerta in Mexico.[105]

Although prospects for quick mediation were rather dim, House went on to Berlin via Paris[106] on March 11, now less in order to talk about terms for peace than to make an effort to improve German-American relations.[107] Since through Zimmermann's letter House knew about the German refusal to discuss the restoration of Belgium, he apparently thought it wiser to strive for an understanding on a different level. In his talks with the German Under Secretary, House therefore did not bring up the Belgian question, and Zimmermann, for his part, preferred not to touch upon the subject. Instead, the conversations turned on generalities about the necessity of finding peace terms which might be acceptable to all parties. In his conversation with Bethmann Hollweg a few days later,[108] House returned, although indirectly, to the Belgian question. On March 27, he wrote to Wilson that he had told the Chancellor that America, like Germany, was interested in the freedom of the seas. If Britain could be brought to an agreement on this question, the German government, he had suggested to Bethmann Hollweg, could inform the public that now, since an arrangement with Britain was possible, Belgium was no longer needed as a base for German naval operations. It may be assumed that House did not choose the example of Belgium by coincidence;[109] but Bethmann Hollweg appears not to have registered the message. Except for sensing the internal German disunity and the oppressive power of the military, House did not bring back much to America. He had recognized, however, that the position of the Emperor had become untenable and that one of the consequences of the war might be "a more democratic Germany."[110]

On May 7 Wilson's peace mediator was sitting down to dinner at the American Embassy in London when a telegram brought the news of the sinking of the *Lusitania*. The political constellation had suddenly changed entirely; the question of peace mediation was now, at least for a time, dismissed, and America's entry into the war on the side of the Entente[111] had become a serious possibility.

FOUR

THE WAR YEARS, 1914–1917

Submarine Warfare and the Possibilities for Peace from May 1915 to the Summer of 1916

The sinking of the *Lusitania* was a turning point in the continually deteriorating relationship between Germany and the United States. Although German submarines had from the beginning ignored the international conventions of naval warfare, the torpedoing of the large British liner demonstrated to the world that Berlin was evidently willing to assume responsibility for such acts. The British blockade, undoubtedly aimed at interrupting the flow of essential supplies also to the German civilian population, somehow seemed more harmless than the deliberate killing of noncombatants. It was not even necessary for the skillful British propaganda to point out this apparent or actual difference, especially to the neutrals. One could only conclude that either the submarine commander had acted contrary to existing orders or that the German government now had decided to pursue its military goals regardless of moral reservations—as much as such scruples are ever recognized in war. Thus Berlin faced the alternative of disavowing Lieutenant Schwieger and trying to quickly handle the matter through diplomatic channels or treating the *Lusitania* case as an incident of war, a regrettable eventuality of this conflict. To its disadvantage, the German government opted for the latter. For the purpose of the present study, it is not of particular importance to investigate which interests prompted Berlin's actions, whether the Chancellor, pushed by the navy and other pressure groups, indeed had no choice, as is often claimed, or whether the Imperial Government was merely unable correctly to appraise the situation. What does seem important here is that Berlin's attitude made it extremely difficult for the United States to mediate with the Allies for Germany in the blockade question. Moreover, those in America who favored a more pro-Allied policy now found a more receptive public for their agitation. One of the unfortunate consequences of Berlin's decision was the severe impairment of Bernstorff's freedom of action in Washington, a development, though, that seemed to cause little concern in German governmental circles. Ultimately it is not surprising that in these circumstances Wilson turned more and more toward the Entente and that as time went on his plans for peace mediation contained less favorable conditions for Germany.

THE U-BOAT WAR ON COMMERCE FROM THE SINKING OF THE *LUSITANIA* UNTIL THE *SUSSEX* CRISIS

On the evening of May 7, Bernstorff was traveling to New York with Paul Warburg when he saw the first reports about the *Lusitania* in the late papers.[1] After Jacob Schiff had confirmed the reliability of the information to the Ambassador at the New York train station, Bernstorff hurried to his suite at the Ritz Carlton, where he was beleaguered by a host of reporters. In the past, Bernstorff had enjoyed being surrounded by journalists and had made it a practice to be available, but those times were long gone. For months now, the German embassy repeatedly had been linked with a number of dubious actions, and his friendly relations with the press, which during the first years of his stay in the United States had produced many a positive comment about the Ambassador, had been disrupted since the late autumn of 1914. There was little to do now but to wait out the night in his hotel suite, and even when he left the Ritz Carlton through a side exit the next morning in order to rush back to Washington, a herd of reporters pursued him to the platform of the train station.[2] Sunday passed without the Ambassador being able to undertake any useful steps. He cabled to Berlin that Wilson to all appearances was taking the matter "calmly,"[3] which was correct, since the President initially took every precaution to avoid reacting to the public excitement. As if to underscore this feigned calmness, Wilson went to his local church and then drove to the country in the afternoon.[4]

President Wilson knew that America would have to offer resistance; but all the same he was determined not to plunge his country irresponsibly into the European war. Bernstorff could consider himself fortunate that Wilson, the pacifist historian, and not the

Roughrider Roosevelt held office in the White House. Wilson's very brief remarks which reached the public on Sunday had suggested that premature drastic reactions were not to be expected: "Of course the President feels the distress and the gravity of the situation to the utmost, and is considering very earnestly, but very calmly, the right course of action to pursue."[5] This was followed by his address before an audience of about 15,000 including a group of 4,000 new citizens in Convention Hall in Philadelphia: "The example of America must be the example, not merely of peace because it will not fight, but of peace because peace is the healing and elevating influence of the world, and strife is not. There is such a thing as a man being too proud to fight. There is such a thing as a nation being so right that it does not need to convince others by force that it is right."[6] It was not until the morning of March 11 that the President met with his cabinet. Wilson presented his own draft of a note to the German government which was cabled with minor changes to Berlin on May 13. A simultaneous special announcement desired by Bryan, which would have declared that the United States would under certain circumstances be willing to submit the *Lusitania* conflict to arbitration, was stopped at the last moment by Lansing's quick action and his secretary Joseph P. Tumulty's personal influence with Wilson.[7] Bryan's proposal was in agreement with the solution that Bernstorff had also suggested in a telegram of May 10 to the Foreign Office following a conversation with the Secretary of State. At that meeting, Bryan had told Bernstorff of his regret that Germany had previously declined to conclude an arbitration treaty with the United States. It may be assumed that Bernstorff, too, now looked at arbitration as a way out and agreed with the Secretary. Two days after this conversation, Bryan had given Wilson his draft of the special announcement.[8]

As it turned out, however, Bernstorff clearly overestimated Bryan's influence with the American President and his political clout. To the Foreign Office, he recommended that Berlin "express in some form regret about the deaths of so many Americans; something which could happen without acknowledging our responsibility."[9] Although he had no doubts about the seriousness of the situation—how could it have been otherwise, given the calls for action by the American press—he nevertheless believed that Bryan's benevolent spirit and influence would determine the course of events, since "Wilson depended on Bryan for his re-election."[10]

The American note of May 13 made it clear that Berlin could not continue submarine warfare as currently practiced without risking a break with Washington. It is true that Wilson refrained from any direct threat, but at the same time the note left no room for misunderstanding:

> The Government of the United States, therefore, desires to call the attention of the Imperial German Government with the utmost earnestness to the fact that the objection to their present method of attack against the trade of their enemies lies in the practical impossibility of employing submarines in the destruction of commerce without disregarding those rules of fairness, reason, justice, and humanity.... American citizens act within their indisputable rights in taking their ships and in traveling wherever their legitimate business calls them upon the high seas.... The Government of the United States cannot believe that the commanders of the vessels which committed these acts of lawlessness did so except under a misapprehension of the orders issued by the Imperial German naval authorities.... It confidently expects, therefore, that the Imperial German Government will disavow the acts of which the Government of the United States complains, that they will make reparation so far as reparation is possible for injuries which are without measure, and that they will take immediate steps to prevent the recurrence of anything so obviously subversive of the principles of warfare.[11]

In spite of contrary opinions of German historians,[12] it would appear that, considering the seriousness of the incident and the aroused public in America, and last but not least, in view of the German declaration that Britain was responsible for the American losses,[13] Wilson's note employed a rather mild tone.[14]

Looking back, it is not easy to understand the naiveté that characterized the reactions of Germany's leaders as well as those of the manipulated German public in view of the catastrophe. Headlines in the large newspapers as well as the local press hailed the purported success.[15] Bernstorff's home newspaper announced: "The strong Britain is trembling.... More and more the world must recognize that Britain's rule over the seas was but a mirage, now dissipating before harsh reality like fog in the victorious sun."[16] Admiral von Pohl wrote: "I am sorry for the passengers, but this is a war and Britain, which wants to starve us, has to be hit in its vital nerve, its trade."[17] Tirpitz felt that especially now one had to be "firm toward America": "concessions ... are only interpreted as weakness abroad and above all in our own country."[18] In this orchestra of irrationality, though, there were some voices of reason, which lacked volume but perhaps nonetheless had some influence. Philip Alfons Baron Mumm von Schwarzenstein, Director of the Zentralstelle für Auslandsdienst in the Foreign Office, for instance, wrote to Otto Hammann: "If it is not too late already, see to it that our answer to America is such that the Americans can digest it. A break with the United States would be the last straw.... The torpedoing of neutral ships is foolish, something the Chancellor has correctly perceived from the very beginning..., and the sinking of the *Lusitania*, despite all the good reasons which I had to put forward in public, was an act which has cost us sympathy all over the world."[19]

After Jagow had informed Gerard on May 15 that Germany was not willing to give up submarine warfare, the Ambassador asked Washington for instructions "for all contingencies."[20] Significantly, even Bryan replied that, while it was necessary first to wait for Germany's answer, the American consuls were to be instructed confidentially to prepare for the possible departure of American citizens from Germany.[21] The widely held German opinion that America's note was no reason for real concern[22] was further strengthened when the Austro-Hungarian Ambassador, Constantin Dumba, cabled from Washington that Bryan had confided to him that the American note had been written under pressure from public opinion and its tone was not intended to be as pointed as it appeared. It is conceivable that because he had failed to persuade the President to publish an offer of a solution through arbitration, Bryan in this way tried indirectly to soften the impact of the note. One is not surprised either by the quick American démenti when Zimmermann somewhat imprudently informed Gerard of Dumba's report. In any event, Bryan was left with the suspicion of intrigue, and the position of Dumba, who in fact should have supported Bernstorff, was further tarnished. Besides, the Austrian's report must have left the impression in Berlin that Bernstorff had appraised the situation in Washington too pessimistically.[23]

Finally, on May 28, two weeks after receiving the American note of protest, the Foreign Office replied.[24] First, Berlin dealt with outstanding disputes over the destruction of other ships; the main body of the text, however, contained little more than the statement that, according to reliable sources, the *Lusitania* had been armed and had transported ammunition and Canadian troops on previous trips.[25] Consequently, the Germans said, the British shipping line, which consciously transported American citizens as guarantee, so to speak, for the safe transport of ammunition, was solely responsible for the death of the passengers. The ship had sunk so quickly, the note said, because the exploding cargo of ammunition had torn her apart. Clearly, as Bernstorff remarks, "the German answer of May 28 did not change the situation at all."[26] The Ambassador was convinced that a war with America, which would result in "Germany's ultimate defeat," absolutely had to be avoided.[27] Besides, he even hoped to be able through possible German concessions on the submarine question to gain a relaxation of the British blockade of food supplies and along with that a new point of departure for possible peace talks. Thus he took the next step that seemed appropriate to him. Without waiting for instructions from Berlin, the records indicate, he asked for a personal audience with President Wilson.[28]

While several studies have taken up these events, one aspect of Bernstorff's difficult situation has received very little attention so far, especially in German historiography. In the early summer of 1915, the Ambassador was also involved in several projects which cannot simply be ignored as unpleasant but expectable actions of a diplomat in time of war. The often complex activities involving sabotage and revolution, which were organized by the Foreign Office in Berlin under the administrative title "Operations and Instigations against Our Enemies" (Unternehmungen und Aufwiegelungen gegen unsere Feinde), were directed from or carried out in a country whose continued neutrality was of great interest to the German Foreign Office and to the Ambassador in Washington. A corps of agents from various German intelligence services operated in the United States by and large with Bernstorff's knowledge and in some cases with his support.[29] In 1915, the broad spectrum of activities ranged from efforts to reestablish General Victoriano Huerta in Mexico to naive bombing schemes, and the organization of ammunition shipments and revolutionary action groups scheduled to be dispatched from the United States to various parts of the British Empire. Although Americans did not learn about the exact details of these operations until much later, Wilson was informed as early as the spring of 1915 about Germany's effort to rekindle the fires of civil war in Mexico as well as about other German projects. Bernstorff, who left no stone unturned in Washington in order to somehow develop a modus operandi in the question of the war on commerce, through his connection with these covert activities indeed must have appeared to the President somewhat compromised. Why the Ambassador let this double role be imputed to him will be examined more closely in a later chapter. The fact, however, that he did play this double role and tried to be on top of both does call for a correction of the picture of Bernstorff as a diplomat who, perhaps motivated by a certain uninformed idealism, here and there overstepped his authority and overestimated America's desire to stay out of the war.

No one doubts that Bernstorff had an audience with the President on June 2, 1915.[30] Circumstantial evidence, however, seems to indicate that the German Ambassador had already seen the President on May 28, possibly as Arthur Link sees it, taking along with him a Dutch citizen named Francis van Gheel Gildemeester, a somewhat mysterious emissary from Berlin. Gildemeester, the son of a well-known Dutch pastor, had appeared in Berlin on May 5 with recommendations from Richard von Kühlmann, the Imperial German Minister at the Hague. He had offered his services to the Germans, in the words of Kühlmann, "to work there [in the United States] for us as an unsuspicious neutral." Kühlmann added to his letter of recommendation: "But the matter must be treated very secretly." The eager emissary apparently impressed the German officials with his "good connections (for instance to the noted Archbishop Ireland of St. Paul, to the Editor of the Saturday Evening Post, to the Chairman of the National Committee of the Democratic Party, and to others) from earlier times." The specific mention in the German records of "his connection with the Dernburg bureau" and Gildemeester's plans to be active "in the Midwest avoiding the German centers (such as Milwaukee, Cincinnati)" actually suggest a propaganda assignment rather than a specific diplomatic mission for the German government in the aftermath of the sinking of the *Lusitania*.[31] The dates of the letter of recommendation from Kühlmann and Gildemeester's appearance in Berlin on May 3 and 5, respectively, would seem to support this impression.[32]

Arthur Link has tried to reconstruct what may have happened on Friday, May 28, 1915. He finds it "strongly possible" that Bernstorff called the President and announced that a secret emissary had arrived from Germany. Wilson, according to Link, may have agreed to see the German Ambassador and the emissary, Francis van Gheel Gildemeester, on the same day. While there is no hint that Gildemeester brought with him a special message from the Imperial Chancellor, Link surmises that Bernstorff's report to Bethmann Hollweg of May 29, speaking of a "most reliable source" ("aus bester Quelle") indeed is referring to Woodrow Wilson himself, supporting the assumption that Bernstorff met with the President prior to the dispatch of the message. According to that "most reliable source," the President would like to solve the *Lusitania* crisis in a favorable way in order to then approach Great Britain to dissuade her from disrupting international trade. If the British would agree to a war at sea in accordance with international law, this might be a good point of departure for a mediation between the warring powers. The President's plan, according to Bernstorff, included the calling of a peace conference with three general conditions being up for discussion: "1. The status quo [presumably ante bellum] in Europe; 2. Freedom of the seas in such a far-reaching way that it would amount to the neutralizing of the sea, 3. Adjustments concerning colonial possessions." According to Link, it is entirely conceivable that Wilson talked in these terms and that Bernstorff therefore correctly reported the President's views rather than inventing matters in support of his own desire to bring about an American mediation.[33]

Another possibility, however, is that Bernstorff gained his knowledge from a "most reliable source," not from Wilson but elsewhere. It is curious that the Ambassador should not have mentioned his encounter with the American President if he actually did see him. While we have no evidence indicating that Bernstorff did not see Wilson on May 28, another source, not often used in the diplomatic history of the period, does seem to suggest that the Dutch citizen Gildemeester at least did not see Wilson prior to May 30, 1915. The secret recordings of the outgoing and incoming telephone calls of the German Embassy in Washington contain several telephone conversations in connection with the mission of Gildemeester. If the notes jotted down by the agents recording these calls can be relied on, Count Bernstorff called the residence of Paul M. Warburg at 10:15 A.M. on Sunday, May 30. To a woman who seems to have been Mrs. Warburg and who told the Ambassador that Paul Warburg was not at home, Bernstorff is recorded to have said: "There is a Mr. Guildemeister [sic] here from Holland, and he has something of importance. I want to bring him around to see your husband. . . . He has something which I think may be of value to us." At 10:45 A.M., according to the same source, a man's voice phoned the German Embassy. The gentleman and Bernstorff agreed to meet on the same day "between 4 and 5." Bernstorff said: "I want this man Guildemeister [sic] to meet you, he wants to get through you to Miller, through Miller to Lane, and through Lane to the President, but at any rate, I do not want it to go through me." The male voice replied: "I shall be glad if I can be of any service." At 11:08 A.M. "Mr. Barber," presumably Warburg, called the German Embassy saying: "I have just found out that Dr. Miller can see us at 6 o'clock, if that will be satisfactory to you." They then agreed that the German Ambassador, who claimed to be tied up with an appointment at 5:30 P.M., would bring Gildemeester to Warburg "a little after 5, and then leave him with you." A further recording of a telephone conversation between Mrs. Warburg and Count Bernstorff at 10:15 A.M. on Thursday, June 3, recorded the Ambassador as saying: "I said yesterday to the President that Guildemeister [sic] is here, and Lane saw him, and Lane need not therefore have any anxiety. If you would tell that to Mr. Warburg. Mr. Warburg could, perhaps, tell Mr. Lane that I spoke to the President. It would be well if Lane said that to him too. Lane you know is a little afraid. I will tell him myself if I see him." However one may be inclined to interpret the events on June 28 and thereafter, Bernstorff's report, in any case, reached Berlin only on June 26, and there is no evidence that Bethmann Hollweg, if ever he had placed any hopes in a mission of Gildemeester, followed up the development.[34]

If the sudden appearance of the presumed go-between Gildemeester leaves many open questions, these are not answered by what we know about the meeting between the President and Bernstorff only a few days later on June 2. Bernstorff evidently was painfully aware that the German note of May 28 had not been satisfactory to the Americans and therefore the worst was to be feared.[35] The Ambassador now had to play for time and hope that the voices demanding action from the President had not gained too much ground. About his conversation with Wilson, Bernstorff reported on the same day to the Foreign Office:

> The seriousness of the situation here caused me to seek an audience with President Wilson. In the course of an extraordinarily friendly conversation, which repeatedly emphasized the wish on both sides to find a way out of the present difficulties, Wilson again and again came back to the idea that for him only the humanitarian aspects of the question were important, compared to which indemnity payment for the Americans

who died on the *Lusitania* was of secondary importance. His efforts [Bernstorff reports Wilson saying] were directed toward the complete halt of the submarine war. In comparison with this final goal, lesser concessions on our part would only be a compromise. By giving up the submarine war we should appeal to morality, since the war could be definitely decided only through an understanding, not through arms. If we would give up the submarine war, then he would press for a suspension of the British starvation policy [the blockade]. According to certain news from London, the present cabinet in London would come to terms. Wilson hopes that with this would be made a beginning for a peace move in grand style, which he, at the head of the neutrals, would like to initiate.[36] ... The very friendly course of the conversation should not deceive us concerning the seriousness of the situation. If we do not succeed in calming matters in the next note, Wilson will not be able to avoid a break in relations. I recommend urgently avoiding this because of effects on the moral interpretation [*wegen moralischer Wirkung*] and because of an immediate increase of the arms exports into immeasurableness as well as the danger of far-reaching financial support of the enemies. In case of an understanding, however, there is a prospect that the existing current in the direction of an arms embargo will win out. Furthermore, then Wilson's intervention in the sense of peace is certainly to be expected.[37]

One result of this meeting was the decision to bring about the desired detente "through personal verbal contact." Following Bernstorff's suggestion, Anton Meyer-Gerhard, who had come to America with Dernburg in 1914 to represent the German Red Cross, was to be sent to Berlin to explain Washington's position. Wilson for his part promised Bernstorff "to take no irrevocable steps until Mr. Meyer-Gerhard's mission had shown some results." Bernstorff remained convinced that his meeting with Wilson helped to save the situation in June 1915, and in his memoirs he rejects the view that the President should have been allowed to go his own way, since it had been in his interest anyway to avoid a war.[38] During the summer of 1915 he indeed succeeded in gaining time, and there is no denying—as is clear from the American note of reply—that at the point of Bernstorff's intervention with Wilson there was every indication of potentially dangerous developments. Decisive for Bernstorff's plans was not his hope, which he also expressed to the Foreign Office, that Wilson would support a relaxation of the blockade if the Germans gave in on the submarine question.³⁹ Instead, his long-range objective clearly was a peace mediation by the President, who in spite of his pro-British sympathies did not want a war but rather saw himself in the altogether plausible role of a peacemaker. He could not adopt this role, however, as long as his hands were tied by German provocations. Consequently, Bernstorff implored the Foreign Office not to reply with more legalistic statements to Wilson's note, which could only be expected to take a strong stance on moral arguments: "Decisive for success whether our note hits right tone for public opinion, which here deciding power factor."⁴⁰

The American reply of June 9 declared that the *Lusitania*, contrary to German allegations, had not been armed and had not transported a Canadian troop contingent. Rather, a principle of humanity was at stake here. The fact that, without prior warning, Germany had sent hundreds of innocent men, women, and children to their deaths could not be explained away.⁴¹ Bryan again had tried to give the note a conciliatory tone by demanding once more that an arbitrational solution to the conflict be offered. Beyond that, he had requested that Americans be denied booking on Allied ships. Moreover, he suggested a simultaneous note of protest to Britain in order to defuse the conflict with Germany. The President's refusal ended the career of the Secretary of State. The often inconsistent, but upright pacifist, who already had felt that he was being bypassed when House went to Europe, submitted his resignation on June 8, following a final fruitless attempt to have the note altered.⁴²

It is difficult to appraise the atmosphere in Berlin on June 11 when Gerard handed the American note to Jagow. Although Bernstorff had warned that the situation was extremely serious and that a break with America caused by poor handling of the American protest could not be ruled out, Dumba's report had given the impression that the American government had opted for a position of strength less out of conviction than in order to soothe public opinion. Bernstorff had done his part to prevent Washington from making stronger demands and thus to keep the door open for diplomatic negotiations; careless German actions, however, could at any moment ruin this even limited readiness to talk. Basically, Bethmann Hollweg also wanted to avoid the break with America, but to all appearances he lacked the personal strength and stature to assume the responsibility for putting an end to the submarine war on commercial shipping. At the same time, the Chancellor enjoyed the support of Jagow, who agreed with him that "in our present position we must try under all circumstances to avoid a war with the United States or even a break of diplomatic relations which in its consequences would be rather the same as war." Jagow very frankly stated his point: "I, for my part, from our political standpoint would not be able to accept responsibility for such a conflict with the most powerful of the still neutral nations."[43]

On June 16, Anton Meyer-Gerhard, thanks to a safe conduct passage arranged by Wilson, reached Berlin and tried to explain Bernstorff's view that it was absolutely necessary to give in to Wilson if a break with America was to be avoided. In his own draft of a note to Washington, Meyer-Gerhard therefore suggested welcoming the American willingness to mediate and guaranteeing the security of American passengers "also on other than passenger ships"[44] if Wilson should succeed in getting Britain to give up the illegal use of neutral flags and the attacks of commercial ships on German submarines.[45] Tirpitz saw this as "a concession which was tantamount to the complete abandonment of submarine warfare,"[46] and on June 22 he underlined his position in the course of a conference with the Chancellor. Bethmann Hollweg, on the contrary, took the view that the United States had a right "to ask something from us," which, of course, as Tirpitz added, presupposed some kind of "disavowal of the torpedoing of the *Lusitania*." Meyer-Gerhard in particular stressed that the German answer would have to be written in a tone which would also meet with the approval of the American public; this, he said, was the opinion of Count Bernstorff, as well as the Naval Attaché, Karl Boy-Ed. Tirpitz, for his part, warned of the unfavorable impression which the tone of the note as proposed by Meyer-Gerhard could evoke among the German public. "The effective continuation of the submarine war," Tirpitz argued, was demanded "by all sectors of the population." Bethmann Hollweg's weak position becomes obvious in his request to Tirpitz to acquiesce for the time being; in six to eight weeks Germany could "take a firmer stand" again if the situation was more favorable.[47] Apparently upset by the blunt comments from Tirpitz, the Chancellor visualized such future actions, even though he must have been aware of the fact that a turn of events in the war so favorable for Germany as to allow a break with the United States was entirely improbable.

The third German *Lusitania* note, transmitted on July 8,[48] contained nothing new other than the offer, prepared with the assistance of Gerard, to permit passage of a certain number of especially marked liners unhindered by submarines in order to allow for sufficient passenger traffic between Europe and North America. Although this was a generally useful proposal, the German reply in no way touched on the heart of the American arguments against the German submarine war. The disappointment in Washington was accordingly great, and a compromise seemed farther removed than ever. Bernstorff let Berlin know that the content of the note did not take care of the *Lusitania* incident, and, after consulting with Lansing, he recommended recognizing Germany's responsibility for the death of neutral passengers while insisting on the justification of the torpedo attack as an act of retribution against Britain. Shortly thereafter, Lansing added the demand that, besides the acknowledgment of German responsibility, it was essential, in order to create a modus vivendi, that such incidents not be repeated.[49] The tone of the third American *Lusitania* note of July 21 clearly reflected Washington's position:

> The Note of the Imperial German Government . . . has received the careful consideration of the Government of the United States and it regrets that it has *found it very unsatisfactory because it* fails to meet the real difference between the two Governments. . . . *Illegal and inhuman acts*, however justifiable they may be thought against an enemy who is believed to have acted in contravention of law and humanity, are manifestly indefensible when they deprive neutrals of *their acknowledged rights*, particularly when they *violate the right of life itself.* . . . They [the German and the American governments] are both contending for the freedom of the seas. The Government of the United States will continue to contend for that freedom from *whatever quarter violated, without compromise at any cost*. It *invites* the practical cooperation of the Imperial German Government at this time. . . . The very value which this Government sets upon the long and unbroken friendship [between Germany and America] . . . *impels it to press very solemnly upon the Imperial German Government the necessity for a scrupulous observance of neutral rights in this critical matter*. . . . *Repetitions by the commanders of German naval* vessels of acts in contravention of those rights must be regarded by the Government of the United States,

when they affect American citizens, *as deliberately unfriendly.*⁵⁰

The jottings of Wilhelm II in the margins of this document illustrate the way in which America's growing power was evaluated in many German quarters and why Bernstorff's constant warnings found so little echo in Berlin: "Utterly impertinent. 24. VII. 15. signed W." was written at the top of the note; "Damn it!" was Wilhelm's comment concerning the remark that the German note had not addressed the real differences; he rejoined with "commands!" next to "invites the practical cooperation"; "outrageous" was added next to "impels it to impress"; and "This is about the most insolent thing in tone and bearing that I have had to read since the Japanese note last August! It ends with a direct threat! signed W." appeared at the end of the text.⁵¹

On the same day that Gerard delivered this note to the Wilhelmstrasse, Bernstorff had a conversation with Lansing. This soberly calculating politician, about whom German historians have little to report except that he sided with the British from the very beginning, had perceived that Bernstorff was Germany's only salvation. The Ambassador had not only succeeded in coming through the *Lusitania* crisis, but his suggestions to Berlin at this point indeed offered the only plausible solution, namely to give in and thereby compel the American President regardless of his better insight to protest against Britain's war tactics. Diplomatically, Wilson thus would have been pushed on to a path which could only have been advantageous for Germany, had it been interested in a status quo ante peace. When Bernstorff went to see Lansing, the American note had just been published by the press, and Lansing intimated to him that Washington had gone a long way toward meeting Germany by dignifying with an answer the note that had in no way addressed the American protest. He felt that he had discerned Bernstorff's attitude toward the submarine war, and later in his memoirs he took up the question of what different course the war might have taken if the German government had paid more attention to Bernstorff's advice. In any case, it was useful for the negotiations in Washington that Lansing had the feeling that Bernstorff understood the situation and was personally convinced that submarine warfare on commercial shipping could not continue as currently practiced.⁵²

In line with the critical situation, Bernstorff, in a long coded report on July 28, summed up his appraisal of the options.[53] Once again he pressed the point "that Mr. Wilson neither wants to bring about a war with us nor wishes to take sides with Britain." If submarine warfare was waged with the expectation "of being able to inflict defeat on Britain," it would be better not to answer the American note at all and to ignore protests by the neutrals. If, however, the purpose of submarine warfare was only "to attain the lifting or relaxation of the British blockade," he would recommend making concessions to the American President in order to enable him to speak up for the freedom of the seas. Since a reply to the note of July 21 was not expected, he would recommend that he himself be authorized to conduct direct negotiations with Wilson. Bernstorff wanted to negotiate three points: the settlement of the *Lusitania* question, Germany's continuation of the submarine war according to the rules of cruiser warfare, and the reestablishment of warfare according to international law, which the President would work for through contacts with Britain. In case the negotiations with Britain failed, the world could at least recognize Germany's innocence, and Wilson would have no other choice but to intercede for Germany.[54]

Bernstorff was advised by Berlin "to negotiate verbally and confidentially with Secretary of State Lansing," something which in principle he deemed pointless as long as Germany continued to insist on sinking ships without warning. But since no passenger ships had been sunk in the past few weeks, he assumed that the submarine war was now being waged with a certain amount of caution.[55] The Ambassador had not been informed about the order to temporarily spare passenger ships, issued after the sinking of the *Lusitania*. In any case, the talks with the State Department which he had been hoping for could begin. They would not have taken place under very promising auspices anyway, since American public opinion just at that time was in a storm of indignation caused by the disclosure of the documents from Heinrich Albert's briefcase and of the operations of Franz Rintelen, an agent of the Admiralty.[56]

Whatever possibilities for negotiation may have existed, they were buried, for the time being, in the Irish Sea off Kinsale by Commander Schneider's *U-24* on August 19, 1915. Captain Schneider had just sunk the British freighter *Dunsley* with cannon fire from his deck gun when the *Arabic* of the White Star Line, weighing over 15,000 tons, appeared on the horizon. Allegedly "warding off an attempted ramming,"[57] *U-24* now chose a torpedo attack, sinking the ship, which on this trip was mainly carrying mail and 423 passengers and crew. Forty-four people, among them two Americans, were lost at sea.[58]

When the news of this deed reached America, the reaction was similar to that after the *Lusitania* incident. There was a wave of excitement, and "a flood of insulting and threatening letters again poured into the embassy."[59] Bernstorff at once got into touch with Colonel House in order at least to tone down the excitement of those immediately surrounding Wilson. He tried to explain Berlin's difficult situation: Wilson, Bernstorff said, prevented the use of German submarines, but, he added, at the same time the United States supported Germany's enemies with war material and credits and remained silent about British violations of current international law. "You know well enough that nobody in Germany believes in the impartiality of the American Government." To the Foreign Office in Berlin he telegraphed the unmistakable message: "Je crains ne pas pouvoir empêcher rupture cette fois, si notre réponse à propos Arabic n'est pas conciliante; je conseille envoyer instructions à moi de suite pour négocier entière question."[60] Once more Bethmann Hollweg had to gather his courage and with his supporters take a stand against the Imperial Navy.[61] It is true that the Chancellor still wanted to avoid a break with the United States and was, therefore, much inclined to take Bernstorff's side, but for the Ambassador, who was almost entirely cut off from Germany, it was not easy to imagine the full extent of the opposition from naval, industrial, and academic circles, and also, by and large, from the press.[62] Particularly disturbing for Bernstorff's mediation efforts were semiofficial and private messages which German representatives in the United States sent to Berlin, often contradicting Bernstorff's own reports. There was very little chance for the Ambassador to stop these messages since several of the letter writers were not clearly his subordinates and in some cases entertained important relations with German power groups.[63]

At a meeting at Pless Castle on August 26, the Chancellor demanded that the order given during the *Lusitania* crisis to spare large passenger liners should now be extended to all passenger ships.[64] This order, together with the offer of an arbitrational solution of the *Lusitania* conflict, was then to be submitted to the American President. Under the impression of loud protests from Tirpitz, however, the Emperor became uncertain, and the decision was postponed.[65] Meanwhile, Bernstorff's above-mentioned cable of

August 20 had arrived in Berlin, and on August 27 the Chancellor, "referring to serious news from Washington," succeeded in wresting from the Emperor approval of the measures demanded by the Foreign Office.[66] While the leaders of the Imperial Navy were infuriated and, not without reason, felt deceived, Bethmann Hollweg undoubtedly had won this round.[67]

On August 28 Bernstorff was instructed[68] to inform Wilson confidentially that the submarines had received orders not to attack any more passenger vessels.[69] The fact, however, that this German measure could only be related confidentially would have prohibited a positive influence on public opinion and the anti-German war agitation in the United States. Accordingly, Bernstorff once more took it upon himself to decide on his own, and he allowed Lansing to publish the news.[70] Earlier, immediately after the sinking of the *Arabic*, he had, also on his own authority, declared "officially and through the press" that Germany would take care of the matter in accordance with the American demands, if it turned out that the U-boat commander had acted incorrectly. Although these steps appear to have been imperative in order to soothe American indignation,[71] German historians to this date are still inclined to write that Bernstorff had succumbed too hastily to the pressure of circumstances and had generally overestimated the danger of war with America.[72] That matters really stood as Bernstorff judged them can be seen from a statement by Wilson published on August 22: "Here is what most likely will happen if the facts are against Germany: The President will recall Ambassador Gerard and all American Consuls from Germany, and give to Ambassador Bernstorff and all of his assistants their passports. That would sever all relations between the two Governments.... The President will act quickly and firmly if the testimony shows that the German Government wantonly disregarded his solemn warning in the last note on the *Lusitania* tragedy."[73] Foreign politicians and historians have spoken with high regard of Bernstorff's resolution and courage and have emphasized that only his quick action mastered the very dangerous situation and that during this crisis he helped immensely to avoid a break with the United States.[74] Expectedly, in circles advocating submarine warfare, the reaction to Bernstorff's policy of appeasement was annoyance bordering on indignation, something unlikely to facilitate the Ambassador's work. An excited inquiry from Jagow read: "We have been placed in unpleasant situation by premature publication in the American press.... I ask Your Excellency for kind clarification."[75] There was little to explain; the Ambassador could only offer his apologies and attempt to describe once again the dangerous situation in America.[76]

For the Ambassador, the problem of having acted somewhat beyond his instructions was at this time a much lesser burden than the Archibald-Dumba affair. The news about this matter unfortunately surfaced just when Bernstorff could have done without the noisy press in order to complete negotiations concerning the *Arabic* and the *Lusitania* without interference. On August 30 the British were able to arrest at Falmouth the American journalist, James F. J. Archibald, who worked for the German embassy. A number of sensitive documents which he was carrying fell into their hands. These papers primarily incriminated the Austro-Hungarian Ambassador Constantin Dumba, whose reports contained details about actions taken to foment trouble among American labor. Since the documents also described the activities of Franz von Papen, Bernstorff's name immediately was drawn into the affair. Thus it happened that only a few days after the Ambassador's notable success, his position was once more seriously endangered, and it was entirely possible that he might be asked to leave. After some consideration of the case, however, the American government decided to make an example of Dumba, since he appeared to be the most heavily incriminated anyway.[77] The extent to which relations between the representative of the Central Powers and influential American circles had worsened is evident from the seemingly unimportant detail that only one American was among the guests at the large farewell dinner which Bernstorff gave for his Austrian colleague.[78]

In the meantime, the Foreign Office in Berlin had furnished Gerard with an explanation about the *Arabic* incident which the Americans were bound to find highly unsatisfactory. The submarine commander, the Germans said, had acted under the impression that the large liner was about to ram his boat. Even if the captain had been in error, the German government did not see itself in a position to acknowledge an obligation to pay damages.[79] Bernstorff immediately cabled to Berlin that the memorandum was not acceptable. He would like to make public, he told the Foreign Office, the exact orders to the submarines so that Washington could see that such incidents would not recur. As long as Germany maintained that the commander had acted according to his instructions, a settlement would be out of the question, because the Americans did not believe in the honesty of German intentions. And he warned: "I do not have the slightest doubt that a break in diplomatic relations will follow if an agreement cannot be reached."[80] A week later he again telegraphed to Berlin: "According to view here, the crucial point of the question is the disavowal of the commander of the U-boat."[81] The warnings had some effect inasmuch as Berlin now instructed Bernstorff to inform Lansing that there was no doubt that Commander Schneider had assumed that his ship would be rammed by the *Arabic*, but that by the same token Germany would not wish to declare the statements of the British eyewitnesses untrue. Therefore, the attack by *U-24*, the Germans said now, had not been in accordance with instructions. "To demonstrate its friendly intentions" and "without acknowledging an obligation according to international law," Germany would be willing to pay damages for the deaths of American citizens. As the instruction did not, however, contain an explicit disapproval of the incident and Washington "absolutely" insisted on such in order to placate public opinion, Bernstorff on his own[82] added the following sentence: "The Imperial Government does not approve of this act and regrets it."[83] Expectedly, this action earned him another rebuke from Berlin, which, however, was not of great concern to him since he was "conscious," in fact, "of having prevented war through my interpretation of the instructions from the Foreign Office."[84] For an ambassador, under normal circumstances, to overstep his instructions and to pursue on his own such policies as might force upon the government he represents certain unplanned modes of procedure would be unacceptable. By the same token, no one would claim that Bernstorff in the United States was representing his country under even remotely normal circumstances. Essentially, one needs to see the situation clearly, which is hardly described by simply showing Bernstorff caught up in the clever game of Robert Lansing, the American Secretary of State.[85] It is necessary to take into consideration the fact that, besides the unfortunately only temporary settlement of the highly sensitive U-boat conflict, Bernstorff also constantly tried to get the Americans to do something against the British blockade.[86] Thus, he not only acted defensively, responding to pressure in Washington, but also his politics were informed by the positive goal of mobilizing America against the British blockade. On the whole, this fully corresponded with the concepts of the Chancellor and the Foreign Office. However, exposed to constant naval opposition and inner-German agitation, the officials in Berlin were hampered in formulating a policy toward the United States that was appropriate to the situation. Concerning the appropriateness of his lone effort, Bernstorff in October 1915 remarked that historians would have to decide "whether the settlement of the *Arabic* question avoided a war with the United States."[87] A half a century later Wilson's biographer, Arthur S. Link, wrote: "The happy conclusion of the *Arabic* crisis on October 5, 1915, averted a break in relations with Germany."[88]

What the German navy thought of the new modus vivendi with America soon became apparent. As early as October 27 Adm. Henning von Holtzendorff deemed "it necessary to wage again the U-boat war with the former severity as soon as possible," and he proposed to inform the American government that on December 10 submarine warfare in the war zone would begin "against all enemy ships." Exceptions should only be made, he argued, for ships whose special markings indicated the presence of American passengers on board. Beyond that, the Admiral demanded that the silhouettes and departure and arrival dates of such ships be submitted to the Admiralty four weeks before the commencement of a journey. Even Bethmann Hollweg, to whom concessions to the United States probably had never been as important as to Bernstorff but who had not lost sight of the goal of keeping America in the camp of the neutrals, recognized the impossibility of the new plan: "The concession not to torpedo liners without warning was not made in September in order to recant in November."[89]

It should be added here that the settlement of the *Arabic* conflict indeed led to concrete results inasmuch as America now took a stand against the British blockade. On October 21 Wilson in principle agreed to a note which had been drafted by Chandler P. Anderson and sharpened by Lansing.[90] In unmistakable language Washington insisted on its rights: "Interference with American ships and cargoes destined in good faith to neutral ports and lawfully entitled have become increasingly vexatious, causing American shipowners and American merchants to complain to this Government of the failure to take steps to prevent an exercise of belligerent power in contravention of their just rights. . . . I believe it has been conclusively shown that the methods sought to be employed by Great Britain to obtain and use evidence of enemy destination of cargoes bound for neutral ports, and to impose a contraband character upon such cargoes, are without justification; that the blockade, upon which such methods are partly founded, is ineffective, illegal, and indefensible ... and that in many cases jurisdiction is asserted in violation of the law of nations. The United States therefore cannot submit to the curtailment of its neutral rights."[91] The American government had thus actually brought itself to openly criticize Britain's violation of international law through the blockade. While an examination of the American motives for this action and the description of indignant British reactions cannot be considered in detail within the framework of this study,[92] it must be remembered, nevertheless, that the unparalleled American move against the British blockade was made possible largely by Bernstorff's overstepping his instructions in the handling of the *Arabic* case. That Germany, during the following months, would destroy the newly created favorable climate by going back to submarine warfare was something the Ambassador could only darkly foresee.

As it was, on November 7 an incident brought about by Max Valentiner, commander of *U-38*,[93] interrupted the short-lived, relatively quiet climate in Washington.[94] The Italian liner *Ancona*, 8,000 tons, had been on her way from Naples to New York when, after a single warning shot, she was sunk off Sicily by a German submarine sailing under the Austrian flag. Valentiner's official notes leave little doubt as to how some U-boat commanders interpreted their orders:

> After the third [hit] liner seemed to stop. ... From a distance of 2,000 meters I shot one shell into the bow in order to speed up the launching [of the lifeboats]. Since no further measures were taken to launch the still numerous lifeboats ... torpedo shot from tube 1 into the front hold. ... I could not wait longer because a steamer ... bearing course on the submarine came into sight ... 1:20 P.M. liner sunk. ... On the upper deck, some passengers from the lower deck were still standing who were in panic. ... I felt obliged to sink the liner, although some passengers were still aboard, because otherwise a situation would have been created according to which no liners could have been sunk anymore if crew and passengers did not abandon ship despite having been requested to do so. It was the liner *Ancona* from Genoa, sailing with a heavy load from Italy.[95]

Among other things the *Ancona* incident certainly contributed to Lansing's reopening the *Lusitania* question, which had never been fully resolved. Wilson had decided that the *Lusitania* affair should be settled in the same manner as the *Arabic* conflict, and he was anxious for Bernstorff to inform Berlin accordingly.[96] It is also evident, though, that Wilson at this point did not want to break with Germany over the issue. The possibility of a rupture of diplomatic relations was also linked to the angry American reaction to the disclosures of covert activities of German intelligence operatives. Austria's acceptance of responsibility for the sinking of the *Ancona* was an additional relief for Bernstorff, who could now limit his action to lending advice to the rather helpless Austrian Chargé d'Affaires, Baron Erich Zwiedineck von Suedenhorst.[97] In fact, it was surmised in Washington that the *Ancona* had fallen victim to the German and not the Austro-Hungarian navy.[98]

On December 7, after some relatively routine reports on various incidents which had caused the American public to become increasingly hostile toward Germany, Bernstorff reported to Berlin that Washington wanted a declaration from Germany that the sinking of the *Lusitania* had been a reprisal and, therefore, not in accordance with international law. Beyond that, he reported, it would be necessary to promise payment of an indemnity. "Whether the *Lusitania* question still has enough practical significance to bring about the rupture of diplomatic relations and a war with the United States because of it, I may leave to Your Excellency's esteemed judgment."[99] On December 13 the Ambassador sounded more impatient: "I am still of the opinion that Mr. Wilson and his advisors do not want war with us. But if the points of friction are not completely removed and the European war continues for a longer period of time, I think a break in the end unavoidable,"[100] and on December 24 he cabled: "Situation very serious ... without recognition that this was a reprisal contrary to international law and without indemnity... solution will be impossible and break... in the long run unavoidable."[101] Bernstorff was not exaggerating. The situation was rapidly deteriorating. The attachés were sent home. News about German sabotage acts multiplied. The press published sensational reports about large funds which allegedly were at the Ambassador's disposal for propaganda and sabotage.

In Germany, the conditions for Bernstorff's plans to settle the U-boat conflicts and thus for a return to peace mediation had not improved. Although the Foreign Office had refused Holtzendorff's suggestion of October 27, the agitation for all-out submarine warfare continued. Bethmann Hollweg's position became even more difficult when the Chief of the General Staff, Erich von Falkenhayn, one of his closest allies against the navy, changed his views now that Serbia had been completely crippled and Bulgaria had joined the Central Powers. Falkenhayn suddenly developed a greater confidence in the effectiveness of the submarine weapon against Britain and also no longer felt that the United States's entry into the war on the side of the Entente would decisively influence Germany's military situation.[102] Even though contrary to the navy's expectations the submarine weapon in the first few weeks of its deployment in the spring of 1915 had not given any reason for hopes of a speedy victory over Britain, Falkenhayn now wrote: "If the navy's definite promises materialize in such a way that unlimited submarine warfare must cause Britain to give in within the year 1916, then even the acceptance of a hostile position on the part of the United States can now be tolerated," and he continued with the underestimation of America's military strength that was so widespread in Germany: "Whether they [the Americans], facing a strong political representation of Germany's standpoint, will decide to proceed to active intervention on the European mainland is doubtful. It is even more doubtful whether they will be able to intervene in time with sufficient force."[103] But more surprising than the low estimation of the United States and the misjudgment of the realities of foreign policy was his approval of unlimited submarine warfare based on the recognition that "he could not bring the war to an end with the thrust of the land forces."[104] Therefore one is led to suspect that Falkenhayn, because of his own hopeless position, was now willing to enter a foreign policy risk through the use of a weapon of whose effectiveness he had not been convinced previously.

For Bethmann Hollweg and the Foreign Office, Falkenhayn's about-face meant that in the fight for America's neutrality they were now confronted with the "combined opposition"[105] of the army and the navy. The Chancellor, who in principle did not have any objections to unlimited submarine warfare, was of the decided opinion that all other possibilities of reaching an honorable peace for Germany had to be exhausted before this weapon was employed. Karl Birnbaum even assumes that perhaps Bethmann Hollweg was hoping to force the United States by diplomatic means to accept the submarine war.[106] While Bernstorff in Washington did all in his power to settle the *Lusitania* case, developments in Berlin lead to a new deterioration in the relationship.

The American government insisted on the admission by Germany that the sinking of the *Lusitania* had been "illegal," something which Admiral Georg Alexander von Müller called a "brazen challenge."[107] Since Germany refused to incorporate such a declaration in a note,[108] Bernstorff tried to avoid the contested wording and, in a long series of drafts and revisions, attempted to formulate a declaration that would be satisfactory to the Americans but at the same time did not literally admit the illegality of the incident.[109] Since the Ambassador had already overstepped his instructions several times during the negotiations regarding the *Arabic* case and his relationship with the Foreign Office therefore was strained anyway, he now had to proceed with special caution to avoid a further weakening of his position.[110] Early in February 1916, he in fact did succeed in drafting a text that between the lines practically admitted the unlawfulness of reprisals, especially when neutrals were involved, but did not contain the words "illegal" and "illegality." Finally, the end of these difficult negotiations seemed to be in sight, and the American government had already declared its readiness to accept this version, when, on February 8, the Germans issued their proclamation of the so-called intensified submarine war. Wilson and Lansing now had no choice but to question the sincerity of the German asseverations.[111] Bernstorff's strenuous efforts had been in vain. "Destiny had ... intended for me the role of Sisyphus.... My hopes of settling the *Lusitania* case and then proceeding to the discussion of the 'freedom of the seas' had failed. This was all the more painful for me since I was convinced that discussion of the latter question would have led the way to peace negotiations."[112]

The fact that Berlin forced this step even before the two still outstanding differences with the United States had been removed and thus played into the hands of Germany's enemies[113] probably can only be explained by the German misjudgment of American power. Bernstorff writes: "In Berlin they were always eager to employ new measures in the U-boat war, although the disadvantages which it brought us outweighed the advantages."[114] After the conference in the Ministry of War in Berlin on December 30, 1915, attended by Falkenhayn, Holtzendorff, Tirpitz, Vice Adm. Reinhard Koch and Lt. Gen. Adolf Wild von Hohenborn, the military, in fact, could no longer back down. While Holtzendorff had claimed that with the submarine Britain could be brought to her knees by the end of 1916, Tirpitz had stressed that the United States had to be counted among Germany's enemies in any case and that the consequences of an American intervention on the European mainland were easily outweighed by the effect to be expected from submarine warfare on Britain. The Minister of War, indeed, had declared that "a hostile America was not to be feared." As a result of such argumentation, it was agreed that the U-boats should be deployed at the beginning of March.[115] The Foreign Office and the Chancellor were less convinced of the insignificance of the consequences of an American entry into the war, although they too lacked a full understanding of the American military capacity. At least Jagow realized that, in the event of the sinking of American ships or the death of American citizens, Wilson would hardly have any choice but to break with Germany. To him it was "logical and probable" that this break "would only be the predecessor of a declaration of war."[116] The Chancellor himself looked at the submarine war as the *ultima ratio* and admitted that in case its aim was not reached, this would mean the *finis Germaniae*. In spite of his desire to gain time in order to exhaust all possibilities of diplomatic negotiation, he gave his approval to the preparation for intensified submarine warfare.[117] Even Wilhelm II, who took the side of his military leaders and gave Holtzendorff permission to prepare the new submarine measures for March 1, ordered the Admiralty once more to look for ways to wage a relentless submarine war against Britain and at the same time to spare the neutrals.[118] Apparently no one in Berlin thought it advisable to first discuss the new steps in the war on commerce with the Ambassador in Washington and perhaps discreetly to query the American government about possible reactions.[119]

The declaration of intensified submarine warfare against all armed commercial enemy vessels thus was a kind of compromise between the demands of the "agitation" for unlimited submarine warfare,[120] which had found favor especially in "conservative circles"[121] and was supported by the navy, and the desire of the Foreign Office to delay the beginning of unrestricted submarine warfare as long as possible in order to gain time for negotiations. British instructions, which had fallen into the hands of Lt. Max Valentiner on November 3, 1915, after the sinking of the British steamer *Woodfield*, had shown that British commercial ships were under order not only to resist enemy attacks with their deck guns, but also to initiate attacks on German submarines.[122] In this respect the German decision to attack armed ships without warning may seem justified; on the other hand, it was known that it would be difficult to ascertain before the torpedo attack whether a commercial steamer was armed. The result of the German deliberations, the proclamation of February 8, 1916, read: "Enemy merchantmen with guns no longer have any right to be considered as peaceable vessels of commerce. . . . German naval forces will receive orders . . . to treat such vessels as belligerents."[123]

Within the limits of this study we cannot examine how various American political groups reacted to the new threat encountered by American citizens traveling on armed British ships. Efforts in the United States to prohibit Americans from traveling on armed commercial vessels did not succeed.[124] Wilson took the only possible position which was open to the President of the United States: he had to insist on the right of every American to enjoy the applicable international rights and privileges on all trade ships everywhere in the world.[125] He had come to the conviction that acceptance of the German war measures could weaken America's position as a neutral power and bring the United States into the war all the sooner.[126] Berlin once again had misjudged the political stance of the big neutral power.

In the meantime, the battle for unlimited submarine warfare continued in Germany with undiminished vehemence.[127] The dissenting positions were clear enough: with the exception of Adm. Georg Alexander von Müller, head of the Imperial Naval Cabinet, who supported Bethmann Hollweg's delaying tactics, and Adm. Henning von Holtzendorff, Chief of the Admiralty Staff, who only approved of submarine warfare if the break with America would be unavoidable anyway, the military leaders worked toward a quick adoption of unrestricted U-boat warfare.[128] The Chancellor and Jagow continued to prefer using diplomatic means to prevent America's entry into the war on the side of the Entente before deploying the ultimate military weapon. Very sceptical about the prognoses of the navy, Bethmann Hollweg in addition thought of the possibility of an acceptable peace mediation, a way out which in all probability would be barred by the unlimited U-boat war.[129] When these viewpoints clashed at the headquarters in Charleville on March 4, 1916, the Chancellor declined to assume responsibility for the steps demanded by the military and in the presence of the Emperor underscored his position by offering his resignation. Once more he won the round; the decision about unlimited submarine warfare was postponed.[130] According to the new orders to the fleet dated March 13, 1916, which had the full approval of the Chancellor,[131] all commercial ships of the enemy in the war zone around the British Isles were to be destroyed without warning; outside the war zone only armed ships were to be sunk without warning. Passenger liners were not to be attacked from underwater in any circumstances.[132] Nevertheless, it was certain that this order sooner or later would create a new incident, pushing German-American relations again to the brink of war.

It was not long before such an event occurred. On March 24, U-29, under the command of Herbert Pustkuchen, encountered the French passenger ship *Sussex* crossing the Channel from Folkstone to Dieppe. Pustkuchen thought he had a mine-layer in front of him and without warning launched a torpedo. Of the 325 passengers, 80 were killed or wounded; four Americans were among the wounded.[133] This time not only were there surviving witnesses[134] to the incident, but the wreck itself could be examined in Boulogne, and the evidence found clearly indicated that the attack had come from a German submarine. Berlin's claim that the ship had not been attacked but had hit a mine[135] proved absurd and only helped to increase American distrust toward Germany and to make Bernstorff's endeavors even more difficult.[136] Wilson's reaction to the German protests of innocence was the equivalent of an ultimatum:

> It has become painfully evident . . . that . . . the use of submarines for the destruction of an enemy's commerce is, of necessity, because of the very character of the vessels employed and the very methods of attack which their employment of course involves, utterly incompatible with the principles of humanity, the . . . rights of neutrals, and the sacred immunities of non-combatants. If it is still the purpose of the Imperial Government to prosecute relentless and indiscriminate warfare against vessels of commerce by the use of submarines without regard to what the Government of the United States must consider the sacred and indisputable rules of international law and the universally recognized dictates of humanity, the Government of the United States is at last forced to the conclusion that there is but one course it can pursue. Unless the Imperial Government should now immediately declare and effect an abandonment of its present methods of submarine warfare against passenger and freight-carrying vessels, the government of the United States can have no choice but to sever diplomatic relations with the German Empire altogether.[137]

Jagow's first reaction to the note, which Gerhard Ritter later was to call "a rude threat,"[138] was the scornful remark: "America is setting itself up as the protector of all neutrals."[139] But a telegram from Bernstorff arriving at the Foreign Office on April 24 should have cleared away any doubts whether Wilson was serious. "Wilson wants rather to risk break than to be ridiculed as an unsuccessful note writer.... Since Wilson needs success [in the presidential election], break seems unavoidable if some sort of mediation does not occur." At the same time, Bernstorff asked the Foreign Office not to write any further notes but to authorize him to conduct direct negotiations. While he believed that Wilson might activate his mediation efforts if Germany ended submarine warfare, he was also afraid that Wilson would refrain from such efforts since "the British would simply laugh at him with his ideas of peace, after he had achieved nothing with us through all his notes."[140]

It was clear from Bernstorff's telegrams that he considered a temporary discontinuation of submarine warfare necessary if Berlin was at all interested in making a peace initiative by Wilson possible. This is not the place to examine in detail whether such a discontinuation of submarine warfare could have been considered; nevertheless there can be no doubt that Bethmann Hollweg and Jagow were exposed to constantly growing pressure from the military leadership, which did not consider "complying with America's demand practicable."[141] The Emperor, evidently under the direct influence of the military, let the Chancellor know that the operations against Verdun could only be carried out in connection with a simultaneous submarine campaign against Britain. Moreover, the successes of the U-boats in March and April, he felt, had shown that Britain could be forced to make peace. By contrast, maintaining relations with America would not bring Germany any measurable advantages, while the rupture of relations would not have to mean war immediately.[142] The Chancellor, already under pressure from Pan-Germans, conservatives, and national-liberals,[143] was thus presented with the unrealistic alternative of a modus vivendi with the United States or the prospect of a successful campaign at Verdun.

The decision in Berlin on May 4 nevertheless to give up submarine warfare came as a consequence of diverse developments. Apparently Bernstorff's opinions had found enough support in the Foreign Office[144] to provide the necessary backing for the Chancellor's difficult negotiations with the Emperor and his military leaders. Jagow had realized that Falkenhayn was out to place the blame for his unsuccessful campaign at Verdun on the Chancellor, and he had immediately advised the latter to put Falkenhayn on the defensive.[145] Adm. Eduard von Capelle, Tirpitz's successor in the Imperial Naval Office, admitted that the submarines had sunk most of the ships in surface attacks anyway and that the total destroyed tonnage in no way justified a war with the United States.[146] Besides, on April 27 Jagow had called Gerard to the Imperial Headquarters at Charleville to allow the American once more personally to explain Wilson's standpoint. What Gerard set forth for the Emperor in a long conversation essentially differed little from the information that Bernstorff had constantly supplied from Washington. Wilhelm II, offended by Wilson's note of April 18, emphasized that as Emperor, as a Christian, and as head of the church of his Empire he had always fostered the desire to lead this war in a chivalrous manner, but that Germany's enemies, who had not hesitated to use cruel weapons, had in fact forced him to respond in kind.[147] The man from Tammany Hall patiently submitted to this Imperial self-justification and in reply stated what the German government knew anyway, namely that the present crisis was not a matter of sudden moral indignation on the part of the American President, but that, after the sinking of the *Lusitania* without warning, the torpedoing of the *Arabic*, which was on a westerly course and therefore not carrying contraband, and after the *Ancona* incident, America's patience had simply reached an end. However unusual the whole episode in Charleville may seem, the exchange undoubtedly contributed to making the Emperor more conciliatory.[148]

Certainly, the German note of reply dated May 4 started[149] with the same sharp tone which several times before had been detrimental to Bernstorff's diplomatic efforts and about which the Ambassador had warned Berlin repeatedly. On the whole, however, Germany gave in to the Americans and promised them that the U-boat war against commercial vessels henceforth would be fought according to the rules of cruiser warfare. Contrary, however, to Bernstorff's explicit counsel,[150] Berlin stressed that President Wilson was expected to intercede with the British for a restoration of the freedom of the seas. In case Washington was not successful in this, Germany would reserve for itself the right to take new steps.[151] Although the resumption of the intensified U-boat war or the declaration of unlimited submarine warfare[152] hung in the air as a sword of Damocles, the *Sussex* crisis thereby was settled for the time being.[153] After brief talks on this matter with Colonel House, Bernstorff reported that the American government would not reply to the German note, but as it turned out, House apparently had judged the situation too optimistically.[154] Washington, in fact, made a point of stating that the international rights and privileges of American citizens could in no way be dependent on the measures of a foreign government.[155] With this firm rejection of the German reservation, "there remained therefore the conflict of opinion which had to turn into a controversy immediately if we proceeded with unlimited submarine warfare,"[156] a situation which was not seen with the necessary clarity by all German leaders.[157]

Nonetheless, through Germany's temporary restraint in the question of submarine warfare and the settlement of the *Sussex* incident, Bernstorff for the time being had succeeded in achieving a political climate that could facilitate his efforts for an American peace mediation, which he "looked upon as the only possible way out of the war."[158] The Ambassador, in contrast to the military leaders in Germany, had recognized America's war potential[159] and had always been of the opinion that submarine warfare could not save Germany, since it would necessarily bring America into the war on the side of the Entente. It was his feeling that "once a [peace] conference had been convened, the United States would no longer be in a position to enter the war, because American public opinion would not have understood this."[160]

MEDIATION POSSIBILITIES FROM THE SPRING OF 1915 UNTIL THE SUMMER OF 1916

Following the sinking of the *Lusitania*, the conditions for American mediation were not as promising either in Washington or in Berlin as they might have looked in the fall and winter of 1914. If Germany's designs for expansion in Western Europe and Great Britain's inflexibility had caused Colonel House to fail in his mission during the first winter of the war, the destruction of a passenger liner and the ensuing exchange of notes between Berlin and Washington had now created a climate which was hardly conducive to a confidential examination of the possibilities for American mediation. Nonetheless, Bernstorff remained steadfast in his conviction that mediation, with the goal of a peace conference, was the only way out of the war for Germany.

While the war propaganda in Germany had gained new ground

and the demands of the various interest groups had become ever more exorbitant,[161] the *Lusitania* incident had convinced a great number of Americans that Berlin could only be dealt with from a position of strength. The victims of the *Lusitania* once more seemed to confirm the assessment of Germany which had gained currency in wide circles of the American population after the rape of Belgium.[162] If Bernstorff in the summer and fall of 1915 never lost sight of the ultimate goal of mediation, even though the political atmosphere continued to deteriorate and submarine incidents provided constant tension, this was not only a consequence of his own political convictions, but also—and this must be kept in mind—a result of poor communication with Berlin and his lack of information about the changing currents of political opinion in Germany. He did receive directives from the Foreign Office which through their content and tone gave him some indication of the situation at home. Through various channels he also corresponded with his wife, who had remained in Germany in 1914.[163] Since the outbreak of the war, however, there had been no opportunity for direct contacts with and information about the opinions of leading and influential personalities in Germany. This is certainly one reason why, in the summer of 1915, he still conducted his talks with House under the totally false assumption that Germany would be willing to consider the evacuation of Belgium and France as a condition of peace.[164] Incidentally, this problem of the unsatisfactory flow of information between Berlin and Washington was recognized on both sides. In Berlin the Foreign Office collected numerous letters and reports of people who in one way or another were able to obtain news about the state of public opinion in the United States.[165] Bernstorff's decision to send Meyer-Gerhard to Berlin in the summer of 1915 was also an effort to transmit his American impressions to the Foreign Office. But since travel between the continents was only possible with false papers and at the risk of being captured or under free passage officially granted by Britain, it was most difficult for special envoys of this kind to cross the Atlantic regularly.[166]

However one judges the possibilities of American mediation, and disregarding the fact that Bernstorff to a certain extent was compromised through his involvement in the so-called "conspiracies," it would appear that, through his energetic approval of peace mediation in the fall of 1914 and his flexible attitude in the U-boat conflict with Washington in 1915, he had proved his aptitude as negotiator between Berlin and the potential mediator Wilson. After conferring with the American President on June 2, at the height of the *Lusitania* crisis,[167] he told Berlin that Wilson was hoping to prepare the way for "a peace move in grand style,"[168] as soon as Britain would declare itself ready to reinstate the "freedom of the seas" in exchange for the abandonment of submarine warfare. Such a way out indeed had seemed feasible. On May 4 House had telegraphed that Grey would consider an end of the blockade as soon as Germany was willing to abandon the submarine war against commerce and gas warfare. Wilson had responded immediately and instructed House to follow up this possibility. Grey also had spoken about the matter in the Cabinet, and House had informed Gerard, who in turn had approached the Foreign Office. But there he had received the negative answer that Germany could only consider such an offer if free passage applied not only to food supplies, but also to raw materials such as cotton, copper, and rubber. Such additional conditions, of course, had been rejected by the British.[169] In spite of it all, Wilson had not lost hope of freeing American trade from the British blockade, and it must have been thoughts of this nature which persuaded him to personally broach the question of mediation with Bernstorff on May 28 and June 2.[170]

While Germany was certainly interested in receiving food supplies as well as raw materials from abroad, it may be assumed that this was not the main reason for the lack of interest in a mediation by the American President. The first winter of the war had been overcome, and a new harvest was ripening in the fields. Apparently very few people suspected that the war could no longer be won militarily. On the contrary, ever more fantastic plans for expansion were constantly being produced by the most diverse interest groups. Belgium, parts of France, perhaps also Poland and large parts of Baltic Russia were to be annexed. The submarine war too seemed to be off to a good start. The sinking of the *Lusitania* in no way had caused people to be alarmed but was seen as a just countermeasure against Britain's naval supremacy and the blockade. Indeed, it is difficult to find any indication that in the early summer of 1915 the desire for a negotiated peace played a discernible role in German policy or public opinion. How little the German government cared about cultivating Wilson's goodwill and readiness to be available as a possible mediator may be surmised from the tone of the German *Lusitania* notes.[171]

In addition to this, Bernstorff's negotiations in Washington were so overshadowed by the threat of a possible rupture of diplomatic relations that the question of suggestions for peace actually could hardly come to the fore. It is true that in spite of constant press and government disclosures about German conspiracies and in spite of the storm of indignation over the *Lusitania* affair Bernstorff had been able to maintain his good relationship with Colonel House. But in view of the seemingly endless and unpleasant submarine war negotiations, there was little opportunity to bring up the subject of peace mediation again. Although House had gradually come to the realization that a war with Germany would be unavoidable in the long run,[172] he had never quite lost hope of eventually being able to resume preparations for a peace move by Wilson. Evidently the settlement of the outstanding U-boat controversies was a conditio sine qua non. Wilson thought along similar lines. Lansing, in contrast, came to a more realistic appraisal of the situation and feared that a possible yielding on the part of Germany might goad the United States into unfriendly negotiations with Great Britain.[173] Thus, the summer passed without any progress toward an American mediation.[174] As one submarine crisis followed another and sensational news about German secret service activities accumulated, in the course of the summer House came to the opinion that Wilson would have to intervene in order to put an end to "German militarism." For the first time, there was the idea that America might no longer offer a peaceful solution but seek to obtain one by force—under the threat of possible military intervention. President Wilson, as head of state of the most powerful neutral nation and in his role as representative of the neutral nations, would call the belligerent parties to the conference table. If one of the two warring parties refused negotiations, America would join the other side—most likely he presumed this to be the Allies—in order to free Europe from militarism. House anticipated that the Allies would not readily agree to the plan, since it was to be feared that Germany would emerge from the war only partially defeated, and a new war would therefore become unavoidable. There was also the fact that relatively poorly armed American forces would not particularly impress the belligerents.[175]

On October 8 House informed the President of his plan. The Allies would be asked whether in principle they would object to an American demand for the discontinuation of hostilities and the commencement of peace negotiations on the basis of "both military and naval disarmament." If the Allies approved, the same demands could be made of Germany. If Germany would not accept a peace conference on this basis, this would bring America and perhaps the other neutral countries in on the side of the Entente.[176] House had already corresponded with Sir Edward Grey during the summer, and, in spite of his continued expectation of a victory by the Entente, the British statesman repeatedly had spoken of the necessity of founding a league of nations with the aim of "eliminating militarism and navalism." Grey frankly inquired: "To me, the great object of securing the elimination of militarism and navalism is to get security for the future against aggressive war. How much are the United States prepared to do in this direction? Would the President propose that there should be a League of Nations binding themselves to side against any Power which broke a treaty . . . ?"[177] With Wilson's approval, on October 17 House wrote a letter to Edward Grey which he thought to be the most important one he had ever written:

> It has occurred to me that the time may soon come when this Government should intervene between the belligerents and demand that peace parlays begin upon the broad basis of the elimination of militarism and navalism.... Whenever you consider the time is propitious for this intervention I will propose it to the President. He may then desire me to go to Europe.... After conferring with your Government, I [would] *should* proceed to Berlin and tell them that it was the President's purpose to intervene and stop this destructive war, provided the weight of the United States thrown on the side that accepted our proposal could do it. I would not let Berlin know of course of any understanding had with the Allies, but would rather lead them to think our proposal would be rejected by [them] *the Allies*. This might induce Berlin to accept the proposal, but if they did not do so it would nevertheless be the purpose to intervene. If the Central Powers were still obdurate, it would *probably* be necessary for us to join the Allies and force the issue.[178]

Clearly, American foreign policy was now about to adopt fundamentally new positions. Wilson's neutrality, which had accepted one unneutral act after the other in his own country and many a questionable incident at sea, now for the first time seemed to give way to the decision to play an active part in the termination of the European war. Direct military intervention of the United States in

Europe had thus become a distinct possibility. An era of restraint in American policy toward Europe appeared to have come to an end.[179]

Bernstorff's reports do not indicate whether he was aware of Washington's new attitude. Considering the widespread underestimation of America's growing power it is doubtful, however, whether such information at this time would have had any impact on opinion in Berlin. Unquestionably, Berlin would have found itself in a relatively disadvantageous starting position at the envisioned negotiations, since the plan was based on the idea of an a priori British-American understanding. The peace, however, that was to be the result of the negotiations desired by Wilson and House was not intended to be a victory for any side. Instead, the main objectives were the termination of the war and the securing of the peace through a league of nations.[180] Even after critical evaluation of the American plan, it is hardly possible to speak, as Gerhard Ritter does, of a "submission of Germany to the will of its enemies with American help."[181] Submission could only come into question if Germany were to refuse to cease hostilities and to evacuate the occupied areas. Although House clearly wished to avoid a defeat for the Entente, because he was afraid a victorious Germany after the war would become engaged in Latin America,[182] he was far from approving a peace through military victory, as some interest groups in the Allied camp had envisioned.[183]

On November 19, 1915, the German Ambassador learned from House that Wilson was considering a mediation on the basis of general disarmament, that is, the abolition of German militarism and British navalism without interference in territorial questions. House told him that Wilson would probably send him to London and, if the German government agreed, he would visit Berlin. Bernstorff expressed great interest and said that he would inform Berlin immediately. He thought the time favorable for such a trip and, in his opinion, House's suggestions were feasible. Although House did not mention any details of his plan, he intimated in the course of a conversation with Bernstorff that it was thoroughly possible that the Allies would bow to Washington's wishes first and thus win American influence for their side. How inaccurate it is to interpret the House scheme merely as a means of subjecting Germany to the will of the Allies with America's help is clear from a letter written by House to Wilson after his conversation with Bernstorff. It stressed that it was time to take measures against the German propaganda in the United States, but that a break with Germany should be avoided since it would make a peace mediation by America impossible. If the sole purpose of the House plan had been to bring America into the war on the side of the Allies to help them achieve their war aims, Wilson and House most certainly could have had a break with Germany much more easily.[184]

On December 22, Bernstorff was able to tell House that he was welcome in Berlin and that, in fact, the Germans would be pleased if he came to Berlin first. House, however, insisted that he had to begin his talks in London, and he explained once more to the Ambassador that it was Wilson's objective to bring the war to an end on the basis of an understanding about general disarmament; American interference in territorial and reparation questions would in no way be intended.[185]

Late in December, House traveled to London, but his first talks with members of the British government brought no new developments. No significant points of departure for an American peace mediation could be discerned, and, on January 20, House went on to Berlin. Encounters with leading personalities and with the Chancellor, however, did not indicate that Berlin's positions had changed appreciably. When House said that he felt the British had more confidence in the Chancellor, Jagow, Zimmermann, and Solf than in the military leaders, Bethmann Hollweg emphasized that "no one and nothing stands between the Emperor and me."[186] The Chancellor intimated that Germany might conceivably be willing to surrender the occupied territories in the West in exchange for appropriate "indemnity."[187] Since the Entente, as the Chancellor must have known, in no case would be ready to pay indemnities for such a troop withdrawal, this offer contained nothing which even in a remote sense might have been interpreted as a basis for a possible peace conference. Bethmann Hollweg indeed did not leave a particularly favorable impression with House, something all the more unfortunate as the American had established very pleasant relations in Britain, particularly with Sir Edward Grey.[188] The report House wrote for Wilson after his departure from Berlin described the German Chancellor as "an amiable, well-meaning man, with limited ability." Otherwise House noted that neither Germany's military leaders nor her Junkers were particularly interested in peace, since the war offered them financial advantages which they would not have had in peacetime. German citizens who thought differently than those in power were serving in action and an uprising in the country itself could only be expected after Germany had lost the war and its army was dissolved. But if Germany emerged victorious from the war, "the warlords will reign supreme and democratic governments will be imperilled throughout the world."[189]

House left Germany with the feeling that the leading figures in Berlin were not yet ready to negotiate about Belgium and Poland and with the conviction that Germany would not agree to even the most lenient peace conditions of the Allies.[190] That his impressions on the whole corresponded to the facts is borne out sufficiently in the German documents of the time. In February 1916, Falkenhayn demanded Belgium "as deployment zone, for the protection of the most important German industrial region and as hinterland for our position on the Flanders coast, which is indispensible for our maritime prestige." From this he concluded "the necessity of absolute military control of Belgium by Germany."[191] One might also look at the Chancellor's much applauded second speech before the Reichstag on December 9, 1915, which hardly left any room for doubt as to the future German plans for Poland and Belgium. The uncalled-for interruption by the Reichstag member Karl Liebknecht, a radical Socialist, "Plans of conquest!" almost went unheard amidst the general approval.[192] As if he feared that the world had not understood him yet, the Chancellor called out in the Reichstag on April 5: "History does not know the status quo ante peace after such dreadful events. The Belgium after the war will not be the same as the old Belgium before the war."[193] Two weeks after House's visit to Berlin, the Foreign Office appraised the situation as follows: "Military situation excellent. Occupied areas will be . . . held against any attack of the enemy. Mood in the country therefore very confident. Food supplies and feed sufficiently available to last at least until the next harvest even in case of complete cut-off from abroad."[194]

The historic meeting in London, in which, besides House, Prime Minister Asquith, Sir Edward Grey, David Lloyd George, Arthur Balfour, and Lord Reading participated, took place on February 14. There was a consensus that, on a date still to be agreed, President Wilson should demand the cessation of the fighting and the calling of a peace conference.[195] The immediate result of this conference was the document which has gone down in history as the House-Grey memorandum. The controversial document reads as follows:

> Colonel House told me that President Wilson was ready, on hearing from France and England that the moment was oppor-

tune, to propose that a Conference should be summoned to put an end to the war. Should the Allies accept this proposal, and should Germany refuse it, the United States would probably enter the war against Germany. . . . If it [the conference] failed to secure peace, the United States would[196] leave the Conference as a belligerent on the side of the Allies, if Germany was unreasonable. . . . If the Allies delayed accepting the offer of President Wilson, and if, later on, the course of the war was so unfavorable to them that the intervention of the United States would not be effective, the United States would probably disinterest themselves in Europe and look to their own protection in their own way.[197]

The rather one-sided appraisal of the House trip to Europe in the spring of 1916 found in most German studies[198] is not only the consequence of a perhaps understandable irritation about America's seemingly unneutral position in the First World War, but, as with other uninformed opinions about America, it has its origins in an underestimation, somewhat popular in Germany, of the United States as a political and military world power. Thus, it was not uncommon to describe the leading neutral nation as being dependent on Britain. The same attitude, as is known now, also was to play a fatal role in the formulation of national-socialist foreign policy before and during the Second World War. Historians still are not in agreement on whether the German government heard about the content of the House-Grey memorandum. Gerhard Ritter claims "that this chance of mediation never became known to the German government."[199] Erwin Hölzle, however, assumes that Jagow "suspected the British-American agreement or that parts of it leaked out." As it is, Hölzle would like to see this suspicion as a plausible explanation for the German refusal of "American mediation under the threat of [America's] entry into the war."[200] Independent of one's evaluation of the militarist or pacifist nuances in Germany and in the countries of the Entente at the time, it needs to be emphasized that Gerhard Ritter's following summary does not correspond to the evidence in the documents: "We already know that Germany's leading statesmen, but also the Emperor and his Chief of Staff, far from any certainty of victory despite all successes on the battlefield, longed for nothing more urgently than an early negotiated peace, if it were only to be had at barely tolerable conditions."[201] As long as the Foreign Office and the Chancellor insisted on far-reaching annexations in the East as well as in the West and demanded reparations for the withdrawal of German troops from territories that had been attacked and occupied by Germany, one can hardly speak of a longing for a negotiated peace. Beyond this, there remains the question how the submarine war, with its embarrassing incidents, and the sabotage campaign, conducted in the United States by the intelligence services with the knowledge of the Foreign Office, could in any way be reconciled with an ostensible desire for a negotiated peace to be brought about by America.

Soon after House returned to Washington, Bernstorff had the opportunity to discuss the situation with him. House of course did not comment on the new understanding initiated in Britain and warned that further incidents like the attack on the *Sussex* could drive America into the war on the side of the Allies, "which Wilson would deplore since in a few months ... he would like to bring about peace." Bernstorff immediately reported the meeting to the Foreign Office and asked for instructions "on the basis of which I can calm down the government here, which now again doubts our good faith."[202] The telegram reached Berlin on April 11, and Jagow's reply of the same day was meant to be a "confidential" message for House: "If President Wilson wishes to arrange for peace, this fully meets the wishes of Germany, which hopes that the course of German-American relations will make possible cooperation for bringing about peace."[203] How the German government envisioned the peace that was to be brought about, Bethmann Hollweg had announced to the world a week earlier before the Reichstag. "Poland, ... which the Russian cossack has left after burning and pillaging, no longer exists.... We will create for ourselves real guarantees that Belgium will not be turned into an Anglo-French vassal state, militarily and economically a bulwark against Germany. Here too there is no status quo ante. Here too fate does not take a step back."[204] That Berlin generally did not want to, or, in view of the manipulated public opinion, could not accept Wilson as peace mediator is evident in Jagow's cable of April 29 to Bethmann Hollweg: "In view of the negative disposition which generally prevails here against America, Wilson as official peacemaker, called upon by us, seems impossible to me. The resulting peace would be suspicious from the very beginning, probably *too* [sic] Anglophile, considering Wilson's tendencies."[205]

When early in May 1916 Gerard visited General Headquarters at Charleville in connection with the *Sussex* crisis, the Chancellor intimated that a peace mediation would now be welcomed, because Germany's position now made it possible to speak of peace without being suspected of weakness. Furthermore, he said, he hoped that House would take up the question of peace and perhaps could return to Germany.[206] Gerhard Ritter has strongly emphasized that on this occasion Bethmann Hollweg favored Wilson's activities as a mediator and that he advocated another trip by House to Berlin.[207] Nonetheless, it is difficult to overlook the critical situation which may have prompted the Chancellor to make what would appear to be concessions. The *Sussex* crisis had not yet been settled; due to the German declaration of intensified submarine warfare, the question of the illegality of the sinking of the *Lusitania* was still unresolved in the spring of 1916. The danger of a rupture of diplomatic relations was therefore still very much a matter of concern. After Gerard's report[208] about his meeting with Bethmann Hollweg arrived in Washington, and after another exchange with House, Bernstorff correctly reported to the Foreign Office that the peace mediation depended "naturally on the smooth progress [of the submarine war negotiations], which could still be reached most easily through an interruption of the U-boat war during negotiations."[209]

Bethmann Hollweg's reply of May 6 is not only of interest because this example shows how differently the same document can be interpreted but also because it truly raises doubt concerning the sincerity of the protestations of the German desire for peace:

> Animosity of public opinion here against Wilson because of tone and content of his note and because of impression of partisanship against us indeed so strong that a publicly recognizable action against Britain has to take place before he would be accepted by the German people as unbiased peace initiator. In that respect, Gerard's telegram [which reported Bethmann Hollweg's alleged desire for mediation] is premature.... Ultimately, of course, initiation [of mediation] remains always desirable. Action against Britain, however, seems also necessary in order to produce compliance there, in order to prevent a peace which would only be favorable to Britain. If it is not possible to induce Britain to talk with us about peace, even perhaps unofficially at first, there will result ... for us a completely untenable position after our major concessions, which in the final analysis includes the abandonment of submarine warfare. House's visit is very welcome here any time.[210]

However one might be inclined to evaluate the Chancellor's motives, this instruction states point-blank that Gerard's report about Germany's readiness to negotiate had been "premature." This, incidentally, was the way Bernstorff understood it, when he informed House accordingly on May 14.[211] The fact that Berlin would be quite ready to talk again with House after an action by Washington against Britain indicates no appreciable change in the German position.[212] One may certainly question whether it is correct to simply speak, as Ritter does, of an "invitation" which remained "unanswered."[213] If indeed the Chancellor should have thought that in the matter of mediation or submarine war he could impose conditions[214] on Wilson, the American note of May 8 must have had a rather sobering effect on Berlin.[215]

In the shadow of the Igel affair[216] and the unsolved *Lusitania* question,[217] and after the exchange of notes concerning the *Sussex*, Bernstorff continued his efforts for a mediation by Wilson with increased ardor.[218] There was little encouragement, however, from Berlin. As Charles Seymour has written, the German government did have a certain interest in keeping alive a general concern about peace in America, something which could be put to work at any time if necessary, but there was no desire to get down to definite peace conditions.[219] On May 11, perhaps fearing another submarine incident and probably under increasing pressure from the naval agitation for a resumption of the U-boat war, the Chancellor expressed to Gerard once again his hope that America would either take some action against Britain or "propose a general peace."[220] Whether the Chancellor in early May desired a general peace initiative by Wilson is open to question; the documents do not bear out such a desire. It has been said that the government at the beginning of the month was still concerned about the supply of food in the country, but that supply forecasts in the course of the month had become more optimistic and the government's interest in peace decreased accordingly.[221] There can be no doubt, however, that the great naval encounter of Jutland, while not producing a decisive result, evoked new confidence in the nation's military strength and in some circles led to a renewed and loudly expressed expectation of victory.[222] Right after this new impetus, the Secretary of the Foreign Office instructed Bernstorff that Wilson's peace initiative was "undesirable to us because too unpopular." Since it was to be expected that his efforts would be directed at the reestablishment of the status quo ante, which was "unacceptable" if the war continued favorably, particularly in view of Germany's plans for Belgium, mediation by the "naive statesman" Wilson was not desired.[223] The subsequent directive for action which Berlin sent to Bernstorff needs no further interpretation: "As soon as Mr. Wilson's mediation intentions threaten to take on a more concrete form and an inclination on the British side to react positively is noticed, it will therefore be Your Excellency's task to prevent President Wilson from approaching us with a positive proposal for mediation. I trust that I may leave to Your Excellency's diplomatic skill the choice of the means of attaining this goal without jeopardizing our relations with the United States."[224] Bernstorff replied on July 13: "At any rate in his above-mentioned meeting with Bethmann Hollweg at the beginning of May he [Gerard] was wrong about the attitude which Your Excellency wants to take toward an American peace initiative. Based on a telegram at that time from Mr. Gerard, Mr. Wilson believed that the Imperial Government would accept his mediation, and I, in my contacts with Mr. House, then corrected [*schwächte ab*] this impression, as instructed."

Bernstorff also made it perfectly clear to Berlin that he "thought it was out of the question to prevent Mr. Wilson from undertaking a peace action." As for Germany's policy toward the United States, Bernstorff listed three choices for the Imperial Chancellor. If Wilson's peace mediation failed because of the Entente's opposition, Germany would be able to reopen the submarine war[225] under more favorable conditions than before, although in that case, he would think "war with the United States probable." If, on the other hand, Germany allowed Wilson's mediation effort to fail and therefore again unleashed the submarines, war with America would be "certain." Thirdly, there would be the possibility that both belligerent parties would accept the mediation. With a view to these prospects, Bernstorff asked the Chancellor for instructions "whether I shall prevent a peace initiative or only a positive proposal which would tie our hands in terms of territorial conditions."[226] It is true that Bethmann Hollweg in his answer of August 18 again declared that Germany would be "very pleased" to accept a mediation by Wilson, but that "naturally we cannot be expected to obligate ourselves to any concrete peace conditions if we accept such mediations."[227]

Although the new directive still left no doubt that Berlin was unwilling to make any concessions in Belgium, France, or Poland before the call for a peace conference, the tone had become somewhat more conciliatory in comparison with previous instructions.

Undoubtedly the military developments in the summer of 1916 had influenced the new political line. The senseless massacre at Verdun had led nowhere; in the East, Brussilov's attack had worsened the German position; and the Austrian offensive in Italy had come to a halt. The Berlin government, moreover, was exposed to growing pressure from the military and other interest groups which vehemently demanded the resumption of submarine warfare. On April 5 the Chancellor had used strong words in the Reichstag in order to take the sting out of the agitation of his enemies,[228] but the yielding to Washington in the *Sussex* conflict had strengthened the opposition again. Increasingly, the Chancellor had become the target of brochures and pamphlets which were printed in spite of the strict censorship. In June, he had been forced to defend himself in the Reichstag, warning "that the people are being poisoned," and from his undermined position he had once again issued an urgent call for the unity of all political parties in Germany, needless to say with the exception of "the gentlemen around Mr. Liebknecht."[229]

Thus even prior to Rumania's declaration of war, which was imminent, the political situation inside Germany appeared less than promising. Against this background the Ambassador, despite his limited freedom of action, attempted to create conditions conducive to a peace initiative by the American President. On July 15, Wilson was again nominated by the Democrats as their candidate for the presidential election of that year. It was quite legitimate to speculate that he would promote a peace mediation in order to conduct the election campaign as a peacemaker. At the same time, one could assume, though with less justification, that Wilson might take more energetic steps against the British blockade in order to curry favor with German-American and Irish-American voters. If, in contrast, Wilson should neither propose a peace conference nor lean on the British, one could expect that the position of the German Chancellor would be further weakened. In that case, the U-boats would be deployed, if not in unlimited warfare, then at least with increased intensity. Such a turn of events, however, would almost certainly lead to a break with Washington and America's entry into the war. Chances that the government in Berlin would sustain its resistance against the pressures of the military and other interest groups on the submarine issue were about as unlikely as the odds for a German peace offer on the basis of the status quo ante.

FIVE

THE WAR YEARS, 1914–1917

Unofficial and Covert Activities of German

Representatives and Agents in the United States

The *Propaganda der Tat* (action propaganda) performed by German representatives and agents in the United States during the First World War deserves special attention. It is true that some authors have mentioned such German activities, and, particularly from the Allied side, we have a considerable number of sensationalistic and more or less tendentious publications. In contrast, there are to date no reliable published scholarly studies concerned with the subject and based on the documentary evidence available.[1] In his well-known Wilson studies, Arthur S. Link repeatedly mentions the illegal German activities and the reactions of the President.[2] Sister Ethel Mary Tinnemann, in her unpublished dissertation on Bernstorff and German-American relations, has devoted an entire section to propaganda and sabotage, but the regrettable damage to the reputation and influence of Count Bernstorff as a consequence of such intelligence activities and the effects of this upon German-American relations have not been sufficiently pursued.[3] A more thorough investigation would appear to be essential for an impartial appraisal of Bernstorff's work in the United States and the entire complex of German-American relations during this period.

This chapter will not include a discussion of the rather unsuccessful German efforts to float a loan in America,[4] the purchases of American war materials by Heinrich Albert and Franz Rintelen,[5] or the attempts to supply German ships on the high seas from American ports.[6] Seen against the background of the war, activities of this nature, although often mentioned in the same breath with German covert intelligence activities, did not represent serious violations of the law and indeed have therefore been described with relative frankness by Albert and Bernstorff in their memoirs. Besides, when compared to the assistance available to the Allies from financial and industrial sources in the neutral United States, these German efforts tend to lose significance. Furthermore, the German economic undertakings, however unusual, as opposed to the sabotage operations and revolutionary projects, neither caused damage to American citizens or goods, nor, as in the case of the formation of paramilitary action groups, were they intended to involve the country in warlike activities.

In addition, it should be said that it is not the purpose of this study to describe in detail individual intelligence work; the point is rather to show Bernstorff's attitude toward certain significant projects and the effects they had on his situation in Washington. Consequently, there will be no attempt made to cover all agents and operations that can be identified from the records. Such a presentation above all would have required a thorough examination of the structure and the areas of responsibility and influence of the German secret services, something beyond the intended scope of this study.[7]

Finally, there is no intention to portray Germany's behavior in America as in any way unique in comparison to that of other nations. A juxtaposition of that nature is not yet possible because the surviving relevant records of the intelligence services and their activities cannot be freely inspected anywhere except in Germany, where the capture of the documents by the Allies at the end of the Second World War and the later return to the German authorities have led to an unusual accessibility.[8]

What this section does aim for is to correct the view that Washington, for purposes of propaganda, grossly exaggerated the activities of the German intelligence services in America.[9] Heinrich Albert, largely responsible through personal negligence for the fact that in the summer of 1915 Wilson became extensively informed about German operations, in 1948 still wrote: "From my own experience and based on my work on these matters, I can state that our entire activity remained strictly within the framework of the American laws."[10] The truth is that influential personalities around Wilson were informed by the autumn of 1914 about the numerous passport forgeries and that Bernstorff and a number of other German representatives were placed under surveillance from that time on.[11] Czechs organized by Emanuel Victor Voska at times cooperated with the British Naval Attaché, Capt. Guy Gaunt, and succeeded in obtaining positions in German offices in America.[12] During the course of the war the Americans also built up their own intelligence organization and thus increasingly became able to observe the activities of German agents.[13] Distrusting the Germans, the U.S. Government even had the telephones of the German embassy tapped.[14] When the Austro-Hungarian Ambassador, Constantin Dumba, employed the American journalist James F. J. Archibald to send rather sensitive documents to Europe, the papers fell into the hands of the British.[15] Through the irresponsible laxness on the part of Franz von Papen and Wolf von Igel, the British and the Americans were able to obtain additional explosive evidence.[16] Thus Washington soon was sufficiently informed about the German *Propaganda der Tat* to leave uncertainty only about the actual extent of the activities. While the American government for some time remained ignorant about details of the German operations and the size of the participating group of agents, Washington was certainly aware that a number of people or organizations were conducting themselves in an unlawful manner, most likely on orders from Berlin, but at least in Germany's interest.

At various times Wilson was called upon by those closest to him to make a clean sweep and, instead of expelling only less important figures, such as Dumba and the German attachés, to declare the German Ambassador himself persona non grata. Only the fact that Wilson and House were hoping to avoid American entry into the war—a likely consequence of Bernstorff's expulsion—and House's conviction that he would need Bernstorff in order to bring about Wilson's peace mediation saved the Ambassador from this fate.[17] One wonders whether Bernstorff was so thoroughly informed about the long-term intentions of the American government that he felt he could afford certain imprudences, or whether, being unable to avoid the *Propaganda der Tat* without taking a strong stand against Berlin, he accepted it as part of his assignment in time of war, even though he was aware of the possible consequences.

In their effect on American public opinion and thereby on the government in Washington, the German intelligence operations must be seen as an important factor in the continuous degeneration of relations between Germany and the United States. In the words of Moritz Julius Bonn, the economist who worked for the German Embassy: "These things poisoned public opinion and were a hindrance everywhere to the real public relations work."[18] How seriously these events were taken in the United States can be seen from a report by Max Warburg to the Under Secretary in the Foreign Office, Hilmar Freiherr von dem Bussche-Haddenhausen, about his talks with Americans in The Hague in March 1918: "The mood in America was so bitter towards Germany [the Americans told him] because so many deceitful things, some of which became known only little by little, had happened. First there had been the various explosions in the factories, which, as evidence had shown, were brought about in America on German orders, at a time when America was not yet at war with us.... The actions of Papen, Igel and others were so unfortunate [his contacts told him] that it was still impossible to appraise the full consequences."[19]

FORGED PASSPORTS FOR RESERVISTS AND AGENTS

Under Secretary Zimmermann probably exaggerated the number of men liable to German military service when, in a conversation with Gerard in the winter of 1914–15, he spoke of 500,000 fully trained German reservists residing in the United States and threatened the American Ambassador with the possibility that these troops could unite with the American Irish and start a revolution.[20] There can be no doubt, however, that a great number of German reservists were living in the United States and that among them were many officers whom the General Staff would have liked to bring back to Germany as quickly as possible.[21] Thus Bernstorff, "in a private letter from the Foreign Office," and the Military Attaché, "officially," received instructions "to send home as many German officers as possible." Since the British would have taken such military persons off the ships if they had traveled to Europe on their own passports, it became necessary to provide them with forged papers. "In the given circumstances," Bernstorff had "no reservations" about supporting the large-scale forgery of passports.[22]

On orders from Berlin, a special office for this task was set up in New York and put under the command of Hans Adam von Wedell, an American notary and former Prussian officer who at the beginning of the war had returned from Berlin. Wedell attempted to purchase as many passports as possible from citizens of neutral countries, most of them sailors, in order to forge them by replacing the pictures with those of the German reserve officers. As it turned out, these documents were not only prepared for reservists willing to do military duty, but also for spies and agents who were dispatched from the neutral United States to other countries.[23]

As could be expected from an operation of this magnitude, the authorities soon found out. Paul Falcke, the German Consul General in New York, reports that a New York politician was approached to help with the procurement of passports. However, the presumed helper of the German cause, who became acquainted with both Wedell and his assistant and successor, the German-American Carl Ruerode, worked together with American legal authorities. When the first disclosures occurred, Wedell hurriedly departed from the United States.[24] Most likely furnished with a passport by his own organization, he failed to clear the British controls and was captured. He was killed when the British vessel *Vinknor*, which had taken him on, hit a mine.[25] Following further revelations, Ruerode together with several of his accomplices, was arrested shortly thereafter and sentenced to three years in the penitentiary.[26]

Just how far Bernstorff went in his support of these passport forgeries can be seen from the fact that he even complained about the New York Consul General who, he said, "felt obliged to raise formalistic doubts."[27] Bernstorff himself wanted "to accept only the one viewpoint . . . that H. von Papen would have to attend to getting as many officers as possible to Germany." In view of these statements, Bernstorff's later depiction of the affair comes as something of a surprise: "Also personal responsibility on my part for the secret office in New York I must emphatically deny." Bernstorff conceded that he had known Wedell as a lawyer (*Advokat*) in New York before the war,[28] but he tries to give the impression of not having been informed about Wedell's and Ruerode's work methods.[29] According to Bernstorff, Wedell, in the summer of 1914, "secretly" and "probably at the instigation of a German military office" had returned to America "in order to disappear just as secretly after an apparently very brief stay."[30] Bernstorff also states in his memoirs that he had "not even known the name" of Ruerode before the latter's arrest, and his description of this case would have the reader believe that he had known nothing about the matter.[31] In fact, however, in March 1915 Bernstorff reported to Bethmann Hollweg about a contract between Papen and Ruerode, according to which Ruerode would plead guilty in court and receive $10,000 in return. Following his release from prison, he was to receive another

$5,000.³² The arrangement had been approved by him, Bernstorff wrote, and he had already paid out the amount.³³

After the Ambassador had reported to the Foreign Office in January 1915 that the American government indeed was conducting investigations, but that a compromising of the embassy was not to be feared, only one month elapsed before the Stegler scandal caused new problems.³⁴ Richard Peter Stegler, a reservist in the German navy who seems to have been hired as a spy by the Naval Attaché Karl Boy-Ed and outfitted with a false passport, disclosed details of his assignment to the American authorities. German protestations of innocence turned out to be futile, when on February 25, 1915, the newspapers published close-up photographs showing Stegler and Boy-Ed together.³⁵

On the whole, it seems that the passport forgeries, inasmuch as they served the purpose of shipping reservists back to Germany, were perhaps justifiable from a military standpoint, even if certain U.S. laws were violated.³⁶ American authorities, who since December 1914 had known of the connection between the forging operation and the German embassy, indeed decided to limit their efforts to prosecuting the less important agents, because Wilson, with some understanding for the motives behind the repatriation of these officers, did not wish a confrontation with Berlin over this affair.³⁷

MEASURES AGAINST THE BRITISH COLONIAL EMPIRE IN INDIA UNDERTAKEN FROM AMERICAN SOIL

These intelligence operations so far have found hardly any attention from German historians. In part this may have resulted from the fact that many documents of the military intelligence services, especially those of the German army, were destroyed in the wake of the revolution of 1918. To complicate matters, the protagonists of this strange interlude have had very little to say about their activities. Walter Nicolai provides no information about his work in this context.³⁸ Rudolf Nadolny is equally taciturn when he talks about the Indian operations.³⁹ Franz von Papen, for his part, is as laconic as he is unreliable in his treatment of the topic.⁴⁰ Bernstorff does mention the Indian conspiracy in the United States, but he disclaims knowledge of any individual project.⁴¹ Outside Germany, a number of more or less sensationalistic reports have been published about so-called German conspiracies in America. Most of them, however, appeared shortly after World War I and are based on the very limited documentary evidence available then and on questionable wartime press stories.[42] In any case, some of these publications contain reproductions of telegrams and reports that had been captured by the Allies during the war, whose authenticity, after checking the archives, in most instances no longer can be doubted.[43]

While some sources give the impression that the German plans to involve the Moslem world and India's Hindu masses in the war were only worked out in the autumn of 1914 after the German armies became stalled in France, the records indicate that revolutionary unrest in Asia had played a role in the deliberations of German governmental circles from the very beginning of the war.[44] On July 30, 1914, Wilhelm II expressed his wish that German consular officials in India and Turkey should incite the Moslems to a "wild uprising" against "this hateful, mendacious, ruthless nation of shopkeepers." The Emperor noted: "If we are to bleed to death, then England shall at least lose India."[45] On August 2 and 5, the Chief of the General Staff, Helmuth von Moltke, also demanded that the Foreign Office instigate "the insurrection of India and Egypt" and arouse the "fanaticism of Islam."[46] Max Freiherr von Oppenheim, who in his function as "resident minister" in the Foreign Office occupied himself with measures against the British colonial empire,[47] on August 18 advised Bethmann Hollweg: "Only when the Turks invade Egypt and flaming uprisings burn in India, will the British become pliable."[48] Statements of this sort do not give the impression that the operations in the Near East and India were only meant to deceive the German public with press reports about supposed rebellions against Britain,[49] but they demonstrate that military and political actions were considered by those in the highest positions.[50] How, in view of the global military constellation, the various authorities in Berlin envisioned a realization of their plans is a question, the answer to which may be found in their general overestimation of German military strength and their underestimation of Britain's endurance. Even if Germany had had sufficient troops at its disposal and if they had been brought to India somehow, it still appears highly improbable that the German government could have successfully incited the people to rise against their colonial masters. The mere fact that many Indians were quite willing to rebel against British rule was no indication that they wished to surrender to German colonialist ambitions.⁵¹ Thus it is not surprising that the revolutionary agents gathered in Germany, Turkey, and the United States were unable to rely on popular support in India.

Even before the war, there had been active cells of revolutionary Indians in the United States. Between 1911 and 1914, the Oxford-educated Har Dayal had organized a group around the periodical *Ghadr* in San Francisco. Their aim was the expulsion of the British from India.⁵² Watched by British intelligence agents and pursued by American authorities, Dayal fled to Germany via Switzerland in the spring of 1914, where he joined the so-called "Indian National Party."⁵³ Most of the Indians who came together in revolutionary circles in Germany were students who, at the outbreak of war, had been caught in Europe rather accidentally. Har Dayal and Virendranath Chattopadhyaya, who had been active against Britain in prewar France, became major figures in this movement and maintained close contacts with the Imperial authorities.⁵⁴ Initially, the Foreign Office assigned Max Freiherr von Oppenheim to attend to the Indians; later they were the responsibility of his successor Otto Günther von Wesendonk, whose activities included arming the revolutionaries and whose offices at the Wilhelmstrasse at times, such as in November 1915, had the appearance of armed camps.⁵⁵ Furthermore, the revolutionaries were in touch with Department IIIb of the General Staff. The students were often recruited and assisted in their propaganda work by professors at German universities.⁵⁶ By the fall of 1914, a connection was established between the Indian groups in Germany and those in the United States. Bernstorff's embassy in Washington was turned into a kind of communication center for the messages between them, the General Staff, the Foreign Office in Berlin, and the agents located all over the Near and Far East.⁵⁷

Generally speaking, Bernstorff was involved in these activities mainly on two levels. By order of the Foreign Office, the embassy saw to it that the Indians were able to travel between Europe, the United States, and Asia, often on forged papers.⁵⁸ Likewise, they were provided the necessary funds for travel expenses and propaganda activities, something which the Foreign Office granted regularly and generously. In addition, the Military Attaché organized revolutionary action groups and arms shipments for the East. Because these operations necessitated the cooperation of several consulates and German-American groups, Bernstorff himself frequently had to intercede and make contact with the leaders of the Indians, especially with Heramba Lal Gupta and Khan Dravanta Chakravarty, leading members of the Indian revolutionary movement, in Germany referred to as the Indian National Party.[59]

The fact that Bernstorff assisted Indian agitators to move between continents is only of interest in so far as large sums were spent, whose actual use, it would appear, was in some cases quite outside the control of the embassy. All Bernstorff could do was to report what from the records would appear to be rather constant financial demands of the Indians to Berlin. There the requests were usually granted without hesitation, since the responsible persons in the Wilhelmstrasse, as well as in the General Staff, obviously placed great confidence in the Indian revolutionaries and their emissaries in America.[60]

If the Indian propaganda schemes did not create much of a stir in the United States prior to 1914 and early in the war, the situation changed when the German government began to organize transports of men and material to Asia.[61] One of the more important undertakings involving the shipment of revolutionary agents from the neutral territory of the United States to foment uprisings in British colonial India was the Wehde expedition. Among the operatives actively participating in this were Albert H. Wehde,[62] who posed as a collector of art objects and jewelry merchant and was supplied with suitable identification papers by the Imperial German consulate in Chicago; the agent, Max Schulze, who worked under the cover name of Sterneck;[63] and Georg Paul Boehm, a former German sergeant. According to Count Bernstorff's reports to the Foreign Office, Wehde was to go to Calcutta in order to support the Indian revolution from there. The Ambassador wanted to deposit the necessary funds for this enterprise in India using the services of American banks. Sterneck and Boehm were to travel to Bangkok "to organize militarily the Indians living there." Later Boehm was supposed to go on to Punjab as part of the same mission.[64] Preparations for this far-flung project were made in New York and Chicago by the Military Attaché Franz von Papen; Gustav H. Jacobsen, a real estate broker in Chicago and head of the American Embargo Conference; and the Indians Heramba Lal Gupta, Dhirenda Nat Sen, and Jodh Singh. A certain William Jarrosch, who probably worked for an American intelligence service at the same time, participated in the preliminary talks in Chicago.[65] After the German Ambassador had reported the financial details of the operation to the Chancellor,⁶⁶ the agents most likely left the United States at the end of April or early in May 1915. In Manila they were expected by the Kaiserliche Zentralstelle für die indische Bewegung in Schanghai (Imperial Central Office for the Indian Movement in Shanghai). A motorized sailing vessel, the *Henry S.*, was purchased and loaded with weapons. When the British authorities refused to clear the vessel, the weapons were left in Manila "in order to conceal the purpose of the expedition," and under Wehde's command the ship headed south on July 15.⁶⁷ After taking on and discharging a mysterious cargo off the coast of Borneo, the *Henry S.* sailed into the Macassar Strait, where a failure of the ship's engine appears to have terminated the journey. Wehde somehow reached Shanghai, and, according to reports from German representatives in Peking, he went to work for the already mentioned Kaiserliche Zentralstelle. Boehm and Sterneck went to Jakarta, where they apparently made contact with German circles, such as the brothers Emil and Theodor Helfferich, who seem to have supported the Imperial German operations in this region.⁶⁸ Altogether this costly adventure seems to have had no tangible results.⁶⁹

The arms shipments organized by the German embassy also had to be discontinued, but they deserve more attention because greater expenditures were involved, and, in the course of these operations, a number of German Imperial officials and agents were dragged into the very limelight they abhorred. The failure, just off the West Coast, of what appears to have been the major arms shipment, led the American government to be all the more watchful. The idea of shipping arms to Asia originated in Berlin at the outset of the war, when it was decided "to hit England's heart in India."⁷⁰ Although some German military leaders indulged in thoughts about a conventional campaign against India, the General Staff apparently came to the more realistic view that the shortage of troops and the nearly impossible logistics of such an operation would rule out any direct military intervention in Southeast Asia. Thus for the time being Berlin seems to have opted for support of the Indian revolutionary movement with war materials. In the autumn of 1914, Indian emissaries appeared in Berlin, and it was agreed that arms and ammunition would be shipped to Java, where they would be taken over by Indian groups.⁷¹ Although the records do not appear to contain evidence concerning the existence of a German military master plan for India,⁷² it is difficult to escape the impression that these arms shipments were part of a loosely defined general military strategy which encompassed an advance against Egypt,[73] the proclamation of the "Holy War" among Moslems in the entire area from North Africa to East Asia,[74] a string of adventurous paramilitary expeditions to Persia and Afghanistan,[75] and an active campaign of sabotage and subversion organized by Imperial German representatives in Peking and Shanghai.[76]

In the middle of October 1914, the embassy received orders from Berlin "[to] buy rifles in larger amounts, up to twenty or thirty thousand, and as much ammunition as possible and to have this shipped to India."[77] With the cooperation of the Krupp representative in the United States, Hans Tauscher, and of Heinrich Albert, Papen succeeded in buying at least $140,000 worth of rifles, pistols, and ammunition,[78] which were stored in various locations. Following consultations with the German representatives in Peking and Shanghai, it was decided in the spring of 1915 to use the German consulate in San Francisco to purchase the steamer *Maverick* in order to transport the arms to Southeast Asia. The plan called for the schooner *Annie Larsen* to bring the arms into Mexican waters, where they were to be transferred to the *Maverick* and then transported to Bangkok under the American flag.[79] A memorandum in the archives of the Imperial Foreign Office of late November 1914, bearing no signature but initialed by the Under Secretary of the Foreign Office, Arthur Zimmermann, and a report from the Military Attaché to the Ministry of War of early March 1915, indicate that the responsibility for the Indian operation was divided between the army and navy. According to the earlier memorandum, Captain von Papen appears to have been in charge of the arms purchases, and the Foreign Office felt that the Attaché might well rely on the Clan na Gael leader, Joseph McGarrity, to arrange the shipment.[80] The later document shows that the purchase of the *Maverick* had to be approved by the Admiralty and that the necessary funds were provided by the Naval Attaché in Washington.[81] Late in January 1915, Bernstorff passed on a request from the German consulate in San Francisco to Berlin to make Captain Othmer, a German from Dortmund, available for this operation. A month later, the Ambassador cabled to Berlin that the Admiralty should authorize the Naval Attaché to spend $150,000 for the vessel needed to transport the arms to India.[82]

As planned, the schooner *Annie Larsen* of the Jebsen Line sailed to Socorro Island off the coast of Mexico and waited for the arrival of the steamer *Maverick* to transfer the cargo of arms. Captain von

Papen's reports on this matter to the General Staff in Berlin were frequent but to all appearances at times less than reliable. In May he wrote that the *Maverick* had met with the *Annie Larsen* in April, but that American and British naval authorities had learned of the transfer of the weapons, which the newspapers speculated were designated for Southwest Africa. Rumors had it, he wrote, that the British cruiser *Newcastle* was on its way to Socorro Island.[83] In late July, Papen had more sobering facts for Berlin. The *Annie Larsen*, he now reported, in fact had missed the *Maverick* at Socorro Island. British warships had stopped and searched the *Maverick* before she could continue her voyage to Hilo. Captain Othmer finally took the *Annie Larsen* into port at Hoquiam, Washington, where American authorities promptly confiscated the vessel and its cargo, which had been falsely declared for Mexico.[84] Othmer managed to escape arrest, but the incident caused a rather unpleasant exchange between the State Department and the German Ambassador. Lansing was informed by the Germans that the arms and ammunition on the *Annie Larsen* were meant for German East Africa and that the transport from San Francisco had been arranged to confuse ever-watchful enemy cruisers. Apart from the incredibility of Bernstorff's statements, the affair was bound to contribute to the further deterioration of the already strained relations between Germany and America.[85]

The total fiasco of this operation, however, did not cause the German diplomatic representatives in the United States to halt their arms shipments to India. Soon after the unsuccessful voyage of the *Annie Larsen*, the Military Attaché, in cooperation with Bernstorff, undertook new arms purchases. In June, a consignment of weapons destined for Jakarta was loaded on the Dutch steamer *Djember*; but through the watchfulness of British consular officials this operation was brought to the attention of the American authorities and the project had to be abandoned.[86] Still not discouraged, Papen and his associates now proceeded to send weapons in postal packages from America to Shanghai, from where they were to be forwarded to the revolutionaries.[87]

In view of the failure of all these efforts, it seems incomprehensible that the German Government continued to seriously consider further proposals worked out by the Indians. The revolutionaries, however, whose sincere motives in the struggle for liberation of India are not questioned here, apparently did not have sufficient military knowledge and experience to realize the futility of their schemes.[88] Bernstorff, too, could hardly be expected to have the expertise and organizational skill to understand the logistics of these operations. The Military Attaché, though, who, besides the Ambassador, bore the main responsibility in Washington for the undertakings and who was in almost constant communication with the General Staff, treated the entire matter with an astonishing degree of dilettantism. The remaining documentary evidence clearly indicates that the German Foreign Office had a similarly distorted picture of political and military conditions in India. As late as April 1916, Jagow notified the Secretary of the Imperial Treasury Office that "news from an absolutely reliable source" in India indicated that a rebellion against Britain was being prepared there which, "in order to get under way," only needed "a push from outside as well as the supply of weapons and ammunition."[89]

Among the more unrealistic projects was also an invasion of the Andaman Islands, planned by Paul von Hintze and his people. For 2,000,000 marks, German authorities in Peking wanted to outfit two large steamers as warships and with them stage an attack on Port Blair. Starting from there, an invasion of India's Orissa Coast was to be the next step in the campaign. The Admiralty, however, apparently thought the plan illusory and called it off.[90] Another scheme was designed to bring about an uprising of the Nepalese, who, it was thought, would join the battle against Britain with the support of Ghurka regiments to be made up of men from German prisoner-of-war camps. This plan, too, had been drawn up by Hintze in Peking and met with the approval of the Military Attaché in Washington.[91] Khan Dravanta Chakravarty and his India Committee in New York advanced their plans for an invasion of the British West Indies. "We can muster," they claimed, "nearly seventy to seventy-five thousand men." In case the British strengthened their garrisons, they would "cross the border and enter into Venezuela." Bernstorff evidently recognized the futility of the project. He told the Foreign Office that, in his view, "a shipment of arms from here [was] impossible" and therefore advised Berlin not to approve the proposal.[92] Looking back, the Ambassador's appraisal appears realistic, and it is not very difficult to imagine how President Wilson in the winter of 1916–17 would have reacted to a military operation in the Caribbean supported by Germany.

The problems besetting the Indian revolutionary schemes were manifold. First of all, the Indians were brought together from different cultural backgrounds and from various parts of the world.

There developed differences concerning the leadership of the group, which, if one follows the documents, consisted of at least three subdivisions, namely, in Europe, North America, and Asia. Leadership positions often were questioned, and the Germans were forced to use pressure to hold the organization together.[93] Communication with each other and with the German officials often broke down. To make matters worse, the British possessed an apparently worldwide network of diplomats and agents, almost constantly on the lookout for the Indians and their German partners.[94] Not surprisingly, London therefore was well informed regarding most German operations in this sector and able to initiate countermeasures. How closely the British followed some German ventures can be seen from the almost continuous flow of information to London concerning the operation of Georg Paul Boehm and Albert Wehde mentioned above.[95]

Although the German representatives in the United States spent large amounts on projects directed at fomenting an Indian revolution, no measurable success could be recorded in any sector of the operations. The arms transports and the groups of agents, apparently, in most cases did not reach their destination. Various operatives, provided with funds by the German embassy in Washington, traveled to a number of points in Asia, but most of them seem to have been apprehended by British authorities or effectively hindered in their undertakings. Indian nationals, who, on orders from the Berlin Foreign Office and with Bernstorff's support, were trained in the use of explosives and weapons, were unable to carry out their assignments or else caused only minor damage.[96] In no case, it would seem, was British colonial rule seriously threatened by German operatives or Indian agents in the service of Berlin.[97]

In the rather voluminous records relating to the German schemes among the Indians we find no evidence that Bernstorff particularly favored these operations. Rather, one gains the impression that the Ambassador considered the efforts against British rule in India as perhaps not always prudent, but nevertheless justifiable, wartime measures and therefore followed the directives from Berlin. Although it is very possible that he was not familiar with all details of the plans of the General Staff and the navy, there can be no doubt that he was rather completely informed about operations originating in the United States and that he made all possible assistance available to the Indians.[98] The Americans knew about Bernstorff's connections with the Indian revolutionaries at least after the unsuccessful attempts at arms shipments on the West Coast; certainly any doubts which may still have existed in Washington were removed after intelligence agents raided Wolf von Igel's office in New York and found among the confiscated documents material about the Indian operations.[99]

SIR ROGER CASEMENT IN THE WEB OF GERMAN WAR POLICY

The events behind the tragic end of Roger Casement until recently have found but scant attention in German historiography. As with the other intelligence operations, the destruction of a great deal of the German records may serve as a partial explanation.[100] However, the main lines of Germany's policy toward Ireland during the First World War can be reconstructed without difficulty from the documents in the German Foreign Office and the writings of Sir Roger Casement available in various publications. Both Rudolf Nadolny, who had been personally instructed by Chief of Staff Gen. Erich von Falkenhayn to take over the "handling of the Irish matter" in Berlin,[101] and Capt. Franz von Papen, who as Military Attaché kept up the German contacts with Sinn Fein until he was declared persona non grata, have given us in their memoirs very limited and misleading information on German-Irish relations.[102] Indeed, with the exception of Franz Rintelen, we have no memoirs from the leading agents who cooperated with the American Irish.

It seems appropriate to mention these connections, not only because the German embassy in Washington managed the flow of information between the Irish underground and Berlin, but also because Bernstorff personally cultivated close contacts with some leading figures of the Irish liberation movement in America. As has been shown above, certain German-American groups had established a relationship with the American Irish before the war and, although it cannot be proved from the documents, one may assume that the possibility of eventual German support of the Irish movement for independence played some role in this rapprochement.[103] Nevertheless, the present state of research does not permit us to speak of a prewar German plan for active cooperation, including a possible German military intervention in Ireland. Although it would appear more than likely that the former Pinkerton man and German agent, Kurt Jahnke, who had established important contacts with Irish-American groups, played his part in the manipulation of Irish revolutionaries for German aims, the records indicate that early significant negotiations with Irish leaders apparently were directed by the Military Attaché. These encounters took place in New York in the summer of 1914 before Count Bernstorff returned from Europe.[104] As soon as the Ambassador arrived in the United States, he was initiated into the various schemes. A first meeting was held at the German Club in New York; besides Bernstorff and a Clan na Gael delegation led by John Devoy,[105] Bernhard Dernburg, Wolf von Igel, Franz von Papen, and Georg von Skal were in attendance. The Irish frankly stated their case to the Ambassador: they wanted to use the opportunity of the war to overthrow British rule in Ireland. They were not in need of financial support, they said, but Germany should supply them with arms and officers. The Irish representatives emphasized that the action which they had planned would tie up a good part of the British troops in Ireland and therefore would reduce Britain's military presence on the battlefields of the Continent. John Devoy recalled later that Bernstorff received the Irish requests "with evident sympathy" and promised to transmit them to Berlin.[106] Just about the same time, Sir Roger Casement, the well-known former British diplomat who was now collaborating with the Irish revolutionaries,[107] was introduced to Bernstorff in Washington, and it was decided that he should be sent to Germany.[108]

Although Devoy and Casement, between the fall of 1914 and the landing in Ireland in April 1916, were not always of the same opinion, Casement clearly went to Berlin as an emissary and confidant of the Clan na Gael.[109] Bernstorff helped to arrange the journey of England's bitter foe and provided him with an official letter of introduction to the Imperial Chancellor.[110] Casement's mission consisted of three assignments which were expected to further the goal of an Irish uprising against Britain. Above all, he was to negotiate German military support for a rebellion in Ireland. Beyond that, he was to influence German public opinion in order to create a broad popular base for eventual steps by Berlin in favor of Ireland. Finally, he was to organize a combat-ready military unit from Irish prisoners of war held in Germany.[111]

Casement left New York on October 15, 1914, disguised as James E. Landy and accompanied by a young Norwegian sailor named Eivind Adler Christensen.[112] Except for an unsuccessful attempt by the British to bribe Casement's traveling companion, the trip went without any incidents worth mentioning.[113] In Berlin, the intelligence services as well as the Foreign Office were prepared for his arrival by telegrams from Papen and Bernstorff. Raketen-Richard (Rocket-Richard) Meyer, a staff member of the Foreign Office,[114] and Georg Count von Wedel[115] took him into their care and turned James E. Landy into Mr. Hammond from New York. Besides the regular meetings with Meyer and Wedel, Casement had talks with the Under Secretary of the Foreign Office, Arthur Zimmermann; the State Secretary of the Colonial Office, Wilhelm Solf; Prince Gebhard Blücher von Wahlstatt, whom he knew well since his stay in Africa;[116] and the historian and political publicist, Theodor Schiemann.[117] Indeed after several attempts, Casement succeeded in meeting with Bethmann Hollweg on December 18, 1914.

Despite some differences of opinion, Casement's initial negotiations[118] with officials of the Foreign Office and with representatives of the intelligence services of the Navy[119] and the General Staff went so smoothly that Zimmermann in November 1914 was able to declare in the name of the Imperial Chancellor and with his approval: "If in the course of this war ... the fortunes of battle should ever bring German troops to the shores of Ireland, they would land there, not as an army of invaders ... but as armed forces of a (friendly)[120] government which is inspired by good will toward a land and people for whom Germany wishes only national prosperity and national freedom."[121] After having met Bethmann Hollweg, Casement was so successful on his mission in Germany that on December 23, 1914, he was able to sign a treaty with the German Foreign Office that was also approved as a valid instrument by the Political Section of the General Staff.[122] The articles of the document above all determined the status of the Irish Brigade, which, for instance, was to fight only for the goals of the Irish liberation movement and in no circumstances was to be used in any other manner for Germany's purposes. Article Six of the treaty promised supplies of weapons and ammunition "to equip the Irish National Volunteers in Ireland," as well as "a supporting body of German officers and men, in German transports," in case a landing in Ireland was feasible. Article Seven of the treaty also conceded the possibility of employing "the Irish Brigade to assist the Egyptian People to recover their freedom by driving the British out of Egypt." The use of the brigade was to be dependent on Roger Casement's approval.[123]

The attempt to raise an Irish unit in a camp near Limburg was rather unsuccessful. To begin with, suitable men had to be found in the prisoner-of-war camps, and, from the beginning, it was important to prevent infiltration of the group by soldiers loyal to Britain. The project was not made easier by the fact that most of the prisoners were not willing to apply for a military unit organized by German authorities and thus to commit treason. Moreover, it would appear that Casement probably was not the ideal person to form such a brigade. In fact, his organizational attempts showed so little progress that John Devoy seriously considered the possibility of sending fifty Irishmen from the United States in order to give some backbone to the project.[124] To turn the Irish volunteers in the camps into a somewhat reliable unit, the Germans decided to assign them politically dependable Irish clergymen, and Bernstorff was instructed to arrange for the dispatch of such priests.[125] In the fall of 1914, Father Canice O'Gorman, "a loyal, devoted nationalist," and Father J. Crotty, a Dominican and an "angry Fenian," came to Germany. They were soon followed by Father John T. Nicholson from America.[126] The financial funding for Casement's activities essentially came from the many small donations of Irish-Americans which were transferred by John Devoy to Casement through Bernstorff and the Foreign Office.[127] The archival sources show clearly that Casement paid back all financial assistance made available by the German Government.[128]

The correspondence between Berlin and Washington regarding Ireland was handled by telegram as well as through couriers and regular mail to cover addresses.[129] As a consequence of the routine exchange of prisoners of war, the British soon learned about Casement's activities in Germany and the attempts to set up the Irish Brigade. Since they also frequently intercepted messages between Berlin and Washington and read some of the clandestine mail between Europe and America, they must have been well informed concerning the cooperation of the Irish and Germans in Europe and in the United States. This took on added importance when preparations for the Irish rising were taking shape in Dublin and New York in 1915.

In April 1915, Joseph Plunkett appeared in Berlin as representative of the Supreme Council of the Irish Republican Brotherhood (IRB) and personally discussed with Bethmann Hollweg the shipment of arms to Ireland in the coming spring.[130] At this stage the exact date of the rising had not yet been decided.[131] It was not until May that the IRB organized the so-called Military Council, of which Plunkett was also a member and which kept in touch with Berlin through Devoy and Bernstorff. In the autumn of 1915, the Irish sent Capt. Robert Monteith, a confidant of the IRB leader Thomas Clarke, a veteran of the British forces in the Boer War, and drill instructor of the Irish Volunteers, to Germany in order to turn the Irish Brigade into an operational unit.[132] He found a sickly and depressed Casement, who spent much of his time in health resorts and, because of his disappointment over the poor results of his labors, had all but given up the recruiting of volunteers from the prisoner-of-war camps.[133] Indeed, the recruiting campaign had been so fruitless that Rudolf Nadolny of the Political Section of the General Staff had already told the Foreign Office in the summer "that from our viewpoint, after the experiences to date, further efforts to form a legion from Irish prisoners are considered to be hopeless."[134]

Early in 1916, the languishing Irish cause in Berlin suddenly was given a new lease on life. On February 5, John Devoy received a message from Dublin that the rebellion was planned for Easter. He immediately passed the information on to Bernstorff, who reported it to Berlin: "Unanimous opinion that action cannot be postponed much longer. Delay disadvantageous to us. . . . We have therefore decided to begin action on Easter Sunday. . . . Must have your arms and ammunition in Limerick between Good Friday and Easter Sunday. We expect German help immediately after the beginning of the action. We might be compelled to unleash action [*losschlagen*] earlier."[135] On March 1 the Foreign Office replied with a text submitted by Nadolny from the General Staff and agreed on by the Admiralty: "Between April 20 and 23 in the evening two or three fishing trawlers could land about 20,000 rifles and ten machine guns as well as ammunition and explosives near Fenit Pier in Tralee Bay. Irish pilot boat shall expect the ships before dawn . . . at entrance to Tralee Bay. . . . Unloading must take place in a few hours. Please wire whether requirements in Ireland can be effected secretly by Devoy, success only possible if all forces are utilized."[136] From a message forwarded to Berlin by Bernstorff on February 16 on behalf of the "Irish Revolutionary Council in America" and received in Berlin shortly after the proposal to land 20,000 rifles, it is quite evident that the German offer of arms in no way corresponded with the expectations of the Irish. This document, signed above Bernstorff's name with "John Devoy, Secretary of the Irish Revolutionary Directory," among other things makes the following points: "If a small expedition with a good supply of arms and ammunition—say from 25 to 50 thousand rifles with a proportionate number of machine guns and field artillery and a few superior officers—could be sent by the northern route, escorted by submarines, it would have a good chance of reaching the west coast of Ireland, especially if simultaneous with a demonstration in the North Sea. . . . We are confident that if we had one hundred thousand rifles we could at once get that number of men . . . and that in a short time the number could be trebled. This force could give occupation to an English army of five hundred thousand."[137]

In the meantime, Monteith had informed the ailing Casement in his hospital in Munich of the latest developments, and the latter had hurried to Berlin to see Nadolny.[138] Apparently Casement had assumed that the operation in question was only an arms shipment for the revolutionaries in Ireland. An open rebellion at this time under the unfavorable conditions offered by Berlin was unthinkable for him. The optimistic Nadolny painted a picture of extraordinary chances for success for the Irish war of independence, but Casement was not willing to consider an invasion of Ireland without adequate German support in the form of arms and officers. Accordingly, at the last moment, he now tried to stop an undertaking that, in his opinion, was in no way consistent with the conditions of the treaty of December 23, 1914, and, in addition, was bound to bring about the most dreadful consequences for Ireland. The Political Section of the General Staff, however, was in no mood to negotiate compromises, and uncouth blackmail was used to force Casement to accept the reckless conditions of the German intelligence services.[139] The idealist who had come to Berlin in 1914 to organize assistance for the Irish liberation movement, who had put his honor at stake by showing the German military representatives and the Foreign Office almost unlimited trust, was now a broken man. Hoping to avoid becoming responsible for the senseless deaths of a handful of Irish volunteers from the Brigade, he now asked for permission to accompany the arms shipment alone.[140] "The *only* thing I can see clearly is that while I *may* sacrifice myself, I am not entitled to sacrifice those who trusted in my honour and good faith, even as I trusted in the honour and good faith[141] of the German Government."[142] How Sir Roger Casement really felt in the spring of 1916 prior to the abortive journey to Ireland can be gleaned from his notes on the back of a letter to him from Father Crotty: "Oh, Ireland—Why did I ever trust in such a Govt. as this—or think that such men would help thee. They have no sense of honour, chivalry generosity.... They are cads.... That is why they are hated by the world and why England will surely beat them."[143] When the Germans realized that Casement was not willing to sacrifice the Irish volunteers, the General Staff did not hesitate to attempt to bribe Casement's last confidant, Captain Monteith, with "a considerable sum of money" to leave Casement behind and to take the brigade to Ireland. The German officers had underestimated the Irish; Monteith was not to be bought.[144]

The decision of the Berlin intelligence services to send a steamer instead of the two fishing vessels to Tralee Bay was transmitted to Devoy through Bernstorff and relayed from New York to Ireland by a courier.[145] On April 14, Philomena Plunkett, the sister of Joseph Plunkett, arrived in New York with a message from Dublin that in no circumstances could the arms be landed before April 23. Devoy immediately notified the embassy through Wolf von Igel, and, on April 15, the change of date was cabled to Berlin. Three days later, during a surprise raid on Igel's New York office, a large number of highly sensitive documents fell into the hands of American intelligence agents. Since the confiscated papers included copies of Bernstorff's telegrams concerning the preparations for the uprising and arms shipments,[146] the often-voiced suspicion that the British Government was informed by the Americans about the impending events in Ireland appears not unjustified.[147]

Bernstorff's vital cable of April 15, 1916, reading "Delivery of weapons must take place exactly on the evening of Sunday, April 23" arrived too late in Berlin.[148] The former British steamer *Castro*, renamed *Aud* by the Germans, was already on the way to Fenit Bay. Commanded by Lt. Karl Spindler and under orders to unload its cargo of arms and ammunition between April 20 and 22, the *Aud* reached Tralee Bay on April 20 and, after a short interval, entered the waters off Fenit, where Spindler searched in vain for a reaction to his signals. Certain that something had gone wrong, he cast anchor and waited for daylight. Instead of the Irish revolutionaries, who were not expecting the ship until Sunday, British Coast Guard vessels appeared the next morning, Good Friday, and put an end to this phase of Germany's Irish expedition. It was only by means of a deceptive maneuver that Spindler managed to sink his ship with its cargo before the eyes of the British navy. The *Aud* did not have a wireless radio, and Berlin apparently had no way to stop the transport after Bernstorff's telegram no. 7 of April 15 had been received.[149]

Also, on the evening of Maundy Thursday, the submarine *U-19* arrived in Tralee Bay. Aboard the vessel were Roger Casement, Robert Monteith, and Daniel Bailey, one of the Irish Volunteers. They had started their voyage on the *U-20* in Wilhelmshaven on April 11 and had changed to the *U-19* at the Helgoland base, where the *U-20* had broken down with engine problems. Why German intelligence had not coordinated the mission of the *Aud* and Casement's landing remains an open question.[150] There is reason to believe, however, that the agents of Department IIIb and their colleagues from the navy had given up all hope in the Casement venture. After the General Staff had made an attempt to ship the Irish Brigade to the war in Syria and only thirty-eight men in Limburg had volunteered, the confidence of the military in the usefulness of the unit was shaken considerably.[151] A low point in the relationship between Casement and the German military, however, was reached when the former quarreled with the intelligence people because he considered the assistance planned by Germany to be totally inadequate for a rebellion.[152] Without informing the Germans, Casement went so far as to send a personal emissary to Ireland with instructions to persuade the IRB at the last moment to stop the operation.[153] It is difficult to avoid the impression that, among other things, Berlin welcomed the opportunity to get rid of the disagreeable Irishman. That Casement even now went to Ireland only to stop the unfortunate uprising was something that Rudolf Nadolny most likely had not taken into consideration.[154] Even though *U-19* had sighted the *Aud* in the evening, the submarine commander made no efforts to contact the vessel. The *Aud* had also been sighted from the shore, but the rebels were not expecting the German arms until Sunday. When the light signals of *U-19* received no answer from the coast, the submarine entered further into the bay and discharged the three Irishmen in a dinghy, equipped only with pistols, binoculars, and knives. Casement was arrested the next morning and after a short interrogation was taken to Dublin. A consideration of the unsuccessful blood-letting at Easter, the brutal retaliatory measures of the British against the Irish civilian population, and the execution of the revolutionary leaders, including Casement, would go beyond the scope of this study. In spite of the British efforts to destroy the image of Casement as a hero of the Irish revolution, it is now generally agreed that the idealistic and self-sacrificing, though perhaps somewhat gullible, man has an important place in the history of the Irish struggle for liberation. Germany's policy toward Ireland

and her treatment of Roger Casement, in contrast, have earned a somewhat less positive appraisal.[155]

For the American Sinn Feiners who had cooperated with the German embassy and the intelligence agents, the bloody suppression of the rising only meant a new incentive to further revolutionary plans. As for the German representatives in America, Wolf von Igel found himself in the embarrassing situation of being suspected of having caused the failure of the Irish uprising by his incredible carelessness.[156] Bernstorff himself faced the less than enviable alternative of demanding from Secretary of State Lansing the return of the documents confiscated in Igel's New York office, or declaring the activities of Igel and Georg von Skal as independent of the embassy and thereby relinquishing the return of the incriminating documents. Since the Americans certainly had already copied or examined the papers, there was little use for Bernstorff to insist on their return.[157]

The cooperation of the Irish Revolutionary Directory in New York with Bernstorff and the German agents was by no means interrupted after the fiasco of Fenit Bay. Shortly after Casement's arrest, Bernstorff notified Berlin: "The Irish leaders here plan to organize themselves once more in Ireland and have renewed the contact with Ireland. They are asking for notification whether upon resumption of the revolution they can count again on support from Germany."[158] Probably with the approval of the Admiralty, which controlled most of the strings of the German intelligence network in America, Nadolny replied on June 11, 1916, that Germany was "basically quite willing to further support the Irish." Consequently, he asked "for timely specification of the kind, time, and extent of the desired help."[159] In early September, Bernstorff was already in a position to inform Berlin about the "kind" of support needed. The Irish Revolutionary Directory not only requested arms shipments, but, as in April, also a simultaneous landing of German troop contingents. When after three months still no reaction had come from Berlin, Bernstorff wired on December 4: "Top secret. Irish leaders here press for answer to Report A no. 415 of September 8."[160] On Christmas Eve 1916, von Hülsen,[161] successor of Rudolf Nadolny as chief of the Political Section of the General Staff since July 1916,[162] told the Foreign Office that 30,000 rifles, 10 machine guns, and 6,000,000 cartridges could be landed in Ireland in February or March. There is, however, no mention of troops in this offer of the General Staff. When Bernstorff informed the American Irish accordingly, they quickly realized that Berlin was basically unwilling to lend stronger support to the revolution, but only welcomed renewed unrest in Ireland as an opportunity to weaken Britain's military operations against Germany. The Irish appeared to have learned from the futile Easter rising. They refused the German offer, as the operation would be "pointless without the landing of sufficient cover troops."[163]

By the autumn of 1916, the relationship between Bernstorff and the Irish must have cooled off considerably, since, in contrast to many German-Americans and radical Irish, he took the stand that Wilson's reelection was in Germany's interest. In his support of Wilson he had gone so far as to keep German-American voices, such as George Sylvester Viereck and his *Fatherland*, from actively campaigning for Charles Evans Hughes. At the same time, many Irish beat their propaganda drums against Wilson as the man who had failed to prevent Casement's execution through timely intervention.[164] Former U.S. Consul in Munich, Thomas St. John Gaffney, who had been Casement's representative in Germany and served as Irish liaison man to the German supporters of Irish independence and Celtic dreams, in August 1916 had returned to the United States in order to campaign for Hughes.[165] Jeremiah A. O'Leary, Irish-American leader and founder of the American Truth Society, wrote to Wilson in a published message that he would not give him his vote, to which the President countered that he was not in the least interested in the vote of someone who had connections with "disloyal Americans."[166] Bernstorff, in any case, did not share the views of such Irish, although only in May he had reported that they had "swept into our camp since last Easter as one man."[167]

In summary, it appears entirely justified to say that from 1914 to 1916 Bernstorff maintained close contacts with the representatives of the Clan na Gael. It is evident from the records that he strongly supported German propaganda activities among the American Irish. There is sufficient evidence to show that he was fully informed about the plans of the Irish rebels; but it is uncertain whether he knew the full details of their temporary cooperation with the agents of the German intelligence services. Besides, it needs to be pointed out that the Ambassador's personal feelings toward Catholicism and the Catholic church were so negative that it appears questionable whether he could have succeeded in developing close personal relations with the largely Catholic Irish. Alfred Noyes's judgment of the German Ambassador is harsh, but it would seem that Bernstorff indeed used the Irish to gain advantages for Germany. He understood the political influence of the American Irish and the significance of the Catholic church as a major institution of this ethnic group. Seen this way, it does not come as a surprise that the Ambassador disregarded his anti-Catholic disposition and in fact made some efforts to utilize Catholic connections for Germany's political purposes.[168] In the final analysis, Bernstorff, after having concluded that an understanding between Britain and Germany for the time being could not be attained, evidently supported the Irish cause in spite of his personal inability to identify with the goals of the Celtic movement and the Irish Catholic circles.

GERMAN INTERESTS AND THE CIVIL WAR SOUTH OF THE BORDER

When war broke out in Europe, Berlin was already fully engaged in Mexico. In contrast to the United States, Germany had supported the government of the reactionary General Victoriano Huerta and underlined its policy by supplying the dictator with arms. Washington had sent its fleet and, among other things, at Veracruz had indicated to the Emperor that within the American sphere of interest he would have to abide by America's rules. Commander Köhler of the *Dresden* had exercised caution, and Albert Ballin's ships had not insisted on docking at Veracruz. Although German arms shipments to Huerta had eroded American confidence in Germany's Latin American policy,[169] this does not seem to have caused any major concern in Berlin; otherwise, in the midst of the European crisis in June 1914, the Emperor would hardly have decided to order the dispatch of the *Panther* to the coast of Mexico, a warship not unknown to the imperialist competition.[170]

July 15 saw the end of the Huerta government, something Wilson had so much hoped for. Accompanied by family and entourage, the General fled his country on board the German cruiser *Dresden* and headed for Spain. Thus Berlin's favorite in Mexico was relieved of his power, forcing Germany to seek an alternative to its Mexican policy.

Since the beginning of the war, the German legation in Mexico had been run by the mission's Secretary, Julius Magnus, because Adm. Paul von Hintze, the previous Minister and an eager supporter of the Huerta clique, had been transferred.[171] His successor, Heinrich von Eckardt, the former envoy in Havana, took office only in March 1915 because Bryan, fearing renewed German meddling in Mexican affairs, had requested a delay in the appointment.[172] Since the summer of 1914, both the embassy in Washington and the German legation in Mexico had been practically cut off from Europe, causing a relatively close cooperation of the two diplomatic missions, a cooperation that took on importance when Berlin began to consider the advantages of entangling the United States in a war with Mexico.[173]

The records for 1914 or earlier do not reveal any evidence of a German military plan that was clearly directed against the United States and included a consideration of Mexico and Japan as allies. While Barbara Tuchman's study of the background of the so-called Zimmermann note could give the impression that there had been concrete plans for a German-Mexican-Japanese operation, the measures taken by Germany rather indicate that Berlin merely tried to tie down America's underestimated army in Mexico by whatever means feasible. This was also the undertone of Bernstorff's reports concerning the situation in Mexico. The "provocation of a war between the U.S. and Mexico"[174] evidently became part of the thinking of some influential people in Berlin in the course of the war. That Bernstorff at any time actively supported such a war, however, cannot be argued from the documents that have become available so far.

Franz von Papen, who until the summer of 1914 was simultaneously accredited as Military Attaché at the embassy in Washington as well as at the legation in Mexico, must have appeared destined to take a hand in the execution of any German operations in Mexico. Not only had he become acquainted with the country and its people, but he had also been able to observe the sabotage methods of the Mexican revolutionaries. The "dashing cavalry officer," who, as Moritz Julius Bonn later recalled, was ready "to take upon himself any risk," but who also lacked "the foresight to judge how the adventure which he had entered into would turn out," was instructed to shut down the oil fields at Tampico, since it was assumed in Berlin that they might be used to supply the British fleet.[175] The sabotage operations, about which Bernstorff was also informed, were prepared by Heinrich von Eckardt, Franz von Papen, and Karl Boy-Ed, who must have had similar instructions from the Admiralty. Eckardt had just finished his last preparatory meetings in Galveston and New Orleans on February 22 and 24, 1915, when the Admiralty suddenly decided that "decisive military damage to Britain by cutting off oil exports from Mexico is not feasible." Consequently, there was "no money available for cut off."[176] Concerning the plans of the General Staff, the documents contain a report by the German Military Attaché, dated New York, March 17, just a few days after the operation had been called off by the navy. Here Papen writes that he had sent a Mr. von Petersdorf to Tampico "in order to cause as much damage as possible by blowing up tanks and pipelines." Papen added confidently: "With the present conditions in Mexico, I am hoping for great success with relatively small means." Whether this reflects the specific opinion of the General Staff, or whether Papen had not been informed in time about the directive of the Admiralty cannot be ascertained. As it was, at this time no specific sabotage projects seem to have been carried out in Tampico, where the Allies also maintained a considerable number of intelligence operatives.[177]

In the spring of 1915, Berlin set out to assist General Huerta in his return to Mexico. The General Staff, as well as the Admiralty, the Foreign Office, and the embassy in Washington all seem to have had a hand in this. The man in charge of the undertaking appears to have been Franz (von) Rintelen, a colorful agent of the Admiralty Staff.[178] Better known to historians for his less than transparent role in the planning of sabotage operations and labor strikes in the United States, he also served as contact man between the German government and the General in exile.[179]

In February 1915, Rintelen met with Huerta in Barcelona and offered him German support for a military coup in Mexico. The Admiralty man then made his way to the United States, where he arrived on April 3.[180] Accompanied by Abraham Ratner and José C. Delgado, Victoriano Huerta landed in New York on April 12 and immediately began a series of meetings and conferences with a great number of Mexican officers and leading generals. To the American press, he announced that a strong man would soon take over the reins in Mexico. In a New York hotel, he conducted secret talks[181] with Rintelen, Papen, and Boy-Ed.[182] German arms shipments and financial support were at the center of the negotiations. An account was opened for Huerta at the Deutsche Bank in Havana with $800,000;[183] another $95,000 were deposited in Mexico. Friedrich Katz puts the total amount held ready by the German government for Huerta's takeover at $12,000,000.[184] Bernstorff was unaware that the man who had been instructed by the embassy to make the arrangements for Huerta's hotel suite was in the service of Thomas Masaryk's agent, Emanuel Victor Voska. Voska's people placed bugs in Huerta's suite and monitored the conspirators' meetings from the adjacent room.[185]

After all preparations for the power struggle in Mexico had been made,[186] General Huerta took a train to El Paso, Texas. Upon his arrival near the border on June 27, he was received not only by his general, Pascual Orozco, but also by an American colonel, who had come to Newman Station some eighteen miles northeast of El Paso with twenty-five soldiers and an intelligence agent. The Americans arrested the General and took him to Fort Bliss, where he was kept prisoner by the army. In his desperation, the Mexican turned to his presumed allies and begged Bernstorff at least to see to it that his wife and children in El Paso were protected. The latter, in his desire to avoid any personal connection with the Mexican conspiracy, forwarded Huerta's letter to the American government.[187] When Huerta fell ill in the fall, the Americans let him go to join his family in El Paso. They thought it inadvisable to have the Mexican die in their custody. But when he did not die as expected, he was again imprisoned at Fort Bliss. When his condition deteriorated again, he was once more released to El Paso, where after two mysterious operations he died on January 13, 1916.[188] No power in the world had lifted a finger for the General during the last months of his life. The German embassy preferred to have had no connections with him; Franz Rintelen was in a prison in England; the attachés Franz von Papen and Karl Boy-Ed had been expelled from the United States at the end of 1915; and President Wilson had just returned from his honeymoon in Hot Springs, Virginia, when the Mexican died.

Thus during 1915 Germany was unable to register any success in its Mexican policy. After Huerta had fled in the summer of 1914, conditions in Mexico had not become normalized, but instead the civil war continued almost unabatingly. Francisco Villa, who once had made common cause with Francisco Madero against the dictator Porfirio Díaz, had no intention of leaving the country to the Constitutionalist, Venustiano Carranza, and his position in fact was strengthened by the temporary support which he received from Washington. Progressives in America had taken to him, and Colonel House, after a conversation with the President, recorded: "We ... agreed that Villa was the only man of force now in sight in

Mexico."[189] It was not until early 1915, when Carranza's General Álvaro Obregón had seized Mexico City from the revolutionary troops of Villa and Emiliano Zapata, that Wilson, after he had withdrawn his troops from Veracruz in late November 1914, reestablished contacts with the Constitutionalists. Soon, however, the situation again deteriorated so much that Washington once more considered using military pressure to bring about order, the reason given being the protection of 2,500 Americans and 23,000 other foreigners in Mexico. When, during the following months, Carranza's soldiers successfully inflicted a decisive defeat on the Villistas, Washington again was on the verge of fully recognizing the Constitutionalists. Simultaneously, however, a strong lobby was active in the United States trying to prepare the ground for a takeover by the counterrevolution in Mexico. The leader of this faction, Eduardo Iturbide, former Chief of Police in Mexico, had escaped the Carranzistas and was hoping to utilize the support of the Catholic church and certain officials in governmental circles in order to win Washington's assistance for his planned coup. But neither Wilson nor Bryan trusted this movement, particularly since they quite understood the political interests of the Church and had received information that Huertista generals and British capital were backing these endeavors.[190] In June 1915 Wilson called upon the leaders of the various factions to work together for a return of order in Mexico. Not leaving it at that, the American President closed his message to the neighbors south of the border with the thinly veiled threat: "If they cannot accommodate their differences and unite for this great purpose within a very short time, this Government will be constrained to decide what means should be employed by the United States in order to help Mexico save herself and serve her people."[191] In September Villa suffered another military defeat, paving the way for Wilson's de facto recognition of Carranza. Whatever course American-Mexican relations would take in the future, Wilson could now claim at least a short-term success: since Veracruz he had, at times against opposition in his own country, avoided direct American intervention.[192]

American intervention in Mexico, however, was just what Germany had hoped for, and Bernstorff only reinforced Germany's incorrect official appraisals of the situation by reiterating in his reports to Berlin the possibility of a Mexican-American confrontation. In July 1915 he wrote to the Imperial Chancellor: "During the next months something will have to happen in regard to Mexico, and every step in this direction must necessarily be to our advantage."[193] When Wilson tried to arrange for a settlement of the Mexican situation by calling a conference of the Latin American states, Bernstorff assumed correctly that this would not be successful, but he was wrong in adding that only "armed intervention" would be left to the American President. "Under the prevailing circumstances," he reported to Berlin, "this for us would be a favorable solution, because the deliveries of arms and ammunition to our enemies would be cut back considerably."[194] Berlin's speculations in this direction, however, were to be disappointed. Wilson's Mexican policy, in fact, meant a double failure for Germany. Neither were America's arms shipments at any time curtailed by the Mexican unrest, nor was Washington's attention ever so completely captivated by the neighbor in the south that Berlin had a free hand on the seas.

The German efforts to involve the United States in a war with Mexico found active support from Bernhard Dernburg who, perhaps because he had not met with any noteworthy success in his two areas of responsibility, namely his financial assignment and the propaganda campaign, developed a penchant for conspiracies and intelligence service operations. Soon after his arrival in the United States he discussed the possibility of German arms purchases in America with his "friend Felix A. Sommerfeld," a native German, who drew his income from different sources and most recently had been head of the secret service of Francisco Madero's short-lived government. After Madero's demise, Sommerfeld had joined Francisco Villa, for whom he was now procuring arms in the United States.[195] Besides these activities, he maintained good relations with American oil companies, who in turn were interested in promoting U.S. intervention in Mexico. Only a few days after the *Lusitania* incident and shortly before his own hurried departure from America, Dernburg presented Berlin with a plan that he and Sommerfeld had concocted to bring about the desired U.S. intervention. Dernburg wrote to Berlin that Sommerfeld would be willing to use Villa to create a situation which would cause America to intervene. Such an opportunity had already presented itself earlier, he wrote, he just had not known whether this would correspond with Germany's wishes. "Except for Mr. Sommerfeld ... only I alone know of his plans. We both have refrained from discussing this matter further with the German Ambassador here because we are convinced that the fewer people who know about this the better, and also, that this delicate matter can only be decided directly by those in authority.... I ask ... to send a 'yes' or 'no' to Sommerfeld through me or directly." At the end of the proposal Sommerfeld and Dernburg gave "our word of honor as German citizens that we ... will talk to no one about this." The plan, which was relayed to the Foreign Office by Adm. Henning von Holtzendorff, found immediate and unhesitating approval from Jagow and Zimmermann; and the Chancellor too opted for a yes, which was passed on to Holtzendorff for transmittal to the United States on May 10, 1915.[196]

Even though the records reveal no evidence as to whether Felix Sommerfeld acted on the message from Berlin, the suspicion has occasionally been voiced that Francisco Villa's attack on Columbus, New Mexico, on March 10, 1916, was a late consequence of the German decision. Although Villa's attack certainly had the purpose of compromising Carranza's government and of inducing a direct American military intervention, a connection between this operation and the conspiracy of Sommerfeld and Dernburg cannot be proved.[197] Right after Villa's attack, Bernstorff, apparently ignorant of the Dernburg-Sommerfeld dealings, reported to Bethmann Hollweg: "It is not surprising that the effort was also made to attribute Villa's invasion to German intrigues and to point Germany out as the true trouble maker. A reason for this false allegation was naturally not given." Adolf Count von Montgelas in the Foreign Office commented the words "false allegation" with "unfortunately" and thereby, as Friedrich Katz sees it, "clearly gave expression to the wishes of German diplomacy."[198] When American troops unsuccessfully tried to hunt down Villa, Bernstorff evidently took delight in Wilson's difficult position. Although the recent sinking of the passenger ship *Sussex* by a German submarine had placed American-German diplomatic relations under great strain, the German Ambassador, in his report to the Foreign Office in early April, remained surprisingly calm: "Development of Mexican question ... stands in foreground of interest here and it appears increasingly that the punitive expedition against Villa will lead to an outright intervention.... As long as the Mexican question remains at this level, we are, I believe, rather safe from aggressive actions by the American Government."[199] The German envoy in Mexico was so thoroughly enthused about the new American military presence in Mexico that he wired to Bernstorff and the Foreign Office at the beginning of April that Carranza seemed "now to think war unavoidable" and that perhaps he would even turn to the German government "for the release of arms which we have at our disposal in the United States."[200]

Speculations on Huerta and the provocation of incidents through Villa, however, were not the only alternatives under consideration by the German authorities. In the spring of 1916 Colonel Gonzaló C. Enrile, who introduced himself as a representative of the "nationalist party in Mexico," arrived in Berlin. Enrile had good contacts with the Huerta people and had played a part in Pascual Orozco's rebellion against Madero in 1912. Before his expulsion from the United States, the German Military Attaché had established contact with the Mexican colonel, and "in agreement with the Ambassador in Washington," Franz von Papen had written a letter of recommendation for the Mexican and sent him to Berlin.[201] When the Foreign Office showed no interest in the emissary because he was unknown in the Wilhelmstrasse, Papen again recommended him and he was finally received. In return for "around 300 million marks," which the Mexican group he claimed to represent would need in order to equip an army against Carranza and to "be able to resist America," he offered:

"1. Initiation of a Mexican policy completely favorable to the German policy and directed against the interests of the United States.
2. Availability of all kinds of concessions to Germany: railroads, oil, mines, and trade.
3. Ousting of the American capital from the country through legislative measures.
4. Formation of a strong army for invasion of American territory at the moment most favorable for Germany and Mexico.
5. Support of the separatist movement which exists already in various southern States of the United States—namely Texas, Arizona, New Mexico, and the south of Upper California.
6. Inducement and maintenance of a political racial revolution in Cuba, Puerto Rico, and Haiti.
7. Guarantees to Germany of payments and deliveries of ammunition and arms in the form desired by Germany."

Enrile's evaluation of the situation in Mexico was also rather optimistic concerning Germany: "The military operations already undertaken . . . make the continuation of the conflict between Mexico and the States seem unavoidable; Germany will be able to keep peace with the States as long as the latter have their hands full with the American differences." The requested weapons would not even have to be shipped from Germany, Enrile said. As Dernburg before him in the spring of 1915, Enrile was probably thinking of the war materiel that Bernstorff, Papen, and Albert, with the help of the Krupp representative, Hans Tauscher, had collected in the United States since the beginning of the war. Neither Jagow nor Zimmermann, so shortly after the miserable failure of the Irish project, was willing, however, to expose Germany. Therefore, on June 17, 1916, Enrile's grand scheme was turned down in no uncertain terms: "The relations between Germany and the United States are quite normal at this time, an interference in the American-Mexican differences—at least at this time—would be out of the question."[202] Colonel Enrile, incidentally, went on to Madrid, where he stayed in contact with the German diplomatic representatives. The records show that he continued to try to find support for his proposal. Of some interest are Enrile's suggestions that it might be possible to win Japanese support for Mexico and thereby draw Japan from the side of the Entente to the Central Powers.[203]

Berlin's efforts to tie up America's army in Mexico were thus doomed to failure.[204] If Bernstorff had hoped that Wilson would stumble over Mexico and give in to those American military and industrial circles who were in favor of intervention, this was not only an erroneous presumption but a gross underestimation of the political farsightedness of the American President, who persistently resisted using military intervention.[205] Not only did Berlin not derive any benefits from the long bloody Mexican revolutionary war, but the German intrigues in Latin America became known in Washington and contributed to an increased American suspicion about Germany's intentions in this region.[206] Moreover, Washington was fully aware that American intervention in Mexico would give Germany a freer hand in its submarine war policy,[207] a point also of some significance in the German deliberations.[208]

As correctly surmised in Washington, German intrigues were not limited to Mexico. Although historical research so far has paid only limited attention to German operations in other Latin American countries, there is sufficient evidence that Berlin did not refrain from playing the powers off against each other elsewhere. A very brief look at Panama may serve as an example. Prior to the war, German industrial circles had tried to gain a foothold there. Through the purchase of land and the construction of railroads, the Panama and Pacific Estates Limited, an enterprise presumably based in London but actually directed from Berlin, wanted to establish itself in Panama.[209] When war came, the European powers became increasingly interested in overseas naval bases, and England and Germany in Washington accused each other of Latin American machinations. The Foreign Office in Berlin sent Antonio Burgos, the Panamanian Chargé d'Affaires in Madrid, to Washington in the summer of 1915 "in order to inform U.S. Government officials about Japanese intrigues against the United States in Panama and . . . to initiate [a press campaign]." Bernstorff was instructed to "lend appropriate support" to Burgos, but "to be sure not to allow the relations with Burgos to become a matter of public knowledge." Whether Bernstorff actually met with the Panamanian cannot be established yet. By way of Matthias Erzberger's network of agents and through the German diplomatic representatives in Madrid, Burgos, however, reported to the Foreign Office that his mission in Washington had been "extraordinarily successful."[210] Bernstorff's assurances that Germany did not have the slightest interest in Latin America had little persuasive power. In view of prewar developments, Washington's suspicion that Germany was looking for coaling stations and bases for its submarines in Latin America certainly was not unjustified, and the wartime policies of Berlin tended to confirm these fears.[211] That rumors and facts were difficult to distinguish from one another, and the fact that other nations were also engaged in Latin America could not alleviate the uneasiness in Washington. Long before the text of the so-called Zimmermann Telegram, confirming these suspicions, found its way to Washington, the American government observed Germany's activities south of the Rio Grande with distrust. Although Bernstorff was careful not to take a public stand on Latin American affairs, Washington looked at him with a jaundiced eye; it was difficult to believe that the compromised Attachés Papen and Boy-Ed could have operated without the Ambassador's knowledge.[212]

IN THE TWILIGHT OF INTELLIGENCE OPERATIONS

It is part of the nature of the organization and operations of intelligence services that is is rather difficult to give a historically accurate picture of them. Without striving for completeness, a broad outline of German intelligence activities in the United States will be sketched to demonstrate the involvement of the diplomatic representatives through some documented projects. The difficulty begins when one tries to draw an organizational chart showing the hierarchy of the agents.

While no significant organization of German intelligence agents seems to have operated in the United States prior to the war, the situation changed abruptly in the summer of 1914. At the outbreak of the war, Capt. Franz von Papen, who as Military Attaché accredited both in Mexico City and in Washington was deeply involved in the German efforts to brace the dictatorship of General Huerta, immediately went to the United States. According to his own memoirs, his first tools were a list of reliable trade firms and a secret code to be used in case of war, which he had received from the General Staff.[213] His first step was to open the clandestine office, operated by Hans Adam von Wedell and Carl Ruerode, that procured forged papers for German reservists and agents. Through this activity, Papen came into contact with a great number of Germans who offered their services to the Fatherland. Only some of them could be transported to Europe; others were used for espionage and sabotage operations. Papen's activities in America along these lines extended from the summer of 1914 until the end of 1915. It is known that during this time a number of operatives sent from Berlin made contact with him and received instructions from him. Similarly, it is known that he maintained an office in Manhattan that directed various intelligence operations. This office was supervised by Wolf von Igel, who after Papen's expulsion continued on his assignment with Bernstorff's explicit approval.[214] In order to pursue his projects, the Military Attaché went on extensive trips throughout the United States, contacting other agents and preparing the execution of espionage and sabotage missions. The records confirm that Papen maintained connections with his superiors in Berlin through the channels of the German embassy as well as directly through the Ministry of War and the General Staff, in other words, often without the Ambassador's knowledge. Although after the war, Bernstorff claimed that instructions from Berlin for the Military Attaché in most cases had been transmitted directly to Papen without his knowledge, it seems unlikely that the Ambassador was uninformed about the content of all these messages, especially since some directives were addressed only to him and in several instances the answers bear only his name.[215] Bernstorff's postwar explanations lose even more in credibility when one thinks of his own numerous reports which dealt with the Irish rising, the incitement of revolt in India, or legal counsel for the agents arrested in America.

While Papen apparently only employed a relatively small number of persons and used German-Americans or agents coming from Germany only for special assignments, a much larger and more diversified but lesser known organization seems to have worked for the Admiralty. The Naval Attaché, Karl Boy-Ed, whose participation in the Huerta affair is often mentioned, though he himself vigorously denied it, was neither the most significant agent nor the head of the naval intelligence service in the United States.[216] At least two other top agents with extensive powers, namely Franz Rintelen and Kurt Jahnke, reported to the Admiralty while working in North America. It is also correct to state that Heinrich von Eckardt, Paul von Hintze's successor in Mexico City, played an important role in naval intelligence.[217] That Boy-Ed at least temporarily cooperated with Rintelen appears evident. The records so far available are less clear on the question of whether Rintelen worked with Jahnke. The surviving documents, however, show clearly that Eckardt and various German consular officials in the southwestern United States were so impressed by Jahnke's actions that Eckardt asked the navy to appoint Jahnke "confidential agent of the Admiralty Staff in Mexico."[218]

The Admiralty agent, Franz Rintelen, who before the war had been in the United States as a representative of a German bank and presumably had made useful business and social contacts,[219] was sent back to America, among other things to engineer General Huerta's return to power in Mexico and to hinder American shipments of war materiel to the Entente. It cannot yet be said with certainty whether he received concrete orders for sabotage and the instigation of strikes while still in Berlin or whether these operations were developed in the United States. Contrary to other diplomats and agents, he did not travel to New York as a stowaway or posing as a sailor, but undertook the journey completely unhindered, with the full knowledge of the Foreign Office and, in fact, of the American embassy in Berlin.[220] Regardless of later official German denials, the various scattered sources indicate that his mission to the United States was supported by highly influential circles in Berlin.[221] In Heinrich Albert's words: "There can be no doubt that on the one hand Rintelen acted with the explicit approval of the military leadership of the time and that on the other hand exclusively patriotic motives were decisive for him."[222] The fact that, after the war, German military leaders like Admiral Paul Behncke[223] and Admiral Hans Zenker[224] defended Rintelen without reservation further confirms that he was in the United States by order of the Admiralty and that he did not work independently or without full knowledge of the authorities in Berlin.[225]

Rintelen's connections to the high echelons of the German military are also evident in the mystery surrounding the recall of Major George T. Langhorne, who served as United States Military Attaché in Berlin until the spring of 1915. Apparently some of Langhorne's coded dispatches to the American Secretary of War were sent through the German Admiralty via the stations at Nauen and Sayville. Rintelen writes in his memoirs that he was able to have Langhorne's cables decoded in the Admiralty and to insert passages of a pro-German nature. It is difficult to believe that this should have been done without authorization from higher up. British intelligence intercepted these cables, apparently decoded them, and promptly complained to the American government. Washington had little choice but to recall the hapless officer.[226]

Placing Kurt Jahnke presents much greater problems. He appeared only briefly at any location, and his identity is not always absolutely clear, yet his apparent lasting contacts in the various centers of power would suggest that he was a top agent in the Empire as well as in the Weimar Republic and under the National Socialists.[227] The irregular traces left by Jahnke in the records of various countries have made it difficult for the historian to draw an accurate picture of the operations in which he was involved. Apparently, Jahnke came to the United States in 1909 and served his military duty in the Philippines. After that, he may have found employment with the international customs service in Peking; his connections to the Pinkerton organization may have been helpful. Following his return to the United States, he is said to have acquired U.S. citizenship and to have been active in various enterprises related to trade with China.[228] One von Alvensleben, functioning as a go-between, apparently arranged for Jahnke to meet Franz Rintelen, and it may have been Rintelen who engaged him for the intelligence service of the Imperial Navy. Since the documents contain no evidence about Jahnke's activities during the first war years, he most likely received his orders directly through couriers and possibly through Rintelen's far-flung network of agents.[229] Contacts between Jahnke and Bernstorff, however, are unlikely. The records contain no hints in this direction, and, as confidants of the Admiralty, Jahnke and Rintelen probably thought of the despised liberal Bernstorff as did their employers in Berlin and therefore steered clear of him. In fact, we know of Rintelen that he avoided Bernstorff and probably only saw him twice in the United States.[230] As it is most unusual to find signed statements from top-level intelligence agents in the records of the Foreign Office, Jahnke's own description of his function in the United States may be of interest: "From August 1914 on I was in California and based in San Francisco, the Central Office for secret military operations of the German government. In March 1916, I took over the western part of the United States as representative of the Admiralty Staff for intelligence and sabotage assignments [für N.- und S.- Angelegenheiten]. In February 1917, I was the representative secret agent [der bevollmächtigte Geheimagent] for the United States. My field of activity, however, also extended to England. I functioned as head of the intelligence and sabotage service until the end of the war."[231]

If Bernstorff emphasizes his unawareness of the intelligence operations in the first volume of his memoirs, published in 1920, this is fully understandable in view of the early date of publication. His assertions, however, that he was unable to find out anything about these matters after his return from the United States and his total silence on this even in the second volume, written in exile in Switzerland in the 1930s, are somewhat astonishing, to say the least. The truth is that he often had information about planned operations and repeatedly turned to the authorities in Berlin to prevent agents from being sent to the United States.[232] In some cases, he openly spoke out against actions that he thought irresponsible and useless.[233]

The records show that the first sabotage operations were aimed at Canada, because Berlin was worried that Japanese troop contingents could be shipped to the European battlefields via Canada.[234] Even if the memoirs of the German operative, Horst von der Goltz,[235] seem unreliable in certain respects, there is sufficient reason to assume that his version of a German operation against Canadian territory, which he claims to have discussed with Papen, is largely consistent with the facts.[236] The plan of an attack on Canada from the State of Washington, using German reservist troops and to be supported by warships, was thwarted by Bernstorff's opposition and the lack of artillery.[237] After that Papen sent Goltz, disguised as Bridgeman H. Taylor, to Baltimore, where Consul Karl Luederitz obtained for him a false passport to fit his new name. Bridgeman Taylor now hired a group of men with whom he took up preparations for the bombing of the Welland Canal.[238] Financial means were placed at his disposal through Papen via the German embassy's straw man, Federico Stallforth,[239] and the Krupp agent, Capt. Hans Tauscher, provided the necessary explosives.[240] For reasons still somewhat unclear, the Military Attaché called off the operation when the agents were in Buffalo, New York, on their way to Canada.[241]

While there was no detailed correspondence between Berlin and Washington regarding the Horst von der Goltz projects, this changed toward the end of 1914.[242] The fact that in London William Reginald Hall's intelligence office, Room 40, in time was able to decode the cables between Berlin and Washington is of more than marginal interest, not only because a vast amount of valuable documentation was created but because during the postwar years the British successfully used the intercepted material to compromise Bernstorff. In December, the Under Secretary of the Foreign Office, Arthur Zimmermann, wired to Bernstorff: "Secret. General Staff wishes energetic action for effective destruction of Canadian Pacific Railway in several places for the purpose of longer disruption of all traffic. Captain Boehm, who is known there and will soon be returning, is informed. Please notify Military Attaché and provide necessary sums."[243] While Papen began to organize groups of fifty to one hundred reservists in several cites such as Chicago, St. Paul, Seattle, and Detroit, to be used as shock troops against Canada,[244] Department IIIb of the General Staff and the Foreign Office took care of the work in Berlin. At the beginning of January, the Admiralty expressed its desire "to incite Irishmen in America with the assistance of Sir Roger Casement to far-reaching sabotage acts in the United States and in Canada. For the purpose of learning what their tasks were" the Irishmen "were to get . . . in touch with the Naval or the Military Attaché in Washington."[245] On January 25, 1915, followed the telegram that after the war was to play such a prominent role in the deliberations of the Mixed Claims Commission as evidence in the American suit for damages:

> Secret. I ask . . . to send the following telegram to the Military Attaché in Washington. From the following persons the names of suitable people for sabotage in the United States and Canada can be obtained: 1) Joseph MacGarrity [sic], 5412 Springfield

Philadelphia, Pa 2) John T. Keating, Maryland avenue, Chicago, 3) Jeremia O'Leary, Park row, New York No. 1 and 2 absolutely reliable and not talking; No. 3 reliable, not always discrete. The sabotage in the United States can extend to all kinds of factories for war material deliveries; railways, dams, bridges are not to be touched there. Embassy must under no circumstances be compromised by sabotage plans nor Irish-German propaganda.[246]

On February 13, Bernstorff was able to report: "The Military Attaché to the General Staff: Back from reconnaissance trip. All preparations made for armed action with purpose of destruction of railway in case of Japanese troops."[247]

From a report by Major Hans Boehm, transmitted to the General Staff's Department IIIb by the Admiralty on February 24, it is evident that the Major, on orders from Papen, was planning five bridge bombings. Apparently the project failed because of the inadequate qualifications of the persons assigned. A new undertaking was limited to three objects. Unfavorable weather conditions thwarted Boehm's own attempt to take care of the bombing of the bridge near Megantic; the second group, scheduled to blast a bridge between Andover and Perth, was equally unsuccessful; the third target was entrusted to Lt. Werner Horn, who managed to set off the explosion at the bridge across the St. Croix River near Vanceboro, but was arrested the next morning on American soil.[248] It is more than likely that Major Boehm, who traveled all across the United States, also had contact with Kurt Jahnke. Both liked to use Americans of Irish descent for their operations, especially members of radical organizations and trade unions, because they were willing "to get at it with utter ruthlessness and blindness." According to Major Boehm, the Irish were "willing to participate in the most daring operations, for instance against Canada, and they have stood at my side in the most unselfish way during the operation against the railways, where the Germans had long failed." In spite of the supposed lack of willingness of the German-Americans, Boehm and Papen used them in various operations. Boehm's most fantastic project was an invasion of Canada at three or four points with troops to be recruited from the many German-American associations in the United States.[249] Following the penetrations of the border with shock troops, recruiting offices were to be set up in

Canada. "The rush undoubtedly would be enormous," Boehm wrote to the General Staff in Berlin, "in any case sufficient to kill [totschlagen] all troops present in Canada, possibly with cudgels." Boehm's bloody campaign never took place.[250] Indications are that the plans for an invasion of Canada were never completely dropped, but rather kept under cover for eventual future implementation.[251]

Besides the attacks on railways in Canada, the plans also called for bombings of locks and grain elevators. The documents contain evidence that a group charged with sabotage and led by the German reservist, Ludwig Schmidt, with the knowledge of the Consul in Chicago, perpetrated attacks on Canadian ammunition factories. When Schmidt was imprisoned, his wife and three children in Detroit were paid a monthly subsidy "with the permission of the Ambassador."[252] The activities of the men organized by the German merchant, Albert Kaltschmidt of Detroit, were of a similar kind. Like other sabotage operations, this case also went down in the records of the German Foreign Office, because after the war the authorities apparently hesitated to reimburse Kaltschmidt and a fellow operative for their expenses. According to his own testimony, Kaltschmidt received orders from Papen to blow up a bridge of the Canadian Pacific Railway, ammunition factories, and a tunnel.[253] The agent, Max Schulze, mentioned previously as a participant in the Wehde expedition under the name of Sterneck, also left some details in the records about his activities with Kaltschmidt's sabotage group.[254] Since Papen told the Imperial Ministry of Finance after the war that Kaltschmidt had indeed received from him the order for the attack on the Canadian railway bridge, one is more than a little surprised to find that, in his memoirs, the Ambassador suggests that Kaltschmidt, who possibly made himself unpopular through the purchases of war materiel, may have been accused unjustly. If the group had indeed carried out the operations mentioned in the indictment, Bernstorff writes, "then they certainly acted on their own initiative and not at the instigation of the Embassy." For reasons unknown, Bernstorff then goes so far as to claim that he had not had the slightest connection with the payments to Kaltschmidt, which American newspapers were blaming him for. From the accounts for the year 1915, prepared by Heinrich Albert and submitted to Berlin by Bernstorff, and from Appendix 8 attached to those accounts and signed by Bernstorff, it is evident that the Ambassador was not only informed by Papen and Consul Reiswitz about Kaltschmidt's sabotage activities, but that he himself deposited a bond in the amount of $10,000 with the Continental and Commercial National Bank in Chicago in case Kaltschmidt was arrested and arranged for a loan of $25,000 secured by shares from the Kaltschmidt corporation.[255]

Considerable German efforts and funds also went into attempts to place bombs on steamers docked in U.S. ports and scheduled to transport war materiel. The explosive devices were set to go off somewhere on the high seas and destroy the ships. It is impossible to determine on how many ships such charges were hidden. Quite a number of steamers were destroyed by explosions at sea, and in the United States the suspicion arose that German agents had had a hand in this.[256] Dr. Walter Theodor Scheele, a German chemist, produced some of these bombs at his New Jersey Agricultural and Chemical Company at 1123 Clinton Street in Hoboken by order of Rintelen. The firm evidently served as a cover for an installation in which Scheele and officers from the German ships interned in American harbors were engaged in various tasks, ranging from preparing foodstuffs for shipment to producing dangerous incendiary bombs.[257] Other explosive devices were produced in Germany, particularly after Rintelen's departure from the United States, and brought to America by agents and couriers. In most instances, the bombs apparently were placed on departing ships by dock workers and longshoremen. It was only after some unexploded devices were found in the cargo at various ports of destination that an attempt was made to thwart this kind of sabotage by increased surveillance in the American ports of departure.

Rintelen used both Irish-Americans and German-Americans as operatives. Besides a few contacts from a prior stay in America, he established close connections with members of the embassy—certainly with Albert, Boy-Ed, and Papen—who placed at least $500,000 at his disposal for various projects. One is struck by the fact that, in contrast to Papen, Rintelen did not resort to amateur groups in his far-flung operations, but instead generally appears to have worked with experienced and unscrupulous men. Through the German Consul General in New York, Horst Falcke, and through Hossenfelder he was introduced to George Freeman[258] and thus gained access to radical Irish-American circles.[259] Through Karl Buenz, Director of the Hamburg-American Line in New York and former Consul in Chicago and New York, Rintelen met Max Weiser, with whom he founded E. V. Gibbons, Inc., an alleged import and export firm.[260] Through another cover firm, the Mexican North-Western Railway Company, he worked with Lt. Robert Fay,[261] an operative who used explosives obtained through Max Breitung, Herbert Kienzle, and Paul Sieps to manufacture time bombs, which under the cover of darkness were attached to the hulls of munitions ships.[262]

Since Rintelen maintained close contact with Irish revolutionaries, it is possible that at times, either on his own initiative or through the mediation of Hossenfelder, Jahnke, or Freeman, he may have worked with the Irish socialist Jim Larkin. "Big Jim" Larkin, the famous labor leader, had come to New York in the fall of 1914 at the bidding of James Connolly[263] and Thomas J. Clarke in order to raise money for the Irish unions and to procure arms for an uprising against England. He had made connections with the powerful Clan na Gael boss, John Devoy, and numerous German and Irish agents. Boy-Ed offered Jim Larkin $200 a week if he would be available to the German intelligence service. Although Larkin later claimed to have turned down the German offers, his quarters in New York apparently were frequented by longshoremen and dock workers, who kept him posted on the munitions transports of the Allies, and by Irish saboteurs, "who cooperated with the German Imperial Government for considerations beneficial to the Irish cause."[264]

Rintelen's abilities, however, were by no means limited to the area of sabotage. Probably with the help of his connections to functionaries of various labor unions and with considerable financial resources, he built up Labor's National Peace Council, whose goal was the organization of wildcat strikes by dockworkers in all the large ports of America. In order to disguise the source of his funds, Rintelen employed the services of David Lamar, who—probably on account of his questionable financial transactions—in the literature is referred to as the "wolf of Wall Street." Capt. Carl von Kleist, who could call on his far-flung connections among the workers on the docks, and Max Weiser were his contact men. On the whole, the organization had much in common with the so-called Liebau Bureau, which was created by Bernstorff and Ambassador Dumba, and we have indications that Rintelen at times cooperated with that office.[265] According to the German Ambassador, the Liebau Bureau was opened in order to find new jobs for German and

Austro-Hungarian workers after they had lost their old ones in war-related industries. While Bernstorff does not recall any organized strikes and claims to have known nothing of Rintelen's efforts, the accounts of the embassy for 1915, however, actually show that "an Irish agent" was paid $39,800 for "direct strike support," and, in a report in April 1915, von Papen mentioned $200,000 that Heinrich Albert had allocated with Dernburg's approval for efforts to create strike conditions in the munitions industry.[266] The strike movement was "also promoted propagandistically particularly by the Church." Among other things, the German press office had a sermon prepared which was sent to 65,000 clergymen "and [according to Bernstorff] used by them."[267] Although such methods of slowing down war production were unlikely to bring noticeable results, they created enough of a sensation to alarm the American government and to arouse anti-German agitation in the press.[268]

The German attempt to bribe members of Congress also belongs in this context. At the beginning of the war, a Berlin professor had suggested "by influencing them with money winning influential members of the American Senate for a prohibition of the export of war material from America." The professor estimated the cost of the project at around $10,000,000 to $20,000,000. Whether proposals of such a nature were turned into instructions for Rintelen or other German agents still remains unknown. In any case, Rintelen succeeded in winning a series of public personalities for Labor's National Peace Council, among them the Representative from Illinois, Frank Buchanan.[269]

How Rintelen's recall from the United States was effected is not entirely clear. Arthur S. Link writes that Rintelen spent a holiday in Kennebunkport, Maine, "during late June or early July" 1915. There, according to Link, he met a young lady, Miss Anne L. Seward, to whom he confided some information concerning his activities as a German agent. The lady wrote a letter to Robert Lansing, relating her unusual encounter. The Americans immediately placed Rintelen under closer surveillance and found their worst suspicions confirmed. Just how the U.S. government reacted to the confirmation that Rintelen was an important German agent remains somewhat in the dark. There appears to be no evidence that he was officially expelled or that an attempt was made to arrest him. Rintelen's own version, related much later in his memoirs, has it that he was handed his orders to report back to Germany on the morning of June 6, 1915 (July 6 seems the more likely date), by Boy-Ed on a street corner in New York City. Why was he recalled? The American government certainly had not intervened diplomatically. The thought, as suggested by Sir William James and Patrick Beesly, that Papen and Boy-Ed saw the high-level, well-financed, and independent agent as a troublesome rival whom they wanted to be rid of seems not entirely impossible. If that had been the case, Papen with his more direct connections to Berlin via Department IIIb of the General Staff could have arranged Rintelen's recall, possibly, as suggested by Beesly, with the agreement of Bernstorff.[270]

Reconstructing his return to Europe from the scattered evidence, it would appear that Rintelen first attempted to obtain an American passport, quite openly, by applying to the Department of State in the name of Edward V. Gates, born in Millersville, Pennsylvania, a wine merchant intent on traveling to England, France, and Germany. According to the United States Secret Service records, the passport was actually issued and sent to New York with the request that Rintelen, or Gates, be identified prior to having the papers handed over to him. Rintelen, probably wishing to avoid a personal confrontation, sent a confidant to fetch the passport. The Secret Service records indicate that this undertaking failed. Rintelen instead then decided to travel on a previously used Swiss passport as Emile Victor Gaché. As such he embarked on the liner *Noordam* of the Holland-America Line on August 3, according to the Secret Service. The journey ended for Rintelen, or Gaché, on August 13 in British coastal waters at Ramsgate, when he was arrested on the Dutch liner by the British navy to be taken ashore and handed over to Captain Hall.[271]

If various people on both sides of the Atlantic were pleased to see Rintelen removed from action, his name was to crop up repeatedly in the coming years in official and often confidential contexts in Britain, the United States, and in Germany before as well as after the demise of the Empire. First, the Germans connected Rintelen's arrest with the American government's declaration that both Papen and Boy-Ed were persona non grata. Shortly thereafter the Berlin Foreign Office instructed Bernstorff to inform Washington that the Imperial Government had never ordered Rintelen to behave illegally, and Bernstorff duly notified Lansing: "With reference to previous letters and conversations I beg to inform you that according to instructions I have just received, my Government disavows Mr.

Franz Rintelen. He never received orders to commit acts contrary to American laws." Lansing's reply indicates that the Americans, at this point, were well enough informed to appraise the situation. A treatment of Rintelen's subsequent tenure in British and American prisons and his often-hinted later personal friendship with Admiral Hall, however interesting, would go beyond the scope of this study.[272]

On the West Coast the previously mentioned intelligence organization run by Kurt Jahnke probably received most directives through couriers of the Admiralty.[273] Although a mammoth trial in the United States, which ended in January 1917, evidently was meant to shed some light on the diversified German operations on the West Coast, Jahnke, at least during the war years, managed to evade all publicity.[274] From 1914 to January 1917, all threads of his network of agents merged in San Francisco. After the war, Bernstorff declared that the Consul General in San Francisco, Franz Bopp, and the persons who were tried with him in the United States had "certainly not acted on instructions of the Embassy or another [German] superior office," and that Bopp had presumably "fallen into an Allied trap."[275] In contrast, in 1925 Bopp recalled that he had found "the personnel increased" when he returned to his post in March 1915. His deputy, Vice-Consul Eckhard von Schack, Bopp testified, had found it necessary to hire several assistants, among whom were "a certain von Brinken" and the "private detective C. C. Crowley." Brincken, Bopp continued, had then engaged Lewis Smith for espionage work.[276] Bernstorff's assertion that he had not been informed about the developments in San Francisco appears unconvincing. Indeed, as early as January 1915, the Ambassador wired to Berlin that, according to reports of the consulate, "Lieutenant of the Territorial Reserve [*Landwehr Reserve*] [Wilhelm von] Brincken is performing inestimable services in Indian and Canadian matters." Brincken's application to have his duty in San Francisco counted as military service, and thus be promoted to a higher pay grade, was commented on by Bernstorff with "I support petition."[277] Bopp's statement before the district court in Berlin, according to which he received "from the former Imperial Ambassador Count von Bernstorff strict orders not to become involved in sabotage activities under any circumstances," even indicates that Bernstorff knew of planned sabotage projects, but wished to prevent the compromising of the official representatives of the Empire.[278]

A motley crew of operatives was assembled at Jahnke's "Central Office for Secret Military Operations."[279] Lieutenant von Brincken, falsely declared an attaché, took over the Press Department and the "Hindu Section" in the Consulate, and, from January 1915, "still other matters of a more dangerous nature" were among his assignments.[280] After the war, Vice-Consul Schack stated that he had "never received an order or an authorization from my superiors to undertake acts of sabotage on American soil, nor [did I] for my part ever give such orders or authorizations," and he emphasized that this applied "especially to Mr. Jahnke." Nevertheless, in the spring of 1915 this same Vice-Consul tried to declare Brincken a member of the consulate staff, in order to prevent his arrest by the American police.[281] The operative Lewis Smith, described by the Consul General as an espionage agent, was, according to later German documents, "one of the persons hired by Consul General Bopp for sabotage purposes."[282] Lothar Witzke, from the fall of 1915 a "special agent" of Kurt Jahnke, toured the United States protected by a Russian passport and evidently was so well informed about German intelligence service operations that, after the war, the authorities in Berlin were seriously concerned about the possibility that he might talk, and they directed Jahnke to help him find a livelihood.[283] According to Bopp's later statement, C. C. Crowley and Lewis Smith toured ports on the Pacific Coast to observe arms shipments. While the two men were in Seattle, a munitions carrier in the harbor happened to explode.[284]

How far the agents of this group participated in German intelligence operations in the Great Lakes industrial region and in the eastern states is still difficult to judge. There is proof, however, that Jahnke's organization and a parallel group from the General Staff under the leadership of a man known as "Delmar" both relocated their headquarters to Mexico at the beginning of 1917 and covered the United States from there.[285]

In spite of the general impression that German intelligence activities in America had reached their peak in 1915, that is, particularly during Franz Rintelen's stay and prior to the expulsion of both attachés, there appears to have been no reduction of operations in 1916. Disregarding here certain individual agents sent from Berlin, the only change seems to have been the constant growth of Kurt Jahnke's sector of responsibility. Moreover, Rintelen apparently had left behind an organization on the East Coast, which even without his leadership continued to undertake rather extensive operations. In this connection, the unsubstantiated claim that Boy-Ed secretly returned to the United States after his expulsion deserves added interest. Whether he established contact with the intelligence group on the East Coast or brought new instructions for Jahnke still remains unknown. He is said to have left the country again on *U-53*.[286]

The two most notorious incidents which have been attributed to German sabotage operations, in fact, did not occur in 1915. The Black Tom Terminal, a huge freight yard in the harbor of New York, was partially demolished during the night of July 29, 1916, and a considerable number of loaded railway cars, several warehouses with war materiel, and a string of other installations were destroyed in the conflagration. The Kingsland Assembly Plant of the Canadian Car and Foundry Company in Kingsland, New Jersey, blew up on January 11, 1917. A large depot of arms and ammunition apparently destined for Russia fell victim to a raging fire. After the war, for many years these events and surrounding evidence occupied the so-called Mixed Claims Commission, which in 1939 declared Germany responsible. Both the drawn-out investigations of these cases and the multifaceted procedures employed by both German and American representatives to locate favorable evidence were of such complicated nature that they cannot be treated in this context.[287] Without a doubt, however, the investigations helped to unearth and preserve a large body of documentary material concerning German intelligence operations, and it is somewhat surprising that historians on both sides of the Atlantic to the present day have paid only very scant attention to these records. Among the operatives who appear to have been connected with the explosions at Black Tom and Kingsland were Lothar Witzke,[288] Friedrich Herrmann,[289] Paul Hilken, Friedrich Hinsch, Raoul Gerdts, Carl Ahrendt, Lieutenant Wilhelm Woehst, and Theodore J. Wozniak.[290] Hinsch evidently continued to run Rintelen's former organization until he moved with other agents to Mexico in 1917 and there, at least for a time, collaborated with Kurt Jahnke.[291] Hilken provided Hinsch with financial resources.[292] Herrmann, who according to his own statement first worked for Papen in America and later was assigned to the Admiralty, admitted in 1930 that he had perpetrated the attack in Kingsland together with Hinsch, Wozniak, and someone named Rodriguez,[293] in accordance with a sabotage assignment from Rudolf Nadolny and Major Maguerre, a sabotage expert of the General Staff.[294] On the basis of a secret text which Herrmann had sent to Hilken in April 1917,[295] the Mixed Claims Commission later decided that the same group of German operatives was responsible for the Black Tom inferno. German protests that the document in question was a forgery were to no avail.

German sabotage activity, incidentally, was by no means limited to the use of explosives. There is sufficient evidence of plans for action on the bacteriological-chemical sector which was intended to slow down the shipment of American supplies to the Allies. Herrmann, Hinsch, and Hilken included in their schemes, among other things, the contamination of American manufacturing plants with influenza virus. The same group paid men for traveling with the horse and mule transports to Europe and infecting the animals with glanders during the trip. In 1930 Herrmann reported that they had received the cultures for these operations in Berlin. Indications are that such measures probably were still organized by Franz Rintelen.[296]

If the treatment of the sabotage agents and their operations in this study must by necessity be very limited, the surviving documents leave no doubt that from the beginning of the war until February 1917 projects were constantly being carried out that egregiously violated American neutrality, in some cases involved the preparation of military actions against other countries from American soil, and in most cases broke American laws. Reflections on the moral aspects of many of these projects do not belong here, but they cannot be ignored entirely, since they quite naturally played a role in the war of propaganda.[297] It was not the task of the Ambassador to inform himself about those intelligence missions in America, which were carried out completely independent of the embassy and its personnel. But in connection with the projects which came to his attention or those which were financed through the embassy, the question of responsibility must be raised. Even completely foregoing a moral judgment and, of course, a more exacting legal examination of the various cases, it seems justified to register doubts as to the wisdom of the Ambassador's silent toleration of most events, as long as it was his serious intention to maintain the formal neutrality of the United States.

The fact that Bernstorff at times energetically resisted orders from Berlin to pay agents and that generally he tried to inform himself as little as possible about the activities of the numerous agents confirms the impression that he was very much aware of the contradictory character of the position into which his government forced him.[298] Undoubtedly, the disclosures of ever new violations and outrages contributed to keeping the American people continuously suspicious of Germany's intentions.[299]

SIX

THE BREAK WITH
THE UNITED STATES

While the early months of the war in the United States were marked by the propaganda campaigns of the belligerents, the period from spring 1915 to May 1916 was largely characterized by submarine war conflicts. During the last year of American neutrality, Bernstorff pursued only one major goal: a negotiated peace, initiated through the mediation of President Wilson. With other critics of the policy of the German government, who since the battle of the Marne no longer believed in a military victory by the Empire, Bernstorff was convinced that he had to bring about a peace initiative from Wilson in order to save his country from a catastrophic defeat.

To be sure, Bernstorff could hardly fail to notice that the German government was not very interested in mediation by the American President and even less in American intervention in possible negotiations. He was aware that Berlin's war aims, even though he did not know them in detail, were unlikely to bring about a negotiated or status quo ante peace. Not unlike Woodrow Wilson he was, however, confident that it would be nearly impossible to resume military actions once a peace conference had been convened. Bernstorff was mistaken in assuming that the Imperial Chancellor and the Secretary of the Foreign Office shared his view. Without going into Bethmann Hollweg's policy on war aims, which has received much attention in recent scholarship, it can now be established on the basis of the records of the Foreign Office that the Chancellor, in contrast to Bernstorff, was not at all convinced of the necessity of American mediation. Bethmann Hollweg was not familiar with the United States, and the documentary evidence shows that many of his closest advisors either knew just as little about America or quite intentionally advised him inadequately. With the growing militarization of Germany, the few warning voices that represented a line similar to Bernstorff's increasingly fell on deaf ears.

In the Foreign Office, too, Bernstorff found little backing. Under Gottlieb von Jagow, this office pursued its irresponsible Mexican policy, and the records contain no evidence that he opposed Department IIIb of the General Staff with the necessary vigor when the matter of carrying out questionable intelligence operations in the United States came up for decision. Complete recklessness and an underestimation of the United States bordering on stupidity, however, only became the rule of the day when Arthur Zimmermann, whom Friedrich von Prittwitz und Gaffron fittingly described as *burschikos* (unreservedly boisterous), took office.[1] It was he who offered Mexico the southwestern American states. Since Zimmermann obtained his knowledge about the United States from associates who shared his nationalistic views and were influenced by the Pan-German spirit of the time, Bernstorff's reports most likely exerted only little influence on him.[2]

In the end, Bernstorff, with his warnings of America's impending entry into the war, stood alone against a front of blinded officials in Berlin,[3] who in their scorn for President Wilson were unable to comprehend the position of the United States. Even toward the end of 1916 and in early 1917, when the Allies were waging their war with increasing material support from the American economy, Berlin officials proclaimed that in the near future the United States would not be in a position to intervene decisively in the European war. However critically one may appraise Bernstorff's decision to cooperate with the intelligence services,[4] German scholarship might do well to recognize the Ambassador's wise foresight and his unselfish efforts in the question of mediation. Long ago, relevant studies outside Germany have acknowledged Bernstorff's engagement.[5]

BERLIN'S URGING FOR AN AMERICAN PEACE APPEAL IN THE EARLY FALL OF 1916

Any discussion of the relations between Berlin and Washington in the second half of 1916 undoubtedly would center around the question of whether the German government, or for that matter Bethmann Hollweg, was at that time seriously interested in American mediation. Whether Germany would have received a general appeal for peace with less displeasure than the wish of the President to bring about a conference with the goal of a status quo ante peace does not seem to be of great significance in this context. The question of Bethmann Hollweg's responsibility also is not of immediate relevance here; instead, the effects of German political decisions on Washington and on Count Bernstorff's not very enviable position will be scrutinized.

The settlement of the *Sussex* crisis had provided a breather for the Ambassador inasmuch as the summer months of 1916 went by without incident. That the dispute over the broader question of submarine warfare was not settled but instead was likely to flare up again at any moment can be seen from a report by Adm. Henning von Holtzendorff to the Imperial Chancellor only a few days after Germany relented on the *Sussex* conflict: "We have the indisputable right to take the same measures against the commerce of our enemies that our opponents are taking against Germany's commerce, and to demand of the neutrals that they put up with our measures just as they tolerate those of the English."[6] To be sure, such a viewpoint was not lacking in vociferous support, above all from Conservatives and National-Liberals.[7] In mid-June, Berlin informed Bernstorff about the growing pressure from "army and navy" for the resumption of submarine warfare, and the Ambassador was asked "whether Wilson following nomination would still push for a break in diplomatic relations and war, even if we spare human lives in a new submarine war."[8] In his response, Bernstorff not only clearly indicated that a German retreat from the assurances given in May would with certainty "lead to the break and to [America's] entry into the war," but he also let Berlin know that the coming elections in America offered no chance for a German gain in the question of the war on commerce. Wilson could not afford to yield now in the submarine conflict, Bernstorff wrote, and Hughes, "who is already suspected of being a German candidate," would be even less in a position to give in.[9] When the German navy then proposed the unrestricted deployment of submarines in the Channel, Bernstorff again warned of the consequences: "In my opinion the government here will not recognize the declaration of the Channel as a war area and will insist on complete adherence to our concessions in the last submarine note. Even if the break should not come immediately, it will certainly occur as soon as a ship with American passengers on board is sunk without warning, etc."[10] The fact that influential personalities in America provided the Foreign

Office with contradictory information, however, had a counterproductive effect and further weakened the Ambassador's already sinking influence in Berlin.[11]

With the Italian and Rumanian declarations of war against the Central Powers in May 1915 and August 1916, the overall strategic situation of the latter deteriorated, and the new Supreme Army Command was not eager to risk America's entry into the war as long as enemy penetrations of the southeastern front were a possibility and the borders with Holland and Denmark were not sufficiently secured. All the same, it was no secret that in principle Hindenburg and Ludendorff advocated the unrestricted use of the submarine. Thus it could only be a matter of time until the army would join in the navy's demands, and until the Chancellor would no longer be able to employ his stalling tactics.[12] It was against this background that Bethmann Hollweg sent his telegram to Bernstorff on September 2, 1916: "Hope for peace before winter through Russia's or France's tiring of the war lessened by this development [Rumania's declaration of war]. If no great catastrophe occurs in the East, does peace mediation by Wilson seem possible and necessary, if we promise conditional restoration of Belgium? Otherwise unrestricted submarine war would have to be seriously considered.[13] Request only your personal view, without giving indications to any side."[14] Belgium, in other words, seemingly became a point of negotiation, though not the freedom of the country, only its "conditional restoration." Whether the Chancellor meant an unoccupied Belgium economically dependent on Germany or whether he was referring to an evacuation of the country except for the important industrial regions and the coastal areas appears immaterial in this context, since the Americans would hardly have felt inclined to condone any German demands on Belgium. Was this telegram indeed "a kind of distress signal" from the Chancellor, who was doing everything "to bring the war to an end diplomatically?"[15] Or was it only an indication of the discernible link between peace mediation, e.g., the possibilities for negotiation, and a return to unrestricted U-boat warfare? After all, already at the beginning of August the Chancellor had held out the prospect of a resumption of unrestricted submarine warfare for February 1917![16] In August, when he spoke to Countess Bernstorff, prior to her departure for the United States,[17] the Chancellor in his "helplessness toward the American problem" made it quite clear that he was fully aware that the unleashing of the submarines would bring about America's entry into the war, but that he was powerless in the face of pressure from the military and the Pan-Germans.[18] Or was the Chancellor, by announcing a supposed readiness to accept Wilson's mediation, using the expected failure of an American peace initiative diplomatically to pave the way for the resumption of submarine warfare?

Although German historians have reproached the Ambassador for not having correctly reported on the situation in the United States, the records of the German Foreign Office clearly demonstrate that in these critical months Bernstorff conveyed a thoroughly realistic and accurate picture. Before the Chancellor's cablegram of September 2 arrived in Washington, Bernstorff had had a conversation with House, about which he reported on September 6: "Wilson's peace mediation delayed for the present because at the moment hopeless due to Rumania's entry and our enemies' resultant confidence in victory. Wilson believes he can no longer mediate before the elections. . . . But in case Wilson wins the elections . . . and war operations have come to a standstill by then, the President wants to bring about mediation immediately. . . . Wilson considers it America's interest that none of the belligerents achieve a decisive victory."[19] In his reply to Bethmann Hollweg's telegram, Bernstorff referred to this report, but then added: "unless Your Excellency should intend to suggest Wilson's mediation yourself," a proposal rejected by the Chancellor, as might be expected.[20] Addressing those governmental circles that wanted to turn Belgium into a vassal state of Germany, he stressed: "If the United States of America will intervene in the territorial question—something I have up to now categorically declined—restoration of Belgium would probably be the main American interest." Finally, addressing those in Germany who were agitating for the submarine war, the Ambassador left no doubt as to his own considered opinion: "Viewed from here, attainment of peace through unrestricted submarine warfare seems hopeless, because that way the United States would certainly be drawn into the war—regardless of how the elections go—and as a consequence, war would only be prolonged."[21]

But the next instructions, evidently a compromise between the Foreign Office, Wilhelm II, and the Supreme Command,[22] openly threatened submarine war if Wilson in the next weeks would not make "a proposal to mediate peace . . . without definite proposals of a territorial nature."[23] Since Bernstorff had explicitly emphasized the importance of the Belgian question, it is striking that Berlin took pains to skirt the issue. On October 3, Bernstorff again met with House and, in line with his instructions, intimated that Germany would welcome an appeal for peace by Wilson.[24] Two days later, most likely after he had also used the Swiss legation to check out the prospects for American action,[25] he cabled to Berlin that the situation remained unchanged and that Wilson would not get a mediation effort under way until after his reelection. Bernstorff was clearly hinting at Germany's search for a possibility to use her submarines without endangering relations with Washington. Therefore he urgently advised that, if unrestricted submarine warfare was "really unavoidable," one ought to wait at least until after the American elections, for "now immediate break with the United States would certainly be expected."[26] After this confirmation that Wilson would take no steps for the time being, Bethmann Hollweg decided to dispatch to Washington the aide-mémoire that was sent by the Emperor to Gerard in Berlin on September 24, but had been held back by the Chancellor. Bernstorff forwarded it to House on October 18. The text of the message, personally drawn up by Wilhelm, left little doubt about German intentions:

> Your Excellency [Gerard] hinted . . . in April that President W. possibly would try toward the end of summer to offer his good services to the belligerents for the promotion of peace. . . . The German Government foresees the time at which it will be forced to regain the freedom of action that it has reserved to itself in the note of May 4th last and thus the President's steps may be jeopardized. The German Government thinks it its duty to communicate this fact to Your Excellency in case you should find that the date of the intended action of the President should be so far advanced toward the end of the season.[27]

Almost as if he were fearful that Bernstorff would not transmit to the Americans with sufficient urgency the German desire for mediation, which, however, one notes, Wilson was not to use as such in his negotiations, on October 14 the Chancellor renewed his request by appealing to Wilson's "duty to put an end to the massacre" and adding almost obtrusively: "If he cannot make a decision by himself, he should take up contact with the Pope, the King of Spain, and European neutrals." The démarche, Bethmann Hollweg thought, would reward the American President with "reelection and historical fame."[28]

Reading these documents superficially, one might indeed gain the impression that Berlin was seriously pursuing the search for a way out of the war through American mediation—an interpretation which has found its exponents in the relevant German literature[29] in spite of the fact that careful scrutiny certainly reveals circumstances in a different light. Thus it would appear justified to inquire whether the German government in the fall of 1916 introduced other initiatives designed to create a climate in Washington that would have allowed Wilson to approach the belligerents with a mediation proposal desired by Germany, but to all appearances originating in America.[30] As it was, American public opinion, which by necessity must have played an important role in every decision of the President in the weeks prior to the elections, was subjected to information about the course of the war that hardly produced the impression of a German desire for peace or even of special consideration for the interests of the United States. The already mentioned giant conflagration at the Black Tom Terminal in the harbor of New York at the end of July 1916 may serve as an example of other developments hardly suited to win the man on the street to the German viewpoint.

It is also noteworthy in this connection that at the same time that Bernstorff was repeatedly urged to encourage Wilson's mediation, the German government decided to take the submarine war to America's East Coast. In July 1916, the commercial submarine *U-Deutschland*, commanded by Capt. Paul König, had appeared in Baltimore and, despite strong protests from the Allies had been treated legally as a commercial vessel. Bernstorff had gone to Baltimore, and a reception was given by the Mayor under the flags of both nations and accompanied by German music had recalled "the good days before the war."[31] On leaving American waters, Captain König noticed that British warships were lying in wait for him. As a result, the Admiralty decided to send the commercial submarine *U-Bremen* under Captain Schwartzkopf to the American coast, to be followed by *U-53* under Lt. Hans Rose, which, among other things, was to attack the Allied ships waiting for the *U-Bremen*.[32] Rose reports that prior to his mission he was told "that under the immediate impression of your appearance before the coast of America the U-boat weapon is to be freed of its chains and the unrestricted submarine war on commerce will be declared." The idea was that the opening of the submarine war through *U-53* would coincide with the victorious entry of German troops into Rumania.[33] On October 7, *U-53* entered the harbor at Newport, Rhode Island, permitted curious military and civilians to come aboard for two and a half hours, and left American waters again. Subsequently and literally under the eyes of the American navy, Rose destroyed neutral and commercial vessels before Nantucket.[34] While the American stock market reacted with panic, press and public opinion were inflamed about the naval war on America's doorstep. One feels inclined to ask how important a peace mediation by President Wilson really was to the Germans when they ordered *U-53* to the American coast. Surely, the possible loss of American lives and the inevitable consequences of such an eventuality would have had to be reckoned with in a military operation of this nature. Since Bernstorff had regularly reported about Washington's standpoint on submarine warfare, Berlin was completely informed about the expectable American reaction. Correspondingly, Wilson also stressed in a conversation with Bernstorff that "he was afraid that waging a submarine war on the American coast would cause such excitement of public opinion here in view of the election campaign that he would not be able to control it."[35] Besides a temporary worsening in the relations between the United States and the Allies[36] and a few sunken ships, the mission of the *U-53* brought Germany no advantages.[37] The records of the German Foreign Office have revealed no evidence indicating that the authorities in Berlin tried to obtain Bernstorff's opinion before sending Rose on his mission.[38]

What, then, were the motives that induced Germany suddenly to press for a peace mediation before the American elections in the fall of 1916? Wolfgang Steglich rightly talks of a "quandary" out of which the peace efforts arose. Steglich considers the uncertainty about the outcome of the war, which was recognized even in Germany, and the "incalculable expansion and ultimate escalation of the war" in the event that the unrestricted use of submarines should bring about the entry of the United States.[39] Karl Birnbaum also writes that in 1916 the Chancellor, contrary to the Supreme Command, seriously hoped for American mediation in order to reach a compromise peace with modest gains.[40] Although the frame of this study does not allow for a detailed investigation of how Bethmann Hollweg's conception of the war aims developed in the late summer and early fall of 1916, the records do not indicate that his policy toward America was really determined by a search for a compromise peace. Perhaps his telegram to Hindenburg on October 1, 1916, casts some light on the motives for his appeal to Wilson:

As is known, we have announced to America that we will wage the submarine war only according to the prize regulations. We can depart from this pledge only through an express statement and in observance of a period of grace. . . . Count Bernstorff is instructed on the personal order of His Majesty to induce President Wilson to issue an appeal for peace.[41] If Wilson can be moved to do so, the probable rejection of the appeal by England and her allies, while we accept it, shall give us the basis to morally justify before the world, particularly also before the European neutrals, our retraction of the pledge given to America. . . . Before the situation is clarified in this regard, an announcement . . . of the submarine war is impossible.[42]

House's comment to Wilson on the Emperor's aide-mémoire of September 24 shows that the Americans saw through Germany's intentions: "The German Memorandum is clearly a threat, their idea being to force you before elections to act, knowing if you are defeated nothing can be done by anyone for many months to come."[43] Wilson's advisor interpreted this document as "clearly a threat to resume submarine warfare, in the event the President does not immediately intervene in the European war."[44]

It is pointless to speculate how the German Emperor and his government would have reacted if Wilson, against expectations, had decided at this time in favor of an action for peace and the Allies had agreed to participate in a first conference. At least the German measures in occupied Belgium, a matter of specific concern to the United States, provide no grounds for assuming that Berlin was thinking of giving in to the expected demands for evacuation and restoration of that country.[45] All in all, German territorial ideas were such that it is readily discernible why Bethmann Hollweg feared and rejected Wilson's participation in a discussion of territorial considerations.

THE SO-CALLED GERMAN PEACE OFFER OF DECEMBER 12, 1916, AND THE REJECTION OF THE AMERICAN MEDIATION ATTEMPT

On November 6, 1916, Americans voted Woodrow Wilson into the White House for a second term. "The die is cast!" Bernstorff reported to his government. "Now that Mr. Wilson owes his reelection to the pacifist element[46] he will have the wish to live in peace with us. If we, for our part, are in a position to refrain from the so-called relentless U-boat war, the success of which would be most uncertain anyway, I certainly believe that Mr. Wilson will do everything in his power to end the world war soon."[47] As a matter of fact, the U-boat weapon had been used only cautiously since the *Sussex* crisis; but this did not mean that the agitation of influential groups in Germany for the unrestrained war on commerce had lost any of its edge. On October 4, Holtzendorff had asked the Emperor once more for permission to employ unrestricted submarine warfare. When Wilhelm II refused to sign because the peace contacts had not been fully explored, the chief of the Admiralty expressed his readiness to order submarine warfare according to the rules of cruiser warfare. Such an order went out on October 6 and served as guideline for submarine operations until the commencement of the U-boat campaign on February 1, 1917.[48] Evidently not even this kind of procedure offered any guarantee against the recurrence of dangerous incidents. The American reaction to the destruction of armed liners such as the *Marina* and the *Arabia*[49] nevertheless indicates that Wilson was determined to advance his peace mediation even if it should become necessary, contrary to the policy desired by his Secretary of State, to treat German transgressions on the high seas with a certain amount of leniency.[50] Bernstorff's reports demonstrate that his estimate of Washington's policy was accurate. On November 14 House had noted in his diary: "The President desires to write a note to the belligerents, demanding that the war cease ..."; a few days later Bernstorff telegraphed to Berlin: "Urgently request to allow no changes in submarine war, until it is decided whether Wilson will enter into peace mediation. I consider this imminent."[51] Then, on November 21, a clear signal came from Washington which needed no interpretation and even suggested a modus procedendi to the German government in the event that it was not seriously interested in Wilson's action: "Wilson spontaneously instructed House to tell me in strict confidence that he wanted to take steps in the peace mediation as soon as possible, presumably between now and the New Year. However, he stipulates that until then we must talk and write as little as possible about a peace mediation in order to prevent a premature refusal on the side of our enemies."[52]

In the meantime, the idea of an independent German peace proposal, separate from the apparent efforts to get Wilson to intervene, had been developed in Berlin. In mid-October, Bethmann Hollweg and the Austro-Hungarian Foreign Minister, Stefan Count Burián von Rajecz, had discussed the latter's plan for a peace move on the part of the Central Powers and the publication of mutual war objectives. In the course of the following weeks, details of the initiative had been agreed upon by Bethmann Hollweg, Burián, and the Supreme Command.[53] On November 16, Jagow had then asked Bernstorff whether and when Wilson would take steps toward mediation, since the "question [is] important for evaluation of possible other steps to the same effect."[54] Following this hint at an imminent separate peace initiative from Berlin, Bernstorff, in his above-mentioned report on November 21, had expressly warned the Foreign Office against unfavorably influencing the international climate of opinion for Wilson's appeal by additional discussions of peace. But in Berlin, where, as Bernstorff was later to write, one "never wanted to believe in Mr. Wilson's intention to bring about peace," the Ambassador's suggestions met with little response.[55] Even before his reply arrived in the Wilhelmstrasse, Jagow had informed him on November 22 that a separate peace initiative was planned "for the near future."[56] Now, after the arrival of the warning from Washington, Zimmermann instructed the Ambassador to exert pressure on the Americans to make their peace move soon, as conditions at the moment favored the Central Powers militarily.[57]

Thus, while the authorities in Berlin continued to work out their own peace offer and its conditions, they also tried to maintain the impression in Washington that an appeal for peace by Wilson would enjoy their support. As in September and October, the alleged desire for American mediation contrasted sharply with the actual demeanor of the Imperial Government. Although Berlin was fully aware of the fact that all measures taken in occupied Belgium were being followed closely in many countries and especially in the United States, at the end of September it was decided to obtain additional labor for German industry by conscripting Belgian civilians. During October and November, a brutal deportation program was developed that in a short period of time brought tens of thousands of Belgians to forced labor in Germany.[58] Even if humane considerations only played a subordinate role in the fall of 1916, Berlin apparently neglected to take into account the negative propaganda effect of this action. When, in mid-November, first reports of the Belgian deportations found their way into the American press, a wave of indignation against Germany, at least as strong as after the

German invasion of Belgium, swept over the American public,[59] and the peace propaganda so eagerly promoted in the United States by Bernstorff and German agents was "strongly impeded." On December 21, 1916, Consul Roh in New Orleans reported to Bernstorff that "the measures against the work-shy Belgians" had hindered his activities on behalf of German benevolent purposes, such as the Red Cross.[60] How much the American President was concerned about his planned peace move can be seen from his own moderate reaction to the reports from Belgium. It is true that Bernstorff was told that the deportations could cause the President further to delay his peace initiative;[61] in reality, however, Wilson was quite determined not to allow Germany's actions to change his course. If news about the events of the war influenced the President at all during those weeks, then it was only, it would appear, because he became all the more convinced of the importance of his plan. On November 25 Wilson drafted the first version of his peace note. Although both House and Lansing feared that the peace initiative was doomed to failure and that America would have to enter the war, they let the President's text stand except for a few minor changes. But, in Lansing's words: "When we do go into this war . . . we must go in on the side of the Allies, for we are a democracy. Suppose, however, Germany listens to the President and the Allies decline to do so, what will be our situation?"[62] Another delaying factor became apparent on December 4, when the domestic situation in England forced Wilson to postpone his actions until a new government could be formed there. After the State Department had approved the draft on December 10, nothing stood in the way of Wilson's plan; Link suggests that the President may have contemplated presenting his appeal for peace "on about December 15."[63]

If Berlin seriously desired a peace initiative by the American President, why would the Germans thwart American intentions on December 12 with a peace note of their own, even though they had been informed by Bernstorff that such an action was to be expected before the end of the year? Steglich emphasizes the unfavorable conditions under which Bethmann Hollweg had to make decisions on foreign policy. The Germans, he writes, were under the impression that Wilson was forever delaying his mediation. He points out the constant pressure from the navy for the unrestricted use of the U-boats, and finally, he argues, German troops were on the advance in Rumania, and the Emperor and his military leaders had decided that the fall of Bucharest would be a suitable moment for a German peace offer. "The events urgently called for action."⁶⁴ The scope of this study does not permit an investigation of whether the situation was indeed so pressing for Germany when Bucharest fell on December 6 or whether the Wilhelmstrasse—where since the end of November the moderate Jagow had been replaced by the unbridled and less talented Arthur Zimmermann—quite purposely launched its presumed peace offer in order to get America to issue an appeal for peace that Berlin from the start viewed as useless.⁶⁵ In contrast, we can be certain that President Wilson's message, delivered by Joseph C. Grew to the Chancellor on December 5, did not have the meaning assigned to it by German officials. The text which the American Chargé d'Affaires read to the Imperial Chancellor said: "What the President is now earnestly desiring is practical cooperation on the part of the German authorities in creating a favorable opportunity for some affirmative action by him in the interest of an early restoration of peace."⁶⁶ Wilson's wish undoubtedly referred to a desired solution of the Belgian deportation problem and the settlement of the submarine incidents; surely the text of the American note did not call upon Germany to rush forward with its own peace proposal. Nonetheless, on reading Bethmann Hollweg's reply to Grew, the suspicion arises that the Chancellor, actually or ostensibly, incorrectly interpreted the American text: "It is with great satisfaction that I have noted that the President of the United States offers to open pourparlers for peace. Negotiations have so far not met with favorable response from the other side. I hope the time will come when Germany's enemies will be more willing to lend an ear to the voice of reason. I am extremely gratified to see . . . that in this eventuality I can count upon the . . . cooperation of the President in the restoration of peace." Here then was the first clear indication for the Americans that a German action had to be expected.⁶⁷

When Bethmann Hollweg came to the Imperial Headquarters in Pless on December 8 to set the date for the German peace move, he found the Supreme Command filled with new confidence resulting from the successful Rumanian campaign. With victory in the East, fresh troops could now be brought to the western front. Hindenburg's conditions for his consent to the German peace feeler now included the demand for the "beginning of unrestricted submarine war at the end of January." But the Chancellor was not quite ready to give in to this demand. There was still hope that Wilson, by his own appeal for peace, which was expected to be rejected by all sides except Germany, would maneuver himself into a position from which he would not be able to do anything against German resumption of unrestricted submarine warfare. Still Bethmann Hollweg, for all matter of speaking, practically agreed to begin the unrestricted submarine campaign against *armed* commercial vessels, should the German peace offer be rejected.[68]

The next day Bernstorff was informed of the impending German peace move. The cable, signed by Under Secretary Wilhelm von Stumm, leaves little room for doubt about the insincerity of German policy toward the United States. Referring to the earlier exchange of views with Grew about "practical cooperation," Stumm closed his instruction to the Ambassador with: "We believe we can assume that our action meets the wishes of the President. Request at any rate that you interpret [matters] this way to President and House."[69] On December 12, the Chancellor personally handed the German peace offer in its French version to the American Chargé d'Affaires.[70] "Fortunately we forestalled him," wrote the Emperor.[71] But the intelligent Maximilian Harden shortly thereafter came to the opinion that "the track on which Mr. Wilson wanted to move forward is now blocked."[72] As was to be expected, Wilson first reacted to the German note with displeasure, but then decided not to be led astray from the path he had embarked upon, and he completed his own appeal for peace.[73] When he noted the negative response of the Allies to the German initiative and simultaneously received reports from Berlin about imminent unrestricted deployment of the U-boats, Wilson felt he had to act immediately to keep the door for a negotiated peace from being shut once and for all by a general rejection of the German offer.[74] On December 18, the State Department issued Wilson's appeal to the governments of the belligerent nations. The document called for the creation of a league of nations after the conflicts of the present war had been resolved. It also contained the modus procedendi for reaching agreement. The central point[75] of Wilson's program was "a comparison of views as to the terms which must precede those ultimate arrangements for the peace of the world. . . . Never yet have the authoritative spokesmen of either side avowed the precise objects which would, if attained, satisfy them and their people that the war had been fought out. . . . It may be that peace is nearer than we know; that the terms . . . are not so irreconcilable as some have feared; that an interchange of views would clear the way at least for conference."[76] With this the American démarche stood in sharp contrast to the German initiative, which was couched in vague generalities.[77]

After publication of Wilson's note, Bernstorff learned from Lansing that Washington would welcome a confidential communication of the terms of peace and that the American government offered to serve as a kind of clearing house. Apparently his report to Berlin of December 21[78] in no way lessened German mistrust toward Wilson. As it was, Berlin wanted to negotiate with the enemy only directly and, therefore, wished to avoid Wilson's intervention at all costs.[79] Without giving a second thought to the serious consequences of a German rebuff of the American offer, which they claimed to have been seeking for months, they snubbed Washington with an undisguised rejection on December 26, two days after the above-mentioned telegram from Bernstorff arrived. Without any reaction to Wilson's basic wish for announcement of the conditions for peace, the German government proposed a conference of the belligerent nations, even though this was evidently impossible without a prior exchange of at least general terms.[80] Berlin's reasons for the rejection of the American mediation offer are quite clear from Zimmermann's instruction to Bernstorff "for [his] exclusively personal information"; "Interference of the President, even in form of a 'clearing house,' would be disadvantageous to our interests, therefore is to be avoided. The basis for a future conclusion of peace we must create through direct agreement with our opponents, *if we do not want to run the risk of being deprived of our desired gains through pressure from the neutrals*. Therefore we also reject the idea of a conference."[81] In other words, for Germany, Woodrow Wilson was only a means to bring its enemies to negotiations or by their refusal to create the diplomatic and moral basis for striking out with the ultimate weapon, the unrestricted submarine war.[82] If the German government had now told Wilson of its extravagant war aims[83] and these had become known to the Allies, Berlin's hopes of breaking up the enemy coalition, either through separate negotiations or through Washington's unyielding neutrality, probably would have been destroyed for good.

Bernstorff's position in Washington became less enviable by the day. Despite his dangerous involvement with and participation in risky intelligence operations, he had worked continuously and earnestly toward an American peace mediation, only to see his final efforts to keep America neutral sabotaged by his own government.

Eager to pave the way for a peace conference and certainly following more his own instinct than Berlin's policy, he permitted a Christmas message signed by him to appear in Ridder's New York *Staats-Zeitung*, which among other things declared: "Germany stands ready to follow him [Wilson]. Certain of its strength, but not arrogant, aware that it drew the sword not because of thirst for conquest but rather in defense of its national existence, it does not seek foreign territory but security against future attack."[84] On December 27, he conferred with House in New York and together they sought a way out of the impasse. Probably on Bernstorff's suggestion,[85] it was agreed that Berlin should convey its terms of peace to Wilson in total secrecy; only Bernstorff and House were to be informed. The records give the impression that both House and Bernstorff spoke with complete sincerity; it should be noted, however, that evidently they were not thinking of the modus procedendi which Lansing had proposed in a wire of December 21 to America's representatives in the warring countries.[86] On December 29, Bernstorff informed his government about the proposed new procedure of mediation. The cable did not arrive in Berlin until January 3. The text quite openly expressed the Ambassador's concern that Berlin might not grant him the necessary authority to negotiate and in fact had perhaps already written off Wilson's mediation as a lost cause: "The more Your Excellency wishes to inform me about our conditions and readiness for guarantees, the better, as viewed from here. However, I do not know whether Your Excellency would not perhaps prefer rather to let the negotiations fail than to accept American help."[87] In his memoirs right after the war, Bernstorff wrote that he considered this telegram about the confidential communication of conditions to Wilson to be the most important of his messages in this connection because it clearly conveyed to the German government an American mediation offer that had to be either accepted or rejected. "In the former case it was necessary to at least postpone the U-boat war; in the latter case we had to create a clear diplomatic situation in Washington, if we wanted to avoid being reproached for having negotiated with Mr. Wilson and simultaneously having planned the submarine war that had to lead to the break with the United States."[88]

As a matter of fact, the political situation in Berlin had changed considerably from December 29 to January 3. Germany's rejection of Wilson's mediation offer on December 26 had made it easier for the Allies to decline the German offer of December 12.[89] With their common refusal, the Entente had once again opened the flood gates for a wave of agitation for the U-boat war. The Emperor, navy and Supreme Command were now prepared to declare unrestricted submarine warfare at the risk of a break with the United States and, with that, its entry into the war on the side of the Allies. Zimmermann's blunt reply of January 7 to Bernstorff's telegram of December 29 reflected this: "For your personal information. American mediation for *genuine* peace negotiations is undesirable to us if for no other reason than public opinion. . . . We are convinced that we can bring the war militarily and economically to a victorious end. The question of communicating our terms of peace should therefore be handled dilatorily by Your Excellency."[90]

Only two days later, on January 9, 1917, the long agitation for the submarine war was to reach its final goal. A letter from the Berlin historian, Dietrich Schäfer, to the Foreign Office on January 3 echoes the contemporary sentiment of large circles in Germany:

> America stands at the center of the situation. That it feels hostile toward us, no one can doubt. Whether it will drive its opposition to the point of open war is a question that cannot be answered with certainty. I do not think so, but I confess that one must count on the possibility. But I also believe that the fear that the possibility could become a reality should not detain us from by all means waging the U-boat war in a manner, the effect of which is certain. For only an effective U-boat war can serve us. . . . Our fatherland can only survive if it is victorious; but victory can now only be achieved by overcoming England, and for that we have the right weapon in the submarine. That above all is also the opinion of those most qualified to judge, the naval experts.[91]

On January 8, the curtain rose on the last act of the U-boat campaign. The military leaders met with Hindenburg to prepare the offensive against the political leadership that was planned for the next day. A brief excerpt from the minutes of this gathering might give an impression of the extent of the presumptuousness and the political naiveté with which the military chiefs recklessly gambled the future of their nation:

> v. Holtzendorff: What will we do if the chancellor does not go along?
> Field Marshal [Hindenburg]: That worries me too.

*Chancellor Theobald von Bethmann Hollweg at Charleroi
(Library of Congress)*

v. Holtzendorff: Then you will have to become chancellor.
Field Marshal: No, I cannot and will not. I cannot deal with the Reichstag.
v. Holtzendorff: I consider Bülow and Tirpitz out of the question because of their relationship to the Emperor.[92]
Exc. Ludendorff: I would not encourage the Field Marshal.
Field Marshal: I cannot talk in the Reichstag. I decline. What about Dallwitz?
Exc. Ludendorff: Does he even want the U-boat war?
v. Holtzendorff: The Chancellor enjoys great confidence abroad.
Field Marshal: So let us stick together. It must be. We are reckoning with the war with America and have made all preparations. It cannot get any worse. The war must be shortened by all means.[93]

The discussion about the overthrow of the Imperial Chancellor, it turned out, was premature. Bethmann Hollweg, in the words of Fritz Stern, "probably... [sharing] the exaggerated faith of his countrymen in the authority of the uniform," went along. Almost without resistance, he gave in to the demands of the military: "Yes, when success beckons, we must act."[94] Thus the meeting of the so-called Crown Council on the evening of January 9 was no more than a formality.[95] Before the end of the day, the order went out from Wilhelm to Admiral von Holtzendorff that unrestricted submarine warfare would begin on February 1, and that preparations were to be made "without delay."[96]

The last vestiges of inhibition were quick to disappear in Berlin. The Emperor was "not at all" interested any more in Wilson's mediation, and in case the break with the United States was unavoidable, he felt "it can't be helped! We shall move ahead."[97] When Bernstorff, in a telegram of January 10, spoke of Wilson's "peace mediation" becoming endangered, Wilhelm II, as if to record it for history, wrote in the margin: "nothing is known of that, nor has [it] been offered or accepted."[98] On January 16, Bethmann Hollweg personally brought an end to the possibilities of mediation by informing Bernstorff that unrestricted submarine warfare would begin on February 1, and that the American Government should be informed about the decision only on that day. "I am well aware that with our action we run the risk of bringing about the break and perhaps war with the United States. We are determined to accept this risk. I ask

Your Excellency, however, to inform me immediately of possible viewpoints for handling matter by which the danger of break could be reduced." Underlining the definitiveness of the decision, the Chancellor notified his Ambassador: "Finally I remind you of the preparation for thoroughly making the German steamers [in U.S. ports] unserviceable. Your Excellency is responsible for getting the necessary code word out early enough and through reliable channels, so that no German steamer falls into foreign hands in usable condition."[99]

BERNSTORFF'S STAND VIS-À-VIS BERLIN IN THE BATTLE FOR THE NEUTRALITY OF THE UNITED STATES

In contrast to his Imperial Chancellor, who on January 9, 1917, capitulated to the pressure of the military leadership, in Washington Bernstorff battled literally until the eleventh hour to maintain American neutrality. After Zimmermann's telegram of January 7, and even more so after Bethmann Hollweg's instructions of January 16, these efforts might well have become a matter of pure formality for him. It would not have been surprising if during these last weeks the Ambassador had tended to avoid exposure and instead had been more concerned to guard his diplomatic reputation. But this is precisely what he did not do. Not having shied away previously from unpleasant and at times, indeed, uncomfortable assignments and tasks such as the collaboration with the intelligence agents, now that Germany's future was really on the line, he took the only honorable position.[100]

When Zimmermann's rejection of Wilson's appeal—dispatched in Berlin on January 7—reached the embassy, Bernstorff evidently had the choice between abandoning his attempts to achieve a Wilsonian mediation and starting all over in Washington in order to be able to place new cards on the table in Berlin. When, early in January, the Foreign Office had informed him that the unrestricted submarine war against armed merchant ships would commence soon, he certainly knew that his time was limited.[101] For reasons unknown, it was only on January 15, five days after the arrival of Zimmermann's message,[102] that he was able to see Colonel House. Since the agreement between the two men led to a new effort of the President to bring about a negotiated peace, it would seem of interest to know what was said at the meeting. Unfortunately, the sources contain only relatively unreliable information, thus making it difficult to determine with certainty whether Bernstorff represented the German position according to his instructions or whether he toned down Berlin's gruff rejection. Our sources are a letter from House to Wilson of January 15 and a telegram of January 16 from Bernstorff to Zimmermann.[103] Zimmermann had informed Bernstorff that Wilson's "mediation for *genuine* [*eigentliche*] peace negotiations [was] . . . not desired"; on the other hand, the Ambassador was authorized to express Germany's readiness to negotiate about questions of international law, such as freedom of the seas, arbitration, and a league for peace. Hence, "in principle" Germany was willing, though with more than two years delay, to enter into negotiations about an arbitration treaty with the United States.[104] From Bernstorff's message of January 16, that House had told him "Wilson views this communication from the Imperial German Government as *extremely* valuable," we can conclude that the Ambassador only made use of the positive part of Zimmermann's telegram. At least he reported no reactions from House concerning the German refusal to state concrete peace terms. For his part, after meeting with Bernstorff House informed the President on January 15 as follows: "(1) His Government are willing to submit to arbitration as a means of peace. (2) They are willing to enter a league of nations. . . . (3) They propose that you submit a program for a peace conference and they agree to give it their approval. (4) To show their good will, they are willing to sign the arbitration treaty immediately (that is the so-called Bryan Treaty). In addition to this, the Chancellor told Bernstorff to say that Germany's terms are very moderate and they did not intend to take any part of Belgium. This was the only definite statement as to actual terms made." To his typed letter to the President, House added that he had taken notes during the conversation, read them to Bernstorff afterwards and that the latter had found them to be correct.[105] If Bernstorff indeed made these statements that did not agree with his instructions, the enthusiasm of House in his closing remarks to Wilson is understandable: "To my mind, this is the most important communication we have had since the war began and gives a real basis for negotiations and for peace." After consultation with the President, in order to reassure himself, on January 17 House wrote Bernstorff a letter indicating that he was not quite certain whether Bernstorff had given the above-mentioned assurances in this manner. Practically listing the points again, House asked Bernstorff: "Going back to paragraph No. 1. [sic] the President wants to know whether we understand you to mean that your Government are willing to submit the terms upon which the war is to be concluded to arbitration, or only that they are willing to conclude arbitration treaties. I regard this communication from your Government as the most important that has been made since the beginning of war and if we have understood it correctly, the President will begin to formulate a plan for further action and from which I sincerely hope peace may be brought about."[106]

The fact that Wilson now wanted to have Bernstorff's message in writing permitted the Ambassador only the most exacting delivery of his instructions from Berlin, something that for obvious reasons he apparently had avoided two days earlier in his conversation with House. He now had to admit that Berlin was willing to submit to arbitration only as "a part of the stipulations contained in No. 2 of your letter [to enter a league of nations, presumably *after* the war]." Point three also could not be passed over in hazy generalities without maneuvering himself into an untenable position: "The idea of my Government was, that the President submit a program *for the general conference* concerning the guarantees for the future. As you know, my Government thinks that a conference *of the belligerents* [therefore without participation of the United States] about the terms of peace should precede the general conference about the guarantees."[107] House could not conceal his disappointment about the fact "that practically everything you said to me ... only had a bearing upon the future and not upon the present"; nevertheless, he asked Bernstorff once again for "peace terms," since more precise information of this kind would put Wilson in a position to undertake a new step toward mediation. At the same time he inquired whether Germany was prepared possibly to submit the deployment of the submarines to the conditions of a Bryan arbitration treaty and thus a waiting period of one year.[108] Under the justified assumption that he could achieve more in a personal talk with House, Bernstorff arranged for a new meeting by telephone. Immediately after this call on January 19, he must have received Bethmann Hollweg's telegram no. 157 of January 16, announcing unrestricted submarine warfare, and in view of the German decision, the Ambassador must have realized the impossibility of continuing his at least partially unauthorized negotiations. Bernstorff's letter to House of January 20 canceled the date arranged over the telephone and was written in an unusually noncommittal and pessimistic tone, particularly for House, who knew nothing of Bethmann Hollweg's instruction that nearly destroyed all hopes for mediation. "I am afraid the situation in Berlin is getting out of our hands," Bernstorff wrote. "The exorbitant demands of our enemies ... seem to have infuriated public opinion in Germany.... In Berlin they seem to believe that the answer of our enemies to the President has finished the whole peace movement for a long time to come, and I am, therefore, afraid that my government may be forced to act accordingly in a very short time.... I am afraid that it will be very difficult to get any more peace terms from Berlin at this time for the reasons I mentioned above."[109]

The Ambassador was in an indescribably difficult position.[110] The military measures announced by Bethmann Hollweg, in Bernstorff's opinion, unavoidably would lead to war with the United States; yet he had been strictly forbidden to make use of this information in any way before February 1. Should he break off his confidential peace talks with House, now that they had lost almost all prospects of success? Bernstorff decided otherwise because he did not want to give up all hope of still finding a modus procedendi for a peace mediation and for arranging a conference. Even in moments when the hopelessness of his efforts must have been clear to him, he may have concluded that, between a peace conference arranged by Washington and America's entry into the war, there was still the—admittedly very improbable—way out, namely, to use submarines in such a way that the United States would acquiesce.[111] This was reason enough to continue negotiating, and at least temporarily it could be seen as a kind of solution, the more so since relations between London and Washington had worsened so much since the fall of 1916 that the attempt to gain some advantage from these Anglo-American conflicts was not mere folly.[112] Curiously, for some unintelligible reason, Anglo-American differences and their implications were not recognized in Berlin.[113] House's first reaction to Bernstorff's retracting statements can hardly be surprising: "They are slippery customers and it is difficult to pin them down to anything definite.... German diplomacy is of the devious kind." He also recognized: "It is possible that they are manoeuvering for position in regard to the resumption of their unbridled submarine warfare. They would like to put the Allies wholly in the wrong and justify Germany in the eyes of the neutrals in resorting to extreme measures."[114]

Of more than secondary interest is the fact that in those hectic weeks of January House also had confidential talks with the colorful British secret service station chief in New York, Sir William Wiseman. The latter had already been informed of Bernstorff's statements of January 15. On January 20, House had further advised the Englishman to win his government for a peace conference, especially since England would otherwise be confronted with the impending unrestricted submarine war. One week later, after British intelligence had intercepted the Foreign Office's telegrams nos. 157 and 158 and thus was probably already fully or partially informed about the planned beginning of the U-boat campaign on February 1, Wiseman brought the news that London was not disinclined toward a conference, as long as Germany also showed interest. The question must remain open whether Britain acted out of fear of the German U-boat war or whether it had calculated that declarations of British readiness for peace might be of advantage in the battle for public opinion, particularly since, with the expected break between Berlin and Washington, there was but small prospect of a conference actually being called.[115]

When Bethmann Hollweg's instructions about the unlimited submarine war jarred Bernstorff in the midst of his negotiations with House on January 19, the Ambassador resolved, as he was later to recall in his memoirs, to work with all his strength against the decision, which he could "only see as a declaration of war on the United States," or "at least . . . [to achieve] a delay of its implementation."[116] Besides continuing his secret negotiations with House, he ventured to warn Berlin unmistakably: "War unavoidable with intended action. . . . Execution of my orders [would] have effect of declaration of war here." Berlin should at least postpone the date for the deployment of the submarines, since Wilson would undertake new steps "in the very near future."[117] Bernstorff's report was quite correct. Wilson knew that he could not afford to lose any time if he did not want the resumption of submarine warfare or intensified measures in the British blockade to make any further attempt at mediation impossible. On January 22, when Bernstorff's telegram with the request for postponement arrived in Berlin, Wilson made a speech before the Senate, which centered on his personal views about the peace to be attained.[118] Undoubtedly, he was addressing the world at large, but he was speaking directly to Germany and her allies when he said: "No peace can last, or ought to last, which does not recognize and accept the principle that governments derive all their just powers from the consent of the governed, and that no right anywhere exists to hand peoples about from sovereignty to sovereignty as if they were property. . . . I am proposing government by the consent of the governed." The peace that Wilson desired was "peace without victory."[119] It is futile to speculate whether such a peace was a real possibility in January 1917, or whether Germany, once it had come to the negotiation table, would have had to accept a peace more like that of Brest-Litovsk or Versailles anyway. The decisive point is that Germany made no attempt to even probe the possibilities indicated in the President's speech.[120] In Berlin, impetuousness and diplomatic incompetence finally had joined hands. The Germans not only had decided to unleash the unrestricted submarine war, but on January 16 they had also sent an offer of alliance, aimed against the United States, to the Mexican President, Venustiano Carranza. When Wilson renewed his call for peace on January 22, Admiral Hall's *Room 40* had already intercepted the Mexico telegram. One week only remained until the submarines would be unchained.

President Wilson was aware that an acceptance of his mediation offer by Germany would decide the future. "I am even more concerned to find out what Germany is thinking,—I mean what those who have the determination of her course of action in their hands are thinking in their hearts. . . . If Germany really wants peace she can get it, and get it soon, *if she will but confide in me and let me have a chance,*" he wrote to House following his speech before the Senate. He asked House to work on Bernstorff once more:

> Tell him that this is the time to accomplish something, if they really and truly want peace; that the indications that come to us are of a sort to lead us to believe that with something reasonable to suggest, as from them, I can bring things about; and that otherwise, with the preparations they are apparently making with regard to unrestrained attacks on merchantmen on the plea that they are for offence, there is a terrible likelihood that the relations between the United States and Germany may come to a breaking point and everything assume a different aspect. . . . Do they [in fact] want me to help? I am entitled to know because I genuinely want to help and have put myself in a position to help without favour to either side.[121]

On January 26, House received the German Ambassador at his home in New York and presented to him the President's last offer of mediation. The Count was obviously depressed and spoke of the heavy influence of the military in Berlin. He was quick, however, to grasp for the possibilities offered by the President's wish for a renewed mediation effort, and, immediately following his visit with House, he urgently cabled Berlin for postponement of the submarine war because of a new possibility of mediation.[122] On January 27, followed his detailed report, telegram no. 239, dispatched to Berlin via the State Department.[123] Once more Bernstorff, who knew little of what was happening in Germany, implored his Government:

> House . . . told me the following as an official message from the President: Wilson offers to begin with confidential peace mediation on the basis of his Senate message, that is, without interference in territorial peace terms. As *not* confidential Wilson would view his simultaneous request to us to communicate peace terms. . . . Wilson would hope that we would communicate peace terms to him which would be permitted to be published here and in Germany. . . . If we only had confidence in him, the President is convinced that he could then arrange the two peace conferences.[124] He would be especially pleased if Your Excellency would at the same time explain that we would be ready to enter the conferences on the basis of his message before the Senate. The motivation for our declaration could be that Wilson had now asked us directly for our terms of peace. The President believes that the Entente note to him, being a bluff, needs not to be taken into consideration. He decidedly hopes to bring about peace conferences and to do it so quickly that unnecessary bloodshed during the spring offensives would be prevented. How far Your Excellency wants to and can meet [*entgegenkommen*] Wilson cannot be judged from here. However, I urgently request to be permitted to present the following. If U-boat warfare is now begun without further ado, the President will view this as a slap in the face, and war with the United States is unavoidable. The war party here will gain the upper hand, and there will be in my opinion no end of the war in sight, since the power resources of the United States, despite all that could be said to the contrary, are very great.[125] Otherwise, if we take up Wilson's proposal, but plans nonetheless fail due to the stubbornness of our opponents, it will be very difficult for the President to go to war against us, even if we then

begin the unrestricted submarine war. In other words, for the time being it is only a matter of a delay of brief duration in order to improve our diplomatic position. *I myself profess the opinion that we will now reach a better peace through conferences than if the United States joins our enemies.*[126]

Still hoping to change the course of events, the Ambassador added: "Since cablegrams always need several days, request immediate wireless instruction in case telegraphed order 157 is not to be executed on February 1."

The telegram reached the Foreign Office by way of the American embassy on January 28. The countdown of the final hours before the presentation of the German submarine note in Washington had begun. Whether, and to what extent, the Chancellor and the Foreign Office went out of their way to argue along the lines proposed by the American President cannot be determined from the records. Although the Chancellor and the Secretary of the Foreign Office went to the headquarters at Pless on January 29, one may well question the seriousness of their efforts.[127] Had they not just recently approved the brash offer to Mexico of an alliance against the United States? Had they not indeed for days already treated the unrestricted deployment of the submarines on February 1 as a fait accompli? At General Headquarters, too, the mood was not exactly in favor of Wilson's mediation offer or Bernstorff's proposal to further postpone the submarine war. The Ambassador's first telegram of January 26 with the request for postponement had already been dealt with curtly: "Regret suggestion impracticable."[128] As it was, Wilhelm II is reported to have suspected that Wilson was only trying to get him to postpone the submarine war because he was concerned about food supplies in Britain.[129] When the news arrived at headquarters on January 29 that Bethmann Hollweg was on his way with an urgent report from Bernstorff, the Emperor was, in the words of Admiral Georg Alexander von Müller "beside himself because again a decision is expected of him." During the audience, the Chancellor read his draft of a reply to Bernstorff, in which he stuck to February 1 as the opening date for the submarine war and which conveyed to Wilson terms of peace which Germany ostensibly would have considered if its offer of December 12, 1916, had been accepted. Admiral von Müller noted the following about the further course of the meeting:

The Chancellor cleverly defended his instruction [to Bernstorff], which, without giving up the submarine war, was to create the possibility that America at least would not enter the war immediately. Perhaps in the meantime the U-boat war would then have had the effect that America totally loses her desire [to enter the war]. Hindenburg was in agreement. The Emperor too, but he would not miss the opportunity to shine with strong language [*Kraftausdrücken*] ('The German Emperor lashes out' [*'Da haut der deutsche Kaiser zu'*]). . . . He demanded that the instruction would have to say clearly that the Emperor would not stand for Mr. Wilson as peace mediator and the participation of America in the peace congress.[130]

The outcome of this strange discussion was telegram no. 65, wired on order of the Chancellor by the Foreign Office to the Ambassador on the evening of January 29. While still at Imperial Headquarters in Pless, Zimmermann cabled instructions to Wilhelm von Stumm in the Wilhelmstrasse to reply to Bernstorff's telegram no. 239. In content and tone the German text of cable no. 65 that went out to Washington is a rather unusual piece of diplomatic correspondence, and the English language version misses some of the color. From the records it would appear that Bernstorff received Bethmann Hollweg's instruction on January 30. One of the English-language texts of the submarine war declaration that the Ambassador had to give to the American government on January 31 has a note in Bernstorff's own handwriting on it, saying "to be copied only on January 30 if until then nothing more arrives from Berlin." This instruction must have been written late on January 29, since only at three o'clock in the afternoon did Bernstorff receive the text of the German government's answer to Wilson's address of January 22 before the Senate, which had been reported to Zimmermann by Gerard in Berlin on the same day. This cable no. 174, transmitted to Bernstorff via the United States embassy in Berlin and the United States State Department, had contained certain detailed instructions regarding the submarine war decision, and Bernstorff was aware that his cable no. 239 of January 27 had not been answered yet. His handwritten note of late January 29 clearly indicates that Bernstorff still had not given up all hope for some change of instruction from Berlin. There is no hint in Bernstorff's memoirs about his reaction to telegram no. 65. The finality of it may have shocked him.

Probably translated into English in the Imperial embassy on January 30, the text of telegram no. 65, which the Ambassador sent by messenger to House in New York on the morning of January 31, contained the following statements:

The Imperial Government has complete confidence in the President and hopes that he will reciprocate such confidence. As proof I am to inform you in confidence that the Imperial Government will be very glad to accept the services kindly offered by the President for the purpose of bringing about a peace conference between the belligerents. My Government, however, is not prepared to publish any peace terms at present, because our enemies have published such terms which aim at the dishonor and destruction of Germany and her allies. My Government considers that as long as our enemies openly proclaim such terms, it would show weakness, which does not exist, on our part if we publish our terms and we would in so doing only prolong the war. However, to show President Wilson our confidence, my Government through me desires to inform him *personally* of the terms under which we would have been prepared to enter into negotiations, if our enemies had accepted our offer of December 12th. "Restitution of the part of Upper Alsace occupied by the French. Gaining of a frontier which would protect Germany and Poland economically and strategically against Russia. Restitution of Colonies in form of an agreement which would give Germany Colonies adequate to her population and economic interest. Restitution of those parts of France occupied by Germany under reservation of strategical and economic changes of the frontier and financial compensations. Restoration of Belgium under special guarantee for the safety of Germany which would have to be decided on by negotiations with Belgium. Economic and financial mutual compensation on the basis of the exchange of territories conquered and to be restituted at the conclusion of peace. Compensation for the German business concerns and private persons who suffered by the war. Abandonment of all economic agreements and measures which would form an obstacle to normal commerce and intercourse after the conclusion of peace, and instead of such agreements reasonable treaties of commerce. The freedom of the seas." The peace terms of our allies run on the same lines. My Government further agrees, after the war has been terminated, to enter into the proposed second International Conference on the basis of the President's message to the Senate. My Government would have been glad to postpone the submarine blockade, if they had been able to do so. This, however, was quite impossible on account of the preparations which could not be canceled.[131] My Government believes that the submarine blockade will terminate the war very quickly. In the meantime my Government will do everything possible to safeguard American Interests and begs the President to continue his efforts to bring about peace, and my Government will terminate the submarine blockade as soon as it is evident that the efforts of the President will lead to a peace acceptable to Germany.[132]

House thought of the confidential talks of the past months and the German peace offer of December 12. Evidently Germany had long been planning the submarine deployment. The German peace offer had only been a diplomatic maneuver to pave the way for the new war measures.[133]

That afternoon Bernstorff went to the State Department and handed the Secretary of State the declaration of unrestricted submarine warfare. Lansing read the German note silently. Bernstorff sat by the side of the Secretary's desk. Then the two men looked at each other, and Bernstorff said: "I am sorry to have to bring about this situation, but my government could do nothing else." Lansing spoke of an "unfriendly and indefensible act." When Bernstorff shook hands with the Secretary of State shortly afterwards, there were tears in his eyes. Lansing felt compassion for him.[134]

The historian could be tempted to end the narrative here—just as one might well view the agreement of the Chancellor to submarine warfare on January 9 as the final act of the drama. The Imperial German Government had challenged the United States to war. As Thomas A. Bailey put it: "Germany . . . virtually declared war on the United States the day she announced her unrestricted submarine warfare."[135] The most powerful of the neutral countries would now join the Allies, and that at a time when, as never before, the American President had pursued the goal of a negotiated peace. Yet, in spite of all indications to the contrary, it appears that the course of events on January 31, 1917, was not yet unalterable. Wilson, regardless of all German provocations, was determined not to lead America into war, as long as he had any other options.

There was no way, however, at this time to avoid breaking off diplomatic relations. At two o'clock in the afternoon of February 3, Lester H. Woolsey, a lawyer from the State Department, appeared in the German embassy and delivered the American answer: "In view of this declaration, which withdraws suddenly and without prior intimation the solemn assurance given in the Imperial Government's note of May 4, 1916, this Government has no alternative consistent with the dignity and honor of the United States but to take the course which it explicitly announced in its note of April 18, 1916. . . . The President has, therefore, directed me to announce to Your Excellency that all diplomatic relations between the United States and the German Empire are severed."[136] From now on, Bernstorff no longer officially represented Germany in Washington; he got in touch with the Swiss Minister, Paul Ritter, and asked him to look after the German interests. Meanwhile, in the German embassy the staff began burning piles of documents and planning for the departure.[137] House's letter to Bernstorff of February 2 reflected the dismal outlook:

> Upon receipt of your letter of January 31st I thought it advisable to take it to Washington and hand it to the President in person. The President is deeply disappointed at the sudden turn in the situation. It seemed as if peace was near by and could be reached by concessions here and there on both sides. The action of your Government in regard to its submarine policy has made it impossible to carry peace negotiations further at present. Even if the submarine issue had not been injected, the proposals that your Government make are, in effect, no proposals at all. They are nullified by the expression "the terms under which we would have been prepared to enter into negotiations, if our enemies had accepted our offer of December 12th." The suddenness with which the new undersea warfare was put into force makes it impossible for the President to propose mediation. I cannot tell you how deeply I regret the turn matters have taken, for there was every reason to believe that within a short time the belligerents would be discussing peace.[138]

Bernstorff answered that same day: "You know how I feel about the matter, so I need not tell you. However, I do not believe that my Government intended to nullify the peace terms I mentioned to you. I understand those terms to be our present ones, and that they will only be changed if the submarine warfare leads to decisive results. I do not wish to close this letter, without expressing to you my most cordial thanks for the kind assistance you have always given me during the last years of stress. I shall never forget the friendship you have shown me."[139] The American, evidently just as moved, responded the next day: "I deeply appreciate your kindly personal expressions. Someday I hope your country will realize, as I do, your endeavors in her behalf."[140] House's hope proved to be false; with the exception of a few very recent publications, the Ambassador's efforts to keep America neutral have not been very highly regarded by German authors.[141] It remained for foreign political writers and historians, even his diplomatic adversaries, to arrive at a positive appraisal of his personal engagement.[142]

While in Germany the final challenge to America, whose formal neutrality had been looked upon with contempt anyway, was generally cheered,[143] Wilson continued his search for a way out of the impasse. Through neutral Swiss channels and approaches to Germany's ally, Austria-Hungary, he undertook final efforts to avoid war. Surprisingly, his endeavors amounted to what many a German politician and the military had often hoped for, namely, the chance of using unrestricted submarine warfare without involving the United States in the war. Only if he were to succeed in modifying the German measures in such a way as to avoid the open conflict with Germany could Wilson hope to continue his activities as mediator. With the consent of the British, who preferred negotiations with Austria-Hungary to those with Germany, Wilson and House, in agreement with Lansing, decided to let Adam Count Tarnowski von Tarnow, Dumba's successor, stay in the country for the time being and not to break off relations with Vienna.[144] When Lansing told the Austrian on February 3 that Washington perhaps might be willing not to break off relations with his government, Tarnowski immediately cabled to Vienna. The reply from Ottokar Count Czernin, the Austro-Hungarian Foreign Minister, on February 5, which incidentally was not discussed with Berlin,[145] was sufficiently diplomatic to raise new hopes in Washington. The Austrians at this stage seem to have understood much better than Berlin how to negotiate with the Americans. They would "be pleased," they wrote, "if the diplomatic relations between the United States and ourselves were maintained." There was talk of a "peace without victory," and the note expressed the Austrian hope that Wilson would "continue the work for peace which he had begun impartially and objectively."[146]

Wilson immediately turned to Lloyd George to persuade Britain to withdraw the Anglo-French threat of January 10 to partition Austria-Hungary. If it were possible to maintain the contact with Vienna, Wilson told the British, he still hoped to be in a position to bring about a peace on the basis of his speech of January 22.[147] But Lloyd George was not prepared to commit himself to any assurances to Austria-Hungary. Judging from the evidence in the German documents, however, it appears doubtful whether London's yielding at this time would have had even the slightest effect on German policy toward Washington. Almost as if to document the German position once again for the historical record, Zimmermann on February 11 unmistakably instructed Botho Count von Wedel, the German Ambassador in Vienna: "I find it important to state and ask you to emphasize to Count Czernin that for us Wilson's role as mediator is played out. Should the President approach us again with such an offer, we would firmly refuse it."[148]

The less than realistic attempt to change the course of events at the last moment through the agency of Austria was not the only peace move undertaken by Washington even after the formal rupture of diplomatic relations with Germany.[149] While Bernstorff's collaboration in the American-Austrian exchange of views cannot be documented, we have evidence that even after February 3 he used his connections in Washington and against all odds continued to work for a negotiated peace. Disguised as a report by the Washington correspondent of the *Kölnische Zeitung*, Georg Barthelme, he sent to Germany a long document by way of the Navy Department as well as through the Swiss representative in Washington.[150] On February 8, Zimmermann received confirmation from the German legation in Bern that Bernstorff indeed had not yet given up: "Urgent! Swiss Government today received following telegram from Washington: 'In agreement with Count Bernstorff for Germany's Government. Here strong urge and active desire to avoid war, from this arose Barthelme's radio wire of yesterday *Kölnische Zeitung*. In case in Berlin inclination to conference with Union on blockade, I would be prepared to pursue matter further here, believe to delay war this way for the time being. No. 79. Minister Ritter.' Romberg."[151] Zimmermann immediately got in contact with General Headquarters and proposed saying to Washington: "Germany now as ever is prepared to negotiate with America, provided that the commercial blockade against our enemies is not thereby interrupted."[152] The reaction from Pless, however, shows that even this noncommittal offer went too far for the Emperor. He demanded that diplomatic relations between Germany and America be restored before resuming negotiations. The Emperor wanted "satisfaction for the affront" of Wilson's break of relations.[153] Zimmermann sent his first draft with the addendum that, before beginning negotiations, diplomatic relations would have to be restored and only the unhindered transport of American passengers, not goods, could be negotiated.[154] Wilson took the only path open to him and demanded the retraction of the declaration of unrestricted submarine warfare of January 31.[155]

On February 10, just a few days before he departed from the United States, Bernstorff once more involved himself personally. Probably through the Swiss envoy, he wired to Berlin:[156] "As there has been no incident since February 1 in which Americans were involved, mood for war is lessened, the country does not want war. If an incident occurs, Wilson will at first only take steps to protect American ships and wait to see what we do; actual war might be delayed still for a long time if we do not proceed against the United States of America itself. Negotiations can, if necessary, still be carried out through Austrian Embassy or Swiss envoy; Wilson will in no case enter an alliance with our enemies." The Emperor's notes in the margins of Bernstorff's telegram speak for themselves. Probably angered anyway by what appeared to be a yielding of the Austrians to the American President, he underlined the words "negotiations" and "Austrian" in the last sentence of the cable and jotted in the margin: "no! definitely not!"[157]

How little Wilhelm II was concerned about an understanding with the United States can be seen from his reaction to an admittedly rather frantic Austrian attempt in March to calm tensions between Washington and Berlin. After the Austrians had, perhaps with a heavy heart, but nevertheless with certainty, turned down an American offer for a separate peace, they evidently still believed they could exert a moderating influence on Germany. Czernin claimed that the American Ambassador, Frederic Courtland Penfield, had suggested to him that "the next American ships travelling to Britain could be 'overlooked' and not torpedoed." Wilson needed this news, he argued, to win public opinion over to his side.[158] Admiral Henning von Holtzendorff, whom the Foreign Office asked for his opinion on the Austrian message, judged that it "would mean ... directly counteracting the aims and the success of the U-boat war, if by admitting American shipments during the present decisive phase we put holes into the trade blockade. As for the formal impudence . . . to officially continue negotiations so to speak incognito after breaking off diplomatic relations, to that the diplomatic advisors of Your Majesty will have to respond."[159] The Emperor himself attended to this matter: "*Negotiations* with America are *finished* now once and for all! If Wilson wants war, then he shall bring it about, and then have it!"[160]

In order to grasp the full extent of the German challenge to the United States in the spring of 1917, it is necessary to cast a brief glance at the most unusual product of Berlin's American policy, the so-called Zimmermann telegram.[161] Not only had Germany frightened the American public by large-scale intelligence service operations and through the submarine war frustrated the earnest wish of the American head of state to bring the war to an end by his peace mediation, but Berlin also did not shy away from an offer to Mexico of an alliance aimed against the United States. As has been indicated earlier in this study, Germany had found itself in opposition to the United States in its Mexican policy since the fall of the Caudillo, Porfirio Díaz. When Berlin's efforts to encourage the counterrevolution and to bring General Victoriano Huerta back to the helm had been decidedly frustrated by American vigilance, the Germans had turned their attention to mobilizing one or the other of the rival political movements against Mexico's northern neighbor. Especially as long as Washington was neutral, but even after the United States had declared war on Germany, Berlin never gave up the unrealistic hope of tying down American armed forces in a military conflict with Mexico and thereby simultaneously checking American arms shipments to Europe. After January 9, 1917, when unrestricted submarine warfare was decided on and, as a consequence, America's entry into the war had to be reckoned with seriously, a large scale military engagement of the United States in Mexico became more desirable to the Germans than ever.[162] The offer to Mexico of an alliance indeed had become a matter of such urgency that the message was not taken to Mexico by a slow but relatively safe submarine as originally planned. Not without reason the authorities in Berlin were worried that in twenty days—the approximate time a submarine would take to complete the voyage— the break with the United States already might be a fait accompli.[163] The German records suggest that the idea originated with Arthur von Kemnitz, an official in the Foreign Office. While among his colleagues he appears to have encountered general opposition to his proposal, he received important backing from Arthur Zimmermann, whose policy toward the United States was characterized by an almost incredible underestimation of American strength.[164] Since only shortly before, the Emperor himself had spoken of the necessity of using Mexico for Germany's purposes in case of war with America, the impression in the Foreign Office may well have been that Wilhelm II would favor the absurd scheme.[165]

On January 16, 1917, Zimmermann dispatched the offer of an alliance as telegram no. 158 for Bernstorff, attached to telegram no. 157 (Bethmann Hollweg's message concerning the unrestricted submarine war) to the American embassy in Berlin for transmission to Washington. When Gerard inquired about the content of the cable, Adolf Count von Montgelas told him that it was a matter of personal information for Count Bernstorff.[166] Bernstorff was instructed to relay "by a safe route" the following text to Heinrich von Eckardt, the German Minister in Mexico:

> Telegram No. 1. Absolutely confidential. To be personally deciphered. It is our purpose on the 1st of February to commence the unrestricted U-boat war. The attempt will be made to keep America neutral in spite of it all. In case we should not be successful in this, we propose Mexico an alliance upon the following terms: Joint conduct of the war. Joint conclusion of peace. Ample financial support and an agreement on our part that Mexico shall gain back by conquest the territory lost by her at a prior period in Texas, New Mexico, and Arizona. Arrangement as to details is entrusted to Your Excellency. Your Excellency will make the above known to the President [Carranza] in strict confidence at the moment the war breaks out with the United States, and you will add the suggestion that Japan be requested to take part at once and that he simultaneously mediate between ourselves and Japan. Please inform the President that the unrestricted use of our U-boats now offers the prospect of forcing England to sue for peace in the course of a few months. Confirm receipt. Zimmermann.[167]

Bernstorff received this message by way of the State Department, took note of it, put his name under it and, as ordered, sent it on to the German legation in Mexico City as telegram no. 130. To be absolutely certain that the instructions would be in Eckardt's hands by January 31, the Foreign Office also sent the message through normal wireless channels as well as via Stockholm and Buenos

Aires.[168] When, on February 3, the United States broke off relations with Germany, the Foreign Office in Berlin was so taken aback[169] that Zimmermann decided to advance the date of an offer of alliance to Mexico. Consequently, Eckardt was instructed to "submit the proposal of alliance to the President already now." Even the possibility that Carranza might not be taken in by the venture had been taken into consideration by the Foreign Office: "Should President refuse for fear of later American retaliation, you are empowered to offer defensive alliance after conclusion of peace, provided that Mexico succeeds in drawing Japan into Alliance."[170]

Like countless other German telegrams between Berlin, Washington, and Mexico, all versions of the Zimmermann note were intercepted by William Reginald Hall's British intelligence service and decoded with the help of various German code books that had fallen into the hands of the Allies.[171] On February 24, the British passed the text of the Zimmermann telegram to Ambassador Page; on March 1, Wilson released the document to the American press. If there had still been any doubts in Washington about the intentions of the German Empire, the Zimmermann telegram swept them away once and for all. Berlin had succeeded in rousing from their apathy even those Americans in the midwestern and western states, who until then had shown little interest in European events.[172] What could only be perceived as German deceit seemed unmasked; Wilson's last hopes for a peaceful reconciliation by mediation were quickly vanishing.[173]

A few weeks later, after German submarines had also sunk American ships, the patience of the United States was exhausted. On March 20, Theodore Roosevelt took it upon himself to call the nation to war: "She [Germany] has sunk our ships. . . . She has asked Mexico and Japan to join with her in dismembering our country. . . . There is no question about 'going to war.' Germany is already at war with us. Let us face the accomplished fact . . . and in our turn wage war on Germany with all our energy and courage."[174] The old Roughrider no longer spoke only for himself and relatively limited interested groups that had criticized Wilson's policy of neutrality almost from the beginning of the war. Once again Theodore Roosevelt represented the nation whose fate he had himself once guided with much different maxims than Wilson, who leaned toward humane pacifism. The chorus of those calling for self-assertion and countermeasures became increasingly louder, and, even from within the cabinet, demands for a declaration of war were heard. During a candid conversation in the White House on March 19 with Frank Cobb, the editor of the *New York World,* Wilson expressed what had worried him the most but now could no longer be averted: "To fight you must be brutal and ruthless, and the spirit of ruthless brutality will enter into the very fibre of our national life."[175] On April 2, Wilson called his country to battle: "We are accepting this challenge of hostile purpose."[176] On April 6, he signed the declaration of war.

The man who had worked harder than any other German official to prevent this course of events and who had even taken a stand against his government in pursuing his elusive objectives had left the United States on February 14.[177] His departure was hardly that of a hated representative from a hostile power.[178] A large crowd of journalists and a number of curious onlookers had turned out on the docks in spite of the early hour. John J. Henry, the United States Secret Service operative in charge of seven agents, who had been ordered to the Hoboken pier to protect the Ambassador, reported that Count Bernstorff and his party arrived at 6:30 and had boarded by 8:15 A.M.[179] When the Danish liner *Frederik VIII* pulled away from the pier at 4:30 in the afternoon, the steam whistles of many other boats sounded a bon voyage. The daily press published friendly farewell articles and many printed the Ambassador's final press release: "When I now leave the United States after a stay of eight years, I wish to express my heartfelt gratitude to my many personal friends for the great friendliness and cordial hospitality which they have shown me. My heart is full of gratitude to those whose personal friendship never wavered during the trying war years. . . . I hope that war be avoided and the former friendly relations between the United States and Germany be restored soon."[180] These were not empty words. The Ambassador rushed back to Germany, where, now that he had become useless in Washington, he wanted to appeal to the Emperor personally. Bernstorff's illusions still had not been entirely destroyed. During his long absence from Berlin he had lost touch with the opinions prevailing in Germany, and he seems not yet to have been fully aware how his country was moving almost unalterably toward disaster. The British must have suspected that the Ambassador still hoped for a final interpellation from the Emperor. Unusual examinations, uncustomary personal searches, and a mixed bag of chicanery were used by British authorities to detain the *Frederik VIII* for twelve days in the port of

Halifax.[181] By these delaying tactics, the Allies in fact were able to incapacitate Bernstorff for nearly a month; his ship did not arrive in Christiania (Oslo) until March 12.[182] But Germany's enemies could have spared themselves the trouble; Berlin showed no inclination to allow the Ambassador to speak freely, not to mention permitting him to intervene through consultations at the highest level.

As the German government was clearly displeased with what was considered an all too friendly departure of the Ambassador from New York, Berlin now took preventive measures to assure at least a proper arrival in Europe. The result was a so-called interview, the text of which had been worked up in advance by the Foreign Office and which the Ambassador would give the journalists who had rushed to be present at his arrival.[183] The text of the interview is of considerable historical interest, precisely because it does not reflect the Ambassador's well-known views, but rather shows the viewpoint that the German government wanted to present to the German people concerning its policy toward the United States. As might be expected, Bernstorff was not the man to be used in this manner. Diplomatic experience and tact evidently caused him to cut some of the most inflammatory statements against the United States from the prescribed text of the interview.[184]

After a brief stay of one day with his cousin, Ulrich Count von Brockdorff-Rantzau, the German Minister in Copenhagen,[185] Bernstorff hurried to Berlin, where he had a meeting with the Imperial Chancellor the day after his arrival. The sources concerning this encounter unfortunately offer very limited information.[186] Bernstorff, who even later always defended Bethmann Hollweg and apparently continued to believe that the Chancellor had sincerely supported his policy toward the United States, reports that they talked about the submarine war and the American mediation efforts. According to Bernstorff, Bethmann Hollweg declared that he had had to agree to the submarine war "because the German people would not have understood it if he had concluded a worthless peace [faulen Frieden] without trying to bring about a favorable solution by using the final and most drastic weapon, which the people had confidence in." An offer of mediation by Wilson, the Chancellor reportedly said, would not have been accepted by anyone in the Reichstag except the Social Democrats. Bernstorff's question why the Chancellor had wanted the American President to mediate if he knew he could not obtain consent from the Reichstag apparently remained unanswered. As for the question whether Bernstorff made a renewed attempt to move the weak and vacillating Chancellor to change Germany's policy toward the United States—that is, to give up unrestricted submarine warfare—and to consider another appeal to Wilson, the available records are so unsatisfactory that a conclusive answer seems impossible.[187]

In the course of the following weeks the Ambassador tried his best to obtain an audience with the Emperor.[188] But Wilhelm II was, as Bethmann Hollweg put it, "very ill-disposed toward Count Bernstorff" and had not the slightest desire to listen to the—in his opinion—incompetent Ambassador[189] who had striven for a negotiated settlement to be obtained through the mediation of the American President and who, what is more, on the political front in Berlin was considered one of the important figures among the Democrats. Constant suspicions cast about more or less publicly in connection with the disclosure of the Zimmermann telegram most likely also had an influence on the Emperor. On March 3, 1917, even before Count Bernstorff arrived back in Europe, Zimmermann made certain that the rumors would gain new currency: "I can only imagine . . . that a crime of some kind was committed. The British and the Americans work with colossal financial amounts; possibly they succeeded in bribing one of our Washington officials and, in this way, [gaining] possession of this telegram." Two days later Zimmermann again fed the rumormongers of the capital by proclaiming: "How the indiscretion was committed, I can today still not say. I cannot imagine that the Imperial Ambassador, as I read in a newspaper story yesterday, gave the instruction to his valet in order that he might deliver it to Mexico. I cannot believe that Count Bernstorff has acted so carelessly."[190] Only when members of the Reichstag began to become openly inquisitive about the reasons why Bernstorff was not received by the Emperor did an invitation emanate from the crown, though not until two months after the Ambassador's arrival in Europe, and at a point when it was no longer possible to change the course of events.[191] Washington had already declared war.

Apparently through the intercession of Major General Max Hoffmann, Lieutenant Colonel Hans von Haeften, and Heinrich Albert, a meeting between Bernstorff and the Supreme Command also came about at General Headquarters on the same day, May 4, 1917.[192] An unusual exchange it was indeed at the encounter of

Count Bernstorff and General Erich Ludendorff. Ludendorff: "Well, so you wanted to make peace in America! You probably thought we were at the end?" Bernstorff: "No, I did not believe we were at the end, but I wanted to make peace before we would be at the end." Ludendorff: "Yes, but we did not want to, and besides, with submarine warfare we will now end the matter in three months."[193]

NOTES

ABBREVIATIONS

AA	Auswärtiges Amt (here referring to Politisches Archiv, Auswärtiges Amt, Bonn)
BA	Bundesarchiv, Koblenz
BAL	*Brewing and Liquor Interests and German and Bolshevik Propaganda*
Bd.	(English: volume) Used only in footnotes referring to German archival sources
B.I.	Bureau of Investigation
DMCC	*Reports of International Arbitral Awards*. Vol. 8, *Decisions of the Mixed Claims Commission*
DRSFM	*Documents Relative to the Sinn Fein Movement*
FO	Foreign Office (here referring to document series at British Public Record Office)
FRUS	*Papers Relating to the Foreign Relations of the United States*
G.A.	Gehorsamste Aufzeichnung
GSA	Geheimes Staatsarchiv, Munich
HAPAG	Hamburg-Amerika Linie (here referring to the archival material of this Hamburg shipping firm)
IMA	*Investigation of Mexican Affairs. Preliminary Report and Hearings of the Committee on Foreign Relations*
IPH	Charles Seymour, ed., *The Intimate Papers of Colonel House*
LAPP	André Scherer and Jacques Grunewald, eds., *L'Allemagne et les Problèmes de la Paix Pendant la Première Guerre Mondiale*
LC	Library of Congress, Washington, D.C.
M.I.D.	Military Intelligence Division
NA	National Archives, Washington, D.C.
NYPL	New York Public Library
OHL	Oberste Heeresleitung
PRO	Public Record Office, London
RG	Record Group
Suppl.	Supplement

UA	Verfassunggebende deutsche Nationalversammlung. 15. Ausschuss. 2. Unterausschuss. Stenographische Berichte über die öffentlichen Verhandlungen des Untersuchungsausschusses
WK	Weltkrieg (documentary series of the Imperial German Foreign Office)
YHC	The Diaries and Papers of Edward M. House (Yale House Collection)

INTRODUCTION

1. Karl E. Birnbaum, *Peace Moves and U-Boat Warfare* (Stockholm, 1958), remains one of the best studies. Ernest R. May's *The World War and American Isolation 1914–1917* (Cambridge, Mass., 1959) is still an impressive overall study, particularly because it covers American relations with both Great Britain and Imperial Germany. It must be remembered though that May, for the German side, solely relies on published sources and on those documents that were available on microfilm. He has not seen the vast amount of unfilmed and unpublished German material. Possibly for this reason, he places much weight on Bernstorff's early memoirs *Deutschland und Amerika* (Berlin, 1920), written immediately after the war and unreliable on many important issues.

2. Fritz Fischer, *Griff nach der Weltmacht* (Düsseldorf, 1961), has been translated into English as *Germany's Aims in the First World War*. The British edition contains an introduction by James Joll (London: Chatto & Windus, 1967), while the American edition contains introductions by Hajo Holborn and James Joll (New York: W. W. Norton & Co., 1967). Both editions are translations of the revised complete German edition of 1964.

3. Gerhard Ritter, *Staatskunst und Kriegshandwerk* (Munich, 1965, 1964, 1968); see my comments in this study.

4. Henry Rollet, review of *Washington-Berlin 1908/1917*, in *Revue d'Histoire Diplomatique* 89 (January–June 1975), pp. 177–79.

5. Critics of Fritz Fischer and some of his students have argued that a relevant appraisal of the events is not possible because the archival material on the Allied side is not as fully available as the German sources. While there is much that remains to be done to assure easier access to archives in several countries, the present study is concerned above all with German-American relations, materials for which abound. Where British interests were concerned, the needed archival sources were also readily available.

6. Cf. Hans E. Riesser, *Haben die deutschen Diplomaten versagt?* (Bonn, 1959), p. 23: "The documents further have shown that neither Bethmann

Hollweg nor Hitler, neither Jagow nor Ribbentrop have listened to the warning reports of the ambassadors."

7. Walter Schmid-Bürckert, "Graf Johann-Heinrich von Bernstorff als deutscher Botschafter in Washington 1908–1917," a 1947 dissertation at Tübingen University, was evidently written without consulting the records, and the author did not interview the numerous contemporaries of Bernstorff still surviving. Erich-Wolfgang Hubrich, "Neutralität und Intervention der Vereinigten Staaten von Amerika 1914–1917," a Kiel University dissertation in 1956, is also based almost entirely on secondary sources. Hans-Jürgen Schwepcke, "U-Boot-Krieg und Friedenspolitik," a Heidelberg University dissertation in 1952, argues that the United States entered the war for economic reasons, emphasizes Bethmann Hollweg's peace endeavors, and portrays Bernstorff as a victim of deceit by Wilson and House. This interpretation of Bernstorff's efforts is also found in Hans Kramer, *Die Grossmächte und die Weltpolitik 1789 bis 1945* (Innsbruck, 1952), p. 555. By comparison, Arnold Meine, *Wilsons Diplomatie in der Friedensfrage 1914–1917* (Stuttgart, 1938), despite a lack of documentation, offers a rather well-rounded picture. The first specialized work on Bernstorff based on records of the German Foreign Office was Sister Ethel Mary Tinnemann's 1960 dissertation "Count Johann von Bernstorff and German-American Relations, 1908–1917." Unfortunately, Tinnemann was limited to the use of microfilms of the records of the German Foreign Office and thus in some cases could not see important documents.

8. Walter LaFeber, *The New Empire* (Ithaca, N.Y., 1968), pp. 323–25.

9. Alfred T. Mahan, *The Influence of Sea Power upon History, 1660–1783* (London, 1965).

10. Indeed, Bernstorff wrote the second volume of memoirs on the basis of his papers and correspondence. Yet, it must be remembered that a large number of persons who had shared his private and public life were still living in National Socialist Germany, and one may conclude that for this reason many of his papers were only used partially. Having been mentioned by Bernstorff in a critical context at that time could easily have ruined a career in Germany or caused other substantial personal damage. It is generally presumed that Countess Bernstorff, fearing a German invasion of Switzerland, destroyed all papers in Geneva before she left for the United States. Count Bernstorff's daughter, Princess zu Loewenstein Wertheim Rosenberg, also informed this author accordingly.

11. Albrecht Count von Bernstorff (1809–73) was Prussian Foreign Minister from 1861 to 1862. He resigned from office when the Prussian government tried to push through the Armed Forces Reform without budget law. Cf. Kurt Freiherr von Stutterheim, *Die Majestät des Gewissens* (Hamburg, 1962), pp. 31–32. He served in London from 1854 to 1861 and again from 1862 until his death in 1873. Cf. Heinz G. Sasse, *100 Jahre Botschaft in London* (Bonn, 1963), pp. 8–11.

12. Georg Ahrens, "Botschafter Graf Bernstorff," *Frankfurter Rundschau*, October 28, 1949, p. 2: "Democracy of the British type ... was something he understood well from his early youth and a personal matter close to his heart."

13. Née Anna Baroness von Koenneritz (1821–93).

14. Album, III. Teil, p. 925, Archiv der Lauenburgischen Gelehrtenschule.

15. Johann Heinrich Graf von Bernstorff, *Erinnerungen und Briefe* (Zürich, 1936), pp. 14–15.

16. Unpublished memoirs of Erika von Watzdorf (privately held), pp. 141–42. Countess Bernstorff was born in New York in 1867 and died in Washington in 1943. The family had two children: Luise Alexandra, born 1888 in Berlin, and Christian Günther, born 1891 in Berlin. In 1911 Alexandra married Raimund Count von Pourtalès, who died as a young man. In a second marriage in 1917, she became the wife of Johannes Prince zu Loewenstein Wertheim Rosenberg. Bernstorff, who was a freethinker, never fully accepted his daughter's conversion to Catholicism in 1919. Princess zu Loewenstein passed away in Switzerland recently. I owe her much gratitude for countless insights into the private life of her father. Günther Count von Bernstorff emigrated to South America and died there several years ago. Family connections between him and his parents had been severed for many years.

17. Bernstorff, *Erinnerungen und Briefe*, pp. 16–19.

18. Ibid., pp. 22–24. On Lichnowsky see now Harry F. Young, *Prince Lichnowsky and the Great War* (Athens, 1977).

19. Bernstorff, *Erinnerungen und Briefe*, p. 26. Pallavicini was later Austro-Hungarian Ambassador in Constantinople when Bernstorff served there again from 1917 to 1918.

20. Ibid., pp. 28–35. Cf. Anton Graf von Monts to Bernhard Fürst von Bülow, January 7, 1898, BA, Bülow Nachlass.

21. Bernstorff to Lujo Brentano, June 3, 1903, BA, Brentano Nachlass.

22. Unpublished memoirs of Erika von Watzdorf, p. 151.

23. Bernstorff, *Erinnerungen und Briefe*, p. 48. Cf. Otto Hammann to Bernstorff, February 24, 1905, ibid., pp. 60–61.

24. Cf. Anton Count von Monts to Bernhard Fürst von Bülow, Highly Confidential, October 31, 1905, AA, England 78, Bd. 38. Monts reports that an American diplomat had told him "that in the person of *Count Bernstorff in London we had a very popular and at the same time highly respected diplomat. The Foreign Office especially had full confidence in him.*" Emphasis in the text represents underlining by the Emperor, who noted in the margin of the document: "correct! in other words *not* the Ambassador! confirms my estimation."

25. Cf. Hammann's appraisal: "Ambassador Count Bernstorff did his best to establish good contacts with respected journalists and to work for a rapprochement with other influential personalities"; Otto Hammann, *Zur*

Vorgeschichte des Weltkrieges (Berlin, 1918), pp. 113–14. One of Bernstorff's valuable contacts in London appears to have been Lucien Wolf with whom he had frequent meetings, exchanged letters, and traded opinions on European politics. When Bernstorff became involved in anti-British propaganda in Washington in 1914, Lucien Wolf was greatly disappointed and saw Bernstorff's earlier professions of British-German common interests as lies and double dealing. Wolf intended to publish Bernstorff's earlier letters and corresponded about this with Sir Eric Barrington and Sir William Tyrrell, Sir Edward Grey's influential private secretary, David Movshowitch Collection, YIVO Institute for Jewish Research. Cf. Paul M. Kennedy, *The Rise of the Anglo-German Antagonism, 1860–1914* (London, 1980), p. 267.

26. Dr. G. Köpke to Georg Ahrens, November 9, 1949, Papers of Georg Ahrens (privately held); unpublished memoirs of Erika von Watzdorf, pp. 165–66.

27. Concerning the first meeting of Bernstorff with Bülow in Petersburg, see Bernstorff, *Erinnerungen und Briefe*, pp. 29–30.

28. Ibid., p. 69.

29. Unpublished memoirs of Erika von Watzdorf, p. 225.

30. Originally there had also been talk about his being sent to Tokyo; ibid., p. 234.

31. Bogdan Count Hutten-Czapski to Bernstorff, November 21, 1908, quoted in Bernstorff, *Erinnerungen und Briefe*, p. 71.

32. Gordon A. Craig, *From Bismarck to Adenauer: Aspects of German Statecraft* (Baltimore, 1958), p. 103.

33. Friedrich von Holstein to Bernhard Fürst von Bülow, October 28, and November 7, 1908, cited in Helmuth Rogge, *Holstein und Harden* (Munich, 1959), pp. 360, 378.

34. Cf. opinion of Friedrich W. von Prittwitz und Gaffron, *Deutschland und die Vereinigten Staaten seit dem Weltkrieg* (Leipzig, 1934), pp. 30–31.

35. Cf. Rudolf Vierhaus, ed., *Das Tagebuch der Baronin Spitzemberg* (Göttingen, 1963), pp. 543, 548; also Albert Ballin to Professor Dr. Ernst Francke, January 8, 1913, in Peter F. Stubmann, *Ballin* (Berlin, 1926), p. 140.

36. Cf. Cecil A. Spring Rice to the British Foreign Office, May 23, 1917, PRO, FO 371, 44171: "Confidential information has been received from American Pressmen who had gone to Germany with Bernstorf [sic].... Small personal group surrounding the Emperor were reactionary. Chancellor, who was abused by all parties, had lost all power while Bernstorf [sic], Harden and Ballin were leaders of the extreme democratic group. Reactionaries had succeeded for a long time in preventing Bernstorf [sic] seeing the Emperor by making him blameable for publication of Mexican note." Max M. Warburg, *Aus meinen Aufzeichnungen* (New York, 1952), p. 55. *Die Ursachen des deutschen Zusammenbruchs im Jahre 1918*, Series 4 (Berlin, 1925–29), 1:110. Minutes of the 150th session of the Ausschuss für den Haushalt, May 1, 1917, AA, Vereinigte Staaten von Amerika 16, Bd. 52.

37. Cf. Karl Boy-Ed (Chief of the Press Section of the Admiralty) to Chief of the Admiralty Staff, October 10, 1917, Highly Confidential, in Wilhelm Deist, ed., *Militär und Innenpolitik im Weltkrieg 1914–1918* (Düsseldorf, 1970), 1:1075–76: "In view of the chancellor crisis that I think undoubtedly exists, I would not wish to leave unmentioned that as new candidates for the post of Imperial Chancellor Max Prince von Baden(!) [*sic*], Prince von Bülow, Count von Bernstorff, and from the side of the Conservatives again General von Gallwitz are being talked about.... Of Count Bernstorff, it is claimed that during his stay in Berlin he has made intensive contacts with influential Members of Parliament and representatives of the press and thereby retroactively has emphasized his democratic views. While acknowledging Bernstorff's many good qualities I personally think him inadequate for the work-intensive, versatile, and responsible post of an Imperial Chancellor. He is among other things too superficial and lacks adroitness in public speaking. The navy should be the last to desire him, since he belongs to those who see the cause of this world war in the existence of the German fleet." Bethmann Hollweg himself, as well as Albert Ballin from the Hamburg-American Line and Rudolf von Valentini, spoke in favor of Bernstorff as a candidate for the post of Chancellor, but the Emperor and his military leaders were opposed to the liberal diplomat. Lamar Cecil, *Albert Ballin* (Princeton, 1967), p. 321.

38. Bernstorff was also considered as successor for his enemy, Arthur Zimmermann. The Berlin *Vossische Zeitung*, July 10, 1917, however, thought an appointment as Secretary of the Foreign Office under Chancellor Bethmann Hollweg "totally impossible" because Bernstorff would "thereby be forced to cover the foreign policy pursued in the past toward the United States under the responsibility of Mr. von Bethmann." Following the resignation of Bethmann Hollweg, the influential newspaper again proposed Bernstorff's candidature. *Vossische Zeitung*, July 14, 1917, p. 1. According to British sources, Bernstorff declined to succeed his cousin in Copenhagen. Sir W. Townley, The Hague, to Foreign Office, July 18, 1917, PRO, FO 371, 2941.

39. The British heard that Richard von Kühlmann, Foreign Secretary from August 1917 to July 1918, had sent him to Constantinople to station the political rival as far away as possible. Sir H. Rumbold, Bern, to Foreign Office, September 7, 1917, PRO, FO 371, 2941.

40. K. B. Militärbevollmächtigter to Bavarian Minister of War, October 8, 1918, Kriegsarchiv Munich, MKr 1832. Similar outgrowths of military irresponsibility were opposed by Bernstorff in Constantinople. The Chief of the Turkish fleet, the German Admiral Hubert von Rebeur-Paschwitz, "in all seriousness and emphatically made the proposal" to destroy the Baghdad Railway tunnel in the Taurus and to "flatten" a palace of the Sultan with the board canons of the *Goeben*. Unpublished memoirs of a German

Diplomat in Constantinople (privately held) who was present at this meeting.

41. As early as July 1918, friends of the Ambassador speculated that he would be called back to Berlin. Marie Rose von Watzdorf, unpublished letters from Constantinople (privately held), p. 32. Bernstorff regretted the change in the Foreign Office "very much for personal reasons." Bernstorff to Georg Ahrens, July 13, 1918, Papers of Georg Ahrens; Bernstorff, *Erinnerungen und Briefe*, p. 174. Cf. K. B. Militärbevollmächtigter to Bavarian Minister of War, September 30, 1918, Kriegsarchiv Munich, Mkr 1832.

42. Bernstorff, *Erinnerungen und Briefe*, pp. 174-77.

43. Unpublished memoirs of a German Diplomat in Constantinople.

44. Cf. Bernstorff, *Erinnerungen und Briefe*, pp. 175-76.

45. Ibid., pp. 176-77. It is interesting to speculate how Bernstorff himself would have acted had he been Chancellor instead of Max Prince von Baden. Bernstorff had been proposed as Chancellor as early as September 29, 1918, in an article by Emil Ludwig in the *Neue Zürcher Zeitung* entitled "Wer führt ein neues Deutschland?" Gustav A. Lang, *Kampfplatz der Meinungen* (Zürich, 1968), p. 86.

46. Bernstorff, *Erinnerungen und Briefe*, pp. 177-79.

47. Bernstorff: "I am willing to be available. What do you want with such a large apparatus in Versailles? You can achieve nothing there. Not in the least. I simply go with one adviser (Geheimrat)." Quoted in Warburg, *Aus meinen Aufzeichnungen*, p. 71; Papers of Max M. Warburg (privately held), 141, Vorbereitung Versailles, Korrespondenz etc. Oct., Nov. 1918-Ende 1918.

48. Cf. Bernstorff to Maximilian Harden, June 26, 1919, BA, Harden Nachlass. Bernstorff: "Now I shall recuperate until the next crisis, and I take comfort in the thought that Bismarck once voiced the desire to see a German who turned down a minister's post."

49. Cf. Klaus Schwabe, "Die Vereinigten Staaten, die deutsche Friedenspolitik und das Scheitern eines 'Wilson-Friedens,'" Habilitationsschrift, University of Freiburg, 1969, p. 26. About this commission, cf. Alma Maria Luckau, *The German Delegation at the Paris Peace Conference* (New York, 1941), and Leo Haupts, *Deutsche Friedenspolitik 1918-19* (Düsseldorf, 1976).

50. Cf. various passages in Erich Brandenburg's manuscript, AA, Brockdorff-Rantzau Nachlass. M. J. Bonn, *So macht man Geschichte* (Munich, 1953), pp. 223-24. Harry Graf Kessler, *Tagebücher 1918-1937*, ed. Wolfgang Pfeiffer-Belli (Frankfurt, 1961), p. 154; Warburg, *Aus meinen Aufzeichnungen*, p. 75.

51. *Berliner Tageblatt*, July 21, 1919, p. 2.

52. Cf. Ch. Appuhn, "L'Ambassade du Comte Bernstorff à Washington," *Revue d'Histoire de la Guerre Mondiale* 3 (October 1925): 297.

53. Otto Baumgarten, *Meine Lebensgeschichte* (Tübingen, 1929), p. 501; Bernstorff, *Erinnerungen und Briefe*, pp. 198–99.

54. A letter from Bernstorff to Maximilian Harden, July 5, 1919, BA, Harden Nachlass, gives us an interesting insight into the political views of Bernstorff: "I am not blind to the weakness of the Democratic Party. I believe, however, that it is the order of the day to reform our party, not to leave it if something does not go according to one's wishes. We need a large middle-class [*bürgerliche*] party as well as a conservative and a socialist party. As it is, according to all my views, I belong to the former. I am not suited to be a November-socialist; I would degrade myself as an opportunist there. I do not believe in socialism. What has made England great? The free initiative of the individual. What has destroyed us? The opportunism that bowed to every authority. *Social* [*sic*] the Democratic Party must be and become, but to put the authoritarian state [*Zwangsstaat*] of the workers in place of the authoritarian state of the military, that I cannot see, not to mention that the other powers will hardly assist us if we do not develop from a socialist to a democratic state."

55. After Brockdorff-Rantzau's demonstrative resignation, the Chancellor Friedrich Ebert had asked Bernstorff to take over the Foreign Ministry. Accepting the offer not only would have meant taking an open stand against his cousin and superior during the Versailles negotiations, but Bernstorff would not even have had the backing of his own party since the DDP was set against the signing of the treaty. Beyond such important considerations, the Allies too exerted pressure on the German government to prevent a further appointment for Bernstorff because he was seen as the chief of German propaganda and sabotage in the United States during the war. Adolf Müller to Foreign Office, Bern, February 11, 1919, AA, Deutschland 135, Nr. 20, Bd. 3; Bernstorff, *Erinnerungen und Briefe*, pp. 192–93; Klaus Epstein, *Matthias Erzberger and the Dilemma of German Democracy* (Princeton, 1959), p. 320. Cf. Sidney Brooks, *America and Germany 1918–1925* (New York, 1925), p. 106.

56. Bernstorff to Georg Ahrens, December 14, 1925, Papers of Georg Ahrens.

57. Rightist radicals and anti-Semitic circles, in some cases the same people who had agitated against him during the war, now organized a smut campaign to ruin his personal reputation. These matters have not been discussed in detail in this study because all the available evidence suggests they had no effect on relations between Washington and Berlin. Cf. among others: the Berlin *Kreuz-Zeitung*, February 17, 1921, newspaper clippings, BA, Akten der Reichskanzlei, Bd. 1019; clipping, *Die Umschau* (publ. in Cincinnati), June 10, 1928, AA, Botschaft Washington, Graf Bernstorff; *Liberty* (February–March, 1931); Folder 33, BA, Nachlass Brönner-Hoepfner. In this context mention should also be made of the telephone conversations of Count Bernstorff in Washington, recorded by U.S. intelligence agents. A

copy of these records is found, among other places, in the Papers of Frank L. Polk, in the Yale University Library, New Haven, Conn.

58. Countess Bernstorff to Georg Ahrens, July 5, 1922, Papers of Georg Ahrens: "What a shame with Rathenau—and now this attack on Harden—Thank God that you don't live in the Grunewald [Berlin] anymore. The area is unsafe. The tactless Brentano thought my husband would soon be next. You can imagine how I suffer from fear when I know that he is in Berlin."

59. Unpublished memoirs of Erika von Watzdorf, p. 474.

60. This verdict appears in a segment entitled "Vom Umsturz zur nationalsozialistischen Revolution 1918–1933" under the subheading "Zur Geschichte der Nachkriegszeit" written by H. Volz in Albert Brackmann and Fritz Hartung, eds., *Jahresberichte für Deutsche Geschichte* 12 (1936): 307.

61. *Historische Zeitschrift* 158 (1938): 381–83. The author was "der Beauftragte des Führers für die Überwachung der gesamten geistigen- und weltanschaulichen Schulung und Erziehung der NSDAP Arbeitsgemeinschaft zur Erforschung der bolschewistischen Weltgefahr" and in the last years of the Second World War "Obereinsatzführer im Stab des Reichsleiters Rosenberg." Photocopy of decision of the Landgericht Frankfurt of September 19, 1973, in the court case Professor Dr. phil. habil. Erwin Hölzle vs. Professor Dr. Georg W. F. Hallgarten. Hölzle's own views on the First World War and its meaning for Germany, as well as on the need for a "new war to finally overcome that dictate [of Versailles]" may be seen among other places in his *Der Osten im Ersten Weltkrieg* (Leipzig, 1944).

62. William L. Langer, "An Honest German Diplomat," *New York Herald Tribune*, October 25, 1936, Sec. X, p. 2. Cf. Charles Seymour, review of Bernstorff, *Memoirs of Count Bernstorff*, *Mississippi Valley Historical Review* 23 (June 1936–March 1937): 589–90: "There are few, if any, statesmen of the war period whose reputations have mounted so impressively in historical retrospect as that of Count Bernstorff." See also Warrington Dawson, ed., *The War Memoirs of William Graves Sharp, American Ambassador to France 1914–1919* (London, 1931), p. 165.

63. Cf. *Neue Zürcher Zeitung*, October 9, 1939, clipping, BA, Presseausschnittsammlung Institut für Weltwirtschaft.

64. Ahrens, "Botschafter Graf Bernstorff."

CHAPTER ONE

1. *Lauenburgische Zeitung*, December 15, 1908. Even abroad, Bernstorff was often considered a friend of the United States who would support good relations between Washington and Berlin. Cf. Maurice F. Egan, *Ten Years near the German Frontier* (New York, 1919), pp. 97–100, for Russian and American opinion. Egan: "In Copenhagen we were deluged with letters

announcing that Count Bernstorff's coming meant a new era; he even excelled Speck in his charm, sympathy, and everything that ought to endear him to us."

2. Roosevelt to Wilhelm II, December 26, 1908, AA, Botschaft Washington, Akten betreffend Präsident und Kabinett, Bd. 6. Cf. Elting E. Morison, ed., *The Letters of Theodore Roosevelt* (Cambridge, Mass., 1951–54) 6: 1441–42.

3. Cf. Alfred Vagts, "Die Juden im amerikanisch-deutschen imperialistischen Konflikt vor 1917," *Amerikastudien/American Studies* 24 (1979), pp. 56–71, who dates the beginning of "the American German estrangement" to the Spanish-American War.

4. Roosevelt to Wilhelm II, January 2, 1909, AA, Botschaft Washington, Akten betreffend Präsident und Kabinett, Bd. 6; Bernstorff to Foreign Office, January 1, 1909, AA, Vereinigte Staaten von Amerika 16, Bd. 24; Bernstorff to Foreign Office, January 1, 1909, AA, Botschaft Washington, Akten betreffend Präsident und Kabinett, Bd. 5. Cf. Joseph B. Bishop, *Theodore Roosevelt and His Time* (London, 1920), 2:284–87.

5. Clipping from the *Chicago Daily Tribune*, December 26, 1908, AA, Vereinigte Staaten von Amerika 16, Bd. 24. Cf. Ethel Mary Tinnemann, "Count Johann von Bernstorff and German-American Relations, 1908–1917" (Ph.D. diss., University of California at Berkeley, 1960), p. 4.

6. Bernstorff to Bülow, February 9, 1909, and Bernstorff to Bülow, February 22, 1909, AA, Vereinigte Staaten von Amerika 16, Bd. 24.

7. Bernstorff to Bülow, March 1, 1909, AA, Botschaft Washington, Akten betreffend Präsident und Kabinett, Bd. 6.

8. Bernstorff, *Deutschland und Amerika* (Berlin, 1920), p. 21.

9. Bernstorff to Bülow, April 15, 1909, AA, Vereinigte Staaten von Amerika 2, secr., Bd. 1. Alfred Vagts, *Deutschland und die Vereinigten Staaten in der Weltpolitik* (London, 1935; New York, 1935), 2:2012.

10. Bernstorff to Bethmann Hollweg, April 4, 1910, AA, Vereinigte Staaten von Amerika 2, secr., Bd. 1. It could not be verified whether J. D. Whelpley is identical with "J. D. Whelpley, Special Agent, G. 2, SOS, AEF" sending reports on Ireland to "Chief Intelligence Officer, Base Section No. 3, SOS, AEF" during September–October 1918. Major A. Campbell Turner, General Staff, to Edward Bell, U.S. Embassy, London, October 5, 1918, NA, RG 59, Dept. of State, Records of the Office of the Counselor.

11. Bernstorff to Foreign Office, June 27, 1909, AA, Botschaft Washington, Akten betreffend England, Bd. 11. The Ambassador asked whether he should publish the article under his own name in case he could not place it in the *Outlook* under the naval authorship.

12. Quoted from the article located in ibid.

13. Gerhart von Schulze-Gaevernitz to Bülow, June 7, 1909; Edward A. Rumely to Schulze-Gaevernitz, May 17, 1909; and Tirpitz to State Secre-

tary in the Foreign Office, May 14, 1909, all in AA, Vereinigte Staaten von Amerika 2, *secr.*, Bd. 1.

14. Bernstorff to Bethmann Hollweg, November 22, 1910, ibid.

15. Bernstorff to Bülow, March 1, 1909, AA, Botschaft Washington, Akten betreffend Präsident und Kabinett, Bd. 6.

16. Bernstorff to Bethmann Hollweg, March 20, 1911, AA, Vereinigte Staaten von Amerika 16, Bd. 29.

17. "Released for the Sunday Papers of November 7th," 1909, AA, Vereinigte Staaten von Amerika 16, Bd. 26.

18. Clippings from the *Houston Daily Post*, November 7, 1909, and the *Philadelphia Public Ledger*, November 8, 1909, in ibid.

19. Clipping from the *Rheinisch-Westfälische Zeitung*, stamped Foreign Office, November 9, 1909, in ibid. Cf. Egan, *Ten Years near the German Frontier* (New York, 1919), p. 98: "And yet I know, at first hand, that the Pan-German hates Bernstorff. If anything approaching to a Liberal Government comes in Germany, Bernstorff will be Minister of Foreign Affairs."

20. Heinrich Class, *Wider den Strom* (Leipzig, 1932), p. 130.

21. Ibid., pp. 146–48.

22. Ibid., p. 148; text of this open letter in AA, Vereinigte Staaten von Amerika 16, Bd. 26, and in *Alldeutsche Blätter* 19(49) (December 4, 1909): 413. The letter in which Bernstorff is accused of having "degraded lightheartedly . . . many thousands of nationally minded Germans in the eyes of foreigners" bore the signatures of Rechtsanwalt H. Class; Superintendent Klingemann; Member of the Reichstag E. von Liebert; Retired Major Freiherr von Stössel; Oberpräzeptor H. Calmbach; A. Fick, M.D.; Professor Dr. Grell; R. Hunsdiecker, M.D.; shipping company owner K. Itzenplitz; Professor P. Langhans; L. Korodi; publisher J. F. Lehmann; Rechtsanwalt Dr. G. Pezoldt; Rechtsanwalt F. Putz; Dr. Reismann-Grone, owner of newspapers; Count E. zu Reventlow, author; Professor Dr. P. Samassa; Privatdozent Dr. F. Solger; Rittergutsbesitzer Schroeder-Poggelow, M.D.; Rechtsanwalt E. Stolte; Professor Dr. L. Viereck; Kaidirektor P. Winter; Major-General von Wrochem; and merchant J. Zeiss. Among other things these signatories believed: " 'Pan-Germans,' as you painted them for the Americans, do not exist in Germany. Rather, they have been invented by foreign anti-German journals in order to agitate against the German Empire and to sow distrust of its political intentions."

23. Cf. Friedrich Meinecke, *Nach der Revolution* (Munich, 1919), p. 57: "However small the actual number of the Pan-Germans remained, they became the strongest manifestation of a spirit which began to spread more and more among the educated classes of the nation."

24. Bernstorff to Bethmann Hollweg, December 28, 1909; clipping from the *New York Times*, December 26, 1909; Bernstorff to Bethmann Hollweg, December 30, 1909; and clipping from the *New York Daily Tribune*, De-

cember 27, 1909, all in AA, Vereinigte Staaten von Amerika 16, Bd. 27.

25. Bernstorff to Bethmann Hollweg, December 30, 1909, ibid.

26. Bernstorff to Lujo Brentano, June 3, 1903, BA, Nachlass Lujo Brentano.

27. "Released for the Sunday Papers of November 7th," 1909, AA, Vereinigte Staaten von Amerika 16, Bd. 26.

28. When General Friedrich von Bernhardi traveled through the United States in the summer of 1912, he attempted to meet with the German Ambassador and the Military Attaché in Washington. Moreover, he wished to attend the Republican convention in Chicago together with Bernstorff. But Bernstorff was "traveling on business," and the Military Attaché, Herwarth von Bittenfeld, was "on vacation." Consul Alfred Geissler in Chicago could "luckily prevent" a scheduled talk by Bernhardi, and tickets for the Republican convention were no longer available through the embassy. Bernstorff could not promise a meeting in Chicago, because he had already made social commitments in Lake Forest. Geissler to Bernstorff, June 12, 1912; Bernhardi to Washington Embassy, June 5, 1912; Bernstorff to Geissler, June 15, 1912; and Washington Embassy to Bernhardi, June 14, 1912; all in AA, Botschaft Washington, Akten betreffend Deutschtum, Bd. 13.

29. Friedrich von Bernhardi, *Deutschland und der nächste Krieg* (Stuttgart, 1912), p. 7. Robert E. Osgood, *Ideals and Self-Interest in America's Foreign Relations* (Chicago, 1953), p. 131, observes that Bernhardi's book was the most widely published propaganda work of this kind. It was translated in 1914 and attracted considerable attention in Britain and the United States. This translation later even appeared in an inexpensive paperback edition. Friedrich Meinecke, *Preussen und Deutschland im 19. und 20. Jahrhundert* (Munich, 1918), pp. 482–83: "The very large edition of the English translation now being spread about in the United States is a dishonest means to turn opinion against us." Gerhard Ritter, *Staatskunst und Kriegshandwerk* (Munich, 1964–68), 2:142–43: "Nothing has been so detrimental to the world-wide reputation of the German General Staff as this publication, which within a few years went through seven editions and was translated . . . into almost every major language." Cf. Walter Görlitz, *Der deutsche Generalstab* (Frankfurt, 1950), pp. 204–5. Fritz Fischer, *Griff nach der Weltmacht* (Düsseldorf, 1961), p. 50.

30. Cf. Meinecke, *Preussen und Deutschland im 19. und 20. Jahrhundert*, p. 482: "He is a well-known military author who has deemed it his duty to inform the German people about its situation and its mission among the world powers and about the dangers which threaten us through England's jealousy and grudge."

31. Cf. among others Heinrich von Treitschke, *Politik* (Leipzig, 1898), 1:39, 72, 75; Adolph Wagner, *Vom Territorialstaat zur Weltmacht* (Berlin, 1900), p. 29; Richard Tannenberg, *Gross-Deutschland* (Leipzig, 1911), pp. 75, 78, 166, 230, 231; and Daniel Fryman [Heinrich Class], *Wenn ich der Kaiser wär'* (Leipzig, 1912), pp. 140–56, 182–83.

32. Although Bülow felt that there was nothing negative about England in the Hale article (Bülow to Metternich, December 11, 1908, AA, Akten des AA im Grossen Hauptquartier 1914–1916, 24, Presse und Journalisten, Bd. 3), the interview did contain such suggestive statements by the Emperor as: "The future belongs to the white race; never fear. . . . It belongs to the Anglo-Teuton, the man who came from northern Europe—where you to whom America belongs came from—the home of the German. It does not belong, the future—to the yellow or the black or the olive-colored; it belongs to the fair-skinned man, and it belongs to Christianity and to Protestantism. We are the only race who can save it. There is no power in any other civilization or any other religion that can save humanity; and the future - belongs - to - us." (Text of the Hale interview, ibid.) Cf. Bernhard Fürst von Bülow, *Denkwürdigkeiten* (Berlin, 1930), 2:374–75.

33. Regarding the *Daily Telegraph* Affair, see Wolfgang J. Mommsen, "Max Weber und die Deutsche Politik, 1890–1920" (Ph.D. diss., Universität Köln, 1959), pp. 165–66; and Wilhelm Schüssler, *Die Daily-Telegraph-Affäre* (Göttingen, 1952).

34. There were at least a complete version in William B. Hale's possession and an abbreviated text for the *Century Magazine*. (Theodore Roosevelt to Theodore Roosevelt, Jr., November 20, 1908, in Morison, ed., *The Letters of Theodore Roosevelt* [Cambridge, Mass., 1951–54], 6:1370–72). Cf. Paul Graf Wolff-Metternich to Bülow (handwritten), January 5, 1909, AA, Vereinigte Staaten von Amerika 6, No. 2., *secr.*, Bd. 2.

35. Bülow to Metternich, December 11, 1908, AA, Akten des AA im Grossen Hauptquartier 1914–1916, 24, Presse und Journalisten, Bd. 3 (Bülow advises Metternich to show the text of the interview to Grey and Asquith in strict confidence). Bernstorff to Bülow, January 5, 1909, and Metternich to Bülow (handwritten), January 5, 1909, AA, Vereinigte Staaten von Amerika 6, No. 2, *secr.*, Bd. 2. Theodore Roosevelt to Elihu Root, August 8, 1908; Roosevelt to Henry White, October 17, 1908; Roosevelt to Theodore Roosevelt, Jr., November 20, 1908; Roosevelt to Whitelaw Reid, January 6, 1909; in Morison, *The Letters of Theodore Roosevelt*, 6:1163–64, 1192, 1370–72, 1465–67. According to Helmuth Rogge, *Holstein und Harden* (Munich, 1959), p. 405, the German Consul General in New York supposedly had already—in November 1908—prevented the publication; however, Rogge reports, "important parts of the interview" had been published in the *New York World* and in German newspapers. (Rogge refers to the *Zukunft*, 65:339.) As might have been expected, there was renewed danger of the interview being published in the autumn of 1914, and Bernstorff had to negotiate again with the *Century Magazine* in order to suppress an article damaging to German interests. Bernstorff to Foreign Office, no Washington date, via Stockholm, November 3, 1914, AA, Vereinigte Staaten von Amerika 6, No. 2, *secr.*, Bd. 2.

36. Bernstorff, *Deutschland und Amerika*, p. 20.

37. Bernstorff to Bethmann Hollweg, April 7, 1913, AA, Botschaft Washington, Akten betreffend Deutschtum, Bd. 13.

38. The Ambassador predicted correctly that after fifty years the German-Americans would "disappear" as a national group "through absorption," since the large waves of immigration would come to an end, and the children would be completely assimilated; ibid.

39. Strictly speaking, this appears exaggerated, because immigrants became citizens only after a certain period of time. Perhaps the Ambassador meant to say that they lived in the United States as if they were citizens. Moreover, he observed that after several generations the immigrants also lost their native language. Bernstorff to Bethmann Hollweg, January 8, 1914, AA, Botschaft Washington, Graf Bernstorff, copy from the "Privateigentum Riesser."

40. Ibid.

41. Bernstorff to Bethmann Hollweg, April 7, 1913, AA, Botschaft Washington, Akten betreffend Deutschtum, Bd. 13.

42. Bernstorff to Bethmann Hollweg, January 8, 1914, AA, Botschaft Washington, Graf Bernstorff, copy from the "Privateigentum Riesser." In part Bernstorff may have been influenced by the positive impression made upon him by the exchange of professors between Germany and America organized earlier. Bernstorff, *Deutschland und Amerika*, p. 16.

43. Cultural relations between Germany and the United States had not always been positive, and often the Ambassador did not have the opportunity to counter this trend. The unhappy episode that prevented the erection of a Carl Schurz monument in Rastatt may serve as an illustration. New York citizens had collected the necessary funds for the monument and had sent the chairman of their association to Germany. As early as 1908, the Municipal Council of Rastatt had approved the project, but in 1913 it was withdrawn under pressure from the Commanding General of the Rastatt garrison. The Department of the Interior of the Grand Duchy of Baden in Karlsruhe had decided that it would not be able to "overlook the weight of the representations of the commanding general," after the latter had declared that the planned monument in Rastatt "could only be interpreted as that of Schurz, the insurgent" and "that realization of the intentions of the monument committee would seriously endanger military interests." Copies of the official rulings that expressed these views were sent to the Schurz family by the commission, and Bernstorff was asked to use his influence in support of the project. When the matter was presented to the Ambassador, he had just a few weeks earlier attended the festive dedication ceremonies of the Carl Schurz Monument on Morning Side Drive in New York and at that occasion told Americans: "I esteem it a high privilege to attend the unveiling of the monument to Carl Schurz, the foremost American citizen of German origin.... My presence here is further a symbol of the reconciliation and blending of the spirits of two successive peri-

ods of German history. Carl Schurz was so consumed with the passion of liberty that he came here in search of freedom after the political movement of 1848 had failed to give our own nation the unity and liberal institutions which we now enjoy." Bernstorff indeed knew well how useless his intervention against the military authorities in Germany would be. All he could do was to tell the Americans that his hands were tied in this matter, "because the same is taking place outside of the sphere of my influence [ausserhalb meines Amtsbezirks]." The documents mentioned here are found in AA, Botschaft Washington, Akten betreffend Deutschtum, Bd. 13.

44. Laudation for Bernstorff by Professor Harry Thurston Peck, University Orator of Columbia University, June 2, 1909, placed at the author's disposal by the Assistant to the President, Columbia University.

45. American newspaper clippings, placed at the author's disposal by the Special Collections Librarian of Brown University.

46. Ira Remsen, President of The Johns Hopkins University, to Bernstorff, February 25, 1910, placed at the author's disposal by the Office of the President, The Johns Hopkins University.

47. Address by Bernstorff, February 22, 1911, Proceedings of "University Day," April 15, 1911. Placed at the author's disposal by the University of Pennsylvania.

48. Laudation for Bernstorff by Dean West, Princeton University, 1913. Placed at the author's disposal by the University Archivist, Princeton University.

49. Bernstorff gave talks on numerous occasions at famous and at lesser-known universities, at academic annual meetings, and at dinner parties that were arranged by the presidents of the Ivy League schools.

50. Alfred H. Fried, *Die moderne Friedensbewegung* (Leipzig, 1907), pp. 88–89: "In the United States the idea of peace has long outgrown the peace societies and become part of politics." Bernstorff, *Deutschland und Amerika*, p. 18: "Nine-tenths of all Americans are pacifists, partly because of their education and a sentimental predilection for the principle, partly out of business-mindedness."

51. Bernstorff's address before the Second National Peace Congress, May 5, 1909, AA, Botschaft Washington, Akten betreffend Internationale Friedensbestrebungen, Bd. 1.

52. Cf. Fried, *Die moderne Friedensbewegung*, p. 90.

53. Alfred von Kiderlen-Wächter to Bernstorff, February 26, 1911: "I believe I may presume that Your Excellency will stay away from the peace congresses in New York, Baltimore, and Lake Mohonk in May . . . in order to prevent false conclusions concerning our position toward the peace movement. It is also to be feared that you might be imposed upon once more to come out of your personal and oratorical reserve." AA, Europa Generalia 40, Die den deutschen Missionen usw. erteilten Instruktionen und Vorhaltungen, Bd. 5. In general, Bernstorff's relationship with Kider-

len-Wächter was not untroubled. It is quite possible that, as Bülow's protégé, Bernstorff agreed with his mentor's judgment that Kiderlen-Wächter was a "vicious dog who should have been chained up in Bucharest"; certainly Bernstorff thought very little of Kiderlen-Wächter's abilities. After the embarrassing *Panthersprung* on July 1, 1911, Kiderlen-Wächter suspected the Ambassador of being behind the negative comments by the American press regarding the German adventure in Morocco. (Bernstorff, *Erinnerungen und Briefe* [Zürich, 1936], p. 77.)

54. Bernstorff to Bethmann Hollweg, May 9, 1910, AA, Vereinigte Staaten von Amerika 1, Bd. 23; Bernstorff to Bethmann Hollweg, February 1, 1911, Botschaft Washington, Akten betreffend Präsident und Kabinett, Bd. 7; Bernstorff, *Deutschland und Amerika*, p. 25.

55. Günther Count von Bernstorff, the Ambassador's son, was temporarily employed by Speyer at his bank.

56. Bernstorff to Bülow, dated March 18, 1909, sent March 22, 1909, AA, Botschaft Washington, Akten betreffend Präsident und Kabinett, Bd. 6.

57. Unofficially, Heinrich von Treitschke had already declared earlier: "Thus it is clear that the international [völkerrechtlichen] treaties, which limit the intentions of a state, are not absolute limits but voluntary self-limitations. From this follows that the establishment of an international court of arbitration as a permanent institution is incompatible with the nature of the state. Only with respect to second- or third-rate questions could the state possibly yield to such a court of arbitration. For vital questions there is no impartial outside power at all." Treitschke, *Politik*, 1:38.

58. Hermann Freiherr Speck von Sternburg to Foreign Office, October 25, 1904, and Bülow to Sternburg, November 2, 1904, AA, Botschaft Washington, Akten betreffend deutsch-amerikanischen Schiedsgerichtsvertrag, Bd. 1. *Die Grosse Politik der Europäischen Kabinette 1871–1918* (Berlin, 1927), 23:15–16.

59. Sternburg to Foreign Office, November 5, 1904, AA, Botschaft Washington, Akten betreffend deutsch-amerikanischen Schiedsgerichtsvertrag, Bd. 1. *Die Grosse Politik der Europäischen Kabinette 1871–1918*, 23:16–17. The text of the Anglo-French treaty, signed in London on October 14, 1903, reads: "Article I. Differences which may arise of a legal nature, or relating to the interpretation of Treaties existing between the two Contracting Parties, and which it may not have been possible to settle by diplomacy, shall be referred to the Permanent Court of Arbitration established at The Hague by the Convention of the 29th July, 1899, provided, nevertheless, that they do not affect the vital interests, the independence, or the honour of the two Contracting States, and do not concern the interests of third Parties. Article II. In each individual case the High Contracting Parties, before appealing to the Permanent Court of Arbitration, shall conclude a special Agreement defining clearly the matter in dispute, the scope of the powers of the Arbitrators, and the periods to be fixed for the formation of the Arbitral

Tribunal and the several stages of the Procedure. Article III. The present Agreement is concluded for a period of five years, dating from the day of signature." *FRUS 1904*, pp. 9–10.

60. Sternburg to Foreign Office, November 17, 1904; Washington Embassy to Foreign Office, November 18, 1904; Bülow to Sternburg, November 20, 1904; and Sternburg to Bülow, November 22, 1904, all in AA, Botschaft Washington, Akten betreffend deutsch-amerikanischen Schiedsgerichtsvertrag, Bd. 1; *Die Grosse Politik der Europäischen Kabinette 1871–1918*, 23:18–21. Cf. Ilse Kunz-Lack, *Die deutsch-amerikanischen Beziehungen 1890–1914* (Stuttgart, 1935), p. 218. Between November 1904 and January 1905, the United States signed identical arbitration treaties with France, Switzerland, Germany, Portugal, England, Italy, Spain, Austria-Hungary, Mexico, Norway, and Sweden. W. Stull Holt, *Treaties Defeated by the Senate* (Baltimore, 1933), p. 204.

61. Sternburg to Bülow, February 13, 1905, *Die Grosse Politik der Europäischen Kabinette 1871–1918*, 23:22–23. The arbitration treaties stipulated that both nations would in any case negotiate a "special agreement" before approaching the Court at The Hague. On a vote of 50 to 9, the Senate changed the arbitration treaty with France by replacing the word "agreement" with the word "treaty." Holt, *Treaties Defeated by the Senate*, p. 204. Cf. William Howard Taft, *The United States and Peace* (London, 1914), pp. 95–96. Heinrich Lammasch, *Die Lehre von der Schiedsgerichtsbarkeit in ihrem ganzen Umfange* (Stuttgart, 1914), p. 93.

62. Elihu Root to Sternburg, January 20, 1908, AA, Botschaft Washington, Akten betreffend deutsch-amerikanischen Schiedsgerichtsvertrag, Bd. 1.

63. Hilmar Freiherr von dem Bussche-Haddenhausen to Sternburg, January 30, 1908, and Wilhelm Freiherr von Schoen to Sternburg, February 4, 1908, ibid.

64. Sternburg to Foreign Office, March 25 and April 3, 1908, ibid.

65. Sternburg to Foreign Office, April 9, 1908, ibid.

66. *Die Grosse Politik der Europäischen Kabinette 1871–1918*, 23:17, editors' note. According to this, Bülow had refused already in 1904, as in the case of Switzerland, to sign arbitration treaties with such smaller states. Cf. Kunz-Lack, *Die deutsch-amerikanischen Beziehungen 1890–1914*, p. 219.

67. Sternburg to Foreign Office, April 26, 1908, AA, Botschaft Washington, Akten betreffend deutsch-amerikanischen Schiedsgerichtsvertrag, Bd. 1. Regarding Root's opinion about Germany's refusal, cf. Richard W. Leopold, *Elihu Root and the Conservative Tradition* (Boston, 1954), p. 100.

68. Schoen to Sternburg, April 28, 1908, AA, Botschaft Washington, Akten betreffend deutsch-amerikanischen Schiedsgerichtsvertrag, Bd. 1.

69. Sternburg to Foreign Office, May 7, 1908, ibid.

70. The records of the German Foreign Office contain lively correspondence from several experts dealing with the question of whether the nego-

tiations should really be considered broken off or not. Sternburg himself used these words: "President told me that he would like to temporarily suspend further negotiations with Germany regarding arbitration treaty." Sternburg to Foreign Office, May 13, 1908, ibid.

71. The German refusal appears all the more incomprehensible in view of a personal letter which President Roosevelt sent to Wilhelm II through Sternburg as late as May 6, 1908: "I hope you can see your way clear to have your Government enter into a treaty of arbitration with the United States. In the form in which the treaty now is I freely admit that it is not as effective as I could wish. Nevertheless good would result from the expression of good will implied in the treaty.... Moreover it would confer a real benefit in the event of any sudden flurry both by providing the executives of the two countries with an excellent reason for demanding cool consideration of any question by their respective peoples, and also by enabling them to make a strong appeal under the sanction of a solemn treaty to both the peoples and their legislatures to accept an honorable arbitration.... Merely to exchange notes of good will between the Governments would be no adequate substitute. On the contrary, it would invite attention to the fact that there is no treaty with Germany whereas there are treaties with the various powers ... ; and indeed might be construed by our people as meaning that Germany did not believe any treaty should be made with us in view of our form of government." Morison, *The Letters of Theodore Roosevelt*, 6:1023.

72. Sternburg to Foreign Office, dated May 14, 1908, mailed May 15, 1908, AA, Botschaft Washington, Akten betreffend deutsch-amerikanischen Schiedsgerichtsvertrag, Bd. 1.

73. Bernstorff to Foreign Office, January 17, 1909: "Neither President nor Secretary of State mentioned to me question of arbitration treaty. In line with my instructions I made no attempt to bring up the matter...," ibid. Cf. however Bernstorff, *Deutschland und Amerika*, p. 21: "When I was appointed ambassador ... [Bülow] also told me that I absolutely had to bring to a good finish the negotiations concerning an arbitration treaty with the United States which, due to my predecessor's death, had remained unfinished. In spite of this clear instruction the German Government stumbled ... later over minor legal technicalities. As it was, Prince Bülow in the meantime had left office." Bülow's resignation did not take place until half a year after the above-quoted cablegram, that is in July 1909.

74. Affidavit signed by "v. Koerner," dated July 12, 1908, AA, Botschaft Washington, Akten betreffend deutsch-amerikanischen Schiedsgerichtsvertrag, Bd. 1. As can be seen from Bussche-Haddenhausen's marginal comments of December 1, 1908, the document was "given [to Bernstorff] for personal, strictly confidential use."

75. Regarding the Georgia Case, see Root to Bernstorff, January 12, 1909, AA, Botschaft Washington, Deutsche Ansprüche gegen den Staat Georgia,

Bd. 1; Foreign Office (without signature) to Bernstorff, April 1, 1909, AA, Botschaft Washington, Akten betreffend deutsch-amerikanischen Schiedsgerichtsvertrag, Bd. 1; Schoen to Bernstorff, February 20, 1910, AA, Botschaft Washington, and Memorandum, State Department to Washington Embassy, February 9, 1914, Deutsche Ansprüche gegen den Staat Georgia, Bd. 1; Bernstorff to Wilhelm von Stumm, February 10, 1912, AA, Botschaft Washington, Akten betreffend deutsch-amerikanischen Schiedsgerichtsvertrag, Bd. 2.

In the Georgia Case, the German Empire, on behalf of a number of German citizens, made certain financial claims against the State of Georgia stemming from promissory notes dating back to 1869. Georgia refused to recognize the claims and Germany turned to Washington. The federal government took the position that an embassy was not permitted to contact the government of a state and that the Georgia Case could not be settled by a court of arbitration. By the same token, the federal government declared that this was a matter to be handled by the State of Georgia. In addition, the Americans gave some indication that they were not necessarily convinced of the justification of the German claims.

76. Bernstorff to Foreign Office, March 18, 1909, AA, Botschaft Washington, Akten betreffend deutsch-amerikanischen Schiedsgerichtsvertrag, Bd. 1.

77. Schoen to Bernstorff, April 18, 1909, ibid.

78. M. J. Bonn, *Was will Wilson?* (Munich, [1918]), p. 24. Cf. Philip C. Jessup, *Elihu Root* ([Hampden, Conn.], 1964), 2:310. Under the impression of his futile efforts to conclude an arbitration treaty with Germany, Root wrote to Andrew Carnegie on April 3, 1909: "The fact is, and no well informed person can doubt it, that Germany, under her present government is the great disturber of peace in the world. At every turn the obstacle to the establishment of arbitration agreements, to the prevention of war, to disarmament, to the limitation of armament, to all attempts to lessen the suspicion and alarm of nations toward each other, is Germany, who stands, and has persistently stood since I have been familiar with foreign affairs against that kind of progress."

79. Bernstorff to Foreign Office, dated December 15, 1909, apparently sent December 17, 1909 (handwritten draft in which Bernstorff replaces "Spitzfindigkeit" with "Bedenken"), AA, Botschaft Washington, Akten betreffend Internationale Friedensbestrebungen, Bd. 1. Bernstorff had had an extended conversation with Andrew Carnegie, who once more had expressed his urgent wish for a German-American treaty. Carnegie emphasized that he would love to pay the debt of the State of Georgia himself if that would bring about the agreement with Germany.

80. Bernstorff to Foreign Office, March 23, 1910, ibid; Bernstorff to Foreign Office, June 1, 1911, and Bernstorff to Foreign Office, arrived Berlin June 10, 1911, AA, Vereinigte Staaten von Amerika 1, Bd. 24; Bernstorff to

Bethmann Hollweg, November 28, 1911, AA, Botschaft Washington, Akten betreffend deutsch-amerikanischen Schiedsgerichtsvertrag, Bd. 1.

81. AA, Botschaft Washington, Akten betreffend deutsch-amerikanischen Schiedsgerichtsvertrag, Bd. 1. Cf. William Howard Taft, *The Proposed Arbitration Treaties with Great Britain and France* (Baltimore, 1912).

82. On the contrary, State Secretary Kiderlen-Wächter roughly reprimanded his Ambassador in Washington when the latter dared to forward to the Foreign Office an "Appeal to the German People" from the German-American National Alliance of the United States of America. The appeal of the German-Americans had stated: "An arbitration treaty like the one suggested signifies a moral victory over old prejudices.... It is precisely the moral impact which makes this treaty so meaningful." Kiderlen-Wächter's blunt reply was: "May I ask [you] to refrain from any prejudicing of this office in the future." The appeal was sent to Bernstorff by Dr. Ernst Richard, Chairman of the German-American Alliance, on June 19, 1911; the appeal and the message from Kiderlen-Wächter to Bernstorff, of July 10, 1911, are found in AA, Botschaft Washington, Akten betreffend deutsch-amerikanischen Schiedsgerichtsvertrag, Bd. 1.

83. Bernstorff to Wilhelm von Stumm, February 10, 1912: "However, I must briefly point out to you that my desire to conclude such a treaty is *simply* an effort not to lose out with public opinion here. In Germany one does not like making such allowances for public opinion, but in dealing with foreign countries we nevertheless have to take into account those factors which are of prime importance in those countries.... The vast majority of Americans are pacifists.... In their judgment they will always take sides against that power which they consider to be the trouble-maker. ... If the other two treaties are ratified and we do not conclude one, our legal objections will have no effect whatsoever on public opinion here.... I would like to ask you to present the matter in higher places in such a way that new instructions ... will be prepared for me." Ibid., Bd. 2.

84. Germany had insisted on including the American states individually in the treaty. There had also been the desire to have the agreement cover already existing differences retroactively. Bernstorff to Stumm, February 10, 1912, ibid.

85. Bernstorff to Bethmann Hollweg, January 31, 1914, AA, Vereinigte Staaten von Amerika 1, Bd. 43.

86. Bernstorff to Bethmann Hollweg, May 23, 1914, AA, Mexico 1, Bd. 48; handwritten comments by the Emperor on the telegram. Cf. Harry Graf Kessler, *Tagebücher 1918–1937*, ed. Wolfgang Pfeiffer-Belli, p. 562.

87. The Bryan Treaties prescribed a waiting period of one year, during which two disagreeing nations would not resort to war in order to settle their differences. It was hoped that tempers would cool off during that period of time and consequently a peaceful solution to the given conflict could be reached. Cf. P., "Influence de la guerre sur les traités d'enquête et

d'arbitrage conclus par les États Unis et sur les rapports entre ces pays et les puissances européennes belligérantes," *Journal du Droit International* 43 (1916): 482–85. Dietrich Schindler, *Die Schiedsgerichtsbarkeit seit 1914* (Stuttgart, 1938), pp. 12–13.

88. Bernstorff, *Deutschland und Amerika*, p. 24.

89. The Austro-Hungarian Ambassador in Washington, Constantin Dumba, writes in his memoirs that in the spring of 1914 he had succeeded in obtaining "the basic approval of my government to conclude a Bryan treaty with the United States." Because of the war, however, he writes, the signing did not take place. But, in his opinion, at least a certain positive impression had been made on Washington. Constantin Dumba, *Dreibund- und Entente-Politik in der Alten und Neuen Welt* (Zürich, 1931), p. 374.

90. *FRUS 1914*, pp. 304–7. J. A. A. J. Jusserand, *Le Sentiment américain pendant la guerre* (Paris, 1931), pp. 38–39. The treaty with France was not ratified until January 1915, the one with England not until November 1915. P., "Influence de la guerre sur les traités d'enquête et d'arbitrage conclus par les États Unis et sur les rapports entre ces pays et les puissances européennes belligérantes," p. 484.

91. Samuel E. Morison and Henry S. Commager, *The Growth of the American Republic* (New York, 1960), 2:449. Dumba, *Dreibund- und Entente-Politik in der Alten und Neuen Welt*, pp. 374–75.

92. Bernstorff, *Deutschland und Amerika*, p. 21. Cf. Tinnemann, "Count Johann von Bernstorff and German-American Relations, 1908–1917," pp. 22–23, who feels that Bernstorff had not engaged himself sufficiently for an arbitration treaty with the United States. Dumba, *Dreibund- und Entente-Politik in der Alten und Neuen Welt*, p. 375, maintains: "If such a treaty between Germany and the United States had materialized, the reconciliation commission would have had to step in when unlimited submarine warfare was declared. Maybe the war could have been avoided, in any case, the *Lusitania* crisis in May 1915 certainly would not have been so acute."

93. The text of Monroe's statement, from his address of December 2, 1823, is given in John B. Moore, *A Digest of International Law* (Washington, D.C., 1906), 6:401–3. Cf. Dexter Perkins, *A History of the Monroe Doctrine* (London, 1960) and *The Monroe Doctrine, 1867–1907* (Gloucester, Mass., 1966). Samuel F. Bemis, *The Latin American Policy of the United States* (New York, 1967).

94. Roosevelt to Cecil A. Spring Rice, August 11, 1897; Roosevelt to McCalla, August 2, 1897; Roosevelt to J. H. Wilson, August 23, 1897; quoted in Bishop, *Theodore Roosevelt and His Time*, 1:78–79.

95. Message of the President to the Senate and House of Representatives, December 6, 1904, *FRUS 1904*, pp. ix–xlviii, and Message from the President to the Senate, February 15, 1905, *FRUS 1905*, pp. 334–42.

96. German efforts were mainly directed at the German population in the United States and in Brazil, because particularly large numbers of Ger-

mans had emigrated there; but attention was paid to other South American countries as well. The official and private German plans for expansion, however, were not unknown in Washington.

97. Bernstorff, *Deutschland und Amerika*, p. 17: "Particularly attacks on the Monroe Doctrine were all too popular in our press. I have always been of the opinion that we should have recognized this American dogma openly and officially. The Monroe Doctrine is not a question of law but of power. We in fact did not have the power to question the Monroe Doctrine, even if we had wanted to. . . . It would have been wiser to acknowledge the Monroe Doctrine." Cf. Perkins, *A History of the Monroe Doctrine*, pp. 381–82: "The German Foreign Office pursued a correct, and even a cautious, policy in the main in the years prior to the First World War; but in no country was opposition to the Monroe Doctrine more violently expressed; and in none were the naval authorities definitely so hostile."

98. William Howard Taft to Helen H. Taft, October 15, 1909, quoted in Henry F. Pringle, *The Life and Times of William Howard Taft* (New York, 1939), 1:462: "I am glad to aid him [Díaz] . . . for the reason that we have two billions American capital in Mexico that will be greatly endangered if Díaz were to die and his government go to pieces. . . . I can only hope and pray that his demise does not come until I am out of office."

99. Cf. Stanley R. Ross, *Francisco I. Madero* (New York, 1955), p. 31.

100. Regarding Orozco, see Michael C. Meyer, *Mexican Rebel* (Lincoln, Neb., 1967). Orozco was captured together with Huerta in 1915 and was shot by American agents and military while fleeing.

101. Shortly before Díaz' escape from Mexico to Paris on the German liner *Ypiranga* (Howard F. Cline, *The United States and Mexico*, Cambridge, 1963, p. 124), William Howard Taft wrote to Horace D. Taft on January 19, 1911: "My own impression has been that Díaz has done more for the people of Mexico than any other Latin American has done for any of his people." Pringle, *The Life and Times of William Howard Taft*, 2:700. *FRUS 1909*, p. 425, Taft to Díaz, June 25, 1909: "It would gratify me very much to meet one in the flesh who has done so much to establish order and create prosperity in his own country and in so doing has won the admiration of the entire world." Among German historical studies dealing with the end of *Porfirismo*, Friedrich Katz' *Deutschland, Diaz und die mexikanische Revolution* (Berlin, 1964) is especially noteworthy. *The Secret War in Mexico* (Chicago, 1981) is a revised and expanded edition.

102. Katz, *Deutschland, Díaz und die mexikanische Revolution*, p. 174. Cline, *The United States and Mexico*, p. 114: "The Madero interests include ranching, agricultural, mining and industrial activities." Ross, *Francisco I. Madero*, pp. 7–11. Cf. Peter Calvert, *The Mexican Revolution, 1910–1914* (Cambridge, 1968).

103. Cf. William Bayard Hale to President Wilson, June 18, 1913, printed

in Arthur S. Link, ed., *The Papers of Woodrow Wilson* (Princeton, 1978–83), 27:536–52. Charles C. Cumberland, *Mexican Revolution* (Austin, Tex., 1952), pp. 239–40. Ross, *Francisco I. Madero*, pp. 335–36. Katz, *Deutschland, Diaz und die mexikanische Revolution*, p. 228: "[H. L.] Wilson's attitude suggests that he not only did not want to take any effective steps to save Madero, but that he wished for the latter's death."

104. Alfred Vagts, *Mexiko, Europa und Amerika* (Berlin, 1928), pp. 167–68. Cline, *The United States and Mexico*, pp. 56–57.

105. Zapata had already broken with Madero when he demanded that the people be given back the land which had been expropriated from them. Now he was fighting to implement the Plan of Ayala, which among other things called for partial expropriation of the large landholders. Historians differ considerably in their appraisal of Zapata. The American historian Howard Cline, for instance, describes Zapata as a symbol of "naked and massive power," and claims that he was "politically naive and socially insensitive" (Cline, *The United States and Mexico*, pp. 125, 137–38). Friedrich Katz, by contrast, arrives at quite different conclusions in 1964. Regarding Zapata, cf. also John Womack, Jr., *Zapata and the Mexican Revolution* (London, 1969).

106. President Taft ordered 20,000 American troops to the Mexican border, supposedly for military maneuvers. Theodore Roosevelt reacted by asking Taft to assign him a cavalry command in the case of American actions in Mexico. Morison, *The Letters of Theodore Roosevelt*, 7:243–44. Pringle, *The Life and Times of William Howard Taft*, 2:701–2. Cline (*The United States and Mexico*, p. 129) believes that Taft sent the troops to the border "to prevent rather than create international difficulties."

107. England and other countries recognized the Huerta regime. Wilson was put under heavy pressure by American industrial interests to do the same. Cf. Katz, *Deutschland, Diaz und die mexikanische Revolution*, pp. 250, 255–56, 262–64. Calvert, *The Mexican Revolution, 1910–1914*, pp. 19–20, 249. Robert E. Quirk, *An Affair of Honor* (Lexington, Ky., 1962), p. 12.

108. Bernstorff, *Deutschland und Amerika*, p. 22.

109. Cf. Quirk, *An Affair of Honor*, pp. 2–3.

110. Sir Francis Stronge was the British Minister in Mexico until the autumn of 1913. He was relieved by Sir Lionel Carden. The latter seems to have held investments in the oil interests of Lord Cowdray, who is thought to have arranged his appointment in Mexico. Calvert, *The Mexican Revolution, 1910–1914*, pp. 218, 237, 277. Katz, *Deutschland, Diaz und die mexikanische Revolution*, pp. 255–56.

111. Louis M. Teitelbaum, *Woodrow Wilson and the Mexican Revolution (1913–1916)* (New York, 1967), p. 78.

112. Regarding the German Empire's plans to extend its military influ-

ence in Mexico, see Warren Schiff, "German Military Penetration into Mexico during the Late Diaz Period," *Hispanic American Historical Review* 39 (August, 1959), 568–79.

113. Bernstorff to Bethmann Hollweg, November 25, 1913: "The present situation as far as Mexico is concerned, is often compared here with the situation before the outbreak of the Spanish War.... President Wilson, however, it seems to me, is more inclined to take up arms than McKinley.... Unfortunately, Europe cannot exert any influence on American policy because it does not have the power to oppose it.... Therefore we must be content with the role of a spectator and see whether the interests of the Democratic party will necessitate intervention in Mexico or not. If it occurs, I am afraid it will be followed by a substantial strengthening of all imperialistic tendencies in this country." AA, Vereinigte Staaten von Amerika 1, Bd. 25.

114. Lichnowsky to Bethmann Hollweg, February 24, 1914, AA, Mexico 1, Bd. 43. The report was written after the murder of William F. Benton, a British subject in Mexico, by Francisco Villa or his men. Details in Katz, *The Secret War in Mexico*, pp. 184–85; Thomas Baecker, *Die deutsche Mexikopolitik 1913/14* (Berlin, 1971), p. 171. Lichnowsky reports views that he has heard from other diplomats in London. The comments are notes in the margin by Wilhelm II. The emphases are his also.

115. Hans-Adolf von Bülow (Prussian Minister in Hamburg) to Foreign Office, April 23, 1914, AA, Mexico 1, Bd. 45. Apparently Ballin himself had told Bülow about the phony destination of the *Ypiranga*. The shipment was consigned to Holst, agent of the Hamburg-based Martin Schröder company. Paul von Hintze to Bethmann Hollweg, June 3, 1914, AA, Mexico 1, Bd. 49. Barbara Tuchman, *The Zimmermann Telegram* (New York, 1958), pp. 46–47, without citing a source, writes that the German Minister in Mexico, von Hintze, had offered arms shipments to Huerta and demanded in return that in case of war the British navy would have its oil faucet turned off. Cf. Quirk, *An Affair of Honor*, p. 98. Baecker, *Die Deutsche Mexikopolitik 1913/14* argues against Barbara Tuchman's viewpoint concerning Berlin's anti-American policy in Mexico and thinks that "political blindness" (p. 183) led to the unloading of the German arms at Puerto México. This seems too simple an explanation of German policy in Mexico and does not alter my considered opinion that Berlin had decided to back the Caudillo Victoriano Huerta, even in the face of opposition from Woodrow Wilson.

116. Handwritten note by Hans A. von Kemnitz, April 24, 1914, AA, Mexico 1, Bd. 45.

117. The so-called Tampico Incident. American sailors had been taken into custody in Tampico for a brief period. Although the responsible local officials had sent an apology to Admiral Henry T. Mayo, who was in command of the American naval forces off Tampico, the latter demanded that

the Mexicans honor the Star Spangled Banner with a cannon salute. President Wilson supported the Admiral's demand. Accounts of the Tampico Incident are found in Quirk, *An Affair of Honor;* Jack Sweetman, *The Landing at Veracruz: 1914* (Annapolis, Md., 1968); and Arthur S. Link, *The New Freedom*, vol. 2 of *Wilson* (Princeton, 1956). The relevant American diplomatic correspondence in *FRUS 1914* conveys the essential details of the incident. Valuable documentation relating to this incident is also contained in Arthur S. Link, *The Papers of Woodrow Wilson*, 29:420 ff.

118. Consul William W. Canada to Secretary of State, April 22, 1914, *FRUS 1914*, pp. 480–81: "Battleships *Florida, Utah, Arkansas, Vermont, New Hampshire, New Jersey, South Carolina,* transport *Prairie,* collier *Orion* now off this port. Transport *Hancock* reported due." Quirk, *An Affair of Honor*, p. 8: "The large number [of U.S. vessels] kept in Mexican coastal waters in 1914 was intended by Wilson to be a constant reminder to the government of Mexico of his displeasure with Huerta."

119. The *Ypiranga* was carrying an especially large cargo. Three trains with ten cars each were waiting at the pier to pick up the German arms. Paul von Hintze to Bethmann Hollweg, June 3, 1914, AA, Mexico 1, Bd. 49, reports the cargo as follows: 15,750 crates with 2,000 cartridges each, approximately 40 machine guns, 717 crates with grenades, 78 caissons, and approximately 10,000 rifles. William Canada, the American Consul in Veracruz, mentions 200 machine guns and 15,000,000 cartridges. Canada to Department of State, April 18, 1914; Canada to Secretary of State, April 20, 1914, Link, *The Papers of Woodrow Wilson*, 29:464, 477. Cf. Ypiranga, Rapporte des Kapitäns, Akte 77, HAPAG. Karl Boy-Ed to State Secretary of the Reichsmarineamt, April 22, 1914, AA, Mexico 1, Bd. 46. Bryan to Canada, April 21, 1914, *FRUS 1914*, p. 477. Apparently the American Admiral had gone beyond his orders when he ordered Captain Bonath of the *Ypiranga* not to leave the harbor of Veracruz. On April 21, 1914, Secretary of State Bryan appeared at the German embassy to deliver an apology from the American President for the action of his admiral. Bryan told Bernstorff that Admiral Fletcher had received instructions to apologize to the captain of the *Ypiranga*. ("The Secretary of State by direction of the President offered to his Excellency the German Ambassador the apology and explanation which Admiral Fletcher was instructed to offer to the captain of the ship [*Ypiranga*].") Nevertheless, Bryan said, the American government hoped the arms destined for Huerta would be unloaded at Veracruz so they could be retained there. Bernstorff to Foreign Office, April 21, 1914, containing memo from Bryan, AA, Mexico 1, Bd. 45. Tuchman, *The Zimmermann Telegram*, pp. 51–52, states that Bryan's backing down was the direct result of an intervention by Bernstorff.

120. Foreign Office (written by Hans A. von Kemnitz) to Bernstorff, April 25, 1914, AA, Mexico 1, Bd. 45. The telegram, also carrying Gottlieb von

Jagow's initials, informed Bernstorff that the *Ypiranga* would receive orders "to unload cargo or keep arms aboard, which probably go back to Hamburg."

121. Bernstorff to Foreign Office, April 25, 1914, AA, Mexico 1, Bd. 45. Bryan knew that the *Ypiranga* had been transferred into the service of the Imperial Navy. Bernstorff asked for instructions as to how he should explain this to the Secretary of State. Cf. Quirk, *An Affair of Honor*, pp. 98–99.

122. Cf. Sweetman, *The Landing at Veracruz: 1914*, p. 155. On May 10, 1914, the *Kölnische Zeitung* published the news that the German liner *Kronprinzessin Cecilie*, also of the Hamburg-American Line, had unloaded arms in Puerto México. Clipping of the *Kölnische Zeitung*, May 10, 1914, AA, Mexico 1, Bd. 46. On May 9, 1914, Bernstorff reported to Bethmann Hollweg (ibid., Bd. 47) that he had heard "liners of the Hamburg-America Line had again landed arms for Huerta in Mexico, namely in Puerto Mexico." Admiral Paul von Hintze, German Minister to Mexico, reported to Bethmann Hollweg (ibid., Bd. 49) on June 3 that he had ordered absolute secrecy toward the Americans concerning the release of the *Ypiranga* from the Imperial Navy. At the same time, according to the Hintze report, the *Bavaria* brought "1400 crates with 2000 Mauser cartridges each." Cf. Ypiranga, Rapporte des Kapitäns, Akte 77, and Kronprinzessin Cecilie, Rapporte des Kapitäns, Akte 78, HAPAG.

123. In telegram no. 30 of April 25, 1914 (see above) from Kemnitz to Bernstorff, it had been suggested that the arms would go back to Hamburg. On April 26 (orally) and on April 29 (in writing), Bryan thanked the German Ambassador for the instructions to the *Ypiranga*. Bernstorff to Foreign Office, April 26, 1914, AA, Mexico 1, Bd. 45; Bryan to Bernstorff, April 29, 1914, ibid., Bd. 46.

124. Bernstorff to Foreign Office, June 10, 1914, ibid., Bd. 48.

CHAPTER TWO

1. The British Ambassador Sir Cecil Arthur Spring Rice had already returned from his vacation in England. Jean Jules Jusserand, the French Ambassador, left Washington on July 1. The Austro-Hungarian Ambassador Constantin Dumba spent the summer in Manchester.

2. Unpublished memoirs of Erika von Watzdorf (privately held), pp. 323–24.

3. Bernstorff, *Deutschland und Amerika* (Berlin, 1920), p. 33.

4. Bernhard Dernburg was not part of the embassy personnel; Heinrich Albert as Commercial Attaché enjoyed diplomatic immunity. The records show that Albert, in fact, was not Commercial Attaché. Cf. Jagow to Secretary of the Interior, October 25, 1915, and Jagow to Bernstorff, October 13,

1915, BA, Personalakte Heinrich Albert. Originally, Berlin had contemplated sending Richard von Kühlmann to America as director of propaganda. Cf. Richard von Kühlmann, *Erinnerungen* (Heidelberg, 1948), p. 421. Unpublished memoirs of Erika von Watzdorf, p. 323.

5. Bernstorff, *Deutschland und Amerika*, pp. 33–34.

6. Warren I. Cohen, *The American Revisionists* (Chicago, 1967), p. 1.

7. Cf. among others Clara E. Schieber, *The Transformation of American Sentiment toward Germany, 1870–1914* (Boston, 1923). Alfred Vagts, *Deutschland und die Vereinigten Staaten in der Weltpolitik* (London, 1935; New York, 1935). Hermann Leusser, *Ein Jahrzehnt deutsch-amerikanischer Politik (1897–1906)* (Munich, 1928). Ilse Kunz-Lack, *Die deutschamerikanischen Beziehungen 1890–1914* (Stuttgart, 1935).

8. Frank P. Chambers, *The War behind the War 1914–1918* (London, 1939), p. 189. Since this opinion, laden with prejudices and heavily influenced by clichés can be traced through the whole of Germany's relations with America, it will not be examined here separately. There is ample evidence, however, that German conceptions of Americans were equally subject to prejudice and misinformation.

9. Bernstorff to Bethmann Hollweg, Secret, October 4, 1914, AA, Vereinigte Staaten von Amerika 2, Bd. 20. See Heinrich Charles to German Ambassador Otto Wiedfeldt, May 19, 1922, about his activities in the summer of 1914. According to this letter, the German-American Chamber of Commerce was organized that year with the support of the German Consul General Paul Siegfried Horst Falcke. NA, T290, Roll 21, AA, Botschaft Washington. See also Ecker to Huldermann, September 21, 1914, HAPAG, Hamburg-Amerika Linie, New York, May 1, 1914–January 15, 1915.

10. Bernstorff (*Deutschland und Amerika*, pp. 37–38) presents the matter as if Dernburg had taken over the direction of the propaganda office more or less by coincidence. Since Dernburg had failed in his financial mission and since he was not fully occupied by his activities for the Red Cross, he could, Bernstorff says, actually have returned to Germany. This had not been possible, however, since he would have risked capture by the British.

11. In the records the office appears as Press Office, news bureau, German Information Service and German Information Bureau. The headquarters of the organization was at 1123 Broadway, New York; *BAL*, p. xv.

12. Bernstorff to Bethmann Hollweg, Secret, October 4, 1914, Minutes of the first business meeting as Enclosure, AA, Vereinigte Staaten von Amerika 2, Bd. 20. Horst P. Falcke, *Vor dem Eintritt Amerikas in den Weltkrieg* (Dresden, 1928), pp. 37–38. Claussen was press agent of the Hamburg-American Line in New York; Fuehr had been interpreter for the German Consulate General in Yokohama and had "extensive experience in press matters"; Viereck was publisher of the magazine *The Fatherland*; Schrader was at least temporarily copublisher of *The Fatherland*. Julius P. Meyer was Director of the Hamburg-American Line in New York. Harvard profes-

sor Hugo Münsterberg, Rittmeister Ewald Hecker, Dr. Mechlenburg (previously also with the diplomatic service in Japan), Professor Kuno Francke, who had immigrated from Germany, Edmund von Mach, and Plage (formerly also with the service in Japan) were also associated with the Press Office. The economist Moritz Julius Bonn, who initially had come to America as an exchange professor, was soon put to work for Heinrich Albert. The American journalist William Bayard Hale, who was personally acquainted with Woodrow Wilson (Mexico mission) and Wilhelm II (Hale interview), supported the group. Cf. among others H. C. Peterson, *Propaganda for War* (Port Washington, N.Y., 1968; 1st ed. 1939), p. 136; Bernstorff, *Deutschland und Amerika*, pp. 46–47. *BAL*, pp. xv–xvi. On Viereck see Niel M. Johnson, *George Sylvester Viereck. German-American Propagandist* (Urbana, Ill., 1972).

13. The quality of the work of Matthew Claussen was disputed among his colleagues in the German propaganda campaign in New York. Cf. Ecker to Huldermann, September 28, 1915, HAPAG, Hamburg-Amerika Linie, New York, July 1, 1915–November 30, 1915 (handwritten section).

14. Bernstorff to Bethmann Hollweg, Secret, October 4, 1914, AA, Vereinigte Staaten von Amerika 2, Bd. 20. Because of military censorship in Germany, telegraphic news transmission to neutral countries was almost impossible at the beginning of the war. "Thus in the neutral areas our enemies had free rein over press matters." G.A. by Zimmermann, September 23, 1914, AA, Akten des AA im Grossen Hauptquartier 1914–1916, Presse und Journalisten, Bd. 2.

15. Bernstorff to Bethmann Hollweg, Secret, October 4, 1914, AA, Vereinigte Staaten von Amerika 2, Bd. 20.

16. The "Zentralstelle für Auslandsdienst" was founded by the German Foreign Office in October 1914 and directed by Otto Hammann. At the outset the following persons were associated with the organization: Erhard Eduard Deutelmoser, Philipp Mumm von Schwarzenstein, Captain Löhlein of the Imperial Naval Office, Consul General J. A. Lettenbaur (formerly in Cincinnati, Ohio) of the Foreign Office, the parliamentarian of the *Zentrum* party Matthias Erzberger, the chief of the picture office (Bilderzentrale) Schumacher, Paul Rohrbach, Ernst Jaeckh, and the Gerichtsassessor Roediger of the Foreign Office. Kurt Koszyk, *Deutsche Pressepolitik im Ersten Weltkrieg* (Düsseldorf, 1968), pp. 240–41. Cf. Klaus Epstein, *Matthias Erzberger and the Dilemma of German Democracy* (Princeton, 1959), pp. 103–4. Hans Barkhausen, *Filmpropaganda für Deutschland im Ersten und Zweiten Weltkrieg* (Hildesheim, 1982), p. 2.

17. Bernstorff, *Deutschland und Amerika*, pp. 38–39. Cf. Bernstorff to Bethmann Hollweg, Secret, October 4, 1914: "Dernburg is now devoting his time exclusively to the press . . . and I have made available to him the necessary means for the office." AA, Vereinigte Staaten von Amerika 2, Bd. 20.

18. Bernstorff too participated in conferences of the Press Office (*BAL*, p. 1391). More specific information regarding Bernstorff's activities and financial support will be supplied below in connection with an investigation of the individual measures taken.

19. The propaganda constantly found itself on the defensive against charges concerning Germany's alleged violation of Belgian neutrality. Reports about German atrocities were rejected and the high standards of the German military were praised.

20. Cf. Arno Spindler, "Der britische Propagandafeldzug gegen die amerikanische Neutralität," in *Berliner Monatshefte* 17 (July 1939): 934. Edgar Stern-Rubarth, *Die Propaganda als politisches Instrument* (Berlin, 1921), p. 3.

21. *BAL*.

22. Such an investigation would not contribute significantly to this study. However, Arthur S. Link expresses the view that German propaganda was "shrewd and subtle." Particularly, German scholars and church leaders, in his opinion, through their prestige, personal contacts, and publications had attained successful results. John Garraty, *Interpreting American History* (London, 1970), 2:126–27; interview with Arthur S. Link. Author's correspondence with Arthur S. Link.

23. Bernstorff, *Deutschland und Amerika*, pp. 54–55.

24. There are indications that Dernburg was not satisfied with Claussen's performance and therefore assigned key functions to Hale (*BAL*, p. 1705). We also have reason to believe that Bernstorff and Dernburg did not always work together smoothly. Whether intentionally or because of incorrect information, part of the American press regarded Dernburg as the Emperor's personal representative. The former chief of the German Colonial Office also had the habit of acting without instructions at times. Heinrich Schnee, *Als letzter Gouverneur in Deutsch-Ostafrika*, ed. Ada Schnee (Heidelberg, 1964), pp. 82–83. Falcke, *Vor dem Eintritt Amerikas in den Weltkrieg*, p. 51. Bernstorff to Foreign Office, March 2, 1915, AA, Vereinigte Staaten von Amerika 2, *secr.*, Bd. 1. Considerable difficulties also arose in the cooperation between Dernburg and the Consul General of New York. Hossenfelder's anti-Semitism played an important role here. Hossenfelder to Bethmann Hollweg, May 4, 1915; Bernstorff to Bethmann Hollweg, May 14, 1915; Hossenfelder to Bethmann Hollweg, May 18, 1915; all in AA, Vereinigte Staaten von Amerika 16, Bd. 34.

25. According to evidence given by himself, Hale was visited by Dernburg personally in December 1914 and asked to actively work for the German propaganda organization. *BAL*, p. 1705. Hale had interviewed the German Emperor in July 1908 after a recommendation by Sternburg and with the agreement of the Foreign Office. His views were known to be friendly to the Germans. In the summer of 1916 Bernstorff sent him to Germany to obtain favorable reports for the American press. Although Hale was tied to

Bernstorff by contract and had received at least $30,000 from the Ambassador, Hearst was not informed about his correspondent's second job. Bernstorff to Foreign Office, no Washington date, Stockholm date June 6, 1916, and Mumm Niederschrift, July 4, 1916, AA, Presseabteilung, Bd. 5, Die Presse in New York; Bernstorff to Foreign Office, July 7, 1916, AA, WK 18, Bd. 19.

26. Cf. Spindler, "Der britische Propagandafeldzug gegen die amerikanische Neutralität," p. 394.

27. Bernstorff, *Deutschland und Amerika*, pp. 45–46. Captain George B. Lester submitted to the American committee of inquiry as "Lester Exhibit No. 5" a list of some of the thirty-one persons who in his opinion had come to America for propaganda purposes. The persons named are: Dr. H. Neumann, Dr. Jos. Stern, Max Ritter, Dr. Hans Mack, Felix Scheibe, Dr. Selbmann, Fritz Hoff, Walter Kuehne, Richard Liskow, A. Neuberger, Hans Schmidt, Keppler, Homann, von Borkowski, and Dr. Karl Fernow. According to Lester's testimony Mack, Fernow, Liskow, and Schmidt went to Mexico in 1914 or 1915. *BAL*, p. 1685. It is quite possible that these names are misspelled, since the minutes of the Subcommittee on the Judiciary often show errors in the rendition of names. Bernstorff (*Deutschland und Amerika*, p. 47) states that Fuehr had assured him that none of the persons listed had worked for the Press Office.

28. Meyer-Gerhard to Solf, October 5, 1914, AA, Akten des AA im Grossen Hauptquartier 1914–1916, Presse und Journalisten, Bd. 3.

29. G. Lechartier, *Intrigues et Diplomaties à Washington (1914–1917)* (Paris, 1918).

30. Peterson, *Propaganda for War*, p. 137.

31. Falcke, *Vor dem Eintritt Amerikas in den Weltkrieg*, p. 51; Peterson, *Propaganda for War*, p. 137.

32. On May 17, 1915 (AA, Vereinigte Staaten von Amerika 16, Bd. 34) Bernstorff reported to Bethmann Hollweg that Dernburg had rendered "exceptional services" as long as he had only written for newspapers, "but when he began to give speeches at German-American gatherings, he entered very dangerous territory. All of us here agreed on that."

33. Dernburg report, August 31, 1914, AA, WK 10, *secr.*, Bd. 1.

34. J. P. Meyer of the Hamburg-American Line in New York to Albert Ballin, Presiding Director of the head office in Hamburg, May 18, 1915, HAPAG, Hamburg-Amerika Linie, New York, January 1, 1915–June 30, 1915. Chambers, *The War behind the War 1914–1918*, pp. 203–5: "The Dernburg incident furnishes only another illustration of the heartless stupidity, the piteous stupidity, with which the Germans sometimes conducted their war." Cf. Dernburg's article in *Independent*, December 7, 1914; Theodore Roosevelt's answer to this article in a letter to Dernburg, in Morison, *The Letters of Theodore Roosevelt*, 8:857–61; Bernhard Dernburg, *Search-Lights on the War* (collection of six articles) (New York, 1915). Rom-

berg to Bethmann Hollweg, December 27, 1915, AA, Vereinigte Staaten von Amerika 16, Bd. 38. Dernburg had already thought of returning to Germany earlier and had proposed releasing the British Admiral Neald from German imprisonment in return for his safe conduct on a neutral ship. Bernstorff to Foreign Office, November 25, 1914, AA, WK 10, secr., Bd. 3. Notes of a meeting with the German Ambassador, May 15, 1915, Houghton Library, Harvard University, Oswald Garrison Villard Papers.

35. Ritter, *Staatskunst und Kriegshandwerk,* 3:170. Ritter does not quote any sources and gives no explanation why Dernburg had to leave the United States. Even Jürgen Möckelmann, *Deutsch-amerikanische Beziehungen in der Krise* (Frankfurt, 1967), p. 16, presents the situation as if Dernburg had left America because he himself considered his continued propaganda work "pointless."

36. Bernstorff, *Deutschland und Amerika,* p. 52. In the fall of 1915 he had reported to Berlin: "If our propaganda ... remained short of what we tried for, this is mainly caused by the developments in German-American relations, public opinion extremely aroused by the incidents of the submarine war, and the attitude of the Government here." Bernstorff to Foreign Office, November 3, 1915, AA, Vereinigte Staaten von Amerika 5, Bd. 16.

37. Cf. copy of "explanatory memorandum prepared by Admiral Hall" sent to Secretary of State, September 1, 1917, NA, RG 59, Records of the Office of the Counselor, Box 200.

38. Dernburg himself started his activities "without any preconceived plan whatsoever." Bernstorff, *Deutschland und Amerika,* p. 46.

39. Berlin's transatlantic cables had been cut by Germany's enemies at the beginning of the war. Wireless communication had not been fully developed yet, and normal postal communication often took very long and was subject to the irregularities and dangers of the war. The HAPAG records contain information concerning the use of wireless messages supplied by the embassy for propaganda purposes. Cf. J. P. Meyer to Bernhard Huldermann, New York, September 23, 1914, HAPAG, Hamburg-Amerika Linie, New York, May 1, 1914–January 15, 1915.

40. Cf. Bernstorff to Foreign Office, June 2 and 5, 1916, English translations, NA, RG 59, Records of the Office of the Counselor, Box 205. J. P. Meyer (and second unreadable signature) to Bernhard Huldermann, HAPAG, Hamburg-Amerika Linie, New York, January 1, 1915–June 30, 1915.

41. For details, see below.

42. Cf. among others M. J. Bonn, *So macht man Geschichte* (Munich, 1953). Heinrich F. Albert, *Aufzeichnungen* (Berlin, [1948]).

43. Bernstorff, *Deutschland und Amerika,* p. 47.

44. Papen to Royal War Ministry in Berlin, November 1914, AA, Vereinigte Staaten von Amerika 5, Bd. 16.

45. Minutes of a conference of the Press Office on November 5, 1914, signed by Fuehr (sent to Berlin by Dernburg on November 9, 1914), AA,

Vereinigte Staaten von Amerika 2, Bd. 21: "Since in this last respect Professor Kühnemann has had considerable success, State Secretary Dr. Dernburg deems it necessary that a second well-known German professor be sent to America for this purpose, and if possible Hermann Oncken in Heidelberg or Dietrich Schäfer in Hamburg or Ernst Marx in Stuttgart." Kühnemann held his "spirited and stirring speeches" before German-American groups of all kinds "and proclaimed prophetically Germany's future position of power." *Monatshefte für deutsche Sprache und Pädagogik*, December 1915, p. 319.

46. Newspaper clippings, *The Seattle German Press*, December 18, 1914, p. 2; December 21, 1914, p. 3, AA Vereinigte Staaten von Amerika 2, Bd. 22. Kühnemann at the Bismarck birthday celebration in Passaic, New Jersey: "We will remain victorious in the field of arms, economy and intellect." *Monatshefte für deutsche Sprache und Pädagogik*, May 1915, p. 160.

47. Robert Lansing to Woodrow Wilson, December 9, 1914, quoted in Arthur S. Link, *The Struggle for Neutrality*, vol. 3 of *Wilson* (Princeton, 1960), p. 162. See full text of Lansing's letter and enclosed lengthy memorandum on Münsterberg and Dernburg in Link, ed., *The Papers of Woodrow Wilson* (Princeton, N.J., 1978–83), 31:432–46. When Münsterberg died in December 1916, and his brother Otto Münsterberg asked for German financial support for the family, the petition was denied by Adolf Count von Montgelas despite Hugo Münsterberg's services for the German cause. AA, Vereinigte Staaten von Amerika 16, Bd. 46.

48. Edmund von Mach is the author of *What Germany Wants* (1914), *Germany's Point of View* (1915), and *Sir Edward's Evidence* (1915).

49. Zimmermann to Bernstorff, October 28, 1914, AA, WK 11k, *secr.*, Bd. 1. Falcke to Bethmann Hollweg, December 7, 1914, AA, WK 11k, Bd. 3; Boehm report, June 24, 1915, AA, WK 11k, Bd. 9.

50. Text here quoted from a leaflet included in the exhibition "Romain Rolland Weltbürger zwischen Frankreich und Deutschland," University Library, Bonn, April/May 1969. The blunt statement of the German intellectual leaders caused James Harvey Robinson to interpret the event in the *New Republic* (December 19, 1914) as "the sign and the seal of the success of German *Kultur* in making all her subjects accept the Kaiser and his decisions." Quoted from George T. Blakey, *Historians on the Homefront* (Lexington, Ky., 1970), p. 32. Charles W. Eliot, the former President of Harvard University, rather unabashedly told his German colleagues what he thought of them: "American sympathies are with the German people in their sufferings and losses, but not with their rulers, or with the military class, or with the professors and men of letters who have been teaching for more than a generation that might makes right." Excerpts from an article written by Eliot for *The New York Times*, from *The Boston Herald*, October 3, 1914, p. 5. (Clipping, AA, Vereinigte Staaten von Nordamerika 2, Bd. 21.) Cf. Fritz Fischer, *Griff nach der Weltmacht* (Düsseldorf, 1961), p. 180.

For a more detailed treatment of the political views of German professors see Klaus Schwabe, "Zur politischen Haltung der deutschen Professoren im Ersten Weltkrieg," in *Historische Zeitschrift* 193 (1961): 601–34.

51. Deputy General Staff of the Army, Department IIIb, to Foreign Office News Department, June 14, 1915, and Röntgen to Deputy General Staff of the Army, July 18, 1915, AA, Presseabteilung, Vereinigte Staaten von Amerika 2, Bd. 1. It was not unusual for Bernstorff to place articles of German origin in the American press. (For instance, articles by General Friedrich von Bernhardi; see Bernstorff to Bethmann Hollweg, December 8, 1915, ibid., Bd. 4.)

52. Bernstorff, *Deutschland und Amerika*, pp. 44–45. Cf. *BAL*, p. 2007. *Monatshefte für deutsche Sprache und Pädagogik*, June 1915, p. 189.

53. The argument that German propaganda activities were especially hampered by shortage of funds was later often mentioned in defense of their failure. Cf. Spindler, "Der britische Propagandafeldzug gegen die amerikanische Neutralität," p. 934.

54. Fuehr to Legationsrat Horstmann, April 24, 1915, AA, Presseabteilung, Vereinigte Staaten von Amerika 2, Bd. 1. Bernstorff's report, June 13, 1915, AA, WK 11k, Bd. 16. Eckardt to Bernstorff, May 26, 1916, and Haniel to Eckardt, June 6, 1916, AA, Botschaft Washington, Akten betreffend Propagandaschriften, Bd. 1.

55. The firm was founded in April 1915 with an initial capital of $10,000. The capital was then increased to $140,000. The business was headed by Fuehr and Claussen, who were supported by Felix Malitz and Adolph Ingel. (The latter two were later sentenced to prison.) The journalist Edward Lyell Fox was also employed here temporarily. Albert maintains that the costs for the fictitious company were covered by "private German-American circles." Bernstorff, *Deutschland und Amerika*, p. 42. *BAL*, pp. xviii–xix, 1664–65.

56. Albert, *Aufzeichnungen*, pp. 51–52. Bernstorff, *Deutschland und Amerika*, p. 54.

57. There were more than 300 German-language newspapers in the country, around 50 of them in Wisconsin and 40 each in Ohio and Illinois. More than 30 German papers were printed in New York. *BAL*, p. 2921. According to Carl Wittke, *The German-Language Press in America* (Lexington, Ky., 1957), p. 243, in 1914 there were approximately 1,300 foreign newspapers and journals in America, of which 40 percent were published in the German language. Among the more than 500 names more than 50 were daily papers.

58. Supposedly already in October 1914 Dernburg paid $15,000 to Adolf Pavenstedt, partner in the finance house of Amsinck & Co. in New York. Pavenstedt is supposed to have contributed $5,000 and to have paid a total of $20,000 to the *Staats-Zeitung* on October 12. John P. Jones and Paul M. Hollister, *The German Secret Service in America 1914–1918* (Boston,

1918), p. 230, shows a photograph of the check written out by Pavenstedt to that amount.

59. Bernstorff to Foreign Office, December 19, 1914, AA, Vereinigte Staaten von Amerika 2, *secr.*, Bd. 1.

60. Zimmermann to Bernstorff, December 24, 1914, ibid.

61. Bernstorff to Foreign Office, December 25, 1914, AA, Deutschland 126a, Bd. 4.

62. Zimmermann to Bernstorff, December 31, 1914, AA, Vereinigte Staaten von Amerika 2, *secr.*, Bd. 1. Ethel Mary Tinnemann, "Count Johann von Bernstorff and German-American Relations, 1908–1917" (Ph.D. diss., University of California at Berkeley, 1960), p. 94, wrongly assumes that Berlin had denied financial support.

63. Bernstorff to Foreign Office, January 15, 1915, and, as enclosure, Pavenstedt to Bernstorff, January 15, 1915; and Bernstorff to Bethmann Hollweg, January 16, 1915, AA, Vereinigte Staaten von Amerika 2, *secr.*, Bd. 1.

64. Regarding the *Staats-Zeitung* see also Link, *The Struggle for Neutrality*, pp. 20–21.

65. Bernstorff to Bethmann Hollweg, November 6, 1915, AA, Presseabteilung, Vereinigte Staaten von Amerika 2, Bd. 4. Carl Wittke was therefore in error when he wrote in 1957: "There is little evidence that any German-language paper in the United States sold its favors for German gold. There was no need for bribery." Wittke, *The German-Language Press in America*, p. 238. That such erroneous information tends to be passed on can be seen from the claims made by Theodore Huebner, *The Germans in America* (Philadelphia, 1962), p. 146: "The German language newspapers were wholly on the German side. The charge that they were bought by German money has not been substantiated. In fact, it would have been unnecessary: their strong emotional response was a natural and a sincere one."

66. Viereck was one of the persons working with the German Information Service. His father was the former Leipzig Member of the Reichstag. *The Fatherland* appeared from August 1, 1914, until February 7, 1917. Viereck also over the years published a number of other papers. For details on Viereck see especially Niel M. Johnson, *George Sylvester Viereck. German-American Propagandist* (Urbana, Ill., 1972).

67. Cf. Theodore Roosevelt to Ralph Montgomery Easley, July 5, 1917, in Morison, *The Letters of Theodore Roosevelt*, 8:1207.

68. Carl Wittke, *German-Americans and the World War* (Columbus, 1936), p. 23.

69. Bernstorff, *Deutschland und Amerika*, p. 36. Jones and Hollister, *The German Secret Service in America 1914–1918*, p. 230.

70. Cf. *BAL*, p. xv.

71. Wittke, *German-Americans and the World War*, p. 23. John Dos Passos, *Mr. Wilson's War* (Garden City, N.Y., 1962), p. 138.

72. Wittke, *German-Americans and the World War*, p. 23, called it "perhaps the most outspoken propaganda sheet in America."

73. Report by Bernstorff, October 27, 1916, AA, Vereinigte Staaten von Amerika 2, Bd. 25. Bernstorff to Lansing, August 18, 1915, *FRUS 1915*, Suppl., p. 930. Tinnemann, "Count Bernstorff and German-American Relations, 1908–1917," pp. 93–94. Cf. C. Hartley Grattan, *Why We Fought* (New York, 1929), p. 86.

74. *BAL*, pp. 1478–79. According to the *Boston Globe*, November 22, 1922, clipping, Daniel F. Cohalan Papers, American Irish Historical Society, New York, Lindheim was codefendant with Edward A. Rumely and S. Walter Kauffman (also spelled *Kaufman*) against charges connected with the *New York Evening Mail* affair.

75. Report by Bernstorff, October 27, 1916, AA, Vereinigte Staaten von Amerika 2, Bd. 25. Cf. *BAL*, p. 1481. Link, *The Struggle for Neutrality*, p. 651.

76. Sielken was an "American businessman [*Grosskaufmann*]" from Baden (Prussian Minister Eisendecher in Karlsruhe to Bethmann Hollweg, November 11, 1916, AA, Vereinigte Staaten von Amerika 2, *secr.*, Bd. 1) with connections to the company "Messrs. Grossman Bros., New York City." T. St. John Gaffney, *Breaking the Silence* (New York, 1930), p. 45.

77. Schulze-Gaevernitz to Zimmermann, March 16, 1915: "I would like to add that ... Rumely is ... my closest friend." AA, Vereinigte Staaten von Amerika 2, *secr.*, Bd. 1.

78. Bernstorff to Foreign Office, January 15, 1915, ibid.

79. Zimmermann to Bernstorff, February 7, 1915, ibid.

80. Bernstorff to Foreign Office, February 21, 1915, ibid. (Here: "price not over 5 million marks.")

81. Apparently in addition to the organization lead by Dernburg.

82. Zimmermann to Bernstorff, March 5, 1915, AA, Vereinigte Staaten von Amerika 2, *secr.*, Bd. 1.

83. Bernstorff to Foreign Office, March 11, 1915, and Bernstorff to Foreign Office, March 20, 1915, ibid. The amounts mentioned vary in the two telegrams.

84. Bernstorff to Foreign Office, March 22, 1915, ibid. Passing on letter from Rumely to Schulze-Gaevernitz.

85. Bernstorff to Foreign Office, March 24, 1915, ibid.

86. Zimmermann to Bernstorff, March 28, 1915, ibid.

87. The author has been unable so far to establish with absolute certainty where this large sum of money came from. According to later information from Albert, "he [Rumely] borrowed the money from German sources." And: "The payments were made from the funds of the Zentral-Einkaufs-Gesellschaft at my disposal under the condition of later repayment from that side which was concerned." After the United States's entry into the war, Rumely settled his debt with the Germans by issuing a

new note in the amount of $100,000. Albert to Minister Adolf Müller in Bern, August 11, 1919, ibid. In January 1920 the German Minister of Finance transferred 1,600,000 marks to the Foreign Office to reimburse the $300,000 spent by the Foreign Office on the *Evening Mail.* Foreign Office to Ministry of Finance, Secret, December 27, 1919, and Minister of Finance to Reichshauptkasse, Secret, January 19, 1920, AA, Presseabteilung, Vereinigte Staaten von Amerika 6, Die Zeitung *Evening Mail,* Bd. 1. Cf. Falcke, *Vor dem Eintritt Amerikas in den Weltkrieg,* pp. 163–64.

88. Albert, *Aufzeichnungen,* p. 48.

89. Bernstorff reported that he had not had "favorable experiences" with Rumely. Report by Bernstorff, October 27, 1916, AA, Vereinigte Staaten von Amerika 2, Bd. 25.

90. Albert, *Aufzeichnungen,* p. 48.

91. The contract is to be found in AA, Presseabteilung, Vereinigte Staaten von Amerika 6. Die Zeitung *Evening Mail,* Bd. 2, prepared in Berlin on October 4, 1916.

92. Hays, Kaufman and Lindheim usually served as lawyers for Heinrich Albert. Falcke, *Vor dem Eintritt Amerikas in den Weltkrieg,* p. 163.

93. Albert, *Aufzeichnungen,* p. 49.

94. *BAL,* p. 1455. O. J. Markel to "Mein lieber Prittwitz," May 31, 1915, AA, Vereinigte Staaten von Amerika 2, Bd. 25.

95. Bernstorff identifies von Hamm as "editor-in-chief of the *New York American.*" Bernstorff to Bethmann Hollweg, Secret, March 27, 1916, AA, Presseabteilung, Vereinigte Staaten von Amerika 4, Propaganda und allgemeine Angelegenheiten, Bd. 1.

96. Ibid.

97. Albert, *Aufzeichnungen,* pp. 49–50. *BAL,* p. 1861. Untermeyer testified that he had met Bernstorff only a few times and that on those occasions only Bernstorff's personal matters had been discussed.

98. Charles Humbert was sentenced to death by a French court and executed. *BAL,* pp. 1945–53, 1960–61. Henry Landau, *The Enemy Within* (New York, 1937), pp. 107–8. George S. Viereck, *Spreading Germs of Hate* (New York, 1930), p. 108.

99. Epstein, *Matthias Erzberger and the Dilemma of German Democracy,* pp. 103–4, does not mention that Bolo Pascha was paid twice for what appears to have been the same operation. Hans Peter Hanssen, *Diary of a Dying Empire* (Bloomington, Ind., 1955), p. 263. Bolo eventually returned to France and in 1918 was tried for high treason, convicted, and executed. Cf. clipping from *New York Evening Sun,* April 17, 1918, Enemy Aliens, scrapbook, Hoboken Public Library, Hoboken, N.J.

100. Report by Bernstorff, October 27, 1916, AA, Vereinigte Staaten von Amerika 2, Bd. 25. Bernstorff writes that Lowe is of German descent, is married to a German and has offered his services. This offer, according to Bernstorff, came at a time when the German officials in the United States

were sorry about the death of John R. McLean, "the former owner of the *Washington Post*," who "had given his paper a quite anti-English character."

101. Lieutenant Colonel Boehm of the Deputy General Staff to Foreign Office, March 2, 1915; Zimmermann to Bernstorff, March 17, 1915; and Schulze-Gaevernitz to Zimmermann, March 16, 1915 (naming Rumely as negotiator in this matter); AA, Vereinigte Staaten von Amerika 2, *secr.*, Bd. 1.

102. Bernstorff to Bethmann Hollweg, October 16, 1916 (arr. Berlin January 3, 1917), AA, WK 10, *secr.*, Bd. 9. The money was paid back. Bernstorff: "May I ask you to treat this transaction as nonexistent, especially also when dealing with Jewish circles."

103. Report by Bernstorff, October 27, 1916, AA, Vereinigte Staaten von Amerika 2, Bd. 25: "Subsidies to American newspapers can never remain secret because there is no discretion in this country. In the end I am always made responsible for all articles."

104. Bernstorff to Bethmann Hollweg, February 18, 1916, AA, WK 10, *secr.*, Bd. 7. This document is Albert's account of the loan for $10,000,000 placed in the United States in 1915. Bernstorff added: "All outlays mentioned in the document have been decided upon in joint consultation by the respective authorities.... In principle all of them were also approved by Your Excellency." In 1915 alone, $1,081,164, or rather, $1,163,664 of the $10,000,000 were "spent for the purchase of newspaper." In the document these transactions appear under the accounts Perez I and Perez II.

105. While this study was being written, the noteworthy work by the German historian Egmont Zechlin, *Die deutsche Politik und die Juden im Ersten Weltkrieg* (Göttingen, 1969), was published. As Zechlin has not used American archives and has not seen the Warburg Papers in London but instead for the American side has relied largely on those Warburg correspondences which Max Warburg chose to pass on to the German Foreign Office, the treatment of the reaction of American Jews, in this context leading American Jewish circles of German descent, remains incomplete. As a consequence, the relevant passages about developments in America tend to be misleading. Zechlin, for instance, states that the German campaign for placing a loan in the United States in the fall of 1915 "morally [broke] the back of German-American agitation" and had "disastrous propagandistic consequences" (p. 500). In fact, as I show below, already in the summer of 1915 German propaganda had suffered such a set-back that the heights of activity of autumn 1914 and spring 1915 were not reached again. In another context, Zechlin apparently confuses the tasks of Heinrich Albert and Bernhard Dernburg (p. 449). Albert, not Dernburg, had been given the assignment to purchase material in the United States.

106. Bernstorff detested the anti-Semitism rampant in some German circles, an attitude which also made him an enemy of similar sentiments at

the time of the Weimar Republic. Kurt Blumenfeld (*Erlebte Judenfrage* [Stuttgart, 1962], pp. 173–74), the chairman of the Pro-Palästina-Komitee, says of him: "It was very fortunate that it was possible [to make] Count Bernstorff . . . a genuine friend of our cause. . . . He felt something of the tragedy of Jewish life in Germany."

107. Cf. Chaim Weizmann's very harsh judgment in *Trial and Error* (London, 1950; 1st ed., 1949), pp. 183–84: "They were the usual type of *Kaiserjuden* [sic], like Albert Ballin and Max Warburg, more German than the Germans, obsequious, superpatriotic, eagerly anticipating the wishes and plans of the masters of Germany."

108. Bernstorff, *Erinnerungen und Briefe* (Zürich, 1936), p. 17.

109. Max Warburg's brother Paul had married Salomon Loeb's daughter in 1895; in 1902 he became partner of his brother-in-law Jacob H. Schiff in the firm Kuhn, Loeb & Co. Felix Warburg, another brother, had married Jacob H. Schiff's daughter Frieda in 1893 and at the same time had become a partner in the company. Paul Warburg under President Wilson became Vice Governor of the Federal Reserve Board and in August 1914 retired as a partner from the banking house M. M. Warburg & Co. in Hamburg. Felix took Paul's place in Hamburg and at the same time remained a partner with Kuhn, Loeb & Co. Eric M. Warburg, "Gedenkrede zum 100-jährigen Geburtstag Max M. Warburgs," in *Max M. Warburg* (Glückstadt, 1967), pp. 13–14. Next to the Morgans, Kuhn, Loeb & Co. was the most important finance house for credits to governments, railways, and big business; Eduard Rosenbaum, *M. M. Warburg & Co. Merchant Bankers of Hamburg* (London, 1962), p. 137. Cf. Morton Tenzer, "The Jews," in *The Immigrants' Influence on Wilson's Peace Policies*, ed. Joseph P. O'Grady (Lexington, Ky., 1967), pp. 289–90.

110. Even Max Warburg, who through his relatives in New York was probably better informed about the American Jews than most influential Germans at the outbreak of the war, thought that Dernburg would succeed in placing a war loan in the United States. Max M. Warburg, *Aus meinen Aufzeichnungen* (New York, 1952), p. 35.

111. Cf. Zechlin, *Die deutsche Politik und die Juden im Ersten Weltkrieg*, p. 481: "The government did ease the disadvantagement of the Jews, but it neither supported total equality for them nor made a serious effort to fight the rampant public prejudices. . . . The Foreign Office did not exert any pressure on either the Imperial Chancellor or the Imperial Ministry of the Interior or the Prussian Ministry of the Interior in support of the suggestions made by Straus, Bernstorff, and Dernburg."

112. The Centralverein deutscher Staatsbürger jüdischen Glaubens was founded in 1893 and "was in its views and attitudes emphatically assimilationist and anti-Zionist." Jacob Dränger, *Nahum Goldmann* (Frankfurt, 1959), 1:215.

113. Proclamation signed: Verband der deutschen Juden (Association of

German Jews). Centralverein deutscher Staatsbürger jüdischen Glaubens (Central Association of German Citizens of Jewish Faith). Dated Berlin, August 1, 1914. In *Im deutschen Reich* 20(9) (September 1914): 339. (The parts of text in italics appear in heavy black print in the original.)

114. In a memorandum to the Foreign Office of 1898, Bodenheimer had already pointed out the importance of the language of the Jews as a "German folk dialect" (*Volksdialekt*) for the Empire. Bodenheimer referred to this memorandum in his petition to the Foreign Office at the beginning of the war. He suggested creating an East European federation with a Polish majority and Ukranians, White Russians, Lithuanians, Estonians, Latvians, Jews, and Germans as minorities. German Jews were supposed to make propaganda for this cause among the "Polish-Russian Jews" and the German army was supposed to appear in the East as a kind of liberation army. The memorandum was positively received, and Bodenheimer was asked to present his case in person. Max I. Bodenheimer, *So wurde Israel* (Frankfurt, 1958), pp. 183–84.

115. Cf. Bogdan Graf von Hutten-Czapski, *Sechzig Jahre Politik und Gesellschaft* (Berlin, 1936), 2:156.

116. Leading members were Max I. Bodenheimer, Franz Oppenheimer, Adolf Friedemann, Alfred Klee, and Hermann Struck. Abraham Robinsohn directed the Berlin office. A wartime newspaper *Kol Mewasser* appeared only twice. Sammy Gronemann and Arthur Hantke also were among the early members. Bodenheimer, *So wurde Israel*, pp. 184–89. Cf. Franz Oppenheimer, *Erlebtes, Erstrebtes, Erreichtes* (Düsseldorf, 1964; 1st ed. Berlin, 1931), p. 223. Minutes of the inaugural meeting at the Eden Hotel, Berlin, on August 17, 1914, AA, WK 11, adh. 2, Bd. 1.

117. Bodenheimer to Foreign Office, attention Minister von Bergen, September 1, 1914, AA, WK 11, adh. 2, Bd. 1. Report by Bodenheimer about his trip to Russian Poland representing the Komitee für den Osten (Committee for the East), late summer 1915, in ibid., Bd. 5: "Since at the beginning of the war an unfriendly opinion prevailed in the Jewish press in America, the committee sent . . . Straus there in order to win over public opinion of the American Jews for the Central Powers."

118. Bodenheimer to Otto Hammann, report about current activities of the German Komitee zur Befreiung der russischen Juden (Committee for the Liberation of the Russian Jews), enclosure to letter of September 28, 1914, ibid., Bd. 1. Cf. Saul Friedländer, "Die politischen Veränderungen der Kriegszeit und ihre Auswirkungen auf die Judenfrage," in *Deutsches Judentum in Krieg und Revolution 1916–1923*, ed. Werner E. Mosse and Arnold Paucker (Tübingen, 1971), pp. 31–33.

119. Spring Rice to Valentine Chirol, November 13, 1914, in Stephen Gwynn, *The Letters and Friendships of Sir Cecil Spring Rice* (London, 1929), 2:242–43. Roosevelt to Spring Rice, February 5, 1915, in Morison, *The Letters of Theodore Roosevelt*, 8:888.

120. Bernstorff had social contacts with the Hamburg branch as well as with the New York branch of the Warburg family. Until the sinking of the *Lusitania*, an "old friendship" linked him to James Speyer. Bernstorff to Bethmann Hollweg, October 20, 1915, AA, WK 11, adh. 2, Bd. 6. Cf. Bernstorff's report about German-Jewish commercial and financial circles. Bernstorff to Bethmann Hollweg, September 28, 1915, ibid., Bd. 5.

121. Cf. Joseph Rappaport, "The American Yiddish Press and the European Conflict in 1914," *Jewish Social Studies* (1957): 115: "Immigrant Jews prayed that the 'more civilized' Germans would free their oppressed brethren in Eastern Europe from Russian persecution." Cf. Roosevelt to Frederick Scott Oliver, July 22, 1915, in Morison, *The Letters of Theodore Roosevelt*, 8:953.

122. Zosa Szajkowski [Szajko Frydman], "Jewish Relief in Eastern Europe 1914–1917," in *Yearbook 10*, Publications of the Leo Baeck Institute (London, 1965), p. 25. Bernstorff to Foreign Office, January 19, 1915; *Hamburger Familienblatt*, January 1915, p. 1; Mumm to Deputy General Staff, January 30, 1915; all in AA, Russland 73, Bd. 10.

123. Cf. Eduard Meyer, *Weltgeschichte und Weltkrieg* (Stuttgart, 1916), p. 173: "If Germany and Austro-Hungary are defeated, Russia's rule over Europe is established; then there is no power anymore to offer resistance to the rule of the Slavs; tsarist despotism and Muscovite barbarism would rule unencumbered on the entire continent and would trample down with brutal force every other nationality, every move oriented by freedom and respecting human dignity. . . . Thus we go into war with the proud awareness that the battle for the preservation of the German nationality is at the same time a battle for the freedom of peoples and for saving civilization from being flooded by the Slavic hordes." (Meant for publication in the United States, but apparently not published there.)

124. Hans Delbrück, *Über den kriegerischen Charakter des deutschen Volkes* (Berlin, 1914), p. 25: "We know now what threat we face from the East, which people is hurtling its waves against us, against which we must defend ourselves, so that high culture will not be crushed by raw force and the suppression of everything fine and noble [*alles Hohen und Edlen*] will not overpower us and humanity with us; and we find nothing more shameful for the cultural peoples of the West than their having united themselves with these semi-barbarians to overpower us, who are among the bearers of the highest culture."

125. Friedrich Meinecke, *Die deutsche Erhebung von 1914* (Stuttgart, 1915), pp. 43, 55.

126. *Im deutschen Reich* 20(9) (September 1914): 348.

127. Newspaper clipping, *Berliner Tageblatt*, December 6, 1914, reprint of a letter from Bernstorff to Bernstein, publisher of *Der Tag*, December 6, 1914, AA, WK 11, adh. 2, Bd. 2.

128. In addition to this group, individual propagandists such as the au-

thor M. F. Seidmann also went to the United States on official propaganda missions. (Memo by Montgelas, November 29, 1914, AA, WK 11, adh. 2, Bd. 2.)

129. Note by Otto von Wesendonk, September 21, 1914, AA, WK 11, adh. 2, Bd. 1. Bodenheimer, *So wurde Israel*, p. 188. The amount involved was 20,000 gold marks, which probably covered more than travel expenses. Szajkowski, "Jewish Relief in Eastern Europe 1914–1917," p. 24, believes that the committee became involved with propaganda activities among the Jews of neutral countries "in order to maintain the goodwill of the German authorities." This is contradicted by the statement of the founder of the committee, Bodenheimer, who declares (*So wurde Israel*, p. 187): "When we were busy with the organization of the office, Friedemann told me that at the request of Meyrowitz, an agent of the North German Lloyd, the Imperial Naval Office wanted to send a trusted person to North America in order to influence the Jews there in favor of the Central Powers. Since this agreed with our intentions we immediately contacted Dr. Jaeckh of the Imperial Naval Office."

130. Draft, Zimmermann to Bernstorff, January 13, 1915, AA, WK 11, adh. 2, Bd. 3.

131. Bodenheimer, *So wurde Israel*, p. 187.

132. There were squabbles with leading Zionists. The Zionist "Aktionskomitee" (action committee) voted against the group around Bodenheimer and Oppenheimer. Arthur Hantke, intermediary of the Komitee zur Befreiung der russischen Juden (Committee for the Liberation of the Russian Jews) to the Zionists, thereupon left the group; ibid., p. 189.

133. Affidavit by Hindenburg for Bodenheimer and Oppenheimer, dated Radom, October 15, 1914, here quoted from ibid., p. 197. In October 1914 the two leaders of the committee had traveled to Radom to visit the German military headquarters at the Eastern front and there had talked with Hindenburg, Ludendorff, and other high-ranking military personnel. The following may serve to illustrate the mentality of the emissaries: Oppenheimer noticed several blond children in a village who were wearing neatly mended clothes. They stood out from the usual dirty children in ragged clothes. Oppenheimer: "It was a German village!" Oppenheimer, *Erlebtes, Erstrebtes, Erreichtes*, p. 231. Bodenheimer for his part told Field Marshall Hindenburg at the headquarters that he hoped "that with the German army also a higher culture would enter this country." Bodenheimer, *So wurde Israel*, pp. 195–96.

134. Schiff to Max Warburg, November 5, 1915, in Cyrus Adler, *Jacob H. Schiff. His Life and Letters* (Garden City, N.Y., 1929), 2:191–92.

135. Bodenheimer to Chief of Deputy General Staff, August 20, 1914, AA, WK 11, adh. 2, Bd. 1. Bodenheimer, *So wurde Israel*, pp. 187–88. Cf. Szajkowski, "Jewish Relief in Eastern Europe 1914–1917," p. 24. Cf. incomplete versions in Richard Lichtheim, *Rückkehr* (Stuttgart, 1970), p. 260,

and Richard Lichtheim, *Die Geschichte des deutschen Zionismus* (Jerusalem, 1954), pp. 212–13.

136. Bodenheimer, *So wurde Israel*, p. 189. Cf. Dränger, *Nahum Goldmann*, 1:186. Oppenheimer, *Erlebtes, Erstrebtes, Erreichtes*, p. 223. Among the new members of the Komitee für den Osten (Committee for the East) were the chairman of the Verband deutscher Juden (Association of German Jews), Eugen Fuchs, the orientalist Moritz Sebastian Sobernheim, Berthold Timendorfer, Julius Magnus, and, for a time, Oskar Cohn as representative of the Jewish socialists. The activities of the committee in the United States were also supported by Leopold Landau, Kurt Blumenfeld, Justizrat Horwitz, Paul Ehrlich, Maximilian Horwitz, and Dr. J. Ginsberg. Komitee to Straus, mailed by the Foreign Office, October 29, 1914, AA, WK 11, adh. 2, Bd. 2.

137. Oppenheimer, *Erlebtes, Erstrebtes, Erreichtes*, p. 226: "This committee has ... handled ... the transfer of financial donations from North American Jews to their relatives living in the occupied territory." Cf. Bodenheimer, *So wurde Israel*, pp. 262–63.

138. The Belgian Jean Fischer was of the opinion that Germany could not win the war. The committee, in his view, had therefore "placed its bet on the wrong horse." Bodenheimer, *So wurde Israel*, p. 189.

139. In America too the various Jewish organizations by no means agreed on their objectives. Here too there were bitter fights which at times were carried out quite openly.

140. Meyrowitz could not return to Germany without risking capture by the British. When the Zentralstelle für Auslandsdienst dropped him in January 1915, he argued that he had been sent to the United States by Ernst Jaeckh of the Imperial Naval Office, and he continued to publish accounts "in the Jewish press, etc., on his own" (Bernstorff). Bernstorff as well as Director Phil. Heineken of the North German Lloyd requested that Meyrowitz after his dismissal should receive financial support in America. Meyrowitz received 350 marks per month from the North German Lloyd. Draft, Zimmermann to Bernstorff, January 13, 1915; Bernstorff to Foreign Office, January 17, 1915; memo by Montgelas, January 28, 1915; in AA, WK 11, adh. 2, Bd. 3; report by Straus from New York of February 1915, sent to Montgelas by Sobernheim, March 27, 1915, in ibid., Bd. 4.

141. Oppenheimer to Bergen, December 5, 1914, AA, WK 11, adh. 2, Bd. 2; report by Straus, February 1915, Sobernheim to Montgelas, March 27, 1915, in ibid., Bd. 4.

142. Bernstorff to Bethmann Hollweg, April 26, 1915, AA, WK 11, adh. 2, Bd. 4.

143. Report by Straus, February 1915, sent to Montgelas by Sobernheim, March 27, 1915, ibid. Cf. Bodenheimer, *So wurde Israel*, p. 188: "Through his connection with the German ambassador Count von Bernstorff, he

(Straus) has rendered valuable services to the Jews of Eastern Europe and Palestine."

144. Straus received money "from the so-called Erzberger fund," paid out through Kuhn, Loeb & Co. and the Warburg bank. Oppenheimer through Foreign Office to Straus, March 29, 1915, AA, WK 11, adh. 2, Bd. 4. *BAL*, p. xvii. Cf. Szajkowski, "Jewish Relief in Eastern Europe 1914–1917," pp. 24–25, according to which the German Government did not cover all expenses of the Straus mission in America. Since 1915 Straus was being reimbursed for "the expenses of his stay" from "embassy funds" in Washington. Komitee für den Osten (Committee for the East) to Bergen, March 20, 1916, AA, WK 11, adh. 2, Bd. 6.

145. Bernstorff to Bethmann Hollweg, October 16, 1916, AA, WK 10, *secr.*, Bd. 9. According to Bernstorff's telegram, this sum was taken from the $10,000,000 loan and paid back prior to the date of this report. See n. 104 above.

146. Among them also Louis Marshall and Oscar S. Straus. American Jewish Committee, *The American Jewish Yearbook 5676*, ed. Joseph Jacobs (Philadelphia, 1915), p. 356.

147. Bernstorff to Foreign Office, September 26, 1914, AA, WK 11, adh. 2, Bd. 1. On November 9, 1914, Jagow rejected issuing a German declaration: "Issuing a proclamation in which Jews are granted complete civic freedom is out of the question in the present situation of war." Jagow to Zimmermann, November 9, 1914, ibid., Bd. 2.

148. Bernstorff to Foreign Office, October 20, 1914, ibid., Bd. 2. Report by Straus from New York, February 1915, Sobernheim to Montgelas, March 27, 1915, in ibid., Bd. 4.

149. Bernstorff to Bethmann Hollweg, October 20, 1915, AA, WK 22, adh. 2, Bd. 6. Albert, *Aufzeichnungen*, pp. 68–69. Cf. Stephen Birmingham, *In unseren Kreisen* (Frankfurt, 1969), p. 308.

150. Rappaport, "The American Yiddish Press and the European Conflict in 1914," pp. 115, 117, 126–29. However Szajkowski, "Jewish Relief in Eastern Europe 1914–1917," p. 26, shows that not all leading Jews sympathized with Germany.

151. Minutes of a conference at the Press Office on November 5, 1914, signed by Fuehr, mailed by Dernburg from New York on November 9, 1914, AA, Vereinigte Staaten von Amerika 2, Bd. 21. Bernstorff was present for part of the meeting. Cf. Falcke, *Vor dem Eintritt Amerikas in den Weltkrieg*, p. 96.

152. Minutes mentioned above of November 5, 1914, AA, Vereinigte Staaten von Amerika 2, Bd. 21.

153. Albert, *Aufzeichnungen*, pp. 50–51.

154. Especially noteworthy also are the letters by Max Warburg, James Simon, and Philipp Schiff to the Foreign Office in 1916. They contain com-

plaints about the unfavorable propaganda of the Straus office in America. Max Warburg sent in a letter of complaint from his brother Felix who writes: "One of the main rabble-rowsers [*Haupt-Hetzer*] and liars has been sent here at the expense of the German Empire and Jewry, and his mouth should be stuffed from over there." Apparently Straus had allowed himself to be used too much for Zionist ends. The Foreign Office through Bernstorff thereupon threatened to withdraw the financial basis for his operations in case he continued his agitation. Max Warburg to Zimmermann, February 5, 1916, July 19, 1916; Felix Warburg to Max Warburg, June 18, 1916; Max Warburg to Zimmermann, October 2, 1916; James Simon to Zimmermann, October 6, 1916; Philipp Schiff to Deputy General Command of the 18th Army Corps, September 13, 1916; Zimmermann to Bernstorff, October 14 or 21, 1916; Bernstorff to Bethmann Hollweg, November 10, 1916; all in AA, WK 11, adh. 2, Bd. 6.

155. Jacob H. Schiff to Zimmermann, on Kuhn, Loeb & Co. company stationery, October 19, 1914, AA, WK 11, adh. 2, Bd. 2. This letter does not appear in Adler, *Jacob H. Schiff. His Life and Letters*. Zechlin, *Die deutsche Politik und die Juden im Ersten Weltkrieg*, pp. 474–75, quotes only short excerpts from the unusual document.

156. S. Adler-Rudel, *Ostjuden in Deutschland 1880–1940* (Tübingen, 1959), p. 37: "None of the promises [of the proclamation] have ever been kept."

157. "Zu die Jiden in Paulen. . . . Unsere Fohnen brengen eich Recht un Freiheit: gleiche Birgerrechte, Freiheit vorn Glauben, Freiheit zu arbeiten ungestert in alle Zweigen vun akonomischen un kulturellen Leben in eier Geist! . . . Gedenkt Kischinew, Homel, Bialystok, Siedletz un viel hunderter andere blutige Pogromes! . . . Mir erwarten, as ihr wet beweisen durch Fakten eier Verschtand un eier Uebergebenheit. . . . Die obere Leitung vun die verbindet deitsche un esterreichisch-ungarische Armees." ("To the Jews in Poland. . . . Our flags bring you justice and freedom: equal civil rights, freedom of religion, freedom to work undisturbed in all areas of economic and cultural life in your spirit! . . . Remember Kischinew, Homel, Bialystok, Siedletz, and many hundred other bloody pogroms! . . . We expect that you will prove through facts your reason and your devotion. . . . The Supreme Command of the united German and Austro-Hungarian Armies") *Im deutschen Reich* (October–December 1914): 409–10, here quoted from the *Israelitisches Familienblatt*. Text also in Adler-Rudel, *Ostjuden in Deutschland 1880–1940*, pp. 156–57.

158. Newspaper clipping, *Berliner Tageblatt*, letter from Bernstorff to Bernstein, editor of *Der Tag*, November 6, 1914, AA, WK 11, adh. 2, Bd. 2.

159. Ibid.: "Germany has given its Jews all civil rights; the few last obstacles will disappear with this war." In reality the opposite was the case. Ernest Hamburger, *Juden im öffentlichen Leben Deutschlands* (Tübingen, 1968), p. 101, speaks of "an intensification of social and political anti-

Semitism, especially during the last war years."

160. Quoted in *Im deutschen Reich* (May–July 1915): 127. Cf. Zechlin, *Die deutsche Politik und die Juden im Ersten Weltkrieg*, pp. 480–81.

161. In the fall of 1915, Julius Berger, Secretary of the World Zionist Organization, traveled to Poland at the request of the American Jewish Relief Committee and became a witness to the bad treatment of the Jews by the German authorities. S. Adler-Rudel, "East European Jewish Workers in Germany," in *Yearbook 2*, Leo Baeck Institute (London, 1957), pp. 143–44.

162. Adler-Rudel, ibid., p. 142: "Wherever the German armies arrived the Jews were the first to suffer." Adler-Rudel, *Ostjuden in Deutschland 1880–1940*, p. 37: "They soon were the victims against whom the German sense of order lashed out in the occupied territory with numerous regulations, threats, and punishments."

163. Bodenheimer, *So wurde Israel*, p. 194: "We suggested to him [Ludendorff] to bring our agents into the occupied territory in order to facilitate the communication between the military and the Jews. When the Jews later had to suffer from the incursions of the German army, we realized how beneficial this would have been. The deeply rooted hatred of the Jews was to blame for the fact that the Jews were met with such great distrust."

164. Bodenheimer, ibid., p. 200.

165. Oppenheimer to Carl-Ludwig Diego von Bergen, December 5, 1914, AA, WK 11, adh. 2, Bd. 2.

166. It was the end of the friendship between Bernstorff and James Speyer. Cf. Jacob Schiff to Charles W. Eliot, March 14, 1917, in Adler, *Jacob H. Schiff. His Life and Letters*, 2:201: "But ever since the sinking of the *Lusitania* and the subsequent ruthless and inhuman acts of the German Government, my attitude has undergone a thorough change, and I now only hope that before very long Great Britain and France will be able to force a peace which shall prevent the return of conditions that have brought upon the world the present ghastly situation."

167. See now this author's comparative ethnic study of Irish and Germans, *Iren und Deutsche in der Neuen Welt* (Stuttgart, 1986). Jürgen Möckelmann, *Deutsch-amerikanische Beziehungen in der Krise*, vol. 6 of *Hamburger Reihe zur neueren Geschichte* (Frankfurt, 1967), treats the problem of the German-Americans but fails to show the close relations between the German propaganda apparatus and organized German-Americans. This omission is particularly serious in the cases of Ridder and Viereck and other such Germans, who worked with funds from the German Embassy and for a time under considerable German influence. As a consequence they did not necessarily express the independently formed public opinion of the German ethnic group. (Möckelmann only mentions the disclosures from Heinrich Albert's papers which fell into the hands of the American Government.)

168. Before publication of the original German edition of this study

(1975) I was not able to see Frederick C. Luebke's *Bonds of Loyalty* (DeKalb, Ill., 1974) which examines the conflict countless German-Americans experienced as a consequence of the war in Europe and in view of American participation after April 1917. Luebke's work is the most thorough investigation of the subject. His portrayal of German-Americans during the First World War is based on broad archival research and expressive of the author's compassion for the troubled ethnic group. My own research in no way contradicts most of the findings of Luebke but places more weight on the negative effects of German propaganda and sabotage projects on U.S. public opinion. Cf. my review of what I have called "a major contribution to German-American studies" in *New Jersey History* (Summer–Autumn 1976): 123–24.

169. Link, *The Struggle for Neutrality*, p. 20, defines as German-Americans such citizens of the United States who had either been born themselves in Germany or who had at least one parent who was born in Germany. He estimates the number of these German-Americans at more than 8,250,000 at the beginning of the war. Cf. Jürgen Möckelmann, "Das Deutschlandbild in den U.S.A. 1914–1918 und die Kriegspolitik Wilsons" (Ph.D. diss., Universität Hamburg, 1965), p. 79.

170. Cf. Wittke, *The German-Language Press in America*, p. 221.

171. After America's entry into the war, a considerable portion of the German-American press even sided with the American government: "Many German language papers denounced the Kaiser and his Junker-dominated government. . . . They pointed with pride to the large number of German names on the rolls of the United States military forces. . . . German-Americans now were as deeply involved in the war as all other Americans." Ibid., p. 266.

172. The German historian Hermann Oncken deplores this fact: "There can be . . . no denial of the grievous fact that the German-Americans are gradually disappearing in an unequalled process of absorption, and this process is all the more curious as it is not a nation of low cultural standing, but the sons of one of the old and great nations of culture and power who are being absorbed." "Die deutsche Auswanderung nach Amerika und das Deutschamerikanertum vom 17. Jahrhundert bis zur Gegenwart," in Hermann Oncken, *Historisch-politische Aufsätze und Reden* (Munich, 1914), 1:115.

173. Wittke, *German-Americans and the World War*, pp. 27–28. Clifton J. Child, *The German-Americans in Politics 1914–1917* (Madison, 1939), pp. 22–23. *Monatshefte für deutsche Sprache und Pädagogik*, October 1914, p. 289.

174. Falcke, *Vor dem Eintritt Amerikas in den Weltkrieg*, pp. 80–81. Albert, *Aufzeichnungen*, pp. 76–77. When the orders for mobilization of the German reservists went out to the diplomatic representatives in America, the authorities apparently had neither expected England's entry into the

war and with it a large-scale blockade of the seas nor had they counted on such a large number of men liable for military service.

175. Rappaport, "The American Yiddish Press and the European Conflict in 1914," p. 115, reports that the German Consulate in New York even asked the Hebrew Immigrant Aid Society to help quarter German reservists before they could be shipped to Europe. Cf. Child, *The German-Americans in Politics 1914–1917*, p. 23.

176. Falcke, *Vor dem Eintritt Amerikas in den Weltkrieg*, p. 37. In fact, Claussen had been engaged in his propaganda activities with the full support of his employer, the Hamburg-American Line office in New York. Ecker to Huldermann, September 28, 1914, HAPAG, Hamburg-Amerika Linie, New York, May 1, 1914–January 15, 1915.

177. The context seems to refer to Dernburg, although the title "Excellency" could refer to Dernburg as well as to Bernstorff.

178. Cf. Wittke, *The German-Language Press in America*, p. 241.

179. Minutes of the meeting of November 5, 1914, signed by Fuehr, sent in by Dernburg on November 9, 1914, AA, Vereinigte Staaten von Amerika 2, Bd. 21.

180. Friedrich von Prittwitz und Gaffron, *Zwischen Petersburg und Washington* (Munich, 1952), p. 215. Hugo Münsterberg was a particularly well-known "hyphenated American" who also worked together with the German Information Service. In his book *The Peace and America* (Leipzig, 1915), he presents a number of typical arguments of some German-Americans. For a specific faction within the German ethnic group see Alan N. Graebner, "The Acculturation of an Immigrant Lutheran Church: The Lutheran Church-Missouri Synod, 1917–1929" (Ph.D. diss., Columbia University, 1965), pp. 33–50.

181. Wittke, *German-Americans and the World War*, p. 40.

182. Ibid.

183. Link, *The Struggle for Neutrality*, pp. 372–73. Cf. Child, *The German-Americans in Politics 1914–1917*, pp. 67–68.

184. Möckelmann, *Deutsch-amerikanische Beziehungen in der Krise*, p. 15.

185. Cf. Jacob H. Schiff to Dernburg, May 12, 1915, in Adler, *Jacob H. Schiff. His Life and Letters*, 2:189–90. Following Dernburg's undiplomatic remarks about the *Lusitania* catastrophe Schiff thought that it would be better for the German chief of propaganda to be silent.

186. Link, *The Struggle for Neutrality*, pp. 374–79.

187. Cf. Möckelmann, *Deutsch-amerikanische Beziehungen in der Krise*, p. 15.

188. Cf. Cecil Spring Rice to Edward Grey, May 20, 1915, in Gwynn, *The Letters and Friendships of Sir Cecil Spring Rice*, 2:270.

189. Bernstorff reported that "the large German American associations which during the war had made their appearance here, in particular the

American Independance [sic] League, the American Truth Society, and the Neutrality League, [were] induced to protest demonstrations of all kinds." Report by Bernstorff, November 3, 1915, AA, Vereinigte Staaten von Amerika 5, Bd. 16. Cf. Arthur S. Link, *Confusions and Crises 1915–1916*, vol. 4 of *Wilson* (Princeton, N.J., 1964), pp. 55–56.

190. Cf. Cohen, *The American Revisionists*, p. 3.

191. Cf. M. J. Bonn, *Amerika und sein Problem* (Munich, 1925), p. 115. Friedrich Luckwaldt, *Geschichte der Vereinigten Staaten* (Berlin, 1920), 2:241.

192. Bernstorff to Bethmann Hollweg, May 17, 1916, AA, Vereinigte Staaten von Amerika 10, Bd. 1. Bonn, *Amerika und sein Problem*, p. 115.

193. Carl Wittke, *The Irish in America* (Baton Rouge, La., 1956), pp. 88–102, 172–80, 216–27. Doerries, *Iren und Deutsche in der Neuen Welt*. German propaganda also catered especially to the Catholic church. Already early in 1915 Bernstorff suggested alerting the Vatican to the dangers of a victory by Orthodox Russia. At the same time it was thought useful to point out to Rome that a victorious Germany combined with Austria and Belgium would represent a predominantly Catholic empire. Bernstorff and Matthias Erzberger even went so far as to attempt to influence the election of a bishop in Ireland. When it came to organizing strikes in America, Catholic priests were also used for German purposes. Bernstorff to Foreign Office, February 27, 1915; Bernstorff to Foreign Office, August 16, 1916; Zimmermann to the Royal Minister in Rome Mühlberg, April 23, 1915; all in AA, Vereinigte Staaten von Amerika 13a, Bd. 6.

194. Wittke, *The Irish in America*, p. 274: "A rapprochement between Irish and German-Americans began to take form about 1898, when the press and spokesmen of both groups believed a secret alliance with England was imminent."

195. Bülow, *Denkwürdigkeiten* (Berlin, 1930), 2:15, had the following to say about Theodor Schiemann, who was to play an unfortunate role in the formulation of some policies of the Foreign Office: "Theodor Schiemann, like some other scholars, did not adjust well to the atmosphere at the Court. More and more, he turned into a lickspittle and a scandalmonger and was to give plenty of trouble to me and, what was worse, to our politics over the years." Regarding Schiemann, cf. also Otto Graf zu Stolberg-Wernigerode, *Die unentschiedene Generation* (Munich, 1968), pp. 216–18.

196. George Freeman to Schiemann (copy), January 23, 1907; and Schiemann to Freeman (copy), February 7, 1907; AA, Vereinigte Staaten von Amerika 10, Bd. 1.

197. As president of the German-American National Alliance, Charles J. Hexamer was one of the key figures of German-American agitation in America during the war.

198. Private letter, Sternburg to Hilmar Freiherr von dem Bussche-Haddenhausen (copy), no date, received by the Foreign Office March 7, 1907;

Freeman to Schiemann (copy), November 3, 1907; and Sternburg to Bülow, May 7, 1908; all in AA, Vereinigte Staaten von Amerika 10, Bd. 1.

199. Bernstorff to Bethmann Hollweg, December 20, 1910, in ibid.

200. Bernstorff to Bethmann Hollweg, January 8, 1914, AA, Botschaft Washington, Graf Bernstorff (copy from the "Privateigentum Riesser").

201. According to the records, in this mostly represented by members of Department IIIb (intelligence service).

202. After Foreign Secretary Gottlieb von Jagow had expressed his doubts: "It should be considered . . . whether through a Government declaration regarding the liberation of Ireland we will not forfeit the sympathies of the British population and the American Government." Jagow from Koblenz to Foreign Office, August 25, 1914, AA, WK 11k, *secr.*, Bd. 1.

203. Bernstorff to Foreign Office, September 25, 1914, ibid. Sir William James, *The Code Breakers of Room 40. The Eyes of the Navy* (New York, 1956), pp. 43–44. Cf. *DRSFM*, p. 3.

204. Basil Thomson, *My Experiences at Scotland Yard* (Garden City, N.Y., 1923), p. 84. Wittke, *The Irish in America*, p. 276. *DRSFM*, p. 3.

205. *BAL*, p. 16. Cf. Falcke, *Vor dem Eintritt Amerikas in den Weltkrieg*, p. 94. James K. McGuire wrote propagandistic literature himself such as *The King, the Kaiser and Irish Freedom* (New York, 1915).

206. Wittke, *The Irish in America*, p. 277.

207. Cf. also Bonn, *Amerika und sein Problem*, p. 115, who speaks of "Imperial German propaganda as it was in particular instigated by the military authorities."

208. See below (Chapter 5) for details of the embarrassing situation in which Bernstorff found himself after the confiscation of Wolf von Igel's papers by American intelligence agents.

209. A declaration giving the impression of having been drafted by the Foreign Office was signed by Boehm on January 12, 1926, probably after he had been summoned by Dr. Johannes G. Lohmann of the Foreign Office; AA, Rechtswesen 6, Sabotage Claims, Bd. 4. According to Boehm's statement, the plan to recruit agents for England among Americans and Irish in America originated with the Admiralty Staff.

210. Most probably men such as Major Boehm were also involved in further plans for armed activities in Ireland. See the treatment of the Casement mission in Chapter 5.

211. Alias Carl Roediger, alias Hajo Schroejers, alias M. Schmidt, alias P. Stamm, alias H. Stamm, alias Dillon, alias Hudson. Jeremiah A. O'Leary, *My Political Trial and Experiences* (New York, 1919), pp. 525–26. Identity of this agent confirmed by his own statements, AA, Rechtswesen 6, Bd. 15.

212. Alias Maria K. de Victorica, alias Maria Victorica, alias Marie de Vussière, alias Clark, alias Maria von Kretschman, alias Baroness von Kretschman. O'Leary, *My Political Trial and Experiences*, pp. 525–26. Regarding this agent, cf. information in Herbert O. Yardley, *The American*

Black Chamber (London, 1931), pp. 53–73. See also Paul Reichardt to Reichswehrministerium, Marineleitung (copy), January 25, 1925, AA, Rechtswesen 6, Bd. 3.

213. Reichardt to Reichswehrministerium, Marineleitung (copy), January 25, 1925, AA, Rechtswesen 6, Bd. 3; Reichardt to Reichswehrministerium, June 22, 1931, ibid., Bd. 20. Commander August Lassen, who took over Reichardt's department (then called N I 11) in the winter of 1917, testified after the war that he had had two agents, "Wessels and Madame Victorica," in America. (Kircheisen had already returned to Germany in the spring of 1917.) In 1925, Lassen only remembered that the two agents had been instructed to disseminate *political* propaganda among the Irish. Lassen to Reichswehrministerium, Marineleitung, Dezernat A 11n, January 8, 1925, Bd. 15.

214. Wittke, *The Irish in America*, p. 278. Link, *The Struggle for Neutrality*, p. 161.

215. Link, *The Struggle for Neutrality*, p. 161.

216. Ibid., p. 23.

217. Bernstorff to Foreign Office, November 3, 1915, AA, Vereinigte Staaten von Amerika 5, Bd. 16. Cf. Wittke, *The Irish in America*, pp. 276–77. O'Leary, *My Political Trial and Experiences*, p. 51. *BAL*, p. xxiii–xxiv.

218. Cf. Wittke, *The Irish in America*, p. 282; Thomas J. Kerr, IV, "German-Americans and Neutrality in the 1916 Election," *Mid-America* 43 (1961): 95–105; Paul L. Murphy, *World War I and the Origin of Civil Liberties in the United States* (New York, 1979), pp. 53–54.

219. Wittke, *The Irish in America*, p. 277. Falcke, *Vor dem Eintritt Amerikas in den Weltkrieg*, p. 94. Kuno Meyer compared what he saw as the splendid development of Alsace-Lorraine with the sufferings of Ireland under England's rule. *Monatshefte für deutsche Sprache und Pädagogik*, March 1915, pp. 88–89.

220. *The Irish World*, one of the more important publications of the American Irish, still supported John Redmond's politics in 1914. Wittke, *The Irish in America*, p. 274.

CHAPTER THREE

1. Especially Karl E. Birnbaum, *Peace Moves and U-Boat Warfare* (Stockholm, 1958), although treating mainly the period from April 1916 to January 1917. Arno Spindler's *Der Handelskrieg mit U-Booten*, vols. 1–5 (Berlin, 1932–66), must still be considered the standard German work on the submarine war on commerce.

2. The relevant archives and memoirs do not contain any pertinent information. One may therefore assume that the Ambassador was not given particular directions or instructions.

3. Spindler, *Der Handelskrieg mit U-Booten*, 1:4–5. According to Spindler the first surprising successes had "enormously increased regard for the submarine" and therefore "blurred the view of what had been and could be attained." Cf. Sir Arthur Hezlet, *The Submarine and Sea Power* (London, 1967), pp. 27–28.

4. Hermann Bauer, *Als Führer der U-Boote im Weltkriege* (Leipzig, 1942), p. 143; Gerhard Ritter, *Staatskunst und Kriegshandwerk* (Munich, 1964–68), 3:146; Alfred von Tirpitz, *Politische Dokumente* (Hamburg, 1926), 2:281.

5. Twelve of the boats were still equipped with older petroleum engines; *U-19–22, U-24, U-27–30* were equipped with Diesel engines. (Spindler, *Der Handelskrieg mit U-Booten*, 1:7.)

6. Cf. ibid., pp. 34–36. Theobald von Bethmann Hollweg, *Betrachtungen zum Weltkriege* (Berlin, 1921), 2:121. The interview was also published in the United States in the late fall of 1914. (Zimmermann to Bethmann Hollweg, March 19, 1915, AA, Akten des AA im Grossen Hauptquartier 1914–1916, Presse und Journalisten, Bd. 5.)

7. Ritter, *Staatskunst und Kriegshandwerk*, 3:146.

8. Bethmann Hollweg to Zimmermann, December 29, 1914, AA, WK 18, *secr.*, Bd. 1. Cf. Tirpitz, *Politische Dokumente*, 2:292–95. Erich von Falkenhayn, *Die Oberste Heeresleitung 1914–1916 in ihren wichtigsten Entschliessungen* (Berlin, 1920), p. 60.

9. Bethmann Hollweg to Zimmermann, December 29, 1914, AA, WK 18, *secr.*, Bd. 1.

10. Tirpitz, *Politische Dokumente*, 2:285–86.

11. Spindler, *Der Handelskrieg mit U-Booten*, 1:58–60. Tirpitz, *Politische Dokumente*, 2:298.

12. Pohl to Bethmann Hollweg, January 20, 1915, AA, WK 18, *secr.*, Bd. 1.

13. Cf. Falkenhayn, *Die Oberste Heeresleitung 1914–1916 in ihren wichtigsten Entschliessungen*, p. 59. Spindler, *Der Handelskrieg mit U-Booten*, 1:66–67.

14. Jagow to Foreign Office for Imperial Chancellor, January 20, 1915, AA, WK 18, *secr.*, Bd. 1.

15. Petition to Imperial Chancellor, January 26, 1915, signed by Sering, Triepel, von Wilamowitz-Möllendorf, Otto von Gierke, Kahl, von Harnack, von Schmoller, and Schiemann, printed in Spindler, *Der Handelskrieg mit U-Booten*, Appendix 24, 1:234–35.

16. Birnbaum, *Peace Moves and U-Boat Warfare*, pp. 25–26.

17. Ritter, *Staatskunst und Kriegshandwerk*, 3:152–53.

18. Present at the meeting at the Imperial Chancellory were the Imperial Chancellor, the Chief of the Admiralty Staff, Zimmermann, Falkenhayn, and State Secretary of the Interior Clemens von Delbrück. Admiral von Pohl declared that difficulties with the neutrals would be avoided since

neutral commercial vessels could be distinguished from enemy vessels. With the U-boat weapon, he said, it would be possible "to move England to give in" within a short period of time. (Spindler, *Der Handelskrieg mit U-Booten,* 1:78–81.)

19. Cf. Bethmann Hollweg (*Betrachtungen zum Weltkriege,* 2:116): "I myself was ... in the winter of 1914–15, not unimpressed by the confidence of the Navy."

20. Spindler, *Der Handelskrieg mit U-Booten,* 1:86–87. Thomas A. Bailey and Paul B. Ryan, *The Lusitania Disaster* (New York, 1975), p. 33. Ritter, *Staatskunst und Kriegshandwerk,* 3:155. Cf. Birnbaum, *Peace Moves and U-Boat Warfare,* p. 24.

21. *FRUS 1915,* Suppl., pp. 95–97. Jagow did declare in a press statement on February 8 that this was not a proclamation of a blockade. He insisted, however, on warning the neutrals against traveling through those areas which had been declared war zones. (Information from Jagow to Associated Press, January 8, 1915, AA, WK 18, secr., Bd. 1.) Cf. the announcement signed by Admiral von Pohl on February 4. (Spindler, *Der Handelskrieg mit U-Booten,* 1:87.)

22. In fact, the American note was sent to Gerard on February 10, who delivered it to Jagow on February 12.

23. Bernstorff, *Deutschland und Amerika* (Berlin, 1920), p. 130. In *The Struggle for Neutrality,* vol. 3 of *Wilson* (Princeton, N.J., 1960), Arthur S. Link says, "News of the German proclamation of February 4 came almost like a bolt out of the blue to Washington" (p. 320).

24. Link, *The Struggle for Neutrality,* pp. 320–22.

25. *FRUS 1915,* Suppl., pp. 98–100. Cf. German translation in Bernstorff, *Deutschland und Amerika,* pp. 131–32. Gerard to Jagow, February 12, 1915, AA, WK 18, secr., Bd. 1.

26. Spindler, *Der Handelskrieg mit U-Booten,* 2:7.

27. Cf. Bernstorff to Foreign Office, February 11, 1915: "Urgently recommend ... most careful examination in cases of liners under American flag ... as well as sparing crews if at all possible. Blunders could have serious consequences." Ibid., 1:100.

28. *FRUS 1915,* Suppl., pp. 112–15. The note was cabled to Washington by Gerard on February 17. Cf. German text in Spindler, *Der Handelskrieg mit U-Booten,* 1:120–26.

29. Spindler, *Der Handelskrieg mit U-Booten,* 1:129–30.

30. Among other things the order said: "His Majesty the Emperor, however, wants to expressly point out to the U-boat commanders that considering the difficult political relationship with the United States and Italy, utmost caution must be observed with regard to American and Italian liners in order to avoid inadvertently sinking them." (Ibid., 1:138–39.)

31. Replying to U.S. note of February 10 (12), Gerard to Bryan, February 17, 1915, *FRUS 1915,* Suppl., pp. 112–15. Cf. Hans Delbrück, "Der Krieg

im Februar," *Preussische Jahrbücher* 159 (January–March 1915): 569–70 regarding the note of February 17: "our often-scorned Foreign Office has masterfully parried this blow [U.S. note of February 10]."

32. Bryan to the American ambassadors in London and Berlin, February 20, 1915, *FRUS 1915*, Suppl., pp. 119–20. The Americans suggested that Germany and Britain should give up the reckless use of drifting mines, that both countries should treat commercial vessels of all nationalities according to international law, and that the misuse of neutral flags should stop. Moreover, the Americans said, Germany should submit to strict controls that would guarantee that imported food only went to "non-combatants." In exchange, Britain should not treat such food as contraband.

33. The conflict regarding the attitude Germany was to take toward the American request reached its climax in the course of a meeting with the Emperor on February 28, 1915. Bethmann Hollweg presented the draft of the German note of reply and declared as useless the Navy's suggestion to use the German ships interned in America for the transport of food under neutral flag. Admiral Bachmann argued that German acceptance of the proposals would in fact mean the abandonment of the submarine war as announced on February 4. In addition, German acquiescence would be interpreted as weakness. Admiral von Müller, however, declared himself in favor of the draft of the Foreign Office, and thus the Emperor approved it, after having pointed out, though, that the whole German people wanted the submarine war and that Bethmann Hollweg would just have to accept that. (Tirpitz, *Politische Dokumente*, 2:322–26.)

34. *FRUS 1915*, Suppl., pp. 129–30. German note of reply of February 28 in Gerard to Bryan, March 1, 1915. Cf. Falkenhayn, *Die Oberste Heeresleitung 1914–1916 in ihren wichtigsten Entschliessungen*, p. 132.

35. Page to Bryan, March 15, 1915, *FRUS 1915*, Suppl., pp. 140–43.

36. Arno Spindler, *Wie es zu dem Entschluß zum uneingeschränkten U-Boots-Krieg 1917 gekommen ist* (Göttingen, n.d.), p. 15.

37. Page to Bryan, March 15, 1915, and "Order of Council of March 11, 1915," *FRUS 1915*, Suppl., pp. 143–45. (All German imports and exports were to be cut off beginning March 1, 1915. The confiscated goods were to be submitted to the jurisdiction of a Prize Court in Great Britain.) Cf. Link, *The Struggle for Neutrality*, pp. 338–39. Ritter, *Staatskunst und Kriegshandwerk*, 3:159. David Lloyd George, *War Memoirs* (London, 1934), 2: 667–68.

38. Bryan to Page, March 30, 1915, *FRUS 1915*, Suppl., pp. 152–56. Link, *The Struggle for Neutrality*, pp. 347–48; quote from Wilson to Mary A. Hulbert, March 7, 1915.

39. Cf. Link, *The Struggle for Neutrality*, p. 368.

40. For Bernstorff's treatment of the matter and the German text see Bernstorff, *Deutschland und Amerika*, pp. 135–39. He dates the notice April 27, 1915. Bailey and Ryan, *The Lusitania Disaster*, p. 74, reproduce

the text as it appeared in the *New York World* on May 1, 1915. Cf. the somewhat different description of the background of the German announcement in Colin Simpson, *The Lusitania* (London, 1972; Boston, 1973), pp. 104–7. The different dates (April 22 and 27) can probably be explained by the postponement of publication.

41. Bernstorff, *Deutschland und Amerika*, p. 137.
42. Link, *The Struggle for Neutrality*, pp. 368–69.
43. Number of victims here according to ibid., p. 372.
44. Bernstorff, *Deutschland und Amerika*, p. 135.
45. Arthur S. Link, *Wilson the Diplomatist* (Baltimore, Md., 1957), p. 31.
46. Bryan to Penfield, August 4, 1914, *FRUS 1914*, Suppl., p. 42. About Wilson's move see also Luigi Albertini, *The Origin of the War of 1914* (London, 1967), 3:699–702.
47. Cf. Lloyd George, *War Memoirs*, 2:674–75.
48. Gerard to Bryan, August 14, 1914, *FRUS 1914*, Suppl., pp. 60–61. James W. Gerard, *My Four Years in Germany* (London, 1917), pp. 138–42. James W. Gerard, *My First Eighty-three Years in America* (Garden City, N.Y., 1951), pp. 217–20. Gerard remembers that the Emperor wrote the answer in his presence and instructed him to wire it to Wilson and to hand it to the press at the same time. Jagow, however, according to Gerard, insisted on being informed about the contents, since difficulties had developed once before as a consequence of an Imperial telegram. After having seen it, the Secretary asked him not to make the telegram public. *IPH*, 1:288–89.
49. House to Zimmermann, September 5, 1914, *IPH*, 1:327–28.
50. See Speyer's own version of the significance of the event in a later letter to Burton J. Hendrick, February 3, 1922, LC, Oscar S. Straus Papers.
51. Cf. Straus' own recollections, LC, Oscar S. Straus Papers, Box 24: "In the course of conversation Bernstorff stated, what is frequently stated by the Germans, that they did not want war. . . . I took occasion to ask whether that sentiment still prevailed. . . . He . . . replied, speaking for himself, he certainly would entertain a proposition for mediation but . . . he could not speak officially." Also Straus to Sir Edward Grey, September 9, 1914, LC, Straus Papers, Box 13: "While this was not his [Bernstorff's] proposition but was mine, the action I took was with his knowledge and consent. In other words, the initiative came from me." Bryan to Page, September 8, 1914, LC, Straus Papers (reproduced in *FRUS 1914*, Suppl., p. 99): "During the conversation Straus asked the Ambassador whether he thought Germany would accept mediation at this time." Link, *The Struggle for Neutrality*, pp. 196–97: "Straus asked the Ambassador . . . Bernstorff replied. . . ."
52. Birnbaum, *Peace Moves and U-Boat Warfare*, p. 93. Tirpitz, *Politische Dokumente*, 2:122.
53. Bernstorff, *Deutschland und Amerika*, p. 67. Bernstorff to Foreign

Office, September 7, 1914, quoted in Link, *The Struggle for Neutrality*, pp. 196–97. Cf. report by Count Adalbert von Sierstorpff, October 13, 1914, in AA, Akten des AA im Grossen Hauptquartier 1914–1916, Presse und Journalisten, Bd. 3.

54. Cf. YHC, House Diaries, September 9, 1914. House writes that he does not approve of the talks between Bernstorff and Straus because this way of dealing with the mediation question "in a semi-public way" would only hamper his own plans. House was afraid that Bernstorff had broached the subject matter with other(s). Oscar S. Straus, *Under Four Administrations from Cleveland to Taft* (Boston, 1922), pp. 378–79. Bryan to Straus, September 23, 1914, LC, Straus Papers: "I am afraid the publicity that attended the matter did not help any. In fact, it made it a little embarrassing for all the countries."

55. In *The World War and American Isolation 1914–1917* (Cambridge, Mass., 1959), pp. 73–74, despite documentary evidence to the contrary, Ernest R. May presents the matter as if the proposal had originated with Bernstorff and then argues that it was Bernstorff's acting without corresponding instructions from Berlin that was largely responsible for the negative outcome of the mediation effort. Because Bernstorff encouraged Bryan, May feels, erroneous presuppositions were created. While it is correct that Bernstorff apparently did not have any instructions, it could be argued that he was justified in supporting the idea of American mediation at least indirectly as long as he could be certain that those in power in Germany would not make their own peace offers. Armin Rappaport, *The British Press and Wilsonian Neutrality* (Stanford, 1951), p. 103, also writes as if Bernstorff had initiated the matter. ("... Oscar Straus ... learned from Bernstorff. ...") See also Bernstorff, *Erinnerungen und Briefe* (Zürich, 1936), p. 101: "In September ... he [Wilson] repeated his efforts [to mediate a peace] with my assistance."

56. Bryan to Gerard, September 7, 1914, *FRUS 1914*, Suppl., p. 98.

57. Bryan to Page and Herrick, September 8, 1914, *FRUS 1914*, Suppl., p. 99. For Grey's reaction to Page's report on the matter see Page to Bryan, September 10, 1914, *FRUS 1914*, Suppl., pp. 100–101. Cf. J. A. A. J. Jusserand, *Le Sentiment américain pendant la guerre* (Paris, 1931), pp. 27–28. When asked by Bryan about his opinion regarding a return to the status quo ante, Jusserand replied: "Mais que ce soit le vrai statu quo; que les Allemands, qui ont envahi notre pays et tué nos gens, rendent la vie à nos morts; sans quoi il n'en saurait être question." See also Spring Rice to Grey, September 8, 1914, in Stephen Gwynn, ed., *The Letters and Friendships of Sir Cecil Spring Rice* (London, 1929), 2:221–23.

58. Bernstorff to Foreign Office, September 7, 1914, *LAPP*, 1:2–3.

59. Page to Bryan, September 20, 1914, *FRUS 1914*, Suppl., pp. 100–101. Cf. Edward Grey, *Twenty-Five Years 1892–1916* (London, 1925), 2:115–17. Grey to Straus, Private, September 26, 1914, LC, Oscar S. Straus Papers: "If

she [Germany] is ready for peace, then I think her Ambassador in Washington ought not to beat about the bush. He ought to make it clear ... that he is authorized to speak on behalf of his Government."

60. Gerard to Bryan, September 14, 1914, *FRUS 1914*, Suppl., p. 104. About the German background of this note see Fischer, *Griff nach der Weltmacht* (Düsseldorf, 1961), pp. 128–30. Fischer speaks of an "American peace feeler" (p. 129) and does not mention Bernstorff's role in this development. Cf. Straus, *Under Four Administrations from Cleveland to Taft*, pp. 384–85.

61. Bernstorff appears to judge the results of the mediation effort somewhat too optimistically: "Nevertheless this intermezzo for us had a favorable result insofar as our readiness to talk contrasted with the refusal of the enemies." (*Deutschland und Amerika*, p. 67.)

62. Generally Wilson trusted his unofficial advisor House more than Secretary of State Bryan. (Link, *Wilson the Diplomatist*, p. 25.)

63. *IPH*, 1:332.

64. Note by House on August 30, 1914, and note by House on November 3, 1914, *IPH*, pp. 299, 304.

65. Cf. Dumba, *Dreibund- und Entente-Politik in der Alten und Neuen Welt* (Zürich, 1931), p. 307. Robert Lansing, *War Memoirs of Robert Lansing* (New York, 1935), pp. 356–58. Link, *The Struggle for Neutrality*, p. 311: "[Bernstorff was] outwardly correct and proper ... wily and imperiously Prussian in appearance and manner." Heinrich Albert remembers, however: "He was free of any arrogance, particularly that supercilious snobism which in those days sometimes characterized the ranking diplomat of noble birth." (Albert, *Aufzeichnungen* (Berlin, [1948]), p. 80.)

66. Matthias Erzberger, who probably had his own motives for agitating against Bernstorff, wrote to the Foreign Office: "My agent ... in Germany's interest considers it necessary that a new ambassador be sent to America before the end of the war, a man who is not a member of the nobility, since this would only be a hindrance in the United States, but rather a man from the practical business world [*Erwerbsleben*]." Erzberger to von Bergen, December 13, 1916, AA, Vereinigte Staaten von Amerika 11a, Bd. 1.

67. Bernstorff to House, February 22, 1929, YHC: "I hope you realize that our relations remain the greatest moment of my life." Bernstorff, *Erinnerungen und Briefe*, p. 97. Cf. George S. Viereck, *The Strangest Friendship in History. Woodrow Wilson and Colonel House* (New York, 1932), pp. 176–77. Charles Seymour, "The House-Bernstorff Conversations in Perspective," in *Studies in Diplomatic History and Historiography in Honour of G. P. Gooch, C.H.*, edited by A. O. Sarkissian (London, 1961).

68. House Diaries, September 21, 1914, YHC: "Spring Rice was altogether distrustful of Bernstorff personally."

69. House to Wilson, September 18, 1914, *IPH*, 1:331.

70. Ritter, *Staatskunst und Kriegshandwerk*, 3:41–42. Fischer, *Griff nach der Weltmacht*, pp. 113–19.

71. Page to Wilson, September 22, 1914, Burton J. Hendrick, *The Life and Letters of Walter H. Page* (London, 1926), 3:141–47. Cf. the well-known German political writer Paul Rohrbach in the autumn of 1914 on Britain: "Our real enemy, however, and not only our enemy, but also the enemy of European culture on the whole, who for his own business profits wanted to deliver Germany to the Muscovites and to destroy German thought in the world, is England. No peace must be made with England, before England's power to injure has been destroyed forever. . . . Down with the English piracy!" Paul Rohrbach, *Der Krieg und die deutsche Politik* (Dresden, 1914), pp. 99–100.

72. Cf. Page to Bryan, September 10, 1914, *FRUS 1914*, Suppl., pp. 100–101.

73. Charles Seymour: "There was at least one German who, in his belief that his country was headed towards destruction and could be saved only by an early peace, laboured incessantly to begin negotiations." *IPH*, 1:344.

74. House to Wilson, September 18, 1914, and House memorandum regarding conversation with Bernstorff, *IPH*, 1:330–32. After House had taken over the negotiations toward peace mediation, Bernstorff repeatedly avoided efforts by Oscar Straus to contact him. This was not altogether easy since Straus, who saw himself as a "messenger of mediation," referred to his connections with Bryan (whom Wilson, however, had taken off the mediation project) and Spring Rice. (Correspondence between Straus and Bernstorff, AA, Botschaft Washington, Friedensvorschläge, Bd. 1.)

75. Spring Rice to Grey, September 22, 1914, in Gwynn, *The Letters and Friendships of Sir Cecil Spring Rice*, 2:224–26. Spring Rice to Grey (with House's approval), September 21, 1914, *IPH*, 1:334–35.

76. House to Wilson, September 22, 1914, *IPH*, 1:335–36. On September 25, Bernstorff reported to the Foreign Office about the status of the negotiations, Bernstorff to Foreign Office, September 25, 1914, AA, WK 10, *secr.*, Bd. 1.

77. Wallace was a prominent friend of House, who in 1919 succeeded William Graves Sharp as American Ambassador in Paris.

78. Memorandum by H. C. Wallace about meeting with Bernstorff, September 25, 1914, *IPH*, 1:338.

79. Link, *The Struggle for Neutrality*, p. 205. (The conversation took place on September 28.)

80. House to Page, October 3, 1914, in Hendrick, *The Life and Letters of Walter H. Page*, 1:413–14.

81. Cf. Stolberg-Wernigerode, *Die unentschiedene Generation* (Munich, 1968), p. 289.

82. Cf. British reaction (Seymour in *IPH*, 1:337).

83. Zimmermann to House, December 3, 1914, ibid., 345–46. It needs to be added that House's note to Zimmermann of September 5 had arrived in Berlin only on October 20.

84. *IPH*, ibid., 344–45; note by House on December 17, 1914, ibid., 346.

85. Note by House on December 20, 1914, ibid., 347. Cf. Lloyd George, *War Memoirs*, 2:668.

86. Note by House on December 23, 1914, ibid., 1:347–49.

87. Grey to Spring Rice, January 22, 1915, ibid., 353–55. Note by House on January 25, 1915, about meeting with Spring Rice, ibid., 363.

88. The meeting took place in the presence of Spring Rice at the home of Assistant Secretary of State William Phillips; ibid., 357–58.

89. Bernstorff to Foreign Office, January 15, 1915, and Bernstorff to Foreign Office, January 21, 1915, *LAPP*, 1:52–53.

90. Bernstorff to Seymour, November 13, 1928, YHC.

91. Bernstorff, *Erinnerungen und Briefe*, p. 95.

92. Bernstorff, *Deutschland und Amerika*, pp. 9–10.

93. Cf. Wilson to House, February 13, 1915, Link, ed., *The Papers of Woodrow Wilson* (Princeton, N.J., 1978–83), 35:231: "Such use of flags plays directly in the hands of Germany in her extraordinary plan to destroy commerce."

94. Note by House on February 5, 1915, *IPH*, 1:367. Cf. Bailey and Ryan, *The Lusitania Disaster*, pp. 48–49.

95. This conversation may be considered significant with regard to the later founding of the League of Nations.

96. House to Wilson, February 9, 1915; note by House about meeting with Grey, *IPH*, 1:368–71. House Diaries, April 30, 1915, YHC: "It is therefore my good fortune that fate has given me two such good friends as Woodrow Wilson and Edward Grey." In a report by Albert Ballin of February 4, which was presented to Bethmann Hollweg on February 5, Hans Niels Andersen, who had just come from London, is quoted as having said that in his conversation with Grey he had "come to the certain conviction that Grey's sympathies are directed toward bringing about peace as soon as possible, yes indeed, that Sir Edward Grey actually can still not quite understand today why it had to come to a war at all." (Report by Ballin, February 4, 1915, *LAPP*, 1:60–62.) Cf. Lloyd George's judgment of Grey (*War Memoirs*, 1:96): "He altogether lacked that quality of audacity which makes a great Minister."

97. Zimmermann to House, February 4, 1915, *IPH*, 1:377. In the meantime House had informed Bernstorff by cable that he was optimistic about the situation in England, but that he had not yet heard from Berlin. Bernstorff thereupon wired to the Foreign Office on February 13 and strongly recommended receiving House "even if question of peace would have to be totally disregarded [*ausgeschaltet*]." Bernstorff to Foreign Office, February 13, 1915, *LAPP*, 1:60.

98. Note by House on February 13, 1915; House to Wilson, February 15, 1915, *IPH*, 1:378–81.

99. Gerard to Bryan, February 11, 1915, *FRUS 1915*, Suppl., pp. 9–10. Gerard: "It is my belief that if you seize the present opportunity you will be the instrument of bringing about the greatest peace which has ever been signed, but it will be fatal to hesitate or wait a moment; success is dependent on immediate action."

100. House to Zimmermann, February 17, 1915, *IPH*, 1:381–82.

101. Fischer, *Griff nach der Weltmacht*, p. 229. Cf. Lloyd George, *War Memoirs*, 2:668.

102. Gerhard Ritter still asked in 1964 (*Der Erste Weltkrieg* [Bonn, 1964], p. 30): "Was it so incomprehensible that he [Bethmann Hollweg] had the desire ... to eliminate France as a great military power for the time being for 15 to 18 years, to strengthen [*verbessern*] the German western border militarily?"

103. Zimmermann to House, March 2, 1915, *LAPP*, 1:67. Text also in *IPH*, 1:395.

104. There were, however, various other German operations whose goal it was to entice one or the other power from the enemy camp. Cf. the efforts regarding an agreement with Russia and the extremely interesting consultations of the Japanese Ambassador in Sweden, Ryohei Uchida, with Austrian and Turkish representatives speaking for Germany and with Hugo Stinnes in the spring of 1915. Frank W. Iklé, "Japanese-German Peace Negotiations during World War I," *American Historical Review* 71 (October 1965): 62–76.

105. Cf. among others especially telegram no. 103, request for "sabotage in the United States," Foreign Office via Stockholm to Washington Embassy, mailed from Berlin January 25, 1915, AA, WK, 11k, *secr.*, Bd. 4. (Not 1916, the year given in many studies!) At the beginning of 1915, the Americans, however, were only partially aware of the planned activities of the German intelligence services, which will be examined in a later chapter.

106. In Paris House held talks with Théophile Delcassé, the French Foreign Minister, and other officials. House to Wilson, March 15, 1915, *IPH* 1:399–401.

107. Ibid., 403. Ritter (*Staatskunst und Kriegshandwerk*, 3:168–69) would like to give the impression that actually no one in Europe approved of House's trip. It is true "that Grey's remarks from London sounded reserved." But what Ritter does not say is that Grey's presupposition for the settlement of the Belgian question was also Bernstorff's presupposition, even if, from the official German standpoint, it may have been an unjustified demand. Ritter's remark, "Moreover, in Berlin House's appearance was viewed with similar apprehension as in London," could also lead to the erroneous impression that the British and the Germans had similar reasons for sabotaging America's peace endeavors. Despite Britain's commitments

to her allies, there was clearly a difference in the war objectives of the two countries.

108. House had also consultations with, among others, State Secretary Gottlieb von Jagow and Walther Rathenau, about whom he noted in his diary: "He is one of the ablest men I have met in Germany. . . . While he believes in Germany, he has views which I am sure are not shared by his fellow countrymen." House Diaries, March 20, 1915, YHC.

109. House to Wilson, March 27, 1915, *IPH*, 1:414–15. Ritter (*Staatskunst und Kriegshandwerk*, 3:170) is therefore mistaken when he writes: "Hence in the talks he had with Zimmermann, Jagow, and Bethmann Hollweg, House did not even mention Belgium." Cf. Fischer, *Griff nach der Weltmacht*, p. 358: "The records show that the Wilhelmstrasse did react positively to the President's inquiry regarding an information-gathering trip of his confidant Colonel House through the European capitals, but that in the matter itself conditions were imposed which would doom House's mission to failure from the very beginning—at least as far as Germany was concerned. . . . From the very beginning the Belgian question thus marked the point where Germany would not withdraw from the position gained in 1914 and which decisively impeded a settlement with Britain, as it would later with America." Karl Birnbaum (*Peace Moves and U-Boat Warfare*, p. 94), too, recognizes the significance of the German standpoint on Belgium and cites a telegram from Gerard to House of April 18, 1915, in which the former relates the German demand for annexation of, among other places, Namur and Liege. Cf. House to Zimmermann, May 1, 1915, *IPH*, 1:433–34: "Of course, you understand that the conversation [with Grey after House's return from Germany] was predicated upon the evacuation of Belgium."

110. House to Wilson, April 11, 1915, *IPH*, 1:417–18. See, by contrast, the interpretation in Ritter, *Staatskunst und Kriegshandwerk*, 3:170.

111. Cf. Lloyd George, *War Memoirs*, 2:668.

CHAPTER FOUR

1. It was later repeatedly claimed that the sinking of the *Lusitania* had been planned. There have also been efforts to connect Franz Rintelen's stay in America with such plans. To date these claims have not been proven. Pastor Martin Niemöller, a U-boat commander who was in contact with Captain Schwieger, has also informed the author that the torpedoing was not planned; Martin Niemöller to author, Wiesbaden, November 21, 1969. Bernstorff emphasizes that he would not have gone to New York if he had expected the sinking of the liner. *Deutschland und Amerika* (Berlin, 1920), p. 138. Cf. Arno Spindler, "Der Lusitania Fall," off-print from *Berliner Monatshefte* (Berlin, 1935), p. 1. Oslo Legation to Foreign Office, April 13,

1931, AA, Länderabteilungen, Vereinigte Staaten von Amerika, WK, Der Lusitania Fall, Bd. 2.

2. Bernstorff, *Deutschland und Amerika*, pp. 138–39.
3. Bernstorff to Foreign Office, May 9, 1915, ibid., p. 143.
4. Cf. Link, *The Struggle for Neutrality*, vol. 3 of *Wilson* (Princeton, N.J., 1960), pp. 380–83.
5. The *New York Times*, May 9, 1915, quoted in ibid., p. 380.
6. The complete text of the address is published in Arthur S. Link, ed., *The Papers of Woodrow Wilson* (Princeton, N.J., 1978–83), 33:147–50. See also Link's interesting footnote (p. 149) on Wilson's deletion of the sentence "There is such a thing as a man being too proud to fight" in a text proposed for publication in late 1915.
7. Link, *The Struggle for Neutrality*, p. 383–89. Also Wilson had apparently been informed about statements by Bernstorff, who expected a mild reaction. Wilson to William Jennings Bryan, May 13, 1915, in Link, *The Papers of Woodrow Wilson*, 33:183–84. Cf. Link, *Woodrow Wilson and the Progressive Era, 1910–1917* (London, 1954), p. 166.
8. Bernstorff to Foreign Office, May 10, 1915, in Bernstorff, *Deutschland und Amerika*, pp. 143–44.
9. Bernstorff to Foreign Office, May 9, 1915, in Bernstorff, *Deutschland und Amerika*, p. 143.
10. Bernstorff to Foreign Office, May 10, 1915, in Bernstorff, *Deutschland und Amerika*, p. 143–44.
11. Bryan to Gerard, May 13, 1915, *FRUS 1915*, Suppl., pp. 393–96.
12. Cf. Gerhard Ritter, *Staatskunst und Kriegshandwerk* (Munich, 1964–68), 3:171.
13. Gerard to Bryan, May 10, 1915, *FRUS 1915*, Suppl., p. 389.
14. In his notes on May 18, 1915, Admiral von Müller speaks about the "frankly insulting note from America in the *Lusitania* case." Walter Görlitz, ed., *Regierte der Kaiser? Kriegstagebücher, Aufzeichnungen und Briefe des Chefs des Marine-Kabinetts Admiral Georg Alexander v. Müller 1914–1918*, 2nd ed. (Göttingen, 1959), p. 102.
15. Under the headline "Cunard liner 'Lusitania' torpedoed," the *Hamburgischer Correspondent* (May 8, 1915, morning edition, p. 1) exclaimed: "Now the sinking of their proudest ship has reminded them [the British] in a terrible way of the seriousness of the situation, and it will fill the entire nation with horror." The same paper said in its evening edition, p. 1: "But only the bragging and disdainful language of the British press, which cannot deride the German submarines enough, is to blame for the passengers not believing in the dangers of a voyage through British waters." The *Hamburger Nachrichten* (May 8, 1915, morning edition, p. 1) found: "Fate and fate's justice have caught up with the Cunard liner." In the evening edition (p. 1) of the same day the newspaper declared that the sinking of the *Lusitania* "also proves that England's legendary rule over the seas is a nothing."

The *Deutsche Tageszeitung* (May 8, 1915, evening edition, p. 1) stated: "They [the owners] alone carry the full responsibility for what had to happen." Even the more liberal *Frankfurter Zeitung* (May 9, 1915, second morning edition, p. 1) called out: "England, the sea-faring nation, the world power, has been overtaken by us younger ones, and there are areas where we are superior." For an extremist view see *Hammer* 312 (June 1915): 278:

> Lusitania
> Das Schiff voll Patronen
> Und oben Kinder!
> Das Schiff voll Granaten
> Und oben Frau'n!
> So wollte England, der alte Sünder,
> Sich ungestört dem Meere vertrau'n!
> Abwehrkanonen blitzend an Deck,
> Neutrale Flagge feig am Heck,
> Ohne Eskorte,
> Voll großer Worte,
> Die Deutschen verlachend
> Mit Hohn und Spott . . .
> Auf einmal erkrachend,
> Ein Schrei nach - Gott,
> Ein Mitleidfleh'n voll Ach und Weh . . .
> Gott *strafe* dich, England,
> Du Lump zur See!
> —Max Bewer
> (Dresden-Laubegast)

16. *Lauenburgische Zeitung,* May 10, 1915, p. 1.

17. Pohl to his wife, May 7, 1915, Hugo von Pohl, *Aus Aufzeichnungen und Briefen während der Kriegszeit* (Berlin, 1920), pp. 126–27.

18. Tirpitz to the chief of the Marinekabinett, May 9, 1915, Tirpitz, *Politische Dokumente* (Hamburg, 1926), 2:335.

19. Mumm to Hammann, May 29, 1915, Otto Hammann, *Bilder aus der letzten Kaiserzeit* (Berlin, 1922), pp. 117–18.

20. Gerard to Bryan, May 15, 1915, and Gerard to Bryan, May 17, 1915, in *FRUS 1915,* Suppl., pp. 396, 398.

21. Bryan to Gerard, May 18, 1915, ibid., pp. 398–99.

22. Mainly due to the refusal to recognize America's military potential.

23. Bryan to Wilson, May 17, 1915, *FRUS, The Lansing Papers,* 1:408–10; Bryan to Dumba, May 24, 1915, and Dumba to Bryan, May 24, 1915, ibid., 413–16. Bernstorff, *Deutschland und Amerika,* pp. 154–55. James W. Gerard, *My Four Years in Germany* (London, 1917), pp. 163–64, and *My First Eighty-Three Years in America* (Garden City, N.Y., 1951), p. 232. Ritter, *Staatskunst und Kriegshandwerk,* 3:173.

24. Gerard to Bryan, May 29, 1915, *FRUS 1915*, Suppl., pp. 419–21.

25. Worth mentioning in this context is an attempt to prove that the *Lusitania* had been armed. A German-American by the name of Gustav Stahl was apparently persuaded by Paul König, an agent of the German intelligence services and of the Hamburg-American Line, to give evidence to this effect. Stahl claimed to have seen cannons on the decks of the *Lusitania*. In the course of a hearing in court Stahl pleaded guilty to perjury and was sentenced. Stahl's report had been one of four affidavits that Bernstorff had presented to the American government. Falcke, *Vor dem Eintritt Amerikas in den Weltkrieg* (Dresden, 1928), pp. 129–31. BAL, 2:1603. Earl E. Sperry, *German Plots and Intrigues in the United States during the Period of Our Neutrality* (Washington, D.C., 1918), pp. 38–40. In connection with the cargo of the *Lusitania* see now Colin Simpson, "A Great Liner with Too Many Secrets," *Life* 73 (October 13, 1972): 60ff, and *The Lusitania* (London, 1972; Boston, 1973). Simpson argues that the U.S. Government was informed about the ammunition carried on the *Lusitania*. Thomas A. Bailey and Paul B. Ryan, *The Lusitania Disaster* (New York, 1975), take issue with Simpson on this and other points.

26. Bernstorff, *Deutschland und Amerika*, p. 147.

27. Walter Schmid-Bürckert, "Graf Johann-Heinrich von Bernstorff als deutscher Botschafter in Washington 1908–1917" (Ph.D. diss., Universität Tübingen, 1947), p. 102.

28. Veit Valentin, *Deutschlands Außenpolitik von Bismarcks Abgang bis zum Ende des Weltkrieges* (Berlin, 1921), p. 284: "Early in June already all preparations for breaking off relations had been made. The Ambassador Count Bernstorff succeeded in bringing about a possibility of bridging over matters [*eine Verständigungsmöglichkeit*] through a direct conversation with President Wilson." Charles Seymour, *American Diplomacy during the World War*, 2nd ed. (Baltimore, Md., 1942), pp. 94–95: "Fortunately Ambassador von Bernstorff was one of the few who did realize the danger of a rupture and the fact that a diplomatic rupture inevitably meant war. . . . To him must go a large share of the responsibility for preventing a break at this time."

29. All indications are that Bernstorff did not see or know of the content of each telegram to or from the attachés, even when the messages officially went through the German Embassy in Washington. Cf. Falcke, *Vor dem Eintritt Amerikas in den Weltkrieg*, p. 119.

30. Cf. Link, *The Struggle for Neutrality*, p. 412.

31. As stated by Kurt Wimer, "Woodrow Wilson and World Order," in *Woodrow Wilson and a Revolutionary World, 1913–1921*, ed. Arthur S. Link (Chapel Hill, N.C., 1982), p. 159.

32. Richard von Kühlmann, Deutsche Gesandtschaft im Haag, to "Lieber Freund" [Adolf Count von Montgelas], May 3, 1915, entry stamp May 5, 1915; office memo by Montgelas, May 5, 1915, with second office memo

on same paper by Montgelas, May 8, 1915, with undated note by the Secretary of the Foreign Office to Jagow "Agreed [Einverstanden] J."; Foreign Office to Bernstorff, May 10, 1915, sent through German consulate in Rotterdam as Dutch mail and through German legation in Copenhagen as Danish mail. All documents in AA, WK 12, Bd. 5. The same sources show that Gildemeester was paid 10,000 marks to defray his expenses.

33. Karl E. Birnbaum, *Peace Moves and U-Boat Warfare* (Stockholm, 1958), pp. 28–29, 343–44, suggests but fails to prove that Bernstorff may have fabricated these conditions. Fritz Fischer, *Griff nach der Weltmacht* (Düsseldorf, 1961), p. 365, also describes these conditions as being proposals of the Ambassador. Gerhard Ritter, *Staatskunst und Kriegshandwerk*, 3:619, refers to Bernstorff's report merely as "a rather mysterious message."

34. Berlin, however, was briefly and indirectly informed on June 3, 1915, through Swedish channels. Note from the Swedish legation, no date, in *LAPP*, 1:119. Text of Bernstorff to Foreign Office, May 29, 1915, in Link, *The Papers of Woodrow Wilson*, 33:279–80. For Link's analysis and reconstruction of the events on May 28, see ibid., 280–82. The records of the telephone calls are in NA, RG 59, Office of the Counselor/Under Secretary and the Chief Special Agent, Leland Harrison's Case Files, Human Espionage Activities, Box 3. They are typed, and errors by the agents in hearing and writing are possible. In addition, the source indicates that these particular conversations were in German, something that can also be seen from the curious English. The agents misspell Gildemeester. Miller is probably Adolph Caspar Miller of the Federal Reserve Board. Lane is most likely Franklin Knight Lane, Wilson's Secretary of the Interior. Gildemeester's letter to Wilson of June 7, incidentally, contains not the slightest hint that they have met previously. Adolph Caspar Miller to William Jennings Bryan, June 3, 1915, confirms the information from the telephone call recorded by the agents, namely that Miller met Gildemeester on Sunday, May 30. Others, such as the British Ambassador in Washington, heard that the Dutch emissary of the Germans saw the President. An otherwise often-used source, the papers of Colonel House, are of no help in this case, because House, according to his diary, only returned to New York from Europe on June 13. Gildemeester's and Miller's letters and Sir Cecil Arthur Spring Rice to Sir Edward Grey, June 7, 1915, in Link, *The Papers of Woodrow Wilson*, 33:332–33, 361–63. *IPH*, 2:4–5.

35. After having seen the entire text of the German note of May 28, 1915, House, still in England, noted in his diary: "I have concluded that war with Germany is inevitable." House Diaries, May 30, 1915, YHC.

36. Concerning Wilson's hope of bringing about a conference of neutrals, see a later letter from the President to Edith Bolling Galt: "We can recall Gerard and give Bernstorff his passports, and note the effect of such a breaking off of all dealings with Germany before we go further. In that case Germany might declare war and the guidance of our policy be taken out of

our hands.... After breaking off diplomatic relations, if we wished to go further, probably the next step would be to call a conference of neutrals ... to consider the present treatment of neutrals by *both* sides in the war and concert some action, to be taken either severally or jointly, calculated to make neutral rights more secure." Wilson to E. B. Galt (after the sinking of the *Arabic*), August 20, 1915, in Link, *The Papers of Woodrow Wilson*, 34:258–61.

37. The second last sentence quoted here from Bernstorff, *Deutschland und Amerika*, p. 152, reads in German: "Ferner ist dann Eingreifen Wilsons im Sinne des Friedens sicher zu erwarten." The same telegram in the Political Archive of the German Foreign Office, reproduced in the original German text (and English translation) in Link, *The Papers of Woodrow Wilson*, 33:316–20, however reads: "Ferner ist dann Eingreifen Wilsons im Sinne der Entsendung Gildemeister [sic] hierher sicher zu erwarten." In other words, it would appear that Count Bernstorff purposely altered the text for publication.

38. Bernstorff, *Erinnerungen und Briefe* (Zürich, 1936), pp. 103–4. About the mission of Meyer-Gerhard see also Link, *The Struggle for Neutrality*, pp. 433–36, and Gerard to House, June 16, 1915, in Link, *The Papers of Woodrow Wilson*, 33:478. With regard to the extent of the danger of war, scholarly opinions still differ widely. Cf. John M. Blum, *Woodrow Wilson and the Politics of Morality* (Boston, 1956), pp. 100–101. Wittke, *German-Americans and the World War* (Columbus, Ohio, 1936), pp. 71–72.

39. At the same time the German government was pressured by Tirpitz and similarly-minded people with the threat "of an outbreak of general resentment throughout the nation," if submarine action were to be limited. Görlitz, *Regierte der Kaiser?*, p. 105.

40. Bernstorff to Foreign Office, June 2, 1915, AA, WK 18, *secr*., Bd. 2.

41. Lansing to Gerard, June 9, 1915, *FRUS 1915*, Suppl., pp. 436–38.

42. House Diaries, June 24, 1915, YHC. Link, *The Struggle for Neutrality*, pp. 413–25. Lawrence E. Gelfand, *The Inquiry* (New Haven, Conn., 1963), pp. 4–5.

43. Jagow to Chief of the Admiralty Staff, June 24, 1915, AA, WK 18, *secr*., Bd. 2.

44. A secret order had already instructed the submarines to spare large enemy passenger liners. Neither Bernstorff nor the American Government knew about this. Tirpitz did not wish to inform the Americans, because Germany's enemies would then also have known about the order.

45. Meyer-Gerhard's draft in Tirpitz, *Politische Dokumente*, 2:363. Bernstorff (*Deutschland und Amerika*, pp. 152–53) declares laconically that Meyer-Gerhard's journey, except for the delivery of his situation report and the fact that some time was gained, had no influence whatsoever on further negotiations.

46. Tirpitz, *Politische Dokumente*, 2:363.

47. Notes of the Chief of the Admiralty Staff about a meeting with the Imperial Chancellor on June 22, 1915, ibid., 364–66. Cf. Rudolf Schmidt-Bückeburg, *Das Militärkabinett der preußischen Könige und deutschen Kaiser* (Berlin, 1933), p. 249.

48. Gerard to Lansing, July 8, 1915, *FRUS 1915*, Suppl., pp. 463–66.

49. Cf. Bernstorff, *Deutschland und Amerika*, pp. 161–62, 164–70. Arno Spindler, *Der Handelskrieg mit U-Booten* (Berlin, 1932–66), 2:176–90.

50. Gerard to Jagow, July 23, 1915, AA, Akten des AA im Grossen Hauptquartier 1915–1919, Vereinigte Staaten von Amerika 3, Bde. 1–2 (emphases by Wilhelm II). *FRUS 1915*, Suppl., pp. 480–82.

51. Gerard to Jagow, July 23, 1915, AA, Akten des AA im Grossen Hauptquartier 1915–1919, Vereinigte Staaten von Amerika 3, Bde. 1–2. (Handwritten jottings by Wilhelm II on the note.) Cf. Tirpitz, *Politische Dokumente*, 2:378–80. German text: "Maßlos unverschämt - Donnerwetter! - commands! - unerhört - Das ist so ungefähr das Unverschämteste in Ton und Gebärde, was ich seit der Japan. [sic] Note im vorigen August zu lesen bekommen habe! Es endigt mit einer direkten Drohung!"

52. Robert Lansing, *War Memoirs of Robert Lansing* (New York, 1935), pp. 40–41.

53. Bernstorff's position in Washington was again made more difficult when on July 24, 1915, American intelligence agents seized Heinrich Albert's briefcase. It contained incriminating records about German propaganda measures and disruptive activities in the United States.

54. Bernstorff, *Deutschland und Amerika*, pp. 167–69. Cf. the similar plan of Helfferich in Karl Helfferich, *Der Weltkrieg*, pt. 2 (Berlin, 1920), pp. 319–20. Helfferich complains that his suggestions were not supported by the Foreign Office. Ritter, *Staatskunst und Kriegshandwerk*, 3:178–79.

55. Bernstorff, *Deutschland und Amerika*, pp. 170–71.

56. For details concerning the activities of German intelligence agents and related events see the following chapter.

57. Gerard to Lansing, September 7, 1915, *FRUS 1915*, Suppl., pp. 539–40. Bodo Herzog and Günter Schomaekers, *Ritter der Tiefe, Graue Wölfe* (Munich, 1965), p. 240.

58. Spindler, *Der Handelskrieg mit U-Booten*, 2:260–61. Link, *The Struggle for Neutrality*, p. 565.

59. Bernstorff to Bethmann Hollweg, August 25, 1915, AA, Vereinigte Staaten von Amerika 16, Bd. 35.

60. Bernstorff to House, August 21, 1915, and Bernstorff to House, August 29, 1915, YHC. Bernstorff, *Deutschland und Amerika*, p. 171.

61. Cf. Lerchenfeld to Royal State Ministry of the Royal House and of the Exterior [Kgl. Staatsministerium des Kgl. Hauses und des Äußeren], August 24, 1915, GSA, MA 95053.

62. Cf. continuous petitions by the Navy. (AA, WK 18, *secr.*) Ballin to

Holtzendorff, June 6, 1915, quoted in Lamar Cecil, *Albert Ballin* (Princeton, N.J., 1967), pp. 285–86.

63. As is evident from the records, Dernburg frequently corresponded with Berlin from America without going through the Embassy. Erich Hossenfelder launched a regular campaign against Bernstorff and in this was supported by contacts in Germany. Apparently anti-Semitic, he supposed that Jewish industrial interest groups wanted to keep peace with America for economic reasons. Cf. Hossenfelder to Bethmann Hollweg, July 19, 1915, and marginal notes by Adolf Count von Montgelas, August 16, 1915, AA, Vereinigte Staaten von Amerika 16. Heinrich Prinz von Preußen to Jagow, June 24, 1915 (AA, WK 18, *secr.*, Bd. 2), writes that "in the long run only the most brutal methods can be useful to us in this war against England." He continues that the American reactions to the sinking of the *Lusitania* were a bluff: "regarding the *Lusitania* case, of which I hope a second similar one will occur as soon as possible." Enclosed are two letters by Heinrich Albert to the Prince. Albert: "I hope that Bernstorff's request to basically abandon submarine warfare will be refused with quiet certainty and dignity" and "I would wish that . . . in Germany . . . one would not be distracted by the fuss of the American press from the path which alone can lead us to our goal, namely from the relentless employment of all means of force—I am thinking in particular of submarines, airships, and airplanes."

64. Cf. Bethmann Hollweg to Treutler, August 25, 1915, AA, WK 18, *secr.*, Bd. 3.

65. Tirpitz, *Politische Dokumente*, 2:402–7. Ritter, *Staatskunst und Kriegshandwerk*, 3:179–80. Bethmann Hollweg to Jagow, August 26, 1915, AA, WK 18, *secr.*, Bd. 2: "Decision . . . not yet made. Hoping to obtain decision along my lines tomorrow, at the latest the day after tomorrow."

66. Spindler, *Der Handelskrieg mit U-Booten*, 2:277. Tirpitz, *Politische Dokumente*, 2:407–8.

67. On August 27 Tirpitz for the second time unsuccessfully asked to be allowed to resign. The Chief of the Admiralty Staff, Admiral Gustav Bachmann, protested against Bethmann Hollweg's going directly to the Emperor and thereupon was replaced by Admiral Henning von Holtzendorff. Cf. Spindler, *Der Handelskrieg mit U-Booten*, 2:281–82. As late as August 29, the Chief of the Admiralty Staff tried unsuccessfully to win Bethmann Hollweg for new measures against the Americans. Bachmann to Bethmann Hollweg, August 29, 1915, and Bethmann Hollweg to Treutler, August 29, 1915, AA, WK 18, *secr.*, Bd. 2.

68. Montgelas to Admiral Paul Behncke, August 28, 1915, in ibid.

69. Treutler to Bethmann Hollweg, August 30, 1915, in ibid., Bd. 3. Cf. Tirpitz, *Politische Dokumente*, 2:412.

70. Cf. Link, *The Struggle for Neutrality*, pp. 583–85.

71. House to Wilson, August 22, 1915, *IPH*, 2:29–31. House's comment,

August 21, 1915: "I would send Bernstorff home and recall Gerard.... I would begin preparations for defence and for war.... I would issue an address to the American people and ... exonerate the Germans as a whole, but I would blister the militant party in Germany.... I would ask the German-Americans to help in redeeming their fatherland from such bloodthirsty monsters." Bernstorff, *Deutschland und Amerika*, pp. 171–72.

72. Cf. for instance Ritter, *Staatskunst und Kriegshandwerk*, 3:182.

73. *New York World*, August 23, 1915, quoted in Link, *The Struggle for Neutrality*, p. 569.

74. Cf. Seymour, *American Diplomacy during the World War*, p. 102: "The credit was largely due to the German Ambassador." Jean-Baptiste Duroselle, *De Wilson à Roosevelt* (Paris, 1960), p. 62: "La paix fut alors sauvée par l'initiative de l'ambassadeur allemand Bernstorff." Lansing, *War Memoirs of Robert Lansing*, p. 49: "A loyal servant of the Kaiser ... he was ready to risk his official position.... He showed a courage most unusual in an official of the German Empire."

75. Jagow to Bernstorff, September 10, 1915, AA, WK 18, *secr.*, Bd. 3. Cf. Tirpitz, *Politische Dokumente*, 2:440–41.

76. Bernstorff to Foreign Office, October 2, 1915, Bernstorff, *Deutschland und Amerika*, pp. 178–80.

77. Bernstorff had thought the risk of sending messages through Archibald too high and consequently had declined to avail himself of the service. Lansing, *War Memoirs of Robert Lansing*, p. 64. Bernstorff to Bethmann Hollweg, September 13, 1915, AA, Vereinigte Staaten von Amerika 16, Bd. 36. Cf. George Harvey, "Dealing with Diplomatic Misfits," *North American Review* (October 1915): 497. Link, *The Struggle for Neutrality*, pp. 645–47. Wilson to House, September 7, 1915, YHC: "If Dumba, why not Bernstorff also? Is there an essential difference?" House to Wilson, September 10, 1915, YHC: "Our people are behind you in this and I believe you can do with Bernstorff and his staff that have been so pernicious as you have with Dumba." *The World's Work* 30(6) (1915): 631.

78. Dumba, *Dreibund- und Entente-Politik in der Alten und Neuen Welt* (Zürich, 1931), p. 117.

79. Gerard to Lansing, September 7, 1915, *FRUS 1915*, Suppl., pp. 539–40. Bernstorff, *Deutschland und Amerika*, pp. 179–80.

80. Bernstorff to Foreign Office, September 15, 1915, AA, WK 18, *secr.*, Bd. 4. Bernstorff, *Deutschland und Amerika*, pp. 180–81. On September 17 he received an instruction allowing him to inform Lansing that the submarines had been ordered to sink passenger liners only "after warning and saving human lives." "Order so definite that in case of doubt attack cannot take place." Foreign Office to Bernstorff, September 17, 1915, AA, WK 18, *secr.*, Bd. 4.

81. Bernstorff to Bethmann Hollweg, September 22, 1915, Bernstorff, *Deutschland und Amerika*, p. 182.

82. The Americans were aware that Bernstorff was again acting on his own. House Diaries, October 6, 1915, YHC.
83. Bernstorff to Lansing, October 2, 1915, *FRUS, The Lansing Papers*, 1:483. Bernstorff, *Deutschland und Amerika*, pp. 185–86. Cf. Tirpitz, *Politische Dokumente*, 2:440. In the generally conciliatory tone of his note Bernstorff also went beyond his instructions from Berlin. English text in *FRUS 1915*, Suppl., p. 560.
84. Bernstorff to Foreign Office, October 19, 1915, AA, WK 18, *secr.*, Bd. 4. Bernstorff, *Deutschland und Amerika*, pp. 185–86.
85. Ritter, *Staatskunst und Kriegshandwerk*, 3:182.
86. Birnbaum, *Peace Moves and U-Boat Warfare*, p. 36.
87. Bernstorff, *Deutschland und Amerika*, p. 187.
88. Link, *Confusions and Crises 1915–1916*, vol. 4 of *Wilson* (Princeton, N.J., 1964), p. 55. Memorandum by Lansing regarding meeting with Bernstorff, October 5, 1915, *FRUS, The Lansing Papers*, 1:485–86.
89. Holtzendorff to Jagow, October 27, 1915, AA, WK 18, *secr.*, Bd. 4. Bethmann Hollweg's comments in the margins of the same document.
90. Link, *The Struggle for Neutrality*, p. 683.
91. Lansing to Page, with enclosures, October 21, 1915, *FRUS 1915*, Suppl., pp. 578–601.
92. Cf. Link, *The Struggle for Neutrality*, pp. 682–93.
93. Commander Valentiner had promised Admiral Holtzendorff in September to sink 50,000 tons on his cruise to the Mediterranean. The 8,210 tons of the *Ancona* constituted a considerable share of the 47,460 tons (14 ships) which he destroyed. Herzog and Schomaekers, *Ritter der Tiefe. Graue Wölfe*, pp. 96–97.
94. Bernstorff had enough other worries. The revelations about the so-called German "conspiracies" had reached a new climax. This development led to the expulsion of the attachés Franz von Papen and Karl Boy-Ed before the end of the year.
95. Excerpt from the logbook of the submarine regarding the sinking of the Italian liner *Ancona* on November 7, 1915, Top Secret, AA, WK 18, *secr.*, Bd. 5. (Less than one hour elapsed between the impact of the torpedo in the cargo section and the sinking of the liner.)
96. Wilson to Lansing, November 21, 1915, *FRUS, The Lansing Papers*, 1:493.
97. Bernstorff, *Deutschland und Amerika*, pp. 208–9. Bernstorff to Bethmann Hollweg, November 15, 1915, AA, WK 18, *secr.*, Bd. 4.
98. Cf. Lansing, *War Memoirs of Robert Lansing*, pp. 88–89. Link, *Confusions and Crises*, pp. 66–67, however: "What ... the American government never knew, was that a German submarine ... had done the deed."
99. Bernstorff to Bethmann Hollweg, December 7, 1915, AA, Vereinigte Staaten von Amerika 16, Bd. 38. Cf. Bernstorff, *Deutschland und Amerika*, pp. 214–15.

100. Bernstorff to Bethmann Hollweg, December 13, 1915, arrived in Berlin January 13, 1916, AA, Vereinigte Staaten von Amerika 16, Bd. 39.

101. Bernstorff to Foreign Office, December 24, 1915, arrived in Berlin the same day, AA, WK 18, *secr.*, Bd. 5.

102. Falkenhayn, *Die Oberste Heeresleitung 1914–1916 in ihren wichtigsten Entschliessungen* (Berlin, 1920), pp. 176–84. Ritter, *Staatskunst und Kriegshandwerk*, 3:191–93. Spindler, *Der Handelskrieg mit U-Booten*, 3:70–71. Tirpitz, *Politische Dokumente*, 2:450–59.

103. Notes by Falkenhayn for a presentation before the Emperor at the end of 1915. Falkenhayn, *Die Oberste Heeresleitung 1914–1916 in ihren wichtigsten Entschliessungen*, pp. 181–82. Cf. Wilhelm Groener, *Lebenserinnerungen*, ed. F. Freiherr Hiller von Gaertringen (Göttingen, 1957), pp. 284–85, 287. Karl-Heinz Janssen, *Der Kanzler und der General* (Göttingen, 1967), pp. 184–89.

104. Notes by Bethmann Hollweg, January 4, 1916. UA Beilagen, pp. 143–44. Rumors concerning doubts of the military leaders about Germany's perseverance and military reserves had already been circulating for some time. Cf. Royal Military Representative (Kgl. Mil. Bevollm.) to Bavarian War Ministry, November 9, 1915, Kriegsarchiv, MKr 1829: "A gentleman of the Foreign Office . . . said that he . . . had heard that the war could not last much longer and that one had to consider concluding peace. . . . There were reports by . . . Falkenhayn, Hindenburg, and Deimling that we were at the end of our strength and that the war had to be ended by the spring. . . . He [Freytag-Loringhoven] too now says that our military strength would be near the end by the spring of 1916 and that a swift conclusion of peace therefore would be necessary."

105. Ritter, *Staatskunst und Kriegshandwerk*, 3:195.

106. Birnbaum, *Peace Moves and U-Boat Warfare*, p. 52.

107. Notes by Müller, January 31, 1916 (Görlitz, *Regierte der Kaiser?*, p. 151): "In agreement with the General Staff, Jagow has refused this humiliation as totally unacceptable."

108. Cf. Lansing's notes on the discussion with Bernstorff, enclosure Foreign Office to Bernstorff, December 31, 1915, given to Lansing on the same day, *FRUS, The Lansing Papers*, 1:510–12.

109. *FRUS, The Lansing Papers*, 1:493–533.

110. Cf. Lansing to Wilson, February 8, 1916, *FRUS, The Lansing Papers*, 1:531.

111. Lansing to Wilson, February 16, 1916, and Wilson to Lansing, February 16, 1916, *FRUS, The Lansing Papers*, 1:531–33.

112. Bernstorff, *Deutschland und Amerika*, pp. 220–21.

113. Cf. Armin Rappaport, *The British Press and Wilsonian Neutrality* (Stanford, Calif., 1951), pp. 80–81: "The British were happy that the *Lusitania* question was thus not solved yet."

114. Bernstorff, *Deutschland und Amerika*, pp. 226–27.

115. Spindler, *Der Handelskrieg mit U-Booten*, 3:70–74. Tirpitz, *Politische Dokumente*, 2:450–55.

116. Notes by Jagow, January 31, 1916, AA, WK 18, *secr.*, Bd. 5. (But Jagow also wrote: " . . . in view of the small military means of the Union. . . .")

117. Spindler, *Der Handelskrieg mit U-Booten*, 3:75.

118. Tirpitz, *Politische Dokumente*, 2:462.

119. Cf. Bernstorff, *Deutschland und Amerika*, p. 234.

120. That is, submarine war against *all* commercial vessels without advance warning to the ships and without recognizing the obligation to take care of passengers and crews.

121. Lerchenfeld to Hertling, February 10, 1916, GSA, MA 95053.

122. Cf. Spindler, *Der Handelskrieg mit U-Booten*, 3:26, 85.

123. Gerard to Lansing, February 10, 1916, *FRUS 1916*, Suppl., pp. 163–66.

124. The question of armed commercial ships already in 1915 had turned into a significant problem in connection with the *Baralong* massacre. Even to Wilson and Lansing the *Baralong* case seemed to give proof that German U-boats could hardly wage war against commercial shipping according to the accepted methods of cruiser warfare as long as commercial vessels of the Entente were equipped for war. On August 19, 1915, *U-27* under the command of Capt. Bernd Wegener had stopped the British steamship *Nicosian*, when the *Baralong* appeared, one of those submarine traps that the British called "Q-ships." The *Baralong* sailed under the American flag. As Wegener approached her, the *Baralong* attacked and sank *U-27*. The crew of the German submarine was then shot by the British. Several American sailors aboard the *Nicosian* had watched the incident and deposited testimonies with Ambassador Page in London, who forwarded them to Washington. Spindler, *Der Handelskrieg mit U-Booten*, 2:250–55. Page to Lansing, August 26 and 29, 1915, *FRUS 1915*, Suppl., pp. 527–29.

125. The resolutions of Rep. [Atkins Jefferson] "Jeff" McLemore from Texas and Sen. Thomas P. Gore from Oklahoma should be mentioned here. The aim of their resolutions was to prohibit Americans from traveling on armed commercial vessels, e.g., on ships of the warring nations and on neutral merchant ships carrying contraband. For a detailed treatment of this question see Link, *Confusions and Crises*, pp. 142–94.

126. Bernstorff, *Deutschland und Amerika*, pp. 235–36. Cf. Link, *Confusions and Crises*, p. 175.

127. Memorandum of the Admiralty Staff, February 12, 1916, AA, WK 18, *secr.*, Bd. 6: "If the new submarine campaign [is conducted] without restrictions . . . , then it can be expected with certainty that Britain . . . will find itself forced to conclude a peace in six months at the most."

128. Birnbaum, *Peace Moves and U-Boat Warfare*, p. 56. (Even Holtzendorff, however, was of the opinion that the break with America would not

be all too serious as long as the submarines were given complete freedom of action.)

129. Ibid., p. 60.

130. Private letter by Bethmann Hollweg to Jagow, March 5, 1916, Tirpitz, *Politische Dokumente*, 2:499–505. Eberhard von Vietsch, *Bethmann Hollweg*, p. 229. Tirpitz' final resignation on March 12 came as a kind of bonus for the Chancellor. Tirpitz, *Politische Dokumente*, 2:508–10. Schmidt-Bückeburg, *Das Militärkabinett der preußischen Könige und deutschen Kaiser*, pp. 249–50. Birnbaum, *Peace Moves and U-Boat Warfare*, pp. 61–63.

131. Spindler, *Der Handelskrieg mit U-Booten*, 3:102–3. Birnbaum, *Peace Moves and U-Boat Warfare*, p. 62.

132. Spindler, *Der Handelskrieg mit U-Booten*, 3:103.

133. Ibid., 125. Birnbaum, *Peace Moves and U-Boat Warfare*, p. 70. Link, *Confusions and Crises*, p. 228.

134. Several witnesses, among them the historian Samuel F. Bemis, had observed the course of the torpedo and submitted testimony. *FRUS 1916*, Suppl., pp. 234–37.

135. Jagow to Gerard, April 10, 1916, AA, WK 18, secr., Bd. 11. Cf. Gerard to Lansing, April 11, 1916, *FRUS 1916*, Suppl., pp. 227–29. Admiral Holtzendorff even went so far as to claim that the *Sussex* had probably been attacked by a British submarine with a German torpedo. Görlitz, *Regierte der Kaiser?*, p. 172. Cf. Ballin to Ernst Francke, April 25, 1916: "We owe the entire situation to the short-legged lies which have been deemed good enough to be used in the *Sussex* as well as in other cases." Quoted in Peter F. Stubmann, *Ballin* (Berlin, 1926), p. 273. Max Weber wrote on April 5: "Yes, the torpedoing of the *Sussex* was admittedly an unequalled mess [*eine Schweinerei sondergleichen*], the most stupid thing that could have happened." Quoted in Marianne Weber, *Max Weber. Ein Lebensbild* (Tübingen, 1926), p. 577.

136. Bernstorff, *Deutschland und Amerika*, pp. 244–45: "especially disastrous and perhaps the most unfortunate official document . . . that ever went from Berlin to Washington."

137. Gerard to Jagow, April 20, 1916, *FRUS 1916*, Suppl., pp. 232–37.

138. Ritter, *Staatskunst und Kriegshandwerk*, 3:209. Falkenhayn, *Die Oberste Heeresleitung 1914–1916 in ihren wichtigsten Entschliessungen*, p. 185.

139. Jagow to Bethmann Hollweg, January 20, 1916, AA, Akten des AA im Grossen Hauptquartier 1915–1919, Vereinigte Staaten von Amerika 3a and 3b, Bd. 1.

140. Bernstorff to Foreign Office, April 23, 1916, AA, WK 18, secr., Bd. 14.

141. Falkenhayn to Bethmann Hollweg, April 25, 1916, in ibid. Cf. Fal-

kenhayn, *Die Oberste Heeresleitung 1914–1916 in ihren wichtigsten Entschliessungen*, pp. 185–87.

142. Bethmann Hollweg to Jagow, April 30, 1916, AA, Akten des AA im Grossen Hauptquartier 1915–1919, Vereinigte Staaten von Amerika 3a and 3b, Bd. 1.

143. Bethmann Hollweg to Treutler, March 22, 1916, AA, Akten des AA im Grossen Hauptquartier 1915–1919, U-Bootkrieg 42. Cf. Max Weber to Foreign Office, March 10, 1916, AA, WK 18, *secr.*, Bd. 9.

144. Dernburg, who had returned to Germany, also supported Bernstorff's efforts and took a stand against submarine warfare. Dernburg to Montgelas, March 24, 1916, AA, WK 18, *secr.*, Bd. 10.

145. Jagow to Bethmann Hollweg, April 30, 1916, ibid., Bd. 14.

146. Spindler, *Der Handelskrieg mit U-Booten*, 3:145. Tirpitz, *Politische Dokumente*, 2:528. Ritter, *Staatskunst und Kriegshandwerk*, 3:210.

147. Wilhelm II spoke as Jagow and Zimmermann had suggested. Notes by Jagow and Zimmermann for the Emperor's talk with Gerard, April 26, 1916, AA, WK 18, *secr.*, Bd. 14.

148. Gerard to Lansing, May 3, 1916, *FRUS 1916*, Suppl., pp. 253–55. Cf. Ritter, *Staatskunst und Kriegshandwerk*, 3:212.

149. Gerard to Lansing, May 4, 1916, *FRUS 1916*, Suppl., pp. 257–60. Tirpitz, *Politische Dokumente*, 2:541.

150. Bernstorff to Foreign Office, April 26, 1916, UA Beilagen, pp. 308–9. Cf. House to Wilson, April 25, 1916, YHC.

151. Bethmann Hollweg had assured Admiral Holtzendorff that the matter could be discussed again in the middle of June. More would be known then about the yields of the harvest, and America would have selected its presidential candidates. Birnbaum, *Peace Moves and U-Boat Warfare*, pp. 90–91.

152. On April 24, following a request from the Chancellor, Holtzendorff had given the order that for the time being the submarine war was to be continued "only according to prize law [*Prisenordnung*]." Since Admiral Reinhard Scheer, Chief of the Maritime Fleet [*Hochseeflotte*], did not want to expose the submarines to cruiser warfare, the U-boat campaign around the British Isles was completely abandoned; ibid., p. 81. Spindler, *Der Handelskrieg mit U-Booten*, 3:140–41. Ritter, *Staatskunst und Kriegshandwerk*, 3:210.

153. Jagow's acknowledgment of the sinking of the *Sussex* by a German U-boat followed on May 8. The injured Americans were offered compensation, and it was announced that Lt. Herbert Pustkuchen would be punished. Gerard to Lansing, May 8, 1916, *FRUS 1916*, Suppl., pp. 265–66.

154. Bernstorff to Foreign Office, May 6, 1916, AA, WK 18, *secr.*, Bd. 16. It is striking that the copy of the text forwarded by Jagow from the Foreign Office to Grünau at General Headquarters leaves out entirely Bernstorff's

remark that new incidents were to be avoided, "particularly since House in the meantime wants to prepare a peace action with Wilson." Jagow to Grünau, May 8, 1916, AA, Akten des AA im Grossen Hauptquartier 1915–1919, Vereinigte Staaten von Amerika 3a and 3b, Bd. 1. Bernstorff to Foreign Office, May 10, 1916, AA, WK 18, *secr.*, Bd. 17.

155. Lansing to Gerard, May 8, 1916, *FRUS 1916*, Suppl., p. 263: "Responsibility in such matters is single, not joint; absolute, not relative."

156. Bernstorff, *Deutschland und Amerika*, pp. 249–50.

157. The Emperor called Wilson's note "the rearguard action of a know-it-all [*Rechthabers*] who still wanted to push his point [*auftrumpfen*]." Grünau to Foreign Office, May 11, 1916, AA, WK 18, *secr.*, Bd. 16. Cf. Birnbaum, *Peace Moves and U-Boat Warfare*, p. 91.

158. Bernstorff, *Deutschland und Amerika*, p. 255.

159. Henry Newbolt, *Naval Operations* (London, 1928), 4:230.

160. Bernstorff, *Deutschland und Amerika*, p. 255.

161. The annexationist demands, rather incredible in their extent in retrospect, repeatedly were the subject of memoranda and petitions supported by numerous signatures. Moreover, far-reaching war goals were frequently discussed in various circles of German leadership.

162. Link, *The Struggle for Neutrality*, pp. 372–73.

163. Countess Bernstorff only joined her husband in the fall of 1916. Aspersions concerning the "taunting faithlessness" of the Countess in 1915, published by Rhodri Jeffreys-Jones in his *American Espionage* (New York, 1977), p. 61, are therefore without foundation. Some of the Ambassador's personal mail reached Europe through the usual clandestine channels such as false addresses in neutral countries or crew members on neutral ships. Since the bulk of the personal papers of Count Bernstorff is still missing, the number of personal letters available to the historian is very small. Some letters, intercepted by British intelligence, have also turned up in the Foreign Office Files at the PRO. Cf. FO 371/2852 and FO 372/950.

164. Notes by House, June 22, 1915, *IPH*, 2:7–8. House also had the impression that Bernstorff was not informed about the full extent of the differences between the government and the military in Berlin.

165. Particularly noteworthy are the many copies of Max Warburg's correspondence with members of his family in America, which he often placed at the disposal of the Foreign Office. In addition, it would appear that a number of routine private letters from America were retained by the German censors. These documents are found scattered throughout the various record series of the German Foreign Office.

166. In spite of it all, several Imperial departments and offices succeeded in smuggling their agents into the United States with false passports. The routes via South America and China do not seem to have been controlled reliably by the Entente.

167. On this occasion Bernstorff was able to obtain Wilson's permission to dispatch ciphered reports to his government via the State Department and the American Embassy in Berlin. This had become necessary because often it would take days before a telegram reached Berlin via Buenos Aires and Stockholm. By contrast, telegrams from the State Department usually arrived on the same day in Berlin. Cf. Bernstorff, *Deutschland und Amerika*, pp. 152–53. Link, *The Struggle for Neutrality*, p. 412.

168. Bernstorff to Foreign Office, June 2, 1915, AA, WK 18, *secr.*, Bd. 2. English translation of Bernstorff's report in Link, *The Papers of Woodrow Wilson*, 33:318–20. Cf. Bernstorff, *Deutschland und Amerika*, pp. 151–52. Link, *The Struggle for Neutrality*, pp. 412–13.

169. Gerard to Bryan, June 4, 1915, *FRUS 1915*, Suppl., pp. 432–33.

170. Gerard to Bryan, May 25, 1915, ibid., p. 415; memorandum by Lansing, May 27, 1915, ibid., pp. 416–17; Bryan to Gerard, May 27, 1915, ibid., p. 418. Link, *The Struggle for Neutrality*, pp. 392–96. Concerning a meeting of Wilson and Bernstorff on May 28, see footnote 34 above.

171. Cf. Gerard to Lansing, July 13, 1915, *FRUS 1915*, Suppl., pp. 43–44.

172. Edward H. Buehrig, ed., *Wilson's Foreign Policy in Perspective* (Bloomington, Ind., 1957), pp. 200–201.

173. Link, *The Struggle for Neutrality*, pp. 395–96. Perhaps if the question of submarine warfare had not overshadowed Washington's relations with Berlin, in the summer of 1915 Wilson might have been willing to take diplomatic steps against Britain's blockade. As matters stood, though, Wilson, Lansing, and House were in agreement that it was inadvisable to put the friendly relations with the Entente at stake since "our friendship with Germany is a matter of the past." Lansing to House, July 30, 1915, quoted in ibid., pp. 596–98.

174. There were a number of less important contacts with various personalities of American public life. Bernstorff avoided most of them in order not to jeopardize his negotiations with House. Worth mentioning is the exchange of letters between Bernstorff and S. H. Church, President of the Carnegie Institute in Pittsburgh. Though it is unlikely that the Ambassador took the efforts of Church very seriously, one notes that in this correspondence Bernstorff declares the evacuation of France and Belgium dependent on the return of the German colonies. The idea of using Belgium and France as a pawn for the reacquisition of a German colonial empire indeed was nothing new among German expansionist circles, but it does not accord with Bernstorff's political views as they are reflected in the records otherwise. The fact that Church also approached Wilhelm II directly in the matter and at the same time submitted a confidential letter Bernstorff had written to him, could only add to the weakening of the Ambassador's position at the court. Documents concerning this contact are located in AA, Botschaft Washington, Friedensvorschläge.

175. *IPH*, 2:81–83.

176. Link, *Confusions and Crises*, pp. 102–3. *IPH*, 2:84–85. Wilson did not give a definite answer at that time, since the discussion was only very short.

177. Grey to House, August 10, 1915, August 26, 1915, September 22, 1915, *IPH*, 2:87–89. Cf. Buehrig, *Wilson's Foreign Policy in Perspective*, pp. 206–7. Link, *Confusions and Crises*, p. 102.

178. Complete text in Link, *The Papers of Woodrow Wilson*, 35:81–82. Words in square brackets were deleted by Woodrow Wilson in the original House draft. Words in italics were inserted by the President.

179. The new direction in American foreign policy was accompanied by a significant program of preparedness. After the navy submitted its first proposals in July, Wilson approved a $500 million naval construction program in October. At the same time the army presented a reorganization plan and requested a reinforcement of almost 50 percent. In November Wilson for the first time presented these plans to the public. As early as December 7 he went before Congress to explain in detail the planned expansion of the navy and the army. At the very latest from this day on, the German government could have no doubt that Americans would not only defend their own rights and territories, "but the rights also of those with whom they have made common cause." Wilson's address to the Manhattan Club, November 4, 1915, and his Annual Message on the State of the Union, December 7, 1915. Texts in ibid., 167–73, 293–310. Link, *Confusions and Crises*, pp. 15–54.

180. Cf. *IPH*, 2:91. Cf. Ritter, *Staatskunst und Kriegshandwerk*, 3:185.

181. Ritter, *Staatskunst und Kriegshandwerk*, 3:184.

182. Notes by House, October 11, 1915, *IPH*, 2:85.

183. Ibid., 86.

184. Bernstorff to Foreign Office, November 23, 1915, UA Beilagen, pp. 297–98. House to Wilson, November 19, 1915, YHC. ("Yet any rupture of diplomatic relations with Germany must not necessarily defeat the general plan to bring about peace.") Link, *Confusions and Crises*, pp. 107–8.

185. House to Wilson, December 22, 1915, *IPH*, 2:106–7. Jagow to Bernstorff, December 20, 1915, UA Beilagen, p. 298.

186. Solf to Jagow, January 28, 1916, and Bethmann Hollweg's note, January 28, 1916, *LAPP*, 1:262–65.

187. According to House, the Chancellor spoke of "indemnities" for the evacuation of France and Belgium. *IPH*, 2:142. Bethmann Hollweg notes that he said: "We would also have to receive an indemnity for Northern France, which France would have to pay." *LAPP*, 1:65.

188. Notes by House about his meeting with the Chancellor and other personalities, *IPH*, 2:140–43.

189. House to Wilson, February 3, 1916, ibid., 146–47; Gerard to House,

December 7, 1915, ibid., 103–4. Concerning his meeting with Bethmann Hollweg on January 28, 1916, House noted: "The Chancellor drank copiously of beer which was served to us from time to time. . . . The beer did not apparently affect him, for his brain was as befuddled at the beginning as it was at the end. Into such hands are the destinies of the people placed." His discussion with Jagow left him equally dissatisfied. His meeting with Zimmermann, whom he thought to be "in some ways, the ablest though not the most trustworthy man in the Government," also brought no results. Notes by House, January 28 and 29, 1916, ibid., 140–43. In his memoirs, *Betrachtungen zum Weltkriege* (Berlin, 1919–21), 2:147, Bethmann Hollweg has little to say about his meeting with House. Cf. notes by Bethmann Hollweg, January 28, 1916, *LAPP*, 1:264–65.

190. *IPH*, 2:153.

191. Falkenhayn to Bethmann Hollweg, February 13, 1916, Top Secret!, *LAPP*, 1:267–68.

192. Friedrich Thimme, ed., *Bethmann Hollwegs Kriegsreden* (Stuttgart, 1919), p. 87.

193. Ibid., p. 97.

194. Zimmermann to Legation Bern, February 11, 1916, *LAPP*, 1:266–67.

195. House's notes about this meeting in *IPH*, 1:179–82. Questions concerning possible territorial changes after a conclusion of peace, that also had come up during House's talks with the Allied leaders, are indeed of interest for an appraisal of the Entente viewpoint, but they do not alter the fact that at this point Wilson had no thought of supporting the war goals of the Entente. A return to the status quo ante certainly cannot be seen as a territorial change. Cf. Ritter, *Staatskunst und Kriegshandwerk*, 3:188–89.

196. Wilson inserted the word "probably" here. Otherwise, he accepted the text of the memorandum. House to Grey, March 8, 1916, quoted in Link, *Confusions and Crises*, p. 138.

197. *IPH*, 2:200–202. Edward Grey, *Twenty-Five Years 1892–1916* (London, 1925), 2:123.

198. Cf. for instance Ritter, *Staatskunst und Kriegshandwerk*, 3:183–91. Even the widely used German historical handbook, Ploetz's *Auszug aus der Geschichte* (Würzburg, 1968), p. 1742, states: "Wilson's peace feeler through Colonel Edward Mandel House with the belligerents to determine their readiness for a peace without victory remains without result as a consequence of the unfulfillable demands of the Allies."

199. Ritter, *Staatskunst und Kriegshandwerk*, 3:189.

200. Hölzle, "Das Experiment des Friedens im Ersten Weltkrieg 1914 bis 1917," *Geschichte in Wissenschaft und Unterricht* 13 (1962): 474.

201. Ritter, *Staatskunst und Kriegshandwerk*, 3:190–91

202. Bernstorff to Foreign Office, April 8, 1916, AA, WK 18, *secr.*, Bd. 12. Tirpitz, *Politische Dokumente*, 2:527.

203. Jagow to Bernstorff, April 11, 1916, AA, WK 18, *secr.*, Bd. 12.
204. Speech before the Reichstag, April 5, 1916, Thimme, *Bethmann Hollwegs Kriegsreden*, p. 97.
205. Jagow to Bethmann Hollweg, April 29, 1916, AA, WK 18, *secr.*, Bd. 14.
206. Gerard to Lansing, May 3, 1916, *FRUS 1916*, Suppl., pp. 253–55.
207. Ritter, *Staatskunst und Kriegshandwerk*, 3:214.
208. Gerard to Lansing, May 3, 1916, *FRUS 1916*, Suppl., pp. 253–55; Gerard to Lansing, May 2, 1916, ibid., p. 27.
209. Bernstorff to Foreign Office, May 4, 1916, UA Beilagen, pp. 5–6. Cf. Tirpitz, *Politische Dokumente*, 2:542.
210. Bethmann Hollweg to Bernstorff, May 6, 1916, UA Beilagen, p. 6. Birnbaum, *Peace Moves and U-Boat Warfare*, pp. 97–98. Tirpitz, *Politische Dokumente*, 2:542.
211. House to Wilson, May 14, 1916, YHC. Bernstorff tried to convince House that it would be expedient to clear away still outstanding controversial questions in order to bring a certain calm to German-American relations. Besides the settlement of the *Lusitania* issue, Bernstorff was hoping to take care of the Igel affair by sending Wolf von Igel back to Germany and in return getting the American government to hand over the compromising Igel papers. Regarding the Igel affair, see Chapter 5.
212. Birnbaum, *Peace Moves and U-Boat Warfare*, pp. 97–98, thinks that Jagow, as well as Bethmann Hollweg, was hoping to reach a separate peace with Britain. He feels, however, that Jagow, in contrast to Bethmann Hollweg, did not consider arranging contacts through America.
213. Ritter, *Staatskunst und Kriegshandwerk*, 3:214.
214. In this connection Jagow told Gerard that Germany had "not voiced any 'condition,' but rather expressed an indeed justified expectation." Notes by Jagow about Gerard's delivery of the American note of May 10, 1916, AA, WK 18, *secr.*, Bd. 16.
215. Lansing to Gerard, May 8, 1916, *FRUS 1916*, Suppl., p. 263.
216. For details of the Igel affair see Chapter 5.
217. Bernstorff to Foreign Office through Lucius, dated Stockholm, May 23, 1916, AA, Vereinigte Staaten von Amerika 16, Bd. 43.
218. Bernstorff to Foreign Office, May 18, 1916, UA Beilagen, pp. 7–8.
219. *IPH*, 2:251–52.
220. Gerard to Lansing, May 11, 1916, *FRUS 1916*, Suppl., p. 267. Gerard to House, May 17, 1916, *IPH*, 2:252. Cf. Birnbaum, *Peace Moves and U-Boat Warfare*, pp. 100–101.
221. Birnbaum, *Peace Moves and U-Boat Warfare*, pp. 99, 103–4; notes by Bethmann Hollweg, May 5, 1916, ibid.
222. Cf. Speech by Bethmann Hollweg, June 5, 1916, Verhandlungen des Reichstags, Bd. 307, p. 1512; Member of the Reichstag Spahn, June 6, 1916, ibid., p. 1521; Member of the Reichstag Bassermann, June 6, 1916, ibid.,

p. 1526: "The supremacy of German seamanship and of our materials has been proven." The naval leaders, however, also made use of the fact that the battleships were in need of repair, in order to put renewed pressure on the Chancellor concerning the resumption of the submarine war. U-boat warfare, they argued, would have to be resumed "on July 1 at the latest." Holtzendorff to Bethmann Hollweg, June 9, 1916, AA, WK 18, *secr.*, Bd. 17; Müller to Bethmann Hollweg, June 10, 1916, ibid., Bd. 18.

223. In his draft of the note, Jagow had used stronger language: "Your Excellency therefore should keep in mind that we must attempt to avoid under all circumstances the mediation of such a naive statesman as President Wilson, who in his entire attitude tends toward the British standpoint." AA, WK 18, *secr.*, Bd. 17, quoted in Birnbaum, *Peace Moves and U-Boat Warfare*, pp. 106–7. Cf. Adolf von Harnack on August 1, 1916: "Looking at it historically, it is also almost impossible for such a war to end with the status quo ante.... We must win back a colonial empire.... But in the west the peace shall assure us against Britain ruling the seas alone and against Belgium remaining its satrapy." Adolf von Harnack, *An der Schwelle des dritten Kriegsjahrs* (Berlin, 1916), pp. 15–16. Cf. Max Weber to Marianne Weber, April 17, 1916: "The mistake not to explain from the very beginning that Belgium would not be kept—now can no longer be repaired." Quoted in Wolfgang J. Mommsen, *Max Weber und die deutsche Politik 1890–1920* (Ph.D. diss., Universität Köln), p. 212.

224. Jagow to Bernstorff, June 7, 1916, not dispatched until June 12 or 13, AA, WK 18, *secr.*, Bd. 17; cf. *LAPP*, 1:359–60. Cf. Jagow to Bernstorff, June 12, 1916, AA, WK 18, *secr.*, Bd. 18.

225. It is not clear whether the "intensified" or the "unrestricted" submarine war is meant here.

226. Bernstorff to Bethmann Hollweg, July 13, 1916, *LAPP*, 1:405–7.

227. Bethmann Hollweg to Bernstorff, August 18, 1916, *LAPP*, 1:438.

228. Cf. text of the speech in Thimme, *Bethmann Hollwegs Kriegsreden*, pp. 90–102; see note 197 above. Cf. Max Weber to Marianne Weber, April 7, 1916: "The Chancellor had to show that he is the 'strong man'—equally as 'strong' as Tirpitz, otherwise he was lost because of the conservative opposition." Quoted in Mommsen, *Max Weber und die deutsche Politik 1890–1920*, pp. 247–48.

229. The Chancellor even allowed himself the ominous threat: "With those, the people will get even after the war." Speech of June 5, 1916, Thimme, *Bethmann Hollwegs Kriegsreden*, p. 121.

CHAPTER FIVE

1. Even broadly conceived studies such as Gerhard Ritter's *Staatskunst und Kriegshandwerk*, vol. 3 (Munich, 1964), have avoided discussing these

matters. David W. Hirst's unpublished dissertation ("German Propaganda in the United States, 1914–1917," Northwestern University, 1962) is the only significant study to use the documents that were available two decades ago.

2. Link, *The Struggle for Neutrality*, vol. 3 of *Wilson* (Princeton, N.J., 1960), especially pp. 31–36, 554–64, 645–51. Link, *Confusions and Crises, 1915–1916*, vol. 4 of *Wilson* (Princeton, N.J., 1964), pp. 55–61. Cf. Thomas A. Bailey, *Woodrow Wilson and the Lost Peace* (New York, 1947), p. 10: "The submarine was clearly the precipitating cause of our war with Germany, but this does not mean that there were not other and highly important contributory causes. German espionage . . . German intrigue . . . and German sabotage as high-lighted by such disasters as the Black Tom explosion, mightily aroused the American people."

3. Ethel Mary Tinnemann, "Count Johann von Bernstorff and German-American Relations, 1908–1917" (Ph.D. diss., University of California at Berkeley, 1960), emphasizes that Bernstorff was probably informed about most of the intelligence services' activities.

4. Only a $10,000,000 loan could be placed. In addition, apparently a small amount was signed for without publicity. Originally, the Reichsschatzamt (Imperial Treasury) had planned to sell German Imperial bonds valued at $175,000,000 in America. The proceeds were supposed to finance the purchase of food supplies, of which Albert was in charge. Evidently, however, the Foreign Office, as opposed to the Reichsschatzamt, had counted on being able to use these funds for other purposes as well. At any rate, Dernburg deemed it necessary to obtain large loans from Kuhn, Loeb & Co.and from Warburg in order to finance his various projects. In this context, see especially Heinrich F. Albert, *Aufzeichnungen* (Berlin, [1948]). Kühn to Jagow, August 9, 1914, AA, WK 10, *secr.*, Bd. 1; Warburg to Reichsschatzamt, October 9, 1914; Kühn to Jagow, October 13, 1914, ibid.; and Bernstorff to Foreign Office, October 16, 1914, ibid., Bd. 2; Helfferich to Jagow, February 15, 1915, ibid., Bd. 4; Bernstorff to Foreign Office, March 31, 1915, ibid., Bd. 5; Bernstorff to Bethmann Hollweg, October 2, 1916, ibid., Bd. 9. Horst P. Falcke, *Vor dem Eintritt Amerikas in den Weltkrieg* (Dresden, 1928), pp. 104–5.

5. Albert tried unsuccessfully to send food supplies and raw materials to Germany on American ships. Cf. Albert, *Aufzeichnungen*, pp. 55–56. Kühn to Secretary of the Interior, September 12, 1914, AA, WK 10, *secr.*, Bd. 1. Bernstorff, *Deutschland und Amerika* (Berlin, 1920), pp. 90–94. In addition, Papen and Albert bought up war materials through firms such as the Bridgeport Projectile Company and the Aetna Powder Company, which had been founded particularly for this purpose by straw men, in order to delay shipments to the Allies. Cf. Bernstorff to Bethmann Hollweg, February 18, 1916, AA, WK 10, *secr.*, Bd. 7. Bernstorff, *Deutschland und Amerika*, pp.

94–97. Franz von Papen, *Der Wahrheit eine Gasse* (Munich, 1952), pp. 61–62.

6. Cf. Falcke, *Vor dem Eintritt Amerikas in den Weltkrieg*, pp. 125–26. Karl Boy-Ed, *Verschwörer?* (Berlin, 1920), pp. 87–94. John P. Jones and Paul M. Hollister, *The German Secret Service in America 1914–1918* (Boston, 1918), pp. 31–42.

7. The following books offer some albeit rather unreliable and incomplete information: Walter Nicolai, *Geheime Mächte* (Leipzig, 1923), mentions neither persons nor assignments in America; and his *Nachrichtendienst, Presse und Volksstimmung im Weltkrieg* (Berlin, 1920) excludes sabotage. Gert Buchheit, *Der deutsche Geheimdienst* (Munich, 1966), gives a superficial treatment. Cf. P.-Louis Rivière, *Un Centre de guerre secrète* (Paris, 1936).

8. Since sabotage in the United States was of no interest to the Allies, this would only be a comparative study of the propaganda and financial efforts. Such a study based on the records available has yet to be written. Information regarding the activities of Sir William Wiseman, Naval Attaché Guy Gaunt, Capt. Norman Thwaites, and other members connected with the British intelligence services in the United States by and large still has to be gathered from the various relevant studies and often cannot be substantiated. Cf. among others Arthur Willert, *The Road to Safety* (London, 1952); W. B. Fowler, *British-American Relations 1917–1918* (Princeton, N.J., 1969); H. C. Peterson, *Propaganda for War* (Port Washington, N.J., 1968); Sir Gilbert Parker, "The United States and the War," *Harper's Magazine* 136 (March 1918): 521–31; Detlef R. Peters, "Das 'US Committee on Public Information'" (Ph.D. diss., Freie Universität Berlin, 1964); James D. Squires, *British Propaganda at Home and in the United States from 1914 to 1917* (Cambridge, Mass., 1935); J. McCarthy, "The British," in *The Immigrant's Influence on Wilson's Peace Policies*, ed. Joseph P. O'Grady (Lexington, Ky., 1967).

9. While still in exile, Bernstorff in his second volume of memoirs spoke of the "infinitely exaggerated so-called German conspiracies in the United States connected with the ammunition trade"; Bernstorff, *Erinnerungen und Briefe* (Zürich, 1936), p. 110.

10. Albert, *Aufzeichnungen*, p. 60. In July 1915, Albert lost his briefcase in a New York elevated train. It fell into the hands of the American Secret Service; ibid., p. 73, contains Albert's own version of the episode. Cf. Link, *The Struggle for Neutrality*, pp. 554–58. Falcke, *Vor dem Eintritt Amerikas in den Weltkrieg*, pp. 223–39. Far from the truth, as the records indicate, is a recent appraisal by Rhodri Jeffreys-Jones, *American Espionage* (New York, 1977), p. 57, that Albert "had authority over the worldwide German spy network outside the 'ring of steel' thrown around the Central Powers by the Allied navies."

11. The U.S. Secret Service kept a close eye on the German seamen stationed on German ships in a number of American ports. German sympathizers were watched. Later a considerable number of telephones of Germans in America, but also of Americans, were tapped. Diverse records in NA, RG 59 and RG 87. Diary of E. M. House, March 10, 1916, YHC. Cf. Arthur Walworth, *Woodrow Wilson* (New York, 1958), 2:22. Link, *The Struggle for Neutrality*, pp. 558–59.

12. Thomas G. Masaryk, *Die Welt-Revolution* (Berlin, 1925), pp. 272–73. Emanuel Victor Voska and Will Irwin, *Spy and Counterspy* (New York, 1940), pp. 17–20, 27, 32–37. (Voska's daughter even became a secretary in Albert's office.)

13. Don Whitehead, *The F.B.I. Story* (London, 1957), pp. 30–43. Link, *The Struggle for Neutrality*, pp. 65, 558–59.

14. Many of these recorded conversations can be found in the Yale House Collection. In the course of the investigations of the Mixed Claims Commission they were brought to light again and surreptitiously even offered to the German Government for a price. Hentig to Foreign Office, October 15, 1930, AA, Rechtswesen 6, Sabotage Claims, Bd. 14.

15. Cf. Link, *The Struggle for Neutrality*, pp. 645–47.

16. When Papen returned to Germany after his expulsion from America, the British checked him on the way, and his papers—among other things, containing financial accounts of sabotage activities—were seized. Igel's office was searched by American agents in the spring of 1916, and secret papers which should either have long been destroyed or taken back to the Embassy were confiscated.

17. House to Wilson, November 19, 1915, YHC; House Diaries, October 8, 1915: "I thought Bernstorff was about the best of his tribe and had done more to bring about a solution of our differences with Germany than perhaps any one man." *IPH*, 2:450. Cf. Link, *The Struggle for Neutrality*, pp. 648–49, 679.

18. M. J. Bonn, *Mußte es sein?* (Munich, 1919), p. 94.

19. Warburg to Bussche-Haddenhausen, March 13, 1918, Papers of Max M. Warburg (privately held). Warburg was in The Hague in order to hold secret negotiations with the Americans, which had been arranged by Rosen, Hahn, and Noeggerath.

20. Gerard to Bryan, telegram, January 24, 1915, YHC.

21. Cf. Karl Jünger, *Deutsch-Amerika mobil . . . !* (Berlin, 1915), p. 57.

22. Bernstorff to Foreign Office, January 7, 1915, AA, Botschaft Washington, Generalkonsulat in New York, Bd. 4.

23. Cf. for instance Foreign Office to Bernstorff, December 2, 1914, AA, WK 11f, Bd. 6. Jones and Hollister, *The German Secret Service in America 1914–1918*, pp. 95–96.

24. Falcke, *Vor dem Eintritt Amerikas in den Weltkrieg*, pp. 85–86.

25. Director of Intelligence Division, Admiralty War Staff, to Foreign Of-

fice, January 13, 1916, PRO, FO 371, 2847. Jagow to Deputy Minister of War, September 3, 1915, AA, Deutschland 141, Nr. 7, Bd. 7. Jones and Hollister, *The German Secret Service in America 1914–1918*, p. 89. Tibor Koeves, *Satan in Top Hat* (New York, 1941), p. 9.

26. On Ruerode's activities, see his testimony before the Chief of the Bureau of Investigation, A. Bruce Bielaski, November 21, 1915, Chief of B.I. to Attorney General, November 21, 1915, NA, RG 59, Box 209. Bail for Ruerode was set at $20,000. As it took some time to secure a bail bond and as Ruerode was not taking well to the conditions in the Tombs prison, the Germans were concerned that he might decide to offer the authorities a statement about his activities. Memorandum from Ch. Schurz for Heinrich Albert, on Hamburg-American Line stationery (New York office), January 30, 1915, NA, Albert Papers, Box 19.

27. Besides other problems it was the "strong difference of opinion" between Bernstorff and Falcke that contributed to Bernstorff's request to the Foreign Office that Falcke be transferred to a South American post. As successor, Bernstorff would have liked to have had Heinrich Albert. Zimmermann refused because of Albert's lack of experience and instead suggested Karl Buenz, the HAPAG director in New York. At age 72 and in bad health, Buenz, however, had no desire to take on additional responsibilities, particularly since besides his commercial activity he had already a contractual relationship with the Reichsmarineamt. Bernstorff to Foreign Office, January 12, 1915, January 18, 1915, January 23, 1915, January 31, 1915; Zimmermann to Bernstorff, January 23, 1915; Buenz to Bernstorff, January 30, 1915; all in AA, Botschaft Washington, Generalkonsulat in New York, Bd. 4.

28. Wedell had been sent to Berlin in the summer of 1914 "with messages and recommendations of the Imperial Embassy." Jagow to Deputy Minister of War, September 3, 1915, AA, Deutschland 141, Nr. 7, Bd. 7. Falcke, *Vor dem Eintritt Amerikas in den Weltkrieg*, p. 85. Jones and Hollister, *The German Secret Service in America 1914–1918*, p. 84. Bernstorff, *Deutschland und Amerika*, p. 104.

29. Cf. Bernstorff to Bethmann Hollweg, draft, probably mailed January 1, 1915, AA, Botschaft Washington, Generalkonsulat in New York, Bd. 4: "Nonetheless I shared Mr. von Papen's opinion that under the prevailing circumstances it is *salus res publicae suprema lex*. Recently I myself have often been in situations where I was forced to take exceptional steps for the cause."

30. Some sources contain a long letter allegedly written by Wedell to Bernstorff on December 26, 1914, before fleeing from America. In this letter he explains that the State Department had discovered his organization and that he had been watched. At the time, he said, he had not volunteered for this work in Berlin but had been persuaded by Count Wedell (probably Count Georg von Wedel, who also took care of other intelligence projects

in the Foreign Office such as Roger Casement's mission). Cf. Bernstorff, *Deutschland und Amerika*, p. 104. Jones and Hollister, *The German Secret Service in America 1914–1918*, pp. 91–92.

31. Bernstorff, *Deutschland und Amerika*, p. 104.

32. In addition Papen paid the legal defense expenses for Ruerode. Papen to Bernstorff, January 8, 1915, AA, Botschaft Washington, Generalkonsulat in New York, Bd. 4.

33. Bernstorff to Bethmann Hollweg, March 6, 1915, quoted in Link, *The Struggle for Neutrality*, p. 560.

34. Bernstorff to Foreign Office, January 7, 1915, AA, Botschaft Washington, Generalkonsulat in New York, Bd. 4.

35. Regarding the Stegler case see Boy-Ed, *Verschwörer?*, pp. 64–69; Falcke, *Vor dem Eintritt Amerikas in den Weltkrieg*, pp. 122–24; Jones and Hollister, *The German Secret Service in America 1914–1918*, pp. 93–95.

36. The Foreign Office recommended the counterfeiters in New York to Bernstorff. Foreign Office to Bernstorff, December 2, 1914, AA, WK 11f, Bd. 6.

37. House Diaries, December 16, YHC. Nonetheless, the American government was aware of the danger from within represented by the great number of German reservists, especially in case of a break in relations with Germany. With this in mind, protective measures for important installations were taken in the large cities. Cf. House Diaries, May 6, 1916, YHC. Link, *The Struggle for Neutrality*, pp. 559–60. Falcke, *Vor dem Eintritt Amerikas in den Weltkrieg*, p. 117.

38. *Nachrichtendienst, Presse und Volksstimmung im Weltkrieg* (1920); *Geheime Mächte* (1923). During the war Nicolai was head of Department IIIb of the Stellvertretender Generalstab (Deputy General Staff). After the war he is said to have been associated with the press office of the Deutschnationale Volkspartei (DNVP), and in Jewish circles he was regarded as an anti-Semite. Reportedly, Adolf Hitler asked him to write down his experiences. In 1945, he, like Kurt Jahnke, is said to have fallen into the hands of the Russians.

39. *Mein Beitrag* (Wiesbaden, 1955). His papers in the German Foreign Office reveal nothing about his activities in the "Sektion Politik" of the Stellvertretender Generalstab. Later he represented Germany in Persia, served as Delegate in Brest-Litovsk, as Minister in Sweden, as Ambassador in Turkey, and from 1933 until 1934 he was Hitler's Ambassador in Moscow.

40. *Der Wahrheit eine Gasse* (Munich, 1952), cf. pp. 63–64.

41. *Deutschland und Amerika* (1920), cf. pp. 111–12.

42. See bibliography. I have discussed some of the problems connected with publications of this nature in "Geheimdienste im 20. Jahrhundert," *Neue Politische Literatur* 3 (1974): 353–64.

43. Mainly telegrams and reports intercepted by the British intelligence

service. Published also, however, were some of the documents which through the negligence of Papen, Albert, Igel, and König fell into the hands of the Americans and the Allies.

44. Cf. Werner Otto von Hentig, *Mein Leben—Eine Dienstreise* (Göttingen, 1963), p. 91.

45. Comments in the margins by Wilhelm II on a telegram from the German ambassador in Petersburg, quoted in Ulrich Gehrke, *Persien in der deutschen Orientpolitik während des Ersten Weltkrieges* (Stuttgart, 1961), 1:1.

46. Fritz Fischer, *Griff nach der Weltmacht* (Düsseldorf, 1961), p. 140. Cf. Gehrke, *Persien in der deutschen Orientpolitik während des Ersten Weltkrieges*, 1:22.

47. Wilhelm Treue, "Max Freiherr von Oppenheim—Der Archäologe und die Politik," *Historische Zeitschrift* 209 (August 1969): 59–60.

48. Oppenheim to Bethmann Hollweg, August 18, 1914, quoted in Fischer, *Griff nach der Weltmacht*, p. 140.

49. Cf. Manabendra Nath Roy, *M. N. Roy's Memoirs* (Bombay, 1964), p. 90.

50. Cf. Colmar Freiherr von der Goltz, *Denkwürdigkeiten*, ed. Friedrich Freiherr von der Goltz and Wolfgang Foerster (Berlin, 1929), pp. 407–8, 421. Goltz to his wife, May 11, 1915: "That military campaign I would still like to take part in."

51. Cf. Daniel Argov, *Moderates and Extremists in the Indian Nationalist Movement 1883–1920* (London, 1967), p. 157. Har Dayal, *Forty-four Months in Germany and Turkey* (London, 1920), p. 67.

52. For a British appraisal of *Ghadr*, see F. David, Censor in Singapore, to Chief Censor in London, Singapore, June 4, 1915, PRO, FO 371, 2493.

53. Spring Rice to Sir Edward Grey, March 5, 1914, ibid., 2154. In this connection Maude Gonne-MacBride approached the well-known Irish-American lawyer John Quinn to prevent the extradition of Dayal to the British. Maude Gonne to John Quinn, Paris, April 1, 1914, NYPL, John Quinn Collection, Box 23. Dayal, *Forty-four Months in Germany and Turkey*, pp. v–vi. Clipping from *San Francisco Examiner*, June 14, 1915, AA, Englische Besitzungen in Asien 2, Bd. 52. In the United States Dayal maintained contacts with the Industrial Workers of the World and for some time probably was influenced by socialist ideology. Horst Krüger, "Har Dayal in Deutschland," *Mitteilungen des Instituts für Orientforschung* 10 (1964): 141–69.

54. Roy, *M. N. Roy's Memoirs*, p. 287.

55. At that time Wesendonk received from the Deutsche Waffen- und Munitionsfabriken 200 army pistols and 20,000 cartridges in the coding office of the Foreign Office (Chiffrier Büro). AA, WK 11f, Bd. 22.

56. Cf. Professor Wilhelm Salomon of the Geological-Paleontological Institute at the University of Heidelberg to Foreign Office, June 11, 1915, WK 11f, Bd. 15.

57. Cf. for instance document series AA, WK 11f. Diwakar Prasad Singh, *American Attitude towards the Indian Nationalist Movement* (New Delhi, 1974), does not include much new information on the German involvement. This may be due to the fact that the author apparently did not use German records and saw only few British documents.

58. Zimmermann to Bernstorff, November 22, 1914, AA, WK 11f, Bd. 5. (Bernstorff was instructed to come up with Persians and Indians, but "Boers we can do without.")

59. Indian Independence Committee to Wesendonk, January 10, 1916, AA, WK 11f, Bd. 24.

60. Since the remaining records are incomplete, the total cost of the Indian projects in America can no longer be established. Substantial sums are mentioned in connection with arms purchases. Cf. Bernstorff to Foreign Office, December 17, 1914, where Bernstorff, on behalf of the "military authorities," most likely Papen, speaks of an arms offer of $2,500,000, AA, WK 11f, Bd. 6. In fact, however, Papen and Tauscher concluded their arms deals for such different purposes as India, Mexico, and the possible invasion of Canada. There is evidence that the Foreign Office had up to 1,000,000 marks available at times. Foreign Office to Washington Embassy, June 10, 1915, AA, WK 11f, Bd. 14. Furthermore, it is evident that from 1914 until his departure in February 1917 Bernstorff regularly paid the Indians considerable amounts for arms, travel expenses, and propaganda. Documentary evidence of such transactions can be found for instance in AA, WK 11f, Bde. 7–37. Payments most of the time were apparently entered in the books under code names so that even the governmental accounts would not yield reliable figures. Reiswitz to Bethmann Hollweg, Secret, April 23, 1917, AA, WK 11f, Bd. 37. A summary of intelligence and propaganda expenses contained in the files of the German Foreign Office supposedly lists such outlays until January 30, 1918. Although Fritz Fischer (*Griff nach der Weltmacht*, p. 176, n. 127) and others seem to accept the figures given here at face value, I have reasonable doubt as to their reliability. The total approved "for Indian purposes" is given here as 5,310,000 marks with 1,797,056.45 marks still being unused as of January 30, 1915. Handwritten account, signed W 3/II, received February 5, 1918, AA, WK 11, Bd. 3.

61. Fliers and brochures were brought into the country by way of the embassy and the consulates. Cf. Bernstorff to Bethmann Hollweg, May 17, 1915, AA, WK 11f, Bd. 14; Bernstorff to Foreign Office, June 13, 1915, ibid., Bd. 16; Foreign Office to Bernstorff, December 1, 1915, ibid., Bd. 22.

62. Wehde's memoirs, *Since Leaving Home* (Chicago, 1923), reveal little about his intelligence assignments. See however Reiswitz to Bethmann Hollweg, April 27, 1917, AA, WK 11f, Bd. 37. Clippings from *Manila Daily Bulletin*, July 12, 1915, PRO, FO 371, 2495.

63. Application for restitution by Max Schulze after his return from China on May 16, 1919, AA, WK 11f, Bd. 48. The agent's names often

appear misspelled, such as Stenneck or Scholz. Cf. British Foreign Office to Spring Rice, January 14, 1916, PRO, FO 371, 2784, where he is referred to as "Steneck (Steinich), a Dutchman(?)."

64. Bernstorff to Bethmann Hollweg, April 20, 1915, April 23, 1915, AA, WK 11f, Bd. 14; Bernstorff to Foreign Office, November 23, 1915, ibid., Bd. 23. Concerning Boehm see also memo by Lohmann, January 19, 1926, AA, Rechtswesen 6, Bd. 4.

65. Statement by Jodh Singh in Singapore, November 15, 1915, PRO, FO 371, 2784. Wehde, *Since Leaving Home*, p. 511. Albert Kaltschmidt to Kommissar des Reichsfinanzministeriums für Rechtsangelegenheiten aus dem Kriege, June 1, 1921, AA, Rechtswesen 15, Kaltschmidt. William Jarrosch also appears in the documents as Jarosch.

66. Wehde received $3,000 for travel expenses and "a credit of $20,000 to start with" for his projects. Bernstorff to Bethmann Hollweg, April 20, 1915, AA, WK 11f, Bd. 14. Papen originally had requested a credit from the embassy for Wehde in the amount of $200,000.

67. Following Papen's order, the *Henry S.* was bought for $17,500 and loaded with arms which had been stored in the harbor on liners of the North German Lloyd. The cargo at first was supposed to go to Chittagong. Papen to Deputy General Staff, July 23, 1915, AA, WK 11f, Bd. 18.

68. Roy, *M. N. Roy's Memoirs*, p. 66: "The Helfferich brothers owned the major share of German interests in the Far East, and would be regarded as pioneers of the abortive German Imperialism. They were to finance the scheme of fomenting an armed uprising in India to embarrass Britain." Cf. Earl E. Sperry, *German Plots and Intrigues in the United States During the Period of Our Neutrality* (Washington, D.C., 1918), p. 47.

69. Regarding this operation cf. Wehde, *Since Leaving Home*. Request for restitution by Max Schulze, AA, WK 11f, Bd. 48; report by Consul Zitelmann of the "Etappe" Manila, June 1918, ibid., Bd. 44; clipping, *The Sunday Times*, Manila; September 12, 1915, ibid., Bd. 22.

70. Hentig, *Mein Leben—Eine Dienstreise*, p. 91.

71. Roy, *M. N. Roy's Memoirs*, pp. 3–4, 286.

72. Ulrich Trumpener, *Germany and the Ottoman Empire 1914–1918* (Princeton, N.J., 1968), p. 22, comes to the same conclusion regarding the operations in the Middle East: "The measures . . . bore all the earmarks of hasty improvisation."

73. Cf. Wilhelm Groener, *Lebenserinnerungen*, ed. F. Freiherr Hiller von Gaertringen (Göttingen, 1957), p. 530, diary, January 21, 1915: "Dr. Jaeckh, . . . with me because of expansion of Baghdad Railway for attack on Egypt, is thinking of putting German artillery and troops on the still-to-be-expanded Baghdad Railway in order to attack Britain via Asia Minor—Arabia—Egypt."

74. Nadolny to Dagobert von Mikusch, September 12, 1936, AA, Nachlass Nadolny. Fischer, *Griff nach der Weltmacht*, p. 147, Gehrke, *Persien in der deutschen Orientpolitik während des Ersten Weltkrieges*, 1:31.

75. The expeditions of Werner Otto von Hentig, Wilhelm Wassmuss, Oskar Niedermeyer, and Fritz Klein. Although in retrospect these operations appear to have been senseless from the very beginning, they were still, "based on the false ideas prevailing in Germany at the time," given a certain chance of success. Interview of the author with Dr. von Hentig.

76. As can be seen from the records, a large part of the telegram exchange of these agencies with Berlin passed through the Embassy in Washington. Bernstorff was thus informed about the activities in China, especially since some of the Indians who were in contact with him traveled between Asia and America with his assistance. Cf. for instance Bernstorff to Foreign Office, January 15, 1915, AA, WK 11f, Bd. 8; Bernstorff to Bethmann Hollweg, June 29, 1915, ibid., Bd. 17. Regarding Hintze's sabotage plans cf. also Elmar Peter, "Die Bedeutung Chinas in der deutschen Ostasienpolitik (1911–1917)" (Ph.D. diss., Universität Hamburg, 1965), pp. 245–50.

77. Foreign Office to Bernstorff, October 11, 1914, AA, WK 11f, Bd. 3. Following Ballin's advice the Ambassador was instructed to contact Minister Hintze in this matter.

78. Papen to Deputy General Staff, October 20, 1914, ibid., Bd. 5; Bernstorff to Foreign Office, December 5, 1914, ibid., Bd. 6.

79. Bernstorff to Foreign Office, February 24, 1915, ibid., Bd. 10; Nadolny to Foreign Office, April 13, 1915, ibid., Bd. 12, Papen report.

80. Cf. memorandum without signature (with Zimmermann's initials), November 24, 1914, ibid., Bd. 5.

81. Papen to War Ministry, March 8, 1915, as a copy from Nadolny to Foreign Office, March 20, 1915, ibid., Bd. 12.

82. Bernstorff to Foreign Office, January 23, 1915, ibid., Bd. 8; Bernstorff to Foreign Office, February 24, 1915, ibid., Bd. 10.

83. Copy of report from Papen, dated May 31, 1915, forwarded by Rudolf Nadolny to Foreign Office, June 20, 1915, ibid., Bd. 15.

84. Papen to General Staff, Dept. IIIb, New York, July 23, 1915, ibid., Bd. 18. Cf. NA, RG 131, Box 3.

85. For the correspondence with the State Department see AA, Botschaft Washington, Maverick und Annie Larsen, July 1915. The Military Attaché in Washington planned to ship the arms to South China as soon as they were freed by the American authorities. Papen to General Staff, Dept. IIIb, New York, July 23, 1915, AA, WK 11f, Bd. 18. See also application of Captain Othmer for reimbursement of his losses (private property left on the *Annie Larsen*) when he fled his ship at Hoquiam; ibid., Bd. 20.

86. Copy of report from Papen, dated May 31, 1915, forwarded by Rudolf Nadolny to Foreign Office, June 20, 1915, AA, WK 11f, Bd. 15; Papen to General Staff, Dept. IIIb, New York, July 23, 1915, ibid., Bd. 18.

87. Papen to Deputy General Staff, November 5, 1915, ibid., Bd. 22.

88. The Indians in Berlin even demanded the deployment of submarines in the Persian Gulf and bombing raids on such cities as Bombay and Kara-

chi. Indian Independence Committee to Wesendonk, November 14, 1915, ibid., Bd. 22.

89. Jagow to State Secretary of the Reichsschatzamt, April 13, 1916, ibid., Bd. 27.

90. Bernstorff to Foreign Office (for Hintze), November 8, 1915, ibid., Bd. 24; Wesendonk memorandum, probably January 14, 1916, ibid.; Foreign Office to Bernstorff (for Hintze), February 29, 1916, ibid., Bd. 26. Cf. Roy, M. N. Roy's Memoirs, pp. 4–5. According to this source, the use of ships interned in Sumatra for the Andamans operation was also considered.

91. Papen to Deputy General Staff, June 22, 1915, AA, WK 11f, Bd. 16.

92. Bernstorff to Bethmann Hollweg, August 5, 1916, ibid., Bd. 34; Bernstorff to Foreign Office, November 7, 1916, ibid.; Foreign Office to Political Section of General Staff, January 6, 1917, ibid., Bd. 35.

93. Heramba Lal Gupta and Khan Dravanta Chakravarty apparently both aspired to leadership and open quarrels developed. Cf. Bernstorff to Bethmann Hollweg, Rye, September 12, 1916, arrived in Berlin January 1, 1917, ibid., Bd. 35.

94. Cf. memo from N.I.D. (Naval Intelligence Division) to British Foreign Office, December 12, 1915, indicating that the British have turned around a German agent and obtained much information. They know of the activities in the German Embassy in Washington, of Indian leaders in San Francisco and New York, and of the work of the Irish-American George Freeman with the Indian groups.

95. See the material in PRO, FO 371, containing consular reports, naval intelligence data, New Scotland Yard memoranda, and information from turned-around agents. Whether the British were correct in assuming that John Brackenridge Starr Hunt, a U.S. citizen from an influential family who was hired by F. Jebsen to join the operation, was the leader of the project seems at least doubtful. Cf. Consul General Beckett to British Foreign Office, Secret, Batavia, October 28, 1915, ibid., 2497. J. L. Starr Hunt to Sir Maurice de Bunsen, Foreign Office, Mexico, D.F., May 20, 1916, ibid., 2787.

96. Foreign Office to Washington Embassy, December 30, 1914, AA, WK 11f, Bd. 7.

97. Cf. André Chéradame, *The United States and Pangermania* (New York, 1918), p. 108.

98. Indian Independence Committee to Wesendonk, April 24, 1916, AA, WK 11f, Bd. 27: "Graf Bernstorff who has been of such valuable assistance to us in our work both in America and in the East."

99. Cf. G.A. from Wesendonk, April 27, 1916, ibid.

100. Nadolny to Papen, December 15, 1951, AA, Nachlass Nadolny. Cf. Robert Monteith, *Casement's Last Adventure* (Chicago, 1952; rpt., Dublin, 1953), p. xi (Foreword by Papen). Karin Wolf's dissertation (University of Munich, 1966), published in 1972 as *Sir Roger Casement und die deutsch-*

irischen Beziehungen (Berlin), did not make sufficient use of the available documents. My own investigation appears in "Die Mission Sir Roger Casements im Deutschen Reich 1914–1916," *Historische Zeitschrift* 222 (1976): 578–625. I have more recently completed a comparative study of Americans of German and Irish descent; see *Iren und Deutsche in der Neuen Welt* (Stuttgart, 1986).

101. Directive from Falckenhayn, November 21, 1914, AA, WK 11k, *secr.*, Bd. 2.

102. Papen, *Der Wahrheit eine Gasse*, p. 59. Nadolny, *Mein Beitrag*, p. 41. See also Papen's foreword to Monteith, *Casement's Last Adventure*.

103. Cf. Theodor Schiemann, *Deutschland und die grosse Politik anno 1908* (Berlin, 1909), p. 135; and *Deutschland und die grosse Politik anno 1910* (Berlin, 1911), pp. 285, 349.

104. Papen to General Staff, August 9, 1914, information transmitted by telephone from General Staff to Zimmermann, August 24, 1914, AA, WK 11k, *secr.*, Bd. 1.

105. This anti-British organization was founded in 1867 by Irish radicals who had been forced to flee from their homeland to America. Carl Wittke, *The Irish in America* (Baton Rouge, La., 1956), p. 159. Cf. Nathan Glazer and Daniel P. Moynihan, *Beyond the Melting Pot* (Cambridge, Mass., 1964), p. 243, where 1869 is given as the date of founding. William O'Brien and Desmond Ryan, *Devoy's Post Bag 1871–1928* (Dublin, 1948), 1:xxxi. Regarding Devoy cf. James Reidy, "John Devoy," *The Journal of the American Irish Historical Society* 27 (1928): 413–25.

106. John Devoy, *Recollections of an Irish Rebel* (New York, 1929), p. 403. Charles Callan Tansill, *America Goes to War* (Boston, 1938), p. 176. Roger McHugh, "Casement and German Help," in *Leaders and Men of the Easter Rising: Dublin, 1916*, ed. F. X. Martin (London, 1967), p. 178.

107. After the world had already been informed through his reports in 1903 about the untenable conditions in the Belgian Congo, he went to Brazil in 1910 to investigate the excesses of the London-based Peruvian Amazon Rubber Company Ltd. against the Indian tribes living on the upper Amazon. He presented his documentation about the cruelties of the white colonists to Edward Grey in the fall of the same year. When returning to the Amazon in 1911, he found that the Indians were still subject to the same inhuman exploitation. It was only after Casement launched a new publicity campaign that serious steps were taken against the oppression of the Indian tribes. Cf. Herbert O. Mackey, *The Life and Times of Roger Casement* (Dublin, 1954), pp. 1–27. Michael Taussig, "Culture of Terror-Space of Death. Roger Casement's Putumayo Report and the Explanation of Torture," *Comparative Studies in Society and History* 26 (July 1984): 467–97.

108. McHugh, "Casement and German Help," p. 179.

109. After he had met leading American Irishmen such as Bourke Cock-

ran, John Quinn, and Joseph McGarrity. Letter by Devoy of November 12, 1915, quoted in Mackey, *The Life and Times of Roger Casement*, pp. 77–78. McHugh, "Casement and German Help," p. 179.

110. Letter of recommendation for Casement written by Bernstorff to Bethmann Hollweg, October 13, 1914, AA, WK 11k, *secr.*, Bd. 1. René MacColl, *Roger Casement* (London, 1956), p. 138.

111. Bernstorff agreed on this point. Bernstorff to Bethmann Hollweg, October 13, 1914, AA, WK 11k, *secr.*, Bd. 1; Bernstorff to Foreign Office, September 25, 1914, ibid.: "The formation of an Irish legion from prisoners of war would be a magnificent idea if it could actually be realized." Devoy, *Recollections of an Irish Rebel*, pp. 431–32. Papen to Deputy General Staff, September 28, 1914, AA, WK 11k, *secr.*, Bd. 1.

112. Prior to his departure another conference between Bernstorff and the Irish leaders took place at the German Club in New York. According to the pencilled notes of Joseph McGarrity it was held on October 10, 1914, in the evening. Others present included Franz von Papen, Bernhard Dernburg, Sir Roger Casement, Daniel Cohalan, and John Devoy. NYPL, The Maloney Collection, Box 15.

113. The so-called Findlay Affair. The British documents in PRO, FO 337, 107, show clearly that London was informed very early on Casement's activities. Intercepted mail and other evidence point to rather close British observation. See PRO, FO 95, 776 for efforts to "capture Casement & his accomplices" (Lord Kitchener to Grey, November 28, 1914) and more specifically for the £5000 promise to informer if Casement is apprehended (A. Nicholson, Foreign Office, to Findlay, Christiania, November 28, 1914). Regarding the efforts of the British chief of mission in Christiania to win E. A. Christensen for a betrayal of Casement, see, for instance, Charles E. Curry, *Sir Roger Casement* (Munich, 1922); B. L. Reid, *The Lives of Roger Casement* (New Haven, Conn., 1976); Brian Inglis, *Roger Casement* (New York, 1974).

114. Richard Meyer dealt with various Irish questions and from time to time worked for Casement as an interpreter. Meyer's testimony before the Amtsgericht (District Court) Berlin-Mitte, July 30, 1929, AA, Rechtswesen 6, Sabotage Claims, Bd. 9. Nadolny to Papen, September 15, 1952, AA, Nachlass Nadolny.

115. Wedel served as an intermediary between Casement and the Foreign Office or Bethmann Hollweg. The letters which Casement addressed to Wedel contain many important references in the Ireland matter. A number of them are located in AA, WK 11k, *secr.*

116. Cf. the remarks in Evelyn Princess Blücher, *An English Wife in Berlin* (London, 1920), which on the basis of the remaining Casement papers can be shown to be unreliable. Princess Evelyn Mary Blücher von Wahlstatt, née Stapleton-Bretherton, was married to Prince Gebhard Lebrecht Blücher von Wahlstatt and met with Casement several times.

117. Through his connections to Eduard Meyer, Casement was also able to meet other noted personalities such as, for instance, the historian Friedrich Meinecke. He also maintained contact with Albert Ballin.

118. At least once he went to the General Headquarters for negotiations.

119. Among others with Captain Walther Isendahl, "Chief of Department N of the Admiralty, who was the head of reconnaissance, counterespionage, and the intelligence services operating abroad." Testimony by Konteradmiral Walther Isendahl before the Amtsgericht (District Court) Berlin-Mitte, August 1, 1929, AA, Rechtswesen 6, Sabotage Claims, Bd. 15.

120. This word was crossed out by Bethmann Hollweg in Zimmermann's draft.

121. Zimmermann to Bethmann Hollweg, November 14, 1914, and Bethmann Hollweg to Zimmermann, November 16, 1914, AA, Akten des AA im Grossen Hauptquartier 1914–1916, Presse und Journalisten, Bd. 4.

122. Although Casement had been sent to Berlin by Devoy officially and following consultation with Bernstorff, and therefore had to be looked upon as the representative of at least the Clan na Gael organization, the IRB did not ratify the treaty. In the United States the document was published in Devoy's *Gaelic American*.

123. The text of the treaty is published in Devoy, *Recollections of an Irish Rebel*, pp. 434–35, and in Monteith, *Casement's Last Adventure*, pp. 264–66. According to Devoy, ibid., p. 435, the Clan na Gael and "our friends in Dublin" objected to Article 7. Nonetheless, in the respective literature one finds erroneous claims that the Casement treaty limited the usage of the brigade to Ireland. Cf. Alfred Noyes, *The Accusing Ghost or Justice for Casement* (London, 1957), p. 89.

124. Charles Duff, *Six Days to Shake an Empire* (London, 1966), p. 139. Devoy, *Recollections of an Irish Rebel*, pp. 438, 441.

125. Bernstorff to Foreign Office, December 12, 1914, AA, WK 11k, *secr.*, Bd. 2. Report by Hans Adam von Wedell, copy without address, received October 1, 1914, AA, Vereinigte Staaten von Amerika 10, Bd. 1.

126. Bernstorff to Foreign Office, December 12, 1914, AA, WK 11k, *secr.*, Bd. 2. Curry, *Sir Roger Casement*, pp. 100, 166. Cf. *DRSFM*, p. 6. For detail on these priests see Doerries, "Die Mission Sir Roger Casements im Deutschen Reich 1914–1916," p. 597.

127. Devoy, *Recollections of an Irish Rebel*, pp. 417–20. Apparently Devoy was having difficulties collecting donations from wealthy Irishmen in the United States. Also, he had counted on the German government picking up the cost of the Irish Brigade. Wedel opened an account for Casement with 8,000 marks at a Berlin bank in February 1915. AA, WK 11k, *secr.*, Bd. 13.

128. Financial data, National Library, Dublin, MS 18081. Reports that Casement accepted German financial assistance appeared in the American press and caused disagreements between him and the Irish-Americans.

Casement to John Quinn, March 20, 1915, NYPL, John Quinn Papers, Box 6. Casement to McGarrity, March 22, 1915, NYPL, The Maloney Collection, Box 15.

129. Besides agents of the German intelligence services, Irish-Americans also traveled back and forth. Moreover, the German Celticist Kuno Meyer was in constant touch with the Clan na Gael as well as with Casement. It was also not unusual for the historian Eduard Meyer to frequently pass on messages. Another line of communication existed through the relations with Edward Rumely, who had been involved with Bernstorff in the acquisition of American newspapers and apparently kept up contacts with the German intelligence services. Connections to the Vatican seem to have played only a relatively minor role in activities with the Irish.

130. Casement was not a member of this inner circle, and it was therefore in Germany's interest to negotiate directly with a top representative of the IRB.

131. Cf. Florence O'Donoghue, "*Ceannt, Devoy, O'Rahilly, and the Military Plan,*" in *Leaders and Men of the Easter Rising: Dublin 1916*, ed. F. X. Martin (London, 1957), p. 195.

132. For Monteith's activities see his *Casement's Last Adventure*. Florence M. Lynch, *The Mystery Man of Banna Strand: The Life and Death of Captain Robert Monteith* (New York, 1959) contains the diary of Monteith during this time. See also much relevant archival material in the Florence Monteith Lynch Collection, Ryan Library, Iona College. The Irish Socialist James Larkin claimed later to have recommended his friend Monteith to the Germans when Berlin had asked him to come to Germany to lend his support to Casement. Emmet Larkin, *James Larkin* (London, 1965), pp. 210–11. It is more than likely that Bernstorff was informed about the connections to James Larkin. Cf. John T. Nicholson to John Devoy by way of the German Foreign Office, January 1915, NA, RG 59, Box 247.

133. Cf. Monteith's diary in Florence M. Lynch, *The Mystery Man of Banna Strand*.

134. Nadolny to Foreign Office, July 17, 1915, AA, WK 11k, secr., Bd. 9.

135. Bernstorff to Bethmann Hollweg, Top Secret, February 10, 1916, ibid., Bd. 11. This message arrived in Berlin only on March 7. Bernstorff to Foreign Office, February 17, 1916, ibid., Bd. 12, which arrived in Berlin some time before March 1, 1916. Doerries, "Die Mission Sir Roger Casements im Deutschen Reich 1914–1916," pp. 610–11. McHugh, "Casement and German Help," pp. 181–82. *DRSFM*, p. 9. Max Caulfield, *The Easter Rebellion* (New York, 1963), p. 40. Devoy, *Recollections of an Irish Rebel*, pp. 458–59.

136. Nadolny to Foreign Office, March 1, 1916, AA, WK 11k, secr., Bd. 12. Unchanged from Foreign Office to Bernstorff, probably March 1, 1916. Caulfield, *The Easter Rebellion*, p. 40. *DRSFM*, p. 10.

137. Bernstorff to Bethmann Hollweg, February 16, 1916, and Igel to

Nadolny, February 16, 1916, AA, WK 11k, *secr.*, Bd. 11. *DRSFM*, p. 12. Monteith also requested 100,000 rifles from the Admiralty. But in Berlin they stuck with the insufficient offer of 20,000 captured Russian rifles. Monteith, *Casement's Last Adventure*, pp. 134–35. Regarding the deployment of German troop contingents, as early as December 1914 Papen (with Bernstorff's knowledge) had recommended an invasion of Ireland with no less than "25,000 men with 50,000 extra rifles." Papen's report via Bernstorff to Foreign Office, December 22, 1914, AA, WK 11k, *secr.*, Bd. 3.

138. Cf. Monteith, *Casement's Last Adventure*, pp. 135–37.

139. Casement to Wedel, March 30, 1916, AA, WK 11k, *secr.*, Bd. 11: "A threat was even held out that unless I submitted to the conditions outlined by Captain Nadolny a telegram would be at once sent to Mr. Devoy to say that . . . the whole plan of helping the Irish revolutionaries in their need had been upset by me and that the blame . . . was wholly mine."

140. Monteith, *Casement's Last Adventure*, p. 139. Charles Callan Tansill, *America and the Fight for Irish Freedom, 1866–1922* (New York, 1957), p. 186. Casement to Wedel, March 30, 1916, AA, WK 11k, *secr.*, Bd. 11.

141. It is striking that a number of foreigners who offered their services to the German Empire for idealistic reasons experienced a similar disappointment in Berlin and felt ruthlessly exploited by the German authorities. Likewise many of them did not succeed in establishing any social contacts in the country which they had praised originally. Some left Berlin as embittered enemies of Germany. Cf. Casement to Wedel, March 30, 1916, AA, WK 11k, *secr.*, Bd. 11: "I am, in this, a passive agent, powerless to act according to my judgment, and with a course of action forced upon me that I wholly deprecate. . . . At the General Staff . . . I was reproached in terms of extraordinary discourtesy and something like a breach of faith or underhand trick." Cf. also Dayal, *Forty-four Months in Germany and Turkey*, p. 23: "Despotism, bureaucracy and caste are the foundations of German society"; p. 63: "The Germans can never inspire confidence in others, for they are dishonourable people. They will ignore others without remorse in order to serve their interests even in small matters"; p. 74: "I was not a free agent."

142. Casement to Wedel, March 30, 1916, AA, WK 11k, *secr.*, Bd. 11.

143. Notes by Sir Roger Casement dated February 6, 1916, on back of letter from Father J. Crotty to Casement, February 4, 1916, NYPL, Maloney Collection, Box 1.

144. Monteith, *Casement's Last Adventure*, p. 140. Cf. Casement Diary, p. 64, NYPL, Maloney Collection, Box 7. According to this source, a Herr von Haugwitz made the bribery attempt. Doerries, "Die Mission Sir Roger Casements im Deutschen Reich 1914–1916," p. 617.

145. Devoy, *Recollections of an Irish Rebel*, pp. 462–63.

146. Bernstorff to Foreign Office, received April 23, 1916, AA, WK 11k,

secr., Bd. 11: "Among the papers . . . confiscated at Mr. von Igel's [office] are some regarding Irish question (cf. my telegrams 7 and 9)." Telegram no. 7 requested arrival of the arms shipment on April 23. Telegram no. 9 of April 17 read: "In connection with telegram no. 7 of April 15. Very urgent. Irish would like to know whether submarine will come to Dublin harbor; if not they intend to block the harbor of Dublin and possibly the harbor of Limerick. Landing of troop contingent, even if ever so small, strongly desired, further they suggest simultaneous strong war demonstration by airships and by sea."

147. Bernstorff to Foreign Office, October 9, 1916, ibid., Bd. 13. Tansill, *America and the Fight for Irish Freedom, 1866–1922*, p. 198. Devoy, *Recollections of an Irish Rebel*, p. 463. Andreas Michelsen, *Der U-Bootkrieg 1914–1918* (Leipzig, 1925), p. 119.

148. Bernstorff to Foreign Office, April 15, 1916, AA, WK 11k, *secr.*, Bd. 11. Cf. *DRSFM*, p. 12.

149. About the journey of the *Aud* see Karl Spindler, *The Mystery of the Casement Ship* (Berlin, 1931).

150. Cf. Monteith, *Casement's Last Adventure*, p. 140.

151. Monteith to Nadolny, January 24, 1916, and Nadolny to Foreign Office, January 26, 1916, AA, WK 11k, *secr.*, Bd. 10.

152. Cf. T. St. John Gaffney, *Breaking the Silence* (New York, 1930), p. 156.

153. Casement to Wedel, March 30, 1916, AA, WK 11k, *secr.*, Bd. 11. Tansill, *America and the Fight for Irish Freedom, 1866–1922*, p. 186.

154. Casement had planned to have the *U-20* drop him off in Tawin, County Galway, and to rush to Dublin in order to prevent the uprising. Mackey, *The Life and Times of Roger Casement*, p. 89.

155. Sean O'Faolain, "Roger Casement. (Born, Dublin, Sept., 1864. Hanged, Pentonville Prison, London, Aug., 1916.)," *American Mercury* (February 1936), in NYPL, Maloney Collection, Box 5. Cf. Tansill, *America and the Fight for Irish Freedom, 1866–1922*, p. 187: "Germany had betrayed him, and was about to betray the Irish people in a miserable effort to evade its commitments to the Irish-Americans by sending a wretched cargo of rifles which would be utterly useless for military purposes."

156. Igel, however, did not hesitate to cast the suspicion of treason on the journalist Karl von Wiegand "in order to exculpate himself." Other persons were also suspected. Note by Montgelas, September 6, 1916, AA, WK 11k, *secr.*, Bd. 12; Romberg to Foreign Office, September 5, 1916, ibid., Bd. 13. AA, Presse-Abteilung, Karl H. von Wiegand, Bd. 1. Hossenfelder for Maltzan, November 29, 1924, AA, Rechtswesen 6, Sabotage Claims, Bd. 1. Royal Bavarian Militärbevollmächtigter (Military Representative) to Bavarian Minister of War, April 28, 1916, Kriegsarchiv, Mkr 8130.

157. Lansing to Bernstorff, April 26, 1916, AA, Botschaft Washington, Prozess von Igel, Bd. 1. Cf. exchange of notes between Bernstorff and Lan-

sing, *FRUS 1916*, Suppl., pp. 807–15. Lansing to Thomas Watt Gregory, Attorney General, December 26, 1917, NA, RG 60, 9-5-163.

158. Bernstorff to Foreign Office, May 6, 1916, AA, WK 11k, secr., Bd. 12.

159. Nadolny to Foreign Office, June 11, 1916, unchanged from Foreign Office to Bernstorff, June 15, 1916, ibid.

160. Bernstorff to Foreign Office, September 8, 1916, and Bernstorff to Foreign Office, December 4, 1916, ibid., Bd. 13.

161. Inger Schuberth, *Schweden und das Deutsche Reich im Ersten Weltkrieg* (Bonn, 1982), p. 146, mentions a Captain Ernst von Hülsen of the Political Section of the General Staff.

162. Statement of Geheimer Oberregierungsrat von Hülsen to Foreign Office, November 25, 1925, AA, Rechtswesen 6, Sabotage Claims, Bd. 3.

163. Hülsen to Foreign Office, December 24, 1916, unchanged from Foreign Office to Bernstorff, and Bernstorff to Foreign Office, January 16 and 17, 1917, AA, WK 11k, secr., Bd. 13. A number of the messages concerned with these plans can also be found (in English) in NA, RG 59, Box 137.

164. George S. Viereck, *Spreading Germs of Hate* (New York, 1930), p. 252. Cf. Tansill, *America and the Fight for Irish Freedom, 1866–1922*, pp. 205, 209.

165. Gaffney, *Breaking the Silence*, p. 180.

166. Wilson: "I would feel deeply mortified to have you or anybody like you vote for me. Since you have access to many disloyal Americans and I have not, I will ask you to convey this message to them." Quoted from Link, *Woodrow Wilson and the Progressive Era, 1910–1917* (London, 1954), p. 247. Cf. John Quinn to George F. Parker, October 5, 1916, NYPL, Maloney Collection, Box 27: "I suppose that consumate [sic] little Irish ass, Jeremiah O'Leary, thought his telegram to Wilson was a 'smart' thing. Wilson's brief answer, two lines and a half, could not be improved on. And has and will make thousands of votes for him." James Kerney, *The Political Education of Woodrow Wilson* (New York, 1926), p. 379. Glazer and Moynihan, *Beyond the Melting Pot*, p. 241.

167. Bernstorff to Bethmann Hollweg, May 17, 1916, AA, Vereinigte Staaten von Amerika 10, Bd. 1.

168. Noyes, *The Accusing Ghost or Justice for Casement*, argues (p. 78) that Bernstorff "for obvious reasons feigned a sympathy for the Irish cause which he did not feel, and held out false hopes and promises." Cf. clipping, *The Times* (London), January 13, 1921, reproducing both a letter from Daniel Cohalan, Bishop of Cork, January 11, 1921, to Editor of *The Times*, and the translated message from Bernstorff to Foreign Office, August 23, 1916, Irish Historical Society, Daniel F. Cohalan Papers.

169. Cf. earlier section about the American landing in Veracruz. The Americans, however, did tolerate arms shipments for Carranza's constitutionalists. They were in part arranged by Felix A. Sommerfeld. Boy-Ed to Reichsmarineamt, June 11, 1914, AA, Mexico 1, Bd. 49.

170. Chief of the Admiralty Staff to State Secretary of the Foreign Office, June 11, 1914, signed "von Pohl": "His Majesty the Emperor has ordered S.M.S. *Panther* following completion of repairs at Danzig (approximately early July) temporarily dispatched to the coast of Mexico." Memo by Adolf Count von Montgelas of the Foreign Office, June 18, 1914: "Freiherr von dem Bussche today made the point that the dispatch of S.M.S. *Panther* to Mexico might, because of the vessel's name and its earlier deployment in Venezuela and at Agadir, cause the American yellow press to publish anti-German diatribes. It might therefore be advisable ... to dispatch ... another vessel." AA, Mexico 1, Bd. 48. See also memo by Hans Arthur von Kemnitz, July 15, 1914, ibid.

171. Alfred von Tirpitz went so far as to propose to the Emperor to replace Gottfried von Jagow with Paul von Hintze as Chief of the Foreign Office. Charles de Gaulle, *La Discorde chez l'ennemi* (Paris, 1924), pp. 16–17. Peter, "Die Bedeutung Chinas in der deutschen Ostasienpolitik (1911–1917)," p. 208. About Hintze's journey from the United States to China in late 1914 see J. P. Meyer to Albert Ballin, New York, December 12, 1914, HAPAG.

172. Friedrich Katz, *Deutschland, Diaz und die mexikanische Revolution* (Berlin, 1964), p. 339.

173. Magnus had succeeded in sending his reports to Germany via the Swedish Embassy, but through an intermediary the British had been able to examine this correspondence. Sir Thomas Hohler, *Diplomatic Petrel* (London, 1942), pp. 222–24.

174. Friedrich Katz, "Die deutsche Verschwörung in Mexiko 1914–1916," in *Politik im Krieg 1914–1918*, ed. project group directed by Fritz Klein (Berlin, 1964), p. 119.

175. M. J. Bonn, *So macht man Geschichte* (Munich, 1953), p. 338. Regarding Papen's simultaneous accreditation in the United States and in Mexico, cf. Papen, *Der Wahrheit eine Gasse*, p. 39.

176. Eckardt to Bethmann Hollweg, February 14, 1915, and Chief of the Admiralty Staff to Jagow, signed "Grasshoff," Top Secret, March 11, 1915, AA, Mexico 1, Bd. 53; Eckhardt to Bethmann Hollweg, Orizaba, July 30, 1915, ibid., Bd. 54. Katz, *Deutschland, Diaz und die mexikanische Revolution*, pp. 350–51, assumes that the Admiralty withdrew the sabotage orders because it was hoped that the Standard Oil Company would supply Germany with oil. Cf. in this context also Friedrich Katz, *The Secret War in Mexico* (Chicago, 1981), pp. 342–44.

177. Papen to Deputy General Staff, March 17, 1915, forwarded by Nadolny to Foreign Office, AA, Mexico 1, Bd. 53. Cf. Katz, *Deutschland, Diaz und die mexikanische Revolution*, p. 349.

178. It is not impossible that the agent Horst von der Goltz was first given the Mexican assignment. Goltz recalls discussing German support measures for Villa with Papen. Kück to Bernstorff, January 9, 1914, AA,

Mexico 1, Bd. 42; Kemnitz note, March 23, 1914, ibid., Bd. 44. Horst von der Goltz, *My Adventures as a German Secret Service Agent* (London, 1918), pp. 108–48, 224–25, 242–43. Michael C. Meyer, "The Mexican-German Conspiracy of 1915," *The Americas* 23 (July 1966): 81–82.

179. Franz Rintelen had acquired experience in banking and was a reserve officer of the German navy. He used a considerable number of aliases.

180. George J. Rausch, Jr., "The Exile and Death of Victoriano Huerta," *Hispanic American Historical Review* 42 (1962): 134–35. Meyer, "The Mexican-German Conspiracy of 1915," p. 82.

181. Franz von Rintelen, *The Dark Invader* (New York, 1933), pp. 175–83.

182. Boy-Ed has insisted that he had seen Huerta only once by coincidence in a passing car in Mexico in the spring of 1914 and that he had never talked to him; Boy-Ed, *Verschwörer?*, p. 83. Bernstorff to Foreign Office, enclosure, received December 5, 1915, AA, Vereinigte Staaten von Amerika 16, Bd. 37.

183. Voska and Irwin, *Spy and Counterspy*, pp. 192–95, mention $500,000 which Boy-Ed put at Huerta's disposal. In addition, they claim Huerta had requested airplanes, but that the German representatives had refused them.

184. Katz, *Deutschland, Diaz und die mexikanische Revolution*, pp. 339–40. Barbara Tuchman, *The Zimmermann Telegram* (New York, 1958), p. 79, also given as a source by Katz, however, has no information on the total amount. The source for this information may be an article in the Sunday edition of the *New York Times* of December 5, 1915, where "the alleged expenditure of more than $27,000,000 in furtherance of German interests in this country" is mentioned. Clipping, *New York Times*, December 5, 1915, AA, Vereinigte Staaten von Amerika 16, Bd. 39. See there also Bernstorff to Lansing, December 6, 1915; Lansing to Bernstorff, December 7, 1915; "For the Press," December 6, 1915, from Lansing. Bernstorff claims that the data about the expenditures are incorrect. He restates (untruthfully) that nobody connected with the German Embassy "had anything to do with Mexican factions."

185. Voska and Irwin, *Spy and Counterspy*, pp. 192–95.

186. Rintelen, *The Dark Invader*, p. 177, claims that he had informed Berlin about the course of his negotiations and that he had received word that the money was supposed to be transferred when military operations against the United States started. In addition, he claims, Berlin had approved the use of submarines and auxiliary cruisers off the Mexican coast.

187. Edith O'Shaughnessy, *Intimate Pages of Mexican History* (New York, 1920), pp. 341–42. Rausch, "The Exile and Death of Victoriano Huerta," p. 147. Tuchman, *The Zimmermann Telegram*, p. 83. Friedrich Katz, "Die deutsche Verschwörung in Mexico 1914–1916," p. 123.

188. Rausch, "The Exile and Death of Victoriano Huerta," p. 150. Speculations that Huerta was in fact murdered cannot be discussed within the

frame of this study. Cf. Meyer, "The Mexican-German Conspiracy of 1915."

189. House Diaries, August 30, 1914, quoted in Link, *The Struggle for Neutrality*, p. 241.

190. Cf. Link, ibid., pp. 471–74, 489.

191. Quoted from Link, *The Papers of Woodrow Wilson*, 33:304. Enclosure to: Woodrow Wilson to William Jennings Bryan, June 2, 1915, for release to the press. For a previous version of this text see ibid.

192. This brief synopsis of Wilson's Mexican policies is mainly based on the presentation in Link, *The Struggle for Neutrality*, pp. 232–66, 456–94, 629–44.

193. Bernstorff to Bethmann Hollweg, July 2, 1915, AA, Mexico 1, Bd. 54.

194. Bernstorff to Bethmann Hollweg, August 10, 1915, ibid.

195. Felix Sommerfeld was not unknown either to the German or to the American government. After Madero's fall in February 1913, he found asylum in the German legation through Hintze, who ultimately assisted him in leaving the country. Rudolf von Kardorff, Secretary of the German Legation in Mexico, in a report to the Foreign Office of the summer of 1913, calls Sommerfeld "an unscrupulous adventurer." In May 1914, Boy-Ed had had contact with the arms dealer, who at that time was working for the Constitutionalists. Kardorff to Bethmann Hollweg, Mexico City, August 15, 1913, AA, Mexico 1, Bd. 37; note by Kemnitz, February 1913, ibid., Bd. 42; Boy-Ed to Reichsmarineamt, May 27, 1914, with copy to Bernstorff, ibid., Bd. 48; Boy-Ed to Reichsmarineamt, June 11, 1914, ibid., Bd. 49. See also U.S. Congress, Senate, *Revolutions in Mexico. Hearings before a Subcommittee of the Committee on Foreign Relations* (Washington, D.C., 1913), pp. 387–91, 447.

196. Letter by Dernburg, reported by Holtzendorff, received May 10, 1915; G. A. Jagow, without date; notes by Zimmermann, May 10, 1915; note by Bethmann Hollweg, May 10, 1915, all in AA, Mexico 1, secr., Bd. 1. Cf. Katz, *Deutschland, Diaz und die mexikanische Revolution*, p. 346. There is no evidence that Bernstorff knew about the matter. There are, however, indications that Dernburg was frequently involved in intelligence work. In 1915, for instance, he is said to have tried to win James Larkin for sabotage operations in American ports; E. Larkin, *James Larkin*, pp. 206–7.

197. James A. Sandos, "German Involvement in Northern Mexico, 1915–1916: A New Look at the Columbus Raid," *Hispanic American Historical Review* 50 (1970). See Friedrich Katz's summary of his thorough research into the matter in "Pancho Villa and the Attack on Columbus, New Mexico," *American Historical Review* 83 (February 1978): 101–30. Cf. Katz, *The Secret War in Mexico*, pp. 336–38.

198. Katz, *Deutschland, Diaz und die mexikanische Revolution*, p. 346. Katz, "Die deutsche Verschwörung in Mexiko 1914–1916," p. 130.

199. Bernstorff to Foreign Office, April 4, 1916, AA, Mexico 1, Bd. 56.

200. Eckardt to Foreign Office, April 5, 1916, ibid.

201. Enrile claims to have also had negotiations with Bernstorff in Washington. Maximilian Fürst von Ratibor und Corvey to Foreign Office, Madrid, February 17, 1916, ibid.

202. The text of the secret treaty or rather the offer of alliance is found in ibid., in document (copy) A. 11153, without date, signed by Enrile and in a document, handed to Montgelas by Enrile, June 15, 1916; see also note by Montgelas, June 27, 1916; Ratibor to Foreign Office, July 14, 1916; note by Montgelas, August 21, 1916; and Ministry of War to Foreign Office, September 3, 1916, all in ibid. The plan of the General Staff to send Enrile as an operative to France was dropped. Apparently the Mexican stayed in Madrid until 1917. Following the rupture of diplomatic relations between Germany and the United States he immediately repeated his offer. But since Berlin was now aiming for an alliance with Carranza, the Foreign Office declined: "Enrile's proposal uninteresting, because he has no influence with the present Mexican government." Ratibor to Foreign Office, February 7, 1917, and Foreign Office to Ratibor, February 10, 1917, ibid., Bd. 57.

203. Ratibor to Foreign Office, July 24, 1916, ibid., Bd. 57. Later, in 1917, he was arrested in Cuba, and the German Minister in Havana warned the Foreign Office not to give out any information, should questions be asked. Ratibor to Foreign Office, February 7, 1917, and Foreign Office to Ratibor, February 10, 1917, ibid.; Ratibor to Foreign Office, August 21, 1917, ibid., Bd. 58.

204. What Germany did not consider was the fact that even before entry into the war, in part because of the Mexican unrest, the American army had reached a relatively high degree of military preparedness. Cf. Thomas G. Frothingham, *The Naval History of the World War* (Cambridge, Mass., 1926), 2:103–4.

205. Cf. Merle E. Curti, *Bryan and World Peace* (Northampton, Mass., 1931), p. 246.

206. Lansing, *War Memoirs of Robert Lansing* (New York, 1935), pp. 19, 75. Louis G. Kahle, "Robert Lansing and the Recognition of Venustiano Carranza," *Hispanic American Historical Review* 38 (August 1958): 353–54.

207. Joseph P. Tumulty, *Woodrow Wilson as I Know Him* (Garden City, N.Y., 1921), p. 159.

208. Bernstorff to Foreign Office, June 24, 1916, AA, WK 18, secr., Bd. 18: "In case of intention to reopen submarine war in its old form, request urgently to postpone beginning until America has firmly gotten its teeth into Mexico." Jagow passed this on to Treutler, who suggested to Bethmann Hollweg to sit on the telegram for the time being, "as long as there is hope that the beginning of the submarine war can be delayed until after the possible beginning of war with Mexico." The Chancellor agreed to this. Jagow to Treutler, June 29, 1916; Treutler to Bethmann Hollweg, June 29,

1916; and Bethmann Hollweg's reply, June 29, 1916, all in AA, Akten des AA im Grossen Hauptquartier 1915–1919, U-Bootkrieg 42, Bd. 2.

209. Almon R. Wright, "German Interest in Panama's Piñas Bay, 1910–1938," *Journal of Modern History* 27 (March–December 1955): 61–66.

210. Zimmermann to Bernstorff, June 29, 1915; Stohrer, Madrid, for Burgos to Foreign Office, August 6, 1915; Krautinger to Erzberger, from Erzberger to Foreign Office, August 9, 1915; and other documents, in AA, Panama 2, secr., Bd. 1.

211. For more details of Imperial German policy and activities in Mexico see Katz, *The Secret War in Mexico*, the most comprehensive study of the triangular European-Mexican-American relations in this period.

212. When Papen was expelled in December 1915, Bernstorff received information from Carranza, indicating "confidentially that Captain von Papen, who was going to Mexico, would not be *persona grata*." Bernstorff to Bethmann Hollweg, December 25, 1915, AA, Deutschland 135, Nr. 20, Bd. 3.

213. Papen, *Der Wahrheit eine Gasse*, p. 55.

214. Even after American agents had confiscated compromising papers in Igel's office, Bernstorff reported to the Foreign Office: "Continued employment [of Igel] indispensible for me." Bernstorff to Foreign Office, September 13, 1916, AA, Vereinigte Staaten von Amerika 16, Bd. 45.

215. Bernstorff, *Deutschland und Amerika*, p. 108: "Coded military telegrams which began with the phrase 'For Military Attaché' ... were ... regularly forwarded immediately to the office of Captain von Papen in New York without my having taken note of their content." In the course of the investigations of the Mixed Claims Commission, Bernstorff also denied (though not under oath) having known about the most important of the telegrams. Karl von Lewinski's (Germany's representative before the Mixed Claims Commission) "Observations concerning the remarks by the Ambassador Count von Bernstorff," October 27, 1925, AA, Rechtswesen 6, Sabotage Claims, Bd. 3: "No one will find it plausible that Papen should not have told the Ambassador about that [telegram of January 1915] unless he intended to keep it secret from him in order to be able to carry it out without hindrance. Also no one will find it plausible that B. should have forgotten such an instruction if it had come to his attention." Cf. *DMCC*, pp. 257–60. Cf. in this context Franz Rintelen's biting comment in his second volume of published memoirs *The Return of the Dark Invader* (London, 1935), pp. 135–38.

216. Boy-Ed, *Verschwörer?*, p. 83.

217. The German records relating to Mexico support this view. Former agents interviewed by the author have confirmed the intelligence connections of Eckardt.

218. Statement by Kapitän a.D. (retired Captain) August Lassen (during the war consultant in Department N of the General Staff) before the Amts-

gericht (District Court) Berlin Mitte, July 18, 1929, AA, Rechtswesen 15, Sabotage Claims, Bd. 15.

219. Franz Dagobert Johannes Rintelen was born in Frankfurt on August 19, 1878, and died in London on May 30, 1949. He was married in 1909 to Emilie ("Milly") Adele von Kaufmann-Asser. Paul and Jost Rintelen, *Das Geschlecht der Rintelen* (Freising, 1977). Tuchman, *The Zimmermann Telegram*, p. 67, has some detail on Rintelen's stay in the U.S. prior to the First World War.

220. The Foreign Office even requested safe conduct for Rintelen from the Americans. James W. Gerard, *My Four Years in Germany* (London, 1917), p. 76. Rintelen, *The Dark Invader*, pp. 73–74. Rintelen to Albert, January 6, 1928, AA, Rechtswesen 20.

221. His dispatch was pushed by the Prussian Deputy Minister of War Franz E. von Wandel, Matthias Erzberger, and Captain Ernst Vanselow. Count Kuno von Westarp and Schiemann were also informed. Verbal note of the Swiss Legation to Foreign Office, November 29, 1919, AA, WK adh. 4, Nr. 3, Bd. 2.

222. HFA (Heinrich F. Albert) to Imperial Minister of Finance, May 21, 1928, AA, Rechtswesen 20, Rintelen.

223. Admiral and Chef der Marineleitung (Chief of the Navy) Behncke to bank director and Kapitänleutnant d.R. (Captain of the Reserve) Rintelen, February 16, 1921, AA, Rechtswesen, Rintelen. Cf. Hossenfelder to Schubert, August 5, 1927, AA, Rechtswesen 6, Sabotage Claims, Bd. 6.

224. Chef der Marineleitung Zenker to Imperial Minister (of Finance?), June 25, 1926, AA, Rechtswesen 20, Rintelen.

225. Bernstorff to Bethmann Hollweg, December 16, 1915; Bernstorff to Lansing, December 13, 1915; Lansing to Bernstorff, December 14, 1915; and Bernstorff to Lansing, December 15, 1915, all in AA, Vereinigte Staaten von Amerika 16, Bd. 39.

226. Papen to General Staff, with agreement of Ambassador, March 26, 1915; Embassy Washington to Foreign Office, April 5, 1915; Moltke of the General Staff to Foreign Office, March 30, 1915, enclosed a clipping from *Daily Telegraph* of March 26, 1915; Bernstorff to Foreign Office, April 5, 1915; Papen to Ministry of War, New York, April 6, 1915; all in AA, Deutschland 127, Nr. 22, Bd. 4. Nicolai, *Nachrichtendienst, Presse und Volksstimmung im Weltkrieg*, p. 64. James W. Gerard, *My First Eighty-three Years in America* (Garden City, N.Y., 1951), p. 227. Other sources refer to the possibility that Major Langhorne may have sent "open," i.e., uncoded messages. Cf. Brig. Gen. H. L. Scott, Chief of Staff, War Department, to Chief, War College Division, February 19, 1915, NA, RG 165, Box 232.

227. As Stresemann's "confidant" Jahnke had good contacts with leading circles in the Weimar Republic. Among other things he directed sabotage activities in the Ruhr region. Cf. Harold J. Gordon, Jr., *The Reichswehr and*

the German Republic 1919–1926 (Princeton, N.J., 1957), pp. 255, 348. Gottfried R. Treviranus, *Das Ende von Weimar* (Düsseldorf, 1968), pp. 57–58. In the Third Reich he was working for Walter Schellenberg. Cf. Walter Schellenberg, *Memoiren*, ed. Gila Petersen (Cologne, 1959), pp. 44, 49, 202–3.

228. Cf. Schellenberg, *Memoiren*, p. 43.

229. Jahnke probably also received new orders through the engineer Karl (also known as Charles) Wunnenberg (in some sources also called Wünnenberg), also known as Son Charles, an agent sent to the United States by the German Naval Intelligence Service from Antwerp on January 1, 1916. Wunnenberg to Foreign Office, December 24, 1915, and note by Montgelas, December 25, 1915, AA, Deutschland 141, Nr. 7, *secr.*, Bd. 8. Testimony by Kapitän a.D. August Lassen before the Amtsgericht (District Court) Berlin Mitte, July 18, 1929, AA, Rechtswesen 15, Sabotage Claims, Bd. 15. Regarding Wunnenberg cf. also testimony by Hermann Wessels before Karl von Lewinski, March 27–29, 1929, AA, Rechtswesen 6, Sabotage Claims, Bd. 15.

230. According to his own statements, Rintelen had orders to avoid contact with Bernstorff. (Verbal note of the Swiss Legation to Foreign Office, November 29, 1919, AA, WK adh. 4, Nr. 3, Bd. 2.) Rintelen speaks of two meetings with Bernstorff; one at the Ritz Carlton in New York, where Bernstorff allegedly demanded to be informed about Rintelen's missions; the second meeting supposedly took place at the German Embassy. On this occasion American agents presumably photographed Rintelen leaving the building with Bernstorff; Rintelen, *The Dark Invader*, pp. 82–84, and *The Return of the Dark Invader*, pp. 37–42. Bernstorff remembered the first meeting, but instead of the second meeting, which according to Rintelen was attended by guests, Bernstorff only mentions an attempt by Rintelen to obtain "credentials" from him. Bernstorff, *Deutschland und Amerika*, p. 122.

231. Jahnke to Reichswehrministerium (Ministry of the Reichswehr), Marineleitung (Naval Command), January 29, 1925, AA, Rechtswesen 6, Sabotage Claims, Bd. 3. James Larkin's claim that Franz Bopp had put him in charge of German intelligence operations from Guatemala to Vancouver in the fall of 1916 appears dubious. Cf. E. Larkin, *James Larkin*, pp. 214–15.

232. From the correspondence concerning the dispatch of Kapitänleutnant Sauerbeck it is clear that the Admiralty attached little importance to these demands and that the Foreign Office apparently submitted to the decisions of the Naval Command. Bernstorff objected to stationing this agent in New York and instructed the German naval personnel there not to make payments without his knowledge, even in the case of an official order of payment, to any persons who by their actions might get into conflict with American law. He asked Berlin "urgently to refrain from issuing orders to S. which could be viewed by local authorities as a violation of neutrality." The Chief of the Admiralty, by contrast, established priorities

in this way: "Kapitänleutnant Sauerbeck is staying in New York to carry out military assignments. He is not registered as a member of the Embassy, and his activities therefore are not the responsibility of the Imp. Ambassador." Chief of the Admiralty Staff to State Secretary of the Foreign Office, August 9, 1916, AA, Rechtswesen 6, Sabotage Claims, Bd. 4; Bernstorff to Foreign Office, June 2, 1916, ibid., Bd. 10; various documents, especially Bernstorff to Marine-Etappe New York, ibid., Bd. 11. Some translated material in NA, RG 59, Box 244.

233. For instance his opposition to the operations in Canada which Franz von Papen and Horst von der Goltz had planned. Falcke, *Vor dem Eintritt Amerikas in den Weltkrieg*, p. 215. Sperry, *German Plots and Intrigues in the United States during the Period of Our Neutrality*, p. 26.

234. Although Papen's reports of that period speak of Japanese troops, he writes in his memoirs that he had worked to delay the transport of Canadian troops; Papen, *Der Wahrheit eine Gasse*, p. 57. Major Boehm in 1926 spoke of attempts "to prevent Japanese and other war transports." Statement by Major a.D. Hans Boehm, probably after talking with Dr. Johannes G. Lohmann on January 12, 1926, without date, AA, Rechtswesen 6, Sabotage Claims, Bd. 4.

235. Prior to his appearance in the United States, Horst von der Goltz, also known as Franz Wachendorf, probably served in the Mexican army. He was recruited for Papen's organization by the German Consul in Chihuahua. The records of the Foreign Office show that Goltz perhaps worked for the revolutionaries in Mexico, was arrested, and later freed by the German Consul. Kemnitz called him an "adventurer without means who is in the service of the Mexican insurgents." Cf. Kück to Bernstorff, January 9, 1914, AA, Mexico 1, Bd. 42; note by Kemnitz, March 23, 1914, ibid., Bd. 44.

236. Allegedly there were also discussions of a plan for an invasion of Jamaica. Goltz, *My Adventures as a German Secret Service Agent*, p. 148.

237. Ibid.

238. Goltz (ibid., pp. 151–55) names Friedrich Busse, Constantine Covani, and A. A. Fritzen. He also worked together with a certain Tucker, alias Tuchhaendler. A. A. Fritzen is Alfred E. Fritzen, identified by the Hamburg-American Line as "an agent of Captain Tauscher." Newsletter no. 6, April 27, 1916, HAPAG New York, HAPAG.

239. According to Albert's statements, Federico (also Frederick) Stallforth was an agent of the Embassy for financial transactions. Albert to Imperial Minister of Finance, May 21, 1928, AA, Rechtswesen 20, Rintelen.

240. Tauscher was acquitted in the Welland Canal trial, according to Bernstorff's memoirs, "because he presented evidence that he had not known about the purpose of the explosives procured by him"; Bernstorff, *Deutschland und Amerika*, p. 118. However, it is evident from the records that this verdict was due to the fact that incriminating documents apparently were not considered. Cf. Igel to Deputy General Staff, forwarded by

Department IIIb to Foreign Office, July 20, 1916, AA, Vereinigte Staaten von Amerika 16, Bd. 44. Cf. Bernstorff to Foreign Office, July 10, 1916, ibid., Bd. 45. By order from Bernstorff, Tauscher's attorneys' fees were paid by Heinrich Albert from funds of the Ministry of War.

241. Concerning the project of Goltz, see Falcke, *Vor dem Eintritt Amerikas in den Weltkrieg*, pp. 214–17. Goltz, *My Adventures as a German Secret Service Agent*, pp. 148–58. Jones and Hollister, *The German Secret Service in America 1914–1918*, pp. 63–69. Newsletter, April 7, 1916, HAPAG New York, HAPAG.

242. In October 1914 Goltz traveled to Berlin. According to his own statements he visited both the Foreign Office and Department IIIb. Apparently, sabotage assignments and other missions in Mexico were discussed. On his return trip to the United States he was arrested by the British. After Papen in January 1916 allowed incriminating checkbooks to fall into the hands of the British, Goltz decided to turn state's evidence. In 1916 he returned to New York following extradition negotiations. Newsletter, March 29, 1916, HAPAG New York, HAPAG. That Goltz did not invent his information can be seen from a letter from Karl von Lewinski to the Foreign Office, Berlin, September 9, 1924, NA, T-290, Roll 36, where the opinion is expressed that Germany will find it difficult to deny the sabotage operations because of the depositions made by Fay, Witzke, and Goltz. Goltz, *My Adventures as a German Secret Service Agent*, pp. 158–99.

243. Hans Boehm, serving in Department IIIb of the General Staff, was sent to the United States at the instigation of the Admiralty. Statement by Major a.D. Hans Boehm, probably after talking with Dr. Johannes G. Lohmann on January 12, 1926, without date, AA, Rechtswesen 6, Sabotage Claims, Bd. 4. Zimmermann to Bernstorff, December 15, 1914, AA, WK 11h, *secr.*, Bd. 1.

244. Papen to Deputy General Staff, February 11, 1915, from Nadolny to Foreign Office, March 11, 1915, AA, WK 11h, *secr.*, Bd. 1. Papen probably obtained arms and ammunition with the help of Tauscher. "A military action against Canada" was often the topic of discussion in Berlin. For instance, in late 1914 Privatdozent Albrecht Wirth from Munich presented a plan to Nadolny "first . . . to occupy . . . Western Canada and then Eastern Canada . . . with Germans, Irish, and Anglo-Americans." Wirth envisioned that the approximately 100,000 reservists living in Canada and the United States would carry out the attack. The operation was to be led by Papen and "some members of the General Staff." Montgelas rejected the plan, because it would violate American neutrality. Montgelas to Wedel, November 12, 1914, as enclosure Wirth's proposal which Montgelas had received from Nadolny, ibid.

245. G.A. written by Richard Meyer, January 5, 1915, AA, WK 11k, *secr.*, Bd. 4.

246. Literal translation of German text. Punctuation here according to

German text. Original to Nadolny, January 23, 1915, initialed illegibly by two persons and by "Mtgs [Montgelas] 23/1" and "23/1 [Richard] Meyer," AA, WK 11k, *secr.*, Bd. 4. In the original the last sentence reads: "Embassy must under no circumstances have knowledge of sabotage plans in the United States; Irish-German propaganda must not be compromised." With this alteration and the addendum: "Persons have been named by Sir Roger Casement," the Foreign Office, under orders from the General Staff, on January 25, 1915, sent out the directive via Stockholm to Washington. The text of this important telegram is reproduced in several publications, although often with the incorrect date of January 25, 1916. See for instance Tansill, *America and the Fight for Irish Freedom, 1866–1922*, pp. 238–39. Sean Cronin, *The McGarrity Papers* (Tralee, 1972), p. 68. Even the official British publication *DRSFM*, p. 8, gives the wrong date of January 26, 1916.

247. One of the planned operations was supposed to be carried out by Lieutenant von Baerensprung and von Alvensleben. Also, an expedition led by von Petersdorf to sabotage a lock on the Panama Canal was planned. Papen to Deputy General Staff, February 11, 1915, from Department IIIb to Foreign Office, March 11, 1915, and Bernstorff to Foreign Office, February 13, 1915, in AA, WK 11h, *secr.*, Bd. 1.

248. Boehm to Admiralty Staff, as copy to Deputy General Staff, February 24, 1915, AA, WK, 11h, *secr.*, Bd. 1. Regarding Horn, cf. Jones and Hollister, *The German Secret Service in America 1914–1918*, pp. 124–25. Bernstorff, *Deutschland und Amerika*, p. 117 (incomplete description). Papen, *Der Wahrheit eine Gasse*, p. 58, mentions the case and remarks that Horn had "volunteered his services for this matter." Newspaper clipping, *New York Times*, February 3, 1915, AA, WK 11h, *secr.*, Bd. 1.

249. For a while the Germans considered also the idea of invading Canada with Indian contingents from the northwest of the United States.

250. Boehm to Deputy General Staff, from Nadolny to Foreign Office, March 2, 1915, AA, WK 11h, *secr.*, Bd. 6. Not only the lack of spirit on the part of the agents but also the security of the installations prevented the execution of various sabotage projects. Papen to Deputy General Staff, March 17, 1915, AA, Mexico 1, Bd. 53.

251. "Incognito" to Frank L. Polk, New York, September 5, 1916, NA, RG 59, Box 219.

252. Reiswitz to Bethmann Hollweg, December 6, 1915, AA, WK 11h, *secr.*, Bd. 1. In January 1916 the Ministry of War accepted responsibility for the payments to the Schmidt family. Ministry of War to Foreign Office, January 24, 1916, ibid., Bd. 2.

253. According to his own statements his collaborators were Carl and Marie Schmidt, Gustav Stephen, Charles Respa, William Jarosch (also Jarrosch), Richard Herrmann, Wilhelm Scholz, William Loeffler, and Fritz Neef. Since most of these names also became known through other intelli-

gence service operations, there is no reason to doubt Kaltschmidt's version. Kaltschmidt to Kommissar of the Reichsfinanzministerium für Rechtsangelegenheiten aus dem Kriege (Commissary of the Imperial Finance Ministry for Legal Questions Deriving from the War), June 1, 1921, AA, Rechtswesen 15, Kaltschmidt.

254. Request for restitution by Max Schulze, who returned from China on May 16, 1919. His collaborator in an unsuccessful Canadian expedition was G. H. Jacobsen; AA, WK 11f, Bd. 48.

255. Kaltschmidt to Kommissar of the Reichsfinanzministerium für Rechtsangelegenheiten aus dem Kriege, June 1, 1921, AA, Rechtswesen 15, Kaltschmidt. Bernstorff, *Deutschland und Amerika*, p. 120. Bernstorff to Bethmann Hollweg, February 18, 1916, here especially enclosure no. 8, AA, WK 10, *secr.*, Bd. 7.

256. The fact that various transports may have run into mines or were lost for other reasons would only change the number of the ships that fell victim to the bombings.

257. Regarding Walter T. Scheele see NA, RG 165, M.I.D., 10546-39. Clipping, *New York Times*, April 29, 1916, PRO, FO 371, 2849. Rintelen, *The Dark Invader*. James B. Scott, ed., *Diplomatic Correspondence between the United States and Germany, August 1, 1914–April 6, 1917* (New York, 1918), p. xiv.

258. Freeman, an American of Irish descent, had good connections to the Embassy. Bernstorff repeatedly mentions him in his reports, though mostly in connection with unofficial projects.

259. Rintelen, *The Dark Invader*, pp. 88–89. Cf. Richard F. Ullner to W. de Haas, September 1, 1927, AA, Rechtswesen 20, Rintelen. Hossenfelder's testimony before the Amtsgericht (District Court) Berlin-Mitte, March 27, 1929, AA, Rechtswesen 6, Sabotage Claims, Bd. 8.

260. It has been claimed that E. V. Gibbons, Inc. succeeded in sending a number of valuable transports to Germany via neutral countries. Jones and Hollister, *The German Secret Service in America 1914–1918*, p. 148.

261. After briefly seeing action at the western front, Fay had been placed at the disposal of the Military Attaché in Washington by Colonel Leopold von Rauch and Kurt Freiherr von Lersner "in order to investigate American ammunition production." According to statements by Rauch and Lersner, which incidentally are almost identical in places, and according to Fay's own statements after the war, neither the intelligence service nor Papen or Boy-Ed had given Fay sabotage orders. According to his own version, he carried out the sabotage activities on his own. Fay's testimony before Examiner Albert Adams, September 19, 1918, AA, Rechtswesen 6, Sabotage Claims, Bd. 1. Fay's testimony before Dr. Johannes G. Lohmann, October 24, 1925, ibid., Bd. 3; statements by Rauch and Lersner, without date, ibid., Bd. 8. It is of some interest to note that Rauch later wished to have the

sentence "There was no talk of sabotage during the negotiations with Fay" deleted from the above-mentioned document. Rauch to Hossenfelder, July 11, 1929, ibid.

262. Other members of this group of operatives were Dr. Karl von Baur-Breitenfeld, who made chemicals available, Captain Wolpert of the Hamburg-American Line, Captain Carl von Kleist, and several engineers and machinists from the German ships interned in American ports.

263. He is said to have made the statement: "Only the Irish working class remain as the incorruptible inheritors of the fight for freedom in Ireland." Nicholas Mansergh, *The Irish Question 1840–1921* (London, 1965), pp. 238–39.

264. On Larkin see especially E. Larkin, *James Larkin*. Benjamin Gitlow, *The Whole of Their Lives* (New York, 1948), pp. 38, 44. Mansergh, *The Irish Question 1840–1921*, pp. 236–40. Among others Larkin had contacts with Franz von Papen, Bernhard Dernburg, Karl Boy-Ed, Wolf von Igel, Sir Roger Casement, Kuno Meyer, Franz Bopp, and Lothar Witzke.

265. Rintelen, *The Dark Invader*, p. 175, writes that upon Dumba's suggestion he had instigated a strike among the mostly Austrian immigrant workers of a Bethlehem Steel plant.

266. At least one strike action was initiated in the fall of 1915 by Papen and Igel in cooperation with John Devoy, James K. McGuire, and the (according to Fuehr) "extremely dangerous Irish anarchist Jim Larkin." Karl Alexander Fuehr later reported that Larkin had been used by the Irish in this operation "against my explicit instructions." Romberg to Foreign Office, September 5, 1917, AA, WK 11k, secr., Bd. 13. Cf. copy without address, signed by Albert, received August 19, 1915, AA, Vereinigte Staaten von Amerika 10, Bd. 1. Regarding James K. McGuire's contacts with Larkin, cf. also E. Larkin, *James Larkin*.

267. Bernstorff to Foreign Office, November 3, 1915, AA Vereinigte Staaten von Amerika 5, Bd. 16.

268. Regarding Labor's National Peace Council and the Liebau Office, cf. Bernstorff to Foreign Office, November 3, 1915, AA, Vereinigte Staaten von Amerika 5, Bd. 16. Falcke, *Vor dem Eintritt Amerikas in den Weltkrieg*, p. 202. Bernstorff, *Deutschland und Amerika*, pp. 116, 123–24. Viereck, *Spreading Germs of Hate*, p. 98. Rintelen, *The Dark Invader*, pp. 171–75. Margaret Hardy, *The Influence of Organized Labor on the Foreign Policy of the United States* (Liège, 1936), pp. 47–48. BAL, 2:1549, 1571–72. Military report by Papen, April 6, 1915, AA, Rechtswesen 6, Sabotage Claims, Bd. 4. Constantin Dumba, *Dreibund- und Entente-Politik in der Alten und Neuen Welt* (Zürich, 1931), p. 402. Papen to Ministry of War, May 10, 1915, BA, Akten des AA, Neutralität Nord-Amerika, Bd. 6881.

269. Note regarding letter of February 24, 1915, from Ministry of War, without date, AA, Deutschland 121, Nr. 19, Bd. 9. (The university professor is here identified as "Prof. Dr. Darmstädter—Berlin.") House Diaries,

March 10, 1916, YHC. Falcke, *Vor dem Eintritt Amerikas in den Weltkrieg*, pp. 127–28. Link, *Confusions and Crises*, pp. 56–57.

270. For Link's earlier (1960) version see his *The Struggle for Neutrality*, pp. 562–63. Link's more recent (1980) reference to this episode appears in *The Papers of Woodrow Wilson*, 33:473–74. Here Anne L. Seward's letter is said to have been addressed to Wilson instead of Lansing, and the editors note: "The letter is missing in all known collections." Several years ago I seem to have come across the missing item in the Records of the Office of the Counselor (RG 59) in the National Archives. What appears to be the original handwritten letter reads:

> July 2nd
> The Copley-Plaza
> Boston
>
> My dear President Wilson,
>
> As a niece of former Secretary of State, William H. Seward, I make bold to write you about a matter of doubtless no weight whatever but of potential seriousness. Last June in Germany I met socially a prominent Berlin banker. He is now here as (I am convinced) a secret but intimate emissary from the Kaiser. Whether his mission be friendly and his presence here harmless his utterances are distinctly offensive and his threats alarming. His national prominence in Germany and his high military rank coupled with his numerous aliases, his frequent changes of address give rise to uncomfortable suspicions. I have recently met him at dinners in New York three times and I feel increasing uneasiness from his sojourn here.
>
> While seeking to do no injustice to a quasi-acquaintance and desiring above all to avoid publicity I nevertheless feel I cannot decently shrink from putting in your way means of probing a sinister situation or one which points to organized antagonism.
>
> I prefer not to write the conversation which caused me to communicate with you but if I knew where to reach Mr. Axson, your brother-in-law, I could easily tell him. My address will be Kennebunkport Maine should you even decide to notice the matter. Having freed my conscience by telling you I can only hope you will understand the spirit in which this is written and believe me
>
> Sincerely at your service
> (Miss) Anne L. Seward.

Together with this letter I found a typed four-page document signed by Chandler P. Anderson and entitled "Memorandum of information communicated by X in regard to Y, July 8, 1915," evidently the information transmitted orally by Anne L. Seward to an interviewer sent to meet her on July 8, 1915. Rintelen, *The Dark Invader*, p. 184. Sir William Reginald Hall and Amos J. Peaslee, *Three Wars with Germany*, ed. Joseph P. Sims (New York,

1944), pp. 6–7. Sir William James, *The Code Breakers of Room 40. The Eyes of the Navy* (New York, 1956), pp. 100–101. Patrick Beesly, *Room 40* (London, 1982), p. 229.

271. Synopsis Franz von Rintelen, August 1918, NA, RG 87, item 55. Beesly, *Room 40*, pp. 229–30. Rintelen, *The Dark Invader*, p. 189 ff.

272. Bernstorff to Foreign Office, via Stockholm, December 10, 1915, AA, Rechtswesen 6, Sabotage Claims, Bd. 4. Bernstorff to Bethmann Hollweg, January 7, 1916; Bernstorff to Lansing, December 13, 1915; Bernstorff to Bethmann Hollweg, December 16, 1915; Lansing to Bernstorff, December 14, 1915; and Bernstorff to Lansing, December 15, 1915, all in AA, Vereinigte Staaten von Amerika 16, Bd. 39.

273. Couriers traveled directly as well as via Latin America. The legation in Mexico and the consulate in San Francisco also served as communication channels to Berlin. Some of the Mexico telegrams were sent through the German embassy in Madrid, which had become a rather important post during the war.

274. It is very likely that British intelligence knew about Jahnke since telegrams from the legation in Mexico apparently were intercepted rather regularly. For 1917 and 1918, cf. Hall and Peaslee, *Three Wars with Germany*, pp. 84–85.

275. Bernstorff, *Deutschland und Amerika*, pp. 120–21.

276. Testimony by Franz Bopp, December 1, 1925, AA, Rechtswesen 6, Sabotage Claims, Bd. 3.

277. Shortly afterwards Bernstorff was instructed to pay Brincken a monthly salary. Bernstorff to Foreign Office, January 20, 1915, AA, WK 11f, Bd. 8; Foreign Office to Bernstorff, March 8, 1915, ibid., Bd. 10.

278. Testimony by Franz Bopp, August 4, 1928, AA, Rechtswesen 6, Sabotage Claims, Bd. 6.

279. Jahnke to Reichswehrministerium, Marineleitung (Naval Command), January 29, 1925, ibid., Bd. 3.

280. Brincken to his father, November 4, 1916, AA, WK 11f, Bd. 34.

281. Testimony by Schack before the Amtsgericht (District Court) Berlin-Mitte, August 4, 1928, AA, Rechtswesen 6, Sabotage Claims, Bd. 6. Brincken to his father, November 4, 1916, AA, WK 11f, Bd. 34. (According to this document Bernstorff prevented Brincken from being employed as attaché.)

282. Lewinski to Foreign Office, *secr.*, May 31, 1930, AA, Rechtswesen 6, Sabotage Claims, Bd. 12.

283. *IMA*, 1:1235, 2:3255. Minutes of a meeting on September 19, 1929, signed by de Haas and Hossenfelder, AA, Rechtswesen 6, Sabotage Claims, Bd. 9; letter from the Reichswehrministerium, (Behncke) Chief of the Marineleitung (Naval Command), December 31, 1922 (regarding Jahnke's report to Behncke), ibid., Bd. 4. Regarding Witzke cf. also Herbert O. Yardley, *The American Black Chamber* (London, 1931), pp. 90–114. My research for

a study of German intelligence operations in the U.S. in both wars indicates that Lothar Witzke stayed with naval intelligence.

284. Testimony by Franz Bopp before the Amtsgericht (District Court) Berlin-Mitte, August 4, 1928, AA, Rechtswesen 6, Sabotage Claims, Bd. 6. Regarding other projects of Crowley cf. Falcke, *Vor dem Eintritt Amerikas in den Weltkrieg*, p. 217.

285. Regarding some of Delmar's activities in Mexico see a number of references in Katz, *Deutschland, Diaz und die mexikanische Revolution*. *DMCC*, pp. 305–10. As late as the spring of 1918 the Chief of the General Staff wished that Delmar "through measures on our part should promote . . . a tying down of American troops on the southern border of the United States." Chief of the General Staff to representative of the Foreign Office at Headquarters, January 11, 1918, forwarded to the Imperial Chancellor on January 12, AA, Akten des AA im Grossen Hauptquartier, 1915–1919, Mexico 20, Bd. 1. "Delmar," Dr. Delmar, or Albert C. Delmar, was Anton Dilger, who is said to have been a physician. Born in Front Royal, Virginia, in 1884, he died in 1918 in Madrid under the name Alberto Donde. Cf. various documents, NA, RG 59.

286. This surprising information is transmitted by Goltz, *My Adventures as a German Secret Service Agent*, p. 252, who aside from a certain amount of braggadocio often appears credible.

287. A thorough investigation of the entire problem in the context of the postwar period has yet to be undertaken. Nevertheless even a fleeting glance at the records and the few existing publications reveals that the uneasy relationship between Germany and the United States between the wars did not remain untouched by this affair. Cf. for instance Hall and Peaslee, *Three Wars with Germany*; James, *The Code Breakers of Room 40. The Eyes of the Navy*; Rintelen, *The Return of the Dark Invader*; and *DMCC*.

288. Cf. minutes of a conference, September 19, 1929, signed by de Haas and Hossenfelder, AA, Rechtswesen 6, Sabotage Claims, Bd. 9: "Lothar Witzke has done much for Germany during the war." For Lothar Witzke's activities after the U.S. entry into the First World War see Charles H. Harris, III, and Louis R. Sadler, "The Witzke Affair: German Intrigue on the Mexican Border, 1917–18," *Military Review* (February 1979): 36–50.

289. Since age 17 Friedrich Herrmann was trained to be an agent for the Imperial German navy. Strempel's notes about meeting with Herrmann in Concepción, February 1930, AA, Rechtswesen 6, Sabotage Claims, Bd. 11. Cf. de Haas to Embassy in Santiago, Chile, July 18, 1929, ibid., Bd. 8. Among others Herrmann also used the names Larssen, Marstrom, Lewis, March, Rasmussen, and Rodriguez.

290. Paul Hilken was a son of the German consul in Baltimore. Friedrich Hinsch (also calling himself Francis Grantnor) was captain on the German steamship *Neckar*. Raoul Gerdts (also called "Cousin Raoul," or Raoul Sala)

was of German and South American background. Carl O. Ahrendt was a native American of German descent, who was employed by a company one of whose partners was Hilken. Wilhelm Woehst (also calling himself Hauten or Rupp) was at least temporarily employed by the same company. After intelligence service training in Italy, he had been sent to the United States by Department IIIb. Theodore J. Wozniak, since the early summer of 1916, worked at the Kingsland factory, apparently with Russian papers. Cf. *DMCC.*

291. Evidently Hinsch's sphere of responsibility was so broadly defined that he went so far as to attempt to bring Jahnke's group under his command. Concerning this fierce power struggle there developed a telegram exchange with Berlin which fell into the hands of the British. Texts of the wires in Hall and Peaslee, *Three Wars with Germany,* pp. 84–85. After U.S. entry into the war, the center of German intelligence activities increasingly tended to move to Mexico. In spite of all difficulties German agents still succeeded in penetrating the Mexican-American border and even in arranging new sabotage projects. Cf. E. Larkin, *James Larkin,* pp. 217–18.

292. Cf. *DMCC,* pp. 345–47.

293. Cf. Hall and Peaslee, *Three Wars with Germany,* p. 124.

294. Lewinski to Foreign Office, April 19, 1930, AA, Rechtswesen 6, Sabotage Claims, Bd. 11; cf. Foreign Office to Nadolny, February 25, 1929, ibid., Bd. 7.

295. Text in Hall and Peaslee, *Three Wars with Germany,* p. 142.

296. Testimony by Hinsch before the Amtsgericht (District Court) Bremerhaven, September 3, 1929, AA, Rechtswesen 6, Sabotage Claims, Bd. 9; Strempel's notes about meeting with Herrmann in Concepción, February 1930, and de Haas to Lewinski, May 15, 1930, ibid., Bd. 11; de Haas to Lewinski, August 1, 1930, ibid., Bd. 13. Cf. Hall and Peaslee, *Three Wars with Germany,* pp. 84–88 (also texts of later telegrams dealing with these activities). In South America Berlin apparently also ordered the large-scale poisoning of food material. Karl Graf Luxburg, *Nachdenkliche Erinnerung* (Schloss Aschach, 1953), p. 98. In further research since the completion of this study I have come upon a number of sources which suggest that germ cultures were brought from Germany to the United States, possibly via Russia, by German agents. Presumably these germs had lost their effectiveness during the long clandestine journey.

297. Cf. Cedric C. Cummins, *Indiana Public Opinion and the World War 1914–1917* (Indianapolis, Ind., 1945), pp. 139–40.

298. Cf. clipping, *Neue Zürcher Zeitung,* February 27, 1918, GSA, MA 95053.

299. Cf. Fred A. Sondermann, "The Wilson Administration's Image of Germany" (Ph.D. diss., Yale University, 1953), p. 342.

CHAPTER SIX

1. Prittwitz und Gaffron, *Zwischen Petersburg und Washington* (Munich, 1952), p. 86.

2. UA, pp. 321–22. Max M. Warburg, *Aus meinen Aufzeichnungen* (New York, 1952), p. 53. Ethel Mary Tinnemann, "Count Johann von Bernstorff and German-American Relations, 1908–1917" (Ph.D. diss., University of California at Berkeley, 1960), pp. 300–301. Barbara Tuchman, *The Zimmermann Telegram* (New York, 1958), p. 112.

3. Cf. Warburg, *Aus meinen Aufzeichnungen*, p. 54.

4. German historians up to now have sidestepped this topic. There is no lack of criticism, however, that Bernstorff did not sufficiently stand up for his government's policies in the United States.

5. Cf. Ch. Appuhn, "L'Ambassade du Comte Bernstorff à Washington," *Revue de d'Histoire de la Guerre Mondiale* 3 (October 1925): 328: "L'attitude prise par le comte Bernstorff dans les derniers mois surtout de son ambassade nous paraît faire honneur à sa clairvoyance. Il a jugé sainement la situation; il a vu beaucoup mieux qu'on ne pouvait le voir en Allemagne le péril que courait son pays; il a, sans plus tergiverser, accepté la paix sans victoire souhaitée par le président Wilson."

6. Holtzendorff to Bethmann Hollweg, May 15, 1916, AA, Akten des AA im Grossen Hauptquartier 1915–1919, U-Bootkrieg 42, Bd. 2.

7. Cf. Members of the Board of the Conservative Party of Pommerania to Bethmann Hollweg, May 16, 1916, and decision of the Zentralvorstand (Central Board) of the National-Liberal Party of May 21, 1916, AA, WK 18, *secr.*, Bd. 17.

8. Jagow to Bernstorff, June 12, 1916, quoted in Bernstorff, *Deutschland und Amerika* (Berlin, 1920), p. 280.

9. Bernstorff to Foreign Office, June 19, 1916, quoted in ibid., pp. 281–82.

10. Bernstorff to Foreign Office, August 8, 1916, AA, WK 18, *secr.*, Bd. 19.

11. Cf. Kuno Meyer (as copy from E. Meyer to Foreign Office), June 17, 1916, AA, WK 18 adh. 2, *secr.*, Bd. 3: "Together with many reasonable people here I am convinced that Germany's decision to resume U-boat warfare will be accepted and approved by all judicious people in the country as well as in Congress. The only question is whether Wilson 1) has the firm desire to break off relations and 2) whether he can get his wish through Congress.... Bernstorff seems to think so; many others, however, do not, and I join them." Cf., however, Fuehr to Consul General Thiel (1912–1914 in Yokohama, then returned to Berlin via the U.S.), received at the Foreign Office, July 19, 1916, AA, WK 18, *secr.*, Bd. 18. Fuehr supports his ambassador: "But there is one thing which we are able to see here without difficulty and which we are obliged to point out emphatically, so that in Germany one is not mislead by illusions in this respect: a renewal of unrestricted U-boat warfare ... would without any doubt bring the

United States immediately to the side of our enemies." Bernd Stegemann, *Die deutsche Marinepolitik 1916–1918* (Berlin, 1970), p. 61.

12. On August 31, 1916, an important meeting took place at General Headquarters. Hindenburg and Ludendorff were in favor of using the submarines, but at this point were not yet ready to assume responsibility for a break with America. Cf. Theobald von Bethmann Hollweg, *Betrachtungen zum Weltkriege* (Berlin, 1919–21), 2:127. Erich Ludendorff, *Meine Kriegserinnerungen 1914–1918* (Berlin, 1919), p. 190. Karl Helfferich, *Der Weltkrieg* (Berlin, 1920), 2:352–53.

13. Bethmann Hollweg's first draft even reads: "Otherwise unlimited U-boat warfare hardly avoidable." Karl E. Birnbaum, *Peace Moves and U-Boat Warfare* (Stockholm, 1958), p. 129.

14. Bethmann Hollweg to Bernstorff, September 2, 1916, mailed September 3, 1916, *LAPP*, 1:465–66.

15. Gerhard Ritter's polemics against Fritz Fischer in this context are not very convincing; the accusation that Bernstorff had "always seen the political situation in the United States too optimistically" is a plain distortion of the facts. To support his argument Ritter also quotes Secretary of State Lansing, but fails to mention that Wilson and House pursued their policy of mediation even *against* Lansing, who in this matter did not enjoy Wilson's absolute confidence. Ritter, *Staatskunst und Kriegshandwerk* (Munich, 1964–68), 3:324, 648. Cf. Arno Spindler, *Der Handelskrieg mit U-Booten* (Berlin, 1932–66), 3:357.

16. Ritter, *Staatskunst und Kriegshandwerk*, 3:322. Holtzendorff too counted on resumption of submarine warfare in the spring of 1917. Birnbaum, *Peace Moves and U-Boat Warfare*, p. 139.

17. From the summer of 1914 to the early fall of 1916 Count Bernstorff was alone in Washington. The documents in the Politisches Archiv of the German Foreign Office clearly show that he had left his family in Germany when he returned to the United States following the beginning of hostilities in Europe in 1914. In the summer of 1916 Countess Bernstorff was able to obtain passage from Copenhagen to New York through the help of Albert Ballin. Her sailing date was most probably August 17, 1916. Prior to her departure she went to Berlin, where she had breakfast with the American Ambassador and a private meeting with the Imperial Chancellor. In order to have a witness, she had asked her very close friend, Erika von Watzdorf, to accompany her. Memoirs Erika von Watzdorf (privately held), p. 348. Cf. Bernstorff to House, New York, August 2, 1916, YHC. Also private letters from Bernstorff to his wife that were intercepted by British intelligence, in PRO, FO 371.

18. Erika von Watzdorf in her memoirs, p. 348: "To Jeanne's [Countess Bernstorff's] repeated warnings that the total submarine war would mean America's entry into the war, Bethmann replied in pain that he knew that but that he was powerless against the will of the Supreme Command and

the Pan-Germans. It was a sad spectacle to see the Chancellor of the German Empire in this helpless, fatalistic condition in the hour of greatest, decisive danger." Countess Bernstorff understood the Chancellor in the same way and transmitted the instruction to the Ambassador to be ready to leave the United States at any time. This verbal order was rescinded by Berlin shortly afterwards. Diary entry of House, September 3, 1916, *IPH*, 2:332–33.

19. Bernstorff to Foreign Office, September 6, 1916, quoted in Bernstorff, *Deutschland und Amerika*, p. 283. Probably mailed September 8, 1916. Cf. *LAPP*, 1:466. Regarding the Bernstorff-House consultation, see *IPH*, 2:332–34. However, the editor Charles Seymour has kept interesting passages of the House diary from the reader. It is evident from the House Diaries, September 3, 1916, YHC, that House had expressed hope that Bernstorff would represent Germany during the coming peace negotiations. The Ambassador in turn suggested his mentor Bernhard Fürst von Bülow. The agreement of the two men in regard to a compromise peace also seems worth noting: "I doubted whether this country could live on amicable terms with either the Central Powers or the Entente should one or the other become entirely triumphant. He [Bernstorff] shared this opinion."

20. Cf. Spindler, *Der Handelskrieg mit U-Booten*, 3:359.

21. Bernstorff to Bethmann Hollweg, September 8, 1916, quoted in Bernstorff, *Deutschland und Amerika*, pp. 284–85.

22. Cf. Ritter, *Staatskunst und Kriegshandwerk*, 3:324–25.

23. Bethmann Hollweg to Bernstorff, September 26, 1916, quoted in Bernstorff, *Deutschland und Amerika*, pp. 285–86. The instruction was mailed by the Foreign Office in three parts on September 26 and 27. Cf. *LAPP*, 1:475–76.

24. Regarding this conversation, see House Diaries, October 3, 1916, YHC. Short excerpt in *IPH*, 2:374.

25. Birnbaum, *Peace Moves and U-Boat Warfare*, p. 162.

26. Bernstorff to Foreign Office, October 5, 1916, *LAPP*, 1:491. He continued: "After the elections, however, in the one case Wilson's mediation is probable, in the other case exists at least a slight possibility of finding a *modus vivendi* through negotiations with the United States."

27. Bethmann Hollweg to Bernstorff, October 9, 1916, in two parts, UA Beilagen, p. 17. Regarding this aide-mémoire, cf. Birnbaum, *Peace Moves and U-Boat Warfare*, pp. 158–65.

28. Bethmann Hollweg to Bernstorff, October 14, 1916, UA Beilagen, pp. 18–19. Bernstorff answered: "As before it is not to be expected that Wilson will take any steps toward peace before the elections. Also not that he will contact the Pope and the King of Spain." Bernstorff to Foreign Office, October 20, 1916, *LAPP*, 1:521.

29. Among others see Ritter, *Staatskunst und Kriegshandwerk*, vol. 3, and Wolfgang Steglich, *Bündnissicherung oder Verständigungsfrieden* (Göt-

tingen, 1958). It is striking that authors who emphasize the sincerity of German readiness for peace often underestimate the importance of the discussion of war aims in Germany for the relations with the United States.

30. Gerard to Lansing, September 25, 1915, *FRUS 1916*, Suppl., p. 55: "If any hint augurs that suggestion comes from here and not as spontaneous act of the President, whole matter will fail and be denied."

31. Bernstorff, *Deutschland und Amerika*, pp. 263–64. For details of the arrival of *U-Deutschland* in Baltimore and the reception of the unusual German ship in America see also the captain's own story in Paul König, *Die Fahrt der Deutschland* (Berlin, 1916), pp. 82–121.

32. The *U-Bremen* never reached the United States. There seems to be much uncertainty about the fate of the ship. See for instance Jesse S. Reeves, "Submarines and Innocent Passage," *American Journal of International Law* 11 (1917): 147–53.

33. Hans Rose, *Auftauchen!* (Essen, 1939), pp. 64–66, 83. Spindler, *Der Handelskrieg mit U-Booten*, 3:237–38, also mentions that the deployment of *U-53* represented a demonstration of "the high standard of the German U-boats."

34. Details in *Der Handelskrieg mit U-Booten*, 3:240–41.

35. Bernstorff to Foreign Office, October 10, 1916, telegram no. 125, AA, WK 18, *secr.*, Bd. 21. Bernstorff to Foreign Office, October 10, 1916, telegram no. 126, AA, WK 2, *secr.*, Bd. 23. Cf., however, Bernstorff, *Deutschland und Amerika*, pp. 265–66, giving October 11, 1916, as the date for telegram no. 126. The records show clearly that telegram no. 126 was composed after telegram no. 125 ("im Anschluss an Telegramm Nr. 125"). Arthur S. Link, *Campaigns for Progressivism and Peace, 1916–1917*, vol. 5 of *Wilson* (Princeton, N.J., 1965), p. 114, first reproduces part of telegram no. 126 and then thinks that telegram no. 125 is Bernstorff's report to Berlin on a further or second meeting with Wilson. The error may have been caused by the translation of "Gelegentlich anderweitiger Besprechung" (telegram no. 125) into "On the occasion of a further interview." It may be assumed that Bernstorff did not have two meetings with Wilson, as Link surmises, but that he reported on one meeting in two consecutive telegrams (125 and 126). "Anderweitig" would then refer not to a second meeting with Wilson but to the fact that the actual reason for the meeting was not the discussion of the submarine war along the American coast but Bernstorff's delivery of a message containing the German agreement to American relief work in Poland. To compound the problem, according to the German records telegram no. 125 arrived in Berlin on October 17, while telegram no. 126 arrived on October 14. Cf. also Birnbaum, *Peace Moves and U-Boat Warfare*, pp. 183–85. *IPH*, 2:334–35, also might mislead one to think that two meetings took place.

36. The Allies had expected a stronger American reaction.

37. Bernstorff, *Deutschland und Amerika*, p. 264: "The episode . . . was,

from a political standpoint, highly undesirable and had no military value whatsoever."

38. Because Rose delivered a letter for Bernstorff in Newport, the Ambassador was unnecessarily connected with the *U-53*. Bernstorff, *Deutschland und Amerika*, p. 264.

39. Steglich, *Bündnissicherung oder Verständigungsfrieden*, p. 17.

40. Birnbaum, *Peace Moves and U-Boat Warfare*, pp. 141–42.

41. Cf. Bethmann Hollweg's distinction between a peace mediation and a peace action by Wilson. According to the Chancellor's postwar testimony, a peace action in the sense of an appeal or an initiative was approved of, but one had not wanted the President to "participate in the arrangement of the conditions for peace." UA, pp. 126–27.

42. Bethmann Hollweg to Grünau, October 1, 1916, UA Beilagen, pp. 190–91. Cf. Fritz Fischer, *Griff nach der Weltmacht* (Düsseldorf, 1961), pp. 369–70: "For Bethmann Hollweg the desired peace initiative by Wilson was less the path toward a peace without victors and vanquished as envisioned by Wilson and Bernstorff, but instead it was to create the springboard and moral-political basis for the resumption of the unrestricted submarine warfare." Cf. *Deutschland im Ersten Weltkrieg*, project group directed by Willibald Gutsche (Berlin, 1968), 2:536. Baldur Kaulisch, "Die Auseinandersetzungen über den uneingeschränkten U-Boot-Krieg innerhalb der herrschenden Klassen im zweiten Halbjahr 1916 und seine Eröffnung im Februar 1917," in *Politik im Krieg 1914–1918*, ed. Fritz Klein (Berlin, 1964), p. 109.

43. House to Wilson, October 20, 1916, quoted in Link, *Campaigns for Progressivism and Peace*, p. 174.

44. *IPH*, 2:337, n.d. As late as 1933, however, Bernstorff insisted that the document did not represent a threat: "The Memorandum . . . was not a menace but a cry for help." Bernstorff to Seymour, May 11, 1933, and June 12, 1933, YHC. Cf. Charles Seymour, "The House-Bernstorff Conversations in Perspective," in *Studies in Diplomatic History and Historiography in Honour of G. P. Gooch, C.H.*, ed. A. O. Sarkissian (London, 1961), pp. 100–101.

45. Regarding the evacuation of Belgian civilians, see below. Germany's long-term plans for Belgium are also recognizable in the administrative measures designed to separate Walloons and Flemish. Cf. Hans W. Gatzke, *Germany's Drive to the West* (Baltimore, 1950), pp. 155–58.

46. On the whole a correct appraisal. German-American voters had been divided. The West and the South had voted for Wilson. Cf. Link, *Campaigns for Progressivism and Peace*, pp. 161–64. See also Thomas J. Kerr, IV, "German-Americans and Neutrality in the 1916 Election," *Mid-America* 43 (1961): 95–105.

47. Bernstorff to Foreign Office, November 12, 1916, UA Beilagen, p. 320.

48. Spindler, *Der Handelskrieg mit U-Booten*, 3:242–45. From the text of

the order: "Commercial vessels, whether they are armed or not, will be dealt with only on the basis of prize law.... Incidents that can lead to justified claims on the side of the neutrals are to be avoided under all circumstances."

49. The *Marina* was torpedoed west of Ireland on October 28, 1916. Six Americans were killed, others were injured. The sinking of the *Arabia* occurred in the Mediterranean, but among the more than fifty dead were apparently no Americans. Cf. Jagow to Bernstorff, November 14, 1916, AA, WK 18, *secr.*, Bd. 22; Zimmermann to Joseph C. Grew, ibid., Bd. 23. Birnbaum, *Peace Moves and U-Boat Warfare*, p. 204.

50. Link, *Campaigns for Progressivism and Peace*, p. 187. That the submarine incidents were nevertheless used to put pressure on Bernstorff does not imply a change in Wilson's basic disposition but rather has to be attributed to tactical considerations and, evidently, the political viewpoints of politicians like Lansing.

51. House Diaries, November 14, 1916, quoted in Link, *Campaigns for Progressivism and Peace*, pp. 187–88. Bernstorff to Foreign Office, without date, received in Berlin, November 24, 1916, UA Beilagen, p. 22.

52. Bernstorff to Foreign Office, November 21, 1916, *LAPP*, 1:575–77. Bethmann Hollweg's statement (*Betrachtungen zum Weltkriege*, 2:162) that Bernstorff had "merely reported" that Wilson "was contemplating . . . a peace action" that did not happen in this way does not correspond to the facts.

53. More about these talks in Steglich, *Bündnissicherung oder Verständigungsfrieden*, pp. 22–93. Ritter, *Staatskunst und Kriegshandwerk*, 3: 333–45. Fischer, *Griff nach der Weltmacht*, pp. 371–72.

54. Jagow to Bernstorff, November 16, 1916, *LAPP*, 1:564–65.

55. Bernstorff, *Deutschland und Amerika*, p. 307.

56. Jagow to Bernstorff, November 22, 1916, UA Beilagen, p. 21.

57. Zimmermann to Bethmann Hollweg, November 26, 1916, in Bernstorff, *Deutschland und Amerika*, pp. 304–5.

58. Early in October Herbert Hoover informed the State Department about the inhumane way in which German occupation authorities selected and treated these Belgian workers. At times conditions were so bad that the American "Relief Commission" had to take care of feeding the forced laborers in transport. Hoover to Lansing, October 10, 1916, *FRUS 1916*, Suppl., pp. 860–61. Cf. extensive American correspondence about the deportations in *FRUS 1916*, Suppl., pp. 858–70.

59. Cf. Link, *Campaigns for Progressivism and Peace*, p. 195.

60. Bernstorff to Foreign Office, December 4, 1916, UA Beilagen, p. 26. Roh to Bethmann Hollweg, December 21, 1916, AA, Botschaft Washington, Akten betreffend Deutschtum, Bd. 15.

61. Robert Lansing, *War Memoirs of Robert Lansing* (New York, 1935), p. 178.

62. Lansing Diaries, December 3, 1916, quoted in Link, *Campaigns for Progressivism and Peace*, pp. 199–200.
63. Ibid., pp. 206–10.
64. Steglich, *Bündnissicherung oder Verständigungsfrieden*, p. 106.
65. Historians have largely come to the conclusion that Jagow pursued more reasonable policies than Zimmermann, whose reputation has suffered irreparable damage because of the so-called Zimmermann telegram. In fact, however, one may speak of a continuity of German policy toward the United States under the two state secretaries. It should not be overlooked that during Jagow's tenure Germany's Mexican policy was directed in such a way that the Zimmermann telegram became possible. The mediation trips of House in 1915 and 1916 in no way had caused the Foreign Office to attempt to make the best of Wilson's interest in offering mediation. The fact that Zimmermann understood the actual international situation even less than his predecessor does not alter the verdict of gross neglect of German-American relations during Jagow's term of office.
66. Lansing to Grew, November 29, 1916, *FRUS 1916*, Suppl., pp. 70–71. Besides unimportant changes—possibly made by Grew—the text printed in UA Beilagen, pp. 322–23, contains an obvious error. Instead of "for some affirmative action" it reads "for soon and affirmative action."
67. Grew to Lansing, December 5, 1916, *FRUS 1916*, Suppl., p. 868; Grew to Lansing, December 7, 1916, ibid., pp. 81–82; Grew to Lansing, December 8, 1916, ibid., p. 82. (Grew had to protest because the Foreign Office had handed the confidential message from Washington to the press.) The version of Bethmann Hollweg's reply to Wilson printed in UA Beilagen, p. 323, is even less encoded. According to the Chancellor's notes (ibid.), Grew also took notes during the encounter. This may have caused the difference between the two texts. Cf. Birnbaum, *Peace Moves and U-Boat Warfare*, pp. 233–34. Steglich, *Bündnissicherung oder Verständigungsfrieden*, p. 141.
68. Notes about the report of Generalfeldmarschall von Hindenburg before the Emperor, December 8, 1916; proclamation to the German Army; and handwritten notes by the Chancellor, in UA Beilagen, pp. 95–96. Ritter, *Staatskunst und Kriegshandwerk*, 3:348. Birnbaum, *Peace Moves and U-Boat Warfare*, pp. 234–42.
69. Stumm to Washington Embassy (via State Department), December 9, 1916, *LAPP*, 1:609–10. Bernstorff wrote to House accordingly. Bernstorff to House, December 12, 1916, YHC; partially reproduced in Link, *Campaigns for Progressivism and Peace*, p. 215.
70. Grew to Lansing, December 12, 1916, text in *FRUS 1916*, Suppl., pp. 89–90; see American note of December 16 to the neutral nations containing English translation. Link, *Campaigns for Progressivism and Peace*, pp. 213–14. Steglich, *Bündnissicherung oder Verständigungsfrieden*, pp. 142–43.

71. Comments in the margin of the American peace note of December 18, December 22, 1916, by Wilhelm II, quoted in Birnbaum, *Peace Moves and U-Boat Warfare*, p. 243. Cf. Zimmermann at a press conference in Berlin: "We issue this peace offer in order to forestall a peace action by Wilson, which probably will be released shortly." UA, pp. 200–201. Cf. Zimmermann's explanation in his statement, ibid., pp. 201–13. Somewhat astonishing is Wolfgang Mommsen's appraisal in "Die deutsche öffentliche Meinung und der Zusammenbruch des Regierungssystems Bethmann Hollweg im Juli 1917," *Geschichte in Wissenschaft und Unterricht* 19 (1968): 660. While one may have no problems agreeing with him that the so-called German peace offer also served to prop up public opinion inside Germany and that the failure of the move may have weakened the Chancellor's position, I find it difficult to see how Mommsen comes to the conclusion that "every chance to reach a peace by way of negotiation" was, for the time being, lost in consequence. The records, by contrast, seem to indicate that Wilson was still open for proposals for mediation if indeed Berlin had desired that. In view of the documents reflecting German intentions, one is even more surprised about Mommsen's assessment that "the transition to unrestricted submarine warfare now became . . . unavoidable if for no reason other than to stabilize the confidence in the Government."

72. Maximilian Harden, "Am tausendsten Tag," *Die Zukunft* (April 28, 1917), p. 109.

73. Link, *Campaigns for Progressivism and Peace*, p. 214. Fischer, *Griff nach der Weltmacht*, p. 386.

74. Link, *Campaigns for Progressivism and Peace*, pp. 216–17. Grew to Lansing, December 13, 1916, *FRUS 1916*, Suppl., p. 89.

75. Cf. Fischer, *Griff nach der Weltmacht*, pp. 380–81.

76. Text of the note *FRUS 1916*, Suppl., pp. 97–99.

77. Harden, "Am tausendsten Tag," p. 109: "expression of a readiness which is silent on all significant issues."

78. Bernstorff to Foreign Office, December 21, 1916, *LAPP*, 1:627–28.

79. Notes by the Emperor in the margins of Zimmermann's telegram of December 22, 1916, and on an Associated Press report, *LAPP*, 1:628–29.

80. Zimmermann to Gerard, December 26, 1916, UA Beilagen, pp. 34–35. Cf. Steglich, *Bündnissicherung oder Verständigungsfrieden*, p. 163.

81. Zimmermann to Bernstorff (via State Department), December 26, 1916, *LAPP*, 1:640–41 (author's emphasis).

82. Cf. John M. Blum, *Woodrow Wilson and the Politics of Morality* (Boston, 1956), p. 126: "But behind this offer [of December 12] superficially so cheering, brooded a militant and corrupted spirit. . . . The Germans had made their gesture not in weakness, not with humanitarian intent, but with confidence in the own impending victory. . . . They had already decided, in the event negotiations failed, to resume unrestricted submarine warfare."

83. The Supreme Command (Oberste Heeresleitung) demanded far-reaching annexations in the East and West, including especially territorial sacrifices from Russia and Belgium. Moreover, Luxemburg and Belgium were to be brought into the German sphere of influence. The Navy, in agreement with the Supreme Command, among other things demanded Belgian coastal territory, the Faroese Islands, Baltic coastal territory (kurländische Küste), an African colonial empire, Dakar with Senegambia, the Azores, Tahiti, and Tsingtau. Hindenburg to Bethmann Hollweg, December 23, 1916, *LAPP*, 1:630–31; Holtzendorff to Bethmann Hollweg, December 24, 1916, ibid., pp. 633–37.

84. Clipping, Sunday edition of the New York *Staats-Zeitung*, December 24, 1916, and Bernstorff's correspondence with the Foreign Office, which disapproved of the publication in AA, Botschaft Washington, Friedensverhandlungen, Bd. 1. A sharp rebuke from Zimmermann was the consequence also of declarations concerning Belgium that Bernstorff had made before representatives of the press shortly before Christmas. Zimmermann to Bernstorff, January 6, 1917, and Bernstorff to Zimmermann, January 8, 1917, both in ibid.

85. House to Wilson, December 27, 1916, YHC: "Bernstorff came to see me this morning by appointment. He was disappointed in his Government's reply to your note. While he does not believe that anyone of the belligerents could state their terms excepting in conference, he thinks that it might be done confidentially." Bernstorff to George Sylvester Viereck, January 13, 1931. See also House Diaries, December 27, 1916, ibid. Cf. Sigmund Freud and William C. Bullitt, *Thomas Woodrow Wilson* (London, 1967), p. 161.

86. *FRUS 1916*, Suppl., p. 112. It reads: "It being understood that the Government of the United States may in its turn convey it [an answer to Wilson's peace appeal, or rather the conditions for peace] in like confidence to the governments of the other group of the belligerents." Likewise, one cannot avoid the impression that Bernstorff may have thought it possible to obtain conditions for peace from Berlin. The German government, however, wanted to present its conditions only at the conference of the belligerent nations.

87. Bernstorff to Foreign Office, December 29, 1916, *LAPP*, 1:649–50. The telegram was probably not sent, as stated here, via the United States Embassy in Berlin but instead via the usual way of Buenos Aires and Stockholm. Cf. Birnbaum, *Peace Moves and U-Boat Warfare*, pp. 275–76.

88. Bernstorff, *Deutschland und Amerika*, p. 324.

89. Text of the Entente note in William Graves Sharp (U.S. Ambassador in Paris) to Lansing, December 29, 1916, *FRUS 1916*, Suppl., pp. 123–25. Link, *Campaigns for Progressivism and Peace*, p. 237.

90. Complete text in Zimmermann to Bernstorff, January 7, 1917, *LAPP*, 1:668–69. Originally both Bethmann Hollweg and the Foreign Office had

formulated an answer to Bernstorff's telegram. The Chancellor's draft authorized Bernstorff to inform the President of relatively modest conditions (cf. Steglich, *Bündnissicherung oder Verständigungsfrieden*, p. 171). Bethmann Hollweg's draft of the instruction for Bernstorff, received January 4, 1917, *LAPP*, 1:659–60. It cannot be established with certainty when the draft of the Foreign Office was approved at General Headquarters and accepted by Bethmann Hollweg. Birnbaum (*Peace Moves and U-Boat Warfare*, p. 309–11) has examined more closely the background and the motives for the two drafts.

91. Schäfer to Zimmermann, January 3, 1917, AA, WK 18, *secr.*, Bd. 24.

92. One is tempted to speculate about a Bülow-Bernstorff (as State Secretary of the Foreign Office) team. It seems very doubtful, however, that against the opposition of the German military leaders, they could have brought about a negotiated peace with England. Curiously, Bülow, although he had been anything but successful in Italy, continued to be mentioned for various positions. In early 1916 American papers speculated that he might replace Bernstorff in Washington. Bernstorff to Countess Bernstorff, intercepted and copied by the British secret service, May 27, 1916, PRO, FO 372, 950.

93. Minutes of the Supreme Command of the meeting of January 8, 1917, UA Beilagen, pp. 334–37. Johann von Dallwitz had been Prussian Minister of the Interior until 1914 and since then served as "Statthalter" in Alsace-Lorraine.

94. Minutes of the Supreme Command of the meeting of January 9, 1917, UA Beilagen, pp. 337–38. Anyway, in advance of the meeting Wilhelm II had decided "that the submarine war was a purely military matter, which was none of the Chancellor's business." Walter Görlitz, ed., *Regierte der Kaiser? Kriegstagebücher, Aufzeichnungen und Briefe des Chefs des Marine-Kabinetts Admiral Georg Alexander v. Müller 1914–1918*, 2d ed. (Göttingen, 1959), p. 247. Fritz Stern, "Das Rätsel Bethmann Hollweg. Die Kunst das Böse zu tun," *Die Zeit* (December 29, 1967), p. 26. In view of the hard evidence from the records, the fact that Germany "faced starvation and defeat" may have been assigned too much weight in this connection in the recent study of the blockade. C. Paul Vincent, *The Politics of Hunger* (Athens, Ohio, 1985), p. 46.

95. Cf. Ritter, *Staatskunst und Kriegshandwerk*, 3:381–82. Birnbaum, *Peace Moves and U-Boat Warfare*, pp. 322–23.

96. Text in Spindler, *Der Handelskrieg mit U-Booten*, 3:378.

97. Lersner to Zimmermann, January 16, 1917, quoting the Emperor, AA, WK 18, *secr.*, Bd. 24.

98. Bernstorff to Foreign Office, January 10, 1917, comments in the margin by the Emperor, ibid.

99. Bethmann Hollweg to Bernstorff, Top Secret, January 16, 1917, UA Beilagen, pp. 45–46.

100. One is tempted to compare the possible consequences of a resignation by either one of the two statesmen, the Chancellor or the Ambassador. Both preferred to stay in office even when they could no longer pursue the policies for which they had stood, at least officially. It is difficult, however, to avoid the impression that Bethmann Hollweg more or less adjusted to the changing political environment (if it was a change) while Bernstorff decided to stand up for his views against the powerful interest groups in Germany.

101. Prior to the decision to engage in unrestricted submarine warfare, only the deployment of the U-boats against armed commercial vessels had been planned. Birnbaum (*Peace Moves and U-Boat Warfare*) examines this decision in detail. On January 4 and 5, 1917, the Foreign Office informed Bernstorff that the measures against armed commercial vessels were to begin "in the immediate future." Bernstorff did not fail to warn at once that this step would "cause the failure of Wilson's peace mediation and instead bring about the rupture of diplomatic relations with the United States." Texts of the correspondence in Bernstorff, *Deutschland und Amerika*, pp. 325–26.

102. January 10, 1917.

103. House to Wilson, January 15, 1917, YHC. Bernstorff to Foreign Office, January 16, 1917, *LAPP*, 1:675–76. Gerhard Ritter, who argues that Bernstorff acted "against his instruction," also can only refer to these documents and has to concede the possibility of a misunderstanding on the part of House. Since we have no notes by Bernstorff, a definitive appraisal of the conversation, for the time being, seems impossible; see Ritter, *Staatskunst und Kriegshandwerk*, 3:388–89.

104. Cf. House to Wilson, January 18, 1917, YHC.

105. House to Wilson, January 15, 1917, YHC.

106. House to Wilson, January 16, 1917; Wilson to House, January 16, 1917; House to Wilson, January 17, 1917; all quoted in Link, *Campaigns for Progressivism and Peace*, p. 257. House to Bernstorff, January 17, 1917, AA, Botschaft Washington, Friedensverhandlungen, Bd. 1. House to Wilson, January 17, 1917, YHC.

107. Bernstorff to House, January 18, 1917, AA, Botschaft Washington, Friedensverhandlungen, Bd. 1.

108. House to Bernstorff, January 19, 1917, ibid.

109. Bethmann Hollweg's telegram no. 157 of January 16, 1917, was received in Washington on January 19. Bernstorff to House, January 20, 1917, AA, Botschaft Washington, Friedensverhandlungen, Bd. 1. The reference is to the Allied note of January 10, 1917, answering Wilson's peace initiative of December 18, 1916. Text in Sharp to Lansing, January 10, 1917, *FRUS 1917*, Suppl. 1, pp. 5–8. The note emphasized the war guilt of the Central Powers ("If there is an historical fact established at the present date, it is the willful aggression of Germany and Austria-Hungary to insure their

hegemony over Europe and their economic domination over the world."), mentioned certain "objects" (i.e., general peace conditions), and, for the rest, stated the mutual decision of the Allies to end the war victoriously. There was no mention of a negotiated peace.

110. Cf. Ritter, *Staatskunst und Kriegshandwerk*, 3:390.

111. It must be underlined, however, that this idea at no time was a decisive motive for his continued efforts regarding an American mediation. Bernstorff's realization that only a negotiated peace, an agreement at a conference, a return to the status quo or a peace without victors could lead Germany out of this conflict went back as far as the fall of 1914, as has been pointed out earlier.

112. The execution of the Irish rebels already had resulted in a bad press for England in the United States. A further impediment to good relations between Britain and the United States was the British publication of the so-called "blacklist" of American companies. Regarding tensions resulting from British measures and American countermeasures in the late summer and fall of 1916, cf. Link, *Campaigns for Progressivism and Peace*, pp. 65–80. In late November the Federal Reserve Board had appealed to member banks to exercise greater caution when extending credits to the belligerent nations. Britain had reason to be seriously concerned about the further financing of the war. Wilson instructed House to "write to Lord Grey in the strongest terms to the effect that he could be sure that . . . her people [the Americans] were growing more and more impatient with the intolerable conditions of neutrality, their feeling as hot against Great Britain as it was at first against Germany." Wilson to House, November 24, 1916; U.S. Congress, Senate, Special Committee on Investigation of the Munitions Industry, *Munitions Industry, Report on Existing Legislation* (Washington, 1936), pp. 212–15. Link, *Campaigns for Progressivism and Peace*, pp. 200–205. Bernstorff, *Deutschland und Amerika*, pp. 329–30.

113. Cf. Arnold Meine, *Wilsons Diplomatie in der Friedensfrage 1914–1917* (Stuttgart, 1938), p. 66.

114. House to Wilson, January 20, 1917, YHC.

115. Telegram no. 157 (German declaration of unrestricted submarine warfare) and telegram no. 158 (the so-called Zimmermann telegram) were both dispatched by the Foreign Office on January 16, 1917. For further detail see below. Concerning the British motivation at this point see Link, *Campaigns for Progressivism and Peace, 1916–1917*, p. 281, and more recently Arthur S. Link, ed., *The Papers of Woodrow Wilson* (Princeton, N.J., 1978–83), 41:26–27, reproducing the notes by Wiseman concerning his meeting with House on January 26, 1917. On Wiseman see especially Arthur Willert, *The Road to Safety* (London, 1952), passim, and Christopher Andrew, *Secret Service* (London, 1985), pp. 208–9.

116. Bernstorff, *Deutschland und Amerika*, p. 358.

117. Bernstorff to Foreign Office, January 19, 1917, quoted in ibid., pp. 358–59.

118. Text in *FRUS 1917*, Suppl. 1, pp. 24–29.

119. Perhaps indicative of Wilson's sometimes unrealistic political viewpoint is the suggestion made in this speech to extend the validity of the Monroe Doctrine over the entire world. If, in this context, he spoke of the self-determination of all nations, this, without any doubt, was meant sincerely but at the same time ignored the fact that the Monroe Doctrine was founded on the superior power of the Union in the Western Hemisphere.

120. Only few influential personalities in Germany understood, for instance, that a clear position on the Belgian question was necessary in order to alleviate the distrust of German intentions. Cf. Max Warburg to Zimmermann, January 20, 1917, AA, WK 20a, *secr.*, Bd. 1: "More or less the European war for them [the Americans], sentimentally as well as politically, is all about Belgium. If therefore, in some form we ... give the Americans an assurance that Belgium will be spared in the final confrontation [Auseinandersetzung], we will remove a reason for the President to declare war on us." Germany should therefore "clearly state that we will allow Belgium to exist again as an independent nation." Cf. Cardinal John Farley (New York) to Prince Hermann von Hatzfeld-Trachenburg, December 9, 1916, AA, Botschaft Washington, Akten betreffend Belgische Deportationen, Bd. 1: "I have ... deemed it my duty ... to urge as earnestly as possible that you recommend to the Imperial Government a change of policy with regard to the deportations of Belgians. It is impossible to convince great masses of the American people that the present policy is not one of great cruelty and that it does not contravene the accepted methods of conducting warfare among modern nations."

121. Wilson to House, January 24, 1917, YHC. The letter is fully reproduced in Link, *The Papers of Woodrow Wilson*, 41:3–4. The two words in brackets are not in the letter copy in Box 121, YHC.

122. House to Wilson, January 26, 1917, *IPH*, 2:432–33. Bernstorff to Foreign Office, January 26, 1917, telegram no. 60, AA, Vereinigte Staaten von Amerika 16, Bd. 48. Bernstorff, *Deutschland und Amerika*, pp. 372–73. In fact, the Ambassador felt that matters were so urgent that at noon, after having seen House, he sent a telegram to his wife in Washington to instruct Edgar Haniel von Haimhausen to cable Berlin to postpone submarine action until his next two wires arrived. Bernstorff to Countess Bernstorff, January 26, 1917, and handwritten note from Countess Bernstorff to Haniel, January 26, 1917, AA, Botschaft Washington, Akten betreffend Friedensverhandlungen, Bd. 1.

123. Bernstorff to Foreign Office, January 27, 1917, *LAPP*, 1:684–85. Also reproduced fully with English translation in Link, *The Papers of Woodrow Wilson*, 41:49–52.

124. The first conference was to bring about peace, the second was to deal with questions of international law.

125. German intelligence services were either insufficiently or wrongly informed. In conservative and national-liberal circles it was very common to make light of America as a military power.

126. Author's emphasis.

127. Cf. Karl Helfferich (*Der Weltkrieg* [Berlin, 1920], pp. 372–73), who saw Bethmann Hollweg on the evening of January 28 and reports that the Chancellor was agitated and appeared to see a last hope to avoid war with the United States and possibly even reach peace negotiations.

128. Zimmermann to Grünau, January 28, 1917, and Grünau to Foreign Office, January 28, 1917, in UA Beilagen, pp. 138–39. Foreign Office to Bernstorff, January 29, 1917, AA, WK 18, *secr.*, Bd. 25.

129. Notes by Georg Alexander von Müller, January 29, 1917, Görlitz, *Regierte der Kaiser?*, p. 253.

130. Notes by Georg Alexander von Müller, January 29, 1917, ibid., p. 254.

131. At Bernstorff's urging the Foreign Office had made an effort to gain a postponement or an extension for neutral ships from the Admiralty. What the Chancellor really thought of the recall of the U-boats at the end of January is reflected in his memoirs: "Without prior testing of this weapon of war, which was considered infallible by the military, the navy, and an enormous portion of public opinion, the German people would then have had to swallow any peace that the President, who had little knowledge of conditions in Germany and in Europe, would have favored and gotten through with the Entente." Theobald von Bethmann Hollweg, *Betrachtungen zum Weltkriege* (Berlin, 1919–21), 2:161.

132. German text of telegram no. 65, Bethmann Hollweg to Bernstorff, January 29, 1917, in AA, WK 18, *secr.*, Bd. 25. It is reproduced in *LAPP*, 1:685–87. The letter from Bernstorff to House, January 31, 1917, translating most of telegram no. 65 into English, is found in YHC, Box 12. It is reproduced in *FRUS 1917*, Suppl. 1, pp. 3–36. Telegram no. 174, Zimmermann to Bernstorff, January 27, 1917, arriving in Washington at 3 P.M. on January 29, 1917, is found in AA, WK 18, *secr.*, Bd. 25; information on date of arrival in AA, Botschaft Washington, Friedensverhandlungen, Bd. 1. Bernstorff's handwritten comment about delaying the copying of the translation of the submarine warfare note is also found there. Cf. Bernstorff's albeit incomplete report on these developments in *Deutschland und Amerika*, pp. 375–78.

133. *IPH*, 2:436–37. Cf. viewpoint of well-known German historian Friedrich Meinecke in *Probleme des Weltkrieges* (Munich, 1917), pp. 135–36: "Because the blinded enemies rejected the compromise peace, we had to get out new sharper weapons, in order to finally bring about peace quickly now. We did not get them out before they had become necessary

and unavoidable and at the same time sharp enough to achieve their goal and hit the enemy at his most sensitive spot."

134. Lansing, *War Memoirs of Robert Lansing*, pp. 210–12. Cf. Bernstorff, *Deutschland und Amerika*, pp. 378–79. Regarding the last negotiations of Bernstorff in Washington, cf. also Z. A. B. Zeman, *A Diplomatic History of the First World War* (London, 1971).

135. Thomas A. Bailey, *Woodrow Wilson and the Lost Peace* (New York, 1947), pp. 8, 11.

136. Lansing, *War Memoirs of Robert Lansing*, p. 216. Lansing to Bernstorff, February 3, 1917, *FRUS 1917*, Suppl. 1, pp. 106–8.

137. Bernstorff to Bethmann Hollweg, on board *Frederik VIII*, March 7, 1917, AA, Mexiko 16, secr., Bd. 1. All codes and material about codes, except code 92705 (German code needed for cable traffic with Swiss Legation) and code 9972 (already known to the U.S. Government) were destroyed. Burned also were political documents including material from the prewar period, the lists of Indian revolutionaries, registers of cover addresses, receipts, account books, and the records of the Military Attaché.

138. House to Bernstorff, February 2, 1917, AA, Botschaft Washington, Friedensverhandlungen, Bd. 1. House Diaries, February 1, 1917, YHC. Cf. *IPH*, 2:441–43.

139. Bernstorff to House, February 3, 1917, AA, Botschaft Washington, Friedensverhandlungen, Bd. 1.

140. House to Bernstorff, February 4, 1917, ibid.

141. See for instance Ritter, *Staatskunst und Kriegshandwerk*, vol. 3. Hans-Jürgen Schwepcke, "U-Boot-Krieg und Friedenspolitik" (Ph.D. diss., Universität Heidelberg, 1952). Otto Graf zu Stolberg-Wernigerode, *Die unentschiedene Generation* (Munich, 1968). Peter Graf von Kielmannsegg, *Deutschland und der Erste Weltkrieg* (Frankfurt, 1968).

142. See for instance Lansing, *War Memoirs of Robert Lansing*. Charles Seymour, "The House-Bernstorff Conversations in Perspective," in *Studies in Diplomatic History and Historiography in Honour of G. P. Gooch, C.H.*, ed. A. O. Sarkissian (London, 1961), pp. 90–106. Appuhn, "L'Ambassade du Comte Bernstorff à Washington." Warrington Dawson, ed., *The War Memoirs of William Graves Sharp, American Ambassador to France 1914–1919* (London, 1931). *Neue Zürcher Zeitung*, October 9, 1939.

143. Cf. letter of February 1, 1917, by the historian Eduard Meyer, who wanted to be regarded as an expert on America and cultivated close connections to the Foreign Office and other political circles: "I ask Your Excellency to accept my most heartfelt thanks on the occasion of the happy news that this morning has brought us and that finally [has] led us to a great and bold decision . . . , and especially for the clear, manly note to America that makes all further vacillation impossible"; AA, WK 18, adh. 2, secr., Bd. 3. *Neue Preussische Zeitung*, Berlin, February 5, 1917, p. 1: "The

final victory cannot be torn away from us anymore. This is guaranteed by our victories to date, the determination for victory of our people and our Army, and the names of our leaders, against whose superior abilities our opponents have nothing of equal value to put forth." *Göttinger Tageblatt*, Göttingen, February 1, 1917, p. 1: "A sigh of relief is going through the German people! Finally, finally, the word has been spoken." Cf. Otto Stadler, "Der U-Bootkrieg gegen England und die deutsche Tagespresse vom 1. August 1914 bis zum 1. Februar 1917" (Ph.D. diss., Universität Heidelberg, 1937), p. 49: "The unrestricted U-boat war had been declared, welcomed by all Germans and the entire German press."

144. House Diaries, February 4, 1917, YHC.

145. In a sharp note, Germany informed Austria on February 6 that "the message ... to Wilson ... hardly corresponds to the spirit of our last note." The Germans moreover made it clear that they had "not called for a peace without victors" because even the "modest demands" could be achieved by Germany "only as victor." Otherwise, Berlin deemed "an all too friendly attitude" toward the United States on the part of Vienna "questionable." UA Beilagen, pp. 343–44.

146. German text in Wedel to Zimmermann, February 5, 1917, UA Beilagen, pp. 341–43. English text of Czernin's note to Lansing in Penfield to Lansing, February 5, 1917, *FRUS 1917*, Suppl. 1, pp. 38–39.

147. Lansing to Page, February 8, 1917, complete text in Link, *Campaigns for Progressivism and Peace*, pp. 316–17.

148. Zimmermann to Wedel, February 11, 1917, UA Beilagen, pp. 346–47.

149. Regarding the Austrian-American contacts, cf. Link, *Campaigns for Progressivism and Peace*, pp. 314–18. Ritter, *Staatskunst und Kriegshandwerk*, 3:406–11. Of some interest also are the efforts of Jacob Noeggerath, a German-American with good American connections, who tried to have the deployment of the U-boats postponed. Among others Noeggerath had contacts with Prince Max von Baden and the Zentralstelle für Auslandsdienst.

150. Text of the communication in Link, *Campaigns for Progressivism and Peace*, p. 319, and in G. Lechartier, *Intrigues et Diplomaties à Washington (1914–1917)* (Paris, 1918), pp. 258–59.

151. Gisbert Freiherr von Romberg, German Minister in Bern, to Foreign Office, February 7, 1917, AA, WK 18, *secr.*, Bd. 28.

152. Zimmermann to Kurt Freiherr von Grünau (at General Headquarters), February 8, 1917, UA Beilagen, p. 345. Zimmermann regarding his suggestion: "With an answer like that we would make no concessions as far as unrestricted submarine warfare is concerned." With "now as ever" he was referring to the German offer to exempt from the submarine war certain passenger liners on the route from the United States to Britain.

153. Grünau to Foreign Office, February 8, 1917, UA Beilagen, p. 346.

154. Report about this in Pleasant Alexander Stovall (American head of

mission in Bern) to Lansing, February 19, 1917, *FRUS 1917*, Suppl. 1, pp. 136–37. Paul Ritter, however, only relayed the contents of the original Zimmermann draft to the American Government. The Emperor's additional conditions apparently were not mentioned. Ritter to Lansing, February 11, 1917, ibid., p. 126. The British Ambassador Cecil Spring Rice seems to have followed Bernstorff's attempts to find a modus vivendi with some nervousness. Cf. Spring Rice to Foreign Office, February 17, 1917: "I think Swiss Minister's proposal was due to intrigue between German Ambassador and Bryan and possibly also Chairman of Senate Committee of Foreign Relations, not to State Department. Object was to influence peace party in Congress"; see also Sir Horace Rumbold, Berne, to A. J. Balfour, February 20, 1917, both in PRO, FO 371, 3109.

155. Lansing to Ritter, February 12, 1917, *FRUS 1917*, Suppl. 1, p. 129. For more detail on the American reaction to these contacts with Germany after the rupture of diplomatic relations see Link, *Campaigns for Progressivism and Peace*, pp. 318ff.

156. The records contain no information on this, but it would appear that this was the only route of communication left for Bernstorff. Strangely enough, though, AA, Vereinigte Staaten von Amerika 16, Bd. 49, still gives the route as via Stockholm.

157. Bernstorff to Foreign Office, February 10, 1917, AA, WK 18, secr., Bd. 30. Printed without the Emperor's comments in UA Beilagen, p. 349. (The telegram was received in Berlin on February 15, 1917, one day after Bernstorff's departure from the United States.)

158. Wedel to Bethmann Hollweg, March 14, 1917, and message by the Austro-Hungarian Embassy in Berlin, March 14, 1917, in UA Beilagen, pp. 352–53.

159. Holtzendorff to the Emperor, March 18, 1917, AA, Vereinigte Staaten von Amerika 16, Bd. 50. Also in UA Beilagen, pp. 353–54.

160. Emperor's comments in the margin of Holtzendorff's telegram quoted above. The Emperor's commentary is reproduced only incompletely in UA Beilagen, p. 354. Careless remarks about Gerard as well as "ist eine Unverschämtheit" (in the margin next to "incognito amtlich") are not printed. Comment by Emperor in German: "Es ist jetzt ein für alle mal *Schluss* mit *Verhandlungen* mit Amerika! Will Wilson Krieg, so soll er ihn herbeiführen und ihn dann haben!"

161. Treated in detail in Friedrich Katz, *Deutschland, Diaz und die mexikanische Revolution* (Berlin, 1964), and Barbara Tuchman, *The Zimmermann Telegram* (New York, 1958).

162. Cf. Arthur Zimmermann, "Fürst Bülows Kritik am Auswärtigen Amt," in *Front wider Bülow*, ed. Friedrich Thimme (Munich, 1931), pp. 233–34. Cf. Michael C. Meyer, "The Mexican-German Conspiracy of 1915," *The Americas* 23 (July 1966): 76: "Zimmermann's proposal to Venustiano Carranza was not a bold and newly devised scheme but rather

the climax of several years of intrigue with various Mexican officials and exile groups."

163. Statement by Zimmermann at the 123d session of the Kommission für den Reichshaushalts-Etat (Commission for the Imperial Budget), March 5, 1917, AA, Deutschland 122, Nr. 2m, Nr. 1.

164. Jordan to Lersner, March 5, 1917, AA, Akten des AA im Grossen Hauptquartier 1915–1919, Mexico 20. Kurt Riezler on March 4, 1917, jotted down: "Kemnitz did this, this fantastic [phantastische] idiot." Karl Dietrich Erdmann, ed., *Kurt Riezler. Tagebücher, Aufsätze, Dokumente* (Göttingen, 1972), p. 412. As Link, *Campaigns for Progressivism and Peace*, p. 344, points out correctly, there are no records containing reliable information regarding discussions in Berlin leading up to the dispatch of the telegram. It is certain, however, that Bernstorff was not asked for his opinion regarding the offer to Mexico.

165. Cf. Katz, *Deutschland, Diaz und die mexikanische Revolution*, pp. 373–74.

166. Memo by Montgelas, January 17, 1917, AA, Mexico 16, secr., Bd. 1. Cf. statement by Zimmermann at the 123d session of the Kommission für den Reichshaushalts-Etat, Berlin, March 5, 1917, indicating that this and other messages were sent through the U.S. Embassy in Berlin and the State Department with the explanation to the American officials that the telegrams were related to the mediation efforts.

167. German text in Zimmermann to Eckardt, January 13, 1917, and Zimmermann to Bernstorff, January 13, 1917, AA, Mexico 16, secr., Bd. 1. Also in UA Beilagen, pp. 355–56. English translation here taken from Link, *Campaigns for Progressivism and Peace*, p. 343, since that text is widely known and readily available in the United States. Cf. literal English translation in Tuchman, *The Zimmermann Telegram*, pp. 201–2.

168. Heinrich von Eckardt, who had close connections with navy circles, was Germany's second most important diplomat on the American continent. The following report from Mexico may serve as an illustration of his outlook: "*Berlin is the kibla*—Mexico is oriented toward Berlin, not Washington, and not yet Tokyo. The legacy [*das Erbe*] of Hernando Cortez, extending far beyond the equator, is up for sale. Humboldt appraised it. Let us seize it, let us intervene, suspending the rule of the law of the strong and the weak neighbor—as on the Bosporus." Eckardt to Georg Count von Hertling, November 30, 1917, AA, Mexico 1, Bd. 58. Cf. Katz, *Deutschland, Diaz und die mexikanische Revolution*, p. 395.

169. Cf. Joseph C. Grew, *Turbulent Era*, ed. Walter Johnson (Boston, 1952), 1:308–9.

170. Zimmermann to Eckardt, February 5, 1917, AA, Mexico 16, secr., Bd. 1. Also in UA Beilagen, p. 356. This note was also drafted by Kemnitz and carried among others the initials of Zimmermann and Montgelas.

171. Inexplicably the Germans continued to use the same codes even

though it must have been known in Berlin that code books had been lost on various occasions during the war. Cf. for instance C. J. Edmonds, "The Persian Gulf Prelude to the Zimmermann Telegram," *Journal of the Royal Central Asian Society* 47 (1960): 58–67.

172. Lansing, *War Memoirs of Robert Lansing*, p. 232. Bailey, *Woodrow Wilson and the Lost Peace*, pp. 7–8. Georg Bernhard in *Vossische Zeitung*, July 8, 1917, pp. 1–2. Marc Ferro, *La Grande Guerre 1914–1918* (Paris, 1969), p. 203: "l'affaire du telegramme Zimmermann, qui agit comme une mèche sur un baril de poudre."

173. M. J. Bonn, *Was will Wilson?* (Munich, [1918]), pp. 48–49. Robert E. Osgood, *Ideals and Self-interest in America's Foreign Relations* (Chicago, 1953), pp. 254–55. Lawrence W. Martin, *Peace Without Victory* (New Haven, Conn., 1958), p. 128.

174. Speech by Roosevelt before the Union League Club, March 20, 1917, in Elting E. Morison, ed., *The Letters of Theodore Roosevelt* (Cambridge, Mass., 1951–54), 8:1163.

175. Link, *Campaigns for Progressivism and Peace*, pp. 398–99.

176. Address of Woodrow Wilson to a Joint Session of Congress, April 2, 1917, in Link, *The Papers of Woodrow Wilson*, 41:525. Cf. Blum, *Woodrow Wilson and the Politics of Morality*, p. 129: "Wilson in the end decided for war because Germany forced him to."

177. Cf. however the Düsseldorf *General-Anzeiger*, March 3, 1917: "Count Bernstorff is on his way to Germany and now has no longer an opportunity to further have his unfortunate hand in the matter of German-American relations." Information indicating that Bernstorff did not want to return to Germany but had planned to go to Cuba could not be confirmed. At any rate, the matter came up for discussion in official government circles in Washington. Cf. House to Wilson, February 4, 1917, YHC: "I am told that he wants to go to Cuba instead of home. They seem to be fearful not only of the voyage but of their reception in Germany. I think it would be a mistake to allow him to remain in the Western Hemisphere if it can be avoided. Even if he did not foment trouble, it would be thought that he was doing so." Cf. M. J. Bonn, *So macht man Geschichte* (Munich, 1953), p. 174: "The German Navy hated the Ambassador; some hothead would have been capable—by accident of course—of torpedoing the ship."

178. Compare the nuisances to which the American Ambassador Gerard was exposed by the Foreign Office before his departure from Berlin. Details, for instance, in *FRUS 1917*, Suppl. 1.

179. John H. Henry to Chief, United States Secret Service, report for Wednesday, February 14, 1917, NA, RG 87, Records of the United States Secret Service, T-915, roll 597. After having been able to examine part of Bernstorff's later correspondence, I do not think it impossible that he told an Associated Press journalist: "I believe that my official career has come to end. I have been sent home by the American Government for something

which I had no power to change, but I think that this is the best moment for me to step down." (The German word *"abzutreten"* could also mean to retire from his professional career altogether.) The Düsseldorf *General-Anzeiger*, February 17, 1917, p. 2, said that these statements of the Ambassador had probably been "altered."

180. *Norddeutsche Allgemeine Zeitung*, February 19, 1917, p. 2. Shortly before sailing, he still handed the customs people a statement to take ashore: "I cannot let the opportunity pass without a last response to the American people for the mass of flowers and presents sent to the Countess and myself. I cannot find sufficient words to express my gratitude for the kindness shown to both of us and no words would be cordial enough to express my farewell greeting"; ibid. Cf. Lechartier, *Intrigues et Diplomaties à Washington (1914–1917)*, pp. 263–64.

181. Details in *Norddeutsche Allgemeine Zeitung*, February 26, 1917, p. 2. Odell to Nachrichtenabteilung of Foreign Office, March 10, 1917, and Wiegand to Presseabteilung of Foreign Office, March 10, 1917, both in AA, Vereinigte Staaten von Amerika 16, Bd. 50. Bonn, *So macht man Geschichte*, pp. 174–75.

182. Cf. UA, pp. 117–18. Bernstorff, *Deutschland und Amerika*, p. 401, gives March 10 as date of arrival. This may be an error, because the press reported the landing at 10:30 A.M. on March 12. Cf. Ulrich Count von Brockdorff-Rantzau (German Minister in Copenhagen) to Foreign Office, March 12, 1917, AA, Vereinigte Staaten von Amerika 16, Bd. 50.

183. Gustav Michahelles, German Minister in Christiania, to Foreign Office, March 6, 1917; Foreign Office to Michahelles, March 6, 1917; Foreign Office to Brockdorff-Rantzau, March 7, 1917; and Brockdorff-Rantzau to Foreign Office, all in AA, Mexico 16, Bd. 1. The prepared, if not to say fictitious, interview was given to the editor-in-chief of the *Hamburger Fremdenblatt*, Felix von Eckardt. His son avoids saying anything about the unusual background of what he calls the "interview, which seemed sensational at the time." Felix von Eckardt, *Ein unordentliches Leben* (Düsseldorf, 1967), p. 36.

184. Compare for instance the text actually published in *Norddeutsche Allgemeine Zeitung*, March 14, 1917, p. 1, and the text drafted by the Foreign Office in AA, Mexico 16, Bd. 1.

185. The two diplomats often had quite different views on basic issues. As a consequence of information from the Navy and "because of domestic political considerations," Brockdorff-Rantzau was clearly in favor of the U-boat war. Memorandum, August 1, 1917, AA, Nachlass Brockdorff-Rantzau, Brandenburg Manuskript.

186. UA, pp. 108–9, 119, 121, 185–86. Bernstorff, *Deutschland und Amerika*, pp. 403–4. Bernstorff arrived in Berlin on March 13, 1917, at 8:25 P.M. *Neue Preussische Zeitung* (March 14, 1917).

187. According to his own statements before the later committee of in-

quiry, Bernstorff did not give the Chancellor any new advice. UA, p. 121. Shortly afterwards, the Chancellor offered Bernstorff to send him to Stockholm "on a special mission" in order to explore new peace possibilities there. But Wilhelm II "categorically refused" such a mission for Bernstorff. Bernstorff, *Deutschland und Amerika*, p. 404. Bethmann Hollweg to Foreign Office, March 21, 1917, AA, Deutschland 135, Nr. 20, Bd. 3.

188. Bernstorff to Lersner, March 29, 1917, and Lersner to Bernstorff, March 31, 1917, AA, Akten des Auswärtigen Amts im Grossen Hauptquartier 1915–1919, Vereinigte Staaten von Amerika 3, Bde. 1 and 2.

189. Bethmann Hollweg to Foreign Office, March 21, 1917, AA, Deutschland 135, Nr. 20, Bd. 3. Gottfried Prinz zu Hohenlohe-Schillingsfürst (Austro-Hungarian Ambassador in Berlin) to Ottokar Count Czernin (Austro-Hungarian Foreign Minister), March 23, 1917, quoted in W. M. Carlgren, *Neutralität oder Allianz* (Stockholm, 1962), pp. 249–50.

190. Speeches by Zimmermann before the 122d and the 123d session of the Kommission für den Reichshaushalts-Etat, March 3 and March 5, 1917, AA, Deutschland 122, 2m, Nr. 1. Wilhelm II, despite the absence of any evidence, seems to have continued to hold Bernstorff responsible for the debacle of the Zimmermann telegram. Cf. the Emperor's reactions in the margins of Hossenfelder to Imperial Chancellor, George Michaelis, October 21, 1917, AA, Vereinigte Staaten von Amerika 16, Bd. 54. In addition to all this, Bernstorff was even held responsible for the breaking off of relations with the United States. Emil Ludwig, *Geschenke des Lebens* (Berlin, 1931), p. 390.

191. Minutes of the 150th session for the Imperial budget (Sitzung für den Reichshaushalt), May 1, 1917, AA, Vereinigte Staaten von Amerika 16, Bd. 52.

192. Bernstorff to Lersner, March 29, 1917, AA, Akten des AA im Grossen Hauptquartier 1915–1919, Vereinigte Staaten von Amerika 3, Bde. 1 and 2. UA, pp. 118–20, 785.

193. Testimony under oath by Bernstorff before the official German committee of inquiry on October 23, 1919. UA, p. 778. Slightly different wording of the testimony in Bernstorff, *Deutschland und Amerika*, p. 412. Cf. Hans E. Riesser, *Haben die deutschen Diplomaten versagt?* (Bonn, 1959), p. 19: "Who before 1917 has recognized the situation in the United States better than Count Bernstorff?"

BIBLIOGRAPHY

I. UNPUBLISHED MATERIAL

A. Federal Republic of Germany

Politisches Archiv, Auswärtiges Amt, Bonn
Kaiserlich Deutsche Botschaft Washington
  Graf Bernstorff (Bd. 1)
  Karl Boy-Ed (Bd. 1)
  Das Kaiserliche Konsulat in Cincinnati (Bd. 1)
  Vorläufige Sammlung von durch die feindseligen Beziehungen
    zwischen V. St. und Mexiko veranlassten Schreiben (Bd. 1)
  Mexiko. Expedition gegen Villa (Bd. 1)
  Deutsche Ansprüche gegen den Staat Georgia (Bd. 1)
  Londoner Seekriegskonferenz (Bd. 1)
  Das Kaiserliche Konsulat in San Francisco (Bde. 1–2)
  Das Kaiserliche Generalkonsulat in New York (Bde. 3–4)
  Geheim. Zusammengehen Deutschlands mit den Vereinigten
    Staaten in Ostasien (Bde. 1–4)
  Militär-Angelegenheiten. Allgemeines (Bd. 1)
  Die antisemitische Bewegung (Bd. 1)
  Friedensvorschläge und Verhandlungen (Bd. 1)
  Internationale Friedensbestrebungen (Bde. 1–2)
  Präsident und Kabinett (Bde. 5–7)
  England (Bde. 9–13)
  Dampfer Maverick und Annie Larsen (Bd. 1)
  Prozess Graves (Bd. 1)
  Friedensverhandlungen (Bd. 1)
  Friedensvorschläge (Bde. 1–3)
  Propagandaschriften (Bde. 1–3)
  Paul Rohrbach (Bd. 1)
  Mittel- und Südamerika (Bde. 2–3)
  Prozess von Igel (Bd. 1)
  Canada (Bde. 1–3)
  Belgische Deportationen (Bd. 1)
  Australien (Bd. 1)
  Südsee-Inseln (Bde. 1–2)

Deutsch-Amerikanischer Schiedsgerichtsvertrag (Bd. 1)
Abbruch (Bd. 1)
Präsidentenwahlen (Bde. 6–7)
Politik—Allgemeines (Bde. 30–32)
Deutschtum (Bde. 12–15)
Trusts (Bde. 5–8)
Staats- und Völkerrechtliche Fragen (Monroe-Doktrin) (Bd. 1)
Professoren- und Lehrer-Austausch (Bde. 1–4)
Handelsvertrag und Zolltarif der Vereinigten Staaten (Bde. 17–20)

Kaiserlich Deutsche Gesandtschaft Stockholm
Konferenz der Neutralen; Tätigkeit der Zionisten; Zentralorganisation für einen dauernden Frieden (Bd. 1)
Friedensangebot (Bd. 1)
Krieg: Transocean (Bd. 1)

Europa Generalia
Die den deutschen Missionen usw. ertheilten Instructionen und Vorhaltungen in geschäftlicher Beziehung (Bde. 5–6)

Deutschland
121, Nr. 19, *secr.*, Angelegenheiten der deutschen Armee: Waffenverkäufe und Allgemeines über Waffenlieferungen deutscher Firmen für Fremde Regierungen (Bde. 6–9)
122, Nr. 2, Das Auswärtige Amt (Bde. 3–4)
122, Nr. 2c, *secr.*, Der Kaiserliche Botschafter von Radowitz (Bd. 1)
122, Nr. 2m, Nr. 1, Parlamentarische Reden des Staatssekretärs Zimmermann (Bd. 1)
126a, *secr.*, Geheime Ausgaben für Presszwecke und Massregeln zur Beeinflussung der Auslandspresse (Bde. 2–5)
127, Nr. 22, Die Botschaft der Vereinigten Staaten von Amerika in Berlin (Bde. 4–6)
127, Nr. 22 adh., Die Veröffentlichungen des ehemaligen amerikanischen Botschafters Gerard (Bd. 1)
135, Die deutschen Missionen im Auslande (Generalia) (Bd. 1)
135, *secr.*, Die deutschen Missionen im Auslande (Generalia) (Bd. 1)
135, Nr. 1, Die Botschaft in Constantinopel (Bde. 1–2)
135, Nr. 2, Die Botschaft in London (Bd. 1)
135, Nr. 4, Die Botschaft in Petersburg (Bde. 1–2)
135, Nr. 4, *secr.*, Die Botschaft in Petersburg (Bd. 1)
135, Nr. 20, Die Botschaft in Washington (Bde. 2–3)
135, Nr. 22, Die Gesandtschaft in Belgrad (Bd. 1)
135, Nr. 23, Die Konsulate (Bd. 5)
141, *secr.*, Staatspolizei (Bd. 1)
141, Nr. 7, *secr.*, Agenten (Bde. 4–10)
144, Die diplomatische Vertretung bei den deutschen Höfen (Bd. 2)
148, *secr.*, Verhandlungen mit England (Bd. 4)

149, Der Geschaeftsgang bei der Politischen Abteilung (Bd. 12)
Preussen
    6a, Dresden (Bd. 1)
    6b, München (Bd. 1)
England
    78, Die politischen Beziehungen Englands zu Deutschland (Bde. 37–38)
Russland
    73, Die Juden in Russland (Bde. 10–11)
Englische Besitzungen in Asien
    2, Britisch Indien (Bde. 51–57)
    2, Nr. 1, Britisch Indien: Militaria (Bd. 18)
Mexico
    1, Allgemeine Angelegenheiten Mexicos (Bde. 36–58)
    1, *secr.*, Allgemeine Angelegenheiten Mexicos (Bd. 1)
    10, Beziehungen Mexicos zu Japan (Bd. 1)
    13, Militär und Marine (Bd. 1)
    16, Beziehungen Mexicos zu Deutschland (Bde. 1–3)
    16, *secr.*, Geheime Handakten des Geh. Legationsrats Dr. Goeppert (Bd. 1)
Panama
    2, *secr.*, Japanisch-Englische Intrigen gegen die Vereinigten Staaten von Amerika in Panama (Bd. 1)
Vereinigte Staaten von Nordamerika
    1, Allgemeine Angelegenheiten von Nordamerika (Bde. 19–28)
    2, Die Presse der Vereinigten Staaten von Nordamerika (Bde. 14–25)
    2, *secr.*, Die Presse der Vereinigten Staaten von Nordamerika (Bd. 1)
    5, Militär-Angelegenheiten (Bde. 13–16)
    5 adh., Begleitberichte zu den Berichten des Militär-Attachés (Bd. 1)
    5a, Marine-Angelegenheiten (Bd. 29)
    6, Nr. 2, Personalien: Journalisten (Bde. 4–6)
    6, Nr. 2, *secr.*, Journalisten (Bde. 1–2)
    6, Nr. 4, Diverse Persönlichkeiten (Bd. 6)
    8, Das diplomatische Corps in Washington (Bd. 6)
    10, Die Irländer in den Vereinigten Staaten (Bd. 1)
    11a, Die Präsidentenwahlen in den Vereinigten Staaten (Bd. 1)
    13, Die Kirche in den Vereinigten Staaten (Generalia) (Bd. 1)
    13a, Die katholische Kirche in den Vereinigten Staaten (Bd. 6)
    14, Das Vereinswesen in den Vereinigten Staaten (Bd. 3)
    15, Sozialisten und Anarchisten in den Vereinigten Staaten (Bde. 5–6)
    16, Beziehungen der Vereinigten Staaten zu Deutschland (Bde. 23–57)
    16, *secr.*, Beziehungen der Vereinigten Staaten zu Deutschland (Bd. 2)
    20a, Die Monroe-Doktrin (Bd. 4)
Internationale Angelegenheiten

Staats- und Völkerrecht adh. Freiheit der Meere (Bd. 1)
Büro-Akten
2, Audienzen beim Reichskanzler und Staatssekretär.
Immediatvorträge des Reichskanzlers und Staatssekretärs (Bd. 10)
Der Weltkrieg
  WK, secr., Der Weltkrieg (Bd. 12)
  WK, adh. 4, Nr. 1, Aburteilung der Schuldigen (Bd. 1)
  WK, adh. 4, Nr. 3, Der parlamentarische Untersuchungsausschuss (Bde. 1–5)
  WK, Nr. 2, Vermittlungsaktionen (Bde. 4–5)
  WK, Nr. 2, secr., Vermittlungsaktionen (Bde. 4–6, 22–23)
  WK, Nr. 10, secr., Finanzielle Massnahmen Deutschlands (Bde. 1–9)
  WK, Nr. 11, Unternehmungen und Aufwiegelungen gegen unsere Feinde. Allgemeines (Bd. 3)
  WK, Nr. 11, adh. 2, Unternehmungen und Aufwiegelungen gegen unsere Feinde durch die Juden (Bde. 1–6)
  WK, Nr. 11e, adh., Entwuerfe von Allerh. Handschreiben an den Emir von Afghanistan und an indische Fürsten (Bd. 1)
  WK, Nr. 11f, Unternehmungen und Aufwiegelungen gegen unsere Feinde in Indien (Bde. 1–48)
  WK, Nr. 11f, adh., Unternehmungen und Aufwiegelungen gegen unsere Feinde in Indien. Personalia (Bd. 1)
  WK, Nr. 11h, secr., Unternehmungen und Aufwiegelungen gegen unsere Feinde in Kanada (Bde. 1–2)
  WK, Nr. 11k, secr., Unternehmungen und Aufwiegelungen gegen unsere Feinde unter den Iren (Bde. 1–13)
  WK, Nr. 12, Gesuche um Verwendung (Bd. 5)
  WK, Nr. 14a, Verwaltung besetzter Gebiete in Russland (Bd. 1)
  WK, Nr. 18, secr., Unterseebootkrieg gegen England und andere feindliche Staaten (Bde. 1–30)
  WK, Nr. 18, adh. 2, secr., Unterseebootkrieg gegen England und andere feindliche Staaten. Sammlung von Privateingaben (Bde. 1–4)
  WK, Nr. 18, adh. 3, Pressestimmen zum U-Bootkrieg (Bd. 1)
  WK, Nr. 20a, secr., Die Zukunft der besetzten Gebiete: Belgien (Bd. 1)
Akten des Auswärtigen Amts im Grossen Hauptquartier, 1915–1919 (Staatssekretär, Vertreter des Amts, Rat im Gefolge) und Akten des Rat im Gefolge S. M. 1917–1918
  3, Vereinigte Staaten von Amerika. Allgemeine Lage (Bde. 1–2)
  3a, Amerika—Sussex Note (Bd. 1)
  3b, Amerika—Friedensvermittlung (Bd. 1)
  20, Mexico (Bd. 1)
  41, Türkei: Allgemeine Politik (Bde. 3–4)
  42, U-Bootkrieg (Bde. 1–2)
Akten des Auswärtigen Amts im Grossen Hauptquartier, 1914–1916

(Reichskanzler, Staatssekretär, Rat im Gefolge)
24, Presse und Journalisten (Bde. 1–5)
31, Amerika (Bde. 1–2)
Rechtswesen 6
    Vereinigte Staaten von Amerika. Rechtliche Beziehungen der Vereinigten Staaten zu Deutschland—Deutsch-Amerikanische Entschädigungsansprüche. Allgemeines (Bde. 1–10)
    Vereinigte Staaten von Amerika. Deutsch-Amerikanische Entschädigungsansprüche. Sabotage Claims (Bde. 1–21)
    Vereinigte Staaten von Amerika. Deutsch-Amerikanische Entschädigungsansprüche. Sabotage Claims. Beiheft: Nadolny-Papen Briefe (Bd. 1)
Rechtswesen 6a
    Vereinigte Staaten von Amerika. Abwicklung der Arbeiten der deutsch-amerikanischen Gemischten Kommission. Aufhebung der Staatsvertretung. Amerikanische Anträge auf Zahlung der late claims. (Bd. 1)
Rechtswesen 15
    Vereinigte Staaten von Amerika. Heft: Kaltschmidt (Bd. 1)
Rechtswesen 19, Nr. 1
    Vereinigte Staaten von Amerika. Heft: Horstmann, Hermann (Bd. 1)
Rechtswesen 20
    Vereinigte Staaten von Amerika. Interimsakte: Zentraleinkaufsgesellschaft (Bd. 1)
    Vereinigte Staaten von Amerika. Schriftwechsel Min.-Dir. de Haas-Rintelen (Bd. 1)
    Vereinigte Staaten von Amerika. Rintelen (Bd. 1)
Länderabteilungen 1920–1936
    Vereinigte Staaten von Amerika—Weltkrieg. Der Lusitania-Fall (Bde. 1–2)
Presse-Abteilung. Vereinigte Staaten von Amerika
    1, Die Presse der Vereinigten Staaten von Amerika (Bde. 1–3)
    2, Die Presse in New York (Bde. 1–5)
    4, Presse-, Propaganda- und allgemeine Angelegenheiten (Bd. 1)
    6, Die Zeitung "The Evening Mail" (Bde. 1–2)
    [unnumbered], Karl H. v. Wiegand (Bd. 1)
    [unnumbered], Maximilian Harden, Herausgeber von "Die Zukunft" (Bd. 1)
Nachlass Brockdorff-Rantzau
    Manuskript der Biographie Brockdorff-Rantzaus von Erich Brandenburg (Bde. 1–4)
    Versailles I
    Versailles II
    Versailles III

Friedensverhandlungen—Abschiedsgesuch
Privatbriefe (Geheime amtliche Papiere)
Nachlass Nadolny
   Selected documents
Nachlass Casement
   Bundle of letters
Bundesarchiv, Koblenz
   Akten des Auswärtigen Amts
   Nachlass Moritz Julius Bonn
   Nachlass Lujo Brentano
   Nachlass Bernhard von Bülow
   Nachlass Brönner-Hoepfner
   Nachlass Eduard David
   Nachlass Hermann Dietrich
   Nachlass Georg Gothein
   Nachlass Maximilian Harden
   Presseausschnittsammlung, Institut für Weltwirtschaft
   Nachlass Erich Koch-Weser
   Zeitungsausschnittsammlung Lauterbach
   Partei- und Verbandsdrucksachen
   Nachlass Friedrich von Payer
   Reichskanzlei-Akten
   Nachlass Hans Wehberg
   Reichskanzlei, Personalakte Heinrich Albert
   Reichskanzlei, Personalakte Meyer-Gerhard
Bayerisches Hauptstaatsarchiv, Geheimes Staatsarchiv, Munich
   MA I, 968, U-Bootkrieg. Tirpitz Krisis. Agitation für unbeschränkten U-Bootkrieg
   MA, 95053, Amerika und Deutsch-Amerikanische Beziehungen, 1912–1918
   MA, 95054, Die Revolution in Mexiko betr. ferner Deutsch-Mexikanische Beziehungen. 1912–[sic]
   MA, 9727, Reise des Iren Sir Roger Casement nach Amerika u. Verwendung zu Gunsten des verhafteten Casement, 1915–1917
   MA, 97528, Seekrieg 1915–1917
   MA, 97533, Seekrieg 1917–1918
   MA, 97568, Das deutsche Friedensangebot 1916–17
Bayerisches Hauptstaatsarchiv, Kriegsarchiv, Munich
   MKr, 1828, 1829, 1830, 1831, 1832, Persönliche Berichte des bayerischen Militär-Bevollmächtigten im Grossen Hauptquartier
HAPAG Archiv, Hamburg
   Hamburg-Amerika Linie, New York vom 1. Mai 1914 bis 15. Januar 1915

Hamburg-Amerika Linie, New York vom 1. Januar 1915 bis 15. Juni 1915
Hamburg-Amerika Linie, New York vom 1. Juli 1915 bis 30. November 1915
Hamburg-Amerika Linie, New York vom 1. März 1917 bis 1918
Ypiranga. Rapporte des Kapitäns, Akte 77
Kronprinzessin Cecilie. Rapporte des Kapitäns. Akte 78
Archiv der Lauenburgischen Gelehrtenschule, Ratzeburg
  Album, 3. Teil
  Zensurenliste der Prima für den Zeitraum von Ostern bis Johannis 1881
Papers of Georg Ahrens. Private possession.
Papers of Max M. Warburg, London. Private possession.
Unpublished Letters from Constantinople (Marie Rose von Watzdorf). Private possession.
Unpublished Memoirs of Erika von Watzdorf. Private possession.
Unpublished Memoirs of a German Diplomat in Constantinople. Inaccessible to public.

B. Great Britain

Public Record Office, London
  Admiralty 137. Items from Intelligence Division.
  War Office 106. Selected items.
  Foreign Office 95. Miscellanea. Items concerning Sir Roger Casement.
  Foreign Office 371. Selected items.
  Foreign Office 372. Selected items.
  Foreign Office 383. Items concerning Rintelen.
  Foreign Office 800. The Private Papers of Sir Francis Bertie (later Lord Bertie of Thame).
  Foreign Office 800. Sir E. (Viscount) Grey's Private Papers.
  Foreign Office 800. Sir C. A. Spring Rice's Private Papers.

C. Republic of Ireland

National Library, Dublin
  Selected items concerning the Easter Rising and Sir Roger Casement.

D. United States of America

National Archives, Washington, D.C., and Suitland, Md.
  RG 38: Records of the Office of the Chief of Naval Operations

RG 59: Records of the Department of State, Records of the Office of the Counselor
RG 60: Records of the Department of Justice, Office of Alien Property Custodian
RG 87: Records of the United States Secret Service
RG 131: Records of the Office of Alien Property
RG 165: M.I.D.
Microfilms:
    T-81, Roll 351, Records of the "Deutsches Ausland-Institut, Stuttgart"
    T-290, Roll 21, Auswärtiges Amt, Botschaft Washington
    T-915, Roll 597, Records of the United States Secret Service

Yale University Library, New Haven, Conn.
    The Diaries and Papers of Edward M. House (Yale House Collection)
    The Papers of Frank L. Polk
    The Charles Seymour Papers
    The William Bayard Hale Papers

Library of Congress, Washington, D.C.
    The Theodore Roosevelt Papers (Reel 335)
    The Oscar S. Straus Papers

Office of United States Secret Service, Washington, D.C.
    Selected items

New York Public Library, New York
    The Maloney Collection
    The John Quinn Collection

Houghton Library, Harvard University, Cambridge, Mass.
    The Oswald Garrison Villard Papers

Ryan Library, Iona College, New Rochelle, N.Y.
    The Florence Monteith Lynch Collection

Hoboken Public Library, Hoboken, N.J.
    Enemy Aliens, Scrapbook

Columbia University Library, New York
    The John W. Burgess Collection
    The William H. Carpenter Collection
    The Random House Collection
    The Henry White Collection

YIVO Institute for Jewish Research, New York
    The David Movshowitch Collection

American Irish Historical Society, New York
    The Daniel F. Cohalan Papers

Milwaukee County Historical Society, Milwaukee, Wis.
    Pamphlet literature

II. PUBLISHED OFFICIAL DOCUMENTS

Ahrens, Georg, and Brinkmann, Carl, eds. *Wilson. Das staatsmännische Werk des Präsidenten in seinen Reden.* Berlin: Dietrich Reimer, 1919.
Austrian and German Papers Found in Possession of Mr. James F. J. Archibald, Falmouth, August 30, 1915. Miscellaneous, no. 16. London: Printed under the Authority of His Majesty's Stationery Office, 1915.
Brewing and Liquor Interests and German and Bolshevik Propaganda. Report and Hearings of the Subcommittee on the Judiciary. United States Senate. 2 vols. Washington, D.C.: Government Printing Office, 1919.
Brooklyn Daily Eagle, *The United States and the War. Eagle Library*, no. 189, vol. 30. Brooklyn, N.Y.: Brooklyn Daily Eagle, 1915.
Committee on Alleged German Outrages. *Report of the Committee on Alleged German Outrages Appointed by His Britannic Majesty's Government and Presided Over by The Right Hon. Viscount Bryce.* London: His Majesty's Stationery Office, 1915.
Committee on Public Information. *German Plots and Intrigues in the United States during the Period of Our Neutrality.* Washington, 1918.
Deist, Wilhelm, ed. *Militär und Innenpolitik im Weltkrieg 1914–1918.* Vols. 1–2. Quellen zur Geschichte des Parlamentarismus und der politischen Parteien. Düsseldorf: Droste, 1970.
Documents Relative to the Sinn Fein Movement. Cmd. 1108. London: His Majesty's Stationery Office, 1921.
Görlitz, Walter, ed. *Der Kaiser... Aufzeichnungen des Chefs des Marinekabinetts Admiral Georg Alexander v. Müller über die Ära Wilhelms II.* Göttingen: Musterschmidt, 1965.
———. *Regierte der Kaiser? Kriegstagebücher, Aufzeichnungen und Briefe des Chefs des Marine-Kabinetts Admiral Georg Alexander v. Müller 1914–1918.* Göttingen: Musterschmidt, 1959.
Die Grosse Politik der Europäischen Kabinette 1871–1914. Vols. 23, 39. Berlin: Deutsche Verlagsgesellschaft für Politik und Geschichte, 1927.
Investigation of Mexican Affairs. Preliminary Report and Hearings of the Committee on Foreign Relations. United States Senate. Vols. 1–2. Washington, D.C.: Government Printing Office, 1920.
Ludendorff, Erich, ed. *Urkunden der Obersten Heeresleitung über ihre Tätigkeit 1916–1918.* Berlin: Mittler, 1920.
Matthias, Erich, ed. *Der Interfraktionelle Ausschuss 1917/18.* Part I. Vol. 1, Quellen und Geschichte des Parlamentarismus und der politischen Parteien. Düsseldorf: Droste, 1959.
Matthias, Erich, and Rudolf Morsey, eds. *Die Regierung des Prinzen Max von Baden.* Vol. 2, Series 1, Quellen zur Geschichte des Parlamentarismus und der politischen Parteien. Düsseldorf: Droste, 1962.

Moore, John B. *A Digest of International Law*. Vol. 6. Washington, D.C.: Government Printing Office, 1906.
Munitions Industry. Report on Existing Legislation. Special Committee on Investigation of the Munitions Industry. United States Senate. Washington, D.C.: Government Printing Office, 1936.
National German-American Alliance. Hearings before the Subcommittee of the Committee on the Judiciary. United States Senate. Washington, D.C.: Government Printing Office, 1918.
Official German Documents Relating to the World War. The Reports of the First and Second Subcommittees of the Committee Appointed by the National Constituent Assembly to Inquire into the Responsibility for the War, together with the Stenographic Minutes of the Second Committee and Supplements thereto. Vols. 1–2. New York: Oxford University Press, 1923.
Papers Relating to the Foreign Relations of the United States. 1904–1917. Washington, D.C.: Government Printing Office, 1905–31.
Papers Relating to the Foreign Relations of the United States. The Lansing Papers 1914–1920. Vols. 1–2. Washington, D.C.: Government Printing Office, 1939–40.
President Wilson's Great Speeches and Other History Making Documents. Chicago: Stanton and Van Vliet, 1917.
Reiss, Klaus-Peter, ed. *Von Bassermann zu Stresemann. Die Sitzungen des nationalliberalen Zentralvorstandes 1912–1917*. Vol. 5, Series 1, Quellen zur Geschichte des Parlamentarismus und der politischen Parteien. Düsseldorf: Droste, 1967.
Reports of International Arbitral Awards. Vol. 7: *Decisions of the Mixed Claims Commission. United States-Germany*. Part 1. United Nations Publications, 1956.
Revolutions in Mexico. Hearing before a Subcommittee of the Committee on Foreign Relations. United States Senate. Washington, D.C.: Government Printing Office, 1913.
Rich, Norman, and M. H. Fischer, eds. *Die Geheimen Papiere Friedrich von Holsteins*. Vol. 4. Göttingen: Musterschmidt, 1963. (German edition by Werner Frauendienst.)
Scherer, André, and Jacques Grunewald, eds. *L'Allemagne et les problèmes de la paix pendant la première guerre mondiale*. Vols. 1–2. Paris: Presses Universitaires de France, 1962, 1966.
Scott, James B., ed. *Diplomatic Correspondence between the United States and Germany, August 1, 1914–April 6, 1917*. New York: Oxford University Press, 1918.
Selection From Papers Found In The Possession Of Captain Von Papen, Late German Military Attaché At Washington, Falmouth, January 2 & 3, 1916. Miscellaneous, no. 6. London: His Majesty's Stationery Office/Harrison and Sons, 1916.

Sworn Statement by Horst von der Goltz alias Bridgeman Taylor. London: His Majesty's Stationery Office/Harrison and Sons, 1916.
Taft, William Howard. *The Proposed Arbitration Treaties with Great Britain and France*. Baltimore, Md.: American Society for Judicial Settlement of International Disputes, February, 1912. (Probably a speech of November 1911.)
Thimme, Friedrich, ed. *Bethmann Hollwegs Kriegsreden*. Stuttgart: Deutsche Verlags-Anstalt, 1919.
Tirpitz, Alfred von. *Politische Dokumente*. Vol. 2. Hamburg: Hanseatische Verlagsanstalt, 1926.
Die Ursachen des deutschen Zusammenbruchs im Jahre 1918. Das Werk des Untersuchungsausschusses der Deutschen Verfassunggebenden Nationalversammlung und des Deutschen Reichstages 1919–1926. Series 4. Vols. 1–12. Berlin: Deutsche Verlagsgesellschaft für Politik und Geschichte, 1925–29.
Verfassunggebende deutsche Nationalversammlung. 15. Ausschuss. 2. Unterausschuss. Beilagen zu den Stenographischen Berichten über die öffentlichen Verhandlungen des Untersuchungsausschusses. Berlin: Norddeutsche Buchdruckerei und Verlagsanstalt, n.d.
Verfassunggebende deutsche Nationalversammlung. 15. Ausschuss. 2. Unterausschuss. Stenographische Berichte über die öffentlichen Verhandlungen des Untersuchungsausschusses. Berlin: Norddeutsche Buchdruckerei und Verlagsanstalt, n.d.
Verhandlungen des Reichstags. Vols. 306–308. Berlin: Norddeutsche Buchdruckerei und Verlags-Anstalt, 1916.

III. PUBLISHED MEMOIRS AND LETTERS AND CONTEMPORARY PUBLICATIONS OF A DOCUMENTARY NATURE

Adler, Cyrus. *Jacob H. Schiff. His Life and Letters*. Vols. 1–2. Garden City, N.Y.: Doubleday, Doran, 1929.
Ahrens, Georg. "Botschafter Graf Bernstorff." *Frankfurter Rundschau* (October 28, 1949).
Albert, Heinrich F. *Aufzeichnungen*. Berlin: W. Büxenstein, [1948].
Alldeutscher Verband. *Zwanzig Jahre alldeutscher Arbeit und Kämpfe*. Leipzig: Dieterich'sche Verlagsbuchhandlung Theodor Weicher, 1910.
"The American Ambassador's Detention in Berlin." *Current History* 5 (March 1917): 974–77.
The American Jewish Committee. *The American Jewish Yearbook 5675*. Edited by Herman Bernstein. Philadelphia: The Jewish Publication Society of America, 1914.
———. *The American Jewish Yearbook 5676*. Edited by Joseph Jacobs.

Philadelphia: The Jewish Publication Society of America, 1915.
———. *The Jews in the Eastern War Zone.* New York: The American Jewish Committee, 1916.
Angell, Norman. *After All.* New York: Farrar, Straus and Young, 1952.
Baden, Max Prinz von. *Erinnerungen und Dokumente.* Berlin: Deutsche Verlags-Anstalt Stuttgart, 1927.
———. *Erinnerungen und Dokumente.* Edited by Golo Mann and Andreas Burckhardt. Stuttgart: Ernst Klett, 1968.
———. *Die moralische Offensive.* Stuttgart: Deutsche Verlagsanstalt, 1921.
Baker, Ray Stannard. *Woodrow Wilson. Life and Letters.* Vols. 3–5. Garden City, N.Y.: Doubleday, Doran, 1931–1938.
———. *Woodrow Wilson. Life and Letters.* Vol. 6. London: William Heinemann, 1938.
Bartholdt, Richard. *From Steerage to Congress.* Philadelphia: Dorrance, 1930.
Baruch, Bernard M. *The Public Years.* New York: Holt, Rinehart & Winston, 1960.
Bauer, Hermann. *Als Führer der U-Boote im Weltkriege.* Leipzig: Koehler & Amelang, 1942.
———. *Reichsleitung und U-Bootseinsatz 1914–1918.* Lippoldsberg: Klosterhaus, 1956.
Baumgarten, Otto. *Meine Lebensgeschichte.* Tübingen: J. C. B. Mohr (Paul Siebeck), 1929.
Behr, Theodor. "Deutschlands Judenpolitik." *Der Jude* 2(9) (1917/1918): 577–86.
Bernhardi, Friedrich von. *Denkwürdigkeiten aus meinem Leben.* Berlin: E. S. Mittler & Sohn, 1927.
———. *Deutschland und der nächste Krieg.* Stuttgart: J. G. Cotta'sche Buchhandlung Nachfolger, 1912.
Bernstorff, Johann Heinrich Graf von. "Abraham Lincoln as the Germans Regard Him." Speech given in Springfield, Illinois, on February 12, 1913.
———. "Address Delivered by the German Ambassador, Count Johann Heinrich von Bernstorff, on the Occasion of the Unveiling of the Statue of General Baron von Steuben, at Washington, D.C., on Wednesday Afternoon, December 7th, 1910." *German American Annals* 8 (1910).
———. "As Between Ambassadors." *Living Age* (February 1923): 441–44.
———. "Die Avant-Garde des Völkerbundes." *Völkerbund-Fragen* 2 (December 1, 1925): 59–63.
———. "Die Biographie eines amerikanischen Botschafters." *Das Demokratische Deutschland* 5 (January 6, 1923): 7–13.
———. "Briefe eines amerikanischen Ministers." *Das Demokratische Deutschland* 5 (February 17, 1923): 145–48.
———. *Deutschland und Amerika.* Berlin: Ullstein, 1920. U.S. edition:

My Three Years in America. New York: C. Scribner's Sons, 1920. British edition: *My Three Years in America*. London: Skeffington, 1920.

———. "Deutschland und der Völkerbund." *Völkerbund-Fragen* 2 (July 31, 1925): 9–17.

———. "The Development of Germany as a World Power." *Supplement to The Annals of the American Academy of Political and Social Science* (January 1910): 7–14.

———. "Eine Engländerin über die Frage der Schuld am Kriege." *Das Demokratische Deutschland* 5 (February 3, 1923): 97–99.

———. *Erinnerungen und Briefe*. Zürich: Polygraphischer Verlag, 1936. U.S. edition: *The Memoirs of Count Bernstorff*. Translated by Eric Sutton. New York: Random House, 1936. British edition: *The Memoirs of Count Bernstorff*. Translated by Eric Sutton. London: W. Heinemann, 1936.

———. "Gedanken des Verfassungstages." *Deutsche Einheit* 7 (August 15, 1925): 972–89.

———. "Gedanken über die Zukunft Deutschlands." In *Deutschlands Zukunft im Urteil führender Männer*, edited by Klemens Löffler, 18–24. Halle: Heinrich Diekmann, 1921.

———. "German Social Problems." In *Proceedings of "University Day" February 22, 1911*. Philadelphia: University of Pennsylvania, 1911.

———. "Germany and the Great War." *The Independent* 79 (September 7, 1914): 333–34.

———. "Germany or France." *The Outlook* 100 (January 20, 1912): 123–25.

———. "Historical Development of the German Empire." (Speech given at The Johns Hopkins University, June 14, 1910.)

———. "Die Memoiren des Obersten House." *Deutsche Einheit* 8 (April 10, 1926): 337–42.

———. "Nochmals die Schuldfrage." *Das Demokratische Deutschland* 5 (June 2, 1923): 491–93.

———. "Nochmals Parlamentariers Wochenende." *Das Demokratische Deutschland* 5 (May 19, 1923): 477–80.

———. "Quosque tandem?" *Völkerbund-Fragen* 2 (September 15, 1925): 45–51.

———. "Social Reforms in Germany." Baccalaureate Address Delivered at the University of Wisconsin, Madison, June 19, 1910.

———. "Wilson und Page." *Deutsche Einheit* 7 (December 19, 1925): 1418–20.

———. "Wilsons Apologie." *Das Demokratische Deutschland* 5 (March 10, 1923): 217–22.

———. "Woodrow Wilson †." *Deutsche Einheit* 6 (February 16, 1924): 145–49.

Bethmann Hollweg, Theobald von. *Betrachtungen zum Weltkriege*. Vols.

1–2. Berlin: Reimar Hobbing, 1919–21.
Binder, Heinrich. *Was wir als Kriegsberichterstatter nicht sagen durften!* Munich: privately printed, 1919.
Bishop, Joseph B. *Theodore Roosevelt and His Time.* Vols. 1–2. London: Hodder & Stoughton, 1920.
Bley, Fritz. *Friedensangebot und U-Boot-Krieg.* Berlin: Reimar Hobbing, 1919.
_____. "Die Zukunft der Deutschamerikaner." In *Kriegshefte der Süddeutschen Monatshefte Oktober 1915 bis März 1916*, edited by Paul N. Cossmann, 33–38. Leipzig: Süddeutsche Monatshefte [1915–16].
Blücher, Evelyn Princess. *An English Wife in Berlin.* London: Constable, 1920.
Blumenfeld, Kurt. *Erlebte Judenfrage.* Stuttgart: Deutsche Verlags-Anstalt, 1962.
"Blundering German Professors." *The Nation* 99 (October 29, 1914): 513.
Bodenheimer, Max I. *So wurde Israel.* Frankfurt: Europäische Verlagsanstalt, 1958.
Bonn, M. J. *Amerika als Feind.* Munich: Georg Müller, 1917.
_____. *Amerika und sein Problem.* Munich: Meyer & Jessen, 1925.
_____. *Mußte es sein?* Munich: Georg Müller, 1919.
_____. *So macht man Geschichte.* Munich, Paul List, 1953.
_____. *Was will Wilson?* Munich: Georg Müller, [1918].
_____. "What Would German Victory Mean?" *Current History* 5 (October 1916): 145–47.
_____. *Wilson.* Berlin: Arbeitsgemeinschaft für staatsbürgerliche und wirtschaftliche Bildung, 1919.
Bonsal, Stephen. "Greater Germany in South America." *North American Review* 88 (January 1903): 58–67.
Bosse, Georg von. *Dr. C. J. Hexamer.* Stuttgart: Chr. Belser, 1925.
Boy-Ed, Karl. *Die Vereinigten Staaten von Amerika und der U-Boot-Krieg.* Berlin: Karl Sigismund, 1918.
_____. *Verschwörer?* Berlin: August Scherl, 1920.
Brecht, Arnold. *Aus nächster Nähe.* Stuttgart: Deutsche Verlags-Anstalt, 1966.
Brentano, Lujo. *Mein Leben im Kampf um die soziale Entwicklung Deutschlands.* Jena: Eugen Diederichs, 1931.
Bryan, William Jennings. "The Genesis of the Munitions Traffic." *Journal of Modern History* 6 (September 1934): 280–93.
_____. *The Memoirs of William Jennings Bryan.* Philadelphia: John C. Winston, 1925.
Bülow, Bernhard Fürst von. *Denkwürdigkeiten.* Vol. 2. Berlin: Ullstein, 1930.
Burian, Stephan Graf. *Drei Jahre.* Berlin: Ullstein, 1923.

Casement, Sir Roger. *The Crime against Ireland and How the War May Right It.* N.p., n.d.
Chamberlain, Houston Stewart. *Kriegsaufsätze.* Munich: F. Bruckmann, 1915.
Chatterton-Hill, George. *Irland und seine Bedeutung für Europa.* Berlin: Karl Curtius, 1917.
Chéradame, André. *The United States and Pangermania.* New York: Charles Scribner's Sons, 1918.
Churchill, Winston S. *The World Crisis 1911–1914.* London: Thornton Butterworth, 1923.
———. *The World Crisis 1915.* London: Thornton Butterworth, 1923.
———. *The World Crisis 1916–1918.* Parts 1–2. London: Thornton Butterworth, 1927.
Class, Heinrich. *Wider den Strom.* Leipzig: K. F. Koehler, 1932.
———. *Zum deutschen Kriegsziel.* Munich, J. F. Lehmann, 1917.
Cohalan, Daniel F. *England gegen Amerika.* Berlin: Karl Curtius, 1921.
Creel, George. *Rebel at Large.* New York: G. P. Putnam's Sons, 1947.
———. *The War, the World and Wilson.* New York: Harper & Brothers, 1920.
Cronon, E. David, ed. *The Cabinet Diaries of Josephus Daniels, 1913–1921.* Lincoln: University of Nebraska Press, 1963.
Curry, Charles E. *Sir Roger Casement.* Munich: Arche, 1922.
Czernin, Ottokar. *Im Weltkriege.* Berlin: Ullstein, 1919.
Daniels, Josephus. *The Wilson Era: Years of Peace 1910–1917.* Chapel Hill: University of North Carolina Press, 1944.
Davis, Arthur N. *The Kaiser I Knew.* London: Hodder & Stoughton, 1918.
Dawson, Warrington, ed. *The War Memoirs of William Graves Sharp, American Ambassador to France 1914–1919.* London: Constable, 1931.
Dayal, Har. *Forty-four Months in Germany and Turkey.* London: P. S. King & Son, 1920.
Deissmann, Adolf. *Der Krieg und die Religion.* Berlin: Carl Heymann, 1914. (Speech on November 12, 1914.)
Delbrück, Hans. "Deutschlands internationale Lage und Amerika." *Preussische Jahrbücher* 112 (April–June 1903): 184–88.
———. "Der Krieg im Februar." *Preussische Jahrbücher* 159 (January–March 1915): 566–70.
———. *Über den kriegerischen Charakter des deutschen Volkes.* Berlin: Carl Heymann, 1914. (Speech on September 11, 1914.)
Delius, Rudolf von. *Deutschlands geistige Weltmachtstellung.* Stuttgart: Die Lese, 1915.
Dernburg, Bernhard. "Germany and the Powers." *North American Review* 200 (December 1914).
———. *Search-Lights on the War.* New York: Fatherland Corporation, 1915.

———. *Von beiden Ufern.* Berlin: Kronen-Verlag, 1917.
Deutelmoser, Erhard. "Die amtliche Einwirkung auf die deutsche Öffentlichkeit im Kriege." *Die deutsche Nation* 1 (Berlin, 1919).
Devoy, John. *Recollections of an Irish Rebel.* New York: Chas. P. Young, 1929.
Dicey, Edward. "England and Germany." *Empire Review and Magazine* 18 (1910): 368–75.
Dirksen, Herbert von. *Moskau Tokio London.* Stuttgart: W. Kohlhammer, 1949.
"Dismissal and Departure of the German Ambassador." *Current History* 5 (1917): 972–74.
Dix, Arthur. *Der Weltwirtschaftskrieg.* Leipzig: S. Hirzel, 1914.
———. "Zentral-Amerika." In *Amerika,* edited by Ernst von Halle, 431–65. Hamburg: Verlag der Hamburger Börsenhalle, 1905.
Dönitz, Karl. *Die U-Bootwaffe.* Berlin: E. S. Mittler & Sohn, 1940.
Dränger, Jacob. *Nahum Goldmann.* Vol. 1. Frankfurt: Europäische Verlagsanstalt, 1959.
Dumba, Constantin. *Dreibund- und Entente-Politik in der Alten und Neuen Welt.* Zürich: Amalthea, 1931.
Eckardstein, Hermann Freiherr von. *Diplomatische Enthüllungen zum Ursprung des Weltkrieges.* Berlin: Karl Curtius, [1918].
———. *Lebenserinnerungen und politische Denkwürdigkeiten.* Vols. 1–2. Leipzig: Paul List, 1919–20.
Eckardt, Felix von. *Ein unordentliches Leben.* Düsseldorf: Econ, 1967.
Edelsheim, Franz Freiherr von. *Operationen über See.* Berlin: R. Eisenschmidt, 1901. U.S. edition: *Operations upon the Sea.* New York: Outdoor Press, 1914. British edition: *Germany's Naval Plan of Campaign against Great Britain and the United States (Operationen Über See).* Translated by Alexander Gray. London: Hodder & Stoughton, 1915.
Egan, Maurice F. *Ten Years near the German Frontier.* New York: George H. Doran, 1919.
Eiffe, Carl Cesar. *Früchte deutscher Arbeit.* Leipzig: Dieterich'sche Verlagsbuchhandlung Theodor Weicher, 1910.
Einhart [Heinrich Class]. *Deutsche Geschichte.* Leipzig: Dieterich'sche Verlagsbuchhandlung Theodor Weicher, 1909.
Ekkehard, E., ed. *Sigilla Veri. (Ph. Stauff's Semi-Kürschner.)* Vol. 1. Erfurt: U. Bodung, 1929.
Erdmann, Karl Dietrich, ed. *Kurt Riezler. Tagebücher, Aufsätze, Dokumente.* Vol. 48, Deutsche Geschichtsquellen des 19. und 20. Jahrhunderts. Göttingen: Vandenhoeck & Ruprecht, 1972.
Eucken, Rudolf. *Die sittlichen Kräfte des Krieges.* Leipzig: Emil Gräfe, 1914.
———. *Die weltgeschichtliche Bedeutung des deutschen Geistes.* Stutt-

gart: Deutsche Verlags-Anstalt, 1914.
Falcke, Horst P. *Vor dem Eintritt Amerikas in den Weltkrieg.* Dresden: Carl Reissner, 1928.
Falkenhayn, Erich von. *Die Oberste Heeresleitung 1914–1916 in ihren wichtigsten Entschliessungen.* Berlin: Ernst Siegfried Mittler & Sohn, 1920.
Faramond de Lafajole, G. M. A. *Souvenirs d'un Attaché Naval en Allemagne et en Autriche 1910–1914.* Preface by Jules Cambon. Paris: Plon, 1932.
Fiedler, Harry A. "Deutschland und die Monroe-Doktrin." *Preussische Jahrbücher* 112 (April–June 1903): 120–37.
Fleischer, Oskar. *Vom Kriege gegen die deutsche Kultur.* Frankfurt: Heinrich Keller, 1915.
Foerster, Friedrich Wilhelm. *Erlebte Weltgeschichte 1869–1953.* Nuremberg: Glock & Lutz, 1953.
_____. *Mein Kampf gegen das militaristische und nationalistische Deutschland.* Stuttgart: Verlag "Friede durch Recht," 1920.
_____. *Weltpolitik und Weltgewissen.* Munich: Verlag für Kulturpolitik, 1919.
Francke, Kuno. *Deutsche Arbeit in Amerika.* Leipzig: Felix Meiner, 1930.
_____. *A German-American's Confession of Faith.* New York: B. W. Huebsch, 1915.
_____. *The German Spirit.* New York: Henry Holt, 1916.
_____. *Germany's Fateful Hour.* Chicago: Germanistic Society of Chicago, 1914.
Friedemann, Adolf. "Die Bedeutung der Ostjuden für Deutschland." In *Kriegshefte der Süddeutschen Monatshefte Oktober 1915 bis März 1916,* edited by Paul N. Cossmann, 674–81. Leipzig: Süddeutsche Monatshefte, [1916].
Frymann, Daniel [Heinrich Class]. *Wenn ich der Kaiser wär'.* 2d ed. Leipzig: Dieterich'sche Verlagsbuchhandlung, 1912.
Fueredi, Arnold. *Deutschland und Amerika Hand in Hand.* Berlin: Concordia Deutsche Verlags-Anstalt, 1914.
Gärtner, Margarete. *Botschafterin des guten Willens.* Bonn: Athenäum, 1955.
Gaffney, T. St. John. *Breaking the Silence.* New York: Horace Liveright, 1930.
Gaunt, Sir Guy. *The Yield of the Years.* London: Hutchinson, 1940.
Gerard, James W. *Face to Face with Kaiserism.* New York: George H. Doran, 1918.
_____. *My First Eighty-three Years in America.* Garden City, N.Y.: Doubleday, 1951.
_____. *My Four Years in Germany.* London: Hodder & Stoughton, 1917.

Gibson, Hugh. *A Diplomatic Diary*. London: Hodder & Stoughton, 1917.
———. *A Journal from Our Legation in Belgium*. Garden City, N.Y.: Doubleday, Page, 1917.
Gierke, Otto von. *Krieg und Kultur*. Berlin: Carl Heymann, 1914. (Speech on September 18, 1914.)
Goebel, Julius. *Das Deutschtum in den Vereinigten Staaten von Nord-Amerika*. Munich: J. F. Lehmann, 1904. (Edited by Alldeutscher Verband as 16th brochure, *Der Kampf um das Deutschtum*.)
Goldmann, Nahum. *Staatsmann ohne Staat*. Cologne: Kiepenheuer & Witsch, 1970.
Goltz, Colmar Freiherr von der. *Denkwürdigkeiten*. Edited by Friedrich Freiherr von der Goltz and Wolfgang Foerster. Berlin: E. S. Mittler & Sohn, 1929.
Goltz, Horst von der. *My Adventures as a German Secret Service Agent*. London: Cassel, 1918.
Graves, Armgaard Karl. *The Secrets of the German War Office*. London: T. Werner Laurie, 1915.
Grew, Joseph C. *Turbulent Era*. Edited by Walther Johnson. Vol. 1. Boston: Houghton Mifflin, 1952.
Grey, Edward (Viscount Grey of Fallodon). *Twenty-Five Years 1892–1916*. Vol. 2. London: Hodder & Stoughton, 1925.
Groener, Wilhelm. *Lebenserinnerungen*. Edited by F. Freiherr Hiller von Gaertringen. Göttingen: Vandenhoeck & Ruprecht, 1957.
Grotthuss, J. E. Freiherr von. "Zwei Botschafter und verschiedene Gedanken." *Der Türmer* 19 (April 1917): 77–87.
Guttmann, Bernhard. *Schattenriss einer Generation 1888–1919*. Stuttgart: K. F. Koehler, 1950.
Gwynn, Stephen, ed. *The Letters and Friendships of Sir Cecil Spring Rice*. Vols. 1–2. London: Constable, 1929.
Haeckel, Ernst, and Rudolf Eucken. "An Appeal from *Eucken and Haeckel*." *The Independent* 79 (September 28, 1914): 439.
Hagedorn, Hermann. *The Hyphenated Family*. New York: Macmillan, 1960.
Hale, William Bayard. *The Exportation of Arms and Munitions of War*. In *Thou Shalt Not Kill*, edited by The Organization of American Women for Strict Neutrality, 5–20. N.p., 1915.
Hall, Thomas C. "Eine amerikanische Charakteristik der englischen Presse." In *Nordamerika und Deutschland*, edited by Eduard Meyer, 71–83. Berlin: Karl Curtius, 1915.
Hall, Sir William Reginald, and Amos J. Peaslee. *Three Wars with Germany*. Edited by Joseph P. Sims. New York: G. P. Putnam's Sons, 1944.
Hammann, Otto. *Bilder aus der letzten Kaiserzeit*. Berlin: Reimar Hobbing, 1922.
———. *Um den Kaiser*. Berlin: Reimar Hobbing, 1919.
———. *Zur Vorgeschichte des Weltkrieges*. Berlin: Reimar Hobbing, 1918.

Hanssen, Hans Peter. *Diary of a Dying Empire*. Bloomington: Indiana University Press, 1955. (Originally published in the Danish language in Copenhagen in 1924.)

Harden, Maximilian. "Am tausendsten Tag." *Die Zukunft*, April 28, 1917.

Harnack, Adolf von. *An der Schwelle des dritten Kriegsjahrs*. Berlin: Weidmann, 1916. (Speech on August 1, 1916.)

———. *Was wir schon gewonnen haben und was wir noch gewinnen müssen*. Berlin: Carl Heymann, 1914. (Speech on September 29, 1914.)

Harris, Frank. *Latest Contemporary Portraits*. New York: Macaulay, 1927.

Harvey, George. "Dealing with Diplomatic Misfits." *North American Review* (October 1915): 497–99.

Helfferich, Emil. *Ein Leben*. Vol. 2. Typescript without date. (University of Göttingen library.)

Helfferich, Karl. *Der Weltkrieg*. Vols. 1–2 in 1 vol. Berlin: Ullstein, 1920.

Hendrick, Burton J. *The Life and Letters of Walter H. Page*. Vols. 1–3. London: William Heinemann, 1925–26.

Hentig, Werner Otto von. *Meine Diplomatenfahrt ins verschlossene Land*. Berlin: Ullstein, 1918.

———. *Mein Leben—Eine Dienstreise*. 2d ed. Göttingen: Vandenhoeck & Ruprecht, 1963.

Hershey, Amos S. "The Deutschland." *The American Journal of International Law* 10 (October 1916): 852–53.

Hertling, Karl Graf von. *Ein Jahr in der Reichskanzlei*. Freiburg: Herdersche Verlagsbuchhandlung, 1919.

Herz, Ludwig. "Marineattachés." *Deutsche Einheit* 7 (January 31, 1925): 110–14.

Heuss, Theodor. *Erinnerungen 1905–1933*. Frankfurt: Fischer, 1965.

Hill, David J. "The Cessation of Diplomatic Relations with Germany." *American Journal of International Law* 11 (1917): 380–84.

Hill, Leonidas E., ed. *Die Weizsäcker Papiere 1933–1950*. Frankfurt: Ullstein (Propyläen), 1974.

Hillard, Gustav [Steinbömer, Gustav]. *Herren und Narren der Welt*. 2d ed. Munich: Paul List, 1955.

Hindenburg, Paul von. *Aus meinem Leben*. Leipzig: S. Hirzel, 1920.

Hinton, Arthur R. "Shall We Annex Northern Mexico?" *The Independent* 79 (July 27, 1914): 124ff.

Hintze, Otto; Friedrich Meinecke; Hermann Oncken; and Hermann Schumacher, eds. *Deutschland und der Weltkrieg*. Vols. 1–2. Leipzig: B. G. Teubner, 1916.

[Hitler, Adolf]. *Hitlers Zweites Buch*. Vol. 7, Quellen und Darstellungen zur Zeitgeschichte, edited by Gerhard L. Weinberg. Stuttgart: Deutsche Verlagsanstalt, 1961.

Hölzle, Erwin. Review of Bernstorff, *Erinnerungen und Briefe*. *Historische Zeitschrift* 158 (1938): 381–83.

Hohler, Sir Thomas. *Diplomatic Petrel*. London: John Murray, 1942.
Holborn, Hajo, ed. *Aufzeichnungen und Erinnerungen aus dem Leben des Botschafters Joseph Maria von Radowitz*. Vols. 1–2. Stuttgart: Deutsche Verlags-Anstalt, 1925.
Holt, W. Stull. *Treaties Defeated by the Senate*. Baltimore: Johns Hopkins Press, 1933.
Hoover, Herbert. *The Memoirs of Herbert Hoover. Years of Adventure 1874–1920*. New York: Macmillan, 1951.
Hosse, Karl. *Das Eingreifen der Vereinigten Staaten in den Weltkrieg und seine Bedeutung für die militärische Lage*. Berlin: Kriegspresseamt, 1917.
Houston, David F. *Eight Years with Wilson's Cabinet, 1913–1920*. Vols. 1–2. London: William Heinemann, 1926.
Huldermann, Bernhard. *Albert Ballin*. Oldenburg: Gerhard Stalling, 1922.
Hutten-Czapski, Bogdan Graf von. *Sechzig Jahre Politik und Gesellschaft*. Vols. 1–2. Berlin: E. S. Mittler & Sohn, 1936.
Ignotus. "Captain von Papen's Ditty Box." *Living Age* (1920): 384–89.
Institut für Marxismus-Leninismus beim Zentralkommittee der Sozialistischen Einheitspartei Deutschlands. *Spartakusbriefe*. Berlin: Dietz, 1958.
Jäckh, Ernst, ed. *Kiderlen-Wächter der Staatsmann und Mensch*. Vol. 2. Stuttgart: Deutsche Verlags-Anstalt, 1924.
Jagow, G. von. *Ursachen und Ausbruch des Weltkrieges*. Berlin: Reimar Hobbing, 1919.
Jahresberichte für Deutsche Geschichte 12 (1936). (Review of Bernstorff, *Erinnerungen und Briefe*.)
Jones, John P. *The German Spy in America*. London: Hutchinson, 1917.
Jones, John P., and Paul M. Hollister. *The German Secret Service in America 1914–1918*. Boston: Small, Maynard, 1918.
Jong van Beek en Donk, B. de. "Der Bryansche Friedensplan." *Zeitschrift für Völkerrecht und Bundesstaatsrecht* 7 (1913): 533–53.
Jünger, Karl. *Deutsch-Amerika mobil . . . !* Berlin: B. Behrs (F. Feddersen), 1915.
Jung, Arthur. *Die 7. Grossmacht im Kriege*. Berlin: Reichsverlag, 1916.
Jusserand, J. A. A. J. *Le Sentiment américain pendant la guerre*. Paris: Payot, 1931.
Kahan, I. "Die nationalen Forderungen des jüdischen Volkes in Russland und seine politischen Parteien." *Jeschurun* 4 (July–August 1917): 353–73.
Kahl, Wilhelm. *Vom Recht zum Kriege und vom Siegespreis*. Berlin: Carl Heymann, 1914. (Speech on October 9, 1914.)
Kessler, Harry Graf. *Tagebücher 1918–1937*. Edited by Wolfgang Pfeiffer-Belli. Frankfurt: Insel, 1961.
King, Rosa E. *Tempest over Mexico*. London: Methuen, 1936.
König, Paul. *Die Fahrt der Deutschland*. Berlin: Ullstein, 1916.

Krumm Heller, Arnold. *Carranzas Mexiko*. Halle: Otto Thiele, 1917.
_____. *Für Freiheit und Recht*. Halle: Otto Thiele, 1918.
Kühlmann, Richard von. *Die Diplomaten*. Berlin: Reimar Hobbing, 1939.
_____. *Erinnerungen*. Heidelberg: Lambert Schneider, 1948.
Kühnemann, Eugen. *Deutschland und Amerika*. Munich: C. H. Beck'sche Verlagsbuchhandlung, 1917.
_____. *Reden an Deutsch-Amerika*. n.d. [publ. by German propagandists in U.S.]
_____. *Vom Weltreich des deutschen Geistes*. Munich: C. H. Beck'sche Verlagsbuchhandlung, 1914.
Lammasch, Heinrich. "Unjustifiable War and the Means to Avoid It." *The American Journal of International Law* 10 (October 1916): 689–705.
Lamprecht, Karl. *Americana*. Freiburg: Hermann Heyfelder, 1908.
_____. *Krieg und Kultur*. Leipzig: S. Hirzel, 1914.
Lancken Wakenitz, Oscar Freiherr von der. *Meine dreissig Dienstjahre 1888–1918*. Berlin: Verlag für Kulturpolitik, 1931.
Lansing, Robert. *War Memoirs of Robert Lansing*. New York: Bobbs Merrill, 1935.
Lechartier, G. *Intrigues et Diplomaties à Washington (1914–1917)*. Paris: Plon, 1918.
Leo, R. *Das Ostjudenproblem und Palästina*. Pro Palästina, no. 6. Berlin: Deutsches Komitee zur Förderung der jüdischen Palästinasiedlung, 1919.
Lichnowsky, Karl Max Fürst. *Auf dem Wege zum Abgrund*. Vols. 1–2. Dresden: Carl Reissner, 1927.
Lichtheim, Richard. *Die Geschichte des deutschen Zionismus*. Jerusalem: Rubin Mass, 1954.
_____. *Rückkehr*. Stuttgart: Deutsche Verlags-Anstalt, 1970.
Liebert, Erich von. "Ziele der deutschen Kolonial- und Auswanderungspolitik." In *Zwanzig Jahre alldeutscher Arbeit und Kämpfe*, edited by Alldeutscher Verband. Leipzig: Dieterich'sche Verlagsbuchhandlung Theodor Weicher, 1910.
Liebmann, Otto, ed. *Die Juristische Fakultät der Universität Berlin*. Berlin: Otto Liebmann, 1910.
Link, Arthur S., ed. *The Papers of Woodrow Wilson*. Vols. 27–42. Princeton, N.J.: Princeton University Press, 1979–83.
A List of Neutral Ships Sunk by the Germans from August 8th, 1914, to April 26th, 1917. London: Alabaster, Passmore & Sons, 1917.
Liszt, Franz von. *Von der Nibelungentreue*. Berlin: Carl Heymann, 1914. (Speech on November 18, 1914.)
Lloyd George, David. *War Memoirs*. Vols. 1–3. London: Ivor Nicholson & Watson, 1933–34.
Lodge, Henry Cabot, ed. *Selections from the Correspondence of Theodore Roosevelt and Henry Cabot Lodge 1884–1918*. Vol. 2. New York: Charles Scribner's Sons, 1925.

———. *The Senate and the League of Nations*. New York: Charles Scribner's Sons, 1925.
Ludendorff, Erich. *Meine Kriegserinnerungen 1914–1918*. Berlin: Ernst Siegfried Mittler & Sohn, 1919.
Ludwig, Emil. *Geschenke des Lebens*. Berlin: Ernst Rowohlt, 1931.
Lützow, Heinrich Graf von. *Im diplomatischen Dienst der k. u. k. Monarchie*. Edited by Peter Hohenbalken. Munich: R. Oldenbourg, 1971.
Der Lusitania Fall im Urteile von deutschen Gelehrten. Breslau: J. U. Kern's Verlag Max Müller, 1915.
Luxburg, Karl Graf. *Nachdenkliche Erinnerung*. Schloss Aschach: privately published, 1953.
Lynch, Florence M. *The Mystery Man of Banna Strand: The Life and Death of Captain Robert Monteith*. New York: Vantage Press, 1959.
McAdoo, William Gibbs. *Crowded Years: The Reminiscences of William Gibbs McAdoo*. Boston: Houghton Mifflin, 1931.
McGuire, James K. *The King, the Kaiser and Irish Freedom*. New York: Devin-Adair, 1915.
Mahan, Alfred Thayer. *The Influence of Sea Power upon History, 1660–1783*. London: Methuen, 1965.
Masaryk, Thomas Garrigue. *Die Welt-Revolution*. Berlin: Erich Reiss, 1925.
Maugham, W. Somerset. *The Summing Up*. Garden City, N.Y.: Doubleday, 1950.
Max M. Warburg. Glückstadt: J. J. Augustin, n.d.
Meinecke, Friedrich. *Friedrich Meinecke Werke*. Edited by Ludwig Dehio and Peter Classen. Vol. 4, *Ausgewählter Briefwechsel*, edited by Hans Herzfeld, Carl Hinrichs, and Walther Hofer. Stuttgart: K. F. Koehler, 1962.
———. *Die deutsche Erhebung von 1914*. Stuttgart: J. G. Cotta'sche Buchhandlung Nachfolger, 1915.
———. *Erlebtes 1862–1919*. Stuttgart: K. F. Koehler, 1964.
———. *Nach der Revolution*. Munich: R. Oldenbourg, 1919.
———. *Preussen und Deutschland im 19. und 20. Jahrhundert*. Munich: R. Oldenbourg, 1918.
———. *Probleme des Weltkriegs*. Munich: R. Oldenbourg, 1917.
———. *Strassburg, Freiburg, Berlin 1901–1919*. Stuttgart: K. F. Koehler, 1949.
———. "Der Ursprung des Weltkrieges." In *Zum geschichtlichen Verständnis des grossen Krieges*. Berlin: Karl Sigismund, 1916.
Melamed, S. M. "Die eingewanderten Juden in Amerika." In *Kriegshefte der Süddeutschen Monatshefte Oktober 1915 bis März 1916*, edited by Paul N. Cossmann, 747–56. Munich: Süddeutsche Monatshefte, 1916.

Meyer, Antonie, ed. *Der Casement-Prozess und seine Ursachen*. Berlin: Karl Curtius, [1916].
Meyer, Eduard. *Der amerikanische Kongress und der Weltkrieg*. Berlin: Karl Curtius, 1917.
_____. *England*. Stuttgart: J. G. Cotta'sche Buchhandlung Nachfolger, 1915.
_____. *Nordamerika und Deutschland*. Berlin: Karl Curtius, 1915.
_____. *Die Vereinigten Staaten von Amerika*. Frankfurt: Heinrich Keller, 1920.
_____. *Weltgeschichte und Weltkrieg*. Stuttgart: J. G. Cotta'sche Buchhandlung Nachfolger, 1916.
Meyer, Kuno. *Der Ententebund der Wissenschaft*. Berlin: Karl Curtius, [1917].
Michaelis, Georg. *Für Staat und Volk*. Berlin: Furche, 1922.
Michelsen, Andreas. *Der U-Bootkrieg 1914–1918*. Leipzig: K. F. Koehler, 1925.
Monteith, Robert. *Casement's Last Adventure*. Rev. ed. Dublin: Michael F. Moynihan, 1953.
Morison, Elting, E., ed. *The Letters of Theodore Roosevelt*. Vols. 1–8. Cambridge: Harvard University Press, 1951–54.
Münsterberg, Hugo. *Amerika und der Weltkrieg*. Leipzig: Johann Ambrosius Barth, 1915.
_____. *The Peace and America*. Leipzig: Bernhard Tauchnitz, 1915.
_____. *The War in America*. New York: D. Appleton, 1914.
Münsterberg, Margaret. *Hugo Münsterberg. His Life and Work*. New York: D. Appleton, 1922.
Nadolny, Rudolf. *Mein Beitrag*. Wiesbaden: Limes, 1955.
"The New German Ambassador in Washington." *Current Literature* 46 (February 1909): 151–54.
Nicolai, Walter. *Geheime Mächte*. Leipzig: K. F. Koehler, 1923.
_____. *Nachrichtendienst, Presse und Volksstimmung im Weltkrieg*. Berlin: Ernst Siegfried Mittler & Sohn, 1920.
Noyes, Alfred. *The Accusing Ghost of Justice for Casement*. London: Victor Gollancz, 1957.
O'Brien, William, and Desmond Ryan. *Devoy's Post Bag 1871–1928*. Vols. 1–2. Dublin: C. J. Fallon, 1948–53.
Ohlinger, Gustavus. *The German Conspiracy in American Education*. New York: George H. Doran, 1919.
Oldenburg-Januschau, Elard von. *Erinnerungen*. Leipzig: Koehler & Amelang, 1936.
O'Leary, Jeremiah. *A German-American War*. New York: American Truth Society, [1915].
_____. *My Political Trial and Experiences*. New York: Jefferson, 1919.
Oncken, Hermann. "Amerika und die grossen Mächte." In *Historisch-*

politische Aufsätze und Reden, by H. Oncken. Vol. 1. Munich: R. Oldenbourg, 1914.

———. "Die deutsche Auswanderung nach Amerika und das Deutschamerikanertum vom 17. Jahrhundert bis zur Gegenwart." In *Historisch-politische Aufsätze und Reden*, by H. Oncken. Vol. 1. Munich: R. Oldenbourg, 1914.

Oppenheimer, Franz. *Erlebtes, Erstrebtes, Erreichtes*. Düsseldorf: Joseph Melzer, 1964.

O'Shaughnessy, Edith. *Intimate Pages of Mexican History*. New York: George H. Doran, 1920.

P. "Influence de la guerre sur les traités d'enquête et d'arbitrage conclus par les États-Unis et sur les rapports entre ces pays et les puissances européennes belligérantes." *Journal du Droit International* 43 (1916): 482–85.

Papen, Franz von. *Der Wahrheit eine Gasse*. Munich: Paul List, 1952.

Parker, Sir Gilbert. "The United States and the War." *Harper's Magazine* 136 (March 1918): 521–31.

Penck, Albrecht. *U.S. Amerika*. Stuttgart: J. Engelhorns Nachfolger, 1917.

Peters, Carl. "Deutschland und Nordamerika." In *Zum Weltkrieg*, by Carl Peters, 169–71. Hamburg: Rüsch'sche Verlagsbuchhandlung, 1917.

Pflug-Harttung, Julius von. *Der Kampf um die Freiheit der Meere. Trafalgar. Skagerrak*. Berlin: R. Eisenschmidt, 1917.

Phillips, William. *Ventures in Diplomacy*. Boston: Beacon, 1952.

Plessen, Leopold [von]. *Begegnungen*. Privately published, 1964.

Pohl, Hugo von. *Aus Aufzeichnungen und Briefen während der Kriegszeit*. Berlin: Karl Sigismund, 1920.

Prittwitz und Gaffron, Friedrich W. von. *Deutschland und die Vereinigten Staaten seit dem Weltkrieg*. Leipzig: B. G. Teubner, 1934.

———. *Zwischen Petersburg und Washington*. Munich: Isar, 1952.

Raeder, Erich. *Mein Leben*. Vol. 1. Tübingen: Fritz Schlichtenmayer, 1956.

Rathenau, Walther. *Tagebuch 1907–1922*. Privately published, 1930.

———. *Walther Rathenau 1867–1922*. Privately published, 1932.

Reeves, Jesse S. "The Prussian-American Treaties." *American Journal of International Law* 11 (1917): 475–510.

———. "Submarines and Innocent Passage." *American Journal of International Law* 11 (1917): 147–53.

Reventlow, Graf Ernst zu. *Deutschlands auswärtige Politik 1888–1914*. Berlin: Ernst Siegfried Mittler & Sohn, 1916.

———. "Die treibenden Kräfte der britischen Politik," In *Zum geschichtlichen Verständnis des grossen Krieges*. Berlin: Karl Sigismund, 1916.

Rheinbaben, Werner Freiherr von. *Kaiser Kanzler Präsidenten. Erinnerungen*. Mainz: v. Hase & Koehler, 1968.

———. "Verpasste Gelegenheiten." *Hannoversche Allgemeine Zeitung* (November 23, 1962): 8.

Riehl, Alois. *1813–Fichte–1914*. Berlin: Carl Heymann, 1914. (Speech on October 23, 1914.)

Riesser, Hans E. *Haben die deutschen Diplomaten versagt?* Bonn: H. Bouvier, 1959.

Rintelen, Franz. *The Dark Invader*. New York: Macmillan, 1933.

———. *The Return of the Dark Invader*. London: Lovat Dickson & Thompson, 1935.

Rintelen, Paul and Jost. *Das Geschlecht der Rintelen*. Freising: Bode, 1977.

Roethe, Gustav. *Wir Deutschen und der Krieg*. Berlin: Carl Heymann, 1914. (Speech on September 3, 1914.)

Rohrbach, Paul. *Der Krieg und die deutsche Politik*. Dresden: "Das Grössere Deutschland," 1914.

Rolland, Romain. *Zwischen den Völkern*. Vols. 1–2. Stuttgart: Deutsche Verlags-Anstalt, 1954–55.

Rolland. Edited by Klaus Dahme. Munich: Süddeutscher Verlag, 1967. (Catalog of Exhibition on Romain Rolland.)

Ronge, Max. *Kriegs- und Industrie-Spionage*. Zürich: Amalthea, 1930.

Roosevelt, Eleanor. *This Is My Story*. New York: Harper & Brothers, 1937.

Rose, Hans. *Auftauchen!* Essen: Essener Verlagsanstalt, 1939.

Rosen, Friedrich. *Aus einem diplomatischen Wanderleben*. Vols. 1–2. Berlin: Transmare, 1931–32. Vols. 3–4. Wiesbaden: Limes, 1959.

Rothenfelder, Franz [Ferdinand Hansen]. *Casement in Deutschland*. Augsburg: Reichel, 1917.

———. *New Yorker Kampf um Wahrheit und Frieden*. Augsburg: J. P. Himmer, 1917.

Roy, Manabendra Nath. *M. N. Roy's Memoirs*. Bombay: Allied Publishers Private Ltd., 1964.

Schellenberg, Walter. *Memoiren*. Edited by Gita Petersen. Cologne: Verlag für Politik und Wirtschaft, 1959.

Schiemann, Theodor. *Die Achillesferse Englands*. Berlin: Georg Reimer, 1914.

———. *Deutschland und die grosse Politik anno 1908*. Berlin: Georg Reimer, 1909.

———. *Deutschland und die grosse Politik anno 1909*. Berlin: Georg Reimer, 1910.

———. *Deutschland und die grosse Politik anno 1910*. Berlin: Georg Reimer, 1911.

———. *Deutschland und die grosse Politik anno 1911*. Berlin: Georg Reimer, 1912.

———. *Deutschland und die grosse Politik anno 1914*. Berlin: Georg Reimer, 1915.

Schnee, Heinrich. *Als letzter Gouveneur in Deutsch-Ostafrika*. Edited by Ada Schnee. Heidelberg: Quelle & Meyer, 1964.

Schoen, Wilhelm Freiherr von. *Erlebtes*. Stuttgart: Deutsche Verlags-Anstalt, 1921.
Schwabach, Paul H. von. *Aus meinen Akten*. Berlin: N.p., 1927.
Scott, James Brown. "The Execution of Captain Fryatt." *American Journal of International Law* 10 (October 1916): 865–77.
Sering, Max. *Die Ursachen und die weltgeschichtliche Bedeutung des Krieges*. Berlin: Carl Heymann, 1914. (Speech on November 6, 1914.)
Seymour, Charles. Review of *Memoirs of Count Bernstorff*. *The Mississippi Historical Review* 23 (June 1936–March 1937): 589–90.
──────, ed. *The Intimate Papers of Colonel House*. Vols. 1–4. London: Ernest Benn, 1926–28.
Sharp, Joseph. *Let There Be Light*. Leipzig: privately published, 1917.
Sharp, William Graves. *War Memoirs of William Graves Sharp, American Ambassador to France 1914–1919*. Edited by Warrington Dawson. London: Constable, 1931.
Skaggs, William H. *German Conspiracies in America*. London: T. Fisher Unwin, 1915.
Smith, Munroe. "American Diplomacy in the European War." *Political Science Quarterly* 31 (1916): 481–518.
Somerville, Boyle. "The Fredrik [sic] VIII at Halifax." *The Living Age* (December 6, 1919): 587–94.
Sperry, Earl E. *German Plots and Intrigues in the United States During the Period of Our Neutrality*. Red, White and Blue Series, no. 10. Washington, D.C.: Committee on Public Information, 1918.
Spindler, Karl. *The Mystery of the Casement Ship*. Berlin: Kribe, 1931.
Stern-Rubarth, Edgar. *Aus zuverlässiger Quellen verlautet*. Stuttgart: W. Kohlhammer, 1964.
Stockhausen, Max von. *Sechs Jahre Reichskanzlei*. Edited by W. Görlitz. Bonn, 1954.
Strantz, Kurd von. "Die irische Hilfe für Deutschland." *Hammer* 14 (February 1915): 61.
Straus, Oscar S. *Under Four Administrations from Cleveland to Taft*. Boston: Houghton Mifflin, 1922.
Strother, French. *Fighting Germany's Spies*. Garden City, N.Y.: Doubleday, Page, 1918.
Stutterheim, Kurt Freiherr von. *Die Majestät des Gewissens*. Hamburg: Hans Christians, 1962.
Taft, William Howard. *The Proposed Arbitration Treaties with Great Britain and France*. Judicial Settlement of International Disputes, no. 7. Baltimore: American Society for Judicial Settlement of International Disputes, 1912.
──────. *The United States and Peace*. London: John Murray, 1914.
Tannenberg, Richard. *Gross-Deutschland*. Leipzig: Bruno Volger, 1911.

Thayer, William Roscoe. *The Life and Letters of John Hay.* Vols. 1–2. Boston: Houghton Mifflin, 1914.
Thimme, Friedrich, ed. *Front wider Bülow.* Munich: F. Bruckmann, 1931.
Thomson, Basil. *My Experiences at Scotland Yard.* Garden City, N.Y.: Doubleday, Page, 1923.
Thwaites, Norman. *Velvet and Vinegar.* London: Grayson & Grayson, 1932.
The Times History of the War. Vol. 5. London: The Times, 1915.
Tirpitz, Alfred von. *Erinnerungen.* Leipzig: K. F. Koehler, 1919.
Toller, Ernst. *Eine Jugend in Deutschland.* Amsterdam: Querido, 1933.
Treitschke, Heinrich von. *Politik.* Vols. 1–2. Leipzig: S. Hirzel, 1898.
Treviranus, Gottfried Reinhold. *Das Ende von Weimar.* Düsseldorf: Econ, 1968.
Troeltsch, Ernst. *Der Kulturkrieg.* Berlin: Carl Heymann, 1915. (Speech on July 1, 1915.)
Tumulty, Joseph P. *Woodrow Wilson as I Know Him.* Garden City, N.Y.: Doubleday, Page, 1921.
Tunney, Thomas J. *Throttled! The Detection of the German and Anarchist Bomb Plotters.* Boston: Small, Maynard, 1919.
Valentiner, Max. *300 000 Tonnen versenkt!* Berlin: Ullstein, 1917.
———. *Der Schrecken der Meere.* Zürich: Amalthea, 1931.
———. *U 38. Wikingerfahrten eines deutschen U-Bootes.* Berlin: Ullstein, 1934.
Viereck, George S. *Spreading Germs of Hate.* New York: Horace Liveright, 1930.
———. *The Strangest Friendship in History. Woodrow Wilson and Colonel House.* New York: Liveright, 1932.
Vierhaus, Rudolf, ed. *Das Tagebuch der Baronin Spitzemberg.* Göttingen: Vandenhoeck & Ruprecht, 1963.
Vietsch, Eberhard von, ed. *Gegen die Unvernunft. Der Briefwechsel zwischen Paul Graf Wolff Metternich und Wilhelm Solf 1915–1918 mit zwei Briefen Albert Ballins.* Bremen: Carl Schünemann, 1964.
Voska, Emanuel Victor, and Will Irwin. *Spy and Counterspy.* New York: Doubleday, Doran, 1940.
Voss, Ernst. *Vier Jahrzehnte in Amerika.* Stuttgart: Deutsche Verlags-Anstalt, 1929.
Wagner, Adolph. *Gegen England.* Berlin: Boll u. Pickardt, 1914.
———. *Vom Territorialstaat zur Weltmacht.* Berlin: Gustav Schade, 1900.
Warburg, Eric M., ed. *Max M. Warburg.* Hamburg: Privately printed, 1967.
Warburg, Max M. *Aus meinen Aufzeichnungen.* New York: Privately printed, 1952. Copyright Eric M. Warburg.
Weber, Marianne. *Max Weber. Ein Lebensbild.* Tübingen: J. C. B. Mohr (Paul Siebeck), 1926.

Weber, Max. *Gesammelte politische Schriften*. Munich: Drei Masken, 1921.
Wehde, Albert. *Since Leaving Home*. Chicago: Tremonia, 1923.
Weizmann, Chaim. *Trial and Error*. London: Hamish Hamilton, 1950.
Westarp, Kuno Graf von. *Konservative Politik im letzten Jahrzehnt des Kaiserreiches*. Vol. 2. Berlin: Deutsche Verlagsgesellschaft, 1935.
Widenmann, Wilhelm. *Marine-Attaché an der kaiserlich-deutschen Botschaft in London 1907–1912*. Göttingen: Musterschmidt, 1952.
Wile, Frederic William. *Men Around the Kaiser*. London: William Heinemann, 1914.
Wilhelm II. *Ereignisse und Gestalten aus den Jahren 1878–1918*. Leipzig: K. F. Koehler, 1922.
Wilson, Henry Lane. *Diplomatic Episodes in Mexico, Belgium and Chile*. London: A. M. Philpot, 1927.
――――. "Errors with Reference to Mexico and Events That Have Occurred There." *International Relations of the United States. The Annals* 54 (July 1914): 148–61.
Wintzer, Wilhelm. *Die Deutschen im tropischen Amerika*. Der Kampf um das Deutschtum, no. 15. Munich: J. F. Lehmann, 1900.
Witte, Emil. *Aus einer deutschen Botschaft*. Leipzig: Zeitbilder-Verlag, 1907.
W. J. [J. Wohlgemuth]. "Deutschland und Ostjudenfrage." *Jeschurun* 3 (January 1916): 1–19.
Wolff, Theodor. *Der Marsch durch zwei Jahrzehnte*. Amsterdam: Allert de Lange, 1936.
Woolsey, T. S. "The Von Igel Case." *American Journal of International Law* 10 (July 1916): 592–93.
Wundt, Wilhelm. "Deutschland im Lichte des neutralen und des feindlichen Auslandes." Off-print from *Scientia* 9 (1915).
――――. *Über den wahrhaften Krieg*. Leipzig: Alfred Kröner, 1914. (Speech on September 10, 1914.)
Yardley, Herbert O. *The American Black Chamber*. London: Faber & Faber, 1931.
Young, Bert Edward. "A Study of Sources. English Influence in Count von Bernstorff's Oration." *The Nation* 99 (December 24, 1914): 737.
Zimmermann, Arthur. "Fürst Bülows Kritik am Auswärtigen Amt." In *Front wider Bülow*, edited by Friedrich Thimme, 221–34. Munich: F. Bruckmann, 1931.
Zweig, Stefan. *Die Welt von Gestern*. Stockholm: Bermann-Fischer, 1944. Reprint. Frankfurt: Fischer, 1970.

IV. BOOKS, ARTICLES, AND DISSERTATIONS

Abrams, Ray H. *Preachers Present Arms.* New York: Round Table Press, 1933.
Achterberg, Erich. *Berliner Hochfinanz.* Frankfurt: Fritz Knapp, 1965.
Adamic, Louis. *Dynamite.* New York: Viking, 1931.
Adams, Henry M. *Prussian-American Relations, 1775–1871.* Cleveland: Press of Western Reserve University, 1960.
Adler, Cyrus, and Aaron M. Margalith. *With Firmness in the Right.* New York: The American Jewish Committee, 1946.
Adler, H. G. *Die Juden in Deutschland.* Munich: Kösel, 1961.
Adler-Rudel, S. "East-European Jewish Workers in Germany." Publications of the Leo Baeck Institute of Jews from Germany. *Year Book* 2 (1957): 136–65.
———. *Ostjuden in Deutschland 1880–1940.* Tübingen: J. C. B. Mohr, 1959.
Ahlswede, Dieter. "Friedensbemühungen zwischen dem deutschen Reich und Grossbritannien 1914–1918." Ph.D. diss., Universität Bonn, 1959.
Albertini, Luigi. *The Origins of the War of 1914.* Vols. 1–3. London: Oxford University Press, 1967.
Alishan, M. "Berlin to India." *Asia* 18 (May 1918): 359–68.
Allen, H. C. *Great Britain and the United States.* London: Odhams, 1954.
Alperovich, M. S. "La Historia de las relaciones entre México y Estados Unidos en la historigrafia mexicana de postguerra." In *Cuatro estudios sovieticos*, edited by M. S. Alperovich, B. T. Rudenko, and N. M. Lavrov, 127–56. Colleccion Reforma-Revolución, no. 2. Mexico: Los Insurgentes, 1960.
Alphaud, Gabriel. *L'Action allemande aux États-Unis.* Paris: Payot, 1915.
Altschuler, Glenn C. *Andrew D. White—Educator, Historian, Diplomat.* Ithaca: Cornell University Press, 1979.
Ambrosius, Lloyd. "The United States and the Weimar Republic: America's Response to the German Problem." In *Perspectives in American Diplomacy*, edited by Jules Davids, 78–104. New York: Arno, 1976.
Andrew, Christopher. *Secret Service.* London: William Heinemann, 1985.
Angermann, Erich. "Ein Wendepunkt in der Geschichte der Monroe-Doktrin und der deutsch-amerikanischen Beziehungen." *Jahrbuch für Amerikastudien* 3 (1958): 22–58.
App, Austin J. "The Germans." In *The Immigrants' Influence on Wilson's Peace Policies*, edited by Joseph P. O'Grady, 30–55. Lexington: University Press of Kentucky, 1967.
Appuhn, Ch. "L'Ambassade du Comte Bernstorff à Washington." *Revue d'histoire de la Guerre Mondiale* 3 (October 1925): 297–329.
Argov, Daniel. *Moderates and Extremists in the Indian Nationalist Movement 1883–1920.* London: Asia Publishing House, 1967.

Assmann, Kurt. *Deutsche Seestrategie in zwei Weltkriegen*. Heidelberg: Vohwinkel, 1957.
———. "Gedanken über die Probleme der deutschen Seekriegführung im Weltkriege." *Militärwissenschaftliche Rundschau* 4 (1939): 187–203, 315–39, 500–528.
Aston, Sir George. *Secret Service*. London: Faber & Faber, 1930.
Aulard, A. (with E. Bouvier and A. Ganem). *1914–1918: Histoire politique de la Grande Guerre*. Paris: Aristide Quillet, 1924.
Baecker, Thomas. "The Arms of the *Ypiranga*: The German Side." *The Americas* 30 (July 1973): 1–17.
———. *Die deutsche Mexikopolotik 1913/14*. Berlin: Colloquium, 1971.
———. "Los Interesses militares del imperio alemán en México: 1913–1914." *Historia Mexicana* 22 (1973): 347–62.
Bailey, Thomas A. *The Man in the Street*. Gloucester: Peter Smith, 1964.
———. *Presidential Saints and Sinners*. New York: Free Press, 1981.
———. "The Sinking of the Lusitania." *American Historical Review* 41 (October 1935): 26–54.
———. *Woodrow Wilson and the Great Betrayal*. New York: Macmillan, 1947.
———. *Woodrow Wilson and the Lost Peace*. New York: Macmillan, 1947.
Bailey, Thomas A., and Paul B. Ryan. *The Lusitania Disaster*. New York: Free Press, 1975.
Baldwin, Hanson. *World War I*. London: Hutchinson, 1963.
Barany, George. "The Magyars." In *The Immigrants' Influence on Wilson's Peace Policies*, edited by Joseph P. O'Grady, 141–72. Lexington: University Press of Kentucky, 1967.
Barkhausen, Hans. *Filmpropaganda für Deutschland im Ersten und Zweiten Weltkrieg*. Hildesheim: Olms, 1982.
Barooah, Nirode Kumar. *India and the Official Germany, 1886–1914*. Frankfurt/Bern: Lang, 1977.
Barry, Colman J. *The Catholic Church and German Americans*. Milwaukee: Bruce, 1953.
Bartlett, Ruhl J. *The League to Enforce Peace*. Chapel Hill: University of North Carolina Press, 1944.
Basler, Werner. *Deutschlands Annexionspolitik in Polen und im Baltikum 1914–1918*. Berlin: Rütten & Loening, 1962.
Bass, Herbert J., ed. *America's Entry into World War I*. New York: Holt, Rinehart & Winston, 1964.
Baum, Loretta. "German Political Designs with Reference to Brazil." *Hispanic American Historical Review* 2 (1919): 586–610.
Baumgart, Winfried. *Deutschland im Zeitalter des Imperialismus (1890–1914)*. Frankfurt: Ullstein, 1972.
Beale, Howard. "Theodore Roosevelt, Wilhelm II. und die deutsch-ameri-

kanischen Beziehungen." *Die Welt als Geschichte* 14 (1954): 155–87.
Beard, Charles A., and Mary R. Beard. *The American Spirit*. New York: Macmillan, 1942.
Beers, Burton F. *Vain Endeavour*. Durham, N.C.: Duke University Press, 1962.
Beesly, Patrick. *Room 40*. London: Hamish Hamilton, 1982.
Bell, A. C. *Die Hungerblockade im Weltkrieg 1914–15*. Veröffentlichungen des Deutschen Instituts für Aussenpolitische Forschung, vol. 14. Essen: Essener Verlagsanstalt, 1943.
Bemis, Samuel F. *The Latin American Policy of the United States*. New York: W. W. Norton, 1967.
———. *The United States as a World Power*. New York: Henry Holt, 1952.
Berg, Hans Walter. "Studien zu Problemen der amerikanischen Neutralitätspolitik." Ph.D. diss., Universität München, 1941.
Berg, Peter. *Deutschland und Amerika 1918–1929*. Historische Studien, no. 385. Lübeck: Matthiesen, 1963.
Berghahn, Volker R. *Der Tirpitz-Plan*. Düsseldorf: Droste, 1971.
Bertram, Rudolf. *Die Ostjuden in Deutschland*. Berlin: Philo, 1924.
Birke, Ernst. "Der Erste Weltkrieg und die Gründung der Tschechoslowakei 1914–1919." In *Handbuch der Geschichte der böhmischen Länder*, Vol. 3, edited by Karl Bosl, 239–447. Stuttgart: Anton Hiersemann, 1968.
Birmingham, Stephen. *In unseren Kreisen*. Frankfurt: Ullstein, 1969. (First published in the United States as *Our Crowd*, 1967.)
Birnbaum, Karl E. *Peace Moves and U-Boat Warfare*. Stockholm Studies in History, no. 2. Stockholm: Almqvist & Wiksell, 1958.
Blakey, George T. *Historians on the Homefront*. Lexington: University Press of Kentucky, 1970.
Bleuel, Hans Peter. *Deutschlands Bekenner*. Bern: Scherz, 1968.
Blood-Ryan, H. W. *Franz von Papen*. London: Rich & Cowan, 1940.
Blum, John M. *Joe Tumulty and the Wilson Era*. Boston: Houghton Mifflin, 1951.
———. *Woodrow Wilson and the Politics of Morality*. Boston: Little, Brown, 1956.
Blumenschein, Ulrich. "Enthüllungen nach 57 Jahren. Die Wahrheit über die 'Lusitania.'" *Stern* No. 45 (1972): 18–24, 28.
Bonhard, Otto. *Geschichte des Alldeutschen Verbandes*. Leipzig: Theodor Weicher, 1920.
Borosini, Victor von. "Mexiko." In *Amerika*, edited by Ernst von Halle, 391–430. Hamburg: Hamburger Börsenhalle, 1905.
Bowden, Tom. *The Breakdown of Public Security*. London and Beverly Hills: Sage, 1977.
Brandenburg, Erich. *Von Bismarck zum Weltkrieg*. Leipzig: Insel, 1939.

Brock, Peter. *Pacifism in the United States.* Princeton, N.J.: Princeton University Press, 1968.
Brooks, Sidney. *America and Germany, 1918–1925.* New York: Macmillan, 1925.
Broszat, Martin. "Die antisemitische Bewegung im Wilhelminischen Deutschland." Ph.D. diss., Universität Köln, 1952.
Brown, Thomas A. *Irish-American Nationalism 1870–1890.* Philadelphia: J. B. Lippincott, 1966.
Buchheit, Gert. *Die Anonyme Macht.* Frankfurt: Akademische Verlagsgesellschaft Athenaion, 1969.
———. *Der deutsche Geheimdienst.* Munich: List, 1966.
———. *Franz von Papen.* Breslau: Bergstadtverlag, 1937.
Buehrig, Edward H. *Woodrow Wilson and the Balance of Power.* Bloomington: Indiana University Press, 1955.
———, ed. *Wilson's Foreign Policy in Perspective.* Bloomington: Indiana University Press, 1957.
Calleo, David. *The German Problem Reconsidered.* Cambridge: Cambridge University Press, 1978.
Calvert, Peter. *The Mexican Revolution, 1910–1914.* Cambridge Latin American Studies, no. 3. Cambridge: Cambridge University Press, 1968.
Canfield, Leon H. *The Presidency of Woodrow Wilson.* Rutherford, N.J.: Fairleigh Dickinson University Press, 1966.
Carlgren, W. M. *Neutralität oder Allianz.* Vol. 6, *Stockholm Studies in History.* Stockholm: Almqvist & Wiksell, 1962.
Carry, E. Malcolm. *Germany and the Great Powers 1866–1914.* Hamden, Conn.: Archon, 1966.
Carsten, F. L. *War Against War.* London: Batsford, 1982.
Caton, William Charles. "Die Rolle des Obersten House im Rahmen der Friedensaktion Wilsons im Jahre 1916/17." Ph.D. diss., Universität Heidelberg, 1937.
Caulfield, Max. *The Easter Rebellion.* New York: Holt, Rinehart & Winston, 1963.
Cecil, Lamar. *Albert Ballin.* Princeton, N.J.: Princeton University Press, 1967.
Chambers, Frank P. *The War behind the War 1914–1918.* London: Faber & Faber, 1939.
Chickering, Roger. *Imperial Germany and a World Without War.* Princeton, N.J.: Princeton University Press, 1975.
Child, Clifton J. "German-American Attempts to Prevent the Exportation of Munitions of War." *Mississippi Valley Historical Review* 25 (1938/39): 351–68.
———. *The German-Americans in Politics, 1914–1917.* Madison: University of Wisconsin Press, 1939.
Clement, Wilhelm. "Die Monroedoktrin und die deutsch-amerikanischen

Beziehungen im Zeitalter des Imperialismus." *Jahrbuch für Amerikastudien* 1 (1956): 153–67.

Clements, Kendrick A. "Woodrow Wilson's Mexican Policy, 1913–15." *Diplomatic History* 4 (Spring 1980): 113–36.

Clendenen, Clarence C. *The United States and Pancho Villa: A Study in Unconventional Diplomacy.* Ithaca: Cornell University Press, 1961.

Cline, Howard F. *The United States and Mexico.* 1953. Rev. ed. Cambridge: Cambridge University Press, 1963.

Clymer, Kenton J. *John Hay.* Ann Arbor: University of Michigan Press, 1975.

Cohen, Hermann. *Jüdische Schriften.* Vol. 2. Berlin: C. A. Schwetschke, 1924.

Cohen, Naomi W. *A Dual Heritage.* Philadelphia: Jewish Publication Society of America, 1969.

Cohen, Warren I. *The American Revisionists.* Chicago: University of Chicago Press, 1967.

———, ed. *Intervention, 1917. Why America Fought.* Boston: D. C. Heath, 1966.

Coletta, Paolo E. *William Jennings Bryan.* Vols. 1–3. Lincoln: University of Nebraska Press, 1964–69.

Conrad, Will C.; Kathleen F. Wilson; and Dale Wilson. *The Milwaukee Journal.* Madison: University of Wisconsin Press, 1964.

Coogan, John W. *The End of Neutrality.* Ithaca: Cornell University Press, 1981.

Cooper, John Milton, Jr. "The British Response to the House-Grey Memorandum: New Evidence and New Questions." *Journal of American History* 59 (March 1973): 958–71.

———. "The Command of Gold Reversed: American Loans to Britain." *Pacific Historical Review* 45 (May 1976): 209–30.

———. *The Vanity of Power.* Contributions in American History, no. 3. Westport, Conn.: Greenwood, 1969.

———. *Walter Hines Page.* Chapel Hill: University of North Carolina Press, 1977.

———. *The Warrior and the Priest.* Cambridge, Mass.: Harvard University Press, Belknap Press, 1983.

Corbett, Sir Julian S. *Naval Operations.* Vols. 1–3. London: Longmans, Green, 1920–29.

Craig, Gordon A. *From Bismarck to Adenauer: Aspects of German Statecraft.* Baltimore: Johns Hopkins Press, 1958.

———. *The Politics of the Prussian Army, 1640–1945.* 1955. New York: Oxford University Press, Galaxy, 1964.

Crighton, John Clark. *Missouri and the World War, 1914–1917: A Study in Public Opinion.* Columbia: University of Missouri, 1947.

Cronin, Sean. *The McGarrity Papers.* Tralee: Anvil Books, 1972.

Cuddy, Edward. "Irish-American Propagandists and American Neutrality, 1914–1917." *Mid-America* 49 (October 1967): 252–75.
Cumberland, Charles. *Mexican Revolution*. Austin: University of Texas Press, 1952.
Cummins, Cedric C. *Indiana Public Opinion and the World War, 1914–1917*. Indianapolis: Indiana Historical Bureau, 1945.
Cunz, Dieter. *The Maryland Germans*. Princeton, N.J.: Princeton University Press, 1948.
Curti, Merle E. *Bryan and World Peace*. Smith College Studies in History. Northampton, Mass.: Dept. of History of Smith College, 1931.
———. *Peace or War*. New York: W. W. Norton, 1936.
Daenell, E. *Geschichte der Vereinigten Staaten von Amerika*. Leipzig: B. G. Teubner, 1907.
Daniels, Jonathan. *The End of Innocence*. Philadelphia: J. B. Lippincott, 1954.
Davids, Jules, ed. *Perspectives in American Foreign Policy*. New York: Arno, 1976.
De Gaulle, Charles. *La Discorde chez l'ennemi*. Paris: Berger-Levrault, 1924.
Dehio, Ludwig. *Deutschland und die Weltpolitik im 20. Jahrhundert*. Munich: R. Oldenbourg, 1955.
Deicke, Gertrud. "Das Amerikabild der deutschen öffentlichen Meinung von 1898–1914." Ph.D. diss., Universität Hamburg, 1956.
Deutschland im Ersten Weltkrieg. Vol. 1. Project group directed by Fritz Klein. Berlin: Akademie-Verlag, 1962.
Deutschland im Ersten Weltkrieg. Vol. 2. Project group directed by Willibald Gutsche. Berlin: Akademie-Verlag, 1968.
Devlin, Patrick. *Too Proud to Fight*. New York: Oxford University Press, 1975.
Dignan, Don K. "The Hindu Conspiracy in Anglo-American Relations during World War I." *Pacific Historical Review* 40 (February 1971): 57–76.
Dittmann, Anneliese. "Die deutschfeindliche Meinungsbildung der Vereinigten Staaten von Nordamerika während des Weltkriegs und 1933/34." Ph.D. diss., Universität Heidelberg, 1938.
Doerries, Reinhard R. "The Americanizing of the German Immigrant: A Chapter from U.S. Social History." *Amerikastudien/American Studies* 23 (1978): 51–59.
———. "Amerikanische Aussenpolitik im Karibischen Raum." *Jahrbuch für Amerikastudien* 18 (1973): 62–82. (With Comment by Klaus Schwabe.)
———. "Empire and Republic: German-American Relations before 1917." In *America and the Germans*, vol. 2, edited by Frank Trommler and Jo-

seph McVeigh, 3–17. Philadelphia: University of Pennsylvania Press, 1985.

———. "Geheimdienste im 20. Jahrhundert." *Neue Politische Literatur* 3 (1974): 353–64.

———. "Imperial Berlin and Washington: New Light on Germany's Foreign Policy and America's Entry into World War I." *Central European History* 11 (March 1978), 23–49.

———. *Iren und Deutsche in der Neuen Welt*. Stuttgart: Franz Steiner Verlag Wiesbaden, 1986.

———. "Die Mission Sir Roger Casements im Deutschen Reich 1914–1916." *Historische Zeitschrift* 222 (1976): 578–625.

———. "The Politics of Irresponsibility: Imperial Germany's Defiance of United States Neutrality during World War I." In *Germany and America: Essays on Problems of International Relations and Immigration*, edited by Hans L. Trefousse, 3–20. New York: Brooklyn College Press, 1980.

———. *Washington-Berlin 1908/1917*. Düsseldorf: Schwann, 1975.

Dos Passos, John. *Mr. Wilson's War*. Garden City, N.Y.: Doubleday, 1962.

Dürking, Irene. "Der amerikanische Senat und der Friede mit Deutschland 1916–1921." Ph.D. diss., Universität München, 1963.

Duff, Charles. *Six Days to Shake an Empire*. London: J. M. Dent, 1966.

Dupuy, Ernest R. *Five Days to War*. Harrisburg: Giniger, 1967.

Duroselle, Jean-Baptiste. *De Wilson à Roosevelt*. Paris: Armand Colin, 1960.

Earle, Edward Meade. "A Half Century of American Foreign Policy. Our Stake in Europe, 1898–1948." *Political Science Quarterly* 64 (1949): 168–88.

Edmonds, C. J. "The Persian Gulf Prelude to the Zimmermann Telegram." *Journal of the Royal Central Asian Society* 47 (1960): 58–67.

Ellis, Edward Robb. *Echoes of Distant Thunder*. New York: Coward, McCann & Geoghegan, 1975.

Epstein, Fritz T. "Germany and the United States: Basic Patterns of Conflict and Understanding." In *Issues and Conflicts*, edited by George L. Anderson, 284–314. Lawrence: University of Kansas Press, 1959.

———. "Zwischen Compiegne und Versailles." *Vierteljahrshefte für Zeitgeschichte* 3 (October 1955): 412–45.

Epstein, Klaus. "Gerhard Ritter and the First World War." *Journal of Contemporary History* 1 (1966): 193–210.

———. *Matthias Erzberger and the Dilemma of German Democracy*. Princeton, N.J.: Princeton University Press, 1959.

Esthus, Raymond A. *Theodore Roosevelt and the International Rivalries*. Waltham, Mass.: Ginn-Blaisdell, 1970.

Eyck, Erich. *Geschichte der Weimarer Republik*. Vols. 1–2. Erlenbach-Zürich: Eugen Rentsch, 1962.

———. *Das persönliche Regiment Wilhelms II.* Erlenbach-Zürich: Eugen Rentsch, 1948.
Falls, Cyril. *The First World War.* London: Longmans, 1960.
Feder, Ernst. *Paul Nathan.* Berlin: Deutsche Verlagsgesellschaft für Politik und Geschichte, 1929.
Feldman, Gerald D. *Army, Industry, and Labor in Germany, 1914–1918.* Princeton, N.J.: Princeton University Press, 1966.
Fellner, Fritz. "Der Plan einer 'Vortragsmission Redlich-Apponyi' in den Vereinigten Staaten von Amerika." In *Beiträge zur neueren Geschichte Österreichs,* edited by Heinrich Fichtenau and Erich Zöllner, 469–88. Wien: Hermann Böhlaus Nachfolger, 1974.
Fernández, Salvador Diego. "La Mision de Conde Bernstorff en Washington." *Revista Mexicana de Derecho International* 2 (1920): 534–42; 3 (1921): 206–11, 543–53; 4 (1922): 104–13, 249–59.
Ferrell, Robert H. *Woodrow Wilson and World War I, 1917–1921.* New York: Harper & Row, 1985.
Ferro, Marc. *La Grande Guerre 1914–1918.* Paris: Gallimard, 1969.
Fest, W. B. "British War Aims and German Peace Feelers during the First World War (December 1916–November 1918)." *Historical Journal* 15 (June 1972): 285–308.
Fischer, Fritz. *Bündnis der Eliten.* Düsseldorf: Droste, 1979.
———. *Griff nach der Weltmacht.* Düsseldorf: Droste, 1961.
———. *Juli 1914: Wir sind nicht hineingeschlittert.* Reinbek: Rowohlt, 1983.
———. *Krieg der Illusionen.* Düsseldorf: Droste, 1969.
———. *Weltmacht oder Niedergang. Deutschland im Ersten Weltkrieg.* Frankfurt: Europäische Verlagsanstalt, 1965.
———. "Weltpolitik, Weltmachtstreben und deutsche Kriegsziele." *Historische Zeitschrift* 199 (October 1964): 265–346.
Forbes, John Douglas. *J. P. Morgan, Jr. 1867–1943.* Charlottesville: University Press of Virginia, 1981.
Fowler, W. B. *British-American Relations, 1917–1918.* Princeton, N.J.: Princeton University Press, 1969.
Fraenkel, Ernst. "Das deutsche Wilsonbild." *Jahrbuch für Amerikastudien* 5 (1960): 66–120.
Freitag, Christian H. "Die Entwicklung der Amerikastudien in Berlin bis 1945 unter Berücksichtigung der Amerikaarbeit staatlicher und privater Organisationen." Ph.D. diss., Freie Universität Berlin, 1977.
Freud, Sigmund, and William C. Bullitt. *Thomas Woodrow Wilson.* London: Weidenfeld and Nicolson, 1967.
———. "Woodrow Wilson." *Encounter* 28 (January 1967): 3–24; (February 1967): 3–24.
Freytag, Dierk. *Die Vereinigten Staaten auf dem Wege zur Intervention.*

Beihefte zum Jahrbuch für Amerikastudien, no. 30. Heidelberg: Carl Winter, 1971.
Fried, Alfred H. *Handbuch der Friedensbewegung*. Parts 1–2. 2d ed. Berlin: "Friedens-Warte," 1911–13.
_____. *Die moderne Friedensbewegung*. Leipzig: B. G. Teubner, 1907.
Friedländer, Saul. "Die politischen Veränderungen der Kriegszeit und ihre Auswirkungen auf die Judenfrage." In *Deutsches Judentum in Krieg und Revolution 1916–1923*, edited by Werner E. Mosse and Arnold Paucker, 27–65. Tübingen: J. C. B. Mohr, 1971.
Friis, Aage. *Die Bernstorffs*. Leipzig: Wilhelm Weicher, 1905.
Frothingham, Thomas G. *The Naval History of the World War*. Vols. 1–3. Cambridge: Harvard University Press, 1925–26.
Fuchs, Lawrence H. *The Political Behavior of American Jews*. Glencoe, Ill.: Free Press, 1956.
Fuller, Joseph Vincent. *William Jennings Bryan*. Vol. 10, *The American Secretaries of State and Their Diplomacy*, edited by Samuel Flagg Bemis. New York: Pageant Book Co., 1958.
Gardiner, Leslie. *The British Admiralty*. Edinburgh: William Blackwood, 1968.
Garraty, John A. *Interpreting American History*. Vol. 2. London: Macmillan, 1970.
_____. *Woodrow Wilson*. New York: Harper & Row, 1970.
Gatzke, Hans W. *Germany and the United States*. Cambridge: Harvard University Press, 1980.
_____. *Germany's Drive to the West*. Baltimore, Md.: Johns Hopkins Press, 1950.
_____. "The United States and Germany on the Eve of World War I." In *Deutschland in der Weltpolitik des 19. und 20. Jahrhunderts*, edited by Imanuel Geiss and Bernd Jürgen Wendt, 271–86. Düsseldorf: Bertelsmann, 1973.
Gehrke, Ulrich. *Persien in der deutschen Orientpolitik während des Ersten Weltkrieges*. Vols. 1–2. Stuttgart: W. Kohlhammer, 1961.
Geiss, Imanuel, ed. *July 1914*. New York: Charles Scribner's Sons, 1967.
_____. "The Outbreak of the First World War and German War Aims." *Journal of Contemporary History* 1 (1966): 75–91.
Gelfand, Lawrence Emerson. *The Inquiry*. New Haven, Conn.: Yale University Press, 1963.
Gelos de Vaz Ferreira, Lilian. *Die Neutralitätspolitik Spaniens während des Ersten Weltkrieges unter besonderer Berücksichtigung der deutsch-spanischen Beziehungen*. Hamburg Dissertations, series 2. Hamburg: Institut für Auswärtige Politik, 1966.
George, Alexander L., and Juliette L. George. *Woodrow Wilson and Colonel House*. New York: John Day, 1956.

Gerschenkron, Alexander. *Bread and Democracy in Germany*. Berkeley: University of California Press, 1943.
Gerson, Louis L. "Immigrant Groups and American Foreign Policy." In *Issues and Conflicts*, edited by George L. Anderson, 171–92. Lawrence: University of Kansas Press, 1959.
Gibson, R. H., and Maurice Prendergast. *The German Submarine War 1914–1918*. London: Constable, 1931.
Gilbert, Charles. *American Financing of World War I*. Contributions in Economics and Economic History, no. 1. Westport, Conn.: Greenwood, 1970.
Gilderhus, Mark T. *Diplomacy and Revolution*. Tucson: University of Arizona Press, 1977.
Gitlow, Benjamin. *The Whole of Their Lives*. New York: Charles Scribner's Sons, 1948.
Glazer, Nathan, and Daniel Patrick Moynihan. *Beyond the Melting Pot*. Cambridge, Mass.: M.I.T. Press, 1964.
Gleich, Albrecht von. *Germany and Latin America*. Santa Monica: Rand Corporation, 1968.
Goblet, Y. M. [Louis Tréguiz]. *L'Irlande dans la crise universelle (1914–1920)*. Paris: Félix Alcan, 1921.
Göhring, Martin. *Bismarcks Erben 1890–1945*. Wiesbaden: Franz Steiner, 1958.
Görlitz, Walter. *Der deutsche Generalstab*. Frankfurt: Frankfurter Hefte, 1950.
Gooch, George P. *Recent Revelations in European Diplomacy*. London: Longmans, 1928.
―――. *Studies in German History*. London: Longmans, 1948.
Gordon, Harold J., Jr. *The Reichswehr and the German Republic, 1919–1926*. Princeton, N.J.: Princeton University Press, 1957.
Graebner, Alan N. "The Acculturation of an Immigrant Lutheran Church: The Lutheran Church-Missouri Synod, 1917–1929." Ph.D. diss., Columbia University, 1965.
Grattan, C. Hartley. *Why We Fought*. New York: Vanguard, 1929.
Gray, Edwin A. *The Killing Time*. New York: Charles Scribner's Sons, 1972.
―――. *The Underwater War*. New York: Charles Scribner's Sons, 1971.
Greenwald, Martin A. "Bernstorff's Prewar View of America, 1908–1914: A German Diplomat's Social Values." Ph.D. diss., Brown University, 1972.
Gregory, Ross. *Walter Hines Page*. Lexington: University Press of Kentucky, 1970.
Grieb, Kenneth J. *The United States and Huerta*. Lincoln: University of Nebraska Press, 1969.

Guinn, Paul. *British Strategy and Politics, 1914 to 1918*. Oxford: Clarendon Press, 1965.
Gutsche, Willibald. *Aufstieg und Fall eines kaiserlichen Reichskanzlers*. Berlin: Akademie-Verlag, 1973.
———. "Der Einfluss des Monopolkapitals auf die Entstehung der aussenpolitischen Konzeption der Regierung Bethmann Hollweg zu Beginn des Ersten Weltkrieges." *Jahrbuch für Geschichte* 5 (1971): 118–73.
Guzmán, Martin Luis. *Memoirs of Pancho Villa*. Austin: University of Texas Press, 1965.
Härtle, Heinrich. *Amerikas Krieg gegen Deutschland*. Göttingen: K. W. Schütz, 1968.
Hamburger, Ernest. *Juden im öffentlichen Leben Deutschlands*. Schriftenreihe Wissenschaftlicher Abhandlungen des Leo Baeck Instituts, no. 19. Tübingen: J. C. B. Mohr, 1968.
Handlin, Oscar. *Adventure in Freedom*. New York: McGraw Hill, 1954.
Harbaugh, William Henry. *The Life and Times of Theodore Roosevelt*. Rev. ed. New York: Collier, 1967.
Hardach, Gerd. *Der Erste Weltkrieg*. Vol. 2, *Geschichte der Weltwirtschaft*. Munich: Deutscher Taschenbuch Verlag, 1973.
Hardy, Margaret. *The Influence of Organized Labor on the Foreign Policy of the United States*. Thése no. 30, Université de Genève. Liége: H. Vaillant-Carmanne, 1936.
Harris, Charles H., III, and Louis R. Sadler. "The Witzke Affair: German Intrigue on the Mexican Border, 1917–18." *Military Review* (February 1979): 36–50.
Hartung, Fritz. "Die geschichtliche Bedeutung des Weltkrieges." *Militärwissenschaftliche Rundschau* 4 (1939): 443–55.
Hashagen, Justus. "Zur Geschichte der amerikanisch-deutschen Beziehungen 1897–1907." *Zeitschrift für Politik* 16 (1927): 122–29.
Haupts, Leo. *Deutsche Friedenspolitik, 1918–19*. Düsseldorf: Droste, 1976.
Hawgood, John A. *The Tragedy of German-America*. New York: G. P. Putnam's Sons, 1940.
Healy, David. *Gunboat Diplomacy in the Wilson Era*. Madison: University of Wisconsin Press, 1976.
Herwig, Holger. "Admirals versus Generals: The War Aims of the Imperial German Navy 1914–1918." *Central European History* 5 (September 1972): 208–33.
———. *The German Naval Officer Corps*. Oxford: Clarendon Press, 1973.
Herzfeld, Hans. *Der Erste Weltkrieg*. Munich: Deutscher Taschenbuch Verlag, 1968.
Herzog, Bodo, and Günter Schomaekers. *Ritter der Tiefe. Graue Wölfe*. Munich: Welsermühl, 1965.

Hess, Gary R. "The 'Hindu' in America: Immigration and Naturalization Policies and India, 1917–1946." *Pacific Historical Review* 38 (1969): 59–79.
Hess, Jürgen C. *"Das ganze Deutschland soll es sein."* Stuttgart: Klett-Cotta, 1978.
Hezlet, Sir Arthur. *The Submarine and Sea Power.* London: Peter Davis, 1967.
Hildebrand, Klaus. *Bethmann Hollweg. Der Kanzler ohne Eigenschaften?* Düsseldorf: Droste, 1970.
Hille, Hans-Joachim. "Vernunft und Geschichte bei Woodrow Wilson." Ph.D. diss., Universität Frankfurt, 1950.
Hillgruber, Andreas. *Deutschlands Rolle in der Vorgeschichte der beiden Weltkriege.* Die deutsche Frage in der Welt, no. 7. Göttingen: Vandenhoeck & Ruprecht, 1967.
Hirsch, Felix. "Stresemann, Ballin und die Vereinigten Staaten." *Vierteljahrshefte für Zeitgeschichte* 3 (January 1955): 20–35.
Hirst, David W. "German Propaganda in the United States, 1914–1917." Ph.D. diss., Northwestern University, 1962.
Hölzle, Erwin. "Das Experiment des Friedens im Ersten Weltkrieg 1914 bis 1917." *Geschichte in Wissenschaft und Unterricht* 13 (1962): 465–522.
Hohlfeld, Johannes. *Der Kampf um den Frieden.* Leipzig: Bibliographisches Institut, 1919.
Holborn, Hajo. "Diplomats and Diplomacy in the Early Weimar Republic." In *The Diplomats 1919–1939*, edited by Gordon A. Craig and Felix Gilbert, 123–71. Princeton, N.J.: Princeton University Press, 1953.
Holbrook, Franklin F., and Livia Appel. *Minnesota in the War with Germany.* Vols. 1–2. St. Paul: Minnesota Historical Society, 1928.
Holt, W. Stull. *Treaties Defeated by the Senate.* Baltimore, Md.: Johns Hopkins Press, 1933.
Hoyt, Edwin P. *Die Vanderbilts.* Frankfurt: Heinrich Scheffler, 1963. (First published 1962 as *The Vanderbilts and Their Fortunes.*)
Hubatsch, Walther. *Der Admiralstab und die obersten Marinebehörden in Deutschland 1848–1945.* Frankfurt: Verlag für Wehrwesen Bernard & Graefe, 1958.
———. *Die Ära Tirpitz.* Göttingen: Musterschmidt, 1955.
———. *Deutschland im Weltkrieg.* Frankfurt: Ullstein, 1966.
———. *Hindenburg und der Staat.* Göttingen: Musterschmidt, 1966.
Hubrich, Erich-Wolfgang. "Neutralität und Intervention der Vereinigten Staaten von Amerika 1914–1917." Ph.D. diss., Universität Kiel, 1956.
———. "Zur amerikanischen Intervention in Europa 1914–1919: Aussenminister Robert Lansing und Präsident Woodrow Wilson im Spiegel der Lansing Papers." In *Historisch-politische Streiflichter*, edited by Kurt Jürgensen and Reimer Hansen, 127–58. Neumünster: Karl Wachholtz, 1971.

Huebner, Theodore. *The Germans in America*. Philadelphia: Chilton, 1962.
Hünseler, Wolfgang. *Die irische Frage in den deutsch-britischen Beziehungen und ihre Beurteilung in der zeitgenössischen Presse und Publizistik 1900–1914*. Frankfurt and Bern: Peter Lang, 1978.
Iklé, Frank W. "Japanese-American Peace Negotiations during World War I." *American Historical Review* 71 (October 1965): 62–76.
Ind, Allison. *A History of Modern Espionage*. London: Hodder & Stoughton, 1965.
Inglis, Brian. *Roger Casement*. New York: Harcourt Brace Jovanovich, 1974.
James, Sir William. *The Code Breakers of Room 40. The Eyes of the Navy*. New York: St. Martin's, 1956.
Janssen, Karl-Heinz. *Der Kanzler und der General*. Göttingen: Musterschmidt, 1967.
———. *Macht und Verblendung*. Göttingen: Musterschmidt, 1963.
———. "Die Mühle von Verdun." *Die Zeit* (February 25, 1966): 32.
Jarausch, Konrad H. *The Enigmatic Chancellor*. New Haven, Conn.: Yale University Press, 1973.
Jerussalimski, A. S. *Die Aussenpolitik und die Diplomatie des deutschen Imperialismus Ende des 19. Jahrhunderts*. Berlin: Dietz, 1954.
Jessup, Philip C. *Elihu Root*. Vols. 1–2. [Hamden, Conn.]: Archon, 1964. (First published 1938.)
Johnson, Niel M. *George Sylvester Viereck. German-American Propagandist*. Urbana: University of Illinois Press, 1972.
Johnson, Thomas M. *Our Secret War*. Indianapolis, Ind.: Bobbs-Merrill, 1929.
Joll, James. *The Origins of the First World War*. London and New York: Longmans, 1984.
Jonas, Manfred. "The Major Powers and the United States: The Case of Germany." In *Perspectives in American Diplomacy*, edited by Jules Davids, 30–77. New York: Arno, 1976.
———. *The United States and Germany*. Ithaca, N.Y.: Cornell University Press, 1984.
Kabisch, Thomas R. *Deutsches Kapital in den USA*. Stuttgart: Klett-Cotta, 1982.
Kahle, Louis G. "Robert Lansing and the Recognition of Venustiano Carranza." *Hispanic American Historical Review* 38 (August 1958): 353–72.
Kahn, David. *The Codebreakers*. New York: Macmillan, 1967.
Katz, Friedrich. "Alemania y Francisco Villa." *Historia Mexicana* 12 (July–September 1962): 88–102.
———. "Die deutsche Verschwörung in Mexiko 1914–1916." In *Politik im Krieg 1914–1918*, edited by project group directed by Fritz Klein, 90–117. Berlin: Akademie-Verlag, 1964.

———. *Deutschland, Diaz und die mexikanische Revolution*. Berlin: VEB Deutscher Verlag der Wissenschaften, 1964.

———. "Pancho Villa and the Attack on Columbus, New Mexico." *American Historical Review* 83 (February 1978): 101–30.

———. *The Secret War in Mexico*. Chicago: University of Chicago Press, 1981. (Translation and revised edition of *Deutschland, Diaz und die mexikanische Revolution*.)

Kaulisch, Baldur. "Die Auseinandersetzungen über den uneingeschränkten U-Boot-Krieg innerhalb der herrschenden Klassen im zweiten Halbjahr 1916 und seine Eröffnung im Februar 1917." In *Politik im Krieg 1914–1918*, edited by project group directed by Fritz Klein, 66–89. Berlin: Akademie-Verlag, 1964.

Keim, Jeanette. *Forty Years of German-American Political Relations*. Philadelphia: William J. Dornan, 1919.

Keller, Phyllis. "George Sylvester Viereck: The Psychology of a German-American Militant." *Journal of Interdisciplinary History* 2 (Summer 1971): 59–108.

———. *States of Belonging*. Cambridge, Mass.: Harvard University Press, 1979.

Kennan, George F. *American Diplomacy, 1900–1950*. Chicago: University of Chicago Press, 1965.

Kennedy, David M. *Over Here*. New York and Oxford: Oxford University Press, 1980.

Kennedy, Paul M. *The Rise of the Anglo-German Antagonism, 1860–1914*. London: George Allen & Unwin, 1980.

———. *The Samoan Tangle*. New York: Harper & Row, 1974.

Kerney, James. *The Political Education of Woodrow Wilson*. New York: Century, 1926.

Kerr, Thomas J., IV. "German-Americans and Neutrality in the 1916 Election." *Mid-America* 43 (1961): 95–105.

Kersten, Dietrich. "Die Kriegsziele der Hamburger Kaufmannschaft im Ersten Weltkrieg." Ph.D. diss., Universität Hamburg, 1963.

Kielmannsegg, Peter Graf von. *Deutschland und der Erste Weltkrieg*. Frankfurt: Akademische Verlagsgesellschaft Athenaion, 1968.

Kimpen, E. *Die Ausbreitungspolitik der Vereinigten Staaten von Amerika*. Stuttgart: Deutsche Verlags-Anstalt, 1923.

Kirchhoff, Hermann D. F. "The Political and Economic Relations between Germany and the United States, 1871–1901." Ph.D. diss., University of Southern California, 1936.

Kitchen, Martin. *The Silent Dictatorship*. London: Croom Helm, 1976.

Klein, Fritz. *Deutschland 1918*. Berlin: Rütten & Loening, 1962.

———, ed. *Die USA und Europa, 1917–1945*. Berlin: Akademie-Verlag, 1975.

Knebel-Doeberitz, Hugo von. *Besteht für Deutschland eine amerikanische*

Gefahr? Berlin: Ernst Siegfried Mittler, 1904.
Knesebeck, Ludolf Gottschalk von dem. *Die Wahrheit über den Propagandafeldzug und Deutschlands Zusammenbruch.* Munich: Privately published, 1927.
Koeves, Tibor. *Satan in Top Hat.* New York: Alliance Book, 1941.
Kohn, Hans. *The Mind of Germany.* New York: Harper Torchbooks, 1965.
Koszyk, Kurt. *Deutsche Pressepolitik im Ersten Weltkrieg.* Düsseldorf: Droste, 1968.
Krakau, Knud. *Missionsbewusstsein und Völkerrechtsdoktrin in den Vereinigten Staaten von Amerika.* Frankfurt: Alfred Metzner, 1967.
Kramer, Hans. *Die Grossmächte und die Weltpolitik 1789 bis 1945.* Innsbruck: Tyrolia, 1952.
Kruck, Alfred. *Geschichte des Alldeutschen Verbandes 1890–1939.* Wiesbaden: Franz Steiner, 1954.
Krüger, Horst. "Har Dayal in Deutschland." *Mitteilungen des Instituts für Orientforschung* 10 (1964): 141–69.
Krüger, Wolfgang. *Der Entschluss zum uneingeschränkten U-Bootkrieg im Jahre 1917 und seine völkerrechtliche Rechtfertigung.* Companion volume no. 5 of *Marine Rundschau* (October 1959).
Kunz-Lack, Ilse. *Die deutsch-amerikanischen Beziehungen 1890–1914.* Stuttgart: W. Kohlhammer, 1935.
Kuropka, Joachim. *Image und Intervention.* Vol. 14, *Historische Forschungen.* Berlin: Duncker & Humblot, 1978.
LaFeber, Walter. *The New Empire.* Ithaca, N.Y.: Cornell University Press, 1968.
Lambach, Frank. *Our Men in Washington.* Bonn: Auswärtiges Amt, 1976.
Lammasch, Heinrich. *Die Lehre von der Schiedsgerichtsbarkeit in ihrem ganzen Umfange.* Stuttgart: W. Kohlhammer, 1914.
———. "Unjustifiable War and the Means to Avoid It." *American Journal of International Law* 10 (October 1916): 689–705.
Landau, Henry. *The Enemy Within.* New York: G. P. Putnam's Sons, 1937.
Lang, Gustav A. *Kampfplatz der Meinungen.* Zürich: Neue Züricher Zeitung, 1968.
Langer, William L. "From Isolation to Mediation." In *Woodrow Wilson and The World of Today*, edited by Arthur P. Dudden, 22–46. Philadelphia: University of Pennsylvania Press, 1957.
———. "An Honest Diplomat." *New York Herald Tribune, Books* (October 25, 1936): Section X, 2.
Langley, Lester D. *Struggle for the American Mediterranean.* Athens: University of Georgia Press, 1976.
Larkin, Emmet. *James Larkin.* London: Routledge & Kegan Paul, 1965.
Laswell, Harold D. *Propaganda Technique in the World War.* New York: Peter Smith, 1938.
Lavrov, N.M. "La Revolución mexicana de 1910–1917." In *La Revolución*

mexicana. Mexico: Editiones Los Insurgentes, 1960.
Leary, William M., Jr. "Woodrow Wilson, Irish Americans, and the Election of 1916." *Journal of American History* 54 (1968): 57–72.
Leopold, Richard W. *Elihu Root and the Conservative Tradition*. Boston: Little, Brown, 1954.
Leusser, Hermann. *Ein Jahrzehnt deutsch-amerikanischer Politik (1897–1906)*. Munich: R. Oldenbourg, 1928.
Liddell Hart, Basil. *A History of the World War*. London: Faber & Faber, 1934. (First published 1930 as *The Real War*.)
Link, Arthur S. *Campaigns for Progressivism and Peace, 1916–1917*. Vol. 5, *Wilson*. Princeton, N.J.: Princeton University Press, 1965.
———. *Confusions and Crises, 1915–1916*. Vol. 4, *Wilson*. Princeton, N.J.: Princeton University Press, 1964.
———. *The Higher Realism of Woodrow Wilson*. Nashville, Tenn.: Vanderbilt University Press, 1971.
———. *The New Freedom*. Vol. 2, *Wilson*. Princeton, N.J.: Princeton University Press, 1956.
———. *The Road to the White House*. Vol. 1, *Wilson*. Princeton, N.J.: Princeton University Press, 1947.
———. *The Struggle for Neutrality*. Vol. 3, *Wilson*. Princeton, N.J.: Princeton University Press, 1960.
———. *Wilson the Diplomatist*. Baltimore, Md.: Johns Hopkins Press, 1957.
———. *Woodrow Wilson and the Progressive Era, 1910–1917*. London: Hamish Hamilton, 1954.
———. *Woodrow Wilson: Revolution, War and Peace*. Arlington Heights: Harlan Davidson, 1979.
———, ed. *Woodrow Wilson and a Revolutionary World*. Chapel Hill: University of North Carolina Press, 1982.
———. *Woodrow Wilson. A Profile*. New York: Hill & Wang, 1968.
Livermore, Seward W. *Politics Is Adjourned*. Middleton, Conn.: Wesleyan University Press, 1966.
Luckau, Alma Maria. *The German Delegation at the Paris Peace Conference*. New York: Columbia University Press, 1941.
Luckwaldt, Friedrich. *Geschichte der Vereinigten Staaten von Amerika*. Vol. 2. Berlin: Walter de Gruyter, 1920.
Luebke, Frederick C. *Bonds of Loyalty*. DeKalb: Northern Illinois University Press, 1974.
Lutz, Ralph Haswell. "Studies of World War Propaganda 1914–33." *Journal of Modern History* 5 (March–December 1933): 496–516.
Lynar, Ernst W. Graf, ed. *Deutsche Kriegsziele 1914–1918*. Frankfurt: Ullstein, 1964.
McCarthy, J. "The British." In *The Immigrants' Influence on Wilson's*

Peace Policies, edited by Joseph P. O'Grady, 85–110. Lexington: University Press of Kentucky, 1967.
MacColl, René. *Roger Casement*. London: Hamish Hamilton, 1956.
MacDonagh, Donagh. "Plunkett and MacDonagh." In *Leaders and Men of the Easter Rising: Dublin 1916*, edited by F. X. Martin, 165–76. London: Methuen, 1967.
McHugh, Roger. "Casement and German Help." In *Leaders and Men of the Easter Rising: Dublin 1916*, edited by F. X. Martin, 177–87. London: Methuen, 1967.
Mackey, Herbert O. *The Life and Times of Roger Casement*. Dublin: C. J. Fallon, 1954.
Mann, Golo. *Deutsche Geschichte des neunzehnten und zwanzigsten Jahrhunderts*. Frankfurt: S. Fischer, 1962.
———. *Vom Geist Amerikas*. Stuttgart: W. Kohlhammer, 1961.
Mansergh, Nicholas. *The Irish Question 1840–1921*. London: George Allen & Unwin, 1965. (First published 1940 as *Ireland in the Age of Reform and Revolution*.)
Martin, F. X., ed. *Leaders and Men of the Easter Rising: Dublin 1916*. London: Methuen, 1967.
Martin, Lawrence W. *Peace without Victory*. New Haven, Conn.: Yale University Press, 1958.
Marwick, Arthur. *The Deluge*. London: Macmillan, 1973.
———. *War and Social Change in the Twentieth Century*. London: Macmillan, 1978.
May, Arthur J. *The Passing of the Hapsburg Monarchy 1914–1918*. Vols. 1–2. Philadelphia: University of Pennsylvania Press, 1966.
———. "Woodrow Wilson and Austria-Hungary to the End of 1917." In *Festschrift für Heinrich Benedikt*, edited by Hugo Hantsch and Alexander Novotny. Wien: Notring der wissenschaftlichen Verbände Österreichs, 1957.
May, Ernest R. "American Policy and Japan's Entrance into World War I." *Mississippi Valley Historical Review* 40 (June 1953–March 1954): 279–90.
———. *The World War and American Isolation 1914–1917*. Cambridge, Mass.: Harvard University Press, 1959.
Mayer, Arno J. *Political Origins of the New Diplomacy, 1917–1918*. New Haven: Yale University Press, 1959.
Meine, Arnold. *Wilsons Diplomatie in der Friedensfrage 1914–1917*. Stuttgart: W. Kohlhammer, 1938.
Meisner, Heinrich Otto. *Militärattachés und Militärbevollmächtigte in Preussen und im Deutschen Reich*. Berlin: Rütten & Loening, 1957.
Meyer, Klaus. *Theodor Schiemann als politischer Publizist*. Frankfurt: Rütten & Loening, 1956.

Meyer, Michael C. "The Mexican-German Conspiracy of 1915." *The Americas* 23 (July 1966): 76–89.

———. *Mexican Rebel*. Lincoln: University of Nebraska Press, 1967.

Millis, Walter. *Road to War*. London: Faber & Faber, 1935.

Mock, James R. "The Creel Committee in Latin America." *Hispanic American Historical Review* 22 (1942): 262–79.

Mock, James R., and Cedric Larson. *Words That Won the War*. New York: Russell & Russell, 1968.

Möckelmann, Jürgen. *Deutsch-amerikanische Beziehungen in der Krise*. Vol. 6, *Hamburger Reihe zur neueren Geschichte*. Frankfurt: Europäische Verlagsanstalt, 1967.

———. "Das Deutschlandbild in den USA 1914–1918 und die Kriegspolitik Wilsons." Ph.D. diss., Universität Hamburg, 1965.

Mommsen, Wolfgang J. "The Debate on German War Aims." *Journal of Contemporary History* 1 (1966): 47–72.

———. "Die deutsche öffentliche Meinung und der Zusammenbruch des Regierungssystems Bethmann Hollweg im Juli 1917." *Geschichte in Wissenschaft und Unterricht* 19 (1968): 656–71.

———. "Der Kanzler im Zwielicht." *Die Zeit* (April 10, 1970): 16.

———. "Max Weber und die deutsche Politik 1890–1920." Ph.D. diss., Universität Köln, 1959.

Morison, Samuel E., and Henry S. Commager. *The Growth of the American Republic*. Vol. 2. New York: Oxford University Press, 1960.

Morrissey, Alice M. *The American Defense of Neutral Rights, 1914–1917*. Cambridge, Mass.: Harvard University Press, 1939.

Murphy, Paul L. *World War I and the Origin of Civil Liberties in the United States*. New York: W. W. Norton, 1979.

Naidis, Mark. "Propaganda of the Gadar Party." *Pacific Historical Review* 20 (1951): 251–60.

Naudé, Kurt. *Der Kampf um den uneingeschränkten U-Boot-Krieg 1914–1917*. Hamburg: Hanseatische Verlagsanstalt, 1941.

Nelson, Keith L. *Victors Divided*. Berkeley and Los Angeles: University of California Press, 1975.

Newbolt, Henry. *Naval Operations*. Vols. 4–5, *History of the Great War*. London: Longmans, 1928–31.

Nowak, Karl Friedrich. *Versailles*. Berlin: Verlag für Kulturpolitik, 1927.

Nowak, Karl Friedrich, and Friedrich Thimme, eds. *Erinnerungen und Gedanken des Botschafters Anton Graf Monts*. Berlin: Verlag für Kulturpolitik, 1932.

O'Connor, Richard. *The German-Americans*. Boston: Little, Brown, 1968.

O'Donoghue, Florence. "Ceannt, Devoy, O'Rahilly, and the Military Plan." In *Leaders and Men of the Easter Rising: Dublin 1916*, edited by F. X. Martin, 189–202. London: Methuen, 1967.

Örvik, Nils. *The Decline of Neutrality 1914–1941.* Oslo: Johan Grundt Tanum, 1953.
O'Grady, Joseph P. "The Irish." In *The Immigrants' Influence on Wilson's Peace Policies,* edited by Joseph P. O'Grady. Lexington: University Press of Kentucky, 1967.
———, ed. *The Immigrants' Influence on Wilson's Peace Policies.* Lexington: University Press of Kentucky, 1967.
Orland, Nachum. "Reichsregierung und Zionismus im Ersten Weltkrieg." *Saeculum* 25 (1974): 56–87.
Osgood, Robert E. *Ideals and Self-Interest in America's Foreign Relations.* Chicago: University of Chicago Press, 1953.
Park, Robert E. *The Immigrant Press and Its Control.* New York: Harper & Brothers, 1922.
Paxson, Frederic L. *Pre-War Years, 1913–1917.* Boston: Houghton Mifflin/Riverside, 1936.
Perkins, Dexter. *A History of the Monroe Doctrine.* London: Longmans, Green, 1960. (First published 1941 as *Hands Off: A History of the Monroe Doctrine.*)
———. *The Monroe Doctrine, 1867–1907.* Gloucester, Mass.: Peter Smith, 1966. (First published 1937.)
Peter, Elmar. "Die Bedeutung Chinas in der deutschen Ostasienpolitik (1911–1917)." Ph.D. diss., Universität Hamburg, 1965.
Peters, Detlef R. "Das 'US Committee on Public Information.'" Ph.D. diss., Freie Universität Berlin, 1964.
Peters, Evelene. *Roosevelt und der Kaiser.* Forschungen zur neueren und neuesten Geschichte, no. 6. Leipzig: Robert Noske, 1936.
Peterson, H. C. *Propaganda for War.* Port Washington, N.Y.: Kennikat Press, 1968.
Peterson, H. C., and Gilbert C. Fite. *Opponents of War, 1917–1918.* Madison: University of Wisconsin Press, 1957.
Pinette, Kaspar. "Albert Ballin und die deutsche Politik." Ph.D. diss., Universität Göttingen, 1936.
Pisney, Raymond F. *Woodrow Wilson in Retrospect.* Verona, Va.: McClure Press, 1978.
Politik im Krieg 1914–1918. Project group directed by Fritz Klein. Berlin: Akademie-Verlag, 1964.
Posani, Riccardo, ed. *La Guerra sottomarina.* La Grande Guerra 1914–18, no. 9. Firenze: Sadea/Sansoni, 1968.
Pratt, Julius W. "Robert Lansing." In *The American Secretaries of State and Their Diplomacy,* edited by Samuel Flagg Bemis, 10:47–175. New York: Pageant Book Co., 1958.
Pringle, Henry F. *The Life and Times of William Howard Taft.* Vols. 1–2. New York: Farrar & Rinehart, 1939.

Quirk, Robert E. *An Affair of Honor.* Lexington: University Press of Kentucky, 1962.
———. *The Mexican Revolution, 1914–1915.* Bloomington: Indiana University Press, 1960.
Rappaport, Armin. *The British Press and Wilsonian Neutrality.* Stanford, Calif.: Stanford University Press, 1951.
Rappaport, Joseph. "The American Yiddish Press and the European Conflict in 1914." *Jewish Social Studies* (1957).
Rathmann, Lothar. *Stossrichtung Nahost 1914–1918.* Berlin: Rütten & Loening, 1963.
Rausch, George J., Jr. "The Exile and Death of Victoriano Huerta." *Hispanic American Historical Review* 42 (1962): 133–51.
Read, James Morgan. *Atrocity Propaganda 1914–1919.* New Haven, Conn.: Yale University Press, 1941.
Reeves, Jesse S. "The Prussian-American Treaties." *American Journal of International Law* 11 (1917): 475–510.
Reid, B. L. *The Lives of Roger Casement.* New Haven, Conn.: Yale University Press, 1976.
Reidy, James. "John Devoy." *Journal of The American Irish Historical Society* 27 (1928): 413–25.
Renouvin, Pierre. *La Crise européenne et la Grande Guerre (1914–1918).* Paris: Félix Alcan, 1934.
Ringhoffer, Karl. *Im Kampfe um Preussens Ehre.* Berlin: Ernst Siegfried Mittler und Sohn, 1906.
Rheinbaben, Werner Freiherr von. "Verpasste Gelegenheiten." *Hannoversche Allgemeine Zeitung* (November 23, 1962): 8.
Ritter, Gerhard. "Bethmann Hollweg im Schlaglicht des deutschen Geschichts-Revisionismus." *Schweizer Monatshefte* 42 (November 1962): 799–808.
———. *Der Erste Weltkrieg.* Bonn: Bundeszentrale für politische Bildung, 1964.
———. *Staatskunst und Kriegshandwerk.* Vols. 2–4. Munich: R. Oldenbourg, 1965, 1964, 1968.
Rivière, P.-Louis. *Un Centre de guerre secrète.* Paris: Payot, 1936.
Rocha, Rodolfo. "The Influence of the Mexican Revolution on the Mexico-Texas Border, 1910–1916." Ph.D. diss., Texas Tech University, 1981.
Rogge, Helmuth. *Holstein und Harden.* Munich: C. H. Beck, 1959.
Rosenbaum, Eduard. "Albert Ballin: A Note on the Style of his Economic and Political Activities." *Publications of the Leo Baeck Institute of Jews from Germany. Year Book* 3 (1958): 257–99.
———. "M. M. Warburg & Co. Merchant Bankers of Hamburg." *Publications of the Leo Baeck Institute of Jews from Germany. Year Book* 7 (1962): 121–49.

Rosenbaum, Eduard, and A. J. Sherman. *Das Bankhaus M. M. Warburg & Co. 1798–1938*. Hamburg: Hans Christians, 1976.
Rosenberger, Homer Tope. *The Pennsylvania Germans, 1891–1965*. Lancaster: The Pennsylvania German Society, 1966.
Ross, Stanley R. *Francisco I. Madero*. New York: Columbia University Press, 1955.
Rudenko, B. T. "México en vísperas de la revolución democrático-burguesa." In *La Revolución Mexicana*. Colleccion Reforma-Revolución, no. 2. Mexico: Ediciones Los Insurgentes, 1960.
Sanders, M. L., and Philip M. Taylor. *British Propaganda during the First World War, 1914–18*. London: Macmillan, 1982.
Sasse, Heinz. *100 Jahre Botschaft in London*. Bonn: Off-print from Mitteilungsblatt der Vereinigung der Angestellten des Auswärtigen Dienstes, 1963.
———. "Zur Geschichte des Auswärtigen Amts." *Mitteilungsblatt der Vereinigung der Angestellten des Auswärtigen Dienstes* 4 (May 1960): 105–18; (June 1960): 133–41; (July 1960): 161–68; (August 1960): 189–95; (September 1960): 213–17.
Schachner, Nathan. *The Price of Liberty*. New York: The American Jewish Committee, 1948.
Schieber, Clara E. *The Transformation of American Sentiment toward Germany, 1870–1914*. Boston: Cornhill, 1923.
Schieder, Theodor. "Europa im Zeitalter der Nationalstaaten und europäischer Weltpolitik bis zum 1. Weltkrieg (1870–1918)." In *Handbuch der Europäischen Geschichte*, edited by Theodor Schieder, 6:1–196. Stuttgart: Union, 1968.
Schieder, Wolfgang, ed. *Erster Weltkrieg. Ursachen, Entstehung und Kriegsziele*. Cologne: Kiepenheuer & Witsch, 1969.
Schiefel, Werner. *Bernhard Dernburg 1865–1937*. Zürich and Freiburg: Atlantis, n.d.
Schiff, Warren. "German Military Penetration into Mexico during the Late Diaz Period." *Hispanic American Historical Review* 39 (August 1959): 568–79.
Schilling, Konrad. "Beiträge zu einer Geschichte des radikalen Nationalismus in der Wilhelminischen Ära 1890–1909." Ph.D. diss., Universität Köln, 1968.
Schindler, Dietrich. *Die Schiedsgerichtsbarkeit seit 1914*. Stuttgart: W. Kohlhammer, 1938.
Schmid-Bürckert, Walter. "Graf Johann-Heinrich von Bernstorff als deutscher Botschafter in Washington 1908–1917." Ph.D. diss., Universität Tübingen, 1947.
Schmidt-Bückeburg, Rudolf. *Das Militärkabinett der preußischen Könige und deutschen Kaiser*. Berlin: E. S. Mittler & Sohn, 1933.

Schnieder, Erich. "Die Vereinigten Staaten von Amerika und das Problem der Neutralität." Ph.D. diss., Universität Göttingen, 1937.
Schreiner, Albert. *Zur Geschichte der deutschen Aussenpolitik, 1871–1945.* Vol. 1. Berlin: Dietz, 1955.
Schröder, Ernst. "Otto Wiedfeldt." Off-print from *Beiträge zur Geschichte von Stadt und Stift Essen* 80 (1964).
Schuberth, Inger. *Schweden und das Deutsche Reich im Ersten Weltkrieg.* Bonn: Ludwig Röhrscheidt, 1982.
Schüssler, Wilhelm. *Die Daily-Telegraph-Affäre.* Göttingen: Musterschmidt, 1952.
Schulz, Gerhard. *Revolutionen und Friedensschlüsse 1917–1920.* Munich: Deutscher Taschenbuch Verlag, 1967.
Schwabe, Klaus. *Deutsche Revolution und Wilson-Frieden.* Düsseldorf: Droste, 1971.
———. "Ursprung und Verbreitung des alldeutschen Annexionismus in der deutschen Professorenschaft im Ersten Weltkrieg." *Vierteljahrshefte für Zeitgeschichte* 14 (April 1966): 105–38.
———. "Die Vereinigten Staaten, die deutsche Friedenspolitik und das Scheitern eines 'Wilson-Friedens.'" Habilitationsschrift, University of Freiburg, 1968.
———. *Wissenschaft und Kriegsmoral.* Göttingen: Musterschmidt, 1969.
———. *Woodrow Wilson.* Vol. 62, *Persönlichkeit und Geschichte.* Göttingen: Musterschmidt, 1971.
———. "Zur politischen Haltung der deutschen Professoren im Ersten Weltkrieg." *Historische Zeitschrift* 193 (1961): 601–34.
Schwepcke, Hans-Jürgen. "U-Boot-Krieg und Friedenspolitik." Ph.D. diss., Universität Heidelberg, 1952.
Seager, Robert, II. *Alfred Thayer Mahan.* Annapolis: Naval Institute Press, 1977.
Seymour, Charles. *American Diplomacy during the World War.* 2d ed. Baltimore, Md.: Johns Hopkins Press, 1942.
———. *American Neutrality 1914–1917.* New Haven, Conn.: Yale University Press, 1935.
———. "The House-Bernstorff Conversations in Perspective." In *Studies in Diplomatic History and Historiography in Honour of G. P. Gooch, C.H.,* edited by A. O. Sarkissian, 90–106. London: Longmans, 1961.
———. Review of *Memoirs of Count Bernstorff. Mississippi Valley Historical Review* 23 (June 1936–March 1937): 589–90.
Sherman, William, and Richard E. Greenleaf. *Victoriano Huerta.* Mexico: Mexico City College Press, 1960.
Silberstein, Gerard E. *The Troubled Alliance.* Lexington: University Press of Kentucky, 1970.
Simpson, Colin. "A Great Liner with Too Many Secrets." *Life* 73 (October

13, 1972): 60, 63–64, 66, 68–72, 74, 76, 79–80.

———. *The Lusitania*. London: Longmans, 1972; Boston: Little, Brown, 1973.

Siney, Marion C. *The Allied Blockade of Germany 1914–1916*. Ann Arbor: University of Michigan Press, 1957.

Singh, Diwakar Prasad. *American Attitude towards the Indian Nationalist Movement*. New Delhi: Munshiram Manoharlal, 1974.

Slosson, Preston William. *The Great Crusade and After, 1914–1928*. Vol. 12, *A History of American Life*. New York: Macmillan, 1946.

Smith, Daniel M. *The Great Departure*. New York: John Wiley & Sons, 1965.

———. "National Interest and American Intervention, 1917: An Historiographical Appraisal." *Journal of American History* 52 (1965): 5–24.

———. "Robert Lansing." In *An Uncertain Tradition*, edited by Norman A. Graebner, 101–27. New York: McGraw-Hill, 1961.

———. *Robert Lansing and American Neutrality, 1914–1917*. Vol. 59, University of California Publications in History. Berkeley and Los Angeles: University of California Press, 1958.

———, ed. *American Intervention, 1917: Sentiment, Self-Interest, or Ideals?* Boston: Houghton Mifflin, 1966.

Smith, Gaddis. *Britain's Clandestine Submarines, 1914–1915*. New Haven, Conn.: Yale University Press, 1964.

Solom, Rudolf. "Die Handelsbeziehungen zwischen Deutschland und den Vereinigten Staaten von Amerika von 1871–1937." Ph.D. diss., Universität Köln, 1949.

Sondermann, Fred A. "The Wilson Administration's Image of Germany." Ph.D. diss., Yale University, 1953.

Spencer, Samuel R., Jr. *Decision for War, 1917*. Rindge, N.H.: Richard R. Smith, 1953.

Spillmann, Kurt R. *Amerikas Ideologie des Friedens*. Bern: Peter Lang, 1984.

———. "Woodrow Wilson's Friedensideologie." In *Festgabe für Leonhard von Muralt*, edited by Martin Haas and René Hauswirth. Zürich: Berichthaus, 1970.

Spindler, Arno. "Der britische Propagandafeldzug gegen die amerikanische Neutralität." *Berliner Monatshefte* 17 (July 1939): 929–43.

———. "Der Eintritt der Vereinigten Staaten in den Weltkrieg." *Berliner Monatshefte* 15 (1937): 283–321.

———. *Der Handelskrieg mit U-Booten*. Vols. 1–5. Berlin: E. S. Mittler & Sohn, 1932–66.

———. "Der Lusitania Fall." Off-print from *Berliner Monatshefte* (1935).

———. "Der Meinungsstreit in der Marine über den U-Bootskrieg 1914–1918." *Marine-Rundschau* 54/55 (1957/1958): 235–45.

———. *Wie es zu dem Entschluß zum uneingeschränkten U-Boots-Krieg 1917 gekommen ist.* Historisch-Politische Hefte der Ranke-Gesellschaft, no. 2. Göttingen: Musterschmidt, n.d.
Squires, James D. *British Propaganda at Home and in the United States from 1914 to 1917.* Cambridge, Mass.: Harvard University Press, 1935.
Stadelmann, Rudolf. "Friedensversuche im ersten Jahre des Weltkrieges." *Historische Zeitschrift* 156 (1937): 485–545.
Stadler, Otto. "Der U-Bootkrieg gegen England und die deutsche Tagespresse vom 1. August 1914 bis zum 1. Februar 1917." Ph.D. diss., Universität Heidelberg, 1937.
Stegemann, Bernd. *Die deutsche Marinepolitik 1916–1918.* Vol. 4, *Historische Forschungen.* Berlin: Duncker & Humblot, 1970.
Steglich, Wolfgang. *Bündnissicherung oder Verständigungsfrieden.* Vol. 28, *Göttinger Bausteine zur Geschichtswissenschaft.* Göttingen: Musterschmidt, 1958.
———. *Die Friedenspolitik der Mittelmächte 1917/18.* Wiesbaden: Franz Steiner, 1964.
Stern, Fritz. *Bethmann Hollweg und der Krieg: Die Grenzen der Verantwortung.* Recht und Staat in Geschichte und Gegenwart, nos. 351–52. Tübingen: J. C. B. Mohr, 1968.
———. *The Failure of Illiberalism.* New York: Alfred A. Knopf, 1972.
———. "Das Rätsel Bethmann Hollweg: Die Kunst, das Böse zu tun." *Die Zeit*, December 29, 1967, 26.
———. *Um eine neue deutsche Vergangenheit.* Konstanz: Universitätsverlag, 1972.
Stern-Rubarth, Edgar. *Graf Brockdorff-Rantzau, Wanderer zwischen zwei Welten.* Berlin: Reimar Hobbing, 1929.
———. *Die Propaganda als politisches Instrument.* Berlin: Trowitzsch & Sohn, 1921.
Stolberg-Wernigerode, Otto Graf zu. "Deutsche Politik von Bismarck bis Ebert." *Politische Bildung* 4 (1952): 221–57.
———. *Deutschland und die Vereinigten Staaten von Amerika im Zeitalter Bismarcks.* Berlin: Walter de Gruyter, 1933.
———. *Geschichte der Vereinigten Staaten von Amerika.* Berlin: Walter de Gruyter, 1956.
———. *Die unentschiedene Generation.* Munich: R. Oldenbourg, 1968.
———. *Wilhelm II.* Colemans Kleine Biographien, no. 6. Lübeck: Charles Coleman, 1932.
Stubmann, Peter. *Ballin.* Berlin: Verlagsanstalt Hermann Klemm, 1926.
Stürmer, Michael, ed. *Das kaiserliche Deutschland.* Düsseldorf: Droste, 1970.
Supple, Barry E. "A Business Elite: German-Jewish Financiers in Nineteenth-Century New York." *Business History Review* 31 (Summer 1957): 143–78.

Sutherland, Sidney. "German Spies in America." *Liberty* 8 (installments, February 21–May 16, 1931).
Sweet, Paul R. "Leaders and Policies: Germany in the Winter of 1914–1915." *Journal of Central European Affairs* 16 (October 1956): 229–52.
Sweetman, Jack. *The Landing at Veracruz: 1914*. Annapolis: United States Naval Institute, 1968.
Szajkowski, Zosa [Szajko Frydman]. "Jewish Relief in Eastern Europe 1914–1917." Publications of the Leo Baeck Institute. *Yearbook* 10 (1965): 24–56.
Tannenbaum, Frank. *The Mexican Agrarian Revolution*. New York: Macmillan, 1929.
_____. *Peace by Revolution: Mexico after 1910*. New York: Columbia University Press, 1966.
_____. "Reflections on the Mexican Revolution." *Journal of International Affairs* 9 (1955): 37–46.
Tansill, Charles Callan. *America and the Fight for Irish Freedom, 1866–1922*. New York: Devin-Adair, 1957.
_____. *America Goes to War*. Boston: Little, Brown, 1938.
Taussig, Michael. "Culture of Terror-Space of Death. Roger Casement's Putumayo Report and the Explanation of Terror." *Comparative Studies in Society and History* 26 (July 1984): 467–97.
Taylor, A. J. P. *The First World War*. Harmondsworth: Penguin, 1966.
_____. *From Sarajevo to Potsdam*. London: Thames and Hudson, 1966.
Teitelbaum, Louis M. *Woodrow Wilson and the Mexican Revolution (1913–1916)*. New York: Exposition, 1967.
Tenzer, Morton. "The Jews." In *The Immigrants' Influence on Wilson's Peace Policies*, edited by Joseph P. O'Grady, 287–317. Lexington: University Press of Kentucky, 1967.
Thimme, Hans. *Weltkrieg ohne Waffen*. Stuttgart: J. G. Cotta'sche Buchhandlung, 1932.
Thompson, William Irwin. *The Imagination of an Insurrection*. New York: Oxford University Press, 1967.
Timmermann, Heinrich. *Friedenssicherungsbewegungen in den Vereinigten Staaten von Amerika und in Grossbritannien während des Ersten Weltkrieges*. Frankfurt and Bern: Peter Lang, 1978.
Tinnemann, Ethel Mary. "Count Johann von Bernstorff and German-American Relations, 1908–1917." Ph.D. diss., University of California at Berkeley, 1960.
Treue, Wilhelm. "Max Freiherr von Oppenheim—Der Archäologe und die Politik." *Historische Zeitschrift* 209 (August 1969): 37–74.
Trevelyan, George M. *Grey of Fallodon*. London: Longmans, Green, 1937.
Trumpener, Ulrich. *Germany and the Ottoman Empire, 1914–1918*. Princeton, N.J.: Princeton University Press, 1968.
_____. "War Premeditated? German Intelligence Operations in July 1914."

Central European History 9 (March 1976): 58–85.
Tuchman, Barbara. *The Guns of August*. New York: Dell, 1963.
———. *The Proud Tower*. New York: Bantam, 1967.
———. *The Zimmermann Telegram*. New York: Viking, 1958.
Turner, Frederick C. "Anti-Americanism in Mexico, 1910–1913." *Hispanic American Historical Review* 47 (1967): 502–18.
Urofsky, Melvin I. *Big Steel and the Wilson Administration*. Columbus: Ohio State University Press, 1969.
Vagts, Alfred. *Defense and Diplomacy*. New York: King's Crown Press, Columbia University Press, 1956.
———. *Deutschland und die Vereinigten Staaten in der Weltpolitik*. Vols. 1–2. London: Lovat Dickson & Thompson; New York: Macmillan, 1935.
———. "Hopes and Fears of an American-German War, 1870–1905." *Political Science Quarterly* 54 (1939): 514–34; 55 (1940): 53–76.
———. "Die Juden im amerikanisch-deutschen imperialistischen Konflikt vor 1917." *Amerikastudien/American Studies* 24 (1979): 56–71.
———. "Die Juden im englisch-deutschen Konflikt vor 1914." In *Imperialismus im 20. Jahrhundert*, edited by J. Radkau and I. Geiss, 113–43. Munich: C. H. Beck, 1976.
———. *Mexico, Europa und Amerika*. Berlin: Walter Rothschild, 1928.
———. "M. M. Warburg & Co.: Ein Bankhaus in der deutschen Weltpolitik 1905–1933." *Vierteljahrsschrift für Sozial- und Wirtschaftsgeschichte* 45 (1958): 289–388.
———. "Staatsmänner und Diplomaten. VI. Colonel House." *Europäische Gespräche* 7 (August 1929): 430–42.
Valentin, Veit. *Deutschlands Außenpolitik von Bismarcks Abgang bis zum Ende des Weltkrieges*. Berlin: Deutsche Verlagsgesellschaft für Politik und Geschichte, 1921.
Vierhaus, Rudolf. "Die politische Mitte in der Weimarer Republik." *Geschichte in Wissenschaft und Unterricht* 15 (1964): 133–49.
Vietsch, Eberhard von. *Bethmann Hollweg*. Schriften des Bundesarchivs, no. 18. Boppard: Harald Boldt, 1969.
Vincent, C. Paul. *The Politics of Hunger*. Athens: Ohio University Press, 1985.
Vogel, Walter. *Die Organisation der amtlichen Presse- und Propagandapolitik des deutschen Reiches von den Anfängen unter Bismarck bis zum Beginn des Jahres 1933*. Berlin: Duncker & Humblot, 1941. Special Issue of *Zeitungswissenschaft*; as such 16 (1941).
Wall, Joseph Frazier. *Andrew Carnegie*. New York: Oxford University Press, 1970.
Walworth, Arthur. *Woodrow Wilson*. Vols. 1–2. New York and London: Longmans, Green, 1958.
Ward, Alan J. *Ireland and Anglo-American Relations, 1899–1921*. London: Weidenfeld and Nicolson, 1969.

Weber, Frank. *Eagles on the Crescent*. Ithaca, N.Y.: Cornell University Press, 1970.
Weber, Hellmuth. *Ludendorff und die Monopole*. Berlin: Akademie-Verlag, 1966.
Wehler, Hans-Ulrich. *Der Aufstieg des amerikanischen Imperialismus*. Kritische Studien zur Geschichtswissenschaft, no. 10. Göttingen: Vandenhoeck & Ruprecht, 1974.
_____. *Das deutsche Kaiserreich 1871–1918*. 4th ed. Göttingen: Vandenhoeck & Ruprecht, 1980.
_____. *Krisenherde des Kaiserreichs 1871–1918*. Göttingen: Vandenhoeck & Ruprecht, 1970.
_____. "Zur Funktion und Struktur der nationalen Kampfverbände im Kaiserreich." In *Modernisierung und nationale Gesellschaft im ausgehenden 18. und im 19. Jahrhundert*, edited by W. Conze, G. Schramm, and K. Zernack, 113–24. Berlin: Duncker & Humblot, 1979.
Weinberg, Gerhard. "National Style in Diplomacy: Germany." In *Oceans Apart?*, edited by Erich Angermann and Marie-Luise Frings, 146–59. Stuttgart: Klett-Cotta, 1981.
Weis, Erwin. *Die Propaganda der Vereinigten Staaten gegen Deutschland im Ersten Weltkrieg*. Essen: Essener Verlagsanstalt, 1943.
Wende, Frank. *Die belgische Frage in der deutschen Politik des Ersten Weltkrieges*. Schriftenreihe zur Auswärtigen Politik, no. 7. Hamburg: Institut für Auswärtige Politik, 1968.
Wernecke, Klaus. *Der Wille zur Weltgeltung*. Düsseldorf: Droste, 1970.
Wheeler-Bennett, John W. *Hindenburg*. London: Macmillan, 1936.
_____. *The Nemesis of Power*. London: Macmillan, 1953.
Whitehead, Don. *The F.B.I. Story*. London: Frederick Muller, 1957.
Wiegand, Wayne A. "Ambassador in Absentia: George Meyer, William II and Theodore Roosevelt." *Mid-America* 56 (January 1974): 3–15.
Willert, Arthur. *The Road to Safety*. London: Derek Verschoyle, 1952.
Wimer, Kurt. "Woodrow Wilson and World Order." In *Woodrow Wilson and a Revolutionary World, 1913–1921*, edited by Arthur S. Link, 146–73. Chapel Hill: University of North Carolina Press, 1982.
Wittke, Carl. *German-Americans and the World War*. Columbus: Ohio State Archaeological and Historical Society, 1936. (Vol. 5, *Ohio Historical Collections*.)
_____. *The German-Language Press in America*. Lexington: University Press of Kentucky, 1957.
_____. *The Irish in America*. Baton Rouge: Louisiana State University Press, 1956.
Wolf, Karin. *Sir Roger Casement und die deutsch-irischen Beziehungen*. Vol. 5, *Historische Forschungen*. Berlin: Duncker & Humblot, 1972.
Womack, John, Jr. *Zapata and the Mexican Revolution*. London: Thames and Hudson, 1969.

Wright, Almon R. "German Interest in Panama's Piñas Bay, 1910–1938." *Journal of Modern History* 27 (March–December 1955): 61–66.
Young, Harry F. *Maximilian Harden.* The Hague: Martinus Nijhoff, 1959.
———. *Prince Lichnowsky and the Great War.* Athens: University of Georgia Press, 1977.
Zechlin, Egmont. *Die deutsche Politik und die Juden im Ersten Weltkrieg.* Göttingen: Vandenhoeck & Ruprecht, 1969.
———. "Friedensbestrebungen und Revolutionierungsversuche." *Aus Politik und Zeitgeschichte* (May 17, 1961): 269–88; (June 14, 1961): 325–37; (June 21, 1961): 341–67; (May 15, 1963): 3–54; (May 23, 1963): 3–47.
Zeman, Z. A. B. *A Diplomatic History of the First World War.* London: Weidenfeld and Nicolson, 1971.
Zmarzlik, Hans Günther. "Der Antisemitismus im Zweiten Reich." *Geschichte in Wissenschaft und Unterricht* 14 (1963): 273–86.
———. *Bethmann Hollweg als Reichskanzler 1909–1914.* Düsseldorf: Droste, 1957.

V. NEWSPAPERS AND JOURNALS NOT SPECIFICALLY CITED IN THE NOTES

Abwehrblätter. Berlin 1925–26, 1930.
Alldeutsche Blätter. Berlin 1909.
Berliner Monatshefte für Internationale Aufklärung (Die Kriegsschuldfrage). Berlin. Various numbers.
Berliner Tageblatt. Berlin. Single numbers.
Das Demokratische Deutschland. Hamburg.
Deutsche Einheit. Hamburg 1923–28.
Deutsche Tageszeitung. Berlin. Single numbers.
Düsseldorfer General-Anzeiger. Düsseldorf, February–April 1917.
Das Echo. Berlin. Single numbers.
The Fatherland. New York 1914–15.
Frankfurter Zeitung. Frankfurt. Single numbers.
The Gaelic American. New York. Single numbers.
Göttinger Tageblatt. Göttingen. Wartime volumes.
Hamburger Nachrichten. Hamburg. Single numbers.
Hamburgischer Correspondent. Hamburg. Single numbers.
Hammer. Leipzig. 1902–5, 1907–9, 1913–15.
Im Deutschen Reich. Berlin 1914–17.
The Independent. New York. Single numbers.
The Irish World. New York. Single numbers.
Jeschurun. Berlin, 1914–17.
Der Jude. Berlin, 1916–19.

Lauenburgische Zeitung. Ratzeburg, Single numbers.
Liberty. New York, 1931.
The Living Age. Boston. Single numbers.
Monatshefte für deutsche Sprache und Pädagogik. Madison, Wisconsin, 1914–17.
Neue Preussische Zeitung. Berlin. Single numbers.
Neue Zürcher Zeitung. Zürich. Single numbers.
The New York Times. New York. Single numbers.
New Yorker Staats-Zeitung und Herold. New York. Single numbers.
Norddeutsche Allgemeine Zeitung. Berlin. January–June, 1917.
The North American Review. New York, 1914–17.
The Outlook. New York, 1912–13.
Pro-Palästina. Berlin. Single numbers.
Revue d'Histoire de la Guerre Mondiale. Paris. Single numbers.
Der Völkerbund. Berlin. Single numbers.
Völkerbund-Fragen. Berlin. Single numbers.
Vossische Zeitung. Berlin. Single numbers.
Die Zukunft. Berlin. Single numbers.

INDEX

Adler-Rudel, S., 277 (n. 162)
Aetna Powder Company, 312 (n. 5)
Agadir, 329 (n. 170)
Aguinaldo y Famy, Emilio, 3
Ahrendt, Carl, 188, 344 (n. 290)
Ahrens, Georg, 13, 236 (n. 12)
Albert, Heinrich Friedrich, 40–41, 43, 49–50, 52–55, 63–64, 71, 112, 141–42, 151, 173, 176, 181–82, 184, 230, 258 (n. 4), 260 (n. 12), 265 (n. 55), 267 (n. 87), 269 (nn. 104, 105), 277 (n. 167), 288 (n. 65), 298 (n. 53), 299 (n. 63), 312 (nn. 4, 5), 313 (n. 10), 315 (n. 27), 317 (n. 43), 337 (n. 240)
Albertini, Luigi, 286 (n. 46)
Alvensleben, von, 177, 338 (n. 247)
American Jewish Committee, 63
American Jewish Relief Committee, 277 (n. 161)
American Truth Society, 76, 164, 280 (n. 189)
Amsinck & Co., 265 (n. 58)
Ancona, 118, 301 (nn. 93, 95)
Andaman Islands, 153, 321 (n. 90)
Andersen, Hans Niels, 290 (n. 96)
Anderson, Chandler P., 117, 341 (n. 270)
Annie Larsen, 151–52, 320 (n. 85)
Appuhn, Ch., 345 (n. 5)
Arabia, 200, 350 (n. 49)
Arabic, 112–18, 121, 126
Archibald, James F. J., 115, 143, 300 (n. 77)
Arkansas, 257 (n. 118)
Armour family, 25

Asquith, Herbert Henry, 95, 134
Aud (Castro), 161–62

Bachmann, Gustav, 81–82, 285 (n. 33), 299 (n. 67)
Bacteriological-chemical warfare, 189
Baden, Maximilian Prince von, 9, 238 (n. 37), 239 (n. 45), 360 (n. 149)
Baerensprung, Lieutenant von, 338 (n. 247)
Baghdad Railway, 238 (n. 40), 319 (n. 73)
Bailey, Daniel, 162
Bailey, Thomas A., 80, 220, 295 (n. 25), 312 (n. 2)
Bakhmeteff, George, 93
Balfour, Arthur, 134
Ballin, Albert, 36, 53, 165, 238 (n. 37), 256 (n. 115), 270 (n. 107), 290 (n. 96), 304 (n. 135), 320 (n. 77), 324 (n. 117), 346 (n. 17)
Baralong, 303 (n. 124)
Barrington, Sir Eric, 237 (n. 25)
Barthelme, Georg, 223
Bassermann, Ernst, 310–11 (n. 222)
Bauer, Hermann, 78
Baumgarten, Otto, 10–11
Baur-Breitenfeld, Karl von, 340 (n. 262)
Bavaria, 258 (n. 122)
Beesly, Patrick, 185
Behncke, Paul, 177, 334 (n. 223), 342 (n. 283)
Belgian Congo, 322 (n. 107)

Belgium, 42, 92, 96, 128–29, 134, 136, 139, 194–95, 199, 201–2, 211, 219, 292 (n. 109), 307 (n. 174), 311 (n. 223), 349 (n. 45), 350 (n. 58), 353 (nn. 83, 84), 357 (n. 120)
Bemis, Samuel Flagg, 304 (n. 134)
Benton, William F., 256 (n. 114)
Bergen, Carl-Ludwig Diego von, 59, 67
Berger, Julius, 277 (n. 161)
Bernhard, Georg, 12
Bernhardi, Friedrich von, 20–21, 244 (nn. 28, 29), 265 (n. 51)
Bernstorff, Albrecht Count von, 5, 235 (n. 11)
Bernstorff, Anna Countess von, 5
Bernstorff, Christian Günther Count von, 39, 236 (n. 16)
Bernstorff, Jeanne Countess von, 6–7, 15, 25, 128, 194, 235 (n. 7), 236 (n. 16), 241 (n. 58), 306 (n. 163), 346 (n. 17), 346–47 (n. 18), 357 (n. 122), 364 (n. 180)
Bernstorff, Luise Alexandra Countess von. *See* Loewenstein Wertheim Rosenberg, Alexandra Princess zu
Bertelli, Charles F., 56
Bethmann Hollweg, Theobald von, 15–17, 19, 32, 36, 62, 66, 79–80, 82, 87, 96, 98, 102, 105, 108–9, 113–14, 117, 119–20, 122–23, 125, 133–40, 145, 147, 150, 157–58, 169, 171, 191–92, 194–96, 198–99, 201–4, 208–14, 217–18, 226, 229–30, 234–35 (n. 6), 235 (n. 7), 238 (nn. 37, 38), 269 (n. 104), 283 (n. 18), 284 (n. 19), 285 (n. 33), 290 (n. 96), 291 (n. 102), 292 (n. 109), 299 (nn. 65, 67), 301 (n. 89), 304 (n. 130), 305 (nn. 151, 152), 308 (nn. 187, 188), 309 (n. 189), 310 (n. 212), 311 (nn. 222, 229), 323 (n. 115), 324 (n. 120), 332–33 (n. 208), 346 (nn. 13, 17), 346–47 (n. 18), 349 (nn. 41, 42), 350 (n. 52), 351 (n. 67), 353–54 (n. 90), 354 (n. 94), 355 (n. 100), 358 (nn. 127, 131), 364–65 (n. 187); and "September Program," 88
Bielaski, A. Bruce, 52
Birnbaum, Karl E., 80, 87, 120, 198, 234 (n. 1), 282 (n. 1), 292 (n. 109), 296 (n. 33), 310 (n. 212), 355 (n. 101)
Bismarck, Herbert Fürst von, 6
Bismarck, Otto Fürst von, 239 (n. 48), 264 (n. 46)
Bismarck family, 6
Bittenfeld, Herwarth von, 244 (n. 28)
Black Tom Terminal, 188–89, 197, 312 (n. 2)
Blücher von Wahlstatt, Evelyn Princess, 323 (n. 116)
Blücher von Wahlstatt, Gebhard Lebrecht Prince, 157, 323 (n. 116)
Blum, John M., 352 (n. 82), 363 (n. 176)
Blumenfeld, Kurt, 270 (n. 106), 274 (n. 136)
Bodenheimer, Max Isidor, 59, 271 (nn. 114, 116, 117, 118), 273 (nn. 129, 132, 133), 274–75 (n. 143), 277 (n. 163)
Boehm, Georg Paul, 149–50, 154, 319 (n. 64)
Boehm, Hans, 75, 179–81, 281 (nn. 209, 210), 337 (n. 243)
Bolo, Madame, 56
Bolo, Paul (Bolo Pascha), 55–57, 268 (n. 99)
Bombay, 320 (n. 88)
Bonath, Captain, 257 (n. 119)
Bonn, Moritz Julius, 143, 166, 260 (n. 12), 363 (n. 177)

Bopp, Franz, 186–87, 335 (n. 231), 340 (n. 264), 343 (n. 284)
Borkowski, von (supposed World War I propagandist), 262 (n. 27)
Boy-Ed, Karl, 109, 119, 143, 146, 151, 166–68, 174, 176, 179, 182, 183, 185, 188, 238 (n. 37), 301 (n. 94), 316 (n. 35), 330 (nn. 182, 183), 339 (n. 261), 340 (n. 264)
Brandenburg, Erich, 239 (n. 50)
Braun, Marcus, 52–53
Breitung, Max, 183
Brentano, Lujo, 7, 19, 241 (n. 58)
Brest-Litovsk, 215, 316 (n. 39)
Bridgeport Projectile Company, 312 (n. 5)
Brincken, Wilhelm von, 186–87, 342 (nn. 277, 281)
Brockdorff-Rantzau, Ulrich K. Count von, 10–11, 229, 240 (n. 55), 364 (n. 185)
Brown, Cyril, 49
Brussilov, Aleksej A., 140
Bryan, William Jennings, 36–37, 80–81, 84, 87, 100, 166, 169, 257 (n. 119), 258 (n. 123), 287 (nn. 54, 55, 57), 288 (n. 62), 289 (n. 74), 361 (n. 154); and arbitration, 32, 108, 211–12, 252–53 (n. 87), 253 (n. 89)
Buchanan, Frank, 184
Buchheit, Gert, 313 (n. 7)
Buenz, Karl, 182, 315 (n. 27)
Bulgaria, 120
Bülow, Bernhard Prince von, 7–8, 16, 19, 27–28, 209, 237 (n. 27), 238 (n. 37), 245 (nn. 32, 35), 248 (n. 53), 249 (n. 66), 250 (n. 73), 281 (n. 195), 347 (n. 19), 354 (n. 92)
Bülow, Hans-Adolf von, 256 (n. 115)
Burgos, Antonio, 174
Burían von Rajecz, Stefan Count, 201

Busch, Mrs. Adolphus, 54
Bussche-Haddenhausen, Hilmar Freiherr von dem, 144, 250 (n. 74), 329 (n. 170)
Busse, Friedrich, 336 (n. 238)
Butler, Nicholas Murray, 23

Cairo, 7–8
Calmbach, H., 243 (n. 22)
Canada, William Wesley, 257 (nn. 118, 119)
Canadian Car and Foundry Company, 188
Capelle, Eduard von, 126
Carden, Sir Lionel, 255 (n. 110)
Carnegie, Andrew, 251 (n. 78)
Carranza, Venustiano, 34, 36, 168–69, 171–72, 215, 227, 332 (n. 202), 333 (n. 212), 361 (n. 162)
Casement, Sir Roger, 73, 155–64, 179, 316 (n. 30), 322 (n. 107), 323 (nn. 110, 112, 114, 115, 116), 324 (nn. 117, 122, 123, 127, 128), 325 (nn. 129, 130), 326 (n. 139), 327 (n. 154), 338 (n. 246), 340 (n. 264)
Central Association of German Citizens of the Jewish Faith (Centralverein deutscher Staatsbürger jüdischen Glaubens), 58, 60, 270 (n. 112), 270–71 (n. 113)
Chakravarty, Khan Dravanta, 149, 153, 321 (n. 93)
Charles, Heinrich, 41, 259 (n. 9)
Charles, Son. See Wunnenberg, Karl
Chattopadhyaya, Virendranath, 148
Chittagong, 319 (n. 67)
Christensen, Eivind Adler, 156, 323 (n. 113)
Church, S. H., 307 (n. 174)
Churchill, Winston, 91
Clan na Gael, 74, 151, 156, 164, 183, 322 (n. 105), 324 (nn. 122, 123), 325 (n. 129)
Clark. See Victorica, Maria

Clarke, Thomas J., 159, 183
Class, Heinrich (pseud. Einhart; Daniel Frymann), 18, 243 (n. 22)
Claussen, Matthew B., 41–43, 69, 259 (n. 12), 260 (n. 13), 261 (n. 24), 265 (n. 55), 279 (n. 176)
Cline, Howard F., 255 (n. 105)
Cobb, Frank Irving, 228
Cockran, Bourke, 322–23 (n. 109)
Cohalan, Daniel, 328 (n. 168)
Cohalan, Daniel F., 74, 323 (n. 112)
Cohn, Oskar, 274 (n. 136)
Columbus Raid, 171, 331 (n. 197)
Committee for the East. See German Committee for the Liberation of the Russian Jews
Connolly, James, 183
Constantinople, 8, 238 (n. 39)
Cortez, Hernando, 362 (n. 168)
Covani, Constantine, 336 (n. 238)
Cowdray, Lord. See Pearson, S. Weetmann
Crotty, J., 158, 160
Crowley, C. C., 186–87
Czernin von und zu Chudenitz, Ottokar Count, 222, 224

Dallwitz, Johann von, 209, 354 (n. 93)
Darmstädter, Professor Dr., 340 (n. 269)
Dawson, Albert, 46
Dayal, Har, 148, 317 (n. 53), 326 (n. 141)
Deimling, Berthold von, 302 (n. 104)
Delbrück, Clemens Gottlieb Ernst, 283 (n. 18)
Delbrück, Hans G. L., 60, 272 (n. 124)
Delcassé, Théophile, 291 (n. 106)
Delgado, José C., 167
Delmar. See Dilger, Anton
Dernburg, Bernhard Jakob Ludwig, 39–45, 47, 51, 53–54, 60–63, 69, 71, 74, 83, 104, 107, 156, 170–71, 173, 184, 258 (n. 4), 259 (n. 10), 260 (n. 17), 261 (nn. 24, 25), 262 (n. 32), 262–63 (n. 34), 263 (nn. 35, 38), 264 (nn. 45, 47), 265 (n. 58), 267 (n. 81), 269 (n. 105), 270 (n. 110), 275 (n. 151), 279 (nn. 177, 185), 299 (n. 63), 305 (n. 144), 312 (n. 4), 323 (n. 112), 331 (n. 196), 340 (n. 264)
Deutelmoser, Erhard Eduard, 260 (n. 16)
Deutsche Bank, 56, 167
Deutsche Demokratische Partei. See German Democratic Party
Deutsche Tageszeitung, 294 (n. 15)
Devoy, John, 74, 76, 156, 158–59, 183, 323 (n. 112), 324 (nn. 122, 127), 326 (n. 139), 340 (n. 266)
Diaz, Porfirio, 4, 33–34, 36, 168, 225, 254 (nn. 98, 101)
Dieckhoff, Hans Heinrich, 9
Dilger, Anton (alias Delmar; Dr. Delmar; Albert C. Delmar; Alberto Donde), 187, 343 (n. 285)
Dillon. See Wessels, Hermann
Dresden, 37, 165
Dumba, Constantin, 49, 86, 102, 108, 115, 143, 183, 222, 253 (nn. 89, 92), 258 (n. 1), 300 (n. 77), 340 (n. 265)
Dunsley, 112
Duroselle, Jean-Baptiste, 300 (n. 74)

Easter Rising, 74, 156, 159–62, 164, 183, 356 (n. 112)
Ebert, Friedrich, 10, 240 (n. 55)
Eckardstein, Hermann Baron von, 7
Eckardt, Felix von, 364 (n. 183)
Eckardt, Heinrich von, 166, 176, 226–27, 333 (n. 217), 362 (n. 168)
Egan, Maurice Francis, 241–42 (n. 1), 243 (n. 19)

Ehrlich, Paul, 274 (n. 136)
Einhart. *See* Class, Heinrich
Eisendecher, Karl J. G. von, 267 (n. 76)
Eliot, Charles W., 264 (n. 50)
Emerson, William E., 1
Enrile, Gonzaló C., 172–73, 332 (nn. 201, 202)
Erzberger, Matthias, 10–12, 56–57, 174, 260 (n. 16), 280 (n. 193), 288 (n. 66), 334 (n. 221)
E. V. Gibbons, Inc., 183, 339 (n. 260)

Fair Play, 52–53
Falcke, Paul Siegfried Horst, 145, 182, 259 (n. 9), 315 (n. 27)
Falkenhayn, Erich von, 119–21, 125–26, 134, 155, 283 (n. 18), 302 (nn. 103, 104)
Farley, John, 357 (n. 120)
Fatherland, The, 41, 52, 164, 259 (n. 12)
Fay, Robert, 183, 337 (n. 242), 339–40 (n. 261)
Fernow, Karl, 262 (n. 27)
Fick, A., 243 (n. 22)
Findlay Affair, 323 (n. 113)
Fischer, Fritz, 1, 2, 234 (nn. 2, 5), 288 (n. 60), 292 (n. 109), 296 (n. 33), 318 (n. 60), 346 (n. 15), 349 (n. 42)
Fischer, Jean, 274 (n. 138)
Fletcher, Frank F., 37, 257 (n. 119)
Florida, 257 (n. 118)
Fox, Edward Lyell, 46, 265 (n. 55)
Francke, Kuno, 260 (n. 12)
Frankfurter Rundschau, 13
Frankfurter Zeitung, 294 (n. 15)
Franz Ferdinand, Archduke, 39
Frederik VIII, 228–29
Freeman, George, 72, 182–83, 321 (n. 94), 339 (n. 258)
Freytag-Loringhoven, Hugo Baron von, 302 (n. 104)

Fried, Alfred H., 247 (n. 50)
Friedemann, Adolf, 62, 271 (n. 116), 273 (n. 129)
Fritzen, Alfred E. (also A. A. Fritzen), 336 (n. 238)
Frymann, Daniel. *See* Class, Heinrich
Fuchs, Eugen, 274 (n. 136)
Fuehr, Karl Alexander, 41, 43, 259 (n. 12), 262 (n. 27), 265 (n. 55), 275 (n. 151), 340 (n. 266), 345–46 (n. 11)

Gaché, Emile Victor. *See* Rintelen, Franz
Gaelic American, 72, 74, 76, 324 (n. 122)
Gaffney, Thomas St. John, 164
Gallwitz, General von, 238 (n. 37)
Gates, Edward V. *See* Rintelen, Franz
Gaunt, Guy, 142, 313 (n. 8)
Geissler, Alfred, 244 (n. 28)
General-Anzeiger, 363 (n. 177), 364 (n. 179)
Georgia Case, 31, 250–51 (n. 75), 251 (n. 79)
Gerard, James W., 80–81, 87, 95, 102, 108, 110–11, 114–15, 126, 129, 136–39, 144, 196, 218, 284 (nn. 22, 28), 286 (n. 48), 291 (n. 99), 292 (n. 109), 296 (n. 36), 300 (n. 71), 305 (n. 147), 310 (n. 214), 346 (n. 17), 348 (n. 30), 361 (n. 160), 363 (n. 178)
Gerdts, Raoul (alias "Cousin Raoul"; Raoul Sala), 188, 343–44 (n. 290)
German-American Chamber of Commerce, 41, 259 (n. 9)
German-American National Alliance, 49, 71, 252 (n. 82), 280 (n. 197)
German Club, 323 (n. 112)

German Committee for the Liberation of the Russian Jews (Deutsches Komitee zur Befreiung der russischen Juden), 59, 62, 67, 271 (n. 118), 274 (n. 136)
German Democratic Party, 10
Ghadr, 148, 317 (n. 52)
Gierke, Otto von, 283 (n. 15)
Gildemeester, Francis van Gheel, 104–6, 296 (nn. 32, 34), 297 (n. 37)
Ginsberg, J., 274 (n. 136)
Goeben, 238 (n. 40)
Goltz, Colmar Baron von der, 317 (n. 50)
Goltz, Horst von der (alias Bridgeman H. Taylor; Franz Wachendorf), 178–79, 329 (n. 178), 336 (nn. 233, 235), 337 (nn. 241, 242), 343 (n. 286)
Gonne-MacBride, Maude, 317 (n. 53)
Gore, Thomas P., 303 (n. 125)
Göttinger Tageblatt, 360 (n. 143)
Grace, E. G., 56
Graebner, Alan N., 279 (n. 180)
Grantnor, Francis. *See* Hinsch, Friedrich
Grell, Professor Dr., 243 (n. 22)
Grew, Joseph C., 203–4, 351 (nn. 66, 67)
Grey, Sir Edward, 21, 87, 91, 93–95, 129, 131, 133–35, 237 (n. 25), 287 (n. 57), 290 (n. 96), 291 (n. 107), 322 (n. 107), 356 (n. 112)
Groener, Wilhelm, 319 (n. 73)
Gronemann, Sammy, 271 (n. 116)
Guaranty Trust Company, 56
Gupta, Heramba Lal, 149, 321 (n. 93)

Haeften, Hans von, 230

Hahn, Kurt, 314 (n. 19)
Haimhausen, Edgar Karl Alfons Haniel von, 41, 357 (n. 122)
Hale, William Bayard, 21, 25, 43, 46, 245 (nn. 32, 34), 260 (n. 12), 261–62 (n. 25)
Hall, William Reginald, 179, 185–86, 215, 227, 263 (n. 37)
Hallgarten, Georg W. F., 241 (n. 61)
Hamburg-American Line (HAPAG), 36–37, 53, 182, 238 (n. 37), 258 (n. 122), 259 (n. 12), 263 (n. 39), 279 (n. 176), 295 (n. 25), 315 (n. 26), 336 (n. 238), 340 (n. 262)
Hamburger, Ernest, 276–77 (n. 159)
Hamburger Fremdenblatt, 364 (n. 183)
Hamburger Nachrichten, 293 (n. 15)
Hamburgischer Correspondent, 293 (n. 15)
Hamm, von (editor), 55, 268 (n. 95)
Hammann, Otto, 102, 236–37 (n. 25), 260 (n. 16)
Hammer, 294 (n. 15)
Hammond. *See* Casement, Sir Roger
Hancock, 257 (n. 118)
Hantke, Arthur, 271 (n. 116), 273 (n. 132)
HAPAG. *See* Hamburg-American Line
Harden, Maximilian, 11, 204, 240 (n. 54), 241 (n. 58), 352 (n. 77)
Hardinge, Lord Charles, 21
Harnack, Adolf von, 283 (n. 15), 311 (n. 223)
Haugwitz, von (bribery attempt), 326 (n. 144)
Hawaii, 3
Hay, John Milton, 27
Hearst, William Randolph, 56, 262 (n. 25)

Hebrew Immigrant Aid Society, 279 (n. 175)
Hecker, Ewald Otto Emil, 260 (n. 12)
Heineken, Phil., 274 (n. 140)
Heinrich, Prince of Prussia, 299 (n. 63)
Helfferich, Emil, and brother, 150, 319 (n. 68)
Helfferich, Karl, 298 (n. 54), 358 (n. 127)
Henry, John J., 228
Henry S., 150, 319 (n. 67)
Hentig, Werner Otto von, 320 (n. 75)
Herrick, Myron Timothy, 87
Herrmann (also Hermann), Friedrich (also Fred) (alias Larssen; Marstrom; Lewis; March; Rasmussen; Rodriguez), 188–89, 343 (n. 289), 344 (n. 296)
Herrmann, Richard, 338 (n. 253)
Hexamer, Charles J., 71, 73, 280 (n. 197)
Hilken, Paul, 188–89, 343–44 (n. 290)
Hill, David Jayne, 31
Hilmi, Abbas, 56
Hindenburg, Paul L. H. A. von Beneckendorff und von, 61, 67, 194, 198, 203, 207, 209, 218, 273 (n. 133), 302 (n. 104), 346 (n. 12), 351 (n. 68)
Hinsch, Friedrich (alias Francis Grantnor), 188–89, 343–44 (n. 290), 344 (nn. 291, 296)
Hintze, Paul von, 8, 153, 165, 176, 256 (n. 115), 257 (n. 119), 258 (n. 122), 320 (nn. 76, 77), 329 (n. 171), 331 (n. 195)
Hirst, David W., 312 (n. 1)
Historische Zeitschrift, 12, 241 (n. 61)

Hitler, Adolf, 2, 12, 234–35 (n. 6), 316 (n. 38)
Hoff, Fritz, 262 (n. 27)
Hoffmann, Max, 230
Hohenborn, Adolf Wild von, 121–22
Holborn, Hajo, 1
Holland-America Line, 185
Holst (agent), 256 (n. 115)
Holstein, Friedrich von, 6, 8
Holtzendorff, Henning von, 117, 119, 121–23, 171, 193, 200, 207, 209, 224, 299 (n. 67), 301 (n. 93), 303–4 (n. 128), 304 (n. 135), 305 (nn. 151, 152), 346 (n. 16), 361 (n. 160)
Hölzle, Erwin, 12, 135, 241 (n. 61)
Homann (supposed World War I propagandist), 262 (n. 27)
Hoover, Herbert, 350 (n. 58)
Hoquiam, 320 (n. 85)
Horn, Werner, 70, 180, 338 (n. 248)
Horwitz, Justizrat, 274 (n. 136)
Horwitz, Maximilian, 274 (n. 136)
Hossenfelder, Erich, 182–83, 261 (n. 24), 299 (n. 63)
House, Edward Mandell, 86, 88–90, 93–95, 97, 108, 129, 134, 168–69, 199–200, 202, 204, 211, 214, 222, 288 (nn. 62, 68), 289 (n. 77), 291 (nn. 106, 107), 292 (n. 109), 296 (n. 34), 306 (n. 154), 307 (nn. 173, 174), 308 (nn. 178, 187, 188), 309 (nn. 189, 195, 198), 346 (n. 15), 351 (n. 65), 356 (n. 112); and Bernstorff, 87–88, 91–92, 94, 113, 126–28, 130–33, 135–39, 143, 195–96, 206, 210–16, 219–22, 287 (n. 54), 288 (n. 67), 289 (n. 74), 290 (n. 97), 299–300 (n. 71), 300 (n. 77), 301 (n. 82), 306 (n. 164), 307 (n. 174), 310 (n. 211), 314 (n. 17), 347 (n. 19),

351 (n. 69), 353 (n. 85), 355 (n. 103), 357 (n. 122), 363 (n. 177)
Hubrich, Erich-Wolfgang, 235 (n. 7)
Hudson. *See* Wessels, Hermann
Huebner, Theodore, 266 (n. 65)
Huerta, Victoriano, 34, 36–37, 96, 103, 165–69, 172, 175–76, 225, 255 (n. 107), 256 (n. 115), 257 (n. 119), 330 (nn. 182, 183), 330–31 (n. 188)
Hughes, Charles Evans, 76, 164, 193
Hülsen, Ernst von, 163, 328 (n. 161)
Humbert, Charles, 56, 268 (n. 98)
Humboldt, Alexander von, 362 (n. 168)
Hunsdiecker, R., 243 (n. 22)
Hutten-Czapski, Bogdan Count, 59

Igel, Wolf Walter Franz von, 75, 138, 143–44, 155–56, 161, 163, 175, 281 (n. 208), 310 (nn. 211, 216), 314 (n. 16), 317 (n. 43), 327 (nn. 146, 156), 333 (n. 214), 340 (nn. 264, 266)
Indians, and German activities, 146–50, 152–54, 186, 316–21 (nn. 38–99), 338 (n. 249), 359 (n. 137)
Industrial Workers of the World (IWW), 317 (n. 53)
Ingel, Adolph, 265 (n. 55)
Ireland, John, 104
Irish, and propaganda, 72–76, 155, 164, 321–28 (nn. 100–168), 338 (n. 246)
Irish Brigade, 73, 157–60, 162, 323 (n. 111), 324 (n. 127)
Irish National Volunteers, 157, 162
Irish Press and News Service, 74
Irish Republican Brotherhood (IRB), 158–59, 162, 324 (n. 122), 325 (n. 130)

Irish World, 74
Isendahl, Walther, 324 (n. 119)
Iturbide, Eduardo, 169
Itzenplitz, K., 243 (n. 22)

Jacobsen, A. D., 16
Jacobsen, Gustav H., 149
Jaeckh, Ernst, 61–62, 260 (n. 16), 273 (n. 129), 274 (n. 140), 319 (n. 73)
Jagow, Gottlieb E. G. von, 54, 66, 81, 102, 108–9, 114–15, 122–26, 133, 136, 153, 171, 173, 191–92, 201, 203, 234–35 (n. 6), 257–58 (n. 120), 275 (n. 147), 281 (n. 202), 284 (nn. 21, 22), 286 (n. 48), 292 (nn. 108, 109), 302 (n. 107), 303 (n. 116), 305 (n. 147), 305–6 (n. 154), 309 (n. 189), 310 (nn. 212, 214), 311 (n. 223), 329 (n. 171), 332 (n. 208), 351 (n. 65)
Jahnke, Kurt, 155–56, 176–78, 180, 183, 186–88, 316 (n. 38), 334 (n. 227), 335 (n. 229), 342 (nn. 274, 283), 344 (n. 291)
Jahresberichte für Deutsche Geschichte, 12
Jamaica, 336 (n. 236)
James, Sir William, 185
Jarrosch (also Jarosch), William, 149, 319 (n. 65), 338 (n. 253)
Jebsen, F., 321 (n. 95)
Jebsen Line, 151
Jeffreys-Jones, Rhodri, 306 (n. 163), 313 (n. 10)
Jews, and German propaganda, 57–67, 269 (nn. 102, 105), 270–77 (nn. 107–66)
Johnson, Niel M., 266 (n. 66)
Juárez, Benito, 33
Jusserand, Jean Adrien Antoine Jules, 93, 258 (n. 1), 287 (n. 57)

Kahl (professor), 283 (n. 15)
Kaltschmidt, Albert, 181–82, 339 (n. 253)
Karachi, 320–21 (n. 88)
Kardorff, Rudolf von, 331 (n. 195)
Katz, Friedrich, 167, 171, 254 (n. 101), 255 (nn. 103, 105), 329 (n. 176), 330 (n. 184), 333 (n. 211), 343 (n. 285)
Kauffman (also Kaufman), S. Walter, 267 (n. 74)
Keating, John T., 180
Kelly, Alfred H., 1
Kemnitz, Hans Arthur W. A. von, 36, 225, 257 (n. 120), 258 (n. 123), 336 (n. 235), 362 (nn. 164, 170)
Keppler (supposed World War I propagandist), 262 (n. 27)
Kiderlen-Wächter, Alfred von, 24, 247–48 (n. 53), 252 (n. 82)
Kienzle, Herbert, 183
Kiliani, Richard, 63
Kingsland Assembly Plant, 188, 344 (n. 290)
Kircheisen (agent), 75
Kitchener, Lord, 323 (n. 113)
Klee, Alfred, 271 (n. 116)
Klein, Fritz, 320 (n. 75)
Kleist, Carl von, 183, 340 (n. 262)
Klingemann, H., 243 (n. 22)
Knox, Philander C., 26, 31
Koch, Reinhard, 121
Koenneritz, Anna Baroness von. See Bernstorff, Anna Countess von
Köhler, Commander, 165
Kol Mewasser, 271 (n. 116)
Kölnische Zeitung, 223
König, Paul (agent), 295 (n. 25), 316–17 (n. 43)
König, Paul (captain), 197, 348 (n. 31)
Korodi, L., 243 (n. 22)

Kramer, Hans, 235 (n. 7)
Kretzschman (also Kretzschmann), Maria von (also Baroness von). See Victorica, Maria
Krieger, Leonard, 1
Kronprinzessin Cecilie, 258 (n. 122)
Kück, Otto, 336 (n. 235)
Kuehne, Walter, 262 (n. 27)
Kühlmann, Richard von, 104, 238 (n. 39), 259 (n. 4)
Kuhn, Loeb & Co., 58, 61, 270 (n. 109), 275 (n. 144), 312 (n. 4)
Kühnemann, Eugen, 47–48, 264 (nn. 45, 46)

Labor's National Peace Council, 183–84, 340 (n. 269)
LaFeber, Walter, 3
Lamar, David, 183
Landau, Leopold, 274 (n. 136)
Landy, James E. See Casement, Sir Roger
Lane, Franklin Knight, 106, 296 (n. 34)
Langer, William L., 12, 241 (n. 62)
Langhans, P., 243 (n. 22)
Langhorne, George T., 177
Lansing, Robert, 81, 84, 110–12, 114, 116–18, 130, 152, 163, 184–86, 200, 202, 220, 222, 264 (n. 47), 300 (nn. 74, 80), 301 (n. 98), 302 (n. 108), 303 (n. 124), 306 (n. 155), 307 (n. 173), 341 (n. 279), 346 (n. 15), 350 (n. 50)
Larkin, James, 183, 325 (n. 132), 331 (n. 196), 335 (n. 231), 340 (nn. 263, 264, 266)
Lassen, August, 282 (n. 213), 333–34 (n. 218)
League of Nations, 10–11, 204, 290 (n. 95)
Lechartier, G., 44
Lehmann, J. F., 243 (n. 22)

Lersner, Kurt Baron von, 339 (n. 261)
Lester, George B., 262 (n. 27)
Lettenbaur, J. A., 260 (n. 16)
Lewinski, Karl von, 333 (n. 215), 337 (n. 242)
Lichnowsky, Karl Max Prince von, 6, 256 (n. 114)
Liebau Bureau, 183–84, 340 (n. 268)
Liebert, E. von, 243 (n. 22)
Liebknecht, Karl, 134, 140
Limburg, 157–58, 162
Lindheim, Norvin R., 53, 267 (n. 74)
Link, Arthur S., 104–5, 117, 141, 184, 202, 257 (n. 117), 261 (n. 22), 278 (n. 169), 284 (n. 23), 288 (n. 65), 293 (n. 6), 296 (n. 34), 297 (n. 38), 331 (n. 192), 341 (n. 270), 348 (n. 35), 356 (n. 115), 361 (n. 155)
Liskow, Richard, 262 (n. 27)
Lloyd George, David, 134, 223, 290 (n. 96)
Loeffler, William, 338 (n. 253)
Loewenstein Wertheim Rosenberg, Alexandra Princess zu, 235 (n. 10), 236 (n. 16)
Loewenstein Wertheim Rosenberg, Johannes Prince zu, 236 (n. 16)
Löhlein, Captain, 260 (n. 16)
Lohmann, Johannes G., 281 (n. 209), 337 (n. 243), 339 (n. 261)
Lowe, Theodore, 57, 268 (n. 100)
Luckemeyer, Jeanne. *See* Bernstorff, Jeanne Countess von
Ludendorff, Erich, 67, 194, 209, 231, 273 (n. 133), 277 (n. 163), 346 (n. 12)
Ludwig, Emil, 12, 239 (n. 45)
Luebke, Frederick C., 278 (n. 168)
Luederitz, Karl, 178–79
Lusitania, 43, 45, 47, 64, 67, 70, 71, 84–85, 94, 97–102, 108–15, 118–21, 126, 128–30, 137–38, 272 (n. 120), 277 (n. 166), 279 (n. 185), 292 (n. 1), 293 (nn. 14, 15), 295 (n. 25), 299 (n. 63), 310 (n. 211)
Luxburg, Karl Count, 344 (n. 296)
Lyon, Walter, 55

McCormick family, 25
McGarrity, Joseph, 151, 179–80, 322–23 (n. 109), 323 (n. 112)
McGuire, James K., 74, 281 (n. 205), 340 (n. 266)
Mach, Edmund von, 48, 260 (n. 12), 264 (n. 48)
Mack, Hans, 262 (n. 27)
McKinley, William, 256 (n. 113)
McLean, John R., 269 (n. 100)
McLemore, Atkins Jefferson ("Jeff"), 303 (n. 125)
Madero, Francisco Indalecio, 34, 170, 172, 255 (nn. 103, 105), 331 (n. 195)
Magnus, Julius, 169, 274 (n. 136), 329 (n. 173)
Maguerre, Major, 189
Mahan, Alfred Thayer, 3
Malitz, Felix, 265 (n. 55)
Manila, 14
Marina, 200, 350 (n. 49)
Marshall, Louis, 275 (n. 146)
Marx, Ernst, 264 (n. 45)
Masaryk, Thomas Garrigue, 168
Maverick, 151–52
Max, Prince. *See* Baden, Maximilian Prince von
May, Ernest R., 234 (n. 1), 287 (n. 55)
Mayo, Henry Thomas, 256–57 (n. 117)
Mechlenburg, Dr., 260 (n. 12)
Meine, Arnold, 235 (n. 7)
Meinecke, Friedrich, 60, 243 (n. 23), 244 (nn. 29, 30), 324 (n. 117), 358–59 (n. 133)

Melamed, S. M., 60, 62
Metternich. See Wolff-Metternich zur Gracht, Paul A. M. H. Count von
Mexico, 32–38, 103, 151, 165–76, 192, 215, 217, 225–27, 254 (nn. 98–103), 255 (nn. 103–12), 256 (nn. 112–17), 257 (nn. 117–20), 258 (nn. 120–24), 318 (n. 60), 328–33 (nn. 169–212), 336 (n. 235), 337 (n. 242), 342 (nn. 273, 274), 344 (n. 291), 351 (n. 65), 361–63 (nn. 161–72)
Meyer, Eduard, 60, 272 (n. 123), 324 (n. 117), 325 (n. 129), 345 (n. 11), 359 (n. 143)
Meyer, Julius P., 41, 259 (n. 12)
Meyer, Kuno, 48, 76, 282 (n. 219), 325 (n. 129), 340 (n. 264), 345 (n. 11)
Meyer, Michael C., 361–62 (n. 162)
Meyer, Richard, 157, 323 (n. 114), 337 (n. 245), 338 (n. 246)
Meyer-Gerhard, Anton, 41, 44, 107, 109, 128, 297 (nn. 38, 45)
Meyrowitz, Arthur, 60, 62–64, 273 (n. 129), 274 (n. 140)
Miller, Adolph Caspar, 106, 296 (n. 34)
Mixed Claims Commission, 179, 188–89, 314 (n. 14), 333 (n. 215)
M. M. Warburg & Co., 270 (n. 109)
Möckelmann, Jürgen, 263 (n. 35), 277 (n. 167)
Moltke, Helmuth Johannes Ludwig von, 147
Mommsen, Wolfgang, 352 (n. 71)
Monroe, James, 253 (n. 93)
Monroe Doctrine, 3, 33, 253 (n. 93), 254 (n. 97), 357 (n. 119)
Monteith, Robert, 159–62, 325 (n. 132), 326 (n. 137)
Montgelas, Adolf Count von, 171, 264 (n. 47), 332 (n. 202), 337 (n. 244), 338 (n. 246), 362 (n. 170)
Monts de Mazin, Anton Count von, 7, 236 (n. 24)
Movshowitch, David, 237 (n. 25)
Müller, Georg Alexander von, 121, 123, 217, 285 (n. 33), 293 (n. 14), 302 (n. 107)
Mumm von Schwarzenstein, Philipp Alfons Baron, 102, 260 (n. 16)
Münsterberg, Hugo, 48, 260 (n. 12), 264 (n. 47), 279 (n. 180)
Münsterberg, Otto, 264 (n. 47)

Nadolny, Rudolf August H., 146, 155, 159–60, 162–63, 188–89, 316 (n. 39), 326 (n. 139), 337 (n. 244)
Nathan, Paul, 61
Neald (British admiral), 263 (n. 34)
Neckar, 343 (n. 290)
Neef, Fritz, 338 (n. 253)
Neuberger, A., 262 (n. 27)
Neue Preussische Zeitung, 359–60 (n. 143)
Neue Zürcher Zeitung, 239 (n. 45)
Neumann, H., 262 (n. 27)
Neutrality League, 280 (n. 189)
Newcastle, 152
New Hampshire, 257 (n. 118)
New Jersey, 257 (n. 118)
New Jersey Agricultural and Chemical Company, 182
New York American, 268 (n. 95)
New Yorker Staats-Zeitung, 15, 51–52, 70, 74, 206, 265 (n. 59)
New York Evening Mail, 53–55, 267 (n. 74), 268 (n. 87)
New York Sun, 55
New York World, 228
Nicholson, John T., 158
Nicolai, Walter, 146, 313 (n. 7), 316 (n. 38)
Nicosian, 303 (n. 124)

Niedermayer, Oskar, 320 (n. 75)
Niemöller, Martin, 292 (n. 1)
Noeggerath, Jakob, 314 (n. 19), 360 (n. 149)
Noordam, 185
Norddeutsche Allgemeine Zeitung, 364 (n. 184)
North German Lloyd, 62, 273 (n. 129), 274 (n. 140), 319 (n. 67)
Noyes, Alfred, 164, 328 (n. 168)

Obregón, Álvaro, 169
O'Gorman, Canice, 158
O'Leary, Jeremiah A., 76, 164, 180, 328 (n. 166)
Oncken, Hermann, 264 (n. 45), 278 (n. 172)
Oppenheim, Max Baron von, 147–48
Oppenheimer, Franz, 61, 67, 270 (n. 116), 273 (nn. 132, 133), 274 (n. 137)
Orion, 257 (n. 118)
Orozco, Pascual, 34, 168, 254 (n. 100)
Osgood, Robert E., 244 (n. 29)
Othmer, Captain, 151–52, 320 (n. 85)

Page, Walter Hines, 87, 89–91, 227, 287 (n. 57), 303 (n. 124)
Pallavicini, Johann Margrave von, 6, 236 (n. 19)
Panama, 173–74, 338 (n. 247)
Pan-Germans, 17–19, 125, 192, 195, 243 (n. 23), 347 (n. 18)
Panther, 165, 248 (n. 53), 329 (n. 170)
Papen, Franz von, 11, 47, 73–75, 119, 143–46, 148–49, 151–53, 155–57, 166–68, 172–75, 178–82, 184–85, 188, 301 (n. 94), 312 (n. 5), 314 (n. 16), 315 (n. 29), 316 (n. 32), 317 (n. 43), 318 (n. 60), 319 (nn. 66, 67), 320 (n. 85), 322 (n. 102), 323 (n. 112), 326 (n. 127), 329 (nn. 175, 178), 333 (nn. 212, 215), 336 (nn. 233, 234, 235), 337 (nn. 242, 244), 339 (n. 261), 340 (nn. 264, 266), 359 (n. 137)
Pavenstedt, Adolf, 52, 56, 265–66 (n. 58)
Pearson, S. Weetmann (Lord Cowdray), 255 (n. 110)
Peck, Harry Thurston, 23
Penfield, Frederic Courtland, 224
Perkins, Dexter, 254 (n. 97)
Persian Gulf, 320 (n. 88)
Peter, Elmar, 320 (n. 76)
Petersdorf, von, 167, 338 (n. 247)
Peterson, H. C., 44
Pezoldt, G., 243 (n. 22)
Phillips, William, 290 (n. 88)
Plage (of German Press Office), 260 (n. 12)
Plunkett, Joseph, 158–59, 160
Plunkett, Philomena, 161
Pohl, Hugo von, 78–79, 101, 283 (n. 18)
Pourtalès, Raimund Count von, 39, 236 (n. 16)
Prairie, 257 (n. 118)
Prittwitz und Gaffron, Friedrich Wilhelm von, 69, 192
Puerto México, 37, 256 (n. 115), 258 (n. 122)
Pustkuchen, Herbert, 124, 305 (n. 153)
Putz, F., 243 (n. 22)

Quinn, John, 317 (n. 53), 322–23 (n. 109), 328 (n. 166)
Quirk, Robert E., 257 (n. 118)

Radolin, Hugo Prince von, 6–7
Radowitz, Joseph Maria von, 6
"Raoul, Cousin." *See* Gerdts, Raoul
Rappaport, Armin, 302 (n. 113)

Rappaport, Joseph, 279 (n. 175)
Rathenau, Walther, 11, 241 (n. 58), 292 (n. 108)
Ratner, Abraham, 167
Rau, A., 41
Rauch, Leopold von, 339–40 (n. 261)
Reading, Lord (Rufus Daniel Isaacs), 134
Rebeur-Paschwitz, Hubert von, 238 (n. 40)
Redmond, John, 76, 282 (n. 220)
Reichardt, Paul, 75, 282 (n. 213)
Reismann-Grone (newspaper owner), 243 (n. 22)
Reiswitz, Consul, 181–82
Remsen, Ira, 23
Respa, Charles, 338 (n. 253)
Reventlow, Ernst Count zu, 18, 243 (n. 22)
Ribbentrop, Joachim von, 234–35 (n. 6)
Richard, Ernst, 252 (n. 82)
Ridder, Herman, 15, 51–52, 70, 76, 206, 277 (n. 167)
Ridder family, 51, 70
Riesser, Hans E., 234–35 (n. 6), 365 (n. 193)
Riezler, Kurt, 362 (n. 164)
Rintelen, Franz (von), 112, 141, 155, 167–68, 176–78, 182–89, 292 (n. 1), 330 (nn. 179, 186), 333 (n. 215), 334 (nn. 219, 220), 335 (n. 230), 340 (n. 265)
Ritter, Gerhard, 2, 45, 78, 124, 132, 135, 137–38, 244 (n. 29), 263 (n. 35), 291 (n. 102), 292 (n. 109), 296 (n. 33), 311–12 (n. 1), 346 (n. 15), 355 (n. 103)
Ritter, Max, 262 (n. 27)
Ritter, Paul, 221, 361 (n. 154)
Robinsohn, Abraham, 271 (n. 116)
Robinson, James Harvey, 264 (n. 50)
Rodriguez (Kingsland attack), 188

Roediger, Carl. *See* Wessels, Hermann
Roediger, Gustav, 260 (n. 16)
Rogge, Helmuth, 245 (n. 35)
Roh, Consul, 202
Rohrbach, Paul, 260 (n. 16), 289 (n. 71)
Rolland, Romain, 264 (n. 50)
Röntgen, Wilhelm Konrad von, 49
Roosevelt, Theodore, 3, 14–15, 21, 24–25, 33, 59, 100, 227, 255 (n. 106), 262 (n. 34); and foreign policy, 4; and Wilhelm II, 14–15, 250 (n. 71); and arbitration, 26–30
Roosevelt Corollary, 33
Root, Elihu, 27–30, 251 (n. 78)
Rose, Hans, 197–98, 349 (n. 38)
Rosen, Friedrich, 314 (n. 19)
Roy, M. N., 319 (n. 68)
Ruerode, Carl, 145–46, 175, 315 (n. 26), 316 (n. 32)
Rumania, 140, 194–95, 202–3
Rumely, Edward A., 16, 53–55, 267 (nn. 74, 77, 84, 85), 268 (n. 89), 269 (n. 101), 325 (n. 129)
Ryan, Paul B., 80, 295 (n. 25)

Sala, Raoul. *See* Gerdts, Raoul
Salomon, Wilhelm, 317 (n. 56)
Samassa, P., 243 (n. 22)
Samoa, 3
Sauerbeck, 335–36 (n. 232)
Schack, Eckhard von, 186–87
Schäfer, Dietrich, 207, 264 (n. 45)
Scheele, Walter Theodor, 182
Scheer, Reinhard, 305 (n. 152)
Scheibe, Felix, 262 (n. 27)
Scheidemann, Philipp, 9
Schellenberg, Walter, 335 (n. 227)
Schiemann, Theodor, 72–73, 157, 280 (n. 195), 283 (n. 15), 334 (n. 221)
Schiff, Jacob Henry, 61, 63, 99, 270

(n. 109), 279 (n. 185)
Schiff, Philipp, 275 (n. 154)
Schmid-Bürckert, Walter, 235 (n. 7)
Schmidt, Carl, 338 (n. 252), 338–39 (n. 253)
Schmidt, Hans, 262 (n. 27)
Schmidt, Hugo, 56
Schmidt, Ludwig, 181
Schmidt, M. *See* Wessels, Hermann
Schmidt, Marie, 338 (n. 253)
Schmoller, von (signer of petition), 283 (n. 15)
Schneider, Commander, 112, 116
Schoen, Wilhelm Baron von, 18
Scholz, Wilhelm, 338 (n. 253)
Schrader, Frederick Franklin, 41, 76
Schröder, Martin, 256 (n. 115)
Schroeder, Reginald, 52
Schroeder-Poggelow (Pan-German sympathizer), 243 (n. 22)
Schroejers, Hajo. *See* Wessels, Hermann
Schuberth, Inger, 328 (n. 161)
Schulze, Max (alias Sterneck), 149–50, 181, 318–19 (n. 63), 319 (n. 69), 339 (n. 254)
Schulze-Gaevernitz, Gerhart von, 16–17, 53–54
Schumacher (chief of picture office), 260 (n. 16)
Schurz, Carl, 246–47 (n. 43)
Schurz, Ch., 315 (n. 26)
Schwabe, Klaus, 265 (n. 50)
Schwartzkopf, Captain, 197
Schwepcke, Hans-Jürgen, 235 (n. 7)
Schwieger, Walter, 70, 84, 98, 292 (n. 1)
Seidmann, M. F., 273 (n. 128)
Selbmann (supposed World War I propagandist), 262 (n. 27)
Sen, Dhirendra Nat, 149
Sering (signer of petition), 283 (n. 15)

Seward, Anne L., 341 (n. 270)
Seward, William H., 341 (n. 270)
Seymour, Charles, 88, 138, 241 (n. 62), 289 (n. 73), 295 (n. 28), 300 (n. 74), 347 (n. 19)
Sharp, William Graves, 289 (n. 77)
Sielken, Hermann, 53–54, 267 (n. 76)
Sieps, Paul, 183
Simon, Frau Dr. *See* Victorica, Maria
Simon, James, 61, 275 (n. 154)
Simpson, Colin, 286 (n. 40), 295 (n. 25)
Singh, Diwakar Prasad, 318 (n. 57)
Singh, Jodh, 149, 319 (n. 65)
Skal, Georg von, 75, 156, 163
Smith, Louis J., 186–87
Sobernheim, Moritz Sebastian, 274 (n. 136)
Solf, Wilhelm, 44, 133, 157
Solger, F., 243 (n. 22)
Sommerfeld, Felix A., 170–71, 328 (n. 169), 331 (n. 195)
South Carolina, 257 (n. 118)
Speyer, James, 25, 86, 272 (n. 120), 277 (n. 166), 286 (n. 50)
Speyer family, 59
Spindler, Arno, 282 (n. 1), 283 (n. 3), 348 (n. 33)
Spindler, Karl, 161
Spring Rice, Sir Cecil Arthur, 33, 59, 87–88, 90–91, 93, 237 (n. 36), 258 (n. 1), 288 (n. 68), 289 (n. 74), 290 (n. 88), 296 (n. 34), 361 (n. 154)
Stadler, Otto, 360 (n. 143)
Stahl, Gustav, 295 (n. 25)
Stallforth, Federico (also Frederick), 179, 336 (n. 239)
Stamm, H. *See* Wessels, Hermann
Stamm, P. *See* Wessels, Hermann
Standard Oil Company, 329 (n. 176)

Starnberg, 8, 39
Starr Hunt, John Brackenridge, 321 (n. 95)
Stegler, Richard Peter, 146, 316 (n. 35)
Steglich, Wolfgang, 198, 202, 350 (n. 53)
Stemrich, Wilhelm, 24
Stephen, Gustav, 338 (n. 253)
Stern, Fritz, 209
Stern, Jos., 262 (n. 27)
Sternburg, Hermann Speck Baron von, 4, 8, 15, 26–30, 242 (n. 1), 261 (n. 25); and Theodore Roosevelt, 14, 250 (n. 71); and Irish, 73
Sterneck. *See* Schulze, Max
Stinnes, Hugo, 291 (n. 104)
Stolberg-Wernigerode, Otto Count zu, 280 (n. 195)
Stolte, E., 243 (n. 22)
Stössel, Baron von, 243 (n. 22)
Straus, Isaac, 59–64, 270 (n. 111), 271 (n. 117), 275 (n. 144), 276 (n. 154)
Straus, Oscar Solomon, 86–87, 275 (n. 146), 286 (n. 51), 287 (nn. 54, 55), 289 (n. 74)
Strempel, 343 (n. 289), 344 (n. 296)
Stresemann, Gustav, 334 (n. 227)
Stronge, Sir Francis, 255 (n. 110)
Struck, Hermann, 271 (n. 116)
Stumm, Wilhelm von, 31, 204, 218
Stutterheim, Kurt Baron von, 235 (n. 11)
Sumatra, 321 (n. 90)
Sussex, 124, 126, 136–38, 140, 193, 304 (n. 135), 305 (n. 153)
Szajkowski, Zosa, 273 (n. 129)

Taft, William Howard, 15, 25–26, 31, 34, 254 (nn. 98, 101), 255 (n. 106)
Tag, Der, 60, 67

Tampico, 256–57 (n. 117)
Tansill, Charles Callan, 327 (n. 155)
Tarnowski von Tarnow, Adam Count, 222
Tauscher, Hans, 151, 173, 179, 318 (n. 60), 336 (n. 238), 336–37 (n. 240), 337 (n. 244)
Taylor, Bridgeman H. *See* Goltz, Horst von der
Thwaites, Norman, 313 (n. 8)
Timendorfer, Berthold, 274 (n. 136)
Tinnemann, Ethel Mary, 141, 235 (n. 7), 266 (n. 62), 312 (n. 3)
Tirpitz, Alfred von, 78–80, 101–2, 109, 113, 121, 126, 209, 297 (nn. 39, 44), 299 (n. 67), 304 (n. 130), 311 (n. 228), 329 (n. 171)
Treitschke, Heinrich von, 248 (n. 57)
Treutler, Carl Georg von, 332 (n. 208)
Triepel (signer of petition), 283 (n. 15)
Trott zu Solz, August B. W. K. von, 48
Trumpener, Ulrich, 319 (n. 72)
Tuchhaendler. *See* Tucker
Tuchman, Barbara W., 166, 256 (n. 115), 330 (n. 184)
Tucker (alias Tuchhaendler; associate of Horst von der Goltz), 336 (n. 238)
Tumulty, Joseph P., 100
Tyrrell, Sir William, 237 (n. 25)

U-9, 78
U-19, 161–62, 283 (n. 5)
U-20, 84, 283 (n. 5), 327 (n. 154)
U-21, 283 (n. 5)
U-22, 283 (n. 5)
U-24, 112, 116, 283 (n. 5)
U-27, 283 (n. 5), 303 (n. 124)
U-28, 283 (n. 5)

U-29, 124, 283 (n. 5)
U-30, 283 (n. 5)
U-38, 118
U-53, 197–98, 348 (n. 33), 349 (n. 38)
U-Bremen, 197, 348 (n. 32)
Uchida, Ryohei, 291 (n. 104)
U-Deutschland, 197, 348 (n. 31)
Untermyer, Samuel, 55, 268 (n. 97)
Utah, 37, 257 (n. 118)

Vagts, Alfred, 242 (n. 3)
Valentin, Veit, 295 (n. 28)
Valentiner, Max, 118, 122, 301 (n. 93)
Valentini, Rudolf von, 238 (n. 37)
Vanderbilt, Alfred Gwynne, 84
Vanselow, Ernst, 334 (n. 221)
Venezuela, 14, 329 (n. 170)
Veracruz, 37, 257 (n. 119), 328 (n. 169)
Verdun, 125
Vermont, 257 (n. 118)
Versailles, 215, 239 (n. 47)
Victorica, Maria (alias Clark; Kretzschmann; Baroness von Kretzschman; Maria von Kretzschman; Dr. Simon; Marie de Vussiere), 75, 281 (n. 212), 282 (n. 213)
Viereck, George Sylvester, 41–42, 52, 70, 76, 164, 259 (n. 12), 266 (n. 66), 277 (n. 167)
Viereck, Louis, 243 (n. 22), 266 (n. 66)
Vierhaus, Rudolf, 1
Villa, Francisco, 34, 36, 168–71, 256 (n. 114), 329 (n. 178)
Villard, Henry, 45
Villard, Oswald Garrison, 45
Vinknor, 145
Voska, Emanuel Victor, 142–43, 168, 314 (n. 12), 330 (n. 183)
Voska family, 314 (n. 12)
Vossische Zeitung, 238 (n. 38)
Vussiere, Marie de. *See* Victorica, Maria

Wachendorf, Franz. *See* Goltz, Horst von der
Waecker-Gotter, Ludwig Baron von, 6
Wallace, Hugh Campbell, 90–91, 289 (nn. 77, 78)
Wandel, Franz E. von, 334 (n. 221)
Warburg, Felix Moritz, 270 (n. 109), 276 (n. 154)
Warburg, Max Moritz, 61, 144, 269 (n. 105), 270 (nn. 107, 110), 275–76 (n. 154), 306 (n. 165), 314 (n. 19), 357 (n. 120)
Warburg, Paul Moritz, 99, 105–6, 270 (n. 109)
Warburg, Mrs. Paul Moritz, 105, 270 (n. 109)
Warburg family, 25, 59, 270 (nn. 109, 110), 272 (n. 120), 275 (n. 144)
Washington Post, 55, 269 (n. 100)
Wassmuss, Wilhelm, 320 (n. 75)
Watzdorf, Erika von, 346 (n. 17), 346–47 (n. 18)
Weber, Max, 304 (n. 135), 311 (nn. 223, 228)
Weddigen, Otto, 78
Wedel, Botho Count von, 223
Wedel, Georg Count von, 157, 315–16 (n. 30), 323 (n. 115)
Wedell, Hans Adam von, 144–45, 175, 315 (n. 28), 315–16 (n. 30)
Wegener, Bernd, 303 (n. 124)
Wehde, Albert H., 149–50, 154, 318 (n. 62), 319 (n. 66)
Weiser, Max, 182–83
Weizmann, Chaim, 270 (n. 107)

Welland Canal, 179, 336 (n. 240)
Wesendonk, Mathilde, 6
Wesendonk, Otto Günther von, 148, 317 (n. 55)
Wessels, Hermann (alias Dillon; Hudson; Carl Roediger; Hajo Schroejers; M. Schmidt; H. Stamm; P. Stamm), 75, 281 (n. 211), 282 (n. 213)
West, Andrew Fleming, 23–24
Westarp, Kuno Count von, 334 (n. 221)
Whelpley, J. D., 16–17, 242 (n. 10)
Wiegand, Karl H. von, 78, 80, 327 (n. 156)
Wilamowitz-Möllendorf, von, 283 (n. 15)
Wilhelm II, 2–3, 8–9, 13, 15, 18–19, 25, 27, 32, 62, 64–65, 69, 79–80, 82, 88, 111, 113, 122–23, 125, 135, 147, 165, 195, 200, 209, 228, 236 (n. 24), 237 (n. 36), 245 (n. 32), 250 (n. 71), 252 (n. 86), 256 (n. 114), 261 (n. 24), 264 (n. 50), 278 (n. 171), 284 (n. 30), 285 (n. 33), 286 (n. 48), 300 (n. 74), 305 (n. 147), 307 (n. 174), 317 (n. 45), 329 (n. 171), 341 (n. 270), 351 (n. 68), 352 (n. 79), 354 (n. 94), 361 (nn. 154, 157, 160), 365 (nn. 187, 190); and Wilson, 86–87, 126, 196, 199, 207, 209, 217–18, 224–25, 298 (n. 51), 306 (n. 157), 352 (n. 71), 361 (n. 160)
Wilson, Henry Lane, 34, 255 (n. 103)
Wilson, Woodrow, 5, 9, 34, 76, 81, 89, 104–6, 108–9, 111, 113–14, 123, 133, 142, 146, 168, 192, 199, 205, 213, 221, 227, 228, 270 (n. 109), 288 (n. 62), 290 (n. 96), 293 (n. 7), 295 (n. 28), 297 (n. 37), 300 (n. 77), 303 (n. 124), 306 (n. 157), 307 (nn. 167, 173), 308 (nn. 176, 178, 179), 311 (n. 223), 328 (n. 166), 341 (n. 270), 345 (n. 11), 346 (n. 15), 348 (nn. 30, 35), 350 (n. 50), 351 (n. 67), 354 (n. 90), 356 (n. 112), 357 (n. 119), 360 (n. 145), 363 (n. 176); and Mexico, 37, 103, 168–71, 173, 255 (n. 107), 256 (n. 113), 260 (n. 12); and mediation, 85–87, 91–92, 106–7, 112, 125–26, 129–32, 134–40, 191, 192–206, 209–12, 215–17, 219, 221–22, 224, 227, 229–30, 287 (n. 55), 289 (n. 74), 296–97 (n. 36), 308 (n. 184), 347 (nn. 26, 28), 349 (nn. 41, 42), 350 (n. 52), 351 (n. 65), 352 (n. 71), 355 (nn. 101, 109), 358 (n. 131); and *Lusitania*, 99–101, 105–7, 112, 114, 118–19, 126
Wimer, Kurt, 295 (n. 31)
Winter, P., 243 (n. 22)
Wirth, Albrecht, 337 (n. 244)
Wiseman, Sir William, 214, 313 (n. 8), 356 (n. 115)
Wittke, Carl, 265 (n. 57), 266 (n. 65), 278 (n. 171), 280 (n. 194)
Witzke, Lothar, 187, 188, 337 (n. 242), 340 (n. 264), 342–43 (n. 283), 343 (n. 288)
Woehst, Wilhelm (alias Hauten; Rupp), 188, 344 (n. 290)
Wolf, Karin, 321–22 (n. 100)
Wolf, Lucien, 237 (n. 25)
Wolff-Metternich zur Gracht, Paul A. M. H. Count von, 7, 21, 245 (n. 35)
Wolpert, Captain, 340 (n. 262)
Womack, John, Jr., 255 (n. 105)
Woodfield, 122
Woolsey, Lester H., 221

Wozniak, Theodore J., 188, 344 (n. 290)
Wrochem, Major-General von, 243 (n. 22)
Wunnenberg (also Wünnenberg), Karl (alias Charles; Son Charles), 335 (n. 229)

Ypiranga, 36–37, 256 (n. 115), 257 (n. 119), 258 (nn. 120–23)

Zapata, Emiliano, 34, 169, 255 (n. 105)
Zechlin, Egmont, 269 (n. 105), 270 (n. 111)
Zeiss, J., 243 (n. 22)
Zenker, Hans, 177
Zimmermann, Arthur, 51, 53–54, 64, 66, 92, 95–96, 102, 133, 144, 151, 157, 171, 173, 179, 192, 201, 203, 205, 207, 210–11, 218, 223–24, 226–27, 230, 238 (n. 38), 283 (n. 18), 292 (n. 109), 305 (n. 147), 309 (n. 189), 315 (n. 27), 320 (n. 80), 324 (n. 120), 351 (n. 65), 352 (nn. 71, 79), 353 (n. 84), 360 (n. 152), 361 (n. 154), 361–62 (n. 162), 362 (nn. 166, 170), 365 (n. 190)
Zimmermann telegram, 77, 166, 215, 217, 225–27, 230, 351 (n. 65), 356 (n. 115), 361–63 (nn. 162–72), 365 (n. 190)
Zukunft, Die, 11
Zwiedineck von Suedenhorst, Baron Erich, 119

Publication of Supplementary Volumes to *The Papers of Woodrow Wilson* is assisted from time to time by the Woodrow Wilson Foundation in order to encourage scholarly work about Woodrow Wilson and his time. All volumes have passed the review procedures of the publishers and the Editor and the Editorial Advisory Committee of *The Papers of Woodrow Wilson*. Inquiries about the Series should be addressed to The Editor, Papers of Woodrow Wilson, Firestone Library, Princeton University, Princeton, N.J. 08540.

Inga Floto, *Colonel House in Paris: A Study of American Policy at the Paris Peace Conference 1919* (Princeton University Press, 1981)

Raymond B. Fosdick, *Letters on the League of Nations. From the Files of Raymond B. Fosdick* (Princeton University Press, 1966)

Wilton B. Fowler, *British-American Relations, 1917–1918: The Role of Sir William Wiseman* (Princeton University Press, 1969)

John M. Mulder, *Woodrow Wilson: The Years of Preparation* (Princeton University Press, 1978)

George Egerton, *Great Britain and the Creation of the League of Nations* (University of North Carolina Press, 1978)

Stephen L. Vaughn, *Holding Fast the Inner Lines: Democracy, Nationalism, and the Committee on Public Information* (University of North Carolina Press, 1980)

Robert C. Hilderbrand, *Power and the People: Executive Management of Public Opinion in Foreign Affairs, 1897–1921* (University of North Carolina Press, 1980)

Edwin A. Weinstein, *Woodrow Wilson: A Medical and Psychological Biography* (Princeton University Press, 1981)

Arthur S. Link (ed.), *Woodrow Wilson and a Revolutionary World, 1913–1921* (University of North Carolina Press, 1982)

Valerie Jean Conner, *The National War Labor Board: Stability, Social Justice, and the Voluntary State in World War I* (University of North Carolina Press, 1983)

Klaus Schwabe, *Woodrow Wilson, Revolutionary Germany, and Peacemaking 1918–1919: Missionary Diplomacy and the Realities of Power* (University of North Carolina Press, 1985)

Frances Saunders, *Ellen Axson Wilson: Between Two Worlds* (University of North Carolina Press, 1985)

Reinhard R. Doerries, *Imperial Challenge: Ambassador Count Bernstorff and German-American Relations, 1908–1917* (University of North Carolina Press, 1989)